THE BROKEN MIRROR:
CHINA AFTER TIANANMEN

THE BROKEN MIRROR: CHINA AFTER TIANANMEN

Edited by
GEORGE HICKS

with contributions by the following:

Asai Motofumi, Geremie Barmé, Michael T. Byrnes,
Joseph Y. S. Cheng, Jerome Alan Cohen, Jürgen Domes,
Fang Lizhi, Thomas B. Gold, Nihal Jayawickrama,
Chalmers Johnson, David Kelly, Michael Lindsay,
Perry Link, Jane Macartney, William McGurn,
Franz Michael, Ramon H. Myers, Jan S. Prybyla,
Lucian W. Pye, Orville Schell, Andrew J. Spano,
Richard C. Thornton, Byron S. J. Weng, Wojtek Zafanolli

**LONGMAN
CURRENT
AFFAIRS**

THE BROKEN MIRROR: CHINA AFTER TIANANMEN

Published by Longman Group UK Limited, Westgate House,
The High, Harlow, Essex, CM20 1YR, United Kingdom.
Telephone (0279) 442601
Telex 81491 Padlog
Facsimile (0279) 444501

Published in the USA and Canada by St James Press,
233 East Ontario Street, Chicago 60611, Illinois, USA

First published 1990. Reprinted 1991.

ISBN 0-582-07485-1 (Longman)

1-55862-069-9 (St James)

A catalogue record for this book is available from the British Library

ISBN 0-582-07485-1

Produced by Longman Group (FE) Ltd.
Printed in Hong Kong.

The Broken Mirror: China After Tiananmen

Foreword

CHALMERS JOHNSON

THE year 1989 not only marked the 200th anniversary of the French Revolution; in future centuries it may be celebrated as a new watershed in revolutionary behavior. A general crisis of communism engulfed the Marxist-Leninist states. The problem of attempting to 'reform' failed economic systems overtaxed the gerontocratic remnants of politburos in most communist systems and left them with the options of either repression or a sharing of power. The Western world, on the other hand, faced with the loss of legitimacy of its communist adversaries, seemed capable only of bumbling, embarrassing responses. The tentativeness and lack of principle in Bush-Quayle Washington or Thatcherite London — e.g., Bush's lack of response early in 1989 to the Chinese regime's hustling Fang Lizhi away from his Beijing dinner party — strongly suggested that Brezhnev-type minds flourished in climates other than Beijing, Bucharest, or Pyongyang.

During 1989, de facto insurrections against communist rule occurred in almost every communist capital, but the least imaginative reaction to its insurrection occurred in China. Until then China had been in the forefront of reform — or at least so its devotees and sycophants wanted to believe. Even before Solidarity in Poland and well before Mikhail Gorbachev came to power in the Soviet Union in March 1985, China had begun to notice a few realities of its so-called revolution. Communism, of course, aims not at economic efficiency but at social justice. But in the modern world, particularly after the advent of the information-based, computer- and microelectronics-driven industrial structure, state-owned and -controlled enterprises cannot operate efficiently enough to finance a modern welfare system. In order for communism to try to distribute benefits equitably, there must be some benefits. By the late 1970s it had become apparent to virtually all Chinese that Mao's 27 years in power had produced nothing more than that: 27 years of Mao's personal dictatorship. The system had run out of benefits.

Dictatorship was the second problem. The communist revolu-

tions of the 20th century differed from the English revolution of
the 17th century or the French revolution of the 18th century in
that they did not culminate in Thermidor. By the concept of
'Thermidor' students of revolution do not mean counterrevolution
but rather that stage in the process of revolution in which the
'masses' (citizens, people, the alleged beneficiaries of the changes
brought about by revolution) assert themselves and send their
revolutionary vanguards back to their customary occupations as
clerks, lawyers, and functionaries. Thermidor means that the peoples whose victimization justified the revolution finally decide to
take their winnings and go home — consolidating the new order
and preserving their gains. Where Thermidor does not occur,
largely because the revolutionary masses, often peasants, are too
unsophisticated to understand what their vanguards are up to, we
see a typical pattern in which the vanguards first attempt to force
their ideology on the masses (the Reign of Terror in the French
Revolution, Stalin's purges, the Great Leap Forward, the Cultural
Revolution) followed by a routinization of vanguard dictatorship.
This latter phase, the sleepy but policed indolence of the Brezhnev
years, is typified by massive cynicism and corruption — the world
of *nomenklatura* and dachas in Russia, the East German communist elites' guarded paradise at Wandlitz north of Berlin, and the
beach resorts and Party stores of China's plutocracy.

Deng Xiaoping tried to restart China's economy without affecting the dictatorship of its entrenched vanguards. Although the
terms had not yet been invented, Deng sought *perestroika* without
glasnost. This was not a particularly unusual project. There are
innumerable historical examples of similarly placed monopolists of
power who wanted economic modernization without political reform, including those of late Manchu China, Czarist Russia, and
Meiji Japan. It does not work. But this is not to say that democracy must necessarily accompany economic reform. There are many
intermediate possibilities, as the cases of postwar Japan (de facto
single-party rule), South Korea (military oligarchy), Hong Kong
(colonialism), Singapore (president for life), and Taiwan (democra-
tizing single-party rule) all illustrate in their different ways. The
Americans who during 1989 immediately projected onto the students of Tiananmen their own values and political procedures were
just as wrong as those who hailed Deng as a liberal in the 1970s;
they were looking into not a broken but a narcissistic mirror.

My point is that reform of a Soviet-type economy, much like

the attempt to achieve an outward orientation among less developed countries, is not a unilinear process. There are different
ways to do it, each with different tradeoffs. Economic reform
certainly must be accompanied by political reform, but that is an
inadequate way to put it. What is needed is a set, or critical mass,
of reforms together with a clear understanding of what it is that
markets do and cannot do for economic systems. This set of
reforms seems to include, in no particular order, the equitable
distribution of the wealth of an economy, a strong commitment to
education, family planning, a pilot agency to guide the economy,
the private ownership of property, performance tests for the nation's households and enterprises, and a relatively autonomous,
meritocratic state. There is nothing easy about this process, but as
the economic dynamism of the non-Communist Pacific reveals,
there are many possible forms of political economy other than
Marxism-Leninism or Adam Smith's capitalism.

China's particular mix of policies for its economic reform was
uninspired to say the least. It was much closer to Manchu China's
(e.g., sending students abroad and inviting in foreign investors)
than, say, to South Korea's or Taiwan's. Foreign scholars and
leaders of the New China lobby (Nixon, Kissinger, Bush, and
their courtiers) who gushed over Deng Xiaoping — 'Deng's reforms turned the drab, gray, fearful China of the Cultural Revolution into a country of many colors' (Kissinger in the *Los Angeles
Times* on the ironic date of 4 June 1989) — should have known
better or else never should have been entrusted with policy-making
toward China. Deng attempted to bring about economic reform
without political change. He was able to make some progress by
exploiting easy reforms, such as lowering agricultural decision-
making to the household, and by inviting investment from overseas Chinese. But neither he nor his hand-picked managers of
reform, Hu Yaobang and Zhao Ziyang, ever touched the privileges
of the old communist vanguards. The difference between Deng on
the one hand and Hu and Zhao on the other is that the latter came
to realize that the reforms were not going to work. Instead of
duplicating South Korea and Taiwan, China seemed to have taken
as a model Ferdinand Marcos's Philippines. And just as in that
case, 'people power' was starting to gather in the wings.

The proximate cause of the Chinese Communist Party's loss of
legitimacy was the close to runaway inflation of 1987–89. This, in
turn, was caused by the disparities between the vibrant private

economy and the depressed state-planned enterprises. Corrupt manipulation of the price differences between the two sectors by Communist Party officials was the major source of fuel for the inflation. Party officials were able to exploit and thereby subvert economic reform in many ways, including as privileged owners and operators of private enterprises, as go-betweens and deal makers in economic transactions, as preferred borrowers from local and central banks for their pet projects, and by illegally shifting commodities from the planned to the market sector of the economy and pocketing the price difference. According to the Chinese government's own statistics, 70 percent of all reported economic crimes during 1987–88 were committed by officials, including officers and enlisted men of the People's Liberation Army.[1]

Corruption extended all the way to the top political leadership, which came to be known as the 14 Big Families. These are the families of Deng, President Yang Shangkun, Premier Li Peng, the deposed party leader Zhao Ziyang, as well as the heirs and descendants of such entrenched or recently deceased old vanguards as Chen Yun, Peng Zhen, Li Xiannian, Hu Yaobang, Liu Shaoqi, Ye Jianying, and Lo Ruixing. Many of the students who gathered in Tiananmen in spring 1989 came from families of lesser officials or professionals on fixed incomes. The inflation both affected them personally and focused their attention on the families who were not troubled by inflation because they were on the take. Their calls for democracy were not so much for the institutions of the West as they were for Thermidor — to get the entrenched old vanguards off the backs of the people and to hold public officials accountable for their actions.

Ironically enough, the 14 Big Families behaved precisely as Marx, Engels, Lenin, and Djilas had predicted such a possessing and ruling class would act under similar circumstances: in their own interest. Instead of compromising with the students (who of course included teachers, bureaucrats, professionals, journalists, workers, and staffs of research institutes) or heeding any of the recent lessons from similar events in Warsaw, Budapest, Manila, Taipei, or Seoul, Deng and company used the army. In so doing they guaranteed themselves a place in history alongside the likes of Leonid Brezhnev, Milos Jakes, and Erich Honecker. It is still difficult to believe, however, that any of these old Stalinists would

have been as inept in the employment of repression as their
Chinese colleagues. With full international media coverage because
of Gorbachev's visit, Deng at first vacillated, then ordered the
army to use tanks and heavy weapons against the unarmed students, and followed up with Big Lie techniques that were easily
exposed. Thousands of Chinese students in foreign countries, as
well as concerned citizens of Hong Kong, transmitted by fax all
over China reports of the Beijing massacre that had been printed in
the Communist Party's own Hong Kong newspapers. 'Truth from
fax,' as John Fincher has reported, became a pun on Deng's 1977
slogan that Chinese should 'seek truth from facts.'[2]

In the world-wide crisis of communism that developed during
1989, China behaved worse than any other communist nation and
with less excuse. Although ostensibly ruled by professional revolutionaries adept at discerning the laws of historical development and
located at the center of the most dynamic economic region on
earth, China still managed to bungle every opportunity. Not only
did the current leaders provoke the largest insurrection in the
history of the Chinese Communist regime against themselves, but
in the process of putting it down they destroyed the military's
reputation within the country even more thoroughly than it had
been in the bungled 1979 invasion of Vietnam. The reply of the
students of Tiananmen was apt: 'Only power grows from the
barrel of a gun; our cause is democracy.'[3] The next time the
students' cause will not be democracy but anti-communism.

The crisis of communism has also proved to be a crisis of
understanding for the non-Communist world. The U.S. in particular, as the other pole of a disappearing bipolar world, faces what
was and is its most serious set of challenges since the consolidation
of the Soviet empire after World War II. What theoretical under-
pinnings guide the Western world's understanding of recent events
in the Marxist-Leninist nations? Are these nations succumbing to
economic or political failures, or a combination of both? What are
the implications for the international system? Is the danger of war
more acute when old and discredited regimes start to collapse than
when they are strong, and can it be avoided? Will ethnicity and
nationalism replace conflicts that were rooted in ideological dis-
putation? Is it true, as such diverse figures as Francis Fukuyama
and Robert Dahl contend, that 'our' form of government is becoming the universal norm (hence, the 'end of history')? Is not this

establishmentarian celebration of the collapse of communism merely a way of distracting ourselves from the thought that the Cold War is over but Japan has won?

Whatever turns out to be the Western response to the collapse of the Soviet empire as a whole, its response to the Chinese dimension of it has been odious. With the possible exception of France, Western governments, and also Japan, have quickly modulated their criticism of China. Winston Lord, U.S. ambassador to China from 1985 to 1989, could hardly wait for the blood to be scrubbed off Tiananmen before he set out the new line. 'Only a small minority of Americans,' he writes, 'have opposed cooperation [with the communist regime in China] and they now point to recent events as vindication of their views. They have it exactly wrong.' The Deng leadership merely feared 'chaos or at least a slippery slope toward a Chinese "Solidarity" movement,' and we must be careful not to 'isolate the Chinese and rip out all the roots that we have so carefully nurtured.'

Perpetuating the role for China as 'the human-rights exception' that the Carter administration started, Lord also instructs us that 'Whatever our anguish for the Tibetans, the U.S. will need to continue to recognize that Tibet is part of China.'[4] With American spokesmen of this sort, it is not really surprising that Deng Xiaoping told Richard Nixon the U.S. was responsible for the 'counter-revolutionary rebellion' and that it was up to the U.S. to make amends.[5]

One of the oddest things about these developments is that the U.S. pursued precisely the opposite policies toward the Soviet Union throughout the Cold War and ended up with a much more satisfactory outcome. Lord seems to suggest that the U.S. has more in common with a repressive China than with a reforming, disarming Soviet Union.

If Tibet has become a taboo subject to raise, so evidently too is the future of Hong Kong. But if Deng Xiaoping achieved nothing else during 1989, he succeeded in finally politicizing 5.5 million of the most apolitical people on earth. The unctiousness of Margaret Thatcher in urging President Bush not to disarm too fast on the eve of his Malta meeting in December 1989 with Gorbachev was surely not lost on Hong Kong households who depend on her for their defense. Without doubt the reassertion of Communist Party despotism in China will accelerate the emigrant flow from Hong Kong. Barring another reversal of politics on the mainland, Hong

Kong's fate is now sealed. The people of Hong Kong know that in 1997 the place they built will be turned over to Chinese Communist management; consequently they have an insistent incentive to relocate elsewhere. While exposing the hypocrisy of Thatcher's rule, this emigrant flow promises also to enrich those nations far-sighted enough to take advantage of it. If indeed there was never anything the nations of the West in general and Britain in particular could do to protect the people of Hong Kong, as Thatcher's spokesmen are forever saying, then the Beijing massacre at least subverted her efforts to mesmerize the people of Hong Kong and send them quietly to their fate. They now know what awaits them; and many will try to get out, one way or another.

One important element of China's response to the crisis of communism has been to expose U.S. policy in the Pacific as bankrupt. The U.S. government is unwilling to stand up for the Tibetans to the extent that it did for the Afghans; it maintains an army in South Korea poised to defend a nation at least twice as large and infinitely richer than its only opponent; it also continues to defend the world's richest nation, Japan, while simultaneously going deeply into debt to it; and it appears to be more concerned about the security of Australia and New Zealand than the more populous and harder working Taiwan. Such policies grow out of an array of anachronistic treaties and relationships dating from World War II and the Korean War. One contribution of the student martyrs of Tiananmen may have been to make this latent situation manifest to concerned citizens of the U.S. and other countries.

What the West desperately needs is not a continuation or a patching-up of old policies, but a new, fresh look at developments in the communist world and, most particularly, in Asia. This book, with its comprehensive coverage of the Chinese dimension of the communist world, is both an analysis of the errors of the Chinese leadership and an intellectual foundation for viewing the developments to come. It is my honor and pleasure to recommend the following essays to you. They concern the lives, politics, and aspirations of the Chinese people.

---

1. Maria Hsia Chang, 'The Meaning of the Tiananmen Incident,' *Global Affairs*, Fall 1989, pp. 12–35, particularly p. 25.

2. John Fincher, 'Zhao's Fall, China's Loss,' *Foreign Policy*, Fall 1989, pp. 4–5.

3. Richard Nations, 'Who Died and Who Didn't,' *The Spectator*, 29 July 1989, p. 13.

4. Winston Lord, 'China and America: Beyond the Big Chill,' *Foreign Affairs*, 68:4 (Fall 1989): 1–26.

5. *New York Times*, 1 November 1989.

Introduction

GEORGE HICKS

THE Beijing massacre of 4 June 1989 was so outrageous, so barbarous, so offensive to every canon of civilized behavior that this book had to be written. It was written in an attempt to seek relief from the sense of anger, impotence, and frustration caused by the massacre. Lacking any other weapon, we took to our pens — or, more accurately, to our word processors and fax machines.

For years a thread of optimism — even wishful thinking — has run through much of Western writing and thinking about China. Tiananmen snapped that thread, and it became clear that the dissenting minority, those who had doubted the reality and durability of China's supposed reforms, had possessed the clearer vision. Many of those dissenters are among the contributors to the present volume, and the massacre made it vital that their post-Tiananmen thinking should be quickly brought together in a wide-ranging assessment of how matters now stand with China.

The title of this book was inspired by the emperor, Taizong. He reigned from 626–649 and is recorded as having said: 'If one uses a bronze mirror one can know how to adjust one's dress; if one uses a mirror of the past, then one may learn the lessons of the rise and fall of dynasties; if one uses others as a mirror, then one may learn of one's achievements and failures.' The mirror of the past can refer to both China's own history (especially from 1949 onward) and the history of failed repressions in the Eastern bloc. The mirror of others is the mirror the students held up to the Communist Party. By carrying out the massacres in June 1989 the Chinese leadership broke both mirrors and must now live with the consequences. On another level, over the past decade the romantic politicians and investors in the West — as well as the overseas Chinese — have been anxious to see China as a mirror which reflected an image of themselves. That image also was destroyed by the Beijing massacre.

It is tempting to believe that all problems have a solution and that in the long run, things will get better. This deeply rooted idea of the inevitability of continuous progress stands as a barrier to understanding China. Another barrier is the related assumption that as China progresses it will become more like us. The West looks at China and sees not what is but an Oriental mirror image of its own hopes and dreams. From 1979–89, China played unerringly to this Western weakness. The West had high hopes, failing to realize that communist systems are inherently incapable of reform. International experience suggests that the overcoming of economic problems must start with the abolition of the communist system, a necessary but far from sufficient condition for economic progress.

What also emerges from this collection of essays is a broadly shared skepticism about many of the 'achievements' of China's recent past and a deep pessimism about its future. (There are, of course, different shades of light and dark to that pessimism.) Communism in China may be doomed but, as Simon Leys puts it, 'the legacy of such a regime can be even more evil than its rule. . . . The poison might outlast the beast.' The collapse of the present government may be inevitable but after 40 years of economic mismanagement, overpopulation, poverty, and a population 'brutalized by four decades of relentless political terror, worse horrors may follow.'

One common illusion of the reform decade was that China was not only successfully modernizing but that it was also going capitalist, democratic, and pluralist. As Miriam London puts it: 'The new notion that China was "going our way," that Deng's economic reforms would necessarily lead to a democratized political system, reflected Western wishful thinking, not Chinese reality.'

Jan Prybyla shows that China's economic and political reforms were largely illusionary. The internal reform of a communist system has never been achieved, he argues, because 'it would require so many simultaneous changes in institutions, property rights, economic policies, and politics, that communism in any meaningful sense could never survive.'

The Western belief in the inevitability of progress has a mirror image in Chinese political culture. As Lucian Pye writes, this is the irrepressible idea that no matter how grim the past and present, 'The future is bright.' An ability to live on hope and wishful thinking may be a psychological necessity in a society where genuine critical analysis could lead only to despair. Pye points out, the 'Chinese revolution has been going on for 150 years. Yet for most of that time the country was getting nowhere and the ways of thinking of the Chinese people had not greatly changed.'

June 4 shattered many illusions; it broke the mirror the West always held up to itself when it thought it was looking at China. Perhaps it even broke the Chinese illusion that 'The future is bright.' It certainly shattered the illusion that China was becoming capitalist and democratic. Yet such is the power of wishful thinking, of Marco Polo romanticism and misplaced *realpolitik*, that by early 1990 the mirror had been largely pieced together again. William McGurn shows that in the eyes of the U.S. authorities, it had hardly cracked.

Recent developments in Eastern Europe and the Soviet Union will almost certainly encourage change in China, even if the first reaction of the authorities has been to crack down. It has proved possible to turn the clock back to Stalinist repression but this will prove increasingly difficult to sustain in the face of deepening ideological isolation. To the regime's lack of domestic legitimacy must now be added a lack of international legitimacy.

Second, changes in the external environment may encourage change in the perceptions of China. Even an event like the June 4 massacre is not sufficient to permanently change Western perceptions of China. As the Cultural Revolution demonstrated, when the West is determined on a romantic view of China there is no limit to the amount of barbarism and anarchy that can be rationalized. Arthur Koestler showed half a century ago in *Darkness at Noon* that there is no reason to believe that appalling events necessarily lead to a loss of faith in the regime perpetuating them. It is only the combination of revolutionary change in Europe with Tiananmen and its aftermath that makes it possible that the mirror will truly be broken beyond repair.

In *Chinese Shadows*, Simon Leys did more than anyone else to shatter the illusions about life in China during the Cultural Revolution. No sooner had these delusions been cleared away than many experts fell under the sway of the new illusion of reform. Deng's reforms required, as London puts it, 'a quick change of illusions behind the scenes. As China itself debunked the miracles of Maoism — the believing China experts managed to switch one set of illusions for another markedly different set with astonishing ease and with no perceptible damage to their reputations.'

China's inability to live with the modern world is its enduring problem. This was as true in the 1840s as it is today. For the last century China has sought 'Western technology with Chinese essence' but has failed to realize that societies which innovate and generate wealth do so in part because they have rule of law, property rights, civil freedoms, and competitive markets. There are many enlightened Chinese who realize this, for example Fang Lizhi. His essay, published here for the first time, defines China's dilemma. China has had some limited success in adopting the technology of the modern world but clings to outmoded attitudes. True modernization will never come to China without a shift toward the universal values which alone free the creative spirit.

The aim of *The Broken Mirror* is not to describe the events of April–June 1989 — a job already well done by journalists who were on the spot — but to analyze their significance. Each author writes on his own area of expertise. In order to integrate the individual efforts into a coherent whole, each contributor received the first draft of every chapter and was then able to relate to other chapters in subsequent drafts. In this way we tried to approach the unity of a single-authored book while keeping the advantages of speed and breadth of expertise that is only possible with teamwork. The 50 or so drafts we edited in Hong Kong were mostly received via fax and many hundreds of shorter notes were sent back and forth the same way.

Modern communications, as miraculous as they are, are still only a tool. The contributors are everything. Without complaint they wrote draft after draft, to a difficult deadline. Unfortunately, not every contributor was at the other end of a phone or fax. After the massacre, Fang Lizhi wisely sought refuge in the U.S. Embassy in Beijing.

Readers should feel free to read the chapters in any order, although there is a loose logic to the arrangement. Part One covers the major actors in the Tiananmen drama: students, intellectuals (with special attention to Fang and literary maverick Liu Xiaobo), rulers, and the military. A decade of being open to the world had armed Chinese intellectuals with the most dangerous weapon of all: ideas. Jane Macartney shows how the students were driven by outside forces which they only dimly understood. Her revisionist account of the students strips them of their halos but leaves them their humanity.

Part Two gives historical and cultural background to the events of 1989: the heritage of communism, the role of Chinese political culture, the socialist economy, authoritarianism, and ideology. The message is that historically and culturally the students were all but doomed from the start. Tom Gold, for example, shows the close affinity of Leninism with a number of central elements in the Chinese political tradition which together give Chinese communism its staying power. Pye points out that the students were 'following in the footsteps of generation after generation of idealistic, but doomed Chinese youth calling for democracy in a society that has yet to shed its authoritarian traditions.'

Part Three focuses on the outside world's reactions to the events in China. Not surprisingly, the impact was greatest in Hong Kong, where the numbing fear of Chinese sovereignty after 1997 could no longer be disguised. As the ultimate economic animal, it was fatally easy for Hong Kong to look at China's growing consumer culture and say, 'They are becoming just like us.' Hong Kong looked at China and saw itself. June 4 smashed this mirror forever. Andrew Spano describes the death of another illusion: the death of the dream of a better China. Teaching in a rural university, his account of the rise and fall of the democracy movement is typical of what happened throughout China.

Part Four deals with China's reaction to the events of June. Although the crackdown on intellectuals was not on the Cultural Revolution scale, the triumph of the left and the return to Stalinist political and economic orthodoxy had been decisively established by early 1990. The irreversible reforms proved easy to reverse — recentralization of economic power and tight money to kill the private sector — and while the open door was not technically slammed shut, fewer cared to walk through. Human rights deteriorated, damaging China's nascent legal system as well as thousands of lives.

Part Five asks the question: Where is China going? Jürgen Domes and Wojtek Zafanolli argue the inevitable, though perhaps long-term, collapse of the Communist Party. Orville Schell points out the changes of the last decade that make the status quo unlikely to endure. Schell argues that the economic and social changes of the recent past had their counterpart in the internal perceptions of the individual. For a decade, people had developed the habit of independent thinking. 'Individuals were now less ready to betray their friends and themselves. Even the Party's grave threats of intimidation and retributions were insufficient to terrorize ...'

Given these crucial changes in the psychology of the individual, any attempt to reintroduce Maoist brainwashing and browbeating will be resisted. At the very least, sullen sabotage will take a fearful economic toll. As the economy declines, resentment and hostility toward the government will broaden and intensify. In the perspective of history, 4 June 1989 will probably be seen not as the end of the decade of reform and increasing freedom but as the beginning of an age of upheaval. Attempts to reform the unreformable led to heightened expectations among the masses which could never be fulfilled and the total alienation of the educated class. But the Communist Party of China will not be easily overthrown: June 4 is likely to prove only the first salvo in a long battle between ideas and bullets.

Hong Kong
24 March 1990

Prologue: On Patriotism and Global Citizenship

FANG LIZHI

YESTERDAY I attended a meeting of the History of Science Society regarding commemorative ceremonies for the 70th anniversary of the May Fourth movement. Current plans for commemorating May Fourth do not include the theme of science and democracy. Of course the student groups would like to talk about science and democracy, but it seems that they will be forced to use 'patriotism' as a substitute. 'Patriotism' is the slogan one hears most often right now. My name probably won't be allowed on the list of official speakers, but I do have a few things to say about patriotism.

Patriotism is a big problem in this country. Criticize someone for being unpatriotic and it will shut them right up. But in my opinion, and I want to say this very clearly, patriotism should not be our most important precept, our first principle. Let me be a little more specific. 'Patriotism' has a range of implications from the purest of emotions to the dirtiest of politics, so the word itself is not too clearly defined. In part it certainly refers to some very pure feelings that spring out of love for your homeland, your mother, your kith and kin. In this sense 'patriotism' is a fine thing, and we should respect it. But when someone says 'patriotism' these days, it by no means carries such a simple meaning. Particularly when you emphasize the '-ism' part, it comes to mean that what you love is the nation-state.

I remember in my younger days joining in on the criticism of our poor old teachers, who would always defend themselves by saying 'At least I'm patriotic; at least I love my country.' Our standard reply was 'But what country do you love? A communist country? Or a Kuomintang country?' Of course what we were implying was that they really weren't patriotic at all. In this context, patriotism obviously does not mean loving your native place, your rivers, your soil, your cities, your kin; it means loving the state. Such a feeling as this clearly won't serve as our guiding principle. After all, what is the state? According to standard Marxist-Leninist teachings, the state is the instrument of repression! The most important tools of the state are police, the courts, the prisons, and the army. That means if we love our country we must love the police, the courts, the prisons, and the army, right? Clearly a patriotism of this sort is no grand, lofty principle. It is just an emotion that is constantly subject to political exploitation.

As far as I know, the first instance of opposition to this kind of nationalistic patriotism came, at least, during the First World War. Of course there were probably even earlier examples, but this one concerns physics and I'm a physicist after all — back to physics again. Anyway, during the war Germany and England were fighting, but the German and British physics communities continued to cooperate. Many felt that nationalistic patriotism was wrong. At that time Einstein was setting out the General Theory of Relativity, and his theoretical predictions were confirmed by the experimental observations of British scientists (led by Sir Arthur Eddington). This was an outstanding act of cooperation. Why shouldn't the same sentiments hold true in China? Certainly there is no way that patriotism, as in 'loving the instrument of the state,' should be exalted as the first principle of the May Fourth commemoration. That's one point I want to make.

Another point is that even very pure and simple feelings of love for home and hearth have their limits. They can be very narrow and are not some sort of absolute criteria on which we can base our judgment. Of course you should love your country, your mother, your land, and so on. But when you encounter something new, do you automatically assume that it's good because it comes from your homeland, or that it's bad because it does not? This attitude creates some serious problems in China, and we need to rethink it very carefully. Einstein was a good model here, as well. He was a Jew, but he did not feel compelled under every circumstance to speak as a Jew, but just as a human being.

In science, we approach a situation by asking if a thing is correct or incorrect, if it is better or worse than what we have at present, if it represents some kind of progress. These are our criteria. We do not ask if a thing originates with our race or nationality. This is extraordinarily clear in natural science: There is no Jewish physics or German physics. There is only physics that gives good answers and physics that doesn't. Where it comes from is irrelevant. There are no national boundaries in scientific thought, and science does not belong to any one race or nation.

In this regard, I think that many scientists have a perspective that transcends their own particular culture. Local cultures should of course be respected, but not as some immutable principle that must be protected to the bitter end. In China, as well as in the West, there has long been a saying to the effect that 'I love my teacher, but I love the truth more.' You should love and respect your teachers, but their ideas shouldn't displace your own judgment and convictions. You have to love the truth more, you simply have to. Whether something is or isn't Chinese is not the issue. You can't go tip-toeing around for fear of challenging anything that is labeled 'Chinese.' Knowledge is just not like this. This issue is whether a thing is true or false, not whether it's Chinese or not.

It is more difficult in the social realm than in natural science, but I think humanity has been slowly evolving in this area as well. As time goes on we are arriving at more and more universally valid concepts, ones that can be applied everywhere. Certainly science was the first such domain. The laws of natural science apply everywhere. But I personally feel that in the domain of the social sciences, in society, we are also increasingly arriving at universally valid concepts. As in science, these truths are not a function of skin color, religion, nationality, and so forth. They transcend such boundaries.

Human rights are such a concept. Human rights aren't the property of a particular race or nationality. Every human being has from birth the right to live, to think, to speak, to find a mate. These are the most fundamental freedoms a human being has. Every person on the surface of the earth should have these rights, regardless of what country they live in. I think humanity is slowly but surely coming to recognize this. It is actually a fairly recent idea in human history; in Lincoln's time, only a century ago, it was just being recognized that black and white people should have the same rights. But we are now confronting just such an issue in China. The validity of human rights does not depend on the particular culture involved. Cultural biases are fine if you are not asking questions of right and wrong. You can like whatever kind of food you want to, and so can I. This is a question of preference, not truth. Taste can be altogether a function of a particular place. But truth cannot. Truth doesn't distinguish between localities.

Of course, when you start asking detailed questions about democracy, such as whether to have a multi-party system, these are things that differ from place to place. The specific framework of democracy in Britain is a constitutional monarchy, in France a republic, and so forth. These can differ. But they all start with the acknowledgment of human rights, and are built on this foundation. In this sense every place is equal, and China is no exception.

The reason we should oppose 'patriotism' is that it seems to become more narrow-minded and parochial as time goes on, and even the purest of patriotic sentiments is too parochial for the world we now live in. Humanity is faced with a very new kind of reality. A century or two ago, a country could be quite isolated or have little contact with the outside. Relationships based on common interests between nations were rare in those days. But if we look from the vantage point of science, the interests of the whole world have become inseparable. We increasingly face common problems. Energy is one example, the environment another. Environmental issues on a global scale include problems of the oceans, the atmosphere, and outer space. Population is also a whole-earth issue. These are truly collective problems, and no nation can go off by itself and solve them. It simply can't be done. If Asia is turned into a desert, the U.S. will suffer. You can't run away from it, not even all the way across the Pacific Ocean. These are global issues, and they demand to be looked at from a global perspective.

In this regard, I would have to say that I personally have been guilty of something common to many scientists, which is believing that science inevitably leads to progress. In fact, you have to acknowledge that science has actually played a major role in creating many world-wide problems. With the advance of medical science came overpopulation, with the development of technology came energy problems, and so on. But at any rate, how do you deal with such problems? I believe that they require a holistic approach, looking at every aspect, including the scientific and technological. Moreover, they demand that we create a truly global civilization.

Patriotism has little to contribute to solving problems of this nature. It is a sentiment belonging to a different stage in history. To restrict your love and concern only to your own country at this stage is completely misguided, and we have to face up to this. Our activities are now intimately linked with what happens in the rest of the world.

You know, the earth is really very, very small. To those of us who work in astronomy it is clear how small it is. People think that the atmosphere and the oceans are so vast that it doesn't matter if you pollute them, but if humanity continues on this course the earth will not be able to withstand it. Under these circumstances, it is very dangerous not to have mutual, balanced management of the world's affairs. We needed to develop a world culture. The concept of national boundaries needs to be weakened, not strengthened.

So you might speak of what China achieved all by itself a millenium or two ago, but in the next century this won't be possible. If things are going to get better for China, they need to get better for the whole world. There are those who speak of the 21st century as being the 'Chinese century,' but I find this unlikely. At least in terms of us doing everything all by ourselves it is not very likely, because the problems we face today don't only involve China.

Einstein's concept of world citizenship was profound. Of course, many of his ideas were badly received while he was alive. Many critics called his work on unified theory, on which he spent the last 30 years of his life, a dead end. Marxist-Leninists blasted his work as philosophical 'idealism.' He had surprisingly few students. But time has shown the true profundity of Einstein's scientific thought. His ideas about world citizenship were also severely criticized at the time; they were called 'cosmopolitanism.' But in the years ahead, the human race will have to come to grips with this idea as well. It is in this vein that I say that patriotism is not of primary importance. I would even call it narrow-minded.

Translated by James H. Williams from a videotape of Fang's speech, made in Beijing 25 February 1989 and transcribed by G.K. Sun.

PART ONE
ACTORS

The Students: Heroes, Pawns, or Power-Brokers?

JANE MACARTNEY

With the current economic problems social unrest is inevitable in China next year, and I expect that at least one leader will fall — probably Zhao Ziyang. But you can't look to the students to do anything, they are too immature.

Wang Juntao, editor, Economic Studies Weekly, *November 1988.*[1]

WANG Juntao, 32, a prominent activist in his student days at Beijing University in the early 1980s, paid great attention to each new campus generation. He was watching to see whether they would pick up the banner of struggle he had raised first in Tiananmen Square in 1976 to mourn the death of Premier Chou Enlai and later in China's first and only university elections in 1981. His disappointment with this student generation was echoed by someone with even closer contacts with the capital's educated youth. Li Shuxian, an associate professor of physics at Beijing University, a school representative to the local branch of the National People's Congress and wife of astrophysicist Fang Lizhi, told me in April 1989 that she saw few signs of political awareness among the current student batch. Their interests focused on playing mahjong and winning a place at a U.S. university, she said. Attendance was poor at the informal 'lawn salon' where several prominent intellectuals were invited to speak on democracy and their political ideas — only a couple of hundred (sometimes a few dozen) in a university of several thousand.

Why were Wang and Li so disillusioned with the students? Who were these young people, what were their aspirations, and what were the motivations that pushed them to confront the might of the Communist Party and its honed apparatus for repression? This article seeks to analyze some of the forces, both conscious and subconscious, abstract and concrete, that prompted the courageous and tragic student demonstrations of April and May

1989. It will focus on some of the students' weaknesses, which diverted vital energies from the movement. It will reflect on the students as human beings with feet of clay and how they differed from the figures of mythology that they have become since the bloodbath of June 4. It will examine the importance of the students' adolescent cult of the hero, which helped contribute to a mounting aura of antagonism and aggression in their peaceful movement, and which was exacerbated by the lack of a clearly thought out ideology beyond the lofty slogans of their banners. And how their failure to remedy the imprecision and formlessness of their ideas left them vulnerable to exploitation and manipulation by various competing political factions, turning them finally into pawns in a greater game that they had set in motion.

The cult of the hero

For many Chinese students, entry to a university, particularly in Beijing, was the culmination of a lifetime of study and sacrifice. Many came from small provincial schools to the most prestigious institutions of higher learning in China. For others, those with powerful, well-connected parents or access to good secondary schools in the capital, a degree from a university in Beijing was easier to attain. All of them had survived an education system that required a great deal of learning by rote but very little emphasis on creative thinking. Little had changed in the form of the education system from imperial times when students learned the classics by heart and regurgitated their learning in examinations set to test the ability of scholars to master those books, not to test their skill in analyzing those texts. Marxism-Leninism-Mao Tse-tung thought had replaced some of the classics in the communist curriculum, but students were not encouraged to exercise independent thought.

That few showed any great interest in the 'lawn salon' — or 'democracy salon' as it was dubbed later — was thus scarcely surprising. With the sudden end to years of pressure from parents, teachers, and peers to enter university, many reacted by having a good time. Drinking parties were common. Dancing gave students an opportunity to meet members of the opposite sex in an atmosphere of freedom from social constrictions they had never before encountered. They had time on their hands to gamble and play cards. Some read. And those who did had access to books that had been unavailable even a few years before. Translations of Milan

Kundera, Max Weber, and Karl Popper lined library shelves. Young professors and research students were delighted to discuss their ideas with anyone who showed an interest.

Few did. After their dance parties or drinking bouts, students returned to squalid and overcrowded dormitories. Most lived six or eight to a room, sleeping in bunkbeds with a line of tables down the middle that served as desks. Their washing dangled in unlit corridors lined with little mounds of rubbish — crumpled paper, biscuit packets, spittle, and rice. An odor of urine drifted from the lavatories and students washed in cold water, leaning over communal, gray concrete sinks. Meals were an unappetizing combination of rice, fried vegetables, and fish or fatty meat. Discomforts pervaded almost every aspect of university life, providing an incentive for students to seek improved conditions in life after graduation and leaving little time for contemplation of ideals.

They expected those improved conditions to come from the economic reforms launched by Deng Xiaoping. Their government hailed the 10-year-old reform and open-door policies as the route to national modernization. This commitment to material modernization seemed to be the only ideology the government could offer to replace increasingly outdated Marxist tenets. Students began to nurture ambitious expectations of a future that China's economy was not yet equipped to provide. They were the nation's elite. Hadn't they won places at China's most famed universities? They felt that this entitled them to a better life. Most wanted material benefits — good jobs, travel abroad, the privileges of Communist Party membership. Asked about their ideals, most were hard pressed for an answer. 'Freedom, democracy,' students said during demonstrations in the winter of 1986–87. Pressed to elaborate, they complained of official corruption and high-level nepotism, poor food and uncomfortable dormitories. Were they talking about universal equality of opportunity or were they merely envious of those who held higher-paying jobs?

That China's tiny educated class appeared more interested in their material well-being than in moral absolutes or political rights was the outcome of 40 years of communist rule and decades of civil war before that. The student was not China's renaissance man. He had emerged from a poverty-stricken society where intellectual prowess was frequently condemned by the Party propaganda machine. Mao Tse-tung had an ambivalent attitude toward them, intermittently cultivating them and calling them the 'stinking ninth category.' But under his rule the ancient Confucian tradition of the scholar as the aristocrat of society had been eroded. With a string of political campaigns and disastrous economic policies, Mao sought to make all Chinese into peasants, whether they worked in fields, factories, government offices, or universities. The students who marched through the streets of Beijing in 1989 were the inheritors of that Maoist tradition — a tradition that had imbued them with a will to escape material poverty while failing to inculcate respect for human rights or to eliminate the Confucian veneration for an educated elite and class divisions.

The average Chinese student at 20 is inexperienced and protected compared to his Western counterpart. He has lived all his life at home. He has read little, he has had access to few Western translations. Domestic publications scarcely touch upon Western political ideas, Marxism being the exception. Few bother to read the newspapers since these are almost never conduits for information but organs of government propaganda. Most find it politically safer, and more entertaining, to browse through translations of Jackie Collins and other Western bestsellers available from street book stalls. The viewing of soft pornographic videos is the main measure of street 'cred' among male students. News restrictions and the barriers of distance have prevented them from gaining a real understanding of the workings of Western democracies.

By early 1989, dissatisfaction was becoming widespread. Intellectuals and students were unhappy with their lot, feeling they were the class that had benefited least from the reforms. Even the official media had begun to discuss a hot topic among students — that doctors and university graduates earned less than cab drivers and hairdressers, and that everyone earned less than private entrepreneurs. Wang Juntao was a man who kept a finger on the pulse of these student sentiments. He was no less surprised than the Beijing residents, the government, and the students themselves at the dimensions the student movement later attained.

Wang had probably underestimated the extent to which China's students were fertile ground for the ideas of Fang Lizhi. While Fang himself, China's boldest advocate of democracy, had maintained a distance from the students for many months, his writings and his ideas were easily accessible. After the government cracked down on the 1986–87 protests, students were required to read and criticize a collection of speeches by Fang distributed by the propaganda organs. The move backfired. Instead of attacking Fang's ideas, the students were spellbound. Never before had they been allowed — let alone ordered — to study such subversive ideas in political study classes. They loved it. The authorities soon realized their error, but the seed had been planted. For students throughout China, Fang became a hero. They saw him as a man who had dared to criticize authority and who had been vilified and purged for his pains. He was the rebel they all wished to be. He had cocked a snook at the government. His ideas and his example gradually carved out a niche in the minds of students.

Fang is the clearest example of a theme underlying the student movement: the cult of the hero. The hero was important to the students because they needed someone to look up to but also they each wanted a share of the limelight, the glory of action. They revered Fang and other intellectuals like him who had suffered at the hands of the government. Those heroes gradually became a powerful motivating force for the students, their defiance in the face of a repressive regime supplying a crucial momentum to the protests and contributing to the bloody denouement.

In the winter of 1986, students in central Hefei, at the university where Fang was vice principal, and in Shanghai raised the slogans of freedom and democracy, corruption and nepotism. But their discussions centered on better food and better job assignments. They wanted to make the government aware of their dissatisfaction, and having achieved that they returned to campus. In the capital, students felt left out, particularly at Beijing University. Students there felt they had betrayed the university's heroic tradition as the center of Chinese campus unrest, a tradition established nearly a century before. That blow to collective pride prompted them to stage a defiant demonstration on New Year's Day as temperatures plunged below zero and snow blanketed the city. They marched through the freezing night to demand the release of some comrades detained earlier in the day. When the hard-line *Beijing Daily* blasted their movement, they lit a bonfire and burned the edition as a gesture of their self-righteousness.

Similarly, a cult of the hero was at work in 1989. The death of Hu Yaobang was hailed as the death of a hero, a man who had apparently confronted the might of senior leader Deng Xiaoping in his desire to open China and boost education and who was purged for it. For the students this was an opportunity to express their dissatisfactions in the guise of mourning. 'This is not just for Hu

Yaobang,' Fang told reporters. 'This is a chance for students to let the government know they are unhappy with the present situation.' It was also a chance for students to prove their mettle. As the protests took off from their tiny beginnings, rivalry soon became apparent. Universities vied for the honor of leading a demonstration. Such was the intensity of competition that some schools followed separate routes toward the city center to avoid giving up the lead of the march to another college. There were even battles among individuals over who should have the honor of carrying the scarlet flag that headed each march. Late, on Tiananmen Square, rival broadcast stations were set up. In a cacophony of competing sounds, the propaganda of Qinghua University vied with statements from the Beijing University loudspeakers. On the rim of the Square, the workers installed a third loudspeaker system.

Their sense of heroism was further stimulated by the knowledge that their action was one of great bravery and bold defiance in the face of a regime that threatened them with an armed police force, with savage punishment, and with an army. Each wanted the opportunity to be a part of the challenge to authority, and to authoritarianism. The hunger strike was one of the clearest manifestations of the cult of the hero. After a shaky start, students flocked to join, swelling the numbers from 300 to more than 3,000. The strike was intended to force the government's hand, to elicit some response, any response, from a leadership that seemed determined to ignore them. Underlying the dramatic action was an excitement that each was taking part in a life or death scenario.

The emergence of identifiable heroes of their own generation also added to the sense of purpose, and drama, of the main body of students. Leaders emerged in the movement, further enhancing their sense of their own glory. One of the most charismatic was a 21-year-old Uighur from Beijing Teachers' University, Wuerkaixi. Another leader was Wang Dan, 24, a Beijing University history student and courageous founder of the 'lawn salon.' The thin, bespectacled youth whose long hair flapped across his face lacked the charm of Wuerkaixi, but more than made up for it with a clearly defined sense of purpose backed by a versatile mind that early on had grasped the significance of the movement. The two, representatives of rival universities, were soon locked in a battle for power as bitter and complex as any inner Party struggle. The power struggles, a signal of ambitions to be recognized as hero of the moment, marred the movement. Undignified bickering broke out as attempts to hold open elections for new student leaders at university playing grounds dissolved into bitter squabbling. Early leaders were ousted amid accusations they were government stooges. The factionalism was not limited to the capital. In Shanghai's Fudan University, for example, four student bodies competed for the top position throughout the demonstrations.

In Beijing, those students who failed to win a place on the leadership or among the potential martyrs, turned out to support the fasters. Encamped on the Square, each felt he was playing his own part on the stage of history. Each school occupied an allotted space, fanning out from the hunger strikers at the center. Visitors were regarded as intruders and turned away with peremptory commands as each student asserted his own role in the movement. Foreign reporters were required to produce some proof of identity, and often that was insufficient to persuade officious teenage sentries to allow the visitors to pass. On several occasions I visited the Square with journalists from the *World Economic Herald*, an outspoken Shanghai newspaper fiercely attacked by the authorities. Our reception upon sight of the *Herald* I.D. card was immediate and reverential. Here, then, were other heroes who had taken on the authorities, people acceptable as their equals in the heroic movement, was the student response. We passed through without difficulty, reaching the spot where the hunger strikers sweltered in the blistering sun, ignored by the government they sought to meet and supported by tens of thousands of anxious Beijing citizens marching on the fringe of that magic inner circle.

At its epicenter, the cult of the hero attained a feverish pitch. The wail of ambulance sirens filled the air as fainting students were snatched away for treatment. Organizers shouted commands, huddled to discuss strategy, and mounted guard over the broadcasting station and key meeting places of the leadership. Access to the inner sanctums was granted only to the Western and Hong Kong press — and even they were required to show makeshift passes scribbled out and stamped by the student leadership.

Although the foreign press was undoubtedly seen as a weapon in their bid to bring pressure on the authorities, it also added to the students' own sense of the heroic proportions of their movement. Wang Dan visited Hong Kong reporters almost daily at the start of the demonstrations to feel out their attitude to the students, to find out whether the outside world was interested in the movement. 'If we stage a demonstration, do you think it will be reported in the foreign press?' he asked *Asiaweek* reporter Kitty Poon in mid-April. On occasion, the students almost played up to the television cameras in their yearning for publicity. They held numerous press conferences on the Square, often with little to say at meetings that disintegrated in argument and disarray among the organizers.

The yearning for heroism extended to the ultimate sacrifice, an almost hysterical desire for blood. Students tied white bands around their heads in a gesture reminiscent of the headbands worn at traditional funerals. Their desperation was compounded by their failure to elicit a response from the government. There was a passion for blood. Before the April 27 march, many students wrote their wills. Intellectuals and students later wrote appeals in blood and the city was patrolled by a daredevil team of motor-cyclists, the 'flying tigers.' Students and workers each set up their own 'dare-to-die' squads ready to take on the army should it move to enter the city. Students lay down in front of tanks and trucks the night before Premier Li Peng declared martial law. Death was in the air.

In the tradition of earlier communist martyrs, the students were almost eager to attain the glory of death. During the hunger strike, 12 students launched a separate fast, denying themselves liquids as well as food. In their gamble with death, they lay in front of the Great Hall of the People, just off Changan Avenne, Beijing's main thoroughfare, in a space guarded by brusque sentries who refused to allow anyone to approach. Pots of pink plastic flowers and dramatic paintings of tormented figures surrounded the sacrificial altar on which they lay. Huge popular demonstrations poured respectfully around them, peering at the prone bodies like Buddhist monks completing a circumambulation around a sacred shrine.

At times the scene took on an air of fanaticism that was whipped up by some of the student leaders themselves. Chai Ling, 23, the only woman prominent in the movement, was the moving force behind a threat by a group of a dozen students to set themselves on fire outside the Zhongnanhai government compound. It was the ultimate sacrifice, fame and glory in death. Her voice rang out almost every day through the students' makeshift broadcasting system. Vibrant with emotion, she harangued the crowds, encouraged them, spread news of political and military developments, and announced new student action.

Despite the growing sense of desperation that excited their suicidal passions, few believed the day of reckoning would come. Countless students and citizens raised the same question in late May. 'You don't think the army will really try to enter the city?' each of them asked. They nurtured a fundamental incredulity that the leadership would turn the army's guns against their people. How would they dare to use force against a movement whose patriotism had already been acknowledged by the 'masses?' But the students also yearned for a grand finale to their movement. Many felt that the entry of the army would give their protest the recognition they believed was their due. Only thus could they perish as martyrs for their cause. 'Both the students and the citizens have failed to develop a sense of their rights. They need a more violent provocation,' Wuerkaixi told reporters on May 29.[3]

So pervasive was the sense of heroics that it seemed at times to override the ideas behind the movement. Why did this emotive stimulus play so important a role? Did the protest lack proper ideas to feed its internal energy?

What did the students want?

What did the students want? Their demands, their slogans, were nebulous and amorphous, a banner of discontent easily recognizable to the man in the street and broad enough to allow him to affix to it his individual grievances. The earliest slogans to appear in the first outpouring of outrage at the death of Hu Yaobang would remain the basis for the movement throughout the ensuing weeks. 'Long live freedom, long live democracy. Down with corruption, down with bureaucracy.' As Lucian Pye points out in this book, the students' slogans provided the acceptable public face for much more mundane and pragmatic complaints that could not be openly expressed without exposing them to the charge of selfishness.

The students made little attempt to debate or analyze the ideas contained in the slogans with which they confronted the government. Apart from more mature activists such as Wang Dan or drama school graduate Ma Shaofang,[4] few explored these complex issues. In fact, many of the slogans and watchwords of the movement came to the students via stage managers hovering on the edge of the set.

In their pleas for democracy the students were not referring to democracy as it is understood in the West. Asked to outline their understanding of the concept, the most commonly heard explanations from students were: 'Freedom of the press,' 'Freedom of expression.' They believed these relaxations were not incompatible with the Communist Party system. In effect, their demand to be heard was an appeal to the government to live up to its promises, as part of the reforms, to improve and expand democratic centralism. 'Aren't we with it?' students would ask rhetorically. 'Our movement is unique in the world,' many said. There seemed to be a sense the movement was unlike any other, partly because it was happening in China. The students wanted democracy with Chinese characteristics. A few mentioned 'supervision of the government.' Most seemed to feel that the right to demonstrate and to meet with the government on terms of equality were the basic criteria. Democracy was a buzzword; accountability was what they meant.

One sign of the paucity of ideas was manifest in the erection of the Goddess of Democracy statue on May 30. Reminiscent of the American Statue of Liberty in its pose and slightly Western features, the statue's appearance on the Square came as a final insolent gesture. The statue's designers insisted it was based on a Chinese peasant, but the similarities to the Statue of Liberty were striking, and the reaction of many Beijing residents ambivalent. 'This is very foolish,' said one middle-aged intellectual who had been a fervent if sometimes skeptical supporter of the movement. 'This is like placing a piece of America in the center of China. It is too provocative.' Some Beijing residents were enthused. Others were puzzled and disappointed, remarking on the alien American influences etched on the plaster and foam figure.

Throughout the movement ran the theme of government recognition. They were demanding the impossible — that the Communist Party grant legality to their independent, unwieldy, volatile, and formless body. The students' demand was not necessarily intended as a challenge to the Party, although that was the reaction of the leadership. In fact, it was their respect for and reliance on the Party that prompted them to ask it for legitimacy. That legitimation — while impossible for the leadership to grant because of such factors as preserving face and not setting a precedent — was basically everything the students wanted. 'Our purpose was to make the government listen to us and talk to us,' Wuerkaixi said after his escape. 'That was our only real demand.'⁵

Freedom of the press meant to them freedom for the press to report on their movement and their demands. They were not demanding an abstract moral absolute. They did not envisage a press that was free to report on such controversial subjects as human-rights abuses or coverage of China's secretive government processes. Rather than challenging the Party for the leadership, the students were adopting the traditional role of the scholar-official in China, making respectful representations to the emperor, ready to sacrifice their lives in an effort to help him see the error of his ways.

Neither did the students have a real sense of building a mass movement. They were thrilled by the participation of the people of Beijing, but also accepted it as their right. They were challenging the government to compromise, to give something to them, but always in return they offered to go back to class and abandon their movement. They did not show a great interest in mobilizing the ordinary man in the street into their protest; he was expected to show support but not to participate. They seemed to be playing a game of ultimata with the government — if you give us what we want, we'll do what you want. Such an approach did not signify demand for structural change to the entrenched communist system. Nor did it reveal recognition of the significance of the huge popular protests of support — which they viewed as peripheral to their action — or an effort to encompass popular demands. Lucian Pye notes that the students would have been content to abandon their protest if the authorities had made the right symbolic gestures.

Within the system one of the students' most fundamental grievances was triggered by a particular government policy. As part of the reforms, the government had decided to end its system of automatic job allocation for university graduates. By 1993 students would be expected to fend for themselves in an open job market.⁶ After smashing the iron rice bowl of a guaranteed lifetime job for workers, the government felt it was time to instill the same freedom — and sense of competition — among the educated elite. Some students welcomed the change. Many, chiefly those in liberal arts departments, were terrified. Students had fiercely criticized the old system, saying that they risked being arbitrarily assigned to remote provinces or unpopular jobs. But they soon realized that the new job freedom brought a new set of problems. All their lives they had expected that the reward for academic achievement would be a solid job in a government ministry, Party organ, or state factory. While not always well paid, they knew that as Party functionaries they would be granted good housing, and possibly even a car, driver, and access to special shops, as well as a place in the hierarchy of power.[7]

The new policy shattered all those expectations. In previous demonstrations, the threat of poor job assignments had generally sent students back to class within days. This time things were different. Students' hopes of a crack at climbing the ladder of political success were dashed by the knowledge that they would have to compete for jobs. As recently as late 1988 in Canton, a city where the impact of market-oriented reform was felt far more profoundly than in the capital, students flocked to join the Party in a bid to guarantee future political success.[8] They were fundamentally not opposed to the system — they wanted a role in the Communist Party. Now it appeared that they were to be denied even this.

Not only were they now living in a system where the risk of competition had been introduced, it was frequently unfair competition. Unlike in the West, where academic achievement or a good interview could clinch employment, in China, good contacts were the prime criterion for finding a job in the Party organ or profitable business venture. The children of high officials, the *gaoganzidi*, started off at an advantage. In addition to their access to a network of connections through their parents, they also possessed the bargaining power of that influence itself. Ability ceased to matter. The key was *guanxi*, or relations.

While this policy affected students nationwide, students in Beijing were subject to an additional disadvantage: They would now have much more difficulty remaining in the capital. Many students at China's most prestigious schools did not hail from Beijing, but from the provinces. In the previous system of job allocation, these students stood a good chance of being assigned a job in the capital and subsequently might even be given a much-coveted Beijing household registration that would guarantee a home in the city, the most cosmopolitan in China. Now, with no household registration to enable them to remain, they would have to go back to their provincial homes to look for work. Most children of Beijing-based parents did not attend the huge, central universities in the city but went to smaller municipal schools, such as the Beijing industrial university, schools that, significantly, played a minor role in the protests.

It must have seemed to many students that they had been rejected by the establishment they once sought to join. What choice did they have but to challenge that establishment and voice their unhappiness? There were very personal reasons why the cries of 'Down with corruption' dominated the movement. The students were starting to feel themselves the victims of abuse of power, a sense of injustice that was easily identified with by people throughout the country and in all levels of society and the Party. Crowds of Beijing residents jostled to read student posters listing the abuse of position by various named *gaoganzidi*. It was a rallying cry that won the hearts of the ordinary people who suffered similar inequalities in their daily lives and who knew the difficulties of getting anything done without greasing the palms of a few officials.

The students felt they had been left out. The solid political career that they believed entry to a university guaranteed them had been snatched away. They were angry and frightened of a future that seemed suddenly shrouded in mist. The establishment had rejected them. They had not rejected the establishment. Rather they simply wanted a dialogue with it. Thus the repeated cry for the government to recognize their movement.

What issues did they want to raise with their leaders? The students set up a special team to represent them in talks. And, working in conjunction with a group of young and middle-aged intellectuals, they had drawn up a list of topics for discussion. The three main issues were to be 1) the impact and nature of the student movement, 2) ways to strengthen reform and 3) article 35 of the Constitution, which guaranteed freedom of expression, publication, association, and the right to demonstrate.[9]

Most of the students believed that despite the legitimacy of their cause, it was unlikely the government would meet them. Thus details of grievances to be raised seemed something of a moot point. They were not demanding detailed fundamental change in their system of government. Foremost was a change of personnel — an end to the lengthy rule of Deng Xiaoping, who was then 84 and whose policies were becoming unpopular.

They were not challenging the right of the Party to rule; rather they were expressing their dissatisfaction with some of its methods. The visit of Soviet leader Mikhail Gorbachev in mid-May provided the students with an opportunity to focus on the political aspect of their demands, and also, tellingly, revealed the limits of those requests. 'We need *perestroika*, too,' read banners held out to greet the Soviet visitor. 'Welcome the initiator of *glasnost*,' read one written in Russian. 'Democracy our common ideal,' ran another. The students wanted Soviet-style 'democracy.' A cry for *glasnost* was a heartfelt cry for more freedom. It was not a call for democracy.

Democracy has become the banner of the tragic student movement. But how important was the idea of democracy for the students? How democratic were the students themselves as they paraded through Beijing, chanting their idealistic slogans? 'In the struggle for a large democracy we can sacrifice a few smaller aspects of democracy,' said Wuerkaixi, asked in late May whether the student movement reflected democratic processes in its own organization.[10] The accuracy of Wuerkaixi's words was evident from a glance at the movement. That they were not trying to challenge the Party but saw themselves as inheritors of the mantle of communist rule was evidenced from their approach to their organization. Their first attempt at free elections for the leadership was abandoned as factions coalesced around individuals and groups.

After that there was little effort to foster participation by the main student body. The leaders took control, seemingly assuming that their emergence in the front line, whether by popular demand or by personal ability and ambition, was enough.

They organized the movement as a microcosm of the Communist Party, or a mini-Communist Youth League. They set up a Propaganda Department, an Organization Department — names and forms borrowed from their Big Brother. It was to be expected that young people, scarcely out of their teens and with scant exposure to any other system beyond the communist structure, should have difficulty conceiving of or executing any other system. But they lacked the creativity even to invent new names for the bodies they formed and copied the methods and practices of the Party hierarchy. Bodyguards protected the leaders from being mobbed by admiring students and autograph hunters, imitating the distance the Politburo kept from the people. While demanding press freedom, the students forbade unauthorized personnel from approaching their broadcasting station and refused to allow a fledgling workers' association to use their equipment. They insisted on maintaining unity, or *tuanjie*,[11] one of the buzzwords of their Marxist rulers. And to ensure that unity, they found that purges were sometimes necessary when independent-minded leaders strayed from the accepted student line or attempted to adopt an unauthorized decision. Almost all the most prominent leaders were purged at least once during the movement. Most fell as a result of internal battles and not by popular demand.

The vital, and eventually tragic decision on whether to withdraw from the Square was not put to a vote. Although Wuerkaixi did say: 'As long as even one student does not want to leave the Square then the leadership must obey,' at the same time Chai Ling seemed to have taken an executive decision that blood would have to flow. 'Only when the Square is washed in our blood will people of the whole country wake up,' she told a U.S. interviewer. She declined to warn the students. 'How can I say such things? The students are so young. I feel responsibility for them. And I feel that I too must continue to fight for the revolution.' On the night of June 3–4, with knowledge of shooting in the west of the city, she made scant attempt to persuade the students to abandon the Square and avoid that bloodshed. In those final hours of darkness on Tiananmen, with soldiers toting sub-machine guns gathering in the night around them, the students took a decision that showed their greatest respect for one another. With all lights in the Square extinguished, they took a voice vote and the majority shouted for retreat. It was the sole vote of that Beijing Spring.

The 'black hands'

Why did the students stay so long on the Square in May and June? It was not just that each harbored a subconscious desire to bask for at least 15 minutes in the glory and excitement of their stupendous, moving, popular demonstrations of a size unprecedented in China. There are other forces at work outside the students and the Square.

From numerous and lengthy interviews in Beijing, it slowly emerged that the student protests triggered by the death of Hu Yaobang were not entirely spontaneous. At Beijing University, two young lecturers were the first to raise banners and big-character posters on the day that Hu died. They provided the spark and took the first step while students, younger, naive, and with less political savvy, jumped in once they had been shown the way. That process was duplicated at the Beijing University of Political Science and Law, the first school to take to the streets. They were led by another young academic who, after stirring the students into action, then took a back seat, preferring to work as a member of a group of intellectuals behind the scenes. As the students marched, and in marching discovered the inadequacy of their ideas and their lack of experience, academics and graduate students in their universities offered guidelines on slogans and organization. Older intellectuals waited on the sidelines, sending out signals to the students that they would be willing to help if asked.

The government later lambasted the 'black hands,' Chinese jargon for behind-the-scenes conspirators, accusing them of orchestrating and using the movement, turning it into counter-revolutionary rebellion. And while for the students their protest was purely peaceful and not aimed at the overthrow of the government — with the exception of Li Peng as the perceived instigator of martial law — there were others involved who had a greater understanding of the threat to the Party contained in the movement and a knowledge of how to exercise it.

In an interview later with a British magazine, escaped student leader Shen Tong said: 'I'd instigated a sort of permanent committee where I was the only student. The others were 30 of the greatest intellectuals in China.'[12] Shen's remark reflects the reverence of students for academics, people like Fang Lizhi, renowned for their scholastic achievements, survivors of a string of Maoist purges against the educated middle classes, and more experienced in the machinations of Chinese political life. Although Fang himself was not a part of this group, it did contain people with equally iconoclastic ideas. Shen's remark also hints at their vulnerability to manipulation by respected elders.

For many students, the encouragement of a group like that came as a great honor and appeared to be proof that their movement was proceeding along the right lines. Yan Jiaqi was the former head of the the Political Science Institute at China's most prestigious think tank, the Chinese Academy of Social Sciences. Like many others, he was an establishment academic rejected by the system he had hoped to improve. Yuan Zhiming was one of the group who produced 'The River Dies Young,' the most controversial and influential television documentary China had seen.

Wang Juntao, jailed for his part in the 1976 Tiananmen outburst of dissent, was a hardened political activist, veteran of the 1979 Beijing Democracy Wall movement and editor of the *Economic Studies Weekly* newspaper. Dai Qing, a well-known reporter and author, did not participate in the group of the most active intellectuals, but was always willing to talk to students who sought her out. There were many more. They were a diverse group, each with different ideas and conflicting plans of what they wanted to achieve and how to do it.

'Together we worked for 15 days on a projection of the future society,' said Shen Tong. 'We had faculty researchers looking out for documents, figures, statistics we needed. It was breathtaking. The demands themselves were not important: The idea was to sit down face to face with the leadership and to show that a new generation was taking hold and thinking differently about China.'

This was what the government most feared: a group of mature, ambitious, and long-repressed intellectuals making use of the energy generated by the huge student movement that showed signs of turning into a popular demonstration. The government's assessment of the so-called black hands was accurate in their terms. Some of the intellectuals were politically ambitious veterans of several political movements who had been awaiting just such an opportunity to impress their own ideas on China. But even someone as well-informed as Shen Tong probably did not realize the full extent of the intellectuals' involvement.

One private organization in the capital in particular was deeply implicated, the Beijing Social, Economic, and Technological Research Institute. This unique body, China's first private think tank, was founded in 1985 by a band of prominent activists from the 1976 Tiananmen incident and run by Chen Ziming. An old friend of Wang Juntao from 1976 and one of the most prominent men of the incident, Chen was building a small private empire. He established lucrative business correspondence schools to finance his think tank, bought a newspaper, the *Economic Studies Weekly*, and engaged in diverse research projects. He carried out opinion polls and market research investigations on commission from government and foreign groups. The Institute was wealthy, well-connected (Chen and his associates had close ties to *gaoganzidi* and high-level Party officials), and ambitious. The academics who prompted the protests at Beijing University and the law school had ties with it. The body moved swiftly to back the students, provid-

ing financing and advice on strategy and slogans from the movement's April inception.[13]

The students probably had little hint of what opinions their
advisers held of them. 'The students are a front for us,' Wang
Juntao told me on May 31. 'We need them because the government may meet with them, never with us, but we have to teach
them what to say.' Wang was not representative of most of the
intellectuals at those meetings. He described himself as a professional revolutionary, someone willing to push the government into
action and into change — and who held a great deal of respect for
Deng Xiaoping, his methods and his achievements. Unlike the
students who banished the workers' association and their tent to
the very corner of the Square, Wang was seeking wider grassroots
participation — one of his old comrades-in-arms was a leader of
the labor group. Wang knew that the intellectuals, divided by their
traditional academic rivalries, lacked the ability to unite. He
looked to the workers and the students to provide the flesh and
bones of protest while he and his colleagues acted as the nerve
center.

Wang was unusual in that he had devoted his entire life since he
was a teenager to political activism. He had a clear understanding
of the eventual communist response to defiant challenge. He knew
that his opponents inside Zhongnanhai were equally well informed
about his own actions. (He was constantly tailed and the State
Security Bureau, China's KGB, requested the telephone exchange
operating his personal beeper to report all names and numbers of
callers.) In early 1988, Zhao Ziyang had ordered the drafting of an
emergency powers law that anticipated the force that would be
required to repress social unrest he foresaw as an inevitable consequence of unpopular aspects of his economic reform program.
Minister of Public Security Wang Fang had issued a secret report
later that year identifying the 10 major threats to communist rule.
He included Fang Lizhi, the authors of 'The River Dies Young,'
and Wang Juntao and Chen Ziming as three separate wells of
potential revolt. The students almost certainly had little understanding that when they invited the intellectuals to become their
advisers, they risked turning themselves into ventriloquists'
dummies.

By the final days, the student demonstrations had taken on a
life of their own and almost gone beyond the reach of anyone to
control. The intellectuals still made an effort to direct those ener-

gies. The final hunger strike staged by Liu Xiaobo and three of his friends on June 2 was intended as the start of a hunger strike relay. 'I have been selected to be one of the next group of hunger strikers,' philosophy researcher Gan Yang told me as the first four began their fast. 'We have a list of dozens of volunteers from among the intellectuals. We are even having to turn people away,' Wang Juntao said to me that afternoon. 'Since we can't persuade the students to leave the Square, we have decided to adopt this means to stimulate the protests further.' Wang was keeping in close contact with the students, even living with the young leaders in hotels and holding daily meetings.[14] The most active intellectuals, such as Wang and a young law academic, were equipped with beepers to allow them to keep in touch. (A beeper was a substantial piece of equipment in China, costing 3,000 yuan, nearly US$700, and came courtesy of their private institute.) They were also in contact with student leaders on the monument and kept tabs on developments on the Square through walkie-talkies.

The intellectuals who met daily with the students in the last days of the movement were not the only group that sought to turn the young protesters into pawns. Another faction included members of Zhao's youthful think tanks. Especially active was the Economic Reform Research Institute led by Chen Yizi — later one of China's seven most-wanted intellectuals. (He escaped to Paris.) The students believed that they had won the sympathies of Party insiders. To some extent they had; the massive popular demonstrations had drawn many Party members. But what these Party officials — particularly Zhao's right-hand man and head of the Political Reform Institute, Bao Tong — hoped to win was student sympathy for the beleaguered Party chief that would persuade the students to leave the Square. Like Zhao, they saw that a bloody end to the protests would set back the reforms to which they had devoted their careers, and frighten away foreign investors. As it became apparent that their mentor was fighting for his political life, these up-and-coming young Party cadres entered the fray. Many were disillusioned with Zhao and his approach to reform, but they knew that their political lives were entwined with his. They leaked information of high-level meetings to the Square and provided the students with copies of internal speeches and documents showing Zhao besieged by enemies.

Another who tried to influence the students was Deng's crippled son, Deng Pufang. Through Wuerkaixi, he issued an appeal to the students to leave the Square. Who knew better than he that the army had been called in to suppress the students? His father had issued the order. The younger Deng apparently disagreed. He, too, believed that the use of force must jeopardize reform.

Politically naive, the students were unable to see behind these various conflicting influences to the motives that prompted them. Throughout, the student leaders repeated that they would not allow themselves to be used in a political power struggle. 'Our movement has absolutely nothing to do with the Party struggle,' Wuerkaixi said later. 'We didn't care anything for their internal struggles. We wanted to found a new democratic system in China; there was no [leadership] faction supporting a democratic system.'[15] They failed to realize that they had become unwitting pawns for the intellectuals, for the Party *apparatchiks* and for the bitter rivals within the highest echelons of the leadership. These groups were playing out their battles in the wings. Each recognized its true opponent. (Said Beijing city Party chief Li Ximing: 'If only we can capture just any one out of three people [Wang Juntao, Chen Ziming, or Chen Yizi], then the truth behind Tiananmen will be exposed.')[16] The students were a tool.

By June the students on the Square had virtually abandoned slogans, ideology, and ideals and were playing a waiting game — there seemed little point trying to seek discussion with a regime that ignored them completely. The students seemed to hope by their presence to force their opponents into decisive action. But because of the movement's directionless internal dynamic, the initiative shifted easily to the invisible backstage players — the generation of new revolutionaries who had inherited the mantle of their communist forefathers. Finally, it was the students and the popular hopes they embodied that were to be sacrificed as the stakes escalated and the movement was overtaken by a struggle for the very mandate of heaven. 'If only they allow us two more weeks, we can achieve so much. We have set so many wheels in motion and our influence is spreading,' Wang Juntao said on May 31.[17] 'But will they let us have those two weeks?'

Conclusion

In defeat, the students have learned much, including the nature of their government. The storming of Beijing on June 4 enraged and alienated a generation of China's brightest and best, not just in the capital but across the country. It outraged the people of Beijing. Sympathy for the students' peaceful protest and anger at the brutality of the government's response have sparked silent, sullen disillusion up to the very highest levels of the Party and bureaucracy. Sporadic instances of campus defiance have hinted at the hatred and anger simmering beneath the surface. The students are awaiting any sign of weakness on the part of the government to raise again their dissenting voices. To prevent that, the authorities have cranked up their propaganda machinery to spread 'The Big Lie.' They have failed to address one of the fundamental problems behind the protest — the lack of an ideology. The materialism of the 'economic reforms' and the 'open-door' policies are not goals to mobilize young students hungry for ideals to the government's side. Zhao's failure to fill the ideology vacuum was one of his biggest mistakes. His successors have tumbled into the same trap: They are trying to govern a disaffected youth for whom they have replaced Marx with that powerful Chinese divinity, the God of Wealth. With reform in retreat, that goal too may be beyond the grasp of China's youth. Their despair will erupt, and next time, remembering the tragedy of their last, peaceful approach, they may meet violence with violence.

1. Author's interview notes.
2. Geremie Barme, 'Blood offering,' *Far Eastern Economic Review*, 22 June 1989.
3. Author's interview notes.
4. 'Renmin bu hui wangji,' Hong Kong Journalists Association, p. 219.
5. Michael Fathers and Andrew Higgins, *Tiananmen: The Rape of Peking*, The Independent, p. 36.
6. Wang Zhichang, State Education Commission director of student affairs, *China Daily*, 14 January 1988.
7. Author's interview notes.
8. Author's interview notes.
9. 'Renmin bu hui wangji,' p. 264.
10. Author's interview notes.
11. 'Renmin bu hui wangji,' p. 262.
12. 'Tiananmen: The Inside Story,' The Face, December 1989.
13. *China Spring*, January 1990, p. 9.
14. Author's interview notes.
15. 'Tiananmen: The Rape of Peking,' p. 57.
16. *China Spring*, January 1990, p. 7.
17. Author's interview notes.

Chinese Intellectuals in the 1989 Democracy Movement

DAVID KELLY

THE cover of the September 1989 edition of *China Spring* showed two neatly suited men lounging amicably against a balustrade. They were Yan Jiaqi and Wuerkaixi, the place was Paris and the occasion the inaugural conference of the Front for a Democratic China (FDC) on September 22–24, which elected them its chairman and vice-chairman, respectively. The FDC represents the continuation offshore of the Chinawide popular movement of April to June 1989. Its guiding principles are to guarantee basic human rights; ensure social justice; promote a market economy (*minying jingji*); and end the dictatorship of a single party.[1] Despite its efforts to distance itself from more radical opposition groups like the U.S.-based Democratic League, the establishment of the FDC was, to say the least, an irritant to the Chinese leadership. The French government was warned that 'short-sighted and reckless' attitudes on the part of foreign countries could close the open door.[2]

China Spring (which is published by a rival organization) paid homage on this cover to two component forces of the movement: the intellectuals and the students. Wuerkaixi became a world celebrity, however briefly, through his role as spokesman of the demonstrating Beijing students, the man who told Premier Li Peng to his face to 'stop wasting time.' But who is Yan Jiaqi? Followers of the Tiananmen story would probably know that he was formerly director of the Institute of Political Science within the Chinese Academy of Social Science (CASS) and the author of several books and many articles on democratic reform. Western audiences would make very little of the fact that Yan Jiaqi has become an international representative of progressive Chinese intellectuals. What is a Chinese intellectual? Why do they matter?

There have been many sociological efforts to define intellectuals, to categorize their species and sub-species and to characterize their role in society.[3] We can only sketch an outline here. In

Western languages, an 'intellectual' is normally thought of as a highly educated person who deals professionally with abstract thought, social justice, the conduct of the state, and so on. We think of an egghead, a writer of books and learned papers, and exclude, rightly or wrongly, most schoolteachers, engineers, and medical practitioners. All of these people are considered intellectuals in China. (Only a fraction of one percent of the population holds a college degree.) Wan Runnan, after the Paris conference the secretary general of the FDC, was until the June crackdown the president of the Beijing Stone Company, a computer company that was a major force behind the student movement. While an entrepreneur and politician in our terms, in China he still counts as an intellectual. More important, he would probably agree with the description. For present purposes we can accept as intellectuals those Chinese who would accept this as a description. It is sufficient to bear in mind that the term carries some specific local associations, deriving both from tradition and from Marxism.

In theory, Marxism regards the working class as the rightful masters of society, and workers are defined in terms of their relationship to the means of production. Knowledge and education were long treated as secondary aspects of social production, and people who dealt with these matters for their livelihood were not members of the working class. They would work for any class in power, but could not be a class on their own. Textbooks defined them as a 'social stratum.' In practice, intellectuals have traditionally been treated with great suspicion by socialist states, and probably nowhere more than in China. In successive waves of persecution, most notably the anti-rightist campaign of 1957 and the Cultural Revolution, they were treated as the lowest order in society and made to suffer both physically and in spirit.

Andrew Spano's account of trainee teachers elsewhere in this volume shows how this prejudice continues to apply despite Deng Xiaoping's vaunted extension of 'working class status' to the intellectuals when he took power in the late 1970s. Of course, not all suffer in this way. An editor of the *People's Daily* or a director of a research institute of the Academy of Social Science would normally hold high Party rank and command authority and privileges equivalent to those of a minister of state. Even at this level, however, life over the past 40 years has been marked by constant insecurity. Elite intellectuals inevitably became identified with Party factions. When political winds shifted, they become prime targets of the opposition, and would often be offered as scapegoats by their erstwhile patrons. For a long time, this has seemed to be the unalterable nature of things. Following the height of the Cultural Revolution, though, there came an awakening to the abnormality of their position in human terms. The shared experiences of terror, wasted potential, and complicity in an inhumane order created unanticipated levels of group sentiment and disaffection among the intellectuals. This process was accelerated by successive campaigns of repression. It came to a head in early 1989 and strongly influenced the democratic movement.

The intellectuals, in the first instance the students, stood up now in a way which had been called for, without much hope, by the physicist Fang Lizhi and a handful of fellow public dissenters — that special inner elite elsewhere referred to as 'heroes' by Jane Macartney — mere months before. Had there been no student movement of April, not to mention the bloody *dénouement*, 1989 would nonetheless have gone down as a signal year, the opening of a new chapter in the history of Chinese intellectuals. The 70th anniversary of the May Fourth movement of 1919 would have brought about a natural peak of consciousness-raising. Even without this, intellectuals were becoming aware as never before of both their own and the nation's predicament and of the need to act in concert to deal with it.[4]

The Chinese government has, in its own way, emphasized the role of intellectuals. One of the key official documents is the speech of July 30 by Beijing Mayor and State Councilor Cheng Xitong, justifying the massacre. This covered pages of the *People's Daily*, sounding a veritable roll-call of independent minds who are held to have conspired to 'stir up turmoil.'[5] There is a weary familiarity in this attempt to reduce a nationwide protest movement to the conspiracy of a few carriers of 'spiritual AIDS.' It is a hallowed tactic of the Communist Party to single out scapegoats for punitive sanctions. Intellectuals have, as usual, been spared the brutality and liquidation to which renegade members of the working class are summarily treated, but they make more suitable candidates for public vilification. Making use of the boundless reserves of resentment to which Lucian Pye has drawn attention in this volume, this tactic intimidates some elements in society while it gratifies others. While repudiating the slanders and fabrications evident in these official accounts, one has to admit that they are at least partially based on fact: Intellectuals are important agents of change in Chinese society. To describe them as influential, however, is by no means to credit them with playing the most active role. Indeed, they required not one but a series of triggers before they moved from postures which, though seeming radical, had been essentially passive and uncertain. While entertaining little hope that the present regime can reform itself, many — including the leadership of the FDC — even now resist all-out opposition.[6] They maintain at a deep level the idea of inducing the government to adopt enlightened principles.

Disintegrating Marxism

Formal education in China has for four decades had the works of Marx, Engels, Lenin, Stalin, and Mao at its core, and throughout this century thinkers of all stripes have dreamed of uniting the ideals of socialism and democracy.[7] Even the most dissident of the figures who inspired the students, such as Fang Lizhi and Liu Xiaobo, share, in addition to their rejection of the regime and its ideology, the experience of having been fervent believers in Marxism in their early years. Their writings have been driven by a double crisis in Chinese Marxism: the first a crisis of orthodoxy, the second a crisis of relevance. Precisely because many of the educated continue to regard Marxism as a fundamental point of reference, its loss of authority over time becomes a vital precipitating factor in the crisis affecting socialist states.

The slogan that 'practice is the criterion of truth' was the starting point of the first of these crises. It was proposed by an article in 1978 by Hu Fuming and utilized by Deng Xiaoping in his campaign against Hua Guofeng and the 'whateverists' — those who sought legitimacy in upholding whatever Mao had said and done. Deng's offensive culminated in the Third Plenum of the Eleventh Central Committee in November 1978. Deng probably had few forebodings that by calling the sacred writ of Mao into question he was divesting Chinese Marxism of its credibility. Marxism was for his generation a sturdy edifice which had withstood practical tests. However, to 'see' this practical success one was best placed at or near the summit of power. It was because they were promised a ringside seat — increased opportunities of Party membership, improved conditions of work, chances to travel, and other benefits — that many intellectuals continued to identify with Marxism. As the 1980s wore on, this support became more and more conditional. The liberalization which Deng seemed to support early in his reign of power released new, highly articulate expressions of discontent with the political system, culminating in the Democracy Wall movement of 1978–79. When Deng suppressed this movement, it came as a dash of cold water to intellectuals who had hoped he would move with the times and honor his apparent promise to allow greater pluralism. Their disillusionment was reflected in Bai Hua's film, 'Unrequited Love' (*Kulian*). In it a returned expatriate artist asks, 'We love our country. Why doesn't our country love us?' The question is really asked on behalf of the intellectuals as a stratum, and levels a judgment on their treatment in successive waves of persecution since the 1950s. This line made Bai Hua the target of yet another campaign.

Earnest Marxism persists, in such critical thinkers as Liu Binyan, Su Shaozhi (who managed to avoid the aftermath of the massacre), Li Honglin, Yu Haocheng, Wang Ruoshui, and Yu Guangyuan (who did not and whose fates are in doubt). This is no longer on the old terms, however. It is they who give legitimacy to the doctrine by virtue of their prestige and their known intellectual honesty. Legitimacy no longer flows from orthodoxy as defined by the supreme rulers, as it did in the Mao era.[8] This alone has meant a sea-change in Chinese attitudes. Its supreme manifestation in the events of 1989 occurred after the death of Hu Yaobang, when gatherings of prominent scholars proclaimed him to have been, as well as a defender of intellectual freedoms, a true Marxist. As Geremie Barmé points out in his paper on Liu Xiaobo, this eulogy struck such a younger activist as hypocrisy, serving only to perpetuate the grip of official values. For those concerned, it was critical that the judgment of who was a Marxist be made by the intellectuals. The angry official reaction indicated that it was equally critical for the government to prevent it.[9] The situation was made even more infuriating by the fact that this time the disaffection was stemming from people who had been expected to be the best pupils of the system, its own children, unlike the targets of previous campaigns of repression who had predominantly been latecomers to Marxism.

Another wave of change came with the debate on humanism and 'socialist alienation' in the early '80s. This can be seen as the Democracy Wall movement carried on by other means, but it registered also the escalating spiritual crisis of the intellectuals themselves. Humanism was meant to give Marxism a renewed lease on life, to enable it to provide spiritual moorings which had been damaged by the Cultural Revolution and late Maoism. Without the writ to define 'higher' values, the intellectuals knew their role would be limited. Some sections of the cadre elite agreed with this some of the time. The critical Marxists — Wang Ruoshui, Su Shaozhi, and so on appeared to have the support of Hu Yaobang and Zhao Ziyang. The stratum which they represented worked for the reforms, indeed seemed set to become an extension of the cadre elite. They were, in fact, essential components of a reform program whose primary strategic objective was relegitimation of the regime. An entire government apparatus was to attempt 'management by objectives,' to be judged by its performance in producing tangible services. Policy research and social science units mushroomed, providing, it was hoped, both legitimacy and vision to the reform faction.

Critical or humanist Marxism, however, was for many a halfway house. A commitment to Marxism, even when sincere, served to sustain another, unstated, commitment of quite different character.[10] What really mattered was to retrace the development of Chinese thought back to the original ideals of science and democracy which had historically been associated with the May Fourth movement in the 1920s. New intellectual leaders emerging in the early 1980s, such as the theoretical historian Jin Guantao, the political scientist Yan Jiaqi and the physicist Fang Lizhi, made use of the enormous respect accorded to science to establish a renegade civil discourse. By this is meant an arena in which, despite the existence of an ideological authority, politics and social norms are treated, not as givens, but as objects of inquiry, dispute and even rejection.[11] They and their many followers hoped that appealing to science would provide immunity from political interference in their work. At the same time they subtly undermined the claims of orthodox Marxists to be the supreme representatives of science.[12]

Cultural re-examination

Science, while perhaps the ideal Trojan horse for ideological transformation, required exposure to specialist training to be properly used and understood. Straining against the straightjacket of the 'Four Cardinal Principles,' reformist intellectuals began to turn to another candidate for civil discourse: culture. Culture — the sphere of underlying values and symbols which differentiate ancient from modern, Chinese from Western institutions — touched everyone, and insight into it was in a sense every intellectual's birthright. No less than science and democracy, 'culture' had been a major concern of the intellectual leaders of the May Fourth movement, who were reacting to the apparent failure of politics in the early Republic. They had popularized the assumption that China could not take its place in the modern world without a transformation of the underlying system of values handed down by tradition.[13] A sign of the 'civil' status of the culture debate was provided when the Academy of Chinese Culture was set up in 1986 as the PRC's first ever non-official academic institution.[14] With the passing of time and the increasing difficulty of carrying through the reform program, however, the debate began to carry an increasingly overt political message.

The 1980s saw the emergence of a still younger generation for whom Marxist thought, even in 'revisionist' or 'critical' form, was no longer a satisfactory tool for exploring one's condition. The theorist most highly respected by intellectuals, Wang Ruoshui, tried with little success to retrieve the initiative for Marxism in a debate over the novel, *When Sunset Clouds Disappear*. This was one of many depicting the spiritual desolation and loss of meaning in the wake of Cultural Revolution, particularly among the generation who had most actively participated in it. Wang lapsed into condescension, urging the young to see these evils in Hegelian-Marxist terms, as the antithesis to their dreams which nonetheless promised a bright synthesis in the future. The novel's author riposted that Wang was out of touch with youth. Wang had in fact begun to concentrate more on the realization of constitutional legality in ways that drew little from Marx and less from Lenin. Even among its exponents, *unorthodox* Marxism was now apparently slipping into irrelevance.[15]

'Cultural re-examination' or 'cultural fever' (*wenhua fansi, wenhua re*) took off in 1985 against the background of this generational shift. As in the case of science, the whole notion of culture called out for fresh appraisal. It was now apparent to many that Marxism could only treat the cultural order as an instrument, as superstructure, a reflection of the class structure of society, or similar terms. In the new models, culture was a subsystem of society on equal footing with politics and economics. In many discussions of the late 1980s, the expression 'traditional culture' may not mean what it appears to. Culture was not sharply distinguished from politics; rather it referred to the whole pattern of interactions between political, economic, moral and other social conceptions. As one writer in *Pacific Review* (an avant-garde theoretical journal inaugurated in early 1989 and edited by intellectual activist Bao Zunxin) put it:

Problems of the economy are closely connected with the ways of behaving and thinking, the conceptual environment controlling Chinese society. The most important of these were products of recent Chinese history, and have little direct relation to so-called Chinese traditional culture. If traditional culture has been a barrier to modernization, it has had to play this role through a whole set of cultural concepts produced by the era of politics [i.e. the Maoist period].[16]

Many levels of irony are invoked when critics use cultural concepts to deal with the contemporary political order. Few Chinese intellectuals would quarrel with Lucian Pye's description of 'Leninist Confucianism' as the dominant political culture in contemporary China.[17] The socialist order was more and more widely understood as being a super-feudal society, one in which feudal relationships are even more important than in feudal society. (In China, 'feudal' refers very generally to pre-modern institutions characterized by patriarchy and dependence; as Michael Lindsay points out, this usage is inconsistent with the technical European sense). In addition, the cadre elite has more than a streak of cultural chauvinism, seeking in this way for support in, for example, the accusation of 'wholesale Westernization' leveled at would-be dissenters.

All this meant that the effort of cultural re-examination was by no means an escapist retreat into 'flogging one's ancestors,' as overseas Chinese critics put it. Virtually all major critics of the regime have taken part in it, as the official blacklists attest.[18] This reflects the fact that it accumulated more and more political content as the late 1980s wore on, and as the nearing of the 70th anniversary sparked excitement about the need to recover and transcend the original May Fourth movement. It was increasingly recognized that the May Fourth movement had erred in treating democratic values as purely a topic of moral exhortation. 'Mr. Democracy' had been conceived in isolation from the concrete freedoms without which democratic reforms would be simply an

ornament for one kind of Oriental despot or another.[19] Without
human rights — characteristic equally of the May Fourth movement and of Marxism-Leninism — democracy was unintelligible as
well as utopian.

Following this rediscovery of culture, the last important transition, an intensification of those already under way, was in the
dimension of self-consciousness, the subjective self. The importance of democracy and even science is not entirely self-evident,
especially to minds spiritually desolated by the Marxism of the
despots. The ideological system had long made these ideals serve
its own purposes, and even educated people could grow up believing that dialectics encompassed all scientific truth, and that the
Constitution embodied genuine democracy. These ideals, it was
now realized, were meaningless without some sense of dignity and
autonomy which only the individual mind could realize by its own
efforts. What was required was an authentic inner break with
dogmatism, increasingly seen as interchangeable with feudalism.

Liu Xiaobo, a widely hated and widely influential maverick of
the younger generation, vividly symbolized this transition to subjective rebellion. Here was someone who castigated not only the
Oriental despots, but also the counter-elite, the humanists like Liu
Binyan and Li Zehou. The latter were implicated in the former's
rule, and contributed to the 'velvet prison' of soft authoritarianism
with which the reform faction were surreptitiously replacing the
older dictatorship over the mind.[20] It is a central argument of Liu
Xiaobo's book, *The Critique of Choice*, that there is no basis for
the modern self — the autonomous individual subject — in
Chinese traditional culture. In attacking the aesthetician and social
theorist Li Zehou for the entire course of this maddeningly repeti-
tive book, Liu is in a sense laying siege to the essential value
structures of directed culture, of soft control. The central message
is that the vaunted humanist emphasis on subjectivity on the part
of Li Zehou and others of the counter-establishment is essentially
in the service of authority. The civil discourse of culture itself
perpetuates an over-socialized, over-politicized ethical world view
which is intrinsic both to tradition on the one hand and ideological
despotism on the other. The two come together in an unholy
alliance.[21] Liu Xiaobo's leap into political action is motivated by
this fear of spiritual subversion. He brings to the Chinese arena a
somewhat self-dramatizing version of the existential social theory
of Central European writers like Vaclav Havel and Míklos Háraz-

ti. This involves above all an emphasis on the sense of the black hole of self-deception by which 'the system' perpetuates itself (see Geremie Barmé's contribution to this volume).

Liu Xiaobo's extremism, though apparently quite congenial to Fang Lizhi, was rejected by the mainstream of the intellectual elite typified by such figures as Jin Guantao, Bao Zunxin, and Yan Jiaqi. Bao, collaborator with Jin on the *Towards the Future* book series as well as the avant-garde highbrow journal *Du shu* ['Reading'], was in the forefront of intellectual supporters of the democracy movement (starting with the open letter campaigns of February and March 1989) and has headed a number of hit lists.

Bao was a leading exponent of highly political exploitation of the cultural issue. In a 1988 article on 'The Confucian tradition and contemporary China,' for example, he analyzed Mao's dictum that ideology and the political line determine 'correctness' in all matters. This, he wrote, was not intrinsically Marxist, but shows an 'internal identity' with the ethical totalism of Confucian tradition. The effects of this identity have been far from academic: In every movement, the minutest aspects of social relationships and private mental life were regarded as expressing political allegiance.[22]

Calls for a return to tradition to provide a basis for modern intellectual values suitable to Chinese society have been advocated by New Confucianists, first offshore (Liu Shu-hsien, Tu Weiming) and later as a flank of the culture debates in the mainland. As one might expect, this tendency came in for heavy criticism for Bao.[23]

Yan Jiaqi is perhaps the supreme example of a member of the reformist intellectual élite who has become radicalized over the course of the 1980s. His initial deviation from the Party standard was in 1979 when at the comparatively early age of 37 he joined Wang Ruoshui and Li Honglin in attacking Party dogmatism.[24] His attacks on the lifetime tenure of position in the Party led to censure by the ideological authorities, who sensed a sympathy for the Democracy Wall agitators. (This not-unfounded charge has now been revived as part of the post-June 4 political campaign against Yan as one of the 'instigators' of the student movement.)[25] In the course of a decade of work to formulate concrete programs of democratic reform, incurring considerable conservative disfavor and the wayward support of the Zhao Ziyang faction, Yan maintained the doctrine of the ultimate power monopoly of the Party.[26]

Signs of a move from this position were characteristically phrased in culture-critical terms. At the end of 1986, he adopted the expression *quan fangwei kaihua* (opening up in all directions). The kernel of this idea is the democratic ethos as a cultural universal:

With the dominance of Marxism in China, China's traditional culture has stubbornly penetrated Marxism...the theory, developed in the course of the Cultural Revolution, that Chinese ideology is the summit of Marxism, was a theory for resisting alien culture...Today, China is carrying out political structural reform; this means abandoning the political theory of feudalism in our political and cultural concepts....[It] means digesting and absorbing the things of the world that are useful to us.[27]

In his *Intellectual Autobiography*, Yan confirms the point made earlier that nativistic appeals to cultural uniqueness were a strong weapon in the hands of conservatives opposing democratic reform. He argued in 1986 that cultural factors could be divided into two levels: those unique to a given race, and those which were essentially universal and differentiated solely by the level to which different nations and groups had absorbed and realized them. Naturally, humanism, democracy, human rights, freedom, and so on, belonged to the latter category of cultural elements.[28] Yan's explanation of backwardness bore a clear political message: Chinese Marxism perpetuated nativistic obscurantism of the feudal period. Fortuitously appearing on the eve of the student movement of December 1986–January 1987, Yan's articles earned the epithet 'bourgeois liberalization' and were included in collections of black documents used in the criticism campaign of early 1987.[29]

Predicament of 1988–89

The sum of the sequence of transitions described in the preceding section was the undermining of all the grounds for believing in the Party: economic, political, cultural, spiritual. Coinciding with that was the first great shock to the system, the student movement of 1985–86. This had been preceded by a rise in intellectual *ésprit de corps*, and the emergence of the first major intellectual figure with the courage to break with the official ideology, Fang Lizhi.[30] The ensuing campaign against bourgeois liberalization in early 1987 failed to halt the drift. Different lessons were drawn from this. Political conservatives, who were increasingly able to prevail upon

Deng Xiaoping, saw that the next intervention against the democratic tide would need to be decisive. Intellectuals for their part
increasingly felt that a return to ideological orthodoxy would cost
them most of what they had gained through the 1980s. The stakes
were rising.

Signs of 'predicament and crisis' — to quote a big-character
poster pasted on a wall in Beijing University in June 1988[31] —
were abundant. Cracks were showing in Zhao Ziyang's political
credibility. Insiders knew that his economic policies had been
checked months before.[32] In the ensuing atmosphere of disillusionment and despair, the nation was galvanized in latter part of 1988
by the television series He Shang, 'The River Dies Young.' This
series was a crystallization of the cultural re-evaluation described
previously; most of its key ideas had been raised in academic
circles some years before. The series debunked many of the
assumptions that Chinese have been encouraged to make about
their own heritage; references to the glories of China's ancient
civilization are so much a part of the Communist Party's claim
to national leadership that the series was seen as literally blas-
phemous.

'The River Dies Young' uses analogy to show that the Communist Party was unable to break with the traditional policy of the
empire, or to nurture a 'maritime' culture equal to the challenge of
the world economy. It defends Zhaoist policies of coastal development and autonomy of scientific and other intellectuals. The cultural chauvinism of the cadre elite, which went hand-in-hand with
anti-intellectualism, comes in for strong criticism. It calls for 'a
democracy based on the middle class.' The traditional intellectual
stratum can gain autonomy by allying itself with the emerging
management professionals, the small entrepreneurs, and the media.
This was an amazingly explicit call for the participation of intellectuals in an emergent civil society rather than the state.

Two important points may be noted here. First, the intellectuals
could only make this statement with official backing. The series
could be shown at prime time only with someone very high up —
Zhao Ziyang, in fact — riding political shotgun. Hence the series
illustrates the continuing dependence of intellectuals on political
patronage, ironically contradicting its own message. Second, however, is the converse dependence of the Zhao faction, at a low
point of its political fortunes, on the intellectuals as a legitimating
force. 'The River Dies Young' represents a desperate attempt at

relegitimation of the Party under a new leadership and program, one which offers an unprecedented share of the action to intellectuals. Zhao could shrug off the more extreme ideas of 'The River Dies Young' about establishing an autonomous intellectual elite as mere rhetoric, the claim of a sectional interest group. The offense taken by the old cadres around Deng was, however, extreme. Aging leaders like Wang Zhen, vice-president of the PRC, reacted violently. Wang made vicious threats against the intellectuals, producing forecasts in the Hong Kong media and elsewhere of violent suppression.[34] This was repeated with added venom after the massacre. It was very helpful in damping down student unrest to be able to insinuate that it was inspired by unpatriotic sentiment.[35]

The ideological crisis was openly described in 'The River Dies Young.' It was also admitted, if tacitly, in the 'new authoritarianism' which helped form the crisis atmosphere of early 1989. This was seen by many intellectuals as another attempt at relegitimating the regime, emanating from opponents of radical reform within the Party school. Significantly, the only mention of Marx came from those older humanists like Yu Haocheng, who regarded the doctrine with alarm. While linked to forces close to Zhao Ziyang (as Thomas Gold notes elsewhere in this volume), the 'new authoritarianism' displayed many ambiguities. Senior reformist intellectuals held grave fears at the time that it would provide the old conservatives with a charter for a return to repressive policies.[36]

Su Shaozhi's denunciation of the Party's constant recourse to repression in late 1988 was another straw in the wind. Su, an authority on Marxism-Leninism Mao Tse-tung thought, and a pioneer of what became Zhao's doctrine of the elementary stage of socialism, had in the past rarely gone directly on the offensive. He preferred to couch his criticisms in the form of theoretical explication, castigating the dictatorship by Party elders as feudalism or dogmatism. He was now asked to celebrate the 10th anniversary of the Third Plenum of the Eleventh CPC Central Committee, but 'not to quibble over the past.' A repeated victim of these movements himself, Su was consciously breaking the rules in expressing his disillusion and anger openly. The publication of his statements by the Shanghai weekly *World Economic Herald* was seen as a political affront and led to predictions of its eventual closure by the conservatives.[37]

From theory to action

Translating the crisis awareness described above into direct political expression, however, was far from straightforward. The stage was set by Fang Lizhi, who opened 1989 on an uncompromising note. His New Year message laid blame for the disappointments of the past 40 years on 'the social system itself.'[38]

On January 6, Fang sent an open letter to Deng Xiaoping demanding the release of the imprisoned Democracy Wall activist Wei Jingsheng. The call was first taken up by a group of 33 intellectual signatories to an open letter of February 13 calling for human rights for all political prisoners.[39] It was the open objective of the 33 to form an independent interest group which, together with private entrepreneurs, would constitute a balancing force in relation to 'politicians' — the hitherto autocratic political elite. The signatories were of mixed origins. They included Party and non-Party figures, artists and theorists, avant-garde café proprietors and a former hack critic used by the Gang of Four, the Beijing University philosopher Tang Yijie. Tang was a living symbol of the historical proclivity of Chinese intellectuals to side with the state against society, and in particular against fellow intellectuals. That he should now join the protest was irony indeed.[40] Next came an open letter of 42 Beijing scientists, who insisted that 'the prerequisite of liberalization and reform is an effort to reform the political system (immediate political democratization) in line with advances in the stage of economic reform.'[41]

This was followed by an open letter of 43 cultural specialists. Beyond amnesty for political prisoners, these letters demanded a wide range of human and civil rights. There were few immediate repercussions beyond the police action to prevent Fang Lizhi attending a reception given by the visiting President Bush on February 26.

Surprising as this show of unity was, it was not without a undertone of bandwagon-jumping. For some years membership of the counter-elite of critical intellectuals had been expanding. Several of these figures had developed international followings and were able to travel abroad and enjoy other trappings of success. The pressure to preserve one's celebrity became an incentive to a kind of brinksmanship. Outside the charmed circle of dissident celebrities, the risks might be much greater. The great majority of intellectuals were still content to express tacit support for radical political reform while keeping up their round of official obligations.

The onset of the student movement following the death of Hu Yaobang on April 15 was a surprise to many of these people. Much as they welcomed it, they had many reasons to hold back. The movement of June 1988 had been abortive. Most intellectuals had disapproved of the students' opportunism and lack of timing. The Beijing people appeared tired of students who protested against the murder of one of their number by 'hooligans.' They asked, 'what's the difference between a student and a hooligan?' thereby questioning the propriety of the students' use of death and mourning to push their own cause. More recent student activism had been chauvinistic, not to say racist demonstrations directed against African students. Fang Lizhi and Li Shuxian were depressed at the students' preoccupation with mahjong and overseas escape. The government, for its part, was gradually stepping up intimidation. Chen Jun, an organizer of the Amnesty '89 group, was deported in early April. There were warnings to abandon the movement

After the failures of 1986 and 1988, the students' ability to stage the moral drama of street protest came as a shock. This provided the intellectuals with the next turning point. When the government finally reacted in issuing the *People's Daily* editorial of April 26 with the imprimatur of Deng Xiaoping, the students stepped up their campaign. Deng began ominously to blame Su Shaozhi, Fang Lizhi, and Yan Jiaqi as 'backstage bosses' guiding the students. There is a great deal of evidence against this. Real activism among the intellectuals followed in the wake of the students' hunger strike of May 12. When Yan Jiaqi, Su Shaozhi, Bao Zunxin, and others put up the big-character poster at Beida declaring that 'We can no longer remain silent,' they would have had reason to feel that in the event of repression they would inevitably share the fate of the students. The poster was followed on May 14 by an 'urgent appeal in the current situation,' when other activists joined in.[42] The May 16 and 17 declarations were issued by a group, once again headed by Bao Zunxin and Yan Jiaqi, and moved the intellectuals into direct confrontation with Li Peng, Yang Shangkun, and ultimately Deng Xiaoping.

Bao Zunxin provides an account of this. He was emphatic throughout that the intellectuals should not attempt to direct the students but to struggle together with them. He constantly reminded the foreign media not to give too much of the credit for the movement to the intellectuals.[43] In a May 31 interview published after his disappearance and Chen Xitong's speech blaming him and others for the turmoil, Bao denied that the 'enlightenment' movement preceding the demonstrations had been anti-Marxist, although it had diverged from orthodoxy. The intellectuals had supported the students from the sidelines in the period immediately after Hu Yaobang's death (April 15-April 20).[44] On April 21, in an open letter to the Party Central Committee, the National People's Congress, and the State Council, the intellectuals formally took a stand supporting the students and calling for dialogue. The letter was not accepted by the government.

Next came major demonstrations following the *People's Daily* April 26 editorial, when Bao and associates used every possible contact with the government to avert violence. This successful effort raised morale. This mood carried over to two major conferences commemorating the 70th anniversary of the May Fourth movement. The atmosphere has been described by Wei Zhengtong, editor of the Taiwanese journal *Zhongguo luntan* (China Tribune). Wei scanned the over 200 papers which were presented at these meetings, from which he abstracted the following leading ideas:

1. May Fourth was essentially a movement of intellectual enlightenment, namely for democracy, freedom, science, and human rights. All major figures and schools of the May Fourth movement should be reappraised and given equal importance. Research had to break out of the dogmas laid down by Mao Tse-tung.
2. Democracy is not bestowed as a gift, it can be won only through sacrifice and struggle.
3. Democracy is one thing and cannot be divided into 'bourgeois' and 'socialist' forms.
4. Criticism of tradition cannot be limited to pre-1949 tradition, but must include the new, post-1949 'tradition.'
5. The May Fourth movement has much in common with the 1976 Tiananmen movement (the April 5 movement), but not with the Cultural Revolution.
6. The May Fourth movement should be both acknowledged and transcended.
7. China's future culture should be a new creation uniting East and West.
8. The thought of Marx and Engels as transmitted by Lenin and

Stalin was a vulgarization that damaged the cause of the May Fourth movement.

9. Forty years of monistic politics have reinforced the slavishness of the Chinese.

Wei says of the righteous conviction with which these conclusions were presented, 'it was hard to believe that this was a nation with socialism as its official ideology.'[45]

On May 13, a meeting of 40 intellectuals drafted the May 16 statement and resolved on a demonstration to be held on May 15. Only hundreds had been expected; some 80,000 intellectuals participated. On the day before, however, the 'reformist' cadre Yan Mingfu called Bao to organize a group to reduce the high tensions in Tiananmen Square. This attempt ended in humiliation for the intellectuals, said Bao: Their intercession was spurned and they lost credibility in the eyes of both students and government. The result was the huge rally of May 15. The 'May 16 Declaration' signed by Bao, Yan Jiaqi, and others was prompted by Zhao Ziyang's revelation (in discussions with Gorbachev) that Deng Xiaoping was the actual political ruler of China. It expressed in the most direct language a denial of the leadership's legitimacy, but did not imply that the system itself was irredeemable.

While dramatic and significant, these actions cannot be considered as totally representative. In general, elite intellectuals of the Academy of Social Science and similar institutions were passive until very late in the movement.[46] As one eye-witness points out, social scientists had, with few exceptions, concentrated on criticism and policy advice within the boundaries of the social and political system. Apart from a small group of activists, the intellectuals waited a month after the death of Hu Yaobang before daring to demonstrate in their own right. They first marched on May 16. The trigger was provided by the student hunger strike, and their central slogan remained 'support the students.' This eye-witness account continues, 'It was possible to actively demonstrate without it being necessary to state the reasons of one's dissatisfaction explicitly by means of slogans, banners, and petitions...the real issue remains unstated.'[47]

The next trigger was provided by the imposition of martial law on May 20. Demonstrations were now forbidden, and to engage in one became a direct political statement. The presence in the streets of groups from research and teaching units which continued until May 25 was a radical departure from the 'rules of the game.' The

eye-witness account points out that the intellectuals were the first
to support the students, thus adding 'a decisive new element to the
repertoire of the movement. Their example pointed out to the rest
of the population that it was possible to demonstrate without
being disloyal to the Party and socialism. Because of this creative
step by the intellectuals, the student demonstrations were able to
develop into a genuine people's movement.'[48] Against this it must
be said that many of the 'masses' had already come out as early as
April. Nevertheless there apparently was some demonstration
effect.

The 'Beijing Association of Intellectuals' was, according to Bao,
established on May 23 in an atmosphere of desperation. There was
nothing left to lose, as the declaration of martial law promised
defeat for the students. 'You are going to die whether you stand
up or lie down, so you might as well stand.'[49] This intervention
was decisive for the intellectuals themselves. Liu Xiaobo and certain others sought to deepen the public impact of the revolt when
it appeared to be faltering. The value of this was, to put it mildly,
questioned by Bao Zunxin among others,[50] for whom the formation of the Beijing Intellectuals Autonomous Union (*Beijing
zhishijie lianhehui*) on May 23 was of great symbolic importance.
Yan Jiaqi and Bao Zunxin were the convenors, and the 90-odd
members included celebrated figures from both inside and outside
the Party. Li Shuxian joined with Bao Zunxin in proclaiming this
the turning of a new leaf for the intellectuals. Bao went on to make
more traditional comments about the students' need for the
theoretical training and coolness of the intellectuals, who would
for the present take up the role of consultants.[51]

Even more pessimistic about the students' strategy was Dai
Qing, a controversial writer and intimate of the cadre elite. An
important contributor to the amnesty movement and leading
eulogist for Hu Yaobang, Dai was a major figure organizing the
demonstration of media workers — a vital substratum of intellectuals — on May 9. Following the declaration of martial law she
diverged from the more radical student and intellectual leaders,
calling for them to give up the hunger strike and accept a compromise. At the time branded a go-between for the authorities, her
role has since been reinterpreted in a more generous light. Go-
between or not, she was arrested after the massacre. Her story
demonstrates the danger of ascribing a single set of motives or
factional interests to the intellectuals as a group.[52] This applies as

well to Wang Juntao, whose activities on the other extreme are described elsewhere in this volume by Jane Macartney.

The role of factional politics in general is far from clear. Elements of Zhao Ziyang's theoretical apparatus, think tanks like the Political Structural Reform Research Centre under Bao Tong, the State Council's Research Institute for the Reform of the Economic Structure under Chen Yizi, and others had advance knowledge of the declaration of martial law and called for the convening of a special session of the National People's Congress.[53] At the same time, they urged the students to end their hunger strike as soon as possible (in his denunciation, Chen Xitong seems oddly to regard this as sinister). The picture is confused further by the fact that members of these units began calling for a life-and-death struggle to be carried out nationally by workers, students, and shopkeepers.[54]

The real factional nature of these groups may have more to do with networks of Cultural Revolution veterans. Following the Cultural Revolution, these former members of rebel Red Guard factions often served years in the countryside as 'sent down educated youth.' Aged in their late 30s and 40s, with the return of formal higher education in 1978, some of the more determined made it by the skin of their teeth back into the universities, bringing with them a passion for all the things they had been denied — had themselves denied — for so long: free thought, legality, democratic politics, liberal economics. Kagami Misuyuki speaks of a Red Guard generation who form the core of the 'reform network.' Since the Cultural Revolution, he claims, this network has worked its way into the power structure in order to dismantle its monolithic structure from within. 'Nobody in the Red Guard generation entertains any possibility of working from outside to create a new party or creating an armed alternative to the People's Liberation Army.' This is certainly consistent with some declarations of the FDC, and at odds with worker rebels like Qiu Wu.[55]

However, Kagami's thesis may reflect the conspiracy theory of the center rather than the whole picture. Many people would fit his description without really belonging to an organized group with a corporate identity and goal. Kagami would need to show that their Red Guard connections outweighed social positions and alliances established in more recent times.

Cao Siyuan, one of the first intellectuals to be arrested, presents a case study. Cao was among those to undertake late graduate training in the Chinese Academy of Social Science, working on political economy under the heretical Marxist Zhang Xianyang and moving on to the Zhao Ziyang think tanks. Specializing in political science and law, he pushed bankruptcy legislation before the NPC in 1984. He left government employment to head the Social Development Research Center of the Beijing Stone Company, a private computer company set up by former Academy of Science technicians, many of whom had checkered pasts like his own. The Stone Company was a quintessential product of the Zhao Ziyang era, and Cao had an obvious interest in supporting the reform faction of the Party. He considerably exceeded any such brief, however, calling in late 1988 for far-reaching political reforms. He was warned to desist when on March 26 he held a 'theoretical discussion meeting for reform of the Constitution.' It has been pointed out that the Stone Company simply provided Cao with a budget and left him to carry out his own programs.[56] His actions display solidarity with the intellectual movement as a whole, when prudence might have led him to keep to the sidelines. He was the leading force in a meeting of Beijing intellectuals which tried to warn the government about impending chaos in April. Following the declaration of martial law, Cao and Hu Jiwei, the former editor of the *People's Daily* and a member of the Standing Committee of the National People's Congress, pursued the attempt to convene an emergency sitting of the NPC to have the order withdrawn. Cao's arrest just prior to the massacre, on June 3, was at the behest of Li Peng and Yang Shangkun, who regarded the right to convene the NPC as the prerogative of the Politburo.

The Stone Company itself contributed enormously to the movement, both financially and organizationally.[57] Its president in exile, Wan Runnan, himself an intellectual in origin, is secretary general of the FDC, and may well be more influential than Yan Jiaqi or Wuerkaixi. Yet another Stone executive, Zhou Duo, was with Liu Xiaobo among the four intellectuals to stage a last minute hunger strike, and to suffer subsequent arrest and torture.[58] The question for many Chinese is, however, how free an organization like the FDC can ultimately be from the links to Zhao Ziyang — the champion of 'soft control' — evident in many of its leaders.

Conclusion — after Tiananmen

The movement which erupted onto the streets of Beijing in April 1989 was as complex in its origins as any significant event in history. Economists, political scientists, and sociologists have offered explanations, and all have been partly correct. However, they often overlook what former Czech dissident Vaclav Havel calls 'the level of human consciousness and conscience, the existential.' Havel — astonishingly now the president of his country — taught that the confrontation between opposition forces and post-totalitarian regimes initially takes place here:

This place is hidden and therefore, from the perspective of power, very dangerous. The complex ferment that takes place within it goes on in semi-darkness, and by the time if finally surfaces to the light of day as an assortment of shocking surprises to the system, it is usually too late to cover them up in the usual fashion. Thus they create a situation in which the regime is confounded, invariably causing panic and driving it to react in inappropriate ways.[59]

While the eventual Beijingwide movement included workers, private entrepreneurs, members of the media, Party and government cadres, and ordinary citizens, its initiators were students, and its first supporters were academics and journalists — either members of or closely linked to the stratum of intellectuals. It was not corruption, inflation, nepotism taken alone that motivated them. Their demands included the resolution of some immediate problems, such as reversal of the official verdict on the earlier student movement of late 1986. They showed also a passionate sense of their right as intellectuals in the making — and thus, in ancient Chinese tradition, bearers of great social responsibility — to deliver judgments on these matters. However, the guiding framework seemed incomparably stronger and more decisive, impelled by an unprecedented sense of crisis. This crisis was as much spiritual as it was economic and political. At work was the mechanism described by Havel, which he describes as 'the singular, explosive, incalculable power of living within the truth.' When given the right opportunity, this power can be issued forth 'in something visible: a real political act or event, a social movement, a sudden explosion of civil unrest, a sharp conflict within an apparently monolithic power structure, or simply an irrepressible transformation in the social and intellectual climate.'[60] The significance of the intellectuals in China derives from the fact that they have been in the front-line for a generation, feeling changes in Havel's 'hidden place' in advance of other sections of society. In addition, they have the training, the discipline, and the organizational links to articulate this irrepressible transformation.

On the other hand, the role of the intellectuals in the 1989 movement, while very important, did not entirely accord with their own self-image. Some, as Jane Macartney emphasizes, sought the role of behind-the-scenes strategists for the students, formulating slogans and strategies without taking serious risks. This was a reflection of their tenuous position in society and an index of the government's success in harnessing them with stick-and-carrot policies. While they had ceased to believe in it, they did not unequivocally refuse any longer to tolerate it. For every Yan Jiaqi who moved from tolerance of the Party's 'leading role' (i.e., absolute domination) to rejection, there were scores who stayed on the fence or on the safe side of it.

In assessing the future role of intellectuals, it is useful to bear in mind Havel's concept of 'living within the truth' as an explosive power for change. It is not intellectuals alone who can claim to do this. However, when this impulse comes to the surface in such a key area of society as the media, the effect may be irreversible. Media workers did this both in their demonstration on May 9 and in their subsequent truthful reporting of events. Under the post-massacre repression, people have returned to sullen cynicism and passive non-cooperation. Nothing, however, can undo the moment in which the reality of the political situation was revealed. The massacre and reign of terror has accomplished a cementing of formerly divided factions, strata, and generations. The events of spring and summer 1989 have taken many intellectuals over a major psychological hump and forced them to complete a process of spiritual emancipation from the established order.

Let us not adopt rose-tinted spectacles, however. Many intellectuals have carried on in their positions without interruption. The traditional alignment of Chinese intellectuals with the state remains a critical issue. Indeed, very little has been done to develop and theorize what intellectuals in Eastern and Central Europe call 'civil society.' The idea has a vital intellectual dimension — civil discourse is a necessary but not sufficient condition for civil society, which is in turn a necessary but not sufficient condition for democracy. However, this cannot occur in isolation from the phenomena described by Thomas Gold under the heading of autonomy. The self-organizing structures which are the vehicles of such autonomy cannot rely on consciousness-raising metropolitan elites, although the latter unquestionably play a significant role in articulating their interests.

Unlike most parallel cases in the socialist world, neither democratic consciousness nor civil society have any clear basis in China's pre-revolutionary tradition: There is, for instance, no clear parallel to the Catholic Church, which nurtured the development of civil society in Eastern Europe. On the other hand, clearly identifiable civil society has recently flourished in Taiwan, posing its demands for autonomy on a Leninist-based 'hard' authoritarian regime which was in many respects little better than its mainland rival.[61] Although one would not explain these differences in terms of differences between Chinese and Taiwanese intellectuals, the comparison is quite revealing. Taiwanese intellectuals are more secularized and professionalized. Self-identification as an ethical elite, still the overwhelming tendency on the mainland, has not disappeared, but for many on Taiwan has come to seem somewhat quaint, the relic of a bygone age.[62]

Fang Lizhi's New Year essay pointed to a rising tide of 'democratic consciousness.' By this he presumably meant 'The River Dies Young,' the salon movement, the New Enlightenment movement to renew the spirit of May Fourth, and the forces who shortly after were to rally around his amnesty letter. We have seen that a new group awareness was forged in the process. The question of what social interest this corporate identity can possibly represent is, however, still a vexing one. Edward Friedman has observed that 'China's intelligentsia seems far more capable of acting to further democracy than does the intelligentsia of the Soviet Union.'[63] The many advances in theory and self-consciousness already noted will leave this potential unfulfilled, however, if they remain within the circle of elite consciousness-raising. Mainland intellectuals, like the students, learned very late in the game that they needed to recognize the rest of the emerging civil society, in particular the workers and private entrepreneurs, and that they would be accorded honor, but not necessarily pride of place within it. The movement from traditional academic and research units into private sector employment in recent years was an important trend supporting the 'extraordinary democratic breakthrough' which Friedman prophesied, but which will no doubt be slowed to a standstill for some time to come. The intellectuals remain, as a stratum, an artifact of the system they oppose. If stronger versions of civil society are to develop, it will be through other strata developing their own intellectual identity rather than through the self-perfection of the educated elite.

---

1. W.L. Chong, 'Recent Activities of the "Front for a Democratic China"', *China Information* (Leiden), 4:2 (Autumn 1989), 1–27; see also *Manifesto of the Federation for a Democratic China*, Paris, 24 September 1989; Cai Yongmei's interview with Federation initiator Ding Xueliang, *Jiefang yuebao* (HK), 10 (October 1988), 20–21; and interview with Wan Runnan, *Zheng ming* (HK), 12 (December 1989), 67–73.

2. *Jiushi niandai* [The Nineties, HK], 11 November 1989, p. 65.

3. For a recent overview see Merle Goldman, Tim Cheek, and Carol Hamrin, eds, *Chinese Intellectuals and the State: In Search of New Relationship*, Cambridge: Harvard University Press, 1987.

4. Pierre Robert, 'Intellectuals and Politics,' *China News Analysis*, no. 1387, 3–9. Perry Link, 'Chinese Intellectuals and the Revolt,' *New York Review of Books*, 29 June 1989, 38–41. Sun Tong, 'Chise kongbu xia de dalu zhishifenzi,' [Mainland intellectuals under the Red Terror], *Zhongguo dalu yanjiu* (Taiwan, 1989), 36–45.

5. 'Report on Checking the Turmoil and Quelling the Counterrevolutionary Rebellion', *Beijing Review*, 17–23 July 1989, I-XX (insert). See translations from the Chinese press in this volume.

6. Chong, 'Recent Activities of the "Front"', *op. cit.*

7. Chi Wen-sun, *Ideological Conflicts in Modern China*, New Brunswick and Oxford: Transaction Books, 1986.

8. I derive this view from discussions with He Baogang. See his 'Legitimacy in Chinese Politics Before and After the Beijing Massacre,' unpublished paper, Department of Sociology, Australian National University, 1989.

9. Tan Wei'er, *et al.*, '*Minyunzhong tingli de zhishifenzi*' [Intellectuals who stood up in the democracy movement], *Renmin buhui wangji — bajiu minyun shilu* [The people won't forget — the democracy movement of 1989], Hong Kong: Xianggang jizhe xiehui, 1989, 270–278. Hu Jiwei, 'Sixiang jiefang de xianqu — diaonian weidade Makesizhuyizhe Hu Yaobang', *Xian guancha*, 9–10 May 1989, pp. 2–4.

10. David Kelly, 'Towards the Future: the Ironic Marxism of Jin Guantao,' unpublished paper, Contemporary China Centre, Australian National University, November 1988.

11. I have been enlightened on this issue by Christopher Buckley.

12. David Kelly, 'Chinese Debates on the Guiding Role of Philosophy over Science,' *Australian Journal of Chinese Affairs*, No. 14, July 1985.

13. Lin Yusheng, *The Crisis of Chinese Consciousness*, 1987.

14. Xiong Zijian, '"*Zhongguo wenhua shuyuan*" de zuzhi yu huodong' [Organization and activities of the Academy of Chinese Culture], *Zhongguo dalu yanjiu* (Taiwan), 31:3 (September 1988), 68–75.

15. Bill Brugger and David Kelly, *Chinese Marxism in the Post-Mao Era*, Stanford: Stanford University Press (forthcoming, 1990), ch. 6.

16. Zhang Yongjie, '*Cong zhengzhi shidai, jingji shidai dao wenhua shidai*' [From the eras of politics and economics to the era of culture], *Taiping yang luntan* [Pacific Forum], no. 4. 1989, 5–8. See also Liu Defu, '*Shehui: quan minzu quan fangwei de fanxing*' [Society: comprehensive national revaluation], *ibid.* 51–2, 63.

17. Lucian Pye, *The Mandarin and the Cadre: China's Political Cultures*, Michigan Monographs in Chinese Studies, no. 59, Ann Arbor, 1988. See also Martin K. Whyte, 'Evolutionary Changes in Chinese Culture', in Charles E. Morrison and Robert F. Dernberger, *Asia-Pacific Report-Focus: China in the Reform Era*, Honolulu: East-West Center, 1989, 93–102.

18. David Kelly, 'Road to crisis — ideological dislocation and "Cultural Revaluation",' unpublished paper, 1989. Luo Rujia '*Wenhua fansi jinru Zhonggong dangnei*' [Cultural reflection enters the CCP itself], *Zheng ming* (HK), 5 May 1988, 36–39. Fang Yingcheng, '*Dalu minzhu sichao jiang riyi shenhua fazhan*' [Democratic thought on the mainland will steadily grow deeper], *Zhongguo dalu* (Taiwan), 22:7 (July 1989), 21–22.

19. The image of Oriental despotism became current though Marxist debates on the 'Asiatic Mode of Production,' later taken up by '*The River Dies Young*' writers and Liu Xiaobo. See Timothy Brook, ed., *The Asiatic Mode of Production in China*, Armonk and London: M.E. Sharpe, 1989; John Rapp, ed., 'China's Debate on the Asiatic Mode of Production,' special issue of *Chinese Law and Government*, 22:2 (Summer 1989).

20. Geremie Barmé, 'The Chinese Velvet Prison: Culture in the 'New Age,' 1976–89', *Issues and Studies*, 25:8 (August 1989).

21. *Xuanze de pipan*, Shanghai: Shanghai renmin chubanshe, 1988.

22. 'The Confucian tradition and contemporary China,' *Zhongguo luntan* (Taipei), 27:1 (October 1988), 27–31.

23. [Intellectuals and the traditional model of 'the integrity of official studies', *Zhongguo luntan*, (Taipei), 25:7 (January 1988), 30–32; '*Rujia lunli yu "Yazhou silong"*' [Confucian ethics and the 'four little dragons,' *Xinhua wenzhai*, 4 April 1988, 157–162.

24. Yan Jiaqi, *Wode sixiang zizhuan* [My intellectual autobiography], Hong Kong: Sanlian Shuju, 1988, 30–37; Li Jiansheng, '*Dongluan "jingying" Yan Jiaqi*' [Yan Jiaqi the 'elite' of the turmoil], *Renmin ribao*, 3 August 1989; Trans. in SWB FE/0527 (5 August 1989), B2/1–4. '*Cong qimeng dao xin qimeng — dui "Wusi" de fansi*' [From enlightenment to New Enlightenment — re-evaluation of the May Fourth Movement], *Zhongguo luntan* (Taipei), 28:2, 25 April 1989, 13–23.

25. *Ibid.*, 34.

26. See Chen Zhangjin, '*Yan Jiaqi ji qi zhengzhi gaige linian*' [Yan Jiaqi and his notion of political reform], *Zhongguo dalu yanjiu* (Taiwan), 29:12 (June 1987), 42–49.

27. [To develop, China must adopt an overall approach of cultural opening up] *Liaowang* (Overseas ed., HK), 6 October 1986; trans. in FBIS, 10 October 1986, K5–7.

28. *Wode sixiang zichuan* [My intellectual autobiography], San Lian Shuju (HK), pp. 59–66.

29. *Ibid.*, p. 65.

30. David Kelly, 'The Chinese Student Movement of December 1986 and its Intellectual Antecedents,' *Australian Journal of Chinese Affairs*, no. 17, July 1987, 127–42.

31. See *'Wenjianli de fandang zuopin'* [Anti-party writings in a Party document], *Dongxiang* (HK), September 1988, 6–11.

32. Arriving in Paris after fleeing the post-massacre purge, Chen Yizi, head of the Institute for Economic Structural Reform, an influential Zhao think tank, said that after the 13th National People's Conference, reformers already knew that the reforms had reached a dead end. See *International Herald Tribune*, Singapore, 5 September 1989.

33. Full text in Su Xiaokang and Wang Luxiang, eds, *He shang*, Beijing: Xiandai chubanshe, 1988. The full translation in JPRS CAR-88-002-L (6 December 1988), to be used with care.

34. 'TV Series Runs into Flak' *Inside China Mainland*, 11:1 (January 1989), 1–10 (Translations of major articles from *Jingbao, Zhengming, Qiushi Zazhi*, etc.; Wang Zhen's statements at p. 9). Geremie Barmé, 'The River Elegy,' *Far Eastern Economic Review*, 1 September 1988, 43–45; 'The Controversy on *The River Elegy*,' *Issues and Studies*, 24:17 (December 1988), 8–11; Chong, W.L., 'Present worries of Chinese Democrats: Notes on Fang Lizhi, Liu Binyan and the film, *'The River Elegy,'* *China Information* (Leiden), 3:4 (Spring 1989), 1–20.

35. Yi Jiayan, 'What did *'The River Dies Young'* Advertise?', *Renmin ribao*, 21 July 1989; FBIS, 21 July 1989, 17–20. Xin Ren, '*Zhao Ziyang tongzhi de jieru shuo he 'He Shang' de "xin jiyuan"'* [Comrade Zhao Ziyang's theory of intervention and *The River Dies Young* 'new epoch'], *Renmin ribao*, 15 August 1989, 4.

36. This was the case with a senior CASS economist visiting Australia early in 1988. He was aghast that his academic hosts should regard the threat of political repression as of little economic consequence. Major writings on the topic are included in Liu Jun, Li Lin, eds, *Xin quanweizhuyi* [New Authoritarianism], Beijing: Jingjixueyuan chubanshe, 1989.

37. Text of Su's speech in FBIS-CHI-89-009 (13 January 1989), 19–23. On Su see Ding Xueliang, 'The Disparity Between Idealistic and Instrumental Chinese Reformers,' *Asian Survey*, 28:11 (November 1988), 1117–39. 'A Severe Cold Winter in Cultural Circles,' *Zheng ming* (HK), no. 136 (February 1989), 11–12; trans. in FBIS, 6 February 1989, 34–5.

38. Fang Lizhi, 'China's Despair and China's Hope,' *New York Review of Books*, 2 February 1989, 3–4. Perry Link, 'Chinese Intellectuals and the Revolt,' *op. cit.*

39. Text in *Inside China Mainland*, April 1989, 14–15; Qi Xin, '*Zhongguo zhishijiede tupoxing xingwei*' [Breakthrough action of Chinese intellectual circles], *Jiushi niandai*, April 1989, 20–21.

40. Interview with Bei Dao, *Jiushi niandai*, March 1989, 22–23, p. 23. Cf *To the Storm*, an autobiography by Tang's wife, Yue Daiyun.

41. '*Beijing kexue si-shi-er ren gongkai xin*' [Open letter of forty-two Beijing scientists], *Jiushi niandai*, (April 1989), 11–12.

42. Chen Xitong, 'Report on Checking the Turmoil and Quelling the Counterrevolutionary Rebellion,' *Beijing Review*, 17–23 July 1989, p. XII.

43. Tan Wei'er, '*Minyun jixianfeng — Bao Zunxin*' [spearhead of the democratic movement — Bao Zunxin], in *Renmin buhui wangji — bajiu minyun shilu* [The people won't forget — the democratic movement of 1989], Hong Kong: Xianggang jizhe xiehui, 1989, 246–48.

44. Zhang Jiefeng, '*Bao Zunxin tan zhishifenzi yu xueyun*' [Bao Zunxin on intellectuals and the student movement], in Zhang Jiefeng, *et al.*, *Xuewo minzhu hua* [Bloodstained blooms of democracy], Hong Kong: Baixing wenhua shiye, 1989, 91–95.

45. *Zhongguo luntan* (Taipei), 26:6 (25 June 1989), 9–11. I have simplified Wei's list slightly.

46. Frank Niming 'Reluctant Revolutionaries: Intellectuals and the Chinese People's Movement, Spring 1989,' unpublished eye-witness account, Leiden, August 1989.

47. *Ibid.*, 5.

48. *Ibid.*, 6–7.

49. Zhang Jiefeng, 'Bao Zunxin,' *op. cit.*, 93.

50. Zhang Jiefeng, 'Bao Zunxin,' *op. cit.*, 94.

51. Tan Wei'er, *et al.*, 'Intellectuals who stood up in the democracy movement,' *op. cit.*, 276.

52. See Li Yi's interview with Su Wei, *Jiushi niandai*, 11 (November 1989, 76–82). Su had denounced Dai publicly: see Cai Yongmei, '*Bei shou zhengyide Dai Qing*' [The controversail Dai Qing], in *Renmin buhui wangji — bajiu minyun shilu* (*op. cit.*), 254–55.

53. Other think tanks concerned were the Development Institute of the China Rural Development Research Centre, the Institute for International Studies of the CITIC, and the Beijing Association of Young Economists. On Chen Yizi see Chong, 'Recent Activities of the "Front",' *op. cit.*, 20–23.

54. Chen Xitong, *op. cit.*

55. Mark Selden and Kagami Misuyuki: 'China: the Roots of Madness,' *AMPO Japan-Asia Quarterly review*, 20:4/21:1, 1989, 104–113; Chong, 'Recent Activities of the "Front",' *op. cit.*, 23–26.

56. Liu Ruishao, '*Changxing fazhide Cao Siyuan*' [Cao Siyuan, advocate of legality], *Renmin buhui wangji — bajiu minyun shilu* [The people won't forget — the democratic movement of 1989], Hong Kong: Xianggang jizhe xiehui, 1989, 249–51.

57. Merle Goldman, 'Vengeance in China,' *New York Review of Books*, 9 November 1989, 5–9. David Kelly, 'Massacre of A Chinese Company: Rise and Fall of the Beijing Stone Group,' *Australian Financial Review*, 4 October 1989, 13.

58. Bei Ling (Huang Beiling), '*Yi ru ji wang — ji zhishifenzi Zhou Duo*' [As always — memoir of the intellectual Zhou Duo], *Jiushi niandai*, no. 11 (November 1989), 98–99.

59. Vaclav Havel, *et al.*, *The Power of the Powerless*, London: Hutchinson, 1985, 41.

60. *Ibid.*, 42.

61. Michael Hsiao, 'Emerging Social Movements and the Rise of a Demanding Civil Society in Taiwan,' *Australian Journal of Chinese Affairs* (forthcoming, 1990).

62. See comparisons made by representatives of the two groups in Beijing in early May 1989: '*Haixia liang'an zhishifenzi de shidai keti*' [Timely topics for intellectuals on both sides of the Taiwan Strait], *Wenxun zazhi* (Taipei), 7 (Taipei July 1989), 26–39.

63. 'Theorizing the Democratization of the Leninist State,' in Arif Dirlik and Maurice Meisner, eds, *Marxism and the Chinese Experience*, Armonk and London: M.E. Sharpe, 1989, 171–189, p. 173.

Confession, Redemption, and Death: Liu Xiaobo and the Protest Movement of 1989[1]

GEREMIE BARMÉ

> *There should be room for my extremism; I certainly don't demand of others that they be like me...*
> *I'm pessimistic about mankind in general, but my pessimism does not allow for escape. Even though I might be faced with nothing but a series of tragedies, I will still struggle, still show my opposition. This is why I like Nietzsche and dislike Schopenauer.*
>
> Liu Xiaobo, November 1988[2]

I

FROM 1988 to early 1989, it was a common sentiment in Beijing that China was in crisis. Economic reform was faltering due to the lack of a coherent program of change or a unified approach to reforms among Chinese leaders and ambitious plans to free prices resulted in widespread panic over inflation; the question of political succession to Deng Xiaoping had taken alarming precedence once more as it became clear that Zhao Ziyang was under attack; nepotism was rife within the Party and corporate economy; egregious corruption and inflation added to dissatisfaction with educational policies and the feeling of hopelessness among intellectuals and university students who had profited little from the reforms; and the general state of cultural malaise and social ills combined to create a sense of impending doom. On top of this, the government seemed unwilling or incapable of attempting to find any new solutions to these problems. It enlisted once more the aid of propaganda, empty slogans, and rhetoric to stave off the mounting crisis.

University students in Beijing appeared to be particularly heavy casualties of the general malaise. In April, Li Shuxian, the astrophysicist Fang Lizhi's wife and a lecturer in physics at Beijing University, commented that students had become apathetic, incapable of political activism. They consisted of two types of people: the mahjong players (*mapai*) and the TOEFL candidates (*tuopai*).³ Thus it came as something of a surprise to the citizens of Beijing — even those who were to participate — when the student demonstrations at the time of Hu Yaobang's death blossomed into a popular protest movement at the end of April.

While the motivations of the students in 1989 are too complex to discuss here, they do reflect a dimension of the thinking of one unique figure of the movement, Liu Xiaobo; a man who has been one of the central targets of official denunciations since his arrest in early June. Liu's career as a renegade critic and cultural nihilist mark him as an unlikely activist in the protests, yet his involvement and the statements he made both before and during the movement reveal an aspect of the protests that may help explain the extraordinary popular energy and enthusiasm that they inspired. Even after the massacre, Liu's suicidal decision not to leave Beijing and in fact to court disaster by traveling around the city openly on a bike, echoes the tragedy of individualistic and heroic Chinese intellectuals of the last century: to travel a course from self-liberation to self-immolation.⁴

II

I'm not famous, but that makes me more clever than any of the famous names. For fame brings with it constant uncertainty. The Chinese love to look up to the famous thereby saving themselves the trouble of thinking; that's why the Chinese rush into things en masse. Occasionally someone stands out from the crowd and lets out a shout: Everyone is astounded. What I'm saying is that there are too few people with their own minds, their own ideas.

Liu Xiaobo, September 1986⁵

In December 1986, as students in Hefei and then other Chinese cities began a series of demonstrations under the rubric 'democracy and freedom,' the Beijing–based literary critic Liu Xiaobo commented:

I can sum up what's wrong with Chinese writers in one sentence: They can't create themselves, they simply don't have the ability, because their very lives don't belong to them. So when young people go off to get involved in politics and all that rubbish, taking part in demonstrations, I see it as something completely superficial. In my opinion, true liberation for the Chinese will only come when people learn to live for themselves, when they realize that life is what you make of it. They should establish this type of a credo: 'Everything I am is of my own doing. If I become famous, that is due to my own efforts; if I'm a failure it's my own fault.'[6]

Although dismissive of the 1986 student demonstrations and the lack of self-awareness that he felt they revealed, Liu not only supported but eventually joined the demonstrators in May 1989.[7] This change in attitude and his activities during the protest movement have placed Liu in the center of the post-massacre purge of Chinese intellectuals. Yet Liu is markedly different from the other intellectuals denounced in the Party press since June. Figures such as the political scientist Yan Jiaqi are establishment intellectuals, reluctant dissidents spurned by a political order that has given in to Stalin-Mao recidivism. Fang Lizhi and Li Shuxian are respected scientists and outspoken political dissidents. Dai Qing, the journalist-cum-historian, was a central figure in the rebellion of China's media workers in May although she strenuously cautioned against the occupation of Tiananmen Square. But Liu Xiaobo has been a loner, and although popular enough with audiences of university students who flocked to hear his lectures, he has never been an accepted or even welcome figure in the Chinese intellectual establishment.

Born in Changchun in the northeast of China in 1955, Liu spent his youth in Changchun with a three-year stint from 1970–73 in Inner Mongolia with his rusticated father. After middle school he spent two years as an 'educated youth' outside Changchun and then a year as a wall-painter for the Changchun Construction Company in 1976–77. Liu said later that he was extremely grateful to the Cultural Revolution because it gave him the freedom to do whatever he pleased; it allowed 'a temporary emancipation from the educational process,' one he declares was then and is today solely concerned with the 'enslavement' of the individual. Secondly, as the only books he had access to were the works of Marx, by reading these — he claims to have read the 40-volume complete works — he was led to study the major Western philosophers.[8] Liu graduated from the Chinese Department of Jilin University in 1982, after which he undertook postgraduate studies at the Beijing Normal University where he also taught. He was awarded the degree of Doctor of Philosophy in July 1988.[9] A prolific writer throughout his postgraduate career, Liu's writings have covered traditional Chinese philosophy and literature, modern and contemporary Chinese literature, and Western philosophy and literature. In late 1988, while traveling overseas, he also wrote a series of articles on politics.

Liu first achieved notoriety in China in September 1986, when he made a devastating critique of post-Cultural Revolution literature during a conference on the subject sponsored by the Literature Research Institute of the Chinese Academy of Social Sciences. Liu's speech, 'Crisis! The Literature of the New Age is Facing Crisis,' was printed shortly afterward in the *Shenzhen Youth Daily*, a controversial newspaper subsequently closed down in the anti-bourgeois liberalization movement of 1987.[10]

In 'Crisis!' Liu passed a series of scathing judgements on virtually every aspect of post-Cultural Revolution literature. He reserved his most acerbic comments for the atavistic 'roots' literature that had been in vogue among both up-market authors and readers since 1984. He saw this literary trend as a dangerous and reactionary retreat into traditionalism.[11] He traced the progress of contemporary Chinese writing

from the nostalgia for the 1950s and affirmation of the early years of Liberation, back further to a longing for the period of the Democratic Revolution (1930s and 1940s), moving gradually from that towards a renewed affirmation of the educated youth in the countryside and those undergoing labor reform. Finally, one arrives at a celebration of traditional classical culture and a return to it.

Liu's speech, a defiant affront to the new godfathers of Chinese literary theory such as Liu Zaifu, while affirming the value of some writers, in particular the 'misty' poets of the late 1970s and a few novelists, managed to sour what had been a cheery gathering exuding an ambience of self-congratulation. Whereas the other participants, mostly the middle-aged authorities who had risen to power since the 1970s, were there to celebrate a new age, Liu Xiaobo and other younger members of the audience wanted to hold a wake for China's stillborn post-Mao culture.

Xu Jingya, the arts editor of *Shenzhen Youth Daily*, added a foreword to the speech pointing out Liu's strengths as a critic. 'To be able to maintain an overall attitude of calm in the laudatory critical atmosphere which exists in the literary world, to have an aggressive, questioning, and challenging approach is all too rare among our critics.' But Liu's unexpected appearance — he was dubbed a 'black horse' (*heima*) — unsettled establishment figures ranging from the most orthodox to the outspoken 'reformers,' the Marxist revisionists or humanists. His personal manner, a gruffness accentuated by a bad stutter, rudeness — he swears freely in his coarse northeastern accent — and his pitiless honesty, not to mention his wildly heterodox views, quickly set him apart from the coteries of Beijing critics and their favored writers. Among his detractors was Wang Meng, the Party novelist who had been appointed Minister of Culture in early 1986. Wang disguised his disquiet in the face of Liu's blistering and perceptive attacks by dismissing him as a mere transient figure; he predicted Liu would fade from the scene as quickly as he had appeared.[12]

Liu Xiaobo reveled in his isolation. After a long period in 1987, the year of the ouster of Hu Yaobang and the purge of 'bourgeois liberalization,' during which he was unable to publish, Liu wrote both a book-length philosophical treatise[13] and an update of his famous 'Crisis!' which appeared in the first issue of *Baijia*, literally 'One Hundred Schools,' a literary bimonthly first published in early 1988.[14] The second issue of the magazine carried another essay by Liu entitled 'On Solitude.' Both articles appeared in a section of the journal provocatively named 'the 101st school,' indicating that the opinions expressed therein were beyond even the range of the '100 contending schools' permitted by Party cultural policy. In what certainly appears to be a mood of self-indulgence, Liu wrote that intellectuals are

the wisdom of the age, the soul of a nation, the fortune-tellers of the human race. Their most important, indeed their sole destiny...is to enunciate thoughts that are ahead of their time. The vision of the intellectual must stretch beyond the range of accepted ideas and concepts of order; he must be adventurous, a lonely forerunner; only after he has moved on far ahead do others discover his worth...he can discern the portents of disaster at a time of prosperity, and in his self-confidence experience the approaching obliteration.[15]

It is a statement of Nietzschean fulsomeness; it is also one with piquant resonance in light of Liu's fate in 1989.[16]

In August 1988, Liu accepted an invitation to travel to Norway where he gave a series of lectures at the University of Oslo and attended an academic conference. Although delighted to have a chance to leave China, he said he found the conference on modern Chinese film and theatre 'agonizingly boring.' His sense of isolation, he commented in a letter to the writer, was little different from that he had experienced in China.[17] His observation of discussions of China's problems in both Norway and the United States may be seen as having played an important role in his eventual decision to return to China and participate in the protest movement. The sojourn in Norway was also important in that it gave him time to consider the direction of his own writing, and after leaving China he embarked on a series of highly political articles markedly different from his earlier work.[18]

He commented that the lectures he gave at the University of Oslo were criticized for shoddy scholarship, and personality clashes with his hosts seem to have made his stay something of a trial for all parties. Indeed, in terms of his scholastic and analytical work, I believe Liu can be easily faulted. His contact with Sinologists in both China and overseas led to scathingly critical comments on Sinology in general, although his remarks on the subject to a Hong Kong journalist in late 1988 would indicate that he had little understanding of contemporary Western Sinology.[19] In fact, Liu's 'nihilistic' style was generally characterized by out-of-hand and dismissive responses, something, as we will see below, quite unlike the measured and positive stance he takes during the protest movement in Beijing.

Liu's extreme and outspoken attitudes had made him generally unpopular with his peers on the Mainland. Notorious in Beijing as an abrasive and even ill-mannered figure, Liu was found intolerable by some people more used to less brusque (although not less demanding) cultural figures. In Beijing, his coarse, stuttering harangues during academic meetings, public lectures or even at sedate dinner parties in which he would assault every aspect of conventional wisdom left few people, either Chinese or foreign, kindly disposed to the fiery critic. His indelicate style was a shock to Sinologists more used to the superficially respectful and cooperative intelligentsia of China. In fact, he enjoyed baiting foreign scholars by making blanket condemnations of Sinology — having made little attempt to study their work.

It is this stance as the 'angry young man,' a bohemian and his anti-social truculence that made him so popular with audiences of Chinese university students since 1986. Honesty, clear-headedness and humor were also the trademarks of Fang Lizhi at the height of his public career. Even before he left China, Liu was both aware and highly critical of the peculiar relationship between the foreign 'discoverers' (be they Sinologists, diplomats, reporters, or teachers)

in Beijing and their Chinese 'cultural pets,' and one of the last
articles he wrote overseas is devoted to the subject.[20] Without
going into the details of the bitter criticisms made of Liu, it is
important to keep in mind that he delighted in being painfully
frank (and opinionated), about both others and himself, and his
unrestrained personality is crucially important in our considerations of his role in the protest movement and his fate after the
massacre.

After three months in Norway, Liu was invited to America for
an extended period where he first visited the East–West Center of
the University of Hawaii. There he luxuriated in the climate and
wrote furiously, producing an impressive series of articles for the
Hong Kong press. 'I even surprise myself,' he wrote, 'I'm writing
at an almost terrifying rate; sometimes I get scared that it's all a
shoddy mess.'[21] Of the essays he produced one is some 60,000
characters in length; entitled 'Contemporary Chinese Intellectuals
and Politics,' which was subsequently serialized in *Cheng Ming*,[22]
and an opus on traditional Chinese culture for *Ming Pao Monthly*,
as well as a number of shorter works for *Emancipation Monthly*,
including 'Two Types of Marxism,' and the essay/introduction 'At
the Gateway to Hell,' a powerful manifesto of political rebellion.[23]
Liu was not the only one surprised by his productivity during
these months. The denunciation published of him in the Beijing
press on June 24, shortly after his arrest, said that his articles were
'a series of anti-communist, anti-people so-called "high-tonnage
bombs." '[24]

In March he moved to New York, where he was sponsored as a
visiting scholar by Columbia University. He was also active in
organizing a petition in support of Fang Lizhi's January call for
the Chinese government to release Wei Jingsheng and other political prisoners. While on the East Coast he lectured and among
other things organized a seminar that carried the title 'Modern
Chinese Intellectuals and Self-reflection.'[25] The theme of self-
reflection is an important one in Liu's writings, and it was central
to his activities in the protest movement. He was also invited to
participate in the China Symposium '89 organized by Orville
Schell, Liu Baifang, and Hong Huang held in Bolinas, California,
in late April 1989. The conference hosted a number of China's
most controversial intellectual figures, including Wang Ruoshi, Po
Yang, Liu Binyan, Chen Ying-chen, and Wu Zuguang, although a
number of those invited from the mainland, such as Fang Lizhi,

Yan Jiaqi, and Su Xiaokang, failed to get permission to leave China. It is reported that other participants already in America, Liu Binyan and his friend the political commentator Ruan Ming, balked at the thought of having to suffer Liu Xiaobo's volatile presence on the West Coast. Liu Binyan in particular had been the subject of some of Liu's scathing remarks only a few months earlier. The two suggested that Liu Xiaobo's connections in America be 'investigated' (diaocha) before he be allowed to attend. It would appear that they wanted to use Liu Xiaobo's friendship with Hu Ping, head of the Chinese Democratic Alliance, and Chen Jun, an activist recently expelled from China, as an excuse to bar him from the conference. It is noteworthy that Liu Xiaobo's Beijing persecutors later jumped on this connection with Hu and Chen as proof of Liu's 'counterrevolutionary' intent.[26] Another aspect of Liu Xiaobo's activities in America could not have failed to disturb Liu Binyan: He was planning a seminar to discuss Liu Binyan in June.[27] On the eve of the Bolinas conference, however, as the demonstrations in Beijing continued, Liu Xiaobo returned to China.

The socialite poet Huang Beiling, a recent exile from the Beijing salons and new-found friend of Liu Xiaobo, claims that Liu returned to China at the request of his thesis adviser who had written to say he had arranged a series of classes for him. Liu returned, Huang says, out of respect for this teacher.[28] Yet the official denunciation of Liu declares that his teachers received a letter from him in early May stating that he would not return until 1990.[29]

Liu certainly was frustrated by the empty talk of Chinese emigrés in America and inspired by the student protests. Chen Jun also talks of the moral pressure Liu had felt at work on him following the burgeoning of the student demonstrations.[30] While other Chinese intellectuals pontificated on the origins, significance and direction of the student movement from the Olympian heights of the West, Liu had the courage of his convictions. Chen quotes Liu as saying: 'Either you go back and take part in the student movement; otherwise you should stop talking about it.'[31] He was critical of Fang Lizhi's reluctance to participate so the movement could maintain its 'purity.' Liu felt it was important for people who had been part of the democracy movement in China in the past or those who had studied it now to come out and direct it. The question of moral pressure is a very important one, and not only in the case of Liu Xiaobo. If the 1989 protest movement as a whole had as one of its motivating forces the deep-seated Chinese desire for moral (and by implication responsible) leadership — something that was momentarily embodied in the person of Hu Yaobang — then the moral energy released first by the students flouting the April 26 *People's Daily* editorial and then engaging in a mass hunger strike in mid-May tapped the most powerful well-springs of political protest in the Chinese mind.

But there was another, more personal level to Liu's desire to return to China. Caught up for years in the intellectual debates of the country, Liu was an important figure in China. In America, he was a nobody. He had a heroic view of himself as quite different from most Chinese intellectuals. His personal philosophy of uniting words with actions, his short but successful career as a controversial figure in China, and the feeling of impotence at being caught in America at such a historic juncture, made involvement a heady lure. This sentiment is encapsulated in a comment he made when pacing the streets of New York with Huang Beiling. 'In China you can't even fart without someone noticing; in America your loudest calls are lost among the innumerable sounds made by others.'[32] Having watched the protests on television, Huang quotes Liu's rather patriotic and sentimental statements on his reasons for returning. Of this, one line in particular rings true: 'Haven't we been preparing for this moment all of our lives?' Liu Xiaobo admired both Rousseau and Nietzsche for their personal courage, their daring, and freedom. 'For them to choose freedom,' he wrote, 'was to choose suffering and danger.'[33]

III

By making a decision to go back [to China in April] Liu Xiaobo was little better than a moth being drawn to a flame.

Liu Binyan, June 1989[34]

Former CCP General Secretary Hu Yaobang's death on 15 April 1989 sparked the student protest movement. The students — many of whom had been used in the purge of Hu in 1987 — mourned the dead man as 'the soul of China' (*Zhongguohun*). The panegyrics for Hu authored by both intellectuals and students who had had little respect for him during his life disgusted Liu Xiaobao. He wrote a powerful critique of the reaction of China's intellectual elite to Hu's passing entitled 'The Tragedy of a Tragic Hero' shortly before leaving America.[35] It provides a number of clues as to why he decided to take part in the protest movement and offers a hint of the role he envisaged for himself.

In the first place, he was dismayed by the 'hysterical response' to Hu's death.[36] Suddenly, Hu Yaobang had gained the status of a tragic hero; the mourning for him seemed to be a replay of the events of April 1976 when Chou Enlai was the focus of popular adulation. 'Why,' he asks, 'do the Chinese constantly re-enact the same tragedy (one starting with Qu Yuan's drowning in the Miluo River)?[37] Why do the Chinese mourn as tragic heroes people like Chou Enlai, Peng Dehuai, and Hu Yaobang, while they forget such tragic figures as Wei Jingsheng?'[38]

He was particularly critical of the people — both students and even Fang Lizhi who produced an enthusiastic epitaph for Hu Yaobang[39] — who now praised Hu whereas in the past they had treated him as either a buffoon or a Party fall guy. For all of his virtues, Hu accepted his demotion with impotent grace — and was lackluster in comparison to Boris Yeltsin, the outspoken ex-mayor of Moscow.[40] Liu argues that Hu was both the product and victim of Party authoritarianism, while Wei Jingsheng, Xu Wenli and the other victims of the 1979 purge of Democracy Wall activ-ists were true democratic reformers. He castigates Liu Binyan, Wang Ruoshui, and Ruan Ming who by paying their condolences to Hu's family were responding like loyal feudal ministers to the passing of their liege. 'How many of China's intellectuals have ever thought of asking after Wei Jingsheng's family as he sits rotting in jail?'[41] While he recognizes the nature of the relationship between Hu Yaobang and China's intellectuals he says it is time to abandon their faith in enlightened reformers within the Party elite; or at least they should support the democratic activists in China (such as Wei and Xu) and overseas (China Spring) at the same time as backing Party reformers.[42] While not rejecting the Party out-right, he was calling for independent popular political action to oppose Party fiat.

In this article Liu combines his stance on the independent intellectual with an awareness that positive group action can act as a catalyst to democratic reform within China. Already in this article he had formulated general principles for democratic agita-tion, which he pursued throughout the movement and dismissed what he saw as the dangerous emotionalism of many intellectuals:

Rationality and order, calmness and moderation must be the rules of our struggle for democracy; hatred must be avoided at all costs. Popular resentment towards authoritarianism in China can never lead us to wisdom, only to an identical form of blind ignorance, for hatred corrupts wisdom. If our strategy in the struggle for democracy is to act like slaves rebelling against their master, assuming for ourselves a position of inequality, then we might as well give up right here and now. Yet that's what the majority of enlightened Chinese intellectuals are doing at this moment.[43]

This principle of rational and democratic process was something he, along with others, repeatedly tried to have implemented by the student leaders on Tiananmen Square. It was central to his 'Six-Point Program for Democracy' devised in the first days after the announcement of martial law, published on May 23 in the name of the Independent Student Union of Beijing Normal University as 'Our Suggestions.'[44] It was seen as a central element of the next stage of the movement, both by Liu and his critics. The program called for the recognition and inclusion of the workers and peasants in a Solidarity-like campaign. It contained the central elements of Liu's approach to the question of 'civil consciousness' in China. Both he and Hou Dejian, the Taiwan-born songwriter who found himself caught up in the protests in late May, were lobbying with the students to get them to hold citywide democratic elections for their organizations, thereby showing in a practical way how democracy worked and could be implemented, first among students and then in independent workers' unions. Hou, who later said he took part in Liu's hunger strike out of sympathy for his friend, spoke of this as being an educational process from which both the students and the electorate, as well as non-student observers, could learn a great deal. This emphasis on process became the core of the 'Hunger Strike Proclamation' of June 2 signed by Liu, Hou, Gao Xin, and Zhou Duo.

Back in China, Liu spent a considerable amount of time with the demonstrators. Students from his own school, Beijing Normal University, were central to the action. A welcome figure, he was known to many Beijing students for his outspokenness in public lectures. Still relatively young — he turned 34 at the end of 1989 — and a recent graduate, Liu mixed with the students easily. In this he was like Lao Mu, the poet who became head of the student propaganda department in Tiananmen, and Wang Juntao and Chen Ziming, activists in both the 1976 Tiananmen incident and the

1978–79 Democracy Wall movement, who were also in their 30s. They were unlike the majority of other 'elite intellectuals' (*gaoji zhishifengzi*) whose self-image as mentors and philosophers generally led them to remain aloof and timorous.

At first, Liu Xiaobo was particularly interested in evaluating the level of popular support for the student movement, and up to the time of the hunger strike in mid-May, he was part of a group that devised a series of questionnaires to gauge public opinion on the events of April and early May. The series found many of those questioned supporting the students' main slogans, which attacked nepotism, corruption, and the lack of democracy.[45] In early May many other writers and intellectuals in the capital were hesitant about taking any direct or public action. Emboldened by the implicit support Zhao Ziyang gave the demonstrators in his speeches of early May, a group of writers did organize their own protest in a comic emulation of the students. Many of the demonstrators were young participants in the Beijing University Lu Xun writers' program, and not wishing to be confused with mere university students, many of the participants put on sashes like competitors in a beauty pageant on which were written their names and the titles of their most famous works. Thus Ke Yunlu appeared with the words 'New Star' on his sash, Lao Gui sported 'Bloody Sunset,' and Zheng Yi advertised 'Old Well.' The Beijing 'entrepreneur novelist' Wang Shuo declined this form of self-promotion; however, he tagged along and later regaled friends with details of his fellow writers' pretensions.

Despite his enthusiastic involvement in the protest movement, Liu, a keen observer of human frailties and foibles, maintained a sardonic view of the students. As with his literary criticism, he chose to view things differently from the general opinion, especially that of other writers and critics. He did not get caught up in the excessive rhetoric of Yan Jiaqi and the other authors of the May 17 proclamation, which was a strident denunciation of Deng Xiaoping, 'the befuddled autocrat' à la the Dowager Cixi. Instead, on that same day, he wrote his own appeal to overseas Chinese and concerned foreigners calling for donations to the student cause and support for the students' demands for the government to withdraw the April 26 *People's Daily* editorial and to engage in 'open, direct, independent, and sincere dialogue' with the students. It avoided the emotive rhetoric of other intellectuals' public petitions (such as the May 16 and May 17 proclamations). He signed the appeal on

Tiananmen Square and left his home telephone number for anyone wishing to contact him.[46]

Many of his own students, or students who had previously listened to his blistering lectures on literature, culture, and philosophy, were involved in the hunger strike that began on the afternoon of May 13. It was the hunger strike, stage-managed by a number of young Beijing intellectuals who were advising the students such as Wang Juntao and Chen Ziming,[47] that changed the nature of the movement and galvanized both the city of Beijing and then many other urban centers. Liu spent most of the hunger strike week (Saturday, May 13, to Friday, May 19) on the Square helping with the logistics of giving the strikers adequate medical help and seeing to their other needs (including fulfilling their request for the purchase of condoms). He also became Wuerkaixi's adviser. As one denunciation notes, quoting another student leader from Beijing Normal University: 'Wuerkaixi is our leader in practical matters, but Liu Xiaobo is our ideological leader.'[48] This statement does, of course, obscure the role of Wang Juntao, et al., of the Beijing Research Institute for Social and Economic Science, claimed by one writer to be the sole truly civilian organization in the capital.[49]

I have known Liu Xiaobo since late 1986, and we met a number of times during my stay in Beijing from May 7–27. The first occasion was on the evening of May 8 with Hou Dejian and after a long talk we all went in Hou's red Mercedes to a small Mongolian hot-pot restaurant in Hufangqiao for a late meal which continued until after 2 a.m. Again, during the hunger strike, he came to where I was staying, talked, had a wash, and asked for a change of clothing — he had been in the same clothes for five days. After martial law was declared on May 20, we met again a number of times, to talk, eat, and so that he and his friends could have a shower.

Our last meeting was on the morning of May 27, when Liu introduced me to Wuerkaixi (a.k.a. Wu Kaixi and Uerkesh Daolet). On May 23, a few days after the declaration of martial law, Liu had told me about Wuerkaixi's call to the students on the Square to retreat. He claimed Deng Pufang, Deng Xiaoping's son, had sent news to him that tanks would be used to crush the student movement. Late on May 22, Wuerkaixi had made a statement through the student broadcasting system on the Square, 'This is Wuerkaixi; this is Wuerkaixi, I now issue the following order...' Liu imitated the opening statement many times for his friends' amusement, commenting that Wuerkaixi spoke just like some self-important bureaucrat. Ironically, it was this same element of brash charisma that led Liu and others to believe Wuerkaixi could be a true leader, one who would benefit from his direction and advice. This final meeting took place in a taxi which traveled from the Palace Hotel in the center of Beijing, out to Beijing Normal University to pick up Wuerkaixi, then back to the Academy of Social Sciences at Jianguomen. At one point, as we approached Jianguomen, Wuerkaixi turned to Liu and said in what was now a familiar imperious tone: 'Eh, Xiaobo, hear you've also written some books. Maybe when this is all over you can give me a few and I'll take a crack at them!' Liu, preoccupied with more weighty matters, grunted his consent.[50]

In private, Liu constantly bewailed the fact that the students were, as he had said elsewhere, 'strong on sloganizing and weak on practical process.'[51] He found the constant power struggles and the corruption involving public donations on the Square depressing.[52] And even at the height of his own involvement, Liu watched out for the elements of farce which he hoped to write about one day. Despite his often bemused observations of the students, the power of the hunger strike in bringing the citizens of Beijing into the streets in support of the protests signified to Liu Xiaobo an important change in the nature of political protest in China; he felt a new opportunity for civil protest was now possible and he was anxious it should not be squandered.

Fang Lizhi had talked of this earlier in the year in his essay 'China's Despair and China's Hope,' where he noted that lobby groups had begun to appear in 1988. Fang also spoke of the extremely negative public reaction to the Party's attempt to 'trace the rumor that top leaders and their children hold foreign bank accounts' late in the year. People were outraged that the government wanted to penalize individuals for bringing this question to light and it was no coincidence that the slogan 'Overthrow official speculators!' (dadao guandao!) was the clarion call of the 1989 protest movement. There was an increased desire for the citizens to be given the right to play a supervisory role in government.

It was during the hunger strike and the early days of martial law, in which the very vocabulary of public discourse changed, that revealed this new attitude. Intellectuals, students, and cadres have always followed the Party delineation of social hierarchy and referred to the 'comrade in the street' as either 'the masses' (*qunzhong*) or 'common people' (*laobaixing*). Now they were spoken of as 'the citizens' (*shimin*), and their role as a positive social force — they brought life in the capital to a standstill, created the unprecedented festive atmosphere of the hunger–strike week, and then closed the city to the People's Liberation Army for two weeks — rather than a lumpen mass requiring direction and leadership, was finally recognized. It is something that certainly caught Liu Xiaobo by surprise. 'Our Suggestions,' a work authored by Liu, expresses perhaps better than any other public document of the early weeks of martial law, the desire of some intellectual activists to turn the protest movement into a broadly based and organized civilian protest. Apart from calling for an end to martial law and an emergency session of the National People's Congress, the thrust of this tract is that organized autonomous groups should be elected by various sectors of the society to represent their interests and to take part in the democratic transformation of the society at every level. The students should analyze their movement, reorganize themselves on a rational and democratic basis, and the eight impotent political parties should push for real political power. Above all, the document emphasized rationality, democratic process, and the growth of civic consciousness (*gongmin yishi*).[53] Liu Xiaobo, a figure labeled in China as the evil champion of nihilism and the irrational was, ironically, now the chief advocate of positive and rational civil action. The enthusiasm he had felt as he witnessed the citizenry of Beijing take the protection of the students and the city into their own hands led him in late May to organize his own hunger strike as the student movement lost momentum and popular interest began to flag.

IV

All of China's tragedies are authored, directed, performed, and appreciated by the Chinese themselves. There's no need to blame anyone else.

Liu Xiaobo, November 1988[54]

On 2 June 1989, what was to be the last group of hunger strikes set up camp in the student tent city at the foot of the Monument to the People's Heroes on Tiananmen Square. The group of four was led by Liu Xiaobo. The other three were Zhou Duo, formerly a lecturer in the Sociology Research Institute of Beijing University, recently the head of planning for the Stone Company, Hou De-jian, and Gao Xin, former editor of the weekly newspaper of Beijing Normal University and a member of the CCP.[55] Sup-posedly the first in a series of strikes by intellectuals which were to continue until the June 20 session of the National People's Con-gress, it was a somewhat feeble, although courageous attempt, to maintain the rage of earlier weeks. The comic aspect of the new strike is described by Michael Fathers and Andrew Higgins, cor-respondents for *The Independent*, in the following way:

> On Friday June 2, they [the students] tried to recapture past magic with a second hunger strike. History repeated itself as farce. It attracted four people, three of whom were prepared to fast for just three days. The fourth, Hou Dejian, a popular songwriter who had defected from Taiwan, said he could go hungry for no more than two days. He would be cutting a new record in Hong Kong the following week, and could not risk his health.
>
> The quartet began melodramatically on the terrace of the Monument [to the People's Heroes], unfurling a huge white banner bearing the words, 'No other way.' The political scientist, Yan Jiaqi, came to give encouragement. 'In the circumstances, there is nothing else we can do,' he said. Others felt differently. No crowds poured into the Square to support this strike. Even the Beijing Municipal Party Committee, not noted for its levity, thought it safe to scoff. It called the event a 'two-bit so-called hunger strike.'[56]

The rubric of the Beijing government was repeated in sub-sequent denunciations of Liu,[57] and although the new strike had elements of farce in it, it bore the unmistakable mark of Liu Xiaobo and his perceptions of the movement. It also attracted greater attention than is credited by Fathers and Higgins.[58]

Liu was highly critical of his fellow 'high-level intellectuals' as they dubbed themselves in the markedly unegalitarian language of the Chinese hierarchy. They had, he observed, made appearances on the Square when it suited them, posing with students after marches, proffering intellectual guidance, play-acting at hunger striking themselves (but never really doing it, unlike Liu et al.), and running for cover when there was any hint of danger. Liu Xiaobo was, as ever, highly dismissive of their role in the preced-ing weeks. But when announcing this new hunger strike he re-served his main criticisms for the student movement. These are best summed up in the joint 'Hunger Strike Proclamation' signed by the four hunger strikers.[59] After commenting on the mistakes made by the government in dealing with the student movement, they went on to analyze the shortcomings of the students:

For their part the errors of the students have been evinced in the internal chaos of their organization, the general lack of efficiency, and democratic process. For example, although their aims are democratic, the means they have employed as well as the processes they have used are undemocratic; their [political] theory is democracy, but in dealing with concrete problems, they have been undemocratic. They lack a spirit of cooperation, their power groups are mutually destructive, which has resulted in the complete collapse of a decision-making process; there is an excess of attention to privilege and a serious lack of equality, etc. Over the last 100 years, most of the struggles for democracy in which the Chinese have been engaged have never got beyond ideology and sloganizing. There's always been a lot of talk about intellectual awakening, but no discussion of practical application; there has been a great deal of talk about ends but a neglect of means and processes. We are of the opinion that the true realization of political democracy requires the democratization of the process, means and structure [of politics]. For this reason we appeal to the Chinese to abandon the vacuous democracy of their traditional simplistic ideology, sloganizing, and end-oriented approach and engage now in the democratization of the political process itself; to turn a democracy movement which has concentrated solely on intellectual awakening into a movement of practicality, to start with small and realistic matters. We appeal to the students to engage in self-reevaluation which will take as its core the reorganization of the student body on Tiananmen Square itself.[60]

Liu Xiaobo was one of the only advocates of a practical application of democratic principles during those final weeks. Even in the early hours of June 4, as the PLA moved on the Square in force, Liu achieved a crucial last-minute implementation of his ideas. As Richard Nations, the correspondent for *The Spectator* who was on the Square at that time reports, in a speech aimed at persuading the remaining students to leave the Square with the minimum of bloodshed, Liu 'turned the question of democracy from a test of courage in some fantasy world of moral absolutes into a practical problem in the immediate present.'[61]

The use of the expression 'self-reevaluation' (*ziwo fanxing*) in the hunger strikers' proclamation is by no means new in mainland political rhetoric. Indeed it has been part of the currency of intellectual debate since the mid-1980s. However, in the context of this proclamation it is interesting that the call for students to review their own movement comes after an earlier and fascinating passage dealing with the question of national reevaluation, even of national repentance in the speech he made at the literary conference which demonstrators declare: 'We are on a hunger strike! We protest! We appeal! We repent!'[62]

They go on to say:

We search not for death, but for true life.

Under the violent military pressure of the irrational Li Peng government, Chinese intellectuals must bring an end to their milennia-old and weak-kneed tradition of only talking and never acting. We must engage in direct action to oppose martial law; through our actions we appeal for the birth of a new political culture; through our actions we repent the mistakes resulting from our long years of weakness. Every Chinese must share in the responsibility for the backwardness of the Chinese nation.[63]

This passage echoes Liu Xiaobo's comments to this writer in 1986. In his 1988 essay 'On Solitude,' he had also emphasized the need for Chinese intellectuals to 'negate' themselves, 'for only in such a negation,' he wrote, 'will we find the key to the negation of traditional culture.' While passing through Hong Kong in late November 1988, Liu repeated this attitude in a conversation with Jin Zhong, the editor of *Emancipation Monthly*. He said:

I'm quite opposed to the belief that China's backwardness is the fault of a few egomaniac rulers. It is the doing of every Chinese. That's because the system is the product of the people. All of China's tragedies are authored, directed, performed, and appreciated by the Chinese themselves. There's no need to blame anyone else. Anti-traditionalism and renewal must be undertaken by every individual, starting with themselves. I'm appalled by [philosopher] Li Zehou's comment that we shouldn't oppose tradition or otherwise we'll negate ourselves. Following the fall of the Gang of Four, everyone has become a victim, or a hero who struggled against the Gang. Bullshit! What were they all doing in the Cultural Revolution? Those intellectuals produced the best big-character posters of all. Without the right environment, Mao Tse-tung could never have done what he did.[64]

By producing the June proclamation and undertaking a hunger strike at a critical time in the period of martial law, which had come into force two weeks earlier, Liu and his fellows were expressing on the one hand that they had been inspired by the actions of the students over the previous weeks and at the same time wishing to engage in an activity which would somehow expiate their own sense of guilt, to free them from the very elements of the intellectual tradition to which they were heir. Of course, knowing Liu and Hou fairly well, I cannot deny that they were also motivated to some extent by personal interest — something alluded to by Chai Ling, another student leader and the rival of Wuerkaixi — a desire to be in the limelight of the movement rather than merely basking in the reflected glory of the student leaders and media stars. Nor were they the first university teachers or 'intellectuals' to join in the fast. Hou was, however, the only member of the Beijing glitterati I know of who took such action. Huang Beiling found a rather grand purpose in the hunger strike and concluded that: 'Their action has become a symbol of the struggle for democracy of both Chinese intellectuals and those from the rest of the world; it washes away the record of humiliation and compromise of contemporary Chinese intellectuals.'[65]

V

True belief is born of sincere and painful repentance.

Liu Xiaobo[66]

The line in the hunger strike proclamation: 'We are on a hunger strike! We protest! We appeal! We repent!' was written up and hung as a banner above the strikers. The last exclamation 'We repent!' was a conscious attempt to add a new dimension to the protest movement, and there is little doubt that Liu Xiaobo was its author.

The concepts of freedom, responsibility, and repentance form a major element of Liu Xiaobo's writings.[67] The importance of assuming responsibility for one's own fate, and sharing in the responsibility for the state of both the society and the nation are among his central concerns. Equally important to his mind was the need for individuals to engage in acts of redemption so that they could affirm their own being. Both Liu and Zhu Dake, a controversial Shanghai critic and a good friend of Liu, had pinpointed the lack of God, of ultimate values, as being the tragic weakness of the Chinese tradition.[68] 'I believe that man is at his most sincere and transparent when he is confessing or admitting that he has sinned. Then he is most vitally alive.' The Chinese, on the other hand, are satisfied with this shore. They find fulfillment in the corporeal; there is no need for God and therefore no need for forgiveness or redemption.[69] In his major article written after Hu

Yaobang's death, Liu criticized Chinese intellectuals for their years of silence regarding the jailed democracy activists Wei Jingsheng and Xu Wenli. He also reflected on his own ignominious past:

Chinese intellectuals have hoped for too much from the government during the past dozen or so years of reform. They have too readily ignored the push for democracy among the people. The cool indifference of everyone in China to Wei Jingsheng's sentencing in 1979 is proof of that attitude. (Here I include myself, for at the time I was just another one of the ignorant mob).[70]

He characterized the petitions of January–March 1989 with the following words:

What is most required of Chinese intellectuals, in particular enlightened intellectuals, now is neither to mourn Hu Yaobang nor eulogize him, but rather to face up to the figures of the imprisoned Wei Jingsheng and Xu Wenli and to engage in a collective act of repentance. The petition movement, rather than being seen as an heroic undertaking, would best be understood as the first step towards such repentance.[71]

What was important was the desire to confess, to find redemption in acts that would negate the disinterested and lethargic attitude to the past, and through that action to find self-fulfillment. Liu had been critical of the 'Confucian personality,' the *kongyan renge*, promoted by such contemporary philosophers as Li Zehou, and was equally dismissive of meaningless self-sacrifice such as that made by the Tang poet Sikong Tu, who starved himself to death out of loyalty to his lord.[72] Equally, he felt that calls by Chinese intellectuals over the years to achieve freedom always had a plaintive tone about them. Like Fang Lizhi, he emphasized that freedom was a natural right and not something to be bestowed by the powerful. 'For so many years now,' he wrote, 'the Chinese have been on their knees [before an emperor] begging for freedom.'[73] He was thus highly critical of the students who had petitioned Premier Li Peng on April 22, the day of the state memorial service for Hu Yaobang, by kneeling on the steps of the Great Hall of the People. It was an example of what he had called 'the Chinese form of death — blind suicide.'[74] However, he saw the mid-May hunger strike of the students as denoting a departure from the mere moral dimension of pressuring the government, and not merely as a throwback to the traditional 'petitioning the throne through death' (*sijian*). Rather it was a form of personal action undertaken for the sake of social advancement and for the development of China's civil society. This is why he decided to emulate the strike in early June, hoping to encourage more intellectuals to pressure people into realizing their role and rights as citizens.

Liu Xiaobo's call for reflection and confession in the June 2 proclamation is not the only example of self-examination that appeared during the student movement. As early as late April a number of confessional-style writings had appeared in Beijing, for example, 'Confessions of a Vile Soul — by a Reborn Ugly Chinaman,' a pamphlet of Beijing Normal University dated late April, and 'The Confession of a Young Teacher — by a young teacher who knows shame.'[75] The authors of both of these essays admit to fear and opportunism at the time of the publication of the April 26 *People's Daily* editorial, which called for suppression of the student protests. The first of these was written as a pointed riposte to the Taiwan writer Bo Yang's controversial speech 'The Ugly Chinaman,' which had been widely reprinted in China in 1986.[76] Liu's fellow hunger striker Hou Dejian also countered Bo Yang's thesis in a song written on Tiananmen Square shortly before the massacre entitled 'The Beautiful Chinese.' The song contains such lines as 'Ugly Chinamen/How beautiful are we today,' and 'Everything can be changed/It is all up to us/Nothing is too distant/ Stand up and see/Everything is before us now.'[77]

Liu was far from being the first mainland writer to talk about the need for repentance or confession in the post-Mao era. The veteran writer Ba Jin has made repentance a central theme of *Random Thoughts*, the collective name for his five volumes of essays/memoirs, and a number of other writers have touched on the need to repent for the dark days of the Cultural Revolution. The establishment literary critic Liu Zaifu, Liu Xiaobo's early nemesis and a comrade of Li Zehou, featured the question of repentance in the speech he made at the literary conference which catapulted Liu Xiaobo to fame in 1986. In his speech, Liu Zaifu made a lengthy analysis of post-1976 literature. Commenting on its limitations, he called for 'national repentance' in regard to the past.

Culturalistic self-reflection is, in the main, an autopsy of the body of the nation. It is a self-examination of the structure of the mass cultural psychology. The enhancing of this kind of self-examination requires the active participation of each and every individual in the nation, and from that participation as soon as each individual undergoes an awakening of self-awareness they will recognize their personal responsibility, they will develop a desire for self-critical reflection, that is, they will [wish to] partake in national confession and joint concern...[78]

However, Liu Zaifu was true to his reformist credo and he points to the positive, social function of confession. Redemption is not part of a personal quest, but rather a prerequisite for the new and correct political and social orientation of the individual:

We engage in self-examination so as to be able to adjust ourselves more readily to modernization, and so we are all the more equipped to participate in it. It is not to be a form of abject self-negation, but rather a positive act whereby we will find value in the lessons of history and be all the more clear-headed as we stride towards the future. The path of self-reflection and criticism is that of self-love and self-strengthening; it is the path of positive change and advancement. Our motherland is at a turning point in history; it wants to free itself of poverty and advance to strength and greatness. Writers who deeply love their country will use their powerful skills to mobilize and encourage our people to join in the struggle, to advance, to create, to offer the light and warmth of their lives to the present great age. Our writers will bring to completion this glorious social task.[79]

I have commented elsewhere on Liu Zaifu's statement in relation to the Chinese Velvet Prison.[80] It is this last statement in particular which is at glaring variance with Liu Xiaobo's view of the confessional. Liu Xiaobo was not interested in using confession to purge himself of the guilt of being a witness of the Cultural Revolution; nor did he wish to engage in a redemptive action merely to align himself better with the forces of reform.

VI

A [destructive] kalpa destiny is now at work, which is called forth by the crimes committed by the tyrannical rulers, and also by the karmic activities of the people developed from immeasurable cycles of transmigration. When I take a look at China, I know that a great disaster is at hand.

Tan Sitong, 1897[81]

The unique thing about man is that he is capable of being aware of his tragic fate; he can be aware of the fact that he will die; he can be aware that the ultimate meaning of the universe and life itself is unknowable. A nation that is without an awareness of tragedy and death is to some extent a nation that is still in the mists of primal ignorance.

Liu Xiaobo[82]

Liu Xiaobo's call for personal confession and repentance repeats attempts at 'self-renewal' made by Chinese intellectuals since the end of the Qing dynasty. An important element of this is the concept of redemptive thought or action as mentioned in the above.

When he wrote in the June 2 proclamation of the hunger strikers, 'Every Chinese must share in the responsibility for the backwardness of the Chinese nation,' Liu Xiaobo was acknowledging the role of the individual in the state of Chinese affairs. It is a central theme also in his essay 'On the Doorstep of Hell.' This is an awareness familiar to Western writers,[83] and one that does not, in fact, mark such a radical departure from the Chinese intellectual tradition of the late 19th and 20th century, as we can see from Tan Sitong's writings at the end of the Qing dynasty. It may be relevant here to quote a few statements made by Huang Yuansheng, an intriguing early Republican writer and the author of a series of confessional writings which in spirit are not unrelated to what Liu Xiaobo has said on the subject.

Huang Yuansheng (zi *Yuanyong*, 1883?–1915) was the author of a fascinating essay entitled 'Confessions' (*Chanhuilu*) published shortly before his death on Christmas Day, 1915. Born in Jiujiang, Jiangxi, into a scholar's family, Huang was the youngest *jinshi* in the last round of imperial exams of the Guangxu reign. He was 21. He immediately went to Japan to study and returned to China shortly after the 1911 Revolution to become a journalist. After a short career as a reporter, one which earned him the reputation as 'a genius of journalism,' he was pressured by President Yuan Shikai, the presumptive emperor, into writing in favor of the new monarchy. After much hesitation, Huang wrote a non-committal piece on the subject. He was directed to make it more to Yuan's liking and instead fled to Shanghai from Beijing to go into hiding. Shortly after this incident he wrote his 'Confessions.'[84]

After being forced to write his 'unlettered essay' on Yuan Shikai he said, 'I have been fortunate enough to escape from all of that and am determined to concentrate all of my energies on being a responsible person (*yiyi zuoren*) and use my utmost efforts to confess the guilt/crimes of my life in the capital.'[85] He also said,

'In a few months I plan to travel around America in an attempt to regain something of the sense of human worth that I have lost.'[86] He says that everything he has written concerning politics and the national character was no more than a parrotting of the opinions of other literati, and that all of it was 'material for a confession.'[87] He went on to say:

All of this is because I had no clear understanding of things; I was not adept in self-cultivation and self-reflection; I lightly gave myself over to the discussion of matters of great import and thought myself to be a superior man of the times. [Faced with] the collapse of the country and the crimes [that have been committed] against the people, I must say that I am in part to blame. In the future, I pledge to exert myself in seeking out knowledge, to become independent and a man of stature.[88]

In 'Confessions,' Huang states that his experience in Beijing under Yuan Shikai, and indeed the years leading up to it, had created in him a feeling of 'schizophrenia.' He feels as though his soul (*hun*) is dead while his body (*xing*) lives on. Huang Yuansheng is also a member of that transitional generation caught between the old and the new; a man who is willing to apportion blame for his dilemma between both society, or history, and himself. Yet, even in his grim despair, he holds to a very positivistic philosophy, one that he announces in no uncertain terms at the end of his confession:

I am of the opinion that the most essential thing is for every aspect [of the society] to undergo reform (*gaige*). Now, to reform the state it is necessary to reform the society, and to do that it is necessary to reform the individual, for the society is the basis of the state, and the individual the foundation of the society. I have no desire to question the state, or society, nor, in fact, other people. But I must first question myself, for if I am incapable of being a man what right do I have to criticize others, let alone the society and the state?[89]

And it is here that we find a fascinating insight into the make-up of a 20th-century Chinese literatus-intellectual. This is a new being, one conditioned by the Confucian tradition of state service and involvement so succinctly stated in the *Great Learning*. He wants to reform himself but thinks very much along the lines of the traditional literatus: The change is for the sake of the society and the country, even if the reform is completely different in content from the past, the structure of tradition remains. The above quotation from Huang Yuansheng is also relevant in our review of Liu Xiaobo's involvement in the 1989 protest movement. Liu was highly critical of the self-dissipating aspect of the student movements since 1979, declaring, 'I see the shadow of China's numerous peasant rebellions in the hot-headed enthusiasm of these movements.'[90] Like Huang Yuansheng, Liu Xiaobo was aware of the need for action not only in the public forum but in one's own life; and like Huang he views the hierarchy of self-reform very much in a Confucian order.

At the same time as staging mass political demonstrations within the wider political sphere, people have to engage in detailed, down-to-earth, and constructive actions in the immediate environment. For example, democratization can start within a student group, an independent student organization, a non-official publication, or even the family. We can also carry out studies of the non-democratic way we live in China, or consciously attempt to put democratic ideals into practice in our own personal relationships (between teachers and students, fathers and sons, husbands and wives, and between friends).[92]

VII

Prior to this [the 1989 protest movement] the students of Beijing University had become extremely degenerate; and the moral standards of the people of Beijing had reached an unprecedented low. The awareness of this all-embracing crisis among people fired a desire for self-destruction. Upon receiving the order to evacuate [Tiananmen] some people slit their wrists with broken glass. For them life was now meaningless; they had no confidence in the nation at all.

Duoduo, June 1989[93]

The concept of 'awakening', *xing* or *juexing*, one common in the writings of Chinese reformers and revolutionaries from the turn of the century, was also a feature of the 1989 protest movement. The movement excited people previously caught in the nihilistic vortex of 1988. Liu Xiaobo expressed the desire for people to participate in protest as part of a civil action of redemption; many people felt that they were being roused by the students' spirit of daring from a long period of social and political apathy.

Banners with the single character '*xing*' writ large on them were prominent.[94] In the streets during the hunger–strike week people excitedly declared that 'the Chinese have woken up'; it was seen as a self-awakening as opposed to the organized standing up of the

Chinese people declared by Mao Tse-tung from the rostrum of Tiananmen in 1949. When people began to realize that this epiphany with Chinese characteristics was doomed to failure and even to be crushed, many participants in the protests became suicidal. The mood of elation turned for some to one of extreme pessimism; having been awakened and redeemed through participation in the movement the sense of loss and hopelessness was now far stronger than it had been in 1988 or early 1989 when the capital was suffused with a fin de siècle ambience. Now the atmosphere was apocalyptic.

Blood and sacrifice were symbols throughout the protest movement. Even in its earliest phase, when writers and intellectuals petitioned the government to release China's political prisoners in February, the poet Bei Dao, one of the organizers of the letter of 33 intellectuals, said he had written a will. Wills were also written by students on the eve of the April 27 march in defiance of the *People's Daily* editorial of the previous day, which had condemned the student demonstrations as 'turmoil' instigated by a small number of plotters. But it was not until the hunger strike of May 13–19 that the specter of death and martyrdom loomed high over Tiananmen Square. The strikers' declarations bespoke death with lines like: 'We use the strength of death to fight for life,' and 'Death awaits the broadest and eternal echo.'[95] Although they claimed that they were too young to wish for death, the symbols of the protest became increasingly sanguine.

Some of the strikers even wrote their oaths in blood, recalling unintentionally the way Chinese Buddhist monks once copied sutras in blood when pledges were made. And it was not long before signs and shirts with gruesome blood markings appeared. For some of the strikers refusing food was not enough. Twelve of them, after toying with the idea of self-immolation, decided to foreswear water as well. This group of students from the Central Drama Academy were separated from the others and isolated in a bus parked at the northern entrance of the Great Hall of the People. A cordon was put up around the area like a giant mandala and supporters circumambulated it often in tearful silence. It was a tragically effective way to elicit an outraged response from the people of the city. The bus had the number of hours during which the students had gone without food and water written up on it. The lighting towers on either side of the Square were occupied by students who hung red-spattered banners with the word 'Sacrifice' (*canlie*) on them.[96] Others wore T-shirts patterned with red, possibly blood, and although the mudra of the movement was the 'V' for victory sign, the red and white headbands worn by the students bespoke rather of a suicidal kamikaze spirit. Indeed, there was something about these young people who had pledged themselves to death for the sake of a cause that now had as much to do with honor and self-esteem as anything; it was reminiscent of that 'splendid death' (*rippa na shi*) pursued by the Japanese *shimpū* pilots.[97] At other times the rhetoric had an unmistakable Chinese resonance. At one point during the hunger strike I saw a group of either workers or local residents circumambulating the strikers' enclosure carrying a large banner on which was written the legend 'Neither bullets nor swords can harm us' (*daoqiang buru*), chilling bravado straight from the Boxer Rebellion of 1900. It was people who expressed such sentiments who presumably went on to form the 'dare to die squads' (*gansidui*).[98]

Sacrifice for the cause, while having a venerable tradition in China, has also been a central feature of Chinese communist education. The role models for Chinese youth were for decades the selfless martyrs Wang Jie, Ouyang Hai and even the red samaritan Lei Feng (who died in far from heroic circumstances: He was felled by a wayward telegraph pole).[99] The sentiments behind the Party slogan, 'Fear neither hardship nor death' (*yi bupa ku, er bupa si*), launched on the nation with the PLA campaign to learn from Wang Jie — a soldier in 1965 who had selflessly sacrificed himself for the safety of his comrades by jumping on a rogue bundle of explosives — were drummed into children in 1969. Twenty years later those children would form the main body of activists in the 1989 protest movement. On October 1, fearful of terrorist retribution for the massacre, the authorities ordered the handpicked revelers who were permitted to dance in Tiananmen Square to emulate Wang Jie. They were instructed to hurl themselves on any explosive device found during the celebrations and make a sacrifice for the nation.

As the protests continued one would hear a new refrain. Perhaps it really was necessary for the blood of the young to anoint the cause of democracy in China! Chai Ling, the 23-year-old who became the last 'commander' of the student mass in Tiananmen Square, was one of those who not only foresaw the bloodshed — as anyone who had taken seriously the dire warnings of the April 26 *People's Daily* editorial could have — she awaited it with grim purpose. In late May, responding to the questions of an American television reporter who asked what would happen next she said, 'Bloodshed. That is what I want to tell them. Only when the Square is washed in our blood will the people of the whole country wake up.' But this was for foreign consumption only. 'How can I say such things,' she continued. 'The students are so young. I feel responsible for them. And I feel that I too must continue to live to fight for the revolution.'[100] Some students were openly expressing the belief that their death would be worth it if they could arouse the nation,[101] and on the evening of June 3 it was Chai Ling who led the remaining students to swear to die on the Square for the sake of democracy.[102] She even disapproved of Hou Dejian's negotiations with the PLA on the edge of the Square and of Liu Xiaobo and Hou's demand that the students vote on a withdrawal.

Tan Sitong was one of the first martyrs for the cause of reform in China in the late Qing, going to his death with equanimity. Similarly, Qiu Jin, the woman revolutionary executed in Shaoxing in 1907, welcomed a martyr's death. In his youth the writer Lu Xun, who died in 1936, offered his blood on the altar of the Yellow Emperor (that is, China) and blood features in many of his classical poems, as it does in the writings and thought of numerous intellectuals before 1949.

The cult of blood offerings and death has been institutionalized in the People's Republic. In language that prefigured the pledge of Chai Ling and her followers, Red Guards in the Cultural Revolution too had sworn to protect China and the revolution with their lives. Post-1949 China had encouraged the love of a martyr's death as an integral part of self-cultivation.[103] The revolutionary tradition of the past century has shrouded death for a cause in a romantic garb. It is a tradition in which 'romanticism and revolutionary impulse fused in a cult of action.'[104] While foreign observers watched the playing out of the tragic plot of the protest movement, many of its participants were drawn almost hypnotically to the cult of death. The suicidal student pledge contained the lines:

I swear that I will devote my young life to protect Tiananmen and the Republic. I may be beheaded, my blood may flow, but the people's Square will not be lost. We are willing to use our young lives to fight to the very last person.[105]

As is usual with revolutionary symbolism, it was a cult that worked both ways. The troops in the martial law invading force took an oath on the eve of the Beijing massacre which read in part:

If I can wake up the people with my blood, then willing I am to let my blood run dry;
If by giving my life the people will awake, then happily do I go to my death.[106]

VIII

Perhaps my personality means that I'll crash into brick walls wherever I go. I can accept it all, even if in the end I crack my skull open. At least I'll have brought it upon myself; I won't be able to blame anyone else.

                                                    Liu Xiaobo, November 1988[107]

Q: Do you know who the three most obstinant men in China are?
A: Deng Xiaoping, Zhao Ziyang, and Liu Xiaobo.

                                                    Post-massacre joke

Liu Xiaobo, while emphasizing in the hunger proclamation that 'We search not for death, but for true life,' realized there was something both vainglorious and even suicidal about the event. Liu's actions after his escape from the square on early June 4 indicate a nearly suicidal nonchalance on his part. He took refuge in a safe house for two days, rejecting suggestions that he consider hiding in the countryside for a while. 'What would I do there?' he retorted. He had lost his passport on the Square and was anxious to go into the streets to see what was happening. While his friends were sinking into despair at the prospects of civil war on June 5, Liu Xiaobo was in high spirits, joking, smoking non-stop, and eating as usual. Despite repeated warnings not to use the telephone, which his fellows were certain was bugged, Liu rang friends constantly, starting every conversation with a blustering, 'This is Xiaobo!' He then went to another house, and from there late on the night of June 6, he decided to take a friend home on his bicycle. They were knocked down by men who jumped out of an unmarked van. Liu was bundled into the vehicle. His detention was not reported in the Chinese press until June 24.[108]

Following the official disclosure of his being taken into custody in June, the mainland Chinese press lavished more newsprint on Liu than any other detainee, including the journalist Dai Qing and the student leader Wang Dan. He has also been the object of a singular honor: The Youth Press of China published a volume of denunciations of him in September — *Liu Xiaobo: the man and his machinations* — with two appendices containing some of his best statements and articles, the latter being reproduced in full. What is so extraordinary is that when Fang Lizhi, Liu Binyan, and Wang Ruowang were denounced in 1987, their speeches, comments, and articles were edited and published in a restricted edition within the Party for criticism. Liu Xiaobo's outrageous writings — in particular devastating political articles such as his long piece on Hu Yaobang, 'Our Suggestions' and 'Hunger Strike Proclamation,' powerful and reasoned critiques of one-party rule — have been on sale to all and sundry.

Liu has been named as one of the 'organizers and planners' of the 'counterrevolutionary insurrection,' and as the key link between the Chinese Democratic Alliance in America (Hu Ping, Chen Jun, et al.), the Stone Company in China (Wan Runnan) and the student movement (Wuerkaixi, etc.).[109] In fact, from early May his alleged role as a liaison man for China Spring was hinted at by State Council spokesman Yuan Mu.[110] During my last meeting with him on May 27, Liu said he had heard the Beijing Municipal Committee was planning to frame him on this account, even though he had no organizational connections with the group.

Criticism and condemnation have been part of the course in Liu Xiaobo's career. One of the exceptional things about him is that he never identified or curried favor with the literary or cultural factions of Beijing. In fact, he condemned the egregious 'cronyism' of the literati in no uncertain terms.

> The famous in China are much taken with acting as benefactors of others who caress and suckle the unknown. They use a type of tenderness which is almost feminine to possess, co-opt, and finally asphyxiate you. This is one of the peculiarites of Chinese culture.... Some people have the talent to excel, but shying from the dangers of going it alone, they instead seek out a discoverer (*Bo Le*). They look for support, for security, so they can sleep easy; lunging into the bosom of some grand authority or other, and doze off in their warm embrace.[111]

Wang Meng, the Party novelist who completed the cycle of transmigration from writer to bureaucrat to writer in September 1989, once said that Liu Xiaobo (although he did not name him) 'would lose popularity as quickly as he gained it.'[112] Indeed, Liu could expect little sympathy or support from the writers and intellectuals of China since he had disparaged them mercilessly, by name, in his writings. Even more devastating than his individual attacks was his summation of the 'cultural industry' of socialist China.

In the Chinese literary scene, factional cronyism is all too common. It is virtually impossible to make a move without the backing of a 'coterie'...In fact, 'coteries' restrain individual artists, they encourage homogenization, lead to mutual admiration societies, and therefore mutual deception. Constantly on the lookout for allies, 'coteries' are the most typical expression of the absence of individuality among Chinese intellectuals...The tragedy of it is that upon discovering one's individual weakness there is no whole-hearted attempt to enrich oneself and seek inspiration, rather people seek desperately to put themselves under the banner of some 'famous person,' which allows them to feel emboldened — even if only momentarily, by their affiliation with a 'coterie.'[113]

Such comments appended to his critique of the leading 'misty' poets, including a number of self-styled dissidents and neo-cultural icons, the 'roots' literature stars such as Ah Cheng, Han Shaogong, and Zheng Yi, and a whole range of older establishment figures, did little to win Liu Xiaobo favor with the stars of the new age or their claques. Passing through Hong Kong in November 1988, he lambasted the notion that Jin Guantao, Li Zehou, and Wen Yuankai were three of the four great intellectual leaders of China (he excluded the fourth, Fang Lizhi altogether, saying he was not a leader), and criticized them for their desire to be 'discoverers.'[114] Liu Zaifu and Li Zehou made their animosity more than clear in a dialogue they had in early 1988, published in the April 14 *People's Daily*. Without naming him they condemn Liu Xiaobo in the tone of elders lecturing some wayward youth: 'I certainly have something to say to those not particularly outstanding but iconoclastic young people,' declared Li Zehou. Liu Xiaobo had dismissed Liu Zaifu in 1986, and he was equally contemptuous of Li Zehou. Not only did he devote a book to a critique of the philosopher, in the copy he sent me he wrote the following inscription: 'There's no need to fear the mediocre; what one must fear is having truck with them. Fortunately, I now understand what's wrong with this book.'[115]

The attacks on Liu by the members of major literary factions or their mates have never ceased. What is relevant here is the fact that because he offended all of these cozy groupings in China and their sympathizers in the higher echelons of the Party, government, and army, there is virtually no one who would be willing to speak out on Liu's behalf, even though his rabid critics have literally called for his blood. He is an ideal sacrifice: Many will make *pro forma* protestations at his treatment, but few will feel any real sympathy for this irascible and unrelenting critic.

By far the most devastating attacks on Liu Xiaobo, however, have come from another quarter, that of the intriguing 'cultural conservative' He Xin. Liu had attacked He Xin as a proponent of cultural atavism in his 1986 manifesto 'Crisis!' and he countered by condemning Liu as a 'cultural nihilist' of evil intent. In late 1988, He cautioned his readers:

> I would like to remind my compatriots that behind the cries of radical anti-traditionalists and iconoclasts so popular today there is a hidden agenda which calls for another Cultural Revolution...
> ...Amidst the miasma of cultural nihilism, radical-anti-traditionalism, as well as among the warped attitudes and extremism of some young intellectuals, if we sit back and consider things calmly and rationally we can discern in their proclamations many familiar shadows of the past. The difference is that the anti-traditionalism and cultural nihilism of those years marched under the banner of Marx and Mao Tse-tung; today it is hidden under the cloak of Freud and Nietzsche. The thing [the two currents of thought] have in common is their zealotry, their absurd theoretical framework, and their wrong-headed and distorted analysis of Eastern and Western culture. (It is here in particular that I suggest people examine and re-evaluate Liu Xiaobo's theories.)[116]

In a strategy paper presented to the Central Committee on 28 April 1989, He Xin actually went so far as to name Liu along with Fang Lizhi as chief instigators of unorthodox thinking (in Liu's case it was 'nihilism') in China over the past few years; Liu was thus identified as a progenitor of the 'turmoil' before he even arrived back in China.[117] It is also interesting to note that in an official comment on the 'micro-environment' or climate of the April–June protest movement in September, Liu and Fang are tarred with the same brush as 'proponents of national nihilism, national betrayal, and wholesale Westernization.'[118]

In July 1989, Jin Zhong, editor of *Emancipation Monthly*, expressed the opinion that Liu was to be the major intellectual victim of the present purge, much in the way that Deng Tuo was among the first victims of the Cultural Revolution. Although an inappropriate comparison, one which would certainly infuriate Liu Xiaobo and horrify the long-dead Marxist Deng, the denunciations

of Liu in the Chinese press since his arrest would indicate that he
is a convenient victim. At the time of writing, Dai Qing and Wang
Ruowang were the only other intellectuals in captivity who had
been attacked in the nationwide press, and although Yan Jiaqi, Ge
Yang, and others have been subject to considerable vilification,
they are, after all, still at large in the West.

In fact, the public condemnation of Liu Xiaobo shows that
he is not only to be dealt with as a rabid proponent of 'bourgeois
liberalization,' but also as a key figure in the 'attempted subversion' and 'armed overthrow' of the People's Republic of China,
which was supposedly being manipulated by counterrevolutionary
forces within and outside China. Liu's connection with Hu Ping of
China Spring,[119] the timing of his return to China in late April, his
friendship with Zhou Duo, an employee of the Stone Company,[120]
all go toward making him a vital link in the government's case
against the 1989 protest movement. Despite headlines in the overseas Chinese press that the authorities are planning to execute
Liu,[121] and he is said to have been tortured by his interrogators at
Qincheng prison in northern Beijing, it is intriguing that he has
been used to counter allegations that Tiananmen Square was
turned into a killing field on the morning of June 4. When quoted
in one 'interview' he was described simply as a 'Chinese lecturer at
Beijing Normal University.' That Liu's comments (along with
those of Zhou Duo and Gao Xin, also both under arrest) were
reproduced in English for foreign consumption in *Beijing Review*
shows a new tack in the manipulation of political non-people.[122]
This is surely an indication of the government's desperation to
improve its image, both in China and overseas, even if that means
employing the services of a named counterrevolutionary. By late
1989, officially Liu has still only been 'detained for questioning,'
and China Spring reported in early 1990 that he was housed in the
relatively salubrious Chaohe Guest House in northwest Beijing.[123]

The international response to Liu's arrest and denunciation has
probably also been a factor in the somewhat irregular treatment of
him in the press. Shortly after his arrest, Mi Qiu, an artist friend
of Liu, set up a Solidarity Group for Liu Xiaobo in Oslo.[124]
In the U.S., scholars at Columbia University wrote to China
expressing concern about Liu's fate, and the provost telexed the
president of Beijing Normal University stating Columbia would
like to have Liu back as soon as possible.[125] In Australia, a petition, which emphasized that at no point during the protest move-

ment had Liu advocated the use of violence, was signed by 41 writers, including Nobel Laureate Patrick White, David Malouf, Thomas Keneally, and Nicholas Jose, was organized by Linda Jaivin.[126] A number of private appeals were also sent to the United Nations.

Liu Xiaobo's unrepentant attitude in the face of his captors has gained him something of a mythological stature in the Chinese capital. Among university students, Liu is now said to be regarded as 'the backbone of Chinese intellectuals.'[127] Overseas, his comments on repentance are even accepted by at least one former critic as being a necessary element of Chinese intellectual debate.[128]

IX

I hope that I'm not the type of person who, standing at the doorway to hell, strikes an heroic pose and then starts frowning with indecision.

Liu Xiaobo[129]

It is interesting that after June 4, in the two days before his arrest, Liu talked constantly about the sense of camaraderie, the *gemer yiqi*, he had discovered on the Square. In particular he felt closely bound to the other three hunger strikers, Hou Dejian, Gao Xin, and Zhou Duo. While the expression *gemer* has a range of meanings, for Liu it indicated a feeling of 'mateship,' a bond with those of his own generation that was marked by equality and respect. It was born of a sense of shared experience; Liu felt united with the others by the enthusiasm of their pledge on June 2 and by the horrors of June 3–4. Previously very much a loner, this new sense of 'community' promised to have quite an impact on Liu's thinking. Now that Liu is in custody that promise has little chance of being realized. The sentiment of mateship is perhaps more easily understood when considered as an aspect of another dimension of Liu's personality: that of the 'knight-errant' or *xia*. Such rakish and strikingly abrasive individuals or vagabonds have been known throughout Chinese history.[130] Liu would possibly be offended by such a comparison, but this aspect of his personality has also struck a Chinese observer of Liu's activities during the protest movement.[131] Liu and his fellows had indicated their commitment to civil society in their 'Hunger Strike Proclamation' of June 2. In fact, they vocalized an attitude that was prominent although only vaguely perceived throughout the protest movement. Both in this statement and many of his writings of 1989, Liu Xiaobo had been moving away from the self-centered, nihilistic world view which had earned him such a name in China. Amazingly, the great theoretical proponent of the irrational became one of the most rational and clear-headed organizers of the protest movement. While remaining true to his credo of 1986 that, 'Everything I am is of my own doing. If I become famous, that is due to my own efforts; if I'm a failure it's my own fault,' he had rejected his earlier blanket dismissal of student demonstrations. To a great extent, I believe that this was because in the 1989 protest movement he was excited by the popular, civilian element of the demonstrations, and saw in them some chance for a new element being introduced into contemporary mainland Chinese political discourse. His interest in confessional thought and repentance now found a vehicle for expression. He realized redemption through action, particularly group action. Ironically, Liu discovered a meaning in his own quest in early June at the very moment when such a quest had become a dangerous impossibility. Perhaps he was, as Liu Binyan had said, like a moth being drawn to a flame.

In post-massacre China, confessions and repentance are again being used as a means for the individual to achieve redemption. On June 4, Beijing mayor Chen Xitong had set the tone by calling on people to surrender, reflect on their role in the turmoil, and undergo a process of 'repentance and self-renewal' *huiguo zixin*.[132] Written confessions — a physical act involving an admission of guilt — have been *de rigueur* in many organizations. The earlier liberating effect of action, participation, and support for the protest movement is wiped out by self-negation. For the moment, the Party, and not history, is to be the judge of individual action; the apparat having taken upon itself the role of 'father confessor.' Hou Dejian, the quirky songwriter and Liu Xiaobo's friend, free once more to speak and protected by his special status as a 'Taiwanese compatriot,' has publicly refused to participate in the charade. He has remained loyal to Liu and in January 1990 authored an extraordinary statement which he would probably delight in. 'You could say I'm the world's stupidest, most amateur dissident,' he said. 'I'm not a politician. I had friends who were dissidents, but...I'm a professional musician. But right now, I'm trying to figure out how to become a passable dissident.'[133]

But this self-liberation may turn out to have been a step on the road to his self-destruction, as with Tan Sitong and so many

Chinese intellectuals of the past century. Indeed, even as He Xin has noted, there is a mechanism within Chinese culture that mitigates against prickly individuals and works toward their elimination.[134]

---

1. This study was written as part of the Tiananmen Square Documentation Project of the Australian National University, Canberra. I would like to thank Linda Jaivin, W.J.F. Jenner, Andrew Nathan, Bonnie S. McDougall, and Jonathan Unger for their comments and criticisms.

2. From an interview given to Jin Zhong, editor of the Hong Kong magazine *Emancipation Monthly* (*Jiefang yuebao*), see 'Liu Xiaobo, "Black Horse" of the Literary World' (*Wentan 'heima' Liu Xiaobo*), *Emancipation Monthly*, 1988:12, pp. 62, 64, respectively.

3. Li Shuxian made these comments to Linda Jaivin, my wife, when they met in April 1989. Jaime Florcruz adds 'dancers,' (*wupai*), and 'drinkers,' (*jiupai*), to the list in 'Long Live the Students!,' his account of the student demonstrations in *Massacre at Beijing: China's Struggle for Democracy*, edited by Donald Morrison, Time/Warner, 1989, p. 134. It is no coincidence that the novelist Shen Rong wrote a fictional summary of 1988 entirely in terms of a game of mahjong. See 'The '88 Syndrome' (*Babanian zonghezheng*), *Renmin wenxue*, 1989:4, pp. 4–11. By September 1989, mahjong once more had become a favorite diversion for both students and urban dwellers. The game was given a slang name: 'Reading the 144th Directive of Deng Xiaoping.' See Nicholas Jose, 'China: What Is Going On?' *The Independent Monthly*, October 1989, p. 15. In October 1989, the government put an official ban on mahjong in universities.

4. See Mark Elvin, *Self-liberation and Self-immolation in Modern Chinese Thought, The 39th George Ernest Morrison Lecture in Ethnology*, Canberra: The Australian National University, 1978. Elvin's comments on the late Qing activist-martyr Tan Sitong are of particular relevance.

5. From 'Crisis! The Literature of the New Age is Facing Crisis' (*Weiji! Xinshiqi wenxue mianlin weiji*), a speech Liu made in September which was subsequently published in *Shenzhen qingnianbao*, 3 October 1986. The value of Liu individualism is perhaps best summed up in the words of the Nobel laureate Joseph Brodsky, who said:

> ...the surest defense against Evil is extreme individualism, originality of thinking, whimsicality, even — if you will — eccentricity. That is, something that can't be feigned, faked, imitated; something even a seasoned impost couldn't be happy with. Something, in other words, that can't be shared, like your own skin: not even by a minority. Evil is a sucker for solidity. It always goes for big numbers, for confident granite, for ideological purity, for drilled armies and balanced sheets. Its proclivity for such things has to do with its innate insecurity, but this realization, again, is of small comfort when Evil triumphs.

See 'A Commencement Address,' in Joseph Brodsky, *Less Than One, Selected Essays*, London: Penguin Books, 1987, p. 385.

6. From an interview with Liu Xiaobo in December 1986. See *Seeds of*

Fire: Chinese Voices of Conscience, edited by G. Barmé and John Minford, New York: Hill & Wang, 1988, p. 397. For the full Chinese transcript of the interview, see Bai Jieming, 'Liberation for the Chinese is in Self-awakening' (*Zhongguorende jiefang zai ziwo juexing*), *The Nineties* (*Jiushi niandai*), 1987:3, pp. 61–65. Of course, here Liu is actually reiterating one of the basic themes of the New Culture Movement of the early Republic, the 'liberation of the individual'.

7. Liu was, however, an admirer of Fang Lizhi, the astrophysicist-dissident who was regarded as one of the instigators of the 1986 student movement. Two books devoted to that movement have been published so far, and both of which deserve the attention of students of the events of 1989. They are *Le dragon et la souris*, Paris: Christian Bourgois, 1987 by Jean-Christophe Tournebise and Lawrence Macdonald, and Zeng Huiyan's *Xuechao: Zhongguo dalu 1986–87*, Taipei: Wansheng chubanshe, 1989.

8. See Jin Zhong, 'Liu Xiaobo, 'Black Horse' of the Literary World,' *Emancipation Monthly*, 1988: 12, pp. 59, 60, 64; also Liu Xiaobo, 'On the Doorway to Hell' (*Zai diyude rukouchu — dui Makesizhuyide zaijian-tao*), *Press Freedom Herald* (*Xinwen ziyou daobao*), No. 11, 30 September, 1989.

9. This information is based on 'Biographical Notes' provided by Liu Xiaobo.

10. See 'Crisis! The Literature of the New Age is Facing Crisis,' *Shenzhen qingnianbao*, 3 October 1986. The editor who had the article printed was Xu Jingya, a friend of Liu's from the northeast and a critic who had been denounced and arrested for his writings on contemporary poetry, in particular his 1983 essay 'A Violent Tribe of Bards,' (*Jueqide shiqun*). Cao Changqing, another editor of *Shenzhen Youth Daily* who was friendly with Liu Xiaobo, founded the weekly *News Freedom Herald* (*Xinwen ziyou daobao*) in America shortly after the June massacre. Cao has been among the activists calling for the release of Liu Xiaobo.

11. Liu's comments on the fiction of writers such as Ah Cheng, Han Shaogong, and Jia Pingwa pointed out their use of rural settings and cultural totems to affirm some form of neo-traditional value structure with which to succor their readers. For a less emotive view of Ah Cheng's fiction, the object of much of Liu's ire, see Kam Louie's 'The Short Stories of Ah Cheng: Daoism, Confucianism, and Life,' in Louie's *Between Fact and Fiction, Essays On Post-Mao Chinese Literature & Society*, Sydney: Wild Peony, 1989, pp. 76–90.

12. See 'Wang Meng Discusses Art and Literature' (*Wang Meng tan wenyi*), *Zhongguo wenhuabao*, 26 November 1986. Many of Wang's comments are clearly directed at Liu Xiaobo.

13. *The Fog of Metaphysics* (*Xing'ershangxuede miwu*), Shanghai: Shanghai renmin chubanshe, 1989, Liu's personal history of Western philosophy. I would like to thank David Kelly of the Contemporary China Centre of the ANU for bringing this work to my attention.

14. See Liu, 'Further Comments on the Crisis Facing the Literature of the New Age' (*Zailun xinshiqi wenxue mianlin weiji*), *Baijia*, 1988:1, pp. 12–26.

15. 'On Solitude' (*Lun gudu*), *Baijia* (Anhui) 1988:2, p. 4. I have quoted this passage in 'Arrière-pensée on an Avant-Garde: The Stars in Retrospect', *The Stars: 10 Years*, Hong Kong: Hanart 2 Gallery, 1989, p. 77.

16. Liu's thinking, especially his discussions of solitude and tragedy, is much influenced by Nietzsche. Liu admired the German philosopher for his courage and uncompromising attitudes. See, for example, Liu's *The Fog of Metaphysics*, pp. 345ff, and 'Metaphysics and Chinese Culture' (*Xing'ershangxue yu Zhongguo wenhua*), *Xinqimeng I*, 1988:10, pp. 73–74, 75. In his study 'The Highest Chinadom: Nietzsche and the Chinese Mind, 1907–1989,' David Kelly discusses Nietzsche's renewed role 'as a source of critical enlightenment' in contemporary China with particular reference to Liu Xiaobo.

17. From a letter dated 23 September 1988.

18. The present writer, although impressed by Liu's earlier literary criticism as reflecting the urban ambience of late 1980s China, had previously suggested to Liu that his work may have been best suited to a column in the *Beijing Evening News*. At the time, I had read little of his philosophical work. The articles that Liu published in the Hong Kong press from late 1988, as well as his April 1989 essay on Hu, however, are a significant departure and are particularly worthy of closer reading.

19. Jin Zhong, 'Liu Xiaobo, 'Black Horse' of the Literary World,' *Emancipation Monthly*, 1988:12, p. 60.

20. See Liu Xiaobo, 'Foreigners' Salons and Cultural Aggression' (*Yangshalong yu wenhua qinlüe*), *Emancipation Monthly*, 1989:3, pp. 79–82. The first part of Liu's article is a riposte to Yang Manke's ill-informed 'Trivia of the Peking Foreigners' Salons' (*Beijing yangshalongde xingxing sese*), *Emancipation Monthly*, 1989:1–2, pp. 14–16. The central questions raised by Yang are, in turn, inspired to some extent by my own 'Peking Foreigners' Salons' (*Beijingde yangshalong*), *The Nineties*, 1988:3, pp. 94–95. Further to this subject, see also Liu Xiaobo in 'Metaphysics and Chinese Culture,' *Xinqimeng I*, 1988:10, pp. 74–75.

21. From a letter to the writer dated 24 January 1989.

22. See Liu Xiaobo, 'Contemporary Chinese Intellectuals and Politics' (*Zhongguo dangdai zhishifenzi yu zhengzhi*), *Cheng Ming* (*Zhengming*), 1989:4, pp. 78–81; 7, pp. 74–77; 8, pp. 90–91; 9, pp. 88–90, and so on.

23. 'At the Doorway to Hell' (*Zai diyude rukouchu — dui Makesizhuyide zaijiantao*), *Press Freedom Herald*, 30 September, 1989.

24. Wang Zhao, 'Grabbing Liu Xiaobo's Black Hand' (*Zhuazhu Liu Xiaobode heishou*), *Beijing ribao*, 24 June 1989.

25. See Bei Ling 'No Other Choice — My Friend Liu Xiaobo' (*Bie wu xuanze — ji wode pengyou Liu Xiaobo*), *Ming Pao Monthly* (*Mingbao yuekan*), 1989:8, pp. 32–33. Bei Ling is the pen name of Huang Beiling. The Chinese title of the seminar was *Zhongguo xiandai zhishi fenzi ziwo fanxing taolunhui*. A tape-recording was made of the proceedings, but I was not been able to consult it when writing this essay.

26. In *Liu Xiaobo, the man and his mainpulations* (*Liu Xiaobo qiren qishi*), the mainland book-length denunciation of Liu edited by Zheng Wang and Ji Kuai (Beijing: Qingnian chubanshe, September 1989), Liu is

named as having written the open letter that Hu Ping, Chen Jun, and eight others sent to the demonstrating students from New York on April 22 (p. 129).

27. See Chen Jun, 'My Days with Liu Xiaobo' (*He Liu Xiaobo zai yiqide rizi*), *Emancipation Monthly*, 1989:7, p. 63.

28. *Ibid.*

29. See Wang Zhao, 'Grabbing Liu Xiaobo's Black Hand.'

30. Chen Jun, '*My Days with Liu Xiaobo*,' p. 63.

31. Chen Jun, p. 26.

32. Bei Ling, '*No Other Choice*,' p. 33. In early 1990, Bei Ling commented, not without some regret, that Liu Xiaobo chose public opposition to authoritarianism instead of continuing with his work in the social sciences. See. 'Choice, a Tragedy of Fate — reflections on the individual and existence,' *China Spring*, 1990:3, p. 96.

33. Liu, 'Metaphysics and Chinese Culture,' *Xinqimeng I*, 1988:10, p. 74.

34. A comment Liu Binyan made to Jin Zhong, editor of *Emancipation Monthly*, during his June trip to Hong Kong. See Jin's essay 'From Black Horse to Black Hand' (*Cong heima dao heishou*), *Emancipation Monthly*, 1989:7, p. 60. See also Chen Jun, 'My Days with Liu Xiaobo,' ibid., where he comments on Liu Binyan's attitude to Xiaobo. 'After Xiaobo had returned [to China], Liu Binyan criticized him for being eager to be in the limelight.'

35. Initially published in the American Chinese language daily *Shijie ribao*, the article was subsequently reprinted in Hong Kong. See 'The Tragedy of a Tragic Hero — Three Critiques of the Phenomena Surrounding Hu Yaobang's Death' (*Beiju yingxiongde beiju — Hu Yaobang shishi xianxiang pinglun zhi yi, er, san*), *Emancipation Monthly* (*Jiefang yuekan*), 1989:5, pp. 30–34. A full translation of this article can be found in *New Ghosts, Old Dreams: Voices from Tiananmen Square*, edited by Geremie Barmé and Linda Jaivin, to be published by Hill & Wang in New York in late 1990. Cao Changqing, editor of the recently established newspaper *Freedom News Herald* (*Xinwen ziyou daobao*) and a former editor of the *Shenzhen Youth Daily*, showed me a copy of this article during the 'China Forum '89,' held in Bolinas from April 25–30. It had been underlined and annotated in many places by Ge Yang, the aged editor of *New Observer* (*Xin guancha*), a senior Party cadre in exile since the June massacre. Her magazine was banned in late June. Ge exclaimed in her comments that Liu's analysis of Chinese intellectuals was outrageous. For the article, see 'The Tragedy of a Tragic Hero — Three Critiques of the Phenomena Surrounding Hu Yaobang's Death' (*Beiju yingxiongde beiju — Hu Yaobang shishi xianxiang pinglun zhi yi, er, san*), *Emancipation Monthly*, 1989:5, pp. 30–34. According to a later *People's Daily* denunciation, this article was broadcast in Beijing on the 'Independent [Student's Union] Station' shortly after Liu returned to China. See Shi Dawen, 'From Being an "Outrageous Man" to Becoming a "Black Hand" — Revealing Liu Xiaobo's Reactionary Mien' (*Cong 'kuangren' dao 'heishou' — jielu Liu Xiaobode fandong mianmu*), *People's Daily*, September 1989.

36. Liu, 'The Tragedy of a Tragic Hero,' p. 30.

37. Qu Yuan (3rd century B.C.), supposed author of the *Chuci*, having been dismissed by his king, is said to have drowned himself in the Miluo River.

38. *Ibid*.

39. Liu, 'The Tragedy of a Tragic Hero,' p. 32.

40. *Ibid*.

41. Liu, 'The Tragedy of a Tragic Hero,' p. 31.

42. *Ibid*.

43. Liu, 'The Tragedy of a Tragic Hero,' p. 33.

44. Liu and Hou Dejian showed me a hand-written version of this program shortly after May 20. The full text of this important document is reprinted in Zheng Wang and Ji Kuai's *Liu Xiaobo: The Man and His Manipulations*, pp. 131–36.

45. These questionnaires were used in three public opinion polls. For a translation of this material see Woei Lien Chong and Fons Lamboo, 'Beijing Public Opinion Poll on the Student Demonstrations Held on 1, 2, and 7 May 1989, Poll Work Group, Psychology Department, Beijing Normal University,' *China Information*, The Documentation and Research Centre for Contemporary China, Leiden, Vol. IV, No. 1 (Summer 1989), pp. 94–124. Sociologists who have seen this material tell me it is both amateurish and unreliable.

46. Liu Xiaobo, 'An Appeal to Overseas Chinese and All Concerned Overseas People' (*Gao haiwai huaren yiji yiqie guanxin wentide haiwai renshi shu*), in *Selected Source Documents from the Chinese Democracy Movement*, Vol. I (*Zhongguo minyun yuan ziliao jingxuan I*), Hong Kong: Shiyue pinglun chubanshe, 1989, p. 14.

47. For details of their activities see Li Yuan's 'Who was the real "black hand" on Tiananmen Square?' (*Shei shi Tiananmen guangchangde zhenzheng 'heishou'*), *China Spring* (*Zhongguo zhi chun*), 1990:1, pp. 7–9, and Jane Macartney's essay in this volume.

48. Quoted in Shi Dawen, 'From Being an "Outrageous Man" to Becoming a "Black Hand" — Revealing Liu Xiaobo's Reactionary Mien', *People's Daily*, 29 September 1989.

49. She Shao Jun, 'The "Independent Kingdom" Under the Nose of the Communist Party' (*Gongchandang bizi xiamiande "duli wangguo"*), *China Spring*, 1990:1, pp. 10–13.

50. Earlier, Wuerkaixi, having been told that I was Australian, commented that he was sure he would get on well with Bob Hawke, because he believed the prime minister had some Tartar ancestors.

51. 'The Tragedy of a Tragic Hero,' p. 33.

52. Details of the unattractive inner workings of the student movement can be found on the front page of the Hong Kong *Ming Pao Daily* of 2 June 1989. Here it is reported that Chai Ling was abducted by a group of students outraged by her conduct. They are said to have extracted a confession from her, and a tape of that confessions is rumored to have found its way to France.

53. See 'Our Suggestions,' *Liu Xiaobo: The Man and His Manipulations*, pp. 131–36. It should be noted that Wang Juntao had been actively

interested in the question of civil society for some years and had been writing on the subject. See Shao Jun's article in *China Spring*, ibid. It is quite possible that 'Our Suggestions' was influenced by Wang and his fellows. Unfortunately, the details of Liu's relationship with Wang are still unclear.

54. Jin Zhong, 'Liu Xiaobo, "Black Horse" of the Literary World,' *Emancipation Monthly*, 1988:12, p. 61.

55. Gao Xin reportedly was detained by the police in late June, while Zhou Duo was captured in Shanghai while planning his escape from China in July. See Wei Mingjian, 'Your Pen is Also a Lethal Weapon!' (*Nide bi ye hui chengwei xiongqi*), *Jiushi niandai*, 1989:8, p. 80. Hou Dejian was, for some 10 weeks, in hiding in the Australian Embassy in Beijing. After obtaining assurances that he would not be arrested, he left the embassy in August. All four hunger strikers are quoted in Qiu Yongsheng, Huang Zhimin, Yi Jianru, Zhang Baorui, and Zhu Yu, 'A Peaceful Retreat, No one Died' (*Heping cheli wu ren siwang — 6 yue 4 ri Tiananmen guangchang qingchang dangshiren fangtanlu*), *People's Daily*, 19 September 1989, evidence that apart from Hou Dejian, the other three ex-strikers were in the hands of the Chinese authorities. Hou, in an interview in early January, said that Gao Xin had been released from custody. See John Kohut, 'Waiting for a peaceful end to suffering,' *South China Morning Post*, 10 January 1990.

56. Michael Fathers and Andrew Higgins, *Tiananmen: The Rape of Peking*, London: The Independent/Doubleday, 1989, p. 90. A more serious account of the strike can be found in Scott Simmie and Bob Nixon's *Tiananmen Square*, Vancouver: Douglas & McIntyre, 1989, pp. 166–69. Official Chinese reports, including Mayor Chen Xitong's speech on the protest movement, called the strike 'a farce' (*naoju*), departing from the strident language usually used to describe 'counterrevolution.'

57. For example in Wang Zhao's, 'Grabbing Liu Xiaobo's Black Hand,' *Beijing ribao*, June 24, 1989.

58. See, for example, Jimmy Ngai (Wei Shaoen), 'Those Tiananmen Days' (*Tiananmen suiyue*), *Esquire* (*Junzi zazhi*), 1989:7, pp. 142–43.

59. 'Hunger Strike Proclamation,' *Emancipation Monthly*, 1989:6, pp. 48–49. While *Emancipation Monthly* has printed the proclamation under Liu's name only, other published versions indicate that it was written by all four hunger strikers. Elsewhere the proclamation is entitled 'June 2 Hunger Strike Proclamation' (*6.2 jueshi xuanyan*). See, for example, *The Tragic Democracy Movement* (*Beizhuangde minyun*), Hong Kong: Ming Pao chubanshe, 1989, pp. 112–13. In the *Time* account account of events, *Massacre at Beijing: China's Struggle for Democracy*, pp. 23–24, Hou Dejian is named as being the most prominent of the group. Scott Simmie and Bob Nixon in *Tiananmen Square*, p. 167, go so far as to claim that the proclamation is the work of Hou Dejian. Hou has denied this to me. Furthermore, a study of Liu Xiaobo's writings and the proclamation indicate that Liu was the guiding intelligence behind the document.

60. From Liu et al, 'Hunger Strike Proclamation,' p. 49. Liu and Hou asked a prominent Beijing translator to write an English version of their

proclamation on June 2. Unfortunately, I have been unable to avail myself of that translation. Liu's critique of the protests once more echoes his comments in 'The Tragedy of a Tragic Hero — Three Critiques of the Phenomena Surrounding Hu Yaobang's Death,' pp. 33–34.

61. Richard Nations, 'Who Died, and Who Didn't,' *The Spectator*, 29 July 1989, p. 12. Hou Dejian wrote about the events of that morning in 'My Personal Account of the Retreat from Tiananmen Square on June 4' (*Liuyue siri cheli Tiananmen guangchangshi wode qinshen jingguo*). In early August, Western military attachés stationed in Beijing reported that they had been shown a video recording by the Chinese Ministry of Defense in which Liu Xiaobo, now in custody, made a statement. Appearing healthy although tired, Liu told his interviewer/interrogator that he had not personally seen anybody die in Tiananmen Square. In August, this video was subsequently screened (and sold) in both Hong Kong and China. See, for example, *Sing Tao Jih Pao*, 24 August 1989. In mid-September, yet another official account of the morning of June 4 was published, quoting Liu Xiaobo and showing a picture of him being interviewed. See Qiu Yongsheng et al, 'A Peaceful Retreat, No one Died,' *People's Daily*, 19 September 1989. Democratic process seemed something of a chore for activists even after the massacre. When exiled Chinese intellectuals gathered in Paris at the end of September to establish the Front for a Democratic China (*Zhongguo minzhu zhenxian*) the process of drafting and adopting a constitution along democratic lines proved to be debilitating. After the endless preparatory meetings and 10 revisions to the draft constitution, it was finally passed. Yuan Zhiming, a philosopher and one of the writers of the controversial pro-Zhao Ziyang television series 'The River Dies Young,' said: 'Democracy is exhausting, especially for people fresh from the mainland: We're now used to all the processes involved in the practice of democracy.' See *Sing Tao Jih Pao* (*Australian Edition*), September 26, 1989.

62. 'Hunger Strike Proclamation', p. 48. These exclamations were also written up on a banner across the monument in the center of the Square. See Donald Morrison, ed., *Massacre at Beijing: China's Struggle for Democracy*, p. 19. The photo album of the movement, *Beijing Spring, Photographs by David and Peter Turnley*, Hong Kong: ASIA 2000, 1989, includes a picture of Liu haranguing a crowd as Hou Dejian and Gao Xin sit in the shade of an umbrella (pp. 124–25); also Ming Pao's *The Tragic Democracy Movement*, p. 111, has a picture of the four with Hou talking; and *The Beijing Student Movement: Witness to History* (*Beijing xueyun: lishide jiangzheng*), Hong Kong: Sing Tao Publishers, 1989, p. 131, shows Wang Dan and Wuerkaixi seated in front of Hou, Zhou and Gao.

63. 'Hunger Strike Proclamation,' p. 48. Liu also talks of the need for re-evaluation and repentance among Chinese intellectuals in 'Arrogance will be Punished by Heaven — on the fatal consequences of moral absolutism in Chinese culture' (*Kuangwang bi zao tianze — lun Zhongguo wenhuade daode zhizhangde zhiming miuwu*), *Ming Pao Monthly*, 1989:8, pp. 35, 37.

64. Jin Zhong, 'Liu Xiaobo, "Black Horse" of the Literary World,' p. 61. This passage echoes Liu's controversial essay 'Mao Zedong, Devil

Incarnate' (*Hunshi mowang Mao Zedong*), *Emancipation Monthly*, 1988:11, pp. 31–34.

65. Bei Ling, 'No Other Choice,' p. 33.

66. From the conclusion to *The Fog of Metaphysics*, p. 433.

67. See, for instance, the introduction to *The Fog of Metaphysics*, pp. 44–46, and the chapter on St. Augustine and repentance, pp. 97–107.

68. See Liu, 'Arrogance will be Punished by Heaven,' op. cit., p. 37, and Zhu Dake, 'Overcoming the Limit' (*Chaoyue daxian*), *Yishu guangjiao*, 1989:1, pp. 20–30.

69. 'Arrogance will be Punished by Heaven,' p. 37.

70. 'The Tragedy of a Tragic Hero — Three Critiques of the Phenomena Surrounding Hu Yaobang's Death,' pp. 33–34.

71. 'The Tragedy of a Tragic Hero — Three Critiques of the Phenomena Surrounding Hu Yaobang's Death', p. 34. A useful digest of the petitions with biographical notes on petitioners and relevant commentaries can be found in Karima Fumitoshi and Yoda Chimei, ed., *Tachiagaru Chûgoku chishikijin: Hô Rekishi to minshûka no koe*, Tokyo: Gaifûsha, 1989, pp. 6–53.

72. Liu Xiaobo, *A Critique of Choice, an exchange with Li Zehou* (*Xuanzede pipan — yu Li Zehou duihua*), Shanghai: Shanghai renmin chubanshe, 1988, p. 103. Li is one of China's much-vaunted philosophers, and Liu attacks Li in this rabid book-length attack. It is not a scholastic analysis of Li's work, but rather a denunciation of Liu's own nightmarish view of 'Marxist-Confucian' intellectuals. Li Zehou is merely used as an icon or symbol in Liu's attack. For his part, Li dismisses Liu's writings out of hand. He responded to Liu's provocations in an interview published in 1989. See *The May Fourth: Pluralistic Reflections* (*Wusi: duoyuande fansi*), Hong Kong: Sanlian shudian, 1989, pp. 252–68. Li Zehou's ill-tempered and racist comments on my own view of Liu Xiaobo in this interview are also highly illuminating.

73. Liu, 'Metaphysics and Chinese Culture,' *Xinqimeng I*, 1988: 10, p. 76. In particular, Liu seems to be referring to the enthusiastic and emotional response among Chinese writers to Politburo ideologue Hu Qili's 'granting' of creative freedom in 1985. Fang Lizhi is famous for his stand on this question. See, for example, 'Democracy Isn't Bestowed' (*Minzhu bushi ciyude*) in Fang Lizhi, *Minzhu bushi ciyude*, Hong Kong: Zhongguo xiandaihua xuehui, 1987, pp. 225–28; 'China's Despair and China's Hope'; and 'Fang Lizhi on the Question of Human Rights in China' (*Fang Lizhi lun Zhongguo renquan wenti*), China Spring (*Zhongguo zhi chun*), 1989:5, p. 12. In the conclusion to their book, Simmie and Nixon quote the quirky literatus Wen Huaisha as saying: 'In China, when you are trying to make some progress, you must make a lot of sacrifices, you must shed your blood. Democracy is not a favor to be conferred on anyone. You must fight for it…' See *Tiananmen Square*, pp. 205–206.

74. *The Fog of Metaphysics*, p. 45.

75. The texts of 'Confessions of a Vile Soul — by a Reborn Ugly Chinaman' (*Choue linghunde zibai — yige fuhuolede chouloude Zhongguoren*) and 'The Confession of a Young Teacher — by a young teacher who knows shame' (*Yige qingnian jiaoshide zibai — yige zhixiude qing-*

nian jiaoshi), written on April 29, can be found in *Selected Source Documents from the Chinese Democracy Movement*, Volume I, pp. 70–71. Another fascinating and well-written 'confession' was published by a Chinese student studying in Australia. See Cong Jian, 'The True Story of Ah P' (*A P zibai*) in *The Tide Newspaper* (*Haichaobao*), 29 June 1989, p. 34.

76. Bo Yang, *Chouloude Zhongguoren*, Taipei: Yiwen tushu gongsi, 1985. A full English version of the speech translated by Don Cohn is available in *Renditions* No. 23, pp. 84–103. For details of the appearance of the speech in mainland China, see Bai Jieming, 'Murder by Tolerance and Bo Yang Fever' (*'Kuanrongsha' yu Bo Yang re*) *The Nineties*, 1987:1, pp. 11–12. Also Barmé, Minford, *Seeds of Fire*, pp. 373–77, for Bo Yang's comments on his mainland debut.

77. Hou Dejian, 'The Beautiful Chinese' (*Piaoliangde Zhongguoren*), *The Nineties*, 1989:6, p. 39.

78. Liu Zaifu, 'The Main Current of the Literature of the New Age' (*Xin shiqi wenxuede zhuchao*), *Wenhuibao* (Shanghai), 8 September 1986.

79. *Ibid.*

80. Barmé, 'The Chinese Velvet Prison: Culture in the "New Age," 1976–89,' *Issues and Studies*, Vol. 25, No. 8, August 1989, p. 63, n. 28.

81. From Tan's treatise *Renxue*, translated by Chan Sin-wai, in *An Exposition of Benevolence, The Jen-hsüeh of T'an Ssu-t'ung*, Hong Kong: The Chinese University Press, 1984, p. 193; the original Chinese can be found on page 284. For the dating of *Renxue*, see Chan, pp. 11–12. For an important analysis of Tan Sitong and his martyrdom, see also Hao Chang, *Chinese Intellectuals in Crisis, Search for Order and Meaning, 1890–1911*, Berkeley: University of California Press, 1987, pp. 66–103, especially pp. 102–103.

82. Liu Xiaobo, *A Critique of Choice, an exchange with Li Zehou*, p. 57.

83. For example, Tillich writes, 'The individual is not guilty of crimes performed by members of his group if he himself did not commit them. The citizens of a city are not guilty as participants in the destiny of man as a whole, and in the destiny of their city in particular; for their acts in which freedom was united with destiny have contributed to the destiny in which they participate. They are guilty, not of committing crimes of which their group is accused but of contributing to the destiny in which these crimes were committed. In the indirect sense, even the victims of tyranny in a nation are guilty of this tyranny.' From Tillich, *Systematic Theology*, Vol. II, pp. 66–68, quoted in John G. McKenzie, *Guilt: Its Meaning and Significance*, London: George Allen & Unwin, 1962, pp. 188–89.

84. These details are taken from Xu Jilin's 'A Look at the Psychology and Personality of Intellectuals from the Perspective of China's Confessions' (*Cong Zhonguode «Chanhuilu» kan zhishifenzide xintai yu renge*), *Dushu*, 1987:1, pp. 11–12.

85. Huang Yuansheng, 'Second Letter to a Reporter of *Jiayin Magazine*' (*Zhi Jiayin zazhi jizhe, qier*), *Posthumous Collection of Huang Yuansheng's Writings* (*Huang Yuansheng yizhu*), Beijing: Shangwu yin-

shuguan, 1984 (facsimile reproduction of the 1920 edition), Vol. II, p. 190. In July 1988, I discussed Huang Yuansheng's work with Liu Xiaobo at some length.

86. Huang, 'First Letter to a Reporter of *Jiayin* Magazine' (*Zhi* Jiayin *zazhi jizhe, qiyi*), *Posthumous Collection of Huang Yuansheng's Writings*, p. 188.

87. Huang, 'First Letter to a Reporter of *Jiayin* Magazine,' p. 189.

88. Ibid.

89. Huang, 'Confessions' (*Chanhuilu*), *Posthumous Collection of Huang Yuansheng's Writings*, Vol. I, p. 134.

90. Liu, 'The Tragedy of a Tragic Hero,' p. 34.

91.

92. Liu, 'The Tragedy of a Tragic Hero,' p. 33. Bo Yang says much the same thing in conversation with Gao Tiansheng. See *The Chinese are Cursed!* p. 275; and also his reflections on democracy during his 1988 trip to the mainland which he presented at a seminar at Beijing University. See *Homeland (Jiayuan)*, Taipei: Linbai chubanshe, 1989, p. 104.

93. The mainland poet Duoduo is a contemporary of Bei Dao. This quotation is taken from a talk he gave at London University, as it was reported in Qiao Lin's 'Duoduo: A Poet from Tiananmen Square' (*Duoduo: laize Tiananmen guangchangde shiren*), *The Nineties*, 1989:8, p. 98. The mood of Beijing in late 1988 and early 1989 is well reflected in pop songs of the time such as 'Don't Crush!,' 'In-house Entrepreneur', 'Officials: Big Eaters and Drinkers,' and Hou Dejian's 'Get off the stage!' For the lyrics of these songs see Yu Jiwen, 'New Rock from Beijing' (*Beijingde xinyaogun*), *The Nineties*, 1989:6, pp. 104–105.

94. See, for example, the *Sing Tao* newspaper's pictorial collection *The Beijing Student Movement: Witness to History*, pp. 50–51.

95. From the pledge of the Beijing University Students, printed in the May 13 extra of *Xinwen daobao* and reprinted in *Selected Source Documents from the Chinese Democracy Movement*, Vol. I, p. 86.

96. The word originally meant 'extreme cold;' it later took on the meaning of pathetic or helpless as well.

97. See Ivan Morris, *The Nobility of Failure: Tragic Heroes in the History of Japan*, New York: Farrar, Straus & Giroux, 1988, pp. 278–334, especially pp. 289, 294. Morris quotes a haiku by one 22-year-old pilot: 'If only we might fall/Like cherry blossoms in the Spring —/So pure and radiant!'

98. The expression 'dare to die' (*gansi*), however, has been in use in Chinese from at least the Han dynasty. Interesingly, the name *gansidui*, while a common modern Chinese translation for the Western word 'commando squad,' was also popular at the end of the Qing dynasty when similar groups appeared. One was the 'Shanghai Women's Northern Expendition Dare to Die Squad' (*Shanghai nüzi beifa gansidui*), founded in November 1911 with 70 members; another was the 'Ying Family Dare to Die Army' (*Yingzi gansijun*) consisting of over 1,000 peasants from Hong Kong, Kowloon, and Huizhou.

99. Since June 4, a new selfless martyr has been promoted as a model for the young. This is the Sichuan adolescent student Lai Ning who died

in a fire in 1988. See 'A Boy Sets the Example,' in *Beijing Review*, 15–21 January 1990, pp. 6–7.

100. Quoted in Fathers and Higgins, *Tiananmen: The Rape of Peking*, pp. 87–88; also in Simmie and Nixon, *Tiananmen Square*, p. 155.

101. Simmie and Nixon, *Tiananmen Square*, pp. 155–156.

102. See Chai Ling's post-massacre statement for the pledge. The Chinese text can be found in *The Tragic Democracy Movement*, p. 123. Jimmy Ngai's account 'Those Tiananmen Days' in *Esquire*, 1989:7, pp. 144–48, also reveals this death-wish mentality.

103. On the subject of thanatopsis and dedication to the revolution in post-1949 and particularly Cultural Revolution China, see Anita Chan, *Children of Mao: Personality Development and Political Activism in the Red Guard Generation*, Seattle: University of Washington Press, 1985, pp. 61, 71, 141–42, 155–56.

104. See Elvin, *Self-liberation and Self-immolation in Modern Chinese Thought*, p. 18, commenting on Guo Moruo.

105. See Chai Ling's post-massacre statement in *The Tragic Democracy Movement*, p. 123.

106. Quoted in Xie Chi and Shi Lu, 'An "Aide-memoire" on the Crushing of the Rebellion' (*Pingbao 'beiwanglu'*), *People's Daily*, July 26.

107. From a letter dated 7 November 1988, and sent to the writer sent from Oslo, Norway. This statement is very similar to what Liu says in his essay 'On the Doorway to Hell.'

108. 'Liu Xiaobo has been Detained by Public Security Organs' (*Liu Xiaobo bei gongan jiguan juliu*), *Beijing Daily*, 24 June 1989. Simmie and Nixon in *Tiananmen Square*, p. 205, follow this report. The Hong Kong weekly *Asiaweek* gave the date wrongly as June 12/13.

109. See, among others, Chen Xitong's speech, and Xie Chi and Shi Lu, 'An "Aide-memoire" on the Crushing of the Rebellion', *People's Daily*, 26 July 1989. For the 'connection' with Stone, see Ye Guang, 'Who did Wan Runnan Play to Crush with his "Stone"?' (*Wan Runnan banqi 'shitou' yao za shei*), *Beijing Daily*, 17 August 1989. Zhou Duo is named as the Stone Company's liaison man with Liu. See also David Kelly, 'Massacre of a Chinese Company', *Financial Review*, 4 October 1989.

110. See 'Spokesman for the State Council Replies to the Questions of Chinese and Foreign Journalists' (*Guowuyuan fayanren da Zhongwai jizhe wen*), *People's Daily*, 4 May 1989. Fang Lizhi is actually named as a 'behind the scenes manipulator' in this press conference.

111. Liu Xiaobo, 'On Solitude,' pp. 5–6.

112. 'Wang Meng Discusses Art and Literature,' *Zhongguo wenhuabao*, 26 November 1989.

113. Liu Xiaobo, 'Further Comments on the Crisis Facing the Literature of the New Age,' p. 18.

114. See Jin Zhong, 'Liu Xiaobo, "Black Horse" of the Literary World', *Emancipation Monthly*, 1988:12, p. 63 for quote.

115. See note 72.

116. He Xin, 'My Perplexities and Concerns' (*Wode kunhuo yu youlü*), *Xuexi yuekan*, 1988:12 pp. 36–37. For the role of He Xin in recent political and cultural debate in China see my article and translation,

'A Word of Advice to the Politburo,' *Australian Journal of Chinese Affairs*, January 1990.

117. He Xin, 'A Word of Advice to the Politburo,' ibid.

118. See 'The Meaning of Micro-Environment' (*Ruhe renshi 'xiao-qihou'*), *Liaowang*, 10 September 1989.

119. Chen Jun, 'My Days with Liu Xiaobo,' *Emancipation Monthly*, 1989:7, p. 63. In fact Liu couldn't tolerate the sectarianism of the organization and was only interested in editing *China Spring* — a job he was supposedly offered when he was in America — if it was freed of its political affiliations. Andrew Nathan comments on Beijing Mayor Chen Xitong's accusation — one based on a mistranslation — that Liu advocated violence in 'Chinese Democracy in 1989: Continuity and Change', *Problems of Communism*, September–October, 1989, p. 26. Linked to the government accusations of Liu's violent intentions is an oft-repeated quote from Liu that 'I have great admiration for Hitler.' Unfortunately, I have not found the origin of this quotation, and none of the mainland criticisms give a source. This statement, however, is worth noting in any lengthier study of the evolution of Liu Xiaobo's thought. It is also noteworthy that in Liu's articles and writings appended to the official book of attacks on Liu Xiaobo, the original article or interview in which this comment is made is not included, which suggests to this writer that it may well have been taken out of context.

120. See Ye Guang, 'Who did Wan Runnan Want to Break with his "Stone"?' ibid.

121. See, for example, the cover story 'The Plot: CCP Plans to Kill Liu Xiaobo' (*Da yinmou: Zhonggong yao sha Liu Xiaobo*), by Lu Bian in *China Spring* (*Zhongguo zhi chun*), 1989:8, p. 6. Also Huang Beiling's announcement on page 7.

122. See 'Eye-witness Accounts of the Clearing of Tiananmen Square,' *Beijing Review*, 23–29 October 1989, p. 27. Interestingly, in this account neither Liu nor Hou Dejian mention the fact that they left the Square before the last students. They told friends later on June 4 that they had been carried out on stretchers with greatcoats over their heads as if corpses. Perhaps these remarks were edited out of their interviews. Gao Xin, on the other hand, says he saw no one killed, while on June 4 he said to friends that he had miraculously survived when a group he was with was mowed down by machine-gun fire.

123. See the inside back cover of *China Spring*, 1990:1. The Chaohe Guest House is in Miyun district near the juncture of the Chao and Bai rivers.

124. See Mi Qiu, 'Save Liu Xiaobo' (*Yuanjiu Liu Xiaobo*), *Dangdai*, 1989:8, pp. 26–29.

125. I would like to thank Andrew Nathan of the East Asian Institute of Columbia University for this information.

126. Reprinted in *South China Morning Post*, 26 July 1989, and *Emancipation Monthly*, 1989:8, p. 58.

127. See *Press Freedom Herald*, No. 10, 19 September 1989, p. 3. See also the virtually hagiographic comments on Liu by the novelist-cum-

editor Ma Jian in his short-lived monthly, 'Liu Xiaobo: The Bravest Man of his Generation' (*Yidai mengshi*), *Daqushi*, 1989:10, p. 85.

128. See Yang Manke, 'Yan Jiaqi's Theory and the Chinese Democratic Front Congress' (*Yan Jiaqide lilun yu Minzhen dahui*), *Emancipation Monthly*, 1989:10, pp. 26–27. As a member of the Chinese mainstream intelligentsia in exile, Yuan Zhiming, one of the authors of the television mini-series 'The River Dies Young,' made one of the most positive evaluations of Liu Xiaobo's role in the protest movement in January 1990. The article is an important (and moving) example of a contemporary Chinese intellectual's 'confession.' Yuan writes: 'Shortly after June 4, the communist press published a major denunciation entitled 'Grabbing Liu Xiaobo's Black Hand.' In fact, Liu Xiaobo's hand was the cleanest of all. He stood forward without fear, and at the most critical moment he started a hunger strike in Tiananmen Square. He always made his appeals directly and without artifice. He didn't play those games where you attack people and then run away when there's a danger of being caught. As for the rest of the intellectual world, if we did get invovled then you could say our hands really were black ...'. See Yudan Zhiming, 'Black Hands and Standard-bearers' (*Heishou Yu qishou*), *News Freedom Herald* (*Xinwen ziyou daobao*), No. 22, 20 January 1990.

129. 'On the Doorstep to Hell,' ibid.

130. For a definition of the *xia*, see James J.Y. Liu, *The Chinese Knight-errant*, London: Routledge and Kegan Paul, 1967, pp. 4–7.

131. This observer has written an account of the protests but has yet to publish them.

132. 'Comrade Chen Xitong's Broadcast Speech' (*Chen Xitong tongzhi guangbo jianghua*), *People's Daily*, 5 June 1989.

133. See Kathy Wilhelm, 'Singer uses songs to spread protest word,' an AP report carried in the *Canberra Times*, 20 January 1990.

134. See He Xin, 'On Eliminating the Elite' (*Lun jingying taotai*) originally published in *Mingbao yuekan* 1988:3, reprinted in *He Xin ji fansi, tiaozhan, chungzao* (Harbin: Heilongjiang jiaoyu chubanshe, 1988).

The Thought and Spirit of Fang Lizhi

PERRY LINK

FANG LIZHI has formidable intelligence. But the first time I met him — at a small dinner party in Beijing in September 1988 — my initial impression was of plainness. Is *this* the famous Professor Fang? Perhaps my expectations were conditioned by the image of Liu Binyan, the outspoken journalist who had been punished together with Fang in January 1987, and whom I had known for years. Liu is tall, lean, handsome, purposefully serious, and projects an appealing 'presence.' Fang Lizhi is shorter and stouter, almost pudgy, and seems quite content to project no image at all. He has a plain round face, slightly buck teeth, and boyish dimples. In group conversation he listens much of the time, and delivers his thoughts simply and briefly when he does speak. Sometimes the best reminder that he is still listening is his explosive laughter, which rings out with joyous gusto at pomposity, hypocrisy, or the ludicrous.

The evening I first met Fang I hardly spoke with him at all, although we did exchange name cards, and shared a car on the trip home because we lived near each other in the northwest part of Beijing. Our first significant contact came two months later, when Fang's permission to travel to the U.S. was abruptly withdrawn by Chinese authorities. My telephone rang at 7:30 one morning, and a voice said, 'This is Fang Lizhi. Can we talk?' I rode my bicycle to his apartment. He had called me because of my role as director of the Beijing office of the U.S. National Academy of Sciences (NAS),[1] on whose programs he had traveled to the U.S. in 1986, and to whom he now wished to appeal for help in again getting travel permission.

When I arrived in Fang's living room he handed me a stack of letters. 'Here are my invitations to the U.S.,' he said, and then waited for me to read them. There was one to give a prestigious Regents' Lecture at the University of California at Santa Cruz, and one to attend an international conference on astrophysics at the University of Colorado, for which Fang himself was a co-organizer. There were other invitations from physics departments at Harvard, Berkeley, Princeton, the University of Texas at Austin, and elsewhere. When I had finished reading, Fang went on to state his case in the clear, direct, and tersely analytical manner that is so characteristic of him. He said, 'Last May I was given approval to attend these events. Yesterday I was told that I could not. I was given three reasons: one, that China's leaders do not like what I said in Australia last August; two, that they do not like what I said to the press in Hong Kong on my way home; and three — although this was expressed to me only vaguely — they do not like me to say things about the overseas bank accounts of the families of top leaders.' He then pointed at his stack of letters. 'I have eight invitations, all entirely non-political. I have three reasons for denial, all entirely political. What do you think of that?' He looked at me with raised eyebrows. I agreed to inform the NAS and the U.S. Embassy of this problem. In follow-up on the matter, I visited him again three or four times.

On 25 February 1989, I attended a meeting in Beijing to plan a conference scheduled for April in California. Fang Lizhi and his wife, Li Shuxian, were also there. Someone at the meeting mentioned Fang's and Li's invitation to a barbecue dinner with President George Bush the next night. My wife and I had also been invited. Again I casually offered, as I had the past September, to share a car. I certainly never imagined — and am certain as well that Fang did not imagine — that this chance occurrence would lead to my wife and I being witnesses as Fang and Li were humiliatingly tailed the next evening through the cold streets of Beijing by bevies of police (some in plain clothes, others in crisp new uniforms and outfitted with revolvers) and repeatedly prevented, on absurd pretexts (such as 'you have defective tail light') not only from riding in cars but even from boarding public buses.

Four hours of such Kafkaesque experiences can leave one disoriented. I wondered, then, how Fang might respond when, around midnight, an aggressive reporter at a large and frenzied gathering of the Western press shouted the question, 'What is the significance of tonight's event, Professor Fang?'

'What, indeed?' I thought to myself, groping among a seeming million of things one might say first.

Fang replied, in halting but clear English, 'I think...tonight ...it's a good example of the state of human rights in China.'

'Your rights were violated?' asked the reporter.

'Not just my rights,' continued Fang. 'Also my wife's rights

...also my American friends'...also many ordinary people
...many people who were waiting for the bus...and the police
did not let the buses stop. Those ordinary people...they could
not get home...their rights were violated.' I marveled not only at
Fang's presence of mind, but at the quality of his answer. Never
mind George Bush and the diplomatic barbecue; or the fatuous
pride of a Li Peng; or the spectacularly clownish behavior of the
Chinese police; or the torrid onslaught of an excited Western press
on the trail of a 'story;' or the multifarious international reverbera-
tions that were sure to come. For Fang the core issue — Can
people have simple, basic human rights? — was best illustrated by
the Beijing common folk who were denied access to buses.

Fang stayed away from Tiananmen Square during the dramatic
events of spring 1989. He did not go to the Square even once. The
student movement was autonomous and broad-based, and Fang
did not wish to lend even the appearance of credibility to government charges that he was a mastermind of it all.

On the morning of June 4, after the massacre, I rode my bicycle
to the homes of several Chinese friends who lived nearby. I
wanted to share impressions about what had just happened, and
to offer my help if that were possible. Around noon I arrived
at the Fangs' apartment, where Li Shuxian answered the door
in a hoarse, urgent whisper: 'They're crazy...they've gone
crazy...' Fang, too, was agitated, but still in control. The next day
I accompanied them to the U.S. Embassy, where, after four hours
of discussion, Fang decided he did not want to ask for refuge,
because it might make the democracy movement vulnerable to
Chinese government charges of 'foreign backing.' (He later did
take refuge in the embassy where he still was at the time of this
writing.) I then escorted them out of the embassy and to a nearby
hotel, where we had dinner and found a room where they could
stay temporarily. That was the last I saw of them.

How should we understand the significance of Fang Lizhi to the
theme of this book, the 'breaking of the mirror' at Tiananmen?
Although Fang was not an active participant at the Square, he did,
in my view, play two important roles in these events: 1) concrete-
ly, as an actor in the earliest genesis of the events; and 2) abstract-
ly, as an inspirational leader and role model for the students.

Fang's concrete role was limited to his open letter of 6 January
1989 to Deng Xiaoping, in which he called for a general amnesty

for Chinese political prisoners, including Wei Jingsheng. Following this letter, three petitions by intellectuals in February and early March echoed Fang's call. The first petition bore 33 signatures, mostly of humanists, including many stellar names in China's literary establishment; the second — a lengthy and carefully written call for wide-ranging democratic reforms — was signed by 42 of Fang's colleagues in the natural sciences; the third was signed by 43 mostly young scholars in the Chinese Academy of Social Sciences. News of the three petitions coursed quickly and widely through the intellectuals' grapevine in Beijing, and soon reached other cities as well. It was the first time since the founding of the People's Republic that intellectuals had opposed their highest rulers publicly and in concert. The three petitions were critically important in preparing the ground for the student movement that followed.

But Fang's letter to Deng, potent though it was, represents the totality of Fang's active involvement in the events of spring. The Chinese government's sporadic charges that he and/or Li Shuxian were 'black hands' who were 'behind the scenes' to 'dictate' strategy and 'manipulate' young students, etc., completely depart from the factual record. Such charges are worthy of study for those who wish to understand the psychology and politics of the Big Lie, but are simply irrelevant to serious study of Fang's significance in the spring movement.

What I call Fang's 'abstract' importance, as an inspiration to the students, was obvious well before the spring of 1989. His bold, plain-speaking lectures around China in 1986 had drawn packed houses everywhere, and were a major cause of the student movement that year, as well as the direct cause of his own expulsion from the Communist Party in January 1987. After 1987, student invitations to him to speak were consistently stymied by the Party — not through any publicly announced ban, but simply through administrative measures such as the denial of the requisite permits. In one case in fall 1988, authorities actually locked the doors of a lecture hall and posted police guards at its entrances to prevent Fang from speaking.

To my knowledge, students at Beijing University were the only ones who managed to foil such obstructionism during 1988, and they did so twice. On 4 May 1988, a large event was convened at Beijing University to commemorate the historic May Fourth movement of 1919. Commissioner of Education Li Tieying, who was highly unpopular with the students, was the keynote speaker. During Li's speech, the students employed one of their standard expressions of sarcasm, called *gudaozhang*, 'ironic clapping,' in which a single loud clap explodes inexplicably in one part of the hall, followed by another single clap in an entirely different part, then a third elsewhere — like a recalcitrant popcorn popper. After Li's speech, the students emerged to find Fang Lizhi among the people outside, and immediately formed a large crowd around him. There, informally, the students enjoyed what they considered to be a more fitting tribute to the ideals of 'science' and 'democracy' espoused by students 70 years ago in the May Fourth movement.

Late in the fall, after student morale had fallen so low that few even bothered to go to class, Beijing University students were somehow able to schedule a room and get Fang Lizhi into it for a speech. Word of this coup spread quickly, and by the time the speech began, it was impossible to squeeze into the hall. Some students were literally hanging on light fixtures. (Embarrassingly for the authorities, one of the university vice presidents was giving a public lecture at the same time upstairs in the very building where Fang spoke; that room was almost empty). Student 'apathy' was clearly shown that night to be a surface phenomenon, a depressed response to official lies. When they had the chance to hear someone like Fang, who spoke the truth plainly, their spirits soared.

What exactly was it, in Fang's person and in his thinking, that appealed so strongly to these Chinese students? Not having done opinion surveys or systematic interviews on this question, I am not in a position to address it with proper social-scientific rigor. Instead, for the remainder of this essay, I will pass along my own first-hand impressions of Fang's thinking and character, and leave to the reader the task of imagining why Chinese students were so attracted.

Although he is widely known as an advocate of democracy, Fang Lizhi's most fundamental commitment is to science. In early 1989 he commented to me that his favorite accomplishment for 1988 was his citation at the Beijing Observatory for the most scientific articles published that year. Fang persisted with his research in astrophysics even after taking refuge in the U.S. Embassy. In fact, during the first three months of confinement there, he produced three articles for publication. During the months I knew Fang, between November 1988 and June 1989, he made a strict rule of going to work at the Beijing Observatory every morning, and returning at 2:00 or 3:00 p.m. Friends and well-wishers, student admirers or Western journalists, could visit only in the late afternoons or evenings.

Fang admires Albert Einstein, both as a fellow physicist and because of his less-well-known social thought.[2] When one entered Fang's Beijing apartment (as it existed before June 1989), the first thing one saw, hanging on the vestibule wall, was a poster of Einstein — with his wildly tousled hair and a steady, benign gaze, as if saying 'Here's the truth, but what will the world do with it?'

Fang's advocacy of democracy and human rights springs from his deep faith in scientific rationalism. In the 1950s, as a young man, he had embraced science and 'scientific Marxism'; later, when he discovered glaring contradictions between 'science' and 'Marxism,' it was the latter that he abandoned, even in the face of great social and political pressure. Science was more fundamental, for Fang, because it was a *method* of discovering truth, not a set of established beliefs. For him a key element in the scientific method was the primacy of fact.

'In science we don't tamper with data no matter what they say,' he once told me. 'Even if the machine is broken, we note the problem with the machine, but keep the data as they are.' Another key element was science's universality. Fang once quoted Einstein as saying, 'I'm not a Jewish scientist — I'm a scientist,' and then added, 'He's right. There's no "Chinese science," either. There's only science.' Fang does allow that cultural characteristics are important, and in many cases valuable. 'In matters of customs, aesthetics, and taste,' he says, 'it is natural, and fine, that there be different preferences. Chinese may like *jiaozi* and Americans hamburgers. Fine. But questions of scientific truth and falsity are not like that. Scientific propositions cannot change from true to false when one crosses national borders.'

Fang holds that the evolution of social organization — including what he regards as the long-term, world-wide transition from autocratic rule to democratic rule — is governed by rules that are universal and scientifically testable. The concept of 'human rights,' for example, may have emerged from the European Enlightenment, and been codified through revolutions that arose in France and America, but should now be viewed as a world-wide legacy, equally valid everywhere. At bottom, it makes no more sense for China's rulers[3] to say human rights are 'a Western thing,' and thus inappropriate to China, than it would for an American president to advise against use of the compass on grounds that it is 'a Chinese thing' that may not work in North America.

In spring 1989, Fang wrote an essay called 'The Progress of Chinese Democracy as Seen from the Beijing Observatory.'[4] In it he points out the difficulties that many generations of Chinese scientists have had in gaining acceptance in China for Western astronomical discoveries. After Matteo Ricci arrived with the ideas of Copernicus in the late 16th century, right through to the early 20th century, Chinese emperors (and even the Nationalist government after 1911) opposed use of the Western calendar, and the astronomy that underlay it, on the grounds that 'China is different.' China's rulers may now accept modern astronomy as a matter of course; but history is littered with examples of scientists who were imprisoned, and even executed, for advocating it.

In the 20th century, the question is 'democracy.' Using the very same language that had been used against astronomy, China's present rulers declare that democracy doesn't fit China's 'national temperament,' *guoqing*.

'Does that mean,' I asked Fang, 'that it will take four centuries for democracy to be accepted, as it did for astronomy?' 'No,' he answered, 'the whole pace of change in modern times has increased so much that acceptance of democracy shouldn't take that long. But it will take a *long* time, and will not be easy.'

Fang's training in science also helps to explain the powerful analyticity, even reductionism, in his thinking and expression. He likes to look straight to the heart of issues, analyze their basic elements, and express his views, as science asks, in the simplest terms the facts will permit. For this reason, I found it not always easy to have conversations with him. I would sometimes ask him a question, even a big question, only to hear him reduce it to its core, answer in one or two sentences, and then look at me with raised eyebrows, as if to say, 'Next question?' When others in the Chinese democracy movement criticize him for 'not paying attention to tactics,' they underestimate him, but indeed have noticed an element of his intellectual style. His preferred manner of argument is not that of the fencer, but more like that of a bowler — roll the ball down the middle, and let the pins fall where they may.

Sometimes watching how the pins fall is, for Fang, rather like watching the results of a scientific experiment. In 1987 a friend who was editing a book commissioned Fang to contribute an essay about conversations that Fang had had with Chinese students abroad during a stay in Italy. But when the book of essays was submitted for publication, Fang's piece was rejected by the political authorities. Fang responded by re-submitting his essay elsewhere, but now adding an account — recorded with the clinical precision of a scientific lab report — of how the essay had been originally solicited and then later rejected. Eventually the essay was rejected again, allowing Fang to write 'An account of an account of an account. . .' The essay ends with this observation:

We have a method in physics whereby we hurl simple particles into the center of complex phenomena. We watch what happens to the simple particles, and from that can infer properties of the complex phenomena. My little essay is like a simple particle. I have hurled it several times into the thick of complex phenomena, and each time learn something new.[5]

It seems to me that Fang's steady rationality, and coolness under pressure, has to do not only with his being a scientist, but with being an astrophysicist in particular. One late afternoon, when he was receiving some foreign journalists at home, I was amused to notice how matter-of-fact he was with them. He fielded questions about Li Peng's mediocrity, about China's human-rights abuses, and about America's 'double standard' problem, as unpretentiously as if he were describing features of the solar system. Suddenly I found it useful to recall that he had, after all, just spent his day at the Beijing Observatory, working in his special field of cosmology, theorizing about a universe that measures billions of light-years across. From a perspective in which the Milky Way is a mere dot, the reporters had brought him back to our minuscule earth, and then to that even smaller part of it called China, and finally to Li Peng. Why would he flinch?

Western journalists often refer to Fang as a 'dissident,' and sometimes as a 'radical.' But these terms are misleading, as are similar terms used in the overseas Chinese press, like *lixin* (literally, 'centrifugal') or *yiyi* ('differently opinioned').[6] The trouble with all such terms is that they suggest that Fang is positioned on the radical fringes of public opinion. But, to judge Chinese public opinion by those measures we have,[7] Fang's core advocacies — such as opposition to corruption, to 'class struggle' as an ideology, and to political oppression, and support for basic freedoms of thought and expression, and for education — are by no means fringe issues. They are formulations of extremely widespread grievances. In fact many others who articulate these grievances, including especially the younger generation of intellectuals, do so in terms that are far more extreme than Fang's own.[8]

Although Fang has clearly decided that China's experiment with communism has been a failure, he is not an extremist even on this score. When the American writer Orville Schell asked him, 'Is there nothing — nothing at all — that China should save from the Maoist period?' Fang replied with this metaphor: 'If China's political structure is like an old brick house, some have advocated keeping the basic architecture the same while remodeling the interior. What I believe is that the whole structure has to be dismantled, reconceived, and rebuilt. But you ask if there's anything to save from the socialist experience. Yes, I would say. There should be some socialist bricks that are worth saving and building into the new structure.'

'Like what bricks?' asked Schell.

'Well,' answered Fang, 'like the principle that we shouldn't allow helpless people to suffer poverty. The state should help such people. That would be a good socialist brick to build into the new house.'

This reply reveals Fang's democratic-spirited populism, a trait he shares with Liu Binyan. Both Fang and Liu often say that their optimism for China does not rely on any faction of the leadership, but on the energy they find, despite periodic crackdowns, inexorably rising from below. They also share a spirit of respect for the little guy, and a 'rooting for the underdog,' that resembles strong traditions in American democratic thought. For example, when we left the U.S. Embassy in June, Fang said, 'I think it would be good if the American Embassy gave protection to some ordinary people — a worker, a student, or just a regular townsperson like the ones who were killed last night. It would be a good statement about the principle of human rights — much better than taking in a famous person.'

In another respect, however, Fang is not a populist. As a modern intellectual, he often expresses himself using terms and concepts (such as 'human rights') that are unfamiliar, and can seem alien to much of the population. The Deng Xiaoping regime has sought to exploit this trait to the full, accusing Fang of advocating 'all-out Westernization,' and trying to provoke xenophobic responses to him. In fact, Fang does not advocate 'all-out Westernization,' and takes great care to avoid explicit comparisons between 'East' and 'West.' When I invited him in early 1989 to contribute an essay to the column called 'East-West Winds' that I was editing for *Eastern Chronicle*, he registered a mild protest at the column's name. 'I don't like to stir up questions of "East" versus "West,"' he said. 'I think the world will be better off if we raise questions of true versus false, and advanced versus backward — but not "East" versus "West." Those terms only tend to stimulate chauvinisms that get in the way. If something's more advanced, then use it — that's all.'

The regime's charge of 'all-out Westernization' also implies that Fang advocates the importing of things without regard for actual conditions in China, but this, too, is a grievous distortion of what he actually thinks and says. How can China implement democracy? 'I think we should start with respect for the basic human rights,' he answers. 'If we have the freedoms of thought, expression, and assembly, we can gradually move toward a full democratic system. But it will take time: I don't know if I can see it in my lifetime.'

But if Fang Lizhi's basic ideas are not extreme, within their context of Chinese public opinion, what has made him stand out so prominently? I would point to two characteristics. One is his readiness to speak out boldly. Nearly all Chinese intellectuals, and many other Chinese as well, censor themselves because of 'personal risk trap.' Privately, they share with one another long lists of bitter grievances against their leaders. At the same time, everyone knows that whoever dares to voice such complaints publicly does so at great personal risk. The result is a pervasive but superficial appearance of public support for officialdom and official policy, a veneer that is maintained only through a well-entrenched system of intimidation. (In Beijing the full extent of the actual discontent of the populace became unmistakably clear for a few days in May 1989, when so many people were in the streets protesting that the 'personal risk trap' lost most of its leverage.)[9]

Fang Lizhi consciously defies the 'personal risk trap.' Some time during the mid-1980s he decided, as a scientist and a democrat, simply to tell the whole truth and take all the consequences. Fortunately his renown, both domestically and internationally, has been sufficient to provide him some protection. What he was saying by 1988 would certainly have brought harsher consequences to less famous people. As a result these people, in great numbers, have generally been obliged to lie low and let voices such as Fang's stand for their own.

Despite the shield an international reputation provides, to speak as boldly as Fang still requires remarkable courage. I sometimes actually felt sorry for Fang as I observed admiring Chinese students, or the overseas Chinese press, almost goading him to make ever-more-bold pronouncements. Did they appreciate, I wondered, that while it may be profoundly satisfying for them to hear such statements, it may be uncomfortable, and lonely, to be the one always having to make them?

There were times, when Fang was under the greatest stress, that I thought I noticed him deliberately firming his resolve by reminding himself to act on principle. On the night when he was blocked from the Bush banquet, after our car had been surrounded by armed police, and after I was able to negotiate permission to exit the car, we began to walk in the direction of the Great Wall Hotel. I noticed that Fang, as he strode along, held his head especially high and his back especially erect. (He reminded me of the stories of Ming dynasty officials who strode into the imperial palace, with backs erect, explicitly to tell the emperor what he did not want to hear — full knowing that their buttocks would be beaten bloody in consequence.) Moments later, Fang was pulled away by a knot of plainclothes police. A similar incident followed later in the evening. About 8:30 when we were finally offered shelter by two Canadian diplomats and were approaching the gate of their residence compound, a group of Chinese police suddenly came forward and gruffly demanded IDs from Fang and his wife. Fang reached into his pocket, produced his ID, held it proudly in front of his chest, and pronounced his name slowly and with unusual precision: 'Fang Lizhi.'

The second characteristic that makes Fang stand out, in my view, is his far-sightedness. Most Chinese intellectuals in recent years have, because of their strong sense of national crisis, become preoccupied with problems of China's immediate situation. Fang also notices these problems, and articulates them with great clarity; but his conceptual framework is much broader. He thinks of China's problems, it seems to me, with the middle of the 21st century in mind. He refers with approval to Albert Einstein's predictions that the world is ultimately destined to see a withering of nationalism as the unity and interdependence of humankind continue to emerge. Humanity is impelled toward interdependence whether we like it or not, he maintains, because of the many complex problems — energy, the environment, population, international business, and security — whose only real solutions will have to be global. More basically, concepts of human rights will continue to emerge as being universally applicable. Basic freedoms of thought and expression, and liberation from oppression and persecution, will more and more come to be regarded as the rights of all human beings, equally and without any distinction. The argument that such matters are the 'internal affairs' of governments will lose credibility as it becomes increasingly accepted that any human being has the right, indeed the duty, to speak out in defense of any other.

One aspect of this vision is the presumption that nationalism will become less and less important. This is a difficult idea for Chinese people to accept, given their immense, and justified, pride in the glories and singularities of China's ancient past, and their anguish at the wars, defeats, and humiliations of the past 150 years. After the crash-landing of the communist revolution, many Chinese feel that patriotism is the one last, and thus precious resource still available to buoy the Chinese spirit. Fang disagrees, stating squarely, but gently, that 'patriotism should not be our top priority.'[10]

Fang further holds that the Communist Party's campaigns in the 1980s to label democratic ideas as 'un-Chinese,' or as 'spiritual pollution' have been aimed at arousing xenophobia, historically one of the most primal impulses in Chinese nationalism, and channeling it into the cause of repression. We must expect, Fang cautions, that China's rulers will continue to employ this tactic, because by now they have lost every other kind of moral and political grounding: Marxist ideology is no longer taken seriously; Maoism remains widely discredited, and is despised by many; and now, the regime has devastated its own moral authority by condoning and participating in the rampant official corruption. Xenophobia is one of the last forces to which it can appeal.

The foregoing sketch of Fang Lizhi's thinking can perhaps suggest why China's students have found him inspiring. That they have felt free to approach him, as an older and acclaimed academic, may well have to do with his open, unassuming style and his charming sense of humor. Everyone who went to his apartment and rang his doorbell (which was an electric device that played 'Happy Birthday') received the same respect from him. He was on friendly, equal terms with ordinary workers in his neighborhood. One day as I was passing Fang's apartment building, on the way to another destination, I noticed his wife, Li Shuxian, standing outdoors in the bitter cold in front of their building. I asked why, and learned that the residents of the building had just had a meeting the night before about how to control a rash of recent burglaries. The group had decided to take turns standing guard outside the main door. 'Fang Lizhi took the first shift,' said Li. 'This afternoon it's my turn.'

Fang's sense of humor, good cheer, and joy in repartee not only survives political adversity, but even, curiously, sometimes seems to thrive on it. In late May 1989, when Beijing was under martial law, Fang returned from a trip to Taiyuan, where he had been tailed by two unmarked police cars wherever he went. 'Now I can guess why they won't let me visit the U.S.' he joked. 'It's probably financial. They can deploy two cars in Taiyuan, but could they afford two cars in Colorado?'

After he wrote his famous open letter of January 6 to Deng Xiaoping, calling for release of all political prisoners, a reporter asked Fang how he had delivered the letter.

'I just put an 8-*fen* stamp on it and put it in a mailbox,' Fang replied.

'Wouldn't a 4-*fen* stamp have been enough?' some clever person asked, since the smaller amount is sufficient postage within Beijing.

'But he winters in Guangdong,' said Fang, 'so I decided to spend the whole 8 *fen*.'

On another occasion, a reporter asked Fang whether he viewed the tapping of his telephone as a violation of his human rights. 'Of course it is,' came the reply. 'But sometimes I look at it a different way. At least they listen to me. How else can I get them to listen?'

---

1. I worked, specifically, for an NAS committee called the Committee on Scholarly Communication with the People's Republic of China (CSCPRC). The views and impressions in this essay are entirely my own, and do not represent the NAS or CSCPRC. The Chinese government's reports (circulated widely inside China but not outside) that say I was 'fired by the U.S. State Department' after June 1989 are laughable. I have never worked for the U.S. State Department, or been fired by anyone.

2. In particular, the belief that universal acceptance of basic human rights is an inevitable consequence of human social development.

3. The word 'ruler' here reflects Fang's preference. In my experience, he consistently referred to the Chinese authorities as *dangquanpai*, 'powerholders' or 'rulers,' not as the more common *lingdao* 'leadership.' Although I never specifically inquired as to this point, I suspect that he wished to avoid the connotation in the word *lingdao* of a followership that is willing.

4. '*Cong Beijing tianwentai kan Zhongguo minzhu jincheng.*' Fang gave me a copy of the essay. I am not sure whether or where it has been published.

5. The latest extant version of this essay had been submitted to a magazine for Chinese intellectuals called *Eastern Chronicle (Dongfang Jishi)*, of which I was a participating editor during 1988–89. Fang had delivered the manuscript to me. Unfortunately it was confiscated from my Beijing office — along with 75 other unspecified 'items' of 'letters, printed matter, and clothing' — by the Chinese police in August 1989. Neither Fang nor I have another copy of the manuscript. I have protested the confiscation to Beijing, but have little hope of recovery under the present regime. I have received a brief official notice of the confiscation, but no itemization or justification.

6. The Communist Party's own special term — *chi butong zhengjian-zhe* ('holders of differing political views') — is simultaneously wordy and vacuous, but everyone understands it as an extremely dangerous political label. Fang, when asked about this term, would usually reply by saying, 'Based on the face-value meanings of the words, I see nothing frightening about it. "Differing political opinions"? There are plenty right in the Politburo.'

7. Public opinion research is difficult in a society where people guard their true feelings under many levels of caution and reserve, and where the opinions of portions of the population — such as urban intellectuals — are much more accessible than those of others — such as peasantry in remote rural areas. But it certainly does not follow, as some have argued, that Chinese opinion is unknowable. In a workshop volume called *Unofficial China: Popular Thought and Culture in Contemporary China*, ed. Perry Link, Richard Madsen, and Paul G. Pickowicz (Boulder: Westview Press, 1989), China scholars from several disciplines, using diverse methodologies, demonstrate how we can understand the thinking, at least on certain questions, of various sectors of the Chinese populace. These essays show how the thought of 'unofficial China' is ofen independent of, divergent from, or even directly opposed to official ideology.

8. At the end of 1988, many young people in Beijing, workers as well as students, were so profoundly cynical about China's system that hyperbolic sarcasm sometimes seemed their only outlet. 'Our country can be summed up in one word,' a young worker said. 'Hopeless!' A young intellectual said, 'China would be better off today if England had colonized it after the Opium War, or even if Japan had won World War II.' Another said China cannot progress 'until it loses half its population, whether by atom bomb, famine, or AIDS doesn't matter.' When one

accounts for this kind of extreme view, whose true constituency is much larger than the Chinese regime wishes us to believe, it becomes obvious that Fang Lizhi does not stand on the fringe.

9. A public opinion survey done during May 1989 by Beijing Normal University found that 96 percent of Beijing residents supported the demands of the students; less than 1 per cent were opposed, and the remainder gave no response. See Nicholas Kristof, 'Beijing Journal,' *The New York Times*, 22 September 1989.

10. A published telephone interview with Fang, entitled *'Aiguozhuyi buying fang zai diyi wei'* (Patriotism should not be put first) appears in the Hong Kong magazine *The Nineties*, January 1989, pp. 96–98.

The Rulers: China's Last Communist Leadership?

Jürgen Domes

When we try to analyze the actors in the system in which the crisis of China in spring 1989 developed, one central question is: Who were the rulers who decided to crack down? Since the Party Statute of the Chinese Communist Party defines the Party as 'the leading core of the Chinese people of all nationalities,' it is appropriate to concentrate on the CCP leadership, for it incorporates all major leading figures of the state machine as well. Moreover, the orders to enact martial law, and to drown the democracy movement in a bloodbath, were decided by Party rather than state organs. I will discuss the position and the composition of the ruling elite by asking four questions:

First, what are the formal central leadership structures of the CCP?

Second, what are the structures of participation in political decision-making within the official political society of the People's Republic of China?

Third, who were the real decision-makers within the CCP elite during the crisis?

Fourth, what is the impact of the decision-making structures that functioned during the crisis on the development of communist rule in China?

The Party Statute defines the National Party Congress, which is supposed to convene once every five years, as the highest organ of the CCP. The last Party Congress, the Thirteenth, convened in Beijing on 25 November 1987, for seven days. It consisted of 1,997 delegates appointed by the Provincial Party Congresses and the People's Liberation Army, 1,953 of whom reported to the meeting.[1]

But the Party Congress, in fact, is only an acclamatory organ. In resolutions, it proclaims the policies decided upon by the inner cores of leadership, and it appoints the Central Committee (CC). The CC is supposed to convene for plenary meetings twice a year to decide personnel reshuffles and major statements of policy, which are usually prepared in advance either by 'Central Work Conferences' or meetings of the Politburo.

The Thirteenth Party Congress appointed 175 full members and 108 non-voting alternate members to the Thirteenth CC, which still officiates today.[2] A number of media reports in early November 1987 insisted that this CC had been thoroughly rejuvenated, and that it contained the highest number of newly elected members since the establishment of the PRC. This was not true. The share of newly appointed full members stood at 35.4 percent in the Thirteenth CC while it had been 46.4 percent in the Eighth in 1956, 80 percent in the Ninth in 1969, 37.4 percent in the Tenth in 1973, 45.3 percent in the Eleventh in 1977, and 46.7 percent in the Twelfth in 1982. Hence, the share of newly appointed full members of the Thirteenth CC was, in fact, the lowest since the establishment of the PRC.

Rejuvenation, too, assumed only moderate proportions. The average age of the 175 full members of the CC in 1987 stood at 57 years. That was three years lower than the average age of 60 in the Twelfth CC in the fall of 1987, yet only one year lower than the 58 years of the Twelfth CC immediately after its appointment in 1982.

Only 5.7 percent of the CC members are women. This share was 4.1 percent in the Eighth and 5.2 percent in the Twelfth CC, but 7.7 percent in the Ninth, 9.2 percent in the Tenth, and 7.0 percent in the Eleventh CC.

As compared to the situation immediately before the Thirteenth Party Congress, the share of representatives of the PLA among the full members of the CC increased slightly from 17.6 percent to 18.3 percent. This is, however, a much smaller number than the 33.6 percent in the Eighth, 50.0 percent in the Ninth, 37.4 percent in the Tenth, and 25.4 percent in the Eleventh CC.

The most dramatic change in the composition of the Thirteenth as compared to the Twelfth CC occurred in the area of Party seniority. Among the members of the Twelfth CC who were in office immediately before the Thirteenth Party Congress, only 29.5 percent had joined the CCP after its victory in the civil war in 1949. In the Thirteenth CC the share of post-revolutionary Party members rose to slightly more than half of the membership, to 50.4 percent.

Yet this same observation cannot be made for the Politburo,

which exerts all powers of the CC when that body is not in session, and which meets at least every four to six weeks. On 2 November 1987, the first plenary meeting of the Thirteenth CC appointed 17 full members and one non-voting alternate member to this leading body of the Party.[3] At the time of appointment, the average age of the full members of the Politburo stood at 61.24 years, which made it the second youngest Politburo; in 1956 it had an average age of 55.7 years, while it was 67.79 years in 1982. Yet despite this remarkable rejuvenation of the Politburo, it still continues to be a group of revolutionary veterans. Only three out of 17 full members and the alternate joined the CCP after 1949, so that — if one includes the alternate — only 22.2 percent of the Politburo belonged to the post-revolutionary generation.

As to the representation of different opinion groups within the Politburo, the decisions of the Thirteenth Party Congress could not be considered a 'triumph of the reformers,' although most media and numerous China specialists in the West proclaimed that in 1987. There were eight reform-oriented revisionists in the new Politburo, but there remained also six orthodox Marxist-Leninists, while the political positions of four full members appeared temporarily unclear, until two of them — the head of the security establishment, Qiao Shi, and the vice premier and former minister of foreign affairs, Wu Xueqian — joined the orthodox coalition in 1988. In early 1989, the head of the Shanghai Municipal Party Committee, Jiang Zemin, followed their move, thus giving the orthodox group the majority on the Politburo.

Different from other ruling communist parties, the CCP since 1956 has, within the Politburo, an official leadership core, which is considered to be the collective leadership of the Party, while the General Secretary cannot be compared to his formal peers in other parties. Mikhail Gorbachev is the General Secretary of the Communist Party of the Soviet Union. The General Secretary in the PRC is only the General Secretary of the CC, a position held by Deng Xiaoping from 1956 through early 1967. This collective leadership organ is the Standing Committee of the Politburo. On 2 November 1987, the CC appointed five politicians to that body:
— Zhao Ziyang, born in 1919, who had joined the CCP in 1938, the general secretary of the CC;
— Li Peng, born in 1928, who had joined the CCP in 1946, and who was acting premier of the PRC in the fall of 1987, and formally appointed premier in April 1988;

— Hu Qili, born in 1929, who had joined the CCP in 1948, and from 1987 to 1989 was a member of the Secretariat of the CC in charge of propaganda and culture;

— Qiao Shi, born in 1924, who joined the CCP in 1940. As chairman of the Central Disciplinary Inspection Commission and of the CC's 'Group on Political and Legal Affairs,' he was the supreme leader of all security, intelligence, and police organs of the PRC; and

— Yao Yilin, born in 1917, who joined the CCP in 1936. He was the first vice-premier and, until December 1989, concurrently chairman of the State Planning Commission of the PRC.

On the Standing Committee, which usually meets at least once a week, Zhao and Hu represented the revisionists, Li and Yao the orthodox Marxist-Leninists, while Qiao wavered for some time until he joined forces with the orthodox group in the summer of 1988.

The major political leaders of the PRC, Deng Xiaoping and Chen Yun, had left the Politburo at the time of the Thirteenth Party Congress. Nevertheless, both continued to wield decisive influence on political decision-making: Deng (born in 1904) in his capacity as chairman of the Central Military Commission, and Chen (born in 1905) in his capacity as chairman of the influential Central Advisory Commission of the Party. Even without formal voting rights, Deng and Chen attended most meetings of the Politburo and the Standing Committee until the fall of 1989. There, Deng, until the summer of 1988, used his authority to promote the policies of economic, but not political, reform, while Chen used his influence to uphold Marxist-Leninist doctrine and to enact a retrenchment of economic reforms.

The first major personnel changes within this official leadership core occurred with the death of Politburo member Hu Yaobang on 15 April 1989, and when the fourth plenary meeting of the Thirteenth CC, on 24 June 1989, decided to remove Zhao Ziyang and Hu Quili from the Politburo and the Standing Committee as well as from the Secretariat, following recommendations by an enlarged meeting of the Politburo, which had been held from June 19 through 21.[4]

At the same time the CC appointed three new members to the Standing Committee of the Politburo:

— Jiang Zemin, born in 1927, who had joined the CCP in 1944, as the new general secretary of the CC;

— Li Ruihuan, born in 1934, who had joined the CCP in 1954, as new secretary of the Secretariat in charge of propaganda and culture; and

— Song Ping, born in 1917, who had joined the CCP during the Long March in 1934, as director of the CC's Organization Department.

Because only Li can be considered a revisionist, the Standing Committee now consists of five orthodox Marxist-Leninists and one revisionist.

No new members were added to the Politburo, and not even the alternate member was promoted to full membership. Hence, in early 1990, the Politburo consists of nine orthodox Marxist-Leninists and four revisionists, while the positions of one full member and the alternate member are still not clear. This formal leadership operates in a hierarchically arranged official political society.

Structures of the official political society

The political society presents itself as a system of seven concentric circles with first gradually and later abruptly increasing degrees of participation in politics.[5] The outermost seventh circle comprises the whole adult population, which is only the object of political decision-making and which, at the end of 1988, consisted of approximately 640 million people over 18 years of age.

The sixth circle includes the members of the official mass organizations. They are being used as elements of mobilization in order to carry through the policies decided upon by the central policy-making bodies. For most of these organizations, no reliable membership figures are available, but it appears safe to assume that, by the end of 1988, they had a total of between 160 and 170 million members, or about 25 percent of the adult population.

In the fifth circle there are the members of the CCP, who numbered approximately 47.7 million in mid-1988, or 7.45 percent of the adult population.[6] This share compares with 9.8 percent in the Soviet Union, and almost 16 percent in East Germany before the events of fall 1989. The organizational density of the CCP was therefore lower than that of other ruling communist parties, but it had also entered the process of transforming itself from a revolutionary cadre Party to a career-oriented mass Party when the spring crisis began. The Party members serve as examples of affirmative attitudinal response to elite stimuli for the population and as a reserve pool for political recruitment, but, as a whole, they are not able to influence political decisions even marginally. From their midst, there arises the structure of the four inner circles of the official political society, of which the fourth through the second can be considered as layers of service hierarchy. Only the first represents a decision-making hierarchy, which in itself, is also structured.

The fourth circle is made up of those persons who are officially called 'cadres'. They number approximately 22 million people, or 3.44 percent of the adult population. The 18 million Party members among them represent 37.7 percent of the CCP membership.[7] These people are responsible for executing the directives of the leadership at the base. In the process, they may be able to change the thrust of the directives in some detail, but they, too, have no influence on the formulation of policy.

In the third circle, there are the recipients of internal Party documents — the serialized 'documents for study' or the circulars of the Party center. They number approximately one million, or 0.16 percent of the adult population, and 2.1 percent of the Party members.[8] This circle, in times of intra-elite conflict, is occasionally addressed by the contending groups and factions, but its members are still not directly involved in such conflicts, although they may become their victims.

The second circle consists of the 'leading cadres.' It includes about 80,000 persons, that is, one for every 8,000 adults, or one for every 596 Party members. This group has close connections with the ruling elite, and in times of intra-elite conflict, the contending groups and factions recruit followers from its members. Yet they are still not involved in political decision-making.

That is the domain of the first and innermost circle, the ruling elite. This group decides the allocation of leadership positions, it co-opts its own new members, and it has a say in policy formulation. It is within this circle of one person for every 795,000 adults or 59,000 Party members, that intra-elite groups form and power and policy conflicts are mainly decided. This political elite includes all leadership personnel down to the level of ministers, governors, and mayors, provincial Party secretaries and alternate secretaries, military district commanders and political commissars. In late 1988, there were 805 persons in this circle. Within this ruling elite, three additional concentric circles can be detected:

1. The executive heads, i.e. those persons who occupy the one

leading position in all major Party, state, and military organs down to the provincial level. They numbered 165 people in late 1988.

2. A decision combine, which includes all political leaders who are directly involved in the preparation of major policy decisions, and who participate in the inner councils of policy making. By the end of 1988, this circle comprised the members and alternates of the Politburo and the Secretariat, the secretaries of the Central Disciplinary Inspection Commission, the members of the presidium and some other members of the Central Advisory Commission, as well as the chairman of the Central Military Commission. At the end of 1988, this circle consisted of 31 persons who, at that time, had an average age of 68.

3. The leadership core, which represents the very heart of rule formulation, and which is identical with the Standing Committee of the Politburo. At the end of 1988, it numbered five people or — if one includes Deng Xiaoping and Chen Yun, seven.

During the spring crisis, this political society displayed distinct tendencies of disintegration. One of the major features of this disintegration was the fact that decision-making was reduced to informal groups within the ruling elite.

Decision-making in the spring crisis

Already after the suppression of the first and still comparatively weak democracy movement of university students in December 1986, the Politburo — at the time that of the Twelfth CC with its 20 full and two alternate members — started to hold 'enlarged meetings,' in which the presidium and selected members of the Central Advisory Commission were not only allowed to participate, as stated in the Party Statute, but also to vote. This procedure was first used on 16 January 1987, when the voting rights of members of the Central Advisory Committee at an 'enlarged meeting' of the Politburo secured an orthodox majority, which decided to dismiss Hu Yaobang from his position as General Secretary of the CC.[9]

After the Thirteenth Party Congress, this method to convene decision-making organs was not only continued, but it became even more frequent. It was at such an 'enlarged meeting' of the Politburo in the northern Chinese sea resort of Beidahe in late July

1988, where a majority of eight out of 16 Politburo members and nine out of 13 members of the Central Advisory Commission present as well as one Party veteran without any institutional position resolved, 18 to nine, with three abstentions, to reject a Zhao Ziyang proposal to accelerate and broaden the policies of economic reform. A second 'enlarged meeting' of the Politburo, which convened in Beijing from August 15–17, then decided to transfer the responsibility for economic policy-making within the Standing Committee from Zhao to Li Peng and Yao Yilin.[10] On 8 April 1989, another 'enlarged meeting' of the Politburo in Beijing discussed educational policies, and it was at this meeting that Hu Yaobang, in a debate with Party veterans, suffered the heart attack from which he died.[11]

From all these 'enlarged meetings,' there emerged gradually a group of eight Party veterans who increasingly influenced the decision-making in the Politburo and even the Standing Committee. Only one is a regular Politburo member, while four of them do not even hold the position of membership in the Central Advisory Commission. Besides Deng Xiaoping and Chen Yun, they are:

— General Yang Shangkun, born in 1907, who joined the CCP in 1926. From 1917 to 1930, Yang studied in the Soviet Union, and he became one of '28 Bolsheviks,' a group of Chinese sent by Stalin to China in order to ensure the 'bolshevization' of the CCP in 1930. He is a member of the Politburo and, since April 1988, the president of the PRC.

— Peng Zhen, born in 1902, who joined the CCP in 1923. From 1945 to 1966 and from 1979 to 1987, he was a member of the Politburo, and from 1983 to 1988 chairman of the Standing Committee of the National People's Congress. Since 1988, he has had no official position.

— Li Xiannian, born, according to official CCP data, in 1909, but according to his own statement to Nym Wales during the 1930s, in 1905. He joined the CCP in 1927 and was a member of the Politburo from 1956–1987, and of the Standing Committee from 1977–1987. From 1983–1988, he served as president of the PRC, and since 1988, as chairman of the Chinese People's Political Consultative Conference. He does not sit on the Central Advisory Commission.

— General Wang Zhen, born in 1908, who joined the CCP in 1927. He was a member of the Politburo from 1978–1985, and he has been vice president of the PRC since April 1988. He does not sit on the Central Advisory Commission.

— Bo Yibo, born in 1908, who joined the CCP in 1925. He was an alternate member of the Politburo from 1956–1966, and has been standing vice-chairman of the Central Advisory Commission since 1982; and

— Song Renqiong, born in 1909, who joined the CCP in 1926. He was a member of the Politburo from 1982–1985, and has been vice chairman of the Central Advisory Commission since 1985.

In its initial stage, which was mainly characterized by students' demonstrations and not yet by manifestations of large parts of the urban population, the democracy movement of 1989 began to preoccupy the ruling elite only after the number of demonstrators on Tiananmen Square swelled to 100,000 on 22 April 1989. The following day, Zhao Ziyang left for a state visit to North Korea. Premier Li Peng, during Zhao's absence in charge of leading the Standing Committee of the Politburo, covened a meeting of that body on April 24, in which President Yang Shangkun participated with voting rights. The meeting decided four votes to one — that of Hu Qili — to outlaw all demonstrations and to attack the movement as a 'riot' in the official media. On April 25, Li and Yang went to Beidahe to see Deng Xiaoping, who was vacationing there, and to secure his agreement. They succeeded.[12]

Deng, who was still wavering between taking a soft and a hard-line approach toward the movement, greatly influenced its branding as a 'riot' instigated by 'a small group of people with ulterior motives' in the editorial of the April 26 edition of the *People's Daily*, to which Zhao had agreed by cable from Pyongyang on April 25.[13] But the reaction to that editorial, a large-scale demonstration of 150,000 students, who were supported by almost 350,000 citizens of the capital, prompted at least parts of the ruling elite to take a more conciliatory approach. On April 28, at an informal meeting of the 11 members of the Politburo who were present in Beijing and some revisionist members of the CC, it was decided that the rulers would shy away from an immediate crackdown on the movement, and try to conduct a 'dialogue' with selected student representatives.[14]

When Zhao returned from North Korea on April 29, he immediately proceeded to Beidahe, where he criticized the April 26 editorial as 'too pointed' in a meeting with Deng, and finally managed to secure Deng's approval that he should attempt to 'stabilize the situation' by means of a conciliatory approach.[15] After returning to Beijing, Zhao immediately legalized the publications that the demonstrating students had published, and on May 6, he ordered the leading cadres of the CC's Propaganda Department to 'support the freedom of the press,' and to order all PRC media to report openly about the activities of the democracy movement.[16] From the next day until May 19, the Party papers and most television and radio stations carried objective accounts of the demonstrations.

Yet the orthodox faction continued to oppose Zhao's conciliatory approach, and its major leaders — Chen Yun, Li Peng, and Yang Shangkun — now began to prepare for an attempt to overthrow Zhao. For this purpose, they had to convince Deng that he should finally turn against his long-time associate and designated successor.

The fact that, since May 4, one group after another of urban society joined the democracy movement, the tremendous impact of the hunger strike, which 3,000 students began on May 13, the continuous occupation of Tiananmen Square, and the impending state visit by Mikhail Gorbachev on May 15–16 forced Deng to choose sides. Beginning on May 16, he supported the orthodox faction, returning openly to the Stalinist positions he had taken in 1957, in the spring of 1979, in late 1986 and early 1987, and never, in fact, entirely relinquished.

In the late afternoon of May 16, the Standing Committee met in the presence of Deng and most probably also Chen Yun, who did not participate in the voting. At this meeting Zhao submitted a proposal to disavow the April 26 editorial, for which he himself offered to assume personal responsibility in public, to establish a special unit under the National People's Congress to investigate corruption, the publication of the income of all Politburo members and other major leaders, and to eliminate all special privileges of the leading cadres. After heated debate, this proposal was defeated by a vote of four — Li Peng, Hu Qili, Qiao Shi, and Yao Yilin against one, Zhao, who was, at that point, totally isolated.[17] But Zhao insisted on a decision by the whole Politburo, which met on May 17 in the presence of Deng, Chen, Vice-President Wang Zhen, Li Xiannian and Bo Yibo, who were given the right to vote. At the meeting, Zhao repeated his proposal from the preceeding day, but although Hu Qili now supported him, the proposal was again rejected. At this point, Zhao offered his resignation as general secretary, but this offer was turned down.[18]

Shortly after midnight on May 19, the Politburo met again, together with the five veterans who had attended the May 17 meeting. Following a motion by Li Peng, this meeting voted, 15–3, to enact martial law in order to suppress the democracy movement. Again, Zhao offered his resignation, and again, it was rejected.[19]

The implementation of martial law, however, stalled. On May 21 and 22, more than two million citizens blocked the entry of armed PLA units into the center of the capital. On these two days and on May 23, the CCP seemed to be threatened by a split. Seven retired senior generals warned May 21 in a letter to the Military Commission that military force should not be used against civilians,[20] and in the evening of the same day, they were joined by two aged marshals of the PLA.[21] Until May 23, 57 of the 135 members of the National People's Congress' Standing Committee had signed a letter to the chairman of that body, the revisionist Politburo member Wan Li, asking him to convene an emergency session in order to 'solve the present crisis,' and implying that this could be done by a recall of Li Peng.[22]

On the other hand, Li, who was now firmly supported by Deng, had secured, between May 21 and 22, the support of the three main units of the PLA General Headquarters — the General Staff, the General Political Department, and the General Rear Services Department — and of the commanders-in-chief of the Navy and Air Force for the implementation of martial law and the use of military force against the democracy movement. The six Military Area Commands of Shenyang, Jinan, Lanzhou, Nanjing, Canton, and Chengdu followed suit. Only the Beijing Military Area Command dragged its heels until May 26.[23]

After the backing of most of the active PLA commanders had been secured, Deng, Li, and Yang moved immediately to reach the solution of the intra-elite conflict. On the afternoon of May 23, Deng and Yang convened a meeting of the Military Commission without inviting Zhao, although he still held the position of first vice chairman. Upon their recommendation, the meeting decided that only Deng and Yang had the right to order the transfer of troops, thus depriving Zhao of any share in the PLA leadership.[24]

In the late evening of that day, a meeting of the Politburo was called, which lasted well into the morning of May 24. Besides the 14 members of the Politburo who were present in the capital — Wan Li was still in the U.S., and Yang Rudai stayed behind in Sichuan — six Party veterans attended the meeting with voting rights: Deng, Chen, Li Xiannian, Peng Zhen, Wang Zhen, and the 85-year-old widow of Chou Enlai. This meeting was the apex of the critical confrontation in the intra-elite conflict.

For some time, it appeared as if Zhao would win the day. He withdrew his offer to resign, and he argued for placating the students by issuing a declaration that, while martial law continued to be implemented, the PLA would not use military force to establish control over the capital, but would wait until the demonstrators voluntarily left Tiananmen Square. Some Politburo members, most notably Hu Qili, supported Zhao's point of view. But then all six Party veterans, one after another, declared that this would mean to 'give in,' and that such concessions would initiate 'the overthrow of the Party and of socialism.' Following a proposal jointly sponsored by Deng, Chen, Yang, and Li Peng, the meeting finally decided that Zhao's and Hu's membership in the Standing Committee of the Politburo and Zhao's position as General Secretary of the CC should be 'temporarily suspended.' Both were confined to their residences in Zhongnanhai, and Li Peng was appointed leader of a 'group in charge of propaganda work.' Zhao Ziyang had been overthrown.[25] Only a few hours later, Yang Shangkun convened an 'enlarged emergency meeting' of the Military Commission, attended by most of the PRC's top brass, where he launched vitriolic attacks against Zhao and called for 'decisive action' against the 'counterrevolutionary riot'.[26]

During the following days, three of the leading Party veterans publicly voiced their support for martial law and their condemnation of the democracy movement in no uncertain terms: Chen Yun on May 26 at a meeting of the Standing Committee of the Central Advisory Commission, Peng Chen on the same day in a discussion with representatives of the non-communist united front parties, and Li Xiannian on May 27 in a meeting of the presidium of the Chinese People's Political Consultative Conference.[27]

Despite these victories of the orthodox faction, those forces in the democracy movement which were still working for political reform within the framework of the socialist system now placed their hope in Wan Li, the chairman of the Standing Committee of the National People's Congress. He had been an ardent supporter of the policies of economic reform for more than 10 years, and had, during his visit to Canada and the U.S., voiced his support for at least some of the demands of the movement. The hope was that he would comply with the proposals of 57 members of the Standing Committee and convene an 'emergency meeting' after his arrival in Beijing. Yet after Wan's plane had landed in Shanghai on May 25, he decided, upon what was afterwards called a recommendation from Deng, to stay in that city 'for health reasons.'[28] On May 27, Wan, in a written statement, declared his full support for martial law and warned against the 'turmoil' in Beijing.[29]

Having thus secured the agreement of large parts of the ruling elite, the leaders of the orthodox faction moved to suppress the democracy movement. The definite decision was made in an informal gathering during the afternoon of June 2, which at its end was converted into a conference of an official organ. In his residence, Deng Xiaoping met with the three remaining members of the Politburo Standing Committee — Li Peng, Qiao Shi, and Yao Yilin — and with Yang Shangkun, Wang Zhen, and Bo Yibo. The seven decided unanimously that, during the night of June 3–4, fully armed PLA units should move with all force into the center of the capital and clear Tiananmen Square and the surrounding area. Their orders were to 'shoot to kill without warning.' Moreover, they resolved, the meeting of the National People's Congress Standing Committee, which had been scheduled for June 20, should be postponed to 'at least June 30,' and that a 'Central Leading Group for Martial Law' should take over the functions of the Politburo, its Standing Committee, and the Secretariat until an 'enlarged meeting' of the Politburo could be held. Li Peng was to act as the convenor of this group, which consisted of 11 members. Besides the seven leaders present, they were: Chen Yun, Li Xiannian, Peng Zhen, and Song Renqiong. After these decisions, they called Chen by phone and secured his agreement. Finally, they decided that this had been an 'enlarged meeting' of the Standing Committee of the Politburo.[30] On the afternoon of June 3, the members of the 'Leading Group' left their residences in Zhongnanhai for undisclosed shelter in a military base in the suburbs of Beijing, to return June 6.

For 17 days, from June 3 until the 'enlarged meeting' of the Politburo convened on June 19, the PRC was ruled by an informal group of four Politburo members and seven Party veterans, of whom three had no official position in the central organs of the Party at all. The average age was 78 years old.

From June 19–21, the 'enlarged meeting' of the Politburo finally met to decide the future composition of the Party leadership. The meeting was attended by all 16 members of the Politburo — including Zhao — and by the seven Party veterans on the 'Leading Group,' who received the right to vote. On the first day, the meeting decided to relieve Zhao of his positions in the Party, and Hu Qili from his positions in the Politburo and the Secretariat. It also removed Yan Mingfu and Rui Xingwen from the Secretariat, as well as Wen Jiabao from his position as alternate secretary, although Yan remained director of the CC's United Front Work Department and Wen director of the CC's General Office.

On June 21, the meeting made its decision concerning the succession of Zhao as Secretary General of the CC. For this position, Chen Yun suggested Yao Yilin, and Peng Zhen opted for Qiao Shi. There seemed to develop a new rift. But then Deng, Li Xiannian, and Li Peng jointly nominated the 62-year-old Party leader of Shanghai, Jiang Zemin, as a compromise candidate. All leaders present — excluding Zhao and Hu, who had been deprived of their voting rights — agreed.[31] It should be noted that among the five leaders who nominated candidates for the position of General Secretary, only Li Peng was a regular Politburo member.

On June 23 and 24, the fourth plenary meeting of the Thirteenth CC assembled in Beijing to ratify the decisions of the 'enlarged' Politburo meeting. This plenum was attended by 170 out of 175 full members and 106 out of 108 alternates, but also by 184 members of the Central Advisory Commission, 68 members of the Central Disciplinary Inspection Commission, and 29 other 'responsible persons,' including Peng Chen, Wang Zhen, and, of course, Deng Xiaoping.[32]

During the following months, the regular leadership organs of the CCP have resumed their work, but there are many indications that the Politburo and its Standing Committee still hold 'enlarged meetings,' which makes between six and eight of the Party veterans an integral part of the newly emerging decision combine and even of the leadership core.

As we have seen, the major decisions during the spring crisis, in particular those to enact martial law and to use full military force to suppress the democracy movement, were either made by 'enlarged meetings' of leading central organs of the CCP, or even by informal groups. Organs of the state apparatus were not at all involved. Hence, the PRC, since May 1989, has been ruled by a combination of official Party leaders and influential veterans without official positions in the Party, and as far as Deng Xiaoping since November 1989, Peng Zhen, and Li Xiannian are concerned — even in Party and state.

This fact will have considerable effect on the development of communist rule in the PRC. In 1985, I argued that

...Communist single-party systems seem to run their historical course through three stages of development:
1. Charismatic rule, as in the Soviet Union under Lenin and in the PRC under the leadership of Mao Tse-tung until the late 1950s;
2. Transitional rule, which assumed the form of monocracy in the Soviet Union under Stalin and which, in an entirely different manner has characterized the political system of the PRC...since late 1958;
3. Institutionalized rule, which the Soviet political system reached in the mid-1950s.[33]

The stage of transitional rule that clearly dominated in the PRC between 1958 and 1982–83, had, in that country, assumed the features of a transitional crisis system. Such a system is based on the interplay between the development of opinion groups within the ruling elite and their condensation into factions, one of which comes out as the victor in each intra-elite conflict, only to split up again as a new crisis cycle begins. Under such conditions, political initiatives are questioned, divided and — with regard to long-term decisions — paralyzed.

Since the Twelfth Party Congress in September 1982, the political system of the PRC seems to have entered into the process of transition to institutionalized rule. The following five criteria serve as indicators that a communist single-party system has reached this stage:
1. The leaders of the Party and the state administrative machine serve their statutory terms of office, the leading organs meet at statutory intervals, and exert their statutory functions.
2. Party decisions concerning the constitutional powers of the state administrative machine are regularly ratified by ensuing decisions of the leading state organs.
3. Promotion within the leading organs of the Party is preceded by promotion in the subsystems of the state administrative machine, the armed forces, or the mass organizations; e.g., a

person becomes first a minister and then, at the next possible date and because of this promotion, a full member of the CC.

4. The subsystems develop their own channels of elite recruitment and career patterns, albeit under the control of the Party center.

5. A generation that joined the Party *after* the establishment of communist rule — the post-revolutionary generation — has taken over the majority of positions in the ruling elite in general, and in the decision combine in particular.[34]

By the summer of 1988 one could conclude that the PRC had not only embarked on, but had already made considerable progress in the process of institutionalization. The first and second of our indicators were already clearly recognizable, and there were signs that the country was moving toward an implementation of the third and the fourth. Only the fifth, generational succession, had not yet really come about. But with the patterns of decision-making and the group of rulers that evolved on the eve of and during the spring crisis, this process of institutionalization has been disrupted. The PRC is back to the stage of a transitional crisis system. Not only has the ruling elite, with the Beijing massacre and the ensuing campaign of Stalinist terror against all dissent, lost the last vestiges of legitimacy, it has also gravely damaged the institutional framework in which it is supposed to operate.

These two factors lead to the conclusion that the rulers who engineered the rape of Beijing on 4 June 1989 may very well turn out to be the last communist ruling elite of China.

---

1. *'People's Daily*, Beijing, 26 November 1987.

2. For a namelist of members and alternate members of the Thirteenth CCP Central Committee, see: *People's Daily*, 2 November 1987.

3. Namelist in: *People's Daily*, 3 November 1987.

4. *People's Daily*, 25 June 1989.

5. For an earlier discussion of the structures of participation in the PRC's official political society, see my *The Government and Politics of the PRC: A Time of Transition* (Boulder, CO and London: Westview Press, 1985), pp. 50–52.

6. Figure computed from: *Peasants' Daily*, Beijing, 1 July 1988.

7. *Workers' Daily*, Beijing, 23 September 1988.

8. This figure can be derived from the press entrances of 17 such documents from 1981 to 1986, which have been seen by the present author.

9. Document *Chung-fa* (1987), no. 3, 17 January 1987 (copy in the

present author's possession). English in: *Inside China Mainland*, Taipei, May 1987, pp. 1–3.

10. The information about both these meetings is based upon reports by Lo Ping in: '*Cheng Ming*' (Debate), Hong Kong (hereafter: *CM*), no. 130, August 1988, 6–10; and: no. 131, September 1988, 6–11; Also: Chou Han-pei, 'The Peitaihe conference amidst runaway inflation', in: *Tide Monthly*, Hong Kong, no. 18, 15 August 1988, pp. 8–10, and the report by Ch'ien Sui, *ibid*., no. 19, 15 September 1988, pp. 6–8; as well as upon information the present author gathered from interviews with leading cadres in Beijing in October 1988.

11. *CM*, no. 139, May 1989, p. 11 f.

12. '*Ching-pao*', Hong Kong, 10 May 1989; quoted by Lowell Dittmer, 'The Tiananmen Massacre,' in: *Problems of Communism*, Washington, DC, September/October 1989, pp. 2–15, a well-documented and reliable narrative of the intra-elite conflict during the spring crisis. Here: p. 6; also: Wang Pi-ch'eng (ed.), Tiananmen i-chiupachiu (Tiananmen 1989) (Taipei: *United Daily News*, 1989), p. 188.

13. Yang Shangkun in a speech on May 24; text in: *Ming Pao* Hong Kong (hereafter: *MP*) and: *China Times*, Taipei (hereafter: *CKSP*), both 29 May 1989. Also: Chang Ching-yu (ed.), *Tzu-yu chih hsüeh, min-chu chih hua: Chung-kuo ta-lu min-chu-te k'an-k'e lu* (The blood of freedom, the flowers of democracy: The rocky road of democracy on the Chinese mainland, Taipei: Institute of International Relations, 1989), p. 376.

14. *MP*, 29 and 30 April 1989.

15. Dittmer, loc, cit., p. 7.

16. *Far Eastern Economic Review*, Hong Kong, 14 December 1989, p. 27.

17. *MP*, 21 May 1989.

18. *MP* and *China Times*, 30 May 1989, C.f.: Dittmer, loc. cit. p. 11.

19. *ibid*.

20. Text in: '*Lien-he pao/United Daily News*', Taipei, 23 May 1989.

21. *The Light*, Beijing, 22 May 1989.

22. *CM*, no. 140, June 1989, p. 89. C.f. Dittmer, loc. cit., p. 11.

23. *People's Daily*, May 22, 24, and 25, 1989.

24. Dittmer, *loc. cit*., p. 11.

25. *China Times* (ed.), *Pei-ching hsüeh-yün wu-shih jih* (50 days of the Beijing students' movement), (Taipei: *China Times*, 1989), p. 111 ff; and: Chang, *op. cit*., p. 376.

26. *Ibid*., p. 375–382.

27. *People's Daily*, 27, 30, and 29 May 1989, respectively.

28. *Central People's Broadcasting Station*, 25 May 1989.

29. *People's Daily*, 29 May 1989.

30. *CM*, no. 141, July 1989, p. 8.

31. *ibid*., p. 7.

32. *People's Daily*, 25 June 1989.

33. Domes, *op. cit*., pp. 249–251 (quote: p. 249)

34. C.f. *ibid*, p. 252.

The Death of a People's Army

MICHAEL T. BYRNES

THE People's Liberation Army men are like fish in the sea of the people.

Mao Tse-tung

This aphorism had substantive meaning until PLA tanks moved into Tiananmen Square in the early morning of 4 June 1989. This use of force not only left hundreds dead on the streets of Beijing, but combined with the events of the next few hours and days, it projected the PLA into the political arena, created a crisis of loyalty within the military, arrested the 10-year professionalism drive, and shattered the cherished image of the PLA as a 'people's army.' This intervention by the army also maintained Deng Xiaoping and the conservative Communist Party leaders in power.

The PLA, or the Red Army as it was initially called, traces its beginnings to 1927. Originated as a people's army, the PLA was urged to support and cherish the people.[1] As such, the PLA was involved not only in fighting, but also in governing areas under its control, supporting local construction projects, participating in agricultural activities, setting up new industries, and managing old ones.[2] In performing these various nation-building tasks, the PLA developed a favorable image as a respected and key element of the Chinese communist structure. In fact, the military and political structures were indistinguishable. The heads of the Party and government organs were military men. Further blurring the distinction between soldiers and civilians, was the Maoist concept that everyone was a soldier.[3]

Relying on revolutionary zeal, the PLA was effective in nation-building and in unconventional warfare, but proved to be deficient in more conventional war scenarios, such as the Korean War.[4] Deficiencies in this war led to the first professionalism drive, launched in the mid-1950s. Under Russian military guidance, this program to improve the operational capability of the PLA was relatively successful. By 1958, the PLA was a more effective military force, and less involved in social, economic, and political affairs.[5]

This attempt to make the PLA a more professional army was a temporary success because it occurred when there was a serious external threat and when the domestic political situation was relatively pragmatic. The changes which affected the military in the mid-1950s were a reflection of the fundamental changes occurring in China at that time. Every time there was a fundamental shift in the nature of Chinese society, the character of the highly politicized Chinese military institution also changed. Because of the interlocking nature of leadership positions, the PLA was subject to the ever-shifting and contending political factions.

This tension between functional and political demands resulted in the development of a multi-dimensional military force. Such a force was neither militarily effective nor efficient.

From the late 1950s to the late 1970s, the PLA's involvement in politics, and the consequent lack of attention to military matters, led to an inevitable decline in military effectiveness. The PLA's political involvement reached a high point when it was called to restore order and halt the anarchy of the Great Proletarian Cultural Revolution. At the Ninth Party Congress in 1969, the military representation on the Politburo and the Central Committee stood at 50 percent. In the provinces the military presence was even greater. Over 75 percent of the first secretaries of the provincial Party committees wore uniforms.[7] This direct involvement, which lasted until the mid-1970s, and the lack of an immediate threat, did not augur well for a non-political and effective military force. In 1979, the shortcomings of the PLA were made obvious in the brief, but disastrous Sino-Vietnamese conflict, in which the PLA was clearly deficient in all facets of combat.[8]

The PLA in the Deng era: The development of a professional military institution

The war with Vietnam served as a spur to much needed military reform. This threat from the south, combined with the overall political and economic changes that Deng was seeking, made professional military reform both urgent and possible.

Deng's wide-ranging reforms, often termed 'the second revolution,' focused on developing a pragmatic social structure less driven by the Maoist standbys of ideology, political reliability, class struggle, and self reliance. His 'New China' relied on pragmatism, technical expertise, economic progress, and relations with the outside world as the basis for shaping society. Deng's military reforms consisted of two primary elements — modernization and professionalism. Focusing on the officer corps as the key link, great advances were made.[9]

In 1978, when Deng began the military reform program, the PLA officer corps was overaged, underqualified, overstrengthened, and highly politicized.[10] Rejuvenation was essential. Old soldiers in the PLA did not fade away — only death removed them from active duty. At the end of the 1970s the PLA was still under the leadership of the Long March and revolutionary war veterans in their 70s and 80s. These veterans rested on their reputations, while they lost touch with modern military developments. The rejuvenation campaign saw all but the most senior officers replaced by younger men so that by the mid-1980s the average age of brigade, division, and group army commanders (38, 45, and 51 years, respectively) was equal to or less than their counterparts in Western armies.[11]

Not only were officers younger, but they were better educated. Civilian education requirements for entry into the army and the officer corps were tightened and the military education system was completely revamped. Instruction focused on improving the officer's functional expertise, while political study was relegated to a minor position.

Streamlining made the PLA smaller and allowed it to focus on a purely military mission. Non-military elements of the PLA, such as the production construction corps, the railway corps, and soldiers involved in civil police duties were removed from the PLA's structure. (The latter group was reorganized as the People's Armed Police.) Additional troop cuts eventually reduced the PLA's overall strength to about three million men from a high of five million in 1979.

Deng's reforms also had the effect of reducing the PLA's involvement in politics. The percentage of active soldiers on the Politburo and the Communist Party Central Committee dropped from approximately 50 percent in 1969 to less than 20 percent in 1987. Finally, time devoted to political study declined relative to tactical training, and the role of the political commissars was reduced. The PLA officer corps had turned its attention to professional military matters. The PLA had become much more capable in its primary mission of providing external security for the state.[12] Combat effectiveness had replaced politics as the PLA's touchstone. However, the last half of the 1980s marked the high tide of the professional military reforms as changes in both the functional and social imperatives began to affect the PLA.

By the end of 1985, the reform pendulum was swinging in a more conservative direction. This had to do with changes in China's perception of the external threat environment and the fact that Deng's reforms had reached their apogee.

The international scene was changing. The U.S. military build–up under President Reagan and the espousal of *glasnost* by Soviet leader Mikhail Gorbachev, led to a gradual restructuring of the international threat environment. In Chinese terms, the world was moving from conflict to cooperation. In 1985, Deng announced that 'war is not inevitable. Although the threat of war always exists, the world's factors for maintaining peace are growing and the factors that check the outbreak of war are also growing.'[13] Without a serious and immediate threat, the PLA's sense of urgency for military matters began to decline. The PLA intensified its involvement in business activities to the detriment of training; many soldiers began to wonder why training was so important if peace were at hand.[14] By 1988, the PLA was in danger of becoming an army without a coherent operational focus — and without this impetus an army poised to return to its multi-dimensional past.

Budget constraints, and the lack of a viable threat, made it increasingly difficult for the PLA to contend for scarce resources and the attention of the national leadership. Military budgets in terms of percentage of GNP declined from 22 percent in 1979 to eight percent in 1989. Responsible individuals in and out of the PLA began to question the need for a large and expensive military force. The PLA was forced to reply with a national defense education campaign.[15]

The reformist policies that underpinned military professionalism were threatened because of the very progress that had been made. The rational and pragmatic political environment in which younger, better educated, and less ideologically motivated experts pushed the reformist programs, was meeting resistance. Not surprisingly, the bulk of this resistance came from within the Communist Party. Specifically, the party elders, such as Chen Yun,

Peng Zhen, Bo Yibo, Li Xiannian, Wang Zhen, and Yang Shang-kun, saw the reforms threatening their positions of power and the ideological status of the revolution.[16]

This put the PLA in a difficult position. Military institutions by their nature are conservative. Armies resist social and political change which could erode their core values and threaten their position. The PLA, especially in the ranks of the senior leaders and the political commissars, had its fair share of conservative ideologues, whose job was to preserve political values.

However, a good portion of the midlevel officers supported the reformist position, which was much closer to the professional ethos of modern military forces. Additionally, under reformist conditions, the PLA stood a better chance of meeting the hardware needs of military modernization, than with conservative policies in command.[17] Within the PLA, loosely organized factions supporting the conservatives on one hand, and the reformists on the other, were making their presence felt. The military commanders and line officers were generally sympathetic to the reformists while the political commissars were closer in political outlook to the conservatives.

The first casualty of this growing tension was Deng's chosen successor, the Communist Party general secretary, Hu Yaobang. Hu's downfall following the student demonstrations in late 1986 and early 1987 has been covered in great detail in other sources.[18] Suffice it to say that the senior military leadership played a part. Furthermore, Hu's dismissal and the subsequent anti-bourgeois liberalization campaign can be viewed in retrospect as a dress rehearsal for Tiananmen. In both cases, one can see virtually the same general scenarios, the same list of players, and the same stakes.[19]

In the Hu affair, not only did a key reformist lose his position, but Deng's position was seriously shaken. The leadership succession issue, or the struggle for position and power, once again became a major force in Chinese politics.[20] In 1987, elements in the senior leadership began jockeying for position to replace the aging Deng and to oust the new Party secretary and appointed successor, Zhao Ziyang. The Party leaders took measures to ensure that it was they who would give new meaning to the Maoist expression, 'Political power grows out of the barrel of a gun.' To make this happen the Party elders stepped up efforts to put their proteges in key positions in the military and in public security organs.

The military leader who played the most critical role in this drama was Yang Shangkun, state president and executive vice-chairman of the Central Military Commission.[21] Yang, a vigorous octogenarian, was a native of Sichuan province and a longtime crony of Deng. A political general whose experience was limited to administrative and party responsibilites, Yang was always considered to be a loyal second in command. By late 1987, he had consolidated his position by political advancement and protege appointment and was no longer satisfied with being number two. He had also elevated his brother, Yang Baibing, to the directorship of the General Political Department.

The PLA is ordered in

The Tiananmen incident began with the death of Hu Yaobang on 15 April 1989. What started out as an issue-oriented political movement quickly became complicated by, and served as a catalyst for, a struggle among the senior leadership for political power and ideological purity. Ostensibly the struggle was between Premier Li Peng and Party General Secretary Zhao Ziyang. In reality, party elders Deng Xiaoping, Chen Yun, Peng Zhen, Li Xiannian, Wang Zhen, Bo Yibo, and Yang Shangkun, in a shifting coalition, provided the conservative backing that determined the shape and direction of the struggle.[22]

From the beginning, the PLA played a part in the response to the growing demonstrations. In late April, the 38th Group Army, headquartered in Baoding, Hebei province, was moved quietly under the guise of a military exercise, to locations around Beijing.[23] One of the PLA's elite units, the 38th, initially demonstrated reluctance to participate in putting down the student demonstrations. The 38th's commander, Xu Qinxian, who reportedly had ties to Zhao Ziyang, was removed, along with a number of his subordinate leaders, as a result of their apparent sympathy for the students.[24]

While the demonstrations were absorbing public attention in China and around the world, the real action was taking place behind the scenes in Zhongnanhai, the walled compound where

China's leaders live and work. The significant stress created by the students in Tiananmen Square and the thought that the workers might join in, brought the simmering power struggle to a boil.[25]

While the 38th Group Army was deployed to positions outside Beijing in late April, other group armies, mostly from Beijing and Shenyang military regions, were alerted and deployed in early and mid-May. Analysts estimate that by May 19, 150,000 to 200,000 PLA soldiers from 10 to 12 different group armies were ringing Beijing.

The eventual deployment of PLA units to Beijing was as much a response to the student activities as it was a response to the power struggle. The sizable military force around Beijing demonstrated that the Party elders were in an unassailable position. That the PLA forces surrounding Beijing included elements from every one of the seven military regions, served to demonstrate the universal support that the Party elders had obtained.[26] Expressions of support, however, did not come easily. Beijing military region appeared to be a reluctant supporter of PLA employment, as did Guangzhou and Nanjing.[27]

Not only were more soldiers than necessary deployed to Beijing, but the PLA was the wrong force to suppress what was in essence, a civil disturbance. The PLA was organized, trained, and equipped for using unrestrained force against external military threats. The armed force specifically organized, trained, and equipped to deal with civil disturbances was the People's Armed Police.

Why the PAP was not employed is one of the major questions of the entire affair. Some observers have pointed out that because the PAP came primarily from Beijing city, it was unreliable. Also, it may be that the PAP was too small to deal effectively with the large demonstrations. Other indicators point to the incredible fact that the PAP was not prepared, in terms of training or equipment, to accomplish such a mission.

The real reason may have more to due with the PAP being an inadequate force to be used to support a power struggle. Only the PLA had the reputation and the capability to effectively execute such a mission. Only the PLA could have mobilized such a large force, from so many locations, so quickly. Finally, only the PLA could have cowered the opposition so completely.

The PLA's role by mid-May was not only to restore order, but to intimidate the reformist faction. For the proper military and political effect, the force had to be large and be drawn from every corner of the land. By the end of May, the PLA forces around Beijing met these criteria. The employment of the PLA in this role was an example of the classical Chinese strategy of using overwhelming force to pre-empt an opponent.

By May 19, when martial law was declared and Zhao Ziyang was ousted, the conservatives had begun to get the upper hand, though opposition by reformists continued to exist in both the military and political sectors. A consensus, however, could not be reached on sending the PLA into the city to restore order forcibly.[28] The PLA made a number of half-hearted attempts to enter Beijing, but the students and city residents successfully turned them back. In this series of confused actions, the PLA showed admirable discipline and restraint. The failure to enter the city was probably due more to the failure of the senior leadership to reach a consensus on the degree of force to be used, than to ineptitude on the part of the PLA.

Between May 20 and June 3, a series of high-level political and military meetings was held in Beijing while troops continued to deploy to areas around the city. In this latter stage, units from Nanjing and Jinan military regions were prominent. By June 4, the forces around Beijing numbered about 200,000 to 250,000 men, from 16 to 18 of the PLA's 25 group armies.[29]

Attempts by the conservatives to portray a united front intensified while rumors of opposition to the use of armed force from within the PLA circulated around the city. Questions about the attitudes of the Navy, the Air Force and several of the military regions were a constant topic of conversation in Beijing.[30]

Retired PLA Marshals Nie Rongzhen and Xu Xiangqian publicly opposed using the PLA to put down the peaceful student demonstrations.[31] A group of seven prominent retired officers, including former Defense Minister Zhang Aiping and Chief of the General Staff Yang Dezhi, wrote a letter to the Central Military Commission protesting the deployment of troops to Beijing.[32] Additionally, reports circulated that Defense Minister General Qin Jiwei was removed for his reluctance to deploy PLA units to Beijing. (This report proved to be untrue.) It is highly likely, however, that General Qin, long an adversary of Yang Shangkun, opposed the moves made by Yang to use the PLA to suppress the demonstrations.[33] Qin probably retained his position in order to maintain the ever important facade of unity and as a counterweight to the growing power of the Yang family.

The final decision to use military force to clear the Square was made on or about May 26. At least several units had been alerted to prepare for movement into Tiananmen Square by May 30.[34] Yang Shangkun, in a speech to an enlarged meeting of the Central Military Commission on May 24 or 25, reportedly said, 'We can no longer retreat. We must launch an offensive.' Yang indicated that troops were to move to predetermined positions, rest a while, then mobilize for action.[35] Other sources reported that as things quieted down, Deng would order troops into the city center by the end of the month.[36] Simultaneously, to test the waters, PLA units began appearing again on Beijing's streets. As time went on, these appearances grew more numerous. The probable intent of these actions was to reassure the students and the residents of Beijing that a military presence in the city was normal.

The appearance of the Goddess of Democracy statue on May 30 was seen as a direct affront to Deng, the Party elders, and to the spirit of the Chinese Revolution. In addition, demonstrations had been breaking out in the provinces. The hard-liners insisted that immediate and forceful action had to be taken to preserve the revolution and to protect their positions. By June 1, the momentum had swung to the Party elders. Some PLA units moved into position closer to the city center. Beginning several days prior to June 1, every organization that meant something in China began issuing declarations of support for martial law and the restoration of order.[37]

An unarmed probe into Tiananmen Square on the night of June 2 was repulsed in hand-to-hand fighting by the combined efforts of students and residents. In an employment of military force that was almost comical, the PLA suffered a blow to its prestige and pride. The purpose of this action remains obscure. Perhaps it was a final attempt to clear the Square peacefully. More cynical observers contend that it was a purposeful attempt to embarrass the PLA to pave the way for PLA revenge in the form of the forceful action that was planned for the next evening. Whatever the purpose, from an operational standpoint, the employment and performance of the PLA was disastrous. Eye-witnesses noted that the PLA units streaming back from Tiananmen early on June 3 looked like a defeated army. Residents of Beijing accosted the retreating soldiers and lectured them on the responsibilities of being Chinese and what it meant to be a 'people's army.'

While these lectures may have had an effect on the young soldiers (few, if any, officers were observed), the senior Chinese leaders were unmoved. PLA forces, spearheaded by the now infamous 27th group army from Shijiazhuang, Hebei province, rolled into Tiananmen Square in the early morning of June 4. The 27th Army was not alone. At least four or five other units, including elements from the 54th, 39th, 24th, and the 14th group armies, participated in the bloody operation.[38] The 27th Group Army, which was reported to have been everywhere and to have done everything on June 4 and the following days, may have gotten more credit than it deserved.

Given the PLA's previous record of discipline and restraint in dealing with the students, the units employed on June 3 and 4 did not represent an army out of control. These troops were disciplined units ordered to perform a mission and to use whatever force was necessary to accomplish that mission. There were examples of bloody excesses, but it was the senior leadership that issued the orders to use maximum force to clear the Square and restore order. The PLA did not act on its own; it followed its orders.

The PLA can be accused of poor execution of a mission that it was not properly equipped, organized, or trained for. Getting to, and clearing, the Square were basically civil disturbance actions requiring a relatively sophisticated and subtle approach. After weeks of being subjected to a strict news blackout, and being thoroughly 'briefed' by their political commissars on the 'unlawful counterrevolutionary activities' of the demonstrators, the PLA used the techniques, that as a military force, it was trained for. It conducted a multi-division assault on Tiananmen Square.[39] The major disconnect was that the PLA was ordered to attack the objective that it was created to defend — the people.

Who ordered in the PLA?

We may never know who gave the order to use military force to clear the streets of Beijing. One could reasonably speculate that this decision resulted from a consensus hammered out by the Party elders in support of the dominant view held by Deng. The most likely candidates pushing to use the PLA would have been Yang Shangkun and the ever-present, former Xinjiang Military Com-

mander, Wang Zhen. President Yang Shangkun, as the Executive
Vice-Chairman of the central Military Commission, had day-to-
day control of the PLA. Wang Zhen's position is a little more
obscure. A former PLA general who had served with Peng
Dehuai's first field army, he was currently serving as the vice-
president of the PRC. Long considered to be a conservative hard-
liner, Wang was present on May 19, when martial law was
announced and he escorted Li Peng on his well-publicized visit to
the martial law troops. Furthermore, Wang occupied a high protocol position at the June 9 meeting held by Deng Xiaoping. Of all
the elder Party members, only Yang Shangkun and Wang Zhen
had substantive military connections and experience (both had
figured prominently in the downfall of Hu Yaobang).[40] As William Whitson pointed out more than 25 years ago, '. . . Wang was a
man to watch, for his power and political acumen increased
throughout the years.'[41] Wang Zhen, in his early 80s but in good
health, is still a man to watch as he has come to exert an influence
in Chinese politics second only to Yang Shangkun.[42]

The crucial question is what role did Deng Xiaoping play in all
of this? Certainly Deng had to put his chop on whatever plan
Yang and the Party elders developed. But it is unlikely, given
Deng's frail health, that he could have taken an active and aggressive role in the tumultuous activities of the previous 45 days. Deng
may have said yes to the bloody employment of the PLA, but it
cannot be ruled out that Deng, the great manipulator, found
himself in the position of being manipulated.

There are indications that Deng was not always kept abreast of
important matters. One report noted that Deng, as chairman of the
CMC, was upset at not being informed of the decision to impose
martial law.[43] The implication is that Yang and Li Peng did not
consult Deng on this matter.

In the days after the assault on Tiananmen, rumors of civil war
involving opposing military factions abounded. While the situation
in Beijing was far from civil war, military opposition to the elders
was not to be ruled out. Public opposition by senior military
leaders, and the reluctance of the 38th Army to forcefully put
down the student demonstrations, were indicators of this opposition. Furthermore, it is highly likely that military officers, trained
to believe that their professional obligations were to protect the
state from the threat of external enemies, would have been sympathetic to the goals and operating style of the reformists.[44] Deng

and Yang were concerned about the army's reliability, especially among army and division-level cadres. Yang, in a speech on May 24 to an enlarged meeting of the Central Military Commission, was quoted as saying, 'The most important thing now is the consolidation of the armed forces. Do the troops support us? This will depend on your work.'[45]

In the final analysis, the martial law troops fell into line, although subsequent press reports indicated that a number of officers were court-martialed or executed for refusing to follow orders to deploy their soldiers against the students. Upwards of 1,000 soldiers shed their weapons and ran away rather than attack the demonstrators.[46] Talk of civil war was more a result of disinformation and wishful thinking than of any deep split within the PLA. When thrust into the crucible of fire, the PLA remained unified.

Unity was also a major theme of the June 9 meeting chaired by Deng Xiaoping. The formal appearance projected at this meeting suggests concern with the slightest indication of disharmony among the leadership. The meeting also created the impression that Deng was in charge and behind the bloody crackdown.

Although Deng was at the head of the table, it was Yang Shangkun who was clearly the host, directing, guiding, and stage-managing the meeting. The protocol seating arrangements shed some light on the relative positions of the Party elders. Li Xiannian, Yang Shangkun, Peng Zhen, Wang Zhen, and Bo Yibo occupied the top positions, even before the Politburo Standing Committee. The military hierarchy, sitting further down the table, included members of the Central Military Commission and the directors of the general staff departments.[47]

This meeting was the symbolic termination of both the civil unrest and the internal power struggle. Normalcy had been restored. The conservatives and Party elders had preserved the socialist ideal, and more importantly, their positions of power. The meeting also symbolized that the PLA was again involved, willingly or not, in internal politics.

The future of the PLA

The PLA's role in maintaining civil order and its renewed involvement in domestic politics differ from its past. With respect to Tiananmen, while the PLA's military intervention was decisive and dramatic, its political involvement was relatively superficial. And while the PLA intervened in great numbers, only a handful of senior military officers were politically involved in any active manner. The lack of more widespread involvement was due to the successful withdrawal of the PLA from politics at all levels during the previous 10 years. Concurrently, the rising level of military professionalism also played a key role in limiting the depth of PLA political involvement. The PLA's participation below the top level of the Central Military Commission resulted more from being ordered to execute a particular mission than from any desire to become involved as political participants. The PLA intervened, but it was not involved in the same way, for example, that it was in the Cultural Revolution.

Theoretically, this means that withdrawing the PLA from its current involvement will be a relatively simple matter if the central Party leadership decides to do so. The PLA of the late 1980s has tended to act more as an agent of the Party than as part of the Party structure or as an independent political actor. The army may be eager to get back to the barracks.

Professionalism is one part of the reason for the low level of political involvement, but the status of military leaders is another. With very few exceptions, group army and military region commanders, and even the general department directors, lack the local ties, the prestige, and the political status to resist orders from the center. The majority of these officers are younger, single-track professionals who have not had the opportunity to build up local bases of power. Nevertheless, the intervention in the events in Beijing has involved the PLA in the political arena, and it is a significant setback to the 10-year professionalism drive and to army-people relations.

In the absence of an external military threat, military reform is not likely to progress as long as the conservative Party elders remain in control. PLA reform is now in jeopardy because the political tenor of the current leadership in Zhongnanhai has mandated a more ideological approach.

As a result of Tiananmen and the subsequent power struggle, the guiding military ethic was shifted from a professional orientation, focusing on expertise, operations, and combat readiness, to a political orientation focusing on revolutionary spirit, ideological purity, and loyalty to the Party. Contrary to Deng's oft-quoted assertion that the color of the cat was not the prime criterion of effectiveness, 'redness' is back.

Political reliability has been elevated to be the primary mission of the PLA, or in the words of Guo Linxiang, the secretary of the CMC Discipline Inspection Committee, 'the armed forces' most important mission is to make sure that they are up to standards politically.' This of course, must be confusing to an army that has been told for the past 10 years that combat training was its most important task.

That the army's obedience to the Party was in question is evident from the campaign launched after Tiananmen to ensure political loyalty. Representative of the tenor of the campaign was the following passage from the PLA newspaper, the *Liberation Army News*. 'At any time, under any circumstances, we must firmly maintain the principle that the Party commands the gun. The army must be subject to the Party's absolute leadership .... The army is a proletarian military force created and led by the Chinese Communist Party, and is an armed group for carrying out the Party's political tasks.'[49] By raising the loyalty issue, the Party, in effect, admitted that there were instances that the army's obedience to orders from the center was in doubt.

In order to ensure that the army would always be politically correct, the strengthening of Party construction has become a major issue both at the military colleges and academies, as well as the grass roots organizations. In an editorial, the *Liberation Army News* directed that 'in order to ensure that our army will always be politically up to standard, we must build and maintain strong Party organizations in the military units at all levels so that the gun will always be firmly held by people who are loyal to the Party.'[50]

Loyalty is also guaranteed by promotions being directly linked to politics and to Party loyalty. Another editorial in the *Liberation Army News* noted that, 'at any time top priority must be given to political quality when cadres are assessed and appointed.'[51]

In practical terms, part of the loyalty issue was to do with defining the army's primary function. The Party's decision following Tiananmen was that due to the attempts of international hostile forces to subvert the country's social system, it is necessary for the armed forces to regard their internal function as the basic function. The Party's newly articulated view is that the army internally serves as a strong pillar to oppose subversion, consolidate political power, and defend the socialist system, and the people's democratic dictatorship.[52]

The emphasis by the PLA on this internal function means that politically conservative military commissars will increase their status and control over the PLA at the expense of military commanders. Certainly, at the very top, the director of the GPD, Yang Baibing, has already benefited from this situation as indicated by his appointment in November 1989 as the Central Military Commission General Secretary and as a member of the secretariat of the Central Committee. Commissars at all levels have gained greater status and power within the PLA. It is unlikely, however, that this will mean a greater role for the army in the political process other than as one of many interest groups seeking a share of the resource pie.

Deng's military reforms sought to control the PLA by separating the army from the Party, and providing the army with an independent sphere of activity. The conservative Party elders are much more likely to attempt to assert control over the PLA by politicizing the military, co-opting the army into the political structure, and involving the PLA in non-military functions. This does not mean that the army as an institution will increase its political power, but that political measures, including ideology, will be used to control the military. Indications of such an approach have already appeared. The president of the PLA Academy of Military Sciences has specifically criticized the 'bourgeois liberal attitude concerning army construction which demands the separation of the Chinese army from the leadership of the Communist Party.'[53]

Where politics is in command, senior military leaders must concern themselves with politics and ideological issues, thus leading to a consequent decline of focus on things military. Concepts such as 'people's war,' Maoist military theory, and stress on the militia, will probably make a comeback. The overall result will be a net decline in combat effectiveness.

Can the people cherish the People's Army?

As a result of Tiananmen, army-to-people relationships and the once high prestige of the People's Liberation Army, have suffered. In the past four to five years, army to people relations were not in the best of shape anyway. Economic improvements and the developing liberalization of Chinese society, led to the erosion of the once-premier status that PLA soldiers held in China. Recruiting had become more difficult just at the time when technical requirements were increasing due to modernization. The Tiananmen incident has made it difficult to conceive of the PLA as an army of the people.

Not surprisingly, the martial law troops in Beijing have borne the brunt of the dramatic downturn in army-people relations. Numerous reports of Beijing residents refusing to assist martial law troops and of merchants refusing to conduct business with the soldiers, have surfaced since June 4. Passive resistance was not the only method used to display the people's discontent with the army. In the three months following the Tiananmen incident, 170 cases of attacks against martial law troops were recorded. During this time, 21 soldiers were killed and 30 vehicles were destroyed.[54]

Tiananmen may also have important external military effects. The unrestrained employment of the PLA in suppressing the student demonstrations has sent a chilling signal to China's neighbors in the Asia-Pacific region.[55] Concern over China's intentions within the region were already at a high level due to the Chinese threat of force along the Sino-Indian border in the summer of 1987, and the use of force in the Spratly archipelago in the spring of 1988. The development of a more powerful PLA with greater force projection capability, controlled by revolutionary leaders who are not bashful about using force, could well lead to an increase in concern and protective reactions by states in the region.

Tiananmen has also hindered the PLA's ability to acquire advanced technology from the West. Exchanges in the areas of tactics, doctrine, strategy, and logistics have come to an abrupt halt. The PLA may turn to the Soviet Union, but there are limits as to what the PLA can obtain from this source, especially in the area of high technology. This cutoff of Western military equipment and assistance may not have an immediate effect, but a prolonged break will slow military modernization. There are, however, a number of Chinese officials who see this break with the West as a positive event as it conforms to their inward-looking view of the world.

One interesting fallout of the Tiananmen crisis was Deng Xiaoping's decision to resign from his last official position as chairman of the Central Military Commission. By submitting his resignation, Deng has temporarily strengthened the position of his chosen successor, Jiang Zemin, who now holds the top positions in both the Party and the army. As Jiang has no military background, his effectiveness in controlling the PLA may be limited. The new makeup of the Central Military Commission also may limit Jiang's ability to parlay his new position into political power.

The real power in the CMC remains with Yang Shangkun, who was elevated to the position of first vice-chairman. Yang's younger brother, Yang Baibing, was appointed to the commission's general secretary position, which gives him control over the PLA.[57]

The Yang family's control is not total, however, as the makeup of the commission is the result of a compromise and an attempt to maintain a delicate balance of power. To counterbalance Yang, the other vice-chairmanship was filled by Liu Huaqing, a former commander of the Navy and a long-time associate of Deng. But as long as Deng is alive and healthy, even though he holds no official position, he will continue to be the final arbiter in important matters.[58]

In fact, Deng has indicated that he will remain involved in the cause of the Party and the state as well as the future of the army.[59] Reports have circulated that a new 'leading group on military affairs' has been organized to advise the CMC and the Ministry of Defense on matters of strategy and planning. Members of this leading group are Deng, Yang Shangkun, Hong Xuezhi, Wang Zhen, Qin Jiwei, and Li Desheng. Some observers have speculated that one of Deng's reasons for setting up the group was to rein in the ambitions of Yang Shangkun.[60] Aligned with Deng in such a scheme would be Hong, Qin, and Li. The conservative hard-liner, Wang Zhen, could swing either way, but he will probably line up with Yang more often than not.

The new CMC and the leading group on military affairs are not only compromise solutions, but they are temporary ones at best. These structural mechanisms will mean very little when Deng's health falters or when he dies.

If Deng were to die soon, leadership contention, military politicization, PLA involvement in maintaining domestic order, and deterioration of army-to-people relations, would intensify. Deng's death will set off a new round of uncertainty and a new power struggle that may increase the political involvement of the PLA.

If the leadership struggle following Deng's death is prolonged, it is conceivable that individual or small groups of military leaders could build up power bases allowing them to compete effectively for political power and even dominate the political process. The threat of 'mountaintopism' that Deng had so successfully negated during his 10-year reign could well re-emerge. The 'man on horseback' may again come to dominate China. One could envision a scenario in which military region commanders would join together with local governors to establish regional power centers in opposition to the central government. The politicization of the PLA would encourage such a situation. The center's push to politicize the PLA could eventually work against its ability to enforce its will on the provinces.

This potential warlordism, combined with other centrifugal forces could lead to a situation of civil war and the eventual dissolution of the PRC as a nation state. Other factors such as economic variations and minority issues carry with them the seeds to support this scenario.

---

1. For good general background see: William Whitson and Chen-Hsia Huang, *The Chinese High Command: A History of Communist Military Politics, 1921–1971* (Praeger, NY) 1973.; Samuel B. Griffith, *The Chinese People's Liberation Army* (McGraw Hill, NY) 1967; John Gittings, *The Role of The Chinese Army* (Oxford University Press, London), 1967.

2. For a review of PLA nation building activities see: Ying-Mao Kao. *The People's Liberation Army and China's Nation Building* (International Arts and Sciences Press, White Plains, NY), 1973.

3. Susan M. Rigdon. *The Chinese Military Ethic* (University of Michigan. PhD Thesis), 1972. p. 26.

4. For an overview of the PLA's participation in the Korean War see: Alexander L. George, *The Chinese Communist Army in Action: The Korean War and Its Aftermath* (Columbia University Press, NY), 1967.

5. A landmark work covering the PLA's first attempt at developing professionalism is: Ellis Joffe, *Party and Army: Professionalism and Political Control in the Chinese Officer Corps, 1949–1964* (Harvard University Press, Cambridge, Mass), 1965.

6. Paul H.B. Godwin, 'People's War Revised: Military Doctrine, Strategy, and Operations,' in Charles D. Lovejoy and Bruce W. Watson, *China's Military Reforms: International and Domestic Implication* (Westview Press, Boulder), 1986.

7. Harlan W. Jencks, from *Muskets to Missiles: Politics and Professionalism in the Chinese Army, 1945–1981* (Westview Press, Boulder 1982), p. 106.

8. Gerald Segal, *Defending China* (Oxford University Press, London. 1985), pp. 218–223 and; Ellis Joffe, *The Chinese Army after Mao* (Harvard University Press, Cambridge, Mass. 1987), p. 97.

9. Lonnie D. Henley, 'China's Military Modernization — A Ten Year

Assessment.' In Larry M. Wortzel, ed., *China's Military Modernization: International Implications* (Greenwood Press, New York, 1988), p. 112.

10. Deng Xiaoping, *Selected Works of Deng Xiaoping: 1975–1982* (Foreign Language Press, Beijing, 1984.)

11. *Liberation Army News* Beijing, 28 August 1988, p. 3.

12. Ellis Joffe, *The Chinese Army After Mao*, pp. 180–183.

13. Deng Xiaoping, 'Deng Talks Freely About Situation At Home and Abroad,' Xinhua, Hong Kong Service, 16 September 1985. In Foreign Broadcast Information Service, Daily Report-China (FBIS), 16 September 1985.

14. 'Division Copes with Indifference in Training,' *Liberation Army News, Beijing*, 8 April 1988.

15. A series of articles in the PLA's *Liberation Army News* and other domestic media highlighted this problem. See: 'PLA Deputies Call for Defense Education,' New China News Agency, 29 March 1988; 'Xin Jiang's National Defense Education Campaign,' Xin Jiang Ribao, 14 May 1988; 'National Defense Education,' Qiu Shi, no. 3, 1 August 1988.

16. Willy Wo Lap Lam, *The Era of Zhao Ziyang: Power Struggle in China, 1986–1988* (AB Books and Stationery, Hong Kong, 1989), pp. 177–179.

17. *Far Eastern Economic Review* (FEER), 22 June 1989, p. 12.

18. Lam, op. cit., pp. 67–88.

19. Lam, Ibid. pp. 72–88. A reading of Lam's account of the Hu Yaobang affair provides a close parallel to the events of April and May 1989.

20. Lam, p. 72.

21. Clare Hollingworth, 'Yang's Political Commissars Back in Authority,' *Pacific Defense Reporter*, July 1989, p. 16.

22. *Ming Pao*, 29 May 1989, p. 2. in FBIS, 30 May 1989.

23. Hong Kong Commercial Radio, 25 April 1989. In FBIS, 25 April 1989.

24. *Ming Pao*, Hong Kong. 16 May 1989, p. 2. In FBIS, 16 May 1989.

25. *South China Morning Post* (SCMP), 25 May 1989, p. 1, 2.

26. 'Special Dispatch,' 'Martial Law Units Have By No Means Withdrawn,' *Ta Kung Pao*, Hong Kong, 24 May 1989, p. 1.

27. *Cheng Ming*, no. 14, 1 June 1989, pp. 6–10.

28. SCMP, 25 May 1989, p. 1, 2.

29. 'Reporter,' 'Initial Exploration of the Background of Surrounding the City with Troops', *Wen Wei Po*, Hong Kong, 25 May 1989, p. 1. In FBIS, 25 May 1989, and *Hong Kong Standard*, 5 June 1989, p. 3.

30. The recounting of events occurring between 20 May and 3 June derive from the author's firsthand observations and discussions with observers on the scene in Beijing; hereafter referred to as 'Personal Notes'.

31. *Hong Kong Standard*, 22 May 1989, p. 1.

32. *Zhong Tong Xun She*, Hong Kong, 22 May 1989. In FBIS, 22 May 1989.

33. SCMP, 29 May 1989, p. 4.

34. *Hong Kong Standard*, 28 May 1989, p. 1.

35. *Ming Pao*, Hong Kong, 29 May 1989, p. 2. In FBIS, 30 May 1989.

36. Kyodo, Toyko, 26 May 1989. In FBIS, 26 May 1989.

37. FBIS 30 and 31 May 1989.

38. *Hong Kong Standard*, 5 June 1989, p. 3, and FEER, 15 June 1989, p. 11.

39. *FEER*, 22 June 1989, p. 12.

40. Lam, op. cit., pp. 72–77.

41. Whitson, op. cit., p. 105.

42. *SCMP*, 7 December 1989, p. 16.

43. *SCMP*, 25 May 1989, p. 1, 2.

44. This conclusion derives from author's personal discussions with a number of PLA officers during the period 1987–1989.

45. *Ming Pao*, 29 May 1989, p. 1, 2. In FBIS, 30 May 1989 and 'Special Dispatch,' *Ming Pao*, 30 May 1989, p. 1. In FBIS, 31 May 1989.

46. *SCMP*, 28 December 1989, p. 1, 10; and *FEER*, 4 January 1990, p. 4.

47. *New York Times*, 10 June 1989, p. 1, 5.

48. 'PLA Involvement in Non-military Tasks Opposed,' *Liberation Army News*, Beijing, 11 September 1988.

49. *Liberation Army News*, Beijing, 1 October 1989, pp. 1, 2. In FBIS, 18 October 1989.

50. Ibid.

51. *Liberation Army News*, 10 October 1989, p. 3. In FBIS, 6 November 1989.

52. 'Uphold the Party's Absolute Leadership...'. op. cit.

53. *People's Daily*, 24 September 1989, p. 2. In FBIS, 30 October 1989.

54. *China Daily*, Beijing, 16 November 1989, p. 4. In FBIS, 16 November 1989.

55. *Cheng Ming*, Hong Kong, 1 October 1989, p. 11. In FBIS, 3 October 1989.

56. *FEER*, 27 July 1989, p. 19.

57. *China Daily*, Beijing, 16 November 1989, p. 4. In FBIS, 16 November 1989.

58. *FEER*, 23 November 1989.

59. *NYT*, 9 November 1989. p. 1, 12.

60. *NYT*, 13 November 1989, p. A-5.

61. *SCMP*, p. 1, 7. In FBIS, 18 October 1989.

PART TWO
HISTORY

After the Massacres

SIMON LEYS

A historian of contemporary China who is considering the events of three years ago, of 10 years ago, of 20 years ago, must feel dizzy: Each time, it is the same story, the plot is identical — one needs only to change the names of a few characters. The grim merry-go-round leads nowhere; it merely spins, ever more squeaky and rickety; the bloody contraption can only crush with increasing brutality a populace thirsting for freedom.

World opinion was revolted by the Beijing massacres of June 1989. Our age, which should be quite blasé in the matter of atrocities, discovered a new dimension to horror as it watched this seemingly unprecedented phenomenon:[1] a government that declares war on its own people, and unleashes an army of murderers against the peaceful and defenseless crowds of its own capital city.

The massacres stunned the world — and yet they should not have surprised anyone.[2] The butchers of Beijing are entitled to feel genuine puzzlement in the face of the indignation expressed by international opinion. Why should foreigners suddenly change their attitude toward them? What was so new in the June atrocities — which, after all, were still performed on a fairly modest scale, when compared with similar operations previously carried out by this same regime?

In fact, it is not the nature of Chinese communism that took a drastic turn for the worse in June; simply, it is the accuracy of Western perceptions that suddenly improved. Well before they took power, the communists considered murder as a basic political device — and I mean murder in its most diverse forms: individual or collective, methodical or random, public or secret, aimed at dissidents to uproot opposition, or aimed at innocents to cow everybody. This method had already been vigorously implemented 20 years before the establishment of the so-called 'people's republic.' (For instance, the notorious massacres of Futian took place in 1930.)

At its beginning, the Chinese communist movement was fired with genuine revolutionary ideals; it sought social justice passionately and succeeded in mobilizing the generosity and courage of a moral and intellectual elite. From the very start, however, it carried within itself the seeds of its eventual corruption; the communists always believed that mankind mattered more than man. In the eyes of the Party leaders individual lives were merely a raw material in abundant supply — cheap, disposable, and easily replaceable. Therefore, quite naturally, they came to consider that the exercise of terror was synonymous with the exercise of power. If, from time to time, a communist government could not kill its citizens, how would you expect it to govern?

William Hinton, the well-known author of several books on contemporary China, was in Beijing at the time of the massacres. I read in the newspapers that he strongly denounced these atrocities. One can only share his indignation — but at the same time, the way in which he expressed his feelings seems to betray a remarkable (yet typical) confusion of ideas. He said that the leaders who ordered the massacres '*are not communists; these people are fascists!*'

One can throw many accusations at the Chinese leaders. If there is one thing they cannot be suspected of it is to have forsaken their unswerving loyalty to communism. Actually the very problem is precisely that they obstinately behaved as pure communists. To brand them as 'fascists' is to borrow a rather dim candle to light up the picture. From a communist point of view, it would not even be possible to condemn the massacres' *stupidity*. Not only were they necessary, but also their logic was impeccably Leninist.

The tactical flexibility of communism is considerable, but it is also entirely subordinated to a strategic imperative that is essential and immutable: In any circumstance and at any cost, political power must be retained in its totality. This rule is absolute, it tolerates no exception and must take precedence over any other consideration. The bankruptcy of the entire country, the ruin of its credit abroad, the destruction of national prestige, the annihilation of all efforts toward overture and modernization — none of these could ever enter into consideration once the Party's authority was at stake. (Besides, in their economic and diplomatic relations with the West, the Chinese leaders were probably not risking much; in this particular occurrence they may have made many miscalculations, but they have shrewdly assessed the actual limits of the memory and the indignation of democratic governments.)

As Bernanos observed, 'Massacres are always committed out of fear.' The great fear that overtook the geriatric rulers in Beijing reached panic proportions when they saw the entire nation rallying round the Tiananmen demonstrators and an alliance being formed between the students and the workers. The day when the demonstrators succeeded in holding martial law in check and in making the army waver in its determination, their fate was sealed. By the use of irreparable violence, a moat of blood was created in order to isolate the soldiers from the people. (It remains to determine what sort of role was played behind the scene by the security organs, which reaped the only benefits that could be derived from the crisis: To what extent was Deng deliberately fed wrong information? The secret police appear to be the real winner of the entire operation.)

The hot violence of the massacres has now given way to a cold terror — even more fearsome, since it is systematic and efficiently organized. In this new stage, there is no more room for messy and random improvisations; an appearance of order has been re-established, the last bloodstains have been carefully scrubbed, the streets look neat and clean; and already a few foreign visitors — businessmen and politicians — are reappearing; they return to sit at the banquet of the murderers, and meanwhile, in the cellars of the secret police, with one bullet in the back of the neck, the youth, the intelligence, and the hope of China are being liquidated.

Twenty years after the storms of the Cultural Revolution, a fragile elite of intellectual and political critics had miraculously emerged again; now, they have been obliterated with one blow. The police, who were keeping records on all the thinking minds of the country, had been waiting for such an opportunity to get rid of them all at once. The talent and expertise which China needs in order to modernize have now gone underground — or they survive only in exile: tens of thousands of scholars and scientists who were abroad at the time of the massacres dare not return home, knowing too well the fate which is awaiting them there. Today China is a nation without brains. What future prospects can a big country on its way to modernization still entertain after suffering such a lobotomy?

This issue does not appear to worry unduly the thugs who are now controlling China's fate. Their only concern is to apply Lenin's recipe: 'A regime which is prepared to use limitless terror cannot be overthrown.' Indeed, nothing else seems to matter now

— this brute repression does not even attempt to cover itself with the scantiest ideological rag; China's senile despots are unable to articulate a single idea. Leading articles in the *People's Daily* can only recycle a dusty jargon that dates to the days of the Cultural Revolution and in order to denounce today's enemies, they have to rehash the very abuse that Mao originally used to hurl at Deng Xiaoping!

In principle, the Beijing massacres were in complete conformity with what could be expected from Chinese communists. Actually, it would have been more surprising had they not taken place, for this would have amounted to the government's announcing its own dissolution. The massacres were new only in one respect, but this particular innovation had momentous repercussions. From beginning to end, the atrocities took place in front of foreign television cameras and under the eyes of the international press. Formerly, in all similar operations, communist leaders always observed carefully the traditional rule which prescribes 'beating the dog behind a closed door' (*guan men da gou*). In June 1989 in Beijing, for the very first time, the gates of the slaughterhouse remained wide open. (Is this perhaps what is called 'the open-door policy'?)

The extraordinary impact of television also has a frightening aspect. For millions of spectators the events that are seen on the small screens take on flesh and carry weight; they can upset world opinion and ultimately affect the policies of democratic governments; conversely, this also means that whatever has escaped the eyes of the camera is virtually erased from reality, or doomed to vegetate in a limbo of the collective consciousness, where it cannot generate emotions or mobilize minds. What happens outside the range of the cameras does not really happen. Thus, for instance, over the years, Chinese communism could liquidate more than a million Tibetans — yet this fact never seriously impaired China's prestige and international credit. Why? There were no television cameras on the spot. Nor were there any cameras to witness the massacres of the Cultural Revolution in which more than half a million lives were lost. In 1968, when the army began its suppression of the Red Guards, slaughters similar to those which we just saw in Beijing took place in dozens of cities. (After one such wave of executions, rivers in southern China were clogged with so many corpses that, on the beaches of Hong Kong, some 80 miles away, the tide would every day bring in scores of dead bodies.) From the beginning these facts were well-known; information was plentiful and easily available. And yet, 10 years after these events, their reality had still not penetrated the consciousness of the Western world; as a result, when Mao died, the leaders of our democracies could wholeheartedly pay a respectful homage to the lunatic old tyrant, whom they described as 'a guiding light for all mankind.'

Shortly before his tragic death, the Soviet dissident Andrei Amalrik became interested in Chinese politics. Some 12 years ago I heard him make a striking observation: He remarked that China was much more 'advanced' politically than the Soviet Union (I should rather use the French word *avancé*, which can also apply to the overripe condition of a cheese; or of a corpse). As Amalrik put it, the misfortune of the Soviet Union was to have won the war, whereas the good luck of China was to have lost the Cultural Revolution. Its victory over Nazi Germany vested Stalinist Russia with a sort of self-righteousness and moral confidence which for a long time precluded any clear awareness of its fundamental failings; the regime found itself confirmed in its worst errors, and as a result, the much-needed reforms were indefinitely postponed. In China, on the contrary, the frightful catastrophe of the Cultural Revolution accelerated the disintegration of the communist system. For a while, the Party was completely destroyed. Though it was eventually rebuilt, it never recovered its prestige and authority; these were irretrievably discredited. Yet the crisis of the Cultural Revolution did not merely expose the moral and political bankruptcy of the regime, it also had positive results: It produced a new breed of citizens — bold and aggressive. People of such caliber can become heroes, they can also become bandits, but certainly it will never be possible again for the regime to cow them into the meek and passive docility of their elders.

The May 1989 demonstrations marked the apex of a long evolution that originally sprang from the Cultural Revolution, and subsequently found its expression in a series of spontaneous movements, with ever-broadening popular support and increasing articulateness. First, there was the earliest of the great Tiananmen demonstrations, on 5 April 1976, which, shortly before Mao's death, dared denounce his tyranny. Then, in 1979, there was the 'Beijing Spring,' with the activities of the 'Democracy Wall,' which represented a deepening of democratic aspirations. Without the previous experiences of the Cultural Revolution, the movement for democracy would probably never have been able to develop on such a scale, and with such speed and audacity — yet its greatest merit is that it succeeded in largely shedding its very origins. In this respect, the personal evolution of a man such as Wei Jingsheng is exemplary: Arrested after writing his eloquent appeal for democracy in China, he was finally to become a hero and a martyr of the Beijing Spring, during the nonviolent struggle for democracy — and yet, 10 years earlier, he had been a leader of the Red Guards.

By a cruel paradox, whereas an elite of China's youth effectively outgrew and discarded the heritage of the Cultural Revolution (which had originally launched them into politics), Deng Xiaoping and his colleagues, after having been the victims of the Cultural Revolution, now remain its prisoners. They fear and hate the Cultural Revolution, yet, at the same time, they have retained its language and methods — as was shown in the Beijing massacres and in the wave of denunciations, lies, and terror that followed it. The ferocity with which they crushed the demonstrators in Beijing cannot merely be explained by the memory of the humiliations which they had suffered at the hands of the Red Guards. How could anyone ever have confused the peaceful and smiling crowds of 1989 with the fanatical hordes of 1967? Could there be anything in common between the young rebels who had dragged them down 20 years earlier and today's nonviolent patriots? A profound metamorphosis has taken place from one generation to the next, but beyond this transformation, Deng and his henchmen confusedly identified a menace — which their blind obstinacy only succeeded in precipitating: They know they are facing the irrepressible surge of the tidal wave which is going to sweep them away tomorrow, together with the last remains of Chinese communism.

Unfortunately, its poison might outlast the beast itself. The legacy of such a regime can be even more evil than its rule. The collapse of the present government is ineluctable; what is to be feared is that, after 40 years of economic mismanagement, in the present circumstances of overpopulation and poverty, with a population brutalized by four decades of relentless political terror, worse horrors may follow.

Reprinted by permission from The New York Review of Books, *where it appeared 12 October 1989.*

1. In fact, it is unfortunately not new — neither in China, nor elsewhere in the world. Yet who remembers the Hama massacres in Syria, where President Assad slaughtered 25,000 fellow citizens in 1982? One has perhaps not yet completely forgotten how, in 1988, the Iraqi government undertook to annihilate with gas and chemical weapons, entire villages of its Kurdish minority — though the only reaction from Washington was to double export credits granted to Iraq, while France, West Germany, and England maintained their friendly relations with Baghdad.

2. Presumably President Bush at least was not surprised — though perhaps not for a very good reason. If I am to believe a report from the *Washington Post* (reproduced in the *Guardian Weekly*, 2 July 1989), President Bush discovered during his stay in China that, owing to 'cultural differences,' 'the Chinese hold life less dear [than those in the West].' Thanks to these wonderful 'cultural differences,' one may also suppose that the Chinese hurt less when they are being crushed by tanks and incinerated alive with flame throwers.

3. It is difficult to determine why this attitude was adopted. Perhaps, within the bureaucracy, some officials who were opposed to the repression deliberately sabotaged the implementation of measures to control the activities of foreign journalists. Perhaps also the gerontocracy in Beijing has become so anachronistic that the leaders are not fully aware of the role being played by the media at the end of the 20th century. For Deng Xiaoping and Yang Shangkun, television is probably a sort of machine that enables you to watch Mickey Mouse at home.

4. The expression was actually used by Mr. Valéry Giscard d'Estaing. It is not even the silliest thing that was said at the time.

Tiananmen and Chinese Political Culture: The Escalation of Confrontation

LUCIAN W. PYE

THE paired dramas of the Beijing Spring of April and May 1989 and the Tiananmen massacre of June 4 encapsulate all too vividly the hope and the despair of modern China. The events were a playing out of the dominant themes of Chinese political culture, both in the students' urge to gain modernity and respectability in the eyes of the world, and the unaltered instincts of authoritarianism of the leadership. Therefore, to write about the relationship of the Tiananmen events to Chinese political culture would seem to call for a summary overview of all the essential characteristics of that tenacious culture. The students in their courageous actions seemed to be following in the footsteps of generation after generation of idealistic, but doomed Chinese youth calling for democracy in a society that has yet to shed its authoritarian traditions. Their blind confidence that virtue should conquer all left them vulnerable to the realities of Chinese authoritarianism. And as for the actions of the leaders, what more is there to say, except to shake our heads sadly and curse, 'There go those Chinese leaders again — so typical of them.'

Indeed the story points to a host of well-established conclusions about Chinese political culture. These include such themes as: the sensitivity of authority to matters of 'face,' the need for authority to pretend to omnipotence; the legitimacy of bewailing grievances; the urge to monopolize virtue and to claim the high ground of morality; the drive to try to shame others; an obsession with revenge; the inability to compromise publicly, and so on. All of which seems to come down to a basic problem in Chinese political culture — the management of aggression. Any conflict arouses hate, and it becomes almost impossible to disagree politically without becoming disagreeable.

Beijing Spring and the Tiananmen massacre brought out in bold relief the basic contradictions of Chinese political culture. The inspiring student demonstrations of April and May were a reminder of the degree to which modern Chinese politics has been carried along more by hope than by accomplishments. It is a politics of becoming, not of being. It was not just Mao Tse-tung but all Chinese leaders who say, no matter what has happened, 'The future is bright.' The Chinese leaders and intellectuals concentrate on describing how wonderful the 'New China' is going to be, how awful the past has been, and thereby they avoid hardheaded analysis of the present. Students of China are equally caught up in this spirit of hope, so that wishful thinking often substitutes for critical analysis. The conventional wisdom, for example, is that a 'Chinese revolution' has been going on for the last 150 years. Yet for most of that time the country was getting nowhere and the ways of thinking of the majority of the Chinese people had not greatly changed. Were a member of the reform movement of the last days of the 19th century to return to China today he could easily pick up on the current discussions of 'building socialism with Chinese characteristics' and other wishful dreams about modernizing China while keeping China somehow 'Chinese.' It is plausible to talk of a Chinese revolution mainly if great weight is given to hope. Thus the stress has been on how at each point in history China was about to become a 'republic,' a 'communist miracle land,' a 'great power,' a 'modernized country,' and even a 'democracy.'

What happened on June 3–4 was appalling, but it was not shocking. The idea that Chinese armies would shoot Chinese people should not have been unthinkable. For that is exactly what Chinese armies have excelled at. The record stands clear: from the Taiping Rebellion to Chiang Kai-shek's troops slaughtering the workers of Shanghai, to the KMT army's arrival in Formosa (no wonder they wanted to change the name), to the killing of landlords, right down to the PLA shooting Tibetans only a year before Tiananmen. In short, the key events of Beijing Spring illustrate essential Chinese traits and fit within the tradition of Chinese political culture.

April 15 — Hu Yaobang dies: death and funerals as spectacles

The Tiananmen demonstrations of 1989 were reminiscent of the Tiananmen incident of 1976, the first spontaneous, and largely student demonstration in the history of the People's Republic. The similarities begin with the fact that both were triggered by the death of a popular leader who never made it to the top. Zhou Enlai, whose death occasioned the first Tiananmen drama, never received the public recognition in life that was his in death. Similarly, Hu Yaobang in life was respected for being a champion of Deng Xiaoping's reforms, but he was also jokingly dismissed as a lightweight by intellectuals who would make a pun by changing the tone in his given name to make it become 'Hu Needs Help.'[1] Before his death he was hardly a popular hero among the students.

Yet the death of Hu, as did the death of Chou Enlai, meant the loss of what the students soon proclaimed was their last hope for a good leader for China. The students' reaction was not despair but activism. (The rule in China is that when the situation is hopeless, take hope.) Indeed, in Chinese political culture, action in hopeless circumstances captures the spirit of the heroic, for the heroic is always flavored with a touch of the tragic. This connection between the heroic and the tragic repeatedly surfaced during Beijing Spring.

Making the grieving over death into a public spectacle is very Chinese. Chinese funerals are public displays, processions through the streets led by wailing mourners. If there are not enough relatives and descendants to make a respectable showing, it is always possible to hire professional mourners with leather lungs and skill at shedding tears. Funeral rituals provide one of the few opportunities Chinese ever have for the public display of emotion. The gap between public grieving and carnival is thus very small. Even as the mobilizations for the first demonstrations were taking place at Tiananmen, wall posters were going up at the various Beijing campuses which combined that distinctive blend of sarcasm and cruel jokes which have been the delight of China's politically weak: 'Those who should not die are dead; those who should not be alive are alive.' 'Mao Tse-tung's son went to the war front. Lin Biao's son plotted a coup. Deng Xiaoping's son toured to get donations. Zhao Ziyang's son speculatd in the sale of color television sets. We have no chance to see Hu Yaobang's son.' And maybe most telling of the mood of the students was one wall poster which read, '[Mr. Hu] was determined to care for the nation and revive the country from its shambles. He was so good at telling the weather by the changes of wind and clouds that he suddenly left for heaven with light steps. As for me, I am only interested in taking the TOEFL [Test of English as a Foreign

Language], purchase a passport and cheat to get a visa so I can quickly leave for the free world with clean hands.'[2]

April 17–22. The students find their voices; concrete concerns give way to lofty sentiments

In Chinese culture, public grieving can legitimize the expression of sentiments that are only vaguely related to any sense of personal loss. Consequently it was not exceptional that as the students began to flock to the center of Beijing and crowd around Zhong-nanhai, the secluded compound of the political elite, their slogans had less and less to do with the death of their newfound hero Hu and more and more with their unhappy lot. The students wanted to know if it was really true that the government would carry out a policy announced in March which stated that on graduation they would be required to spend time in the countryside and that they would no longer be able to avoid being assigned to their first jobs. The students had a host of other complaints. Their living conditions were abominable, six or more students to a room. The food was inedible, the lighting inadequate. They knew that their professors were paid less than waitresses and cab drivers, and that China ranked with the lowest 20 countries in the world in percentage of GNP devoted to education.

Yet, and this is an important feature of Chinese political culture, the students could not concentrate their complaints on such pragmatic, concrete personal problems because this would expose them to the criticism of being selfish. They had to escalate their demands to more abstract, lofty, and essentially idealistic themes. In Chinese political culture, the ultimate sin is selfishness — hence the Chinese abhorrence of individualism. It is this deep hostility toward individualism which makes the culture so blissfully insensitive to many human rights issues. People are expected to willingly make sacrifices for the collective while forgetting their own interests. The group is idealized, not the individual.

Needless to say it is lowly people who are expected to sacrifice everything for the collectivity, while the lofty ones, whether they are the grandfathers or political leaders, know that rank has its privileges. There are few political cultures in which there is greater sensitivity to matters of status and gradations of hierarchy. Yet how can a culture that glorifies the leaders, making emperors, chairmen, and a paramount leader without formal office into supermen and objects of personality cults, really believe that the collectivity is greater than the individual? Who must be selfless and who is entitled to an enlarged ego is a matter of status. The common people, such as students, are expected to be selfless. Yet within any significant Chinese public institution, the dominant tone is not that of selflessness, but rather envy — the driving force of so much of elite behavior.

The practice of publicly classifying selfishness as an ultimate sin has other troublesome consequences for Chinese politics. It contributes, for example, to an inflated style of political rhetoric. Prohibited from advocating their own concrete, down-to-earth interests, people have to act as though they are only concerned with matters of propriety and general well–being. Every issue has to be dressed up as being in the collective interest. There is no room for respecting individual rights. This helps to explain why expressions of patriotism have become such a hackneyed part of Chinese political language. Whereas other cultures can acknowledge that patriotism may be the last refuge of scoundrels, in Chinese political culture, patriotism is the first refuge for anyone who has a grievance.

This practice also means that in China, public rhetoric rarely has a down-to-earth quality, and there is little open discussion about practical solutions to specific problems. In the two years leading up to the Tiananmen drama, the Chinese political economy was sinking into even deeper troubles: Inflation was rampant, inequalities were growing, price reform stalled betwixt and between two contradictory systems, the peasants were increasingly unhappy as the agricultural reforms were no longer working, and the political leadership was adrift. Yet, even with so much going wrong, public discourse in China never came down to the level of examining concrete proposals. The rhetoric remained lofty, symbolic, and moralistic. The rule in Chinese public life usually is, 'Don't analyze, just moralize.' Hard thinking barely goes beyond complaining about corruption. The one absolutely predictable certainty that runs throughout Chinese political history is that whenever there are difficulties, the Chinese reaction will be to declare the rulers corrupt. Once that has been done, it is no longer necessary to think much about the substantive problems. Individuals may come up with concrete proposals, but there is no general engaging of issues to produce a forum for real public debate. The rhetoric of public discourse is intellectually spongy. Indeed, one of the risks of being a student of Chinese politics is that prolonged immersion in the language of Chinese politics may dim one's wits to the point that it becomes impossible to recognize fuzzy thinking.

As a counter-balance to the increasingly lofty sentiments the students felt compelled to express, and as a surrogate for their concrete interests, which they could no longer express for fear of appearing to be 'selfish,' the students' substitute for substantive reality became the circulation of elaborate and detailed rumors about the circumstances of Hu Yaobang's death. The aura of the inexplicable, so naturally associated with death, readily fueled the rumors which in their richness of detail helped to demystify Hu's death and to suggest what should be done next. This was not an odd development. In Chinese political culture, the need to suppress concrete interests and to use moralistic sentiments means that there is a void in the description of reality which usually can only be filled with rumors and speculation. It was not peculiar that the students in Tiananmen were soon passing around stories about how the 'bad' other leaders had caused Hu's death. Li Peng was said to have insulted Hu before the Politburo. Then the story was that attacks of the conservative leaders had so enraged Hu that his heart gave way. This led to the more sinister rumor that when Hu had his heart seizure, none of the other leaders called for help. This was topped by saying that Jiang Zemin gave him the wrong medicine.

The rumors thus went from speculations about what Hu had uttered in his last gasps, to the failure of the leadership to help him, to killing him. The escalation is understandable given Chinese notions about the omnipotence of authority. All good things, and hence also all bad things, can be traced to the acts of the highest authorities. Since political authorities are supposed to be endowed with almost magical capabilities, when something bad happens it probably reflects the hidden wishes and preferences of the top leaders. What this meant was that the anger the students felt over their personal grievances and their inability to articulate their real complaints had become legitimized hostility in their own eyes because they now knew that the leaders had acted evilly toward Hu Yaobang.

There was thus an escalating sequence of psychological states which inevitably brought the students into direct conflict with the topmost leadership. It began with the spirit of playfulness of the earliest wall posters which in turn opened the way to the articulation of fantasies that were clearly related to barely suppressed real grievances which, however, could not be fully articulated for fear of appearing to be selfish. To escape from the charge of selfishness, the students had to give voice to more lofty sentiments. In doing so, they set themselves on a collision course with the top leadership who believed that they were the sole fountainhead of such sentiments.

This was the situation in April 22 when the leadership was inside the Great Hall of the People listening to carefully crafted eulogies, and some 80,000 students were outside demanding that the premier meet with them. Deng Xiaoping was reported to have been angered that in the service Hu had been called a 'great Marxist.' He is supposed to have said, 'Even when I die they will not call me a great Marxist. Who do they think that turtle egg Yaobang was?' Accurate or not, the remark probably reflected Deng's mood. On the students' side, what they didn't hear was what angered them: There was no suggestion that in death Hu was to be rehabilitated.

The students' reaction was in line with the classic Chinese tradition of aggrieved parties wailing before the Yamen door, of publicly dramatizing their unhappiness by petitioning officialdom — and they expected that the louder the wailing the more likely their petition would be heard. Thus, student leaders went up the steps of the Great Hall on their knees, holding written petitions above their heads while surrounded by other tearful students who sincerely believed that the officials would have to respond. Li Peng, however, failed to play the role of the good magistrate of old; he refused to come out. Instead, police appeared and got the students to return to their campuses. As one student later said of her experience that day, 'I always believed I was a Mao Tse-tung. Now I know I am nobody.'[3]

April 24–26 — The Editorial: 'While sticks and stones may merely break my bones, words can totally shatter me.'

The situation seemed at that point to have reached a stage at which in other cultures it should have been possible to defuse the tension and return to a state of unhappy normalcy. But in terms of what is important in Chinese political culture this was not possible. There was instead an inexorable movement toward confrontation. In the eyes of the leaders, the students had already gone too far. There-

fore, the leaders had to take on what in Chinese political culture is
a prime responsibility of government, that of teaching the lessons
of correct behavior. The students, in seeking to find fig leaves to
cover their 'improper' selfishness, had been driven to proclaim
their superior moral righteousness; but in doing so they were
acting in ways which the leadership saw as attempts to strip the
authorities of their fig leaves. One might wonder if there were
enough fig leaves to go around since the 'leaves' seemed to be
made of nothing more than the cheap fluff which in other cultures
would be merely the rhetorical window dressings associated with
preambles and ritual statments. In China, however, the students'
rhetorical claim to the highest moral sensitivities was a direct
challenge to the leadership because it threatened the very basis of
its claim to legitimacy. Rulers in China are supposed to have the
monopoly on teaching the ways of virtue. To question this is to
challenge their status.

The Standing Committee of the Politburo could not abide such
an insulting challenge, and so on the night of April 24 it decided
that the students were an evil, anti-socialist movement which
threatened the sacred Party. The next day Deng reinforced the
committee's decision with a speech which showed that he was
worried that the Chinese Communist Party might lose its
monopoly of power. 'Those people who have been influenced by
the free elements of Yugoslavia, Poland, Hungary, and the Soviet
Union have a reason to create turmoil. Their motive is to overthrow the Party.'[4] Deng went on to make what has been called his
'Three Don't-Be-Afraid' remarks: Don't be afraid of domestic
reactions, don't be afraid of foreign opinion, and don't be afraid of
bloodshed. Whether he actually made the remarks or not, it is
certain that he was fully behind the next step of trying to publicly
shame and humiliate the students.

This decision to use shame and to rely upon words rather than a
low level of police intimidation was typical of Chinese political
culture. Whereas in the West the rule is that, 'While sticks and
stones may break my bones, words can never hurt me,' in China
this is turned upside down in that people act as though 'Words can
utterly shatter me.' Acting on this assumption, the leadership
believed that the student movement could be demolished by merely issuing a fierce editorial. In organizing the drafting of the
editorial the leadership also practiced a classic Chinese political
tactic. They decided the person to supervise the drafting of the

editorial should be the member of the Standing Committee whose loyalty was the most suspect. Such a vulnerable person could be counted upon either to reveal his disloyalty or to cover his vulnerability by being more thorough and nasty than others would be.

So Hu Qili, then a recognized moderate and ally of Zhao Ziyang, was assigned to produce the April 26 editorial for the *People's Daily*. The result was a document which instantly became the symbolic bone of contention in the next stage of the battle. Just to make sure everyone recognized its importance, the editorial was read in its entirety on the national television news. The language repeated verbatim the phrases used to denounce the student demonstrations of 1987, the event which everybody remembered had brought Hu Yaobang's downfall. It said that the students had been 'incited by a very small number of people with evil purposes,' and that in 'creating chaos' the students were behaving unpatriotically.

The editorial, however, failed in its calculated purpose of shattering the student movement. Instead, it enraged the students, and led them to escalate their challenge to the leadership. The students became in their own eyes a governmental authority as they formed the Beijing Federation of Autonomous Student Unions for 10 universities and colleges, and promptly issued 'Order Number 1,' which called for marches on Tiananmen Square in support of 'communism' and the 'socialist order' and in opposition to 'bureaucracy, corruption, and special privileges.' They played the classic Chinese game of usurping the role and the pretensions of state power by outmoralizing the leadership. By trying to capture the moral high ground, they were asserting that they were the ones who most deserved to govern. They were not, however, calling for a revolution or for the destruction of the system. They only wanted a more righteous, moral, and purer leadership.

The editorial also elevated the students into a position of personal conflict with Deng Xiaoping. In Chinese political culture, public insults have to be redressed publicly, and since the editorial directly attacked the students they were compelled to demand that the authorities 'reverse the verdict' of the editorial. In calling for a 'reversal of the verdict,' all knowledgeable Chinese recognized that they were mocking Deng Xiaoping because in his return from disgrace after Mao's death he had made a major issue of 'reversing the verdict' of the first Tiananmen incident. The students soon proved that they could be as stubborn as Deng. With May Day and the 70th anniversary of May Fourth movement coming up, it was impossible for the government to tell the students to go back to school and treat what had happened as water over the dam.

Thus after the April 26 editorial the students were in that advantageous position in Chinese politics in which they could freely use idealistic rhetoric to achieve a very concrete goal, one that would also have the payoff of humiliating their opponents.

May 1–15 — May Day, May Fourth, the hunger strike, and Gorbachev's visit. Heroism and tragedy; the battles to shame the other; and politics as symbols and theater

The combination of the challenge of the editorial and the upcoming possibilities for great drama on May Day, the 70th anniversary of May Fourth, and the world media's attention on Gorbachev's impending visit, all helped to galvanize the students and to escalate their demonstrations. The conflict was fully joined, and the students and the government acted in terms of three significant themes in Chinese political culture. First, their battle became one of each trying to shame the other, under the assumption that humiliation is an absolute weapon. Second, the students in particular, knowing that they were engaged in a conflict with a superior force, sought the rewards of heroic posturing, which they linked in the Chinese manner with tragedy and visions of death. Third, in the Chinese tradition of ascribing great power to the manipulation of symbols, they sought to make politics into theater.

The Confucian tradition of rule by moral example implicitly attributes extraordinary powers to the act of shaming others. In the Chinese socialization process children are constantly shamed into proper conduct. The power of parents is the power to shame, and to teach children the supreme importance of not losing 'face.' As children learn the power of shaming, they are quick to try to shame their parents for doing wrong things to them. Shaming is thus seen as not only a potent weapon for both the authority and the weak, but also as a pleasurable activity, for it certifies that one is in the advantaged position of the superior.

The students sought to shame the government, especially during Gorbachev's visit, into 'reversing the verdict' of the editorial and into admitting that the students were indeed patriotic and selfless.

The Party leadership was just as energetically engaged in trying to shame the students by characterizing them as the dupes of a few 'hooligans' and 'bad elements.' Each was seeking to be more virtuous than the other, each was trying to depict the other as needing to mend its ways.

The Chinese leadership in particular has almost an obsession with the presumed advantage of shaming others, an obsession that is reinforced by a conviction that everybody else has a compelling need to have good relations with them. Note how in foreign relations the Chinese government is prone to tell other governments that their relations with China are not as good as they should be because the other party's actions have 'cast a shadow over the relationship,' and that if there is to be an improvement in their relations the other party must change. The Chinese seem oblivious that such self-righteous scolding can be the cause of mirth in chancelleries throughout the world. The tactic seems to work with only a few countries, but one of these is the U.S., since its Puritan instincts for guilt make it quick to believe that if somebody is angry with it, it must be America's fault.

Since there is no way of compromising in a battle of shaming, the struggle could only intensify. The students' response was to adopt ever more heroic posturing, and since the ultimate act of heroism is tragic death, by early May they were acting as though they should prepare for just such an ending. Students began to write their wills, but since they were quick to display publicly what they had written, it seems that they were not really anticipating death but only savoring the thrill of heroics. We know that this probably was the case because after more than a month of talking about getting ready for death the students were dumbfounded when the actual shooting began on June 4. Wall posters at Beida publicized the wills of some of the students:

I am willing to go over boiling water and burning fire for democracy and freedom. I will not have any regrets about dying for the Chinese people. My country, my people, when are you going to wake up and stand up as a man?

For democracy and freedom I am not afraid of anything. I am ready to fight for my own life.

In order to fight for my motherland which is in great trouble, I am going to pay with my blood and life. I will have no regrets if I die.

Mother, I am sorry that I let you down.... If you do not understand, history will.

I am going for the future and hope of the Chinese people. I am not going to listen to my parents any more.[5]

It was clearly the rhetoric of adolescent fantasy about heroic glory. All of this might have passed as a part of the posturing of the two sides if the students had not come up with a tactic that captured the imagination of the civilian population of Beijing. On May 13, two days before Mikhail Gorbachev was due to arrive for his historic meeting with Deng Xiaoping, the students came up with the ingenious tactic of a hunger strike. It was a statement that they found the government to be illegitimate. For in the legendary history of the Zhao dynasty an upright official, Boyin Suqi, had starved himself to death rather than recognize a usurper, and then in the Yuan and Qing dynasties some scholars had emulated Boyin to dramatize the illegitimacy of the non-Han emperors. However, the practice of a hunger strike was foreign to contemporary Chinese political culture. Yet some Chinese in the city must have recognized the message. For quite unexpectedly the announcement of the hunger strike electrified the population of Beijing, causing people to practically ignore Gorbachev's visit as they rallied to the students' cause. It was the hunger strike which suddenly brought the citizens into the drama on the side of the students. In the previous student demonstrations for democracy in 1986–7 the Chinese population had been impassive.

What was it about the hunger strike that stirred up the people of Beijing to the point that their participation in the events quickly led to what may have been the largest demonstrations for democracy in all of history? In part it was no doubt the language of the vow which the hunger strikers took:

Under the bright sunshine of May, we are going on a hunger strike. We have to throw away the beauty of our youth, even though we are very reluctant to do so. Our nation has reached a critical turning point. We are plagued by inflation, corruption and the abuses of power.... We are the purest patriots. We are the brightest and most innocent children. Yet we are accused of creating chaos, of harboring evil purposes, and of being used by a very small minority of people.... Our parents, please do not be sad when we are hungry. Our uncles and aunts, please do not cry when we say goodbye. We only have one hope, that is, that after we die, our people will have a better life... Death is then waiting with the most extensive and longlasting echoes. Goodbye, our fellow students, the dead and the living are equally loyal, our homes, we do not like to leave you, but we have to. Goodbye, our parents, please forgive us because we cannot be loyal citizens and filial sons and daughters at the same time. Goodbye our people, please forgive us for the way we choose to show our loyalty....[6]

The initiation of the hunger strike, a non-violent act, seems paradoxically to have been accompanied by the expression of a heightened degree of aggression. Wall posters went up expressing heated anger: 'Hang Li Peng,' 'Death to Li Peng and Deng Xiaoping.' After Zhao Ziyang was reported to have told Gorbachev that Deng was in full command of China's policies, there were calls for the 'resignation' of 'Emperor' Deng, a 'senile and fatuous autocrat.' The combination of heightened aggression and the symbolism of self-destruction may suggest an added explanation for why the Chinese population responded so dramatically to the hunger strike. The reason may be that in Chinese culture suicide is a well-recognized act used to shame authority. The emotional logic is that even though feelings of aggression cannot be directed against an authority figure, aggression can still be turned inward against the self, and the result will still be an attack against authority. 'Even if I can't hurt you, I can hurt myself, and this will make you feel awful, which is what I want to accomplish.' In traditional China, an aggrieved party might commit suicide at the door of an offending official in the belief that the official would be humiliated and the public would curse the official and think well of the one who was driven to suicide. The score would be settled, or so went the logic of the compelling fantasy.

The Chinese public was certainly moved by what they perceived as a sign of the students' sincerity. For the first time in the history of the People's Republic of China, workers joined the students in criticizing the government and the Party. This was the dangerous development that Deng Xiaoping saw as directly threatening the legitimacy of his regime. He responded by preparing the military for martial law.

The hunger strike as a symbolic act of suicide was one of many imported symbolic acts that reinforced traditional Chinese symbols and thereby strengthened the students' appeal among the people of Beijing. The flowing banners were classic revolutionary drama, but also reminiscent of the heroic operas of the Mao era.

The headbands around the foreheads of the shouting, fist-waving students were taken from South Korean and Japanese demonstrations, and they certainly evoked a readiness for suicidal actions. The slogans of 'people power' and the offering of flowers and gifts of food and drink to soldiers seemed directly out of the Philippine democratic revolution. And, of course, there was the statue to the 'Goddess of Democracy.' All this seemed to the Chinese public to make the students honorable heroes who could certainly help create 'democracy with Chinese characteristics.' They had apparently found the formula for realizing the long-sought Chinese goal of gaining greatness in the eyes of both the world and the Chinese people. The students seemed to be overcoming national humiliation by humiliating the national leaders; they were thus acting in the best of the May Fourth tradition.

Finally, when Li Peng agreed on May 18 to meet with a student delegation in the Great Hall and before the television cameras, Wuerkaixi further played to the symbolism of the hunger-striking Gandhi by appearing in his pajamas much as the loin-clothed Mahatma had appeared in confronting the British authorities. The spirit of the meeting was not, however, one of non-violence but filled with the passion of aggression and hatred.

May 20–June 4 — Martial law and power from the barrel of the gun: the Chinese art of war and the paramountcy of revenge

The authorities found themselves caught up in the classic contradictions of a Chinese government under stress as it sought to move in two directions at once. In one direction, the government sought to exaggerate the extent of 'chaos' and disorder, painting a picture of the imminent collapse of the 'Chinese revolution.' At the same time, it tried to minimize the extent of the opposition, saying that it was all the work of a few 'troublemakers,' 'hooligans' and 'bad elements.' Without reversing the verdict of the April 26 editorial, the leaders did acknowledge that most of the students were misguided but good people.

Thus when martial law was imposed on May 20 it was not clear what the government's intent was or who exactly was the enemy. The students' response was again the classic Chinese tactic of mocking authority by seeking to appear more virtuous and more pure-hearted. They even went so far as to take over the task of maintaining order in Beijing, the job of the confused government, organizing themselves into a quasi-government of a highly bureaucratic nature. They began to direct traffic and check the identities of those who entered their territory. In their actions they were saying to the government, 'You lie, there is no chaos, there are no hooligans.'

The students also showed that they were prepared to settle if only the right *symbolic* gestures were made by the authorities. They did this when they gave up their hunger strike after Zhao Ziyang made his tearful visit May 19 to Tiananmen Square to meet with them, a visit that lost Zhao his job and maybe more. After the authorities gave the students a deadline to clear the square by 5 a.m. on May 22, the students again responded by writing their 'last wills' and swearing a new oath:

For the progress of democracy and the prosperity of our motherland, for the lives of one billion people, I swear that I am going to defend Tiananmen Square and the republic with my youthful life. I would rather be beheaded or shed blood for the defense of the people's square. We are going to fight with our lives until the last one of us dies.[7]

Once again, there was the drama of approaching death that was more a heroic gesture than any actual expectation of death, and once more the people of Beijing were moved by the thought of the students' gesture of suicide. Moreover, the arriving troops seemed more vulnerable than threatening. They came almost unarmed and seemingly unwilling to do harm. For nearly two weeks it appeared that the declaration of martial law only revealed the impotence of the government. In a vague way, the students seemed to have 'won' in that they had not been defeated, and therefore the Party would have to accept the idea of a new China with more political liberties. At the same time the students were exhausted, ready to call it a completed event. In a sense a happy party was coming to a warmhearted ending, a story with a peaceful but undramatic conclusion. The Party leadership, by holding back its power, seemed to be tacitly acknowledging the merits of some of the students' demands.

Then came the sudden, brutal slaughter of the June 3–4 massacre. What happened then may have been on a par with what had happened the year before in Tibet or what the Burmese army had done the year before to the students in Rangoon. The setting, however, was totally different because before it unleashed its savage fire, the People's Liberation Army in Beijing had appeared to be a 'people's army,' benign in spirit, incapable of doing harm to its own people.

In terms of Chinese political culture, there are only three things which need to be said with respect to the tragedy of the massacre and its aftermath. First, the act was a gross violation of the most basic principles of Confucianism, which holds that a ruler should always be benevolent and kind to the people. Second, the army relied upon the traditional Chinese tactic of surprise and deception in preparation for an attack. And third, the aftermath reflected the importance of revenge, always a driving force in Chinese politics.

Aside from inventing gunpowder, China's main contribution to the science of warfare has been to highlight the importance of deception and surprise, of lulling the enemy before attacking. From the writings of Sun Wu to those of Mao Tse-tung, the main doctrine has been to hit the enemy when he least expects it, to appear weak when actually strong, and to press any advantage. The rules are that of the schoolyard fight: 'Hit him when he is not looking; run if he hits back; and kick him when he is down.' Moreover, don't ever be embarrassed if you have superior fire power. Those were roughly the rules the PLA followed in carrying out the Tiananmen massacre of June 3–4.

The conclusion of the story of Beijing Spring and the Tiananmen massacre is that Chinese politics in the years immediately ahead will be overwhelmingly driven by revenge. Everybody has scores to settle. Within the leadership the hard-liners want revenge against the reformers who for the last few years had been insulting them, saying that they did not understand how to manage China's economy. The reformers must seek revenge against the hard-liners for pushing them aside and saying that they brought China to chaos. The dissidents, of course, need revenge, and the officials who were humiliated will be out to settle their scores. Anger and hatred will be legitimized by the Chinese cultural appreciation of the absolute need for revenge. As Geremie Barmé has pointed out, the rampancy of revenge in Chinese public life today will certainly damage the social fabric.[8] He notes that the Beijing Public Security Bureau reported that by the end of July it had received some 16,000 calls on its informer 'hot line' denouncing 'counterrevolutionaries' which had resulted in 5,000 arrests — 4,000 of them turned out to involve neighbors or husbands or wives. Deng

Xiaoping finally had to issue an order that arrest should only be made on the basis of two phone calls. People who lost out during the decade of private money-making will seek revenge against those who prospered under the reforms. Indeed, in offices and factories the men and women who, as Barme notes, thrived in the atmosphere of the political campaigns of the Mao era will become the watchdogs of the new morality, for they are 'the mediocrities who are inept at everything but betrayal.' The police who were embarrassed during Beijing Spring will also have their days of sweet revenge. And of course the secret police kept their files up to date through it all.

The outside world has shown its horror over what happened and its contempt for the Deng-Li clique, but the Chinese leadership, adhering to the tradition that China is the center of the world, believes that the world will soon get over its zeal for criticism, and that foreigners will flock back to China and its wonders. In the meantime it is only necessary to take note as to who are the real 'friends' of China. The logic that the Chinese elite follows which convinces them that Tiananmen will not seriously damage their relations with, for example, Washington, was spelled out in some detail in a secret article in the Internal Reference Selection (*Neican Xuanpian*), a copy of which was obtained by the *New York Times*. The article stated that although the Bush administration says that it wishes to balance support of the democracy movement with the need to protect Chinese–American relations, it will in fact have to tilt to the latter because of five fears:

First, that China will be forced into isolation and hostility toward the West. Second, that China will be pushed into the embrace of the Soviet Union, thus costing the U.S. the use of an important political and military power to check the Russians. Third, China might back away from its reform and opening policies, thus destroying American efforts to encourage China to evolve peacefully to capitalism. Fourth, if China and the U.S. quarrel, then Japan, West Germany, and South Korea will jump into China's huge market on an unprecedented scale and cause colossal damage to American businesses. Fifth, a divided and weak China would not have the power to check Japan economically and militarily, and that might complicate the process of maintaining peace and stability in the Asia-Pacific region.[9]

In short, the Chinese elite reasons that if China commits suicide, the U.S. will feel hurt. It is also true that Beijing, after so many years of hearing American officials propound the Nixon-

Kissinger thesis about the geopolitical importance of China, has probably correctly judged Washington's instincts.

In the larger sense, the tragedy of Tiananmen was a Chinese version of a Greek tragedy. There was an inevitability in the escalating confrontation. The students' progression from playfulness to moralizing, to shaming the government, to acting as a more righteous government was a sequence that could not have been better designed to cause maximum pain for the Chinese leaders. The best and the brightest of China's youth succeeded in driving their father figure, Deng Xiaoping, into a fit of rage. In an all too vivid way the 'children' had caused Deng to destroy himself and his once honored place in history. The tragedy was also a uniquely Chinese one, for once again China's political leadership had acted in a way that would keep China from regaining the qualities of greatness that it has strived so hard for in modern times. The Chinese style of politics has again obstructed progress, and all the great hopes of the Beijing Spring have turned to despair.

---

1. Frederic E. Wakeman, Jr., 'The June Fourth Movement in China,' *Items*, Vol. 43, No. 3, September 1989, footnote 4.

2. *China Spring*, July 1989, p. 50 and *United Daily*, 29 April 1989. I am indebted to Lu-tao Sophia Wang for this and the quotations from student wallposters that will be cited below.

3. Interview with Chai Ling, *Central Daily*, 2 June 1989.

4. Merle Goldman, 'Vengeance in China,' *New York Review of Books*, Vol. XXXVI, No. 17, 9 November 1989, p. 5.

5. *China Times Weekly*, 26 August 1989, p. 39.

6. *China Spring*, August 1989, p. 12.

7. *Central Daily*, 12 June 1989.

8. Geremie Barme, 'The Politics of Revenge,' *The Independent Monthly* (Sydney), 14 September 1989.

9. Nicholas D. Kristof, 'Strained U.S. Ties Reported in China,' the *New York Times*, 5 October 1989.

China's Socialist Economy: A Broken System

JAN S. PRYBYLA

LIKE all social organisms, whatever their systemic family, China's economy suffers from and tries to remedy problems, many of them extremely serious. These problems can be traced to three sources. Although in practice the sources overlap, they are conceptually distinct, and it is helpful in searching for workable remedies to identify with as much precision as possible the origins of the problems.

The first, not necessarily the most important, source of problems is what one might call 'acts of God,' or 'objective' causes. These are natural handicaps that plague the economy, some of them quite disabling. Something can usually be done about them, but not all that much and certainly not quickly. Blaming problems on objective causes is popular with politicians. The miserable state of socialized farming in Russia has long been ascribed by the *apparatchiks* to the severe climate in which much Soviet farm activity unfolds. But while there is chronic shortage of decent food in Leningrad, there is no shortage a few miles north across the border in Finland. Unless we are dealing with different sets of gods, the objective-causes explanation is not convincing in this instance. In China the 'acts of God' explanation focuses on the staggering number of people and the massiveness of the natural population increase: a net addition of 30 people every minute. It is argued that this, in combination with shrinking farmland due in part to urban sprawl caused by the rising flood of people, confronts policy makers with an awesome challenge and helps to explain the low level and the slow rise of income per head. In this instance, too, troubling reservations can be made. There are other places where rapid increases of population (not due primarily to prolific conception) have occurred and the farmland/population ratio was worse than in China. Next door Hong Kong is a case in point, its six million people sitting one on top of the other on a rock, enjoying a per capita income 30 times that of China.

The second source of problems is policy mistakes. Policy is premeditated action within a given institutional structure. Everybody makes mistakes, democrats as well as autocrats, except that autocratic mistakes tend to be bigger than democratic mistakes because autocracy lacks democracy's checks and balances that minimize the harmful effects of erroneous decisions. The Great Leap Forward in China, which brought millions of unnatural deaths and dreadful degradation of the natural environment, was declared by its author, Mao, to have been a mistake. Mao's successors adjudged the Cultural Revolution a mistake. Policy mistakes, also known as errors of workstyle, are another explanation of the source of economic problems popular with communist elites. Policy mistakes are merely misunderstandings of, or deviations from, a basically sound doctrine and institutional setup. Not to worry: Mistakes can be corrected by replacing bad policies and personnel with good ones. The mistake is Stalinism, Khrushchevism, Brezhnevism, Honeckerism, Ceausescuism, Maoism, Zhaoism, maybe one day (as twice before) Dengism, but not socialsim.

The third, possibly the most important source of economic problems is the system. Like other social organisms, economic systems consist of an institutional structure and principles. The institutional structure is a package of interdependent, interacting, compatible, integrated, socially agreed-on, and legally recognized and protected ways of doing things (allocating resources among competing alternative uses), a holistic operation, not a random collection of unrelated parts.[1] The principles that refer to this institutional structure are of two kinds: positive and normative. Positive theory or economic analysis explains the functioning of the institutional structure: what is. Normative theory lays down the ethical rules governing the institutional structure: what should be. No structure is faultless: Institutional failures do occur and the same holds for the explanatory theories and the ethical principles attaching to social structures. Thus, the system can be and, in fact, often is, the source of problems. Reluctance to acknowledge the systemic origin of problems, much in evidence among communist elites everywhere until the 1980s, is due in large measure to the understanding that solutions to such problems require a fundamental restructuring of the system's institutions and a concurrent revolutionary transformation of ideas. If the problems are deadly, nothing short of uprooting the system will do.

China's systemic problems

The primary purpose of a modern economic system is to provide increasing quantities and qualities of goods that people want at prices they are able and willing to pay and to do this efficiently, that is, with the least possible expenditure of resources at a point in time and over time. The first part of the purpose (provision of useful, affordable goods) is what makes the system economic. The system's *raison d'être* is to alleviate scarcity, to lessen the tautness between means and ends, between supply and demand, not to add to scarcity. No human system can banish scarcity. To postulate that this can be done is to invite trouble on the way to an unrealizable utopia. The human devastation brought about by socialism since 1917 is philosophically traceable in large part to the Marxist millenialistic illusion that the purpose of a historically correct economic system is to guide people to the stage of absolute abundance (*Überflussgesellschaft*). In pursuit of this objective all means are justified, including wickedness and rascality and the indefinite deferment of consumption improvements in the ever-lengthening transitional period. The second part of the purpose (efficiency, especially dynamic efficiency) is what makes the system modern. It involves primarily the application to the everyday business of making a living of novel social and engineering techniques (technological innovation).

At the end of the 1970s, the post-Mao leadership conducted a critical wide-ranging review of China's economic performance since 1957 to help policy makers launch the country on the 'four modernizations' of agriculture, industry, science-technology, and national defense. The review, assisted by academic economists brought back from forced employment in the countryside, came up with two major findings.

The first conclusion was that China's economy from 1957 through the late 1970s produced chronic shortages of useful goods side by side with chronic surpluses of useless goods, adding up to massive allocative waste, which the country — given its poverty — could ill afford. That this is not a peculiarly Chinese phenomenon is brought out by the fact that in 1989, 1,000 of the 1,200 goods that make up the standard Soviet basket of consumer goods were in short supply and that 60 percent of the apartment fires in Moscow are caused by defective Soviet-made TV sets (useless goods). In 1989 a study carried out by the Soviet Statistical Office showed that in 83 percent of the 420 cities and villages surveyed, there was a shortage of boots. The Soviet Union has three million tractors: 250,000 of them are broken at any one time.[2] In China, like elsewhere in the socialist family, lunatic incentives to workers and managers were generated, resulting in low labor productivity. They also affected capital productivity through technological stagnation of the engineering kind and aberrant social innovation of the Great Leap Forward and Cultural Revolution types. The economy was thus unable to make the necessary transition to intensive, factor productivity-based growth and risked remaining permanently mired in shortage-flation, stuck in underdevelopment, falling farther behind its dynamic East Asian market economy neighbors — particularly and most gallingly, behind Taiwan. Growth was attended by frightening ecological destruction that in the absence of remedial reformist measures seriously put to question the economy's future ability to grow and modernize. Similar environmental destruction is documented for the Soviet Union and Eastern Europe. According to the World Resources Institute, environmental conditions there 'are so bad they affect the very possibility of economic growth.' A quarter of Poland's farmland is so polluted with lead, zinc, cadmium, and mercury that it is dangerous to grow anything on it. In Hungary, air pollution accounts for one in 17 deaths.

The second conclusion reached by the post-Mao review was that while acts of God and policy mistakes were partly responsible for the economy's grim impasse, the principal reason was systemic. The fault lay with the system of central administrative command planning which China adopted from the Soviets in the early 1950s, to which were added some less attractive native traits (e.g., bizarre bureaucratism), and which for 30 years had been ineffectually tinkered with. It followed that one had to reform the system, meaning that the web of institutionalized irrationalities and scientological theories had to be reconstructed from first principles. Ideological contortions, intrasystemic policy adjustments, and body shuffling (e.g., arresting the Gang of Four) would not do on the principle that you can't stick your finger in the dike when the dike is broken, a principle with which Soviet system tinkerers are intimately familiar.

Now what do we have here? We have a system that in the normal course of its operation produces chronic shortages of useful goods at very high real cost (the cost in want satisfactions sacrificed through waste), and we have a system that fails to generate and apply technological innovation to growth. In other words, the system does not address the economic problem of scarcity: It is noneconomic. In fact, by making scarcity worse, by manufacturing shortage as its principal product, the system is anti-economic. Moreover, its apparent inability to move beyond extensive growth (growth through the addition of qualitatively unimproved factors of production), makes the system premodern. Stifling innovation where innovation naturally occurs — where real people are, at the grassroots — by, among others, restricting the free flow of and adulterating information in order to centrally control economic agents, makes the system retarding. After years of political mass mobilization under Mao, the Dengist clansmen began to emphasize economics, or at least less subservience of economics to politics, and they wanted modernization. Clearly, the systemic vehicle they had to work with was not only unsuitable for but inimical to both economizing and modernization.

If the system, defined by bureaucratic resource allocation (central administrative planning) and socialized (state-collective) property, is noneconomic and premodern, or more accurately, anti-economic and retarding, what *is* its rationale? History is full of pseudoeconomic systems, the basic purposes of which had little or nothing to do with relieving scarcity by qualitative means, that is, through social and engineering inventiveness applied to product growth. Such systems were designed to produce things other than useful goods efficiently. The bullionist system, for example, strove to maximize specie hoards (and in the process reduced Spain to Third World status). The mercantilist system used by most Western European countries for three centuries strove to secure for each nation a trade surplus in the belief that a positive balance of trade was the key to enhancing the power of emerging nation states. The national socialist variant of the command system set out to achieve military-secret police supremacy for world conquest in the cause of Aryan-Germanic racial superiority. The fundamental purpose of Marxist-Leninist socialism, to which all is subservient, is the preservation of the monopoly power of the Communist Party elite, the top echelons of the *nomenklatura*.

The purpose is not, contrary to propaganda, the efficient provision of increasing quantities and qualities of affordable useful goods. To preserve and perpetuate what euphemistically is called the 'leading role' of the Party, resources are allocated by the planners to the production of weapons and the gadgetry of domestic snooping. One of every 80 East Germans was for 40 socialist years either in the direct employ of the secret police or a paid informant. In Romania the proportion was much higher. Until recently, when the practice was suspended, the annual cost to the Soviet bloc of jamming Radio Free Europe broadcasts was $200 million a year on top of the $250 million it cost to build the jammers. British-made cameras paid for by the World Bank (i.e., by free-world taxpayers) and delivered to China for traffic-count purposes were used to photograph and hunt down participants in the Tiananmen 'counterrevolutionary rebellion.' They are still used to see who talks to foreigners in the streets of Beijing. Most staggering of all, between 1966 and 1976, almost half of state capital construction investment went into military-related projects in remote areas of the country as part of the so-called 'Third Front' (*san xian*) strategy intended to provide interior provinces with industrial infrastructures deemed necessary by the planners to withstand foreign invasion or domestic revolution, in violation of every notion of economic rationality and the calculus of comparative advantage. This strategy was adhered to for almost 20 years, beginning in 1965.

Whatever merit there may be to the socialist system's basic purpose, it is cap-and-bell economics. As the events of 1989 in Eastern Europe and the Soviet Union demonstrate, the system has trouble fulfilling this purpose. Nowadays it delivers neither useful good nor unchallenged Party control. It is, as Lech Walesa put it in his address to the U.S. Congress, a 'system of economy incompatible with rationality and common sense.'

Reform dilemmas

After the traumatic experience of the Cultural Revolution, with memories of the Great Leap disaster still painfully fresh, Mao embalmed, and the four gangsters in jail, the born-again bureaucrats newly returned from long stints in the rice paddies were not inclined to seek systemic remedies to the left of the radicalized command system they inherited. The fragile consensus was to head for the right, to decentralize the system by tolerating, indeed encouraging, some spontaneous movement at the base and not cry 'Chaos!' whenever anything so much as stirred without official permission.

If taken seriously, the conclusions emerging from the review of the Chinese economy would require fundamental changes in property rights and of the system's coordinating mechanism, and corresponding changes in explanatory theories and economic ethics. If reform is to be effective, property rights must be privatized, resource allocation has to be marketized, the *nomenklatura* has to be dismissed, Marxist economic theories and their 'creative' additions and extensions by the likes of Lenin, Stalin, and Mao have to be discarded, and the socialist code of economic ethics (egalitarianism, collectivism, anti-private property animus, hierarchically structured 'unity', i.e., power monopoly, lifelong and full employment, subsidized price stability) has to be recoded to accommodate income differentials reflecting marginal factor productivities, individual initiative and responsibility for decisions, voluntariness and horizontality of transactions, competition, rightness of profit-making, free entry and exit, price flexibility, and other normatives of the market system. The necessary and sufficient condition of real systemic reform that successfully tackles the socialist problem of terrible quality (waste, perverse incentives, technological stagnation), is the dismantling of the socialist system from top to bottom and its replacement, in its entirety, by the market system.

The transition from producer- to consumer-driven growth, from a chronic state of excess demand to a buyers' market, and from intensive to extensive growth — from socialism to a functioning modern economic system — has to be no less than the complete replacement of one system with another, not a hodgepodge of partial, unintegrated, alogical, inconsistent, incompatible transplants. Halfway measures of the socialist-market or market-socialism 'mixed' variety are conceptually deficient and unworkable in practice. They cannot cure the planning system's structural ills or correct socialism's intellectual errors that Friedrich Hayek masterfully dissects in *The Fatal Conceit*. Its elegant analytical trappings notwithstanding, Oskar Lange's model of market socialism remains a utopian vision — like full communism — and equally mischievous and misleading. Marx's vision of communism gave gangsters like Stalin and Mao an intellectual excuse for their outrages against humanity. The model of market socialism provides the successors of Stalin, Mao, Honecker, and Ceausescu with a theoretical justification for their refusal to dismember the system of central administrative command planning and replace it, and themselves, with free markets, free wills, and free elections as the people demand. They will build, they say, a new system that is superior to capitalism, one that retains the essence of socialism unsullied by past errors of workstyle, a socialism with a human face: some sort of Dubčekism serviced by the reserve army of 'good' and lenient communists, where regulated markets and socially truncated private property rights are used in subsidiary and subservient ways to improve ('perfect') the job being done by the dominant central plan and state-cooperative ownership in a political framework of single-party pluralism.

They are encouraged and supported in this endeavor by many Western academics (not just Galbraithian socialists) and under-utilized clerics unreconciled to the volume and assortment of goods produced by the market system ('vulgar consumerism') and opposed to the market ethic ('greed'). The broken mirror must be put together again, they say, to form a different market socialist pattern. But the image reflected in the rearranged pieces will be the same, only more grotesquely distorted. Attempts to give body to the ideal of market socialism (or socialist market) in which elements of plan and market, socialized and private property, and quasi-Weberian (rational) bureaucratic and individual decision-making are nicely balanced, but still with the plan, socialized property, and bureaucracy having the edge, result in what Hungary's Janos Kornai calls 'dual dependence.' In this condition a state-owned firm depends vertically on the bureaucracy and horizontally on its suppliers and customers. In such a situation,

the 'rules of the game' are not generated in a natural, organic way by economic and social processes; rather, they are elaborated artificially by officers and committees of the administrative authorities...The role of the state is not restricted to determining a few macroaggregates or economy-wide parameters like the exchange rate or interest rate...There are millions of microinterventions in all facets of economic life; bureaucratic *microregulation* [continues] to prevail.[3]

China's experience with partial economic changes and halfway reforms since 1979, culminating in the Tiananmen massacre and systemic recidivism, is an object lesson in the futility of taking the capitalist road without going all the way to advanced democratic capitalism. (Another instructive, if for the time being — but probably not for long — less bloodstained object lesson is Yugoslavia, whose labor-managed quasi-market economy, once admired by many social democrats in the West, has fallen apart in advance of its polity). When the late Chairman Mao denounced the 'Party persons in authority taking the capitalist road' (the Liuists and Dengists), and sent some of them off to set their ideas straight through manual labor in the countryside and others to see Marx, he was only half right in his assessment of the alleged deviationists' ultimate intent. As demonstrated by Deng in his latest reincarnation, the capitalist roaders' destination was not modern capitalism (the market system), nor was it democracy.

True to their appellation, the capitalist roaders merely wanted to saunter down the capitalist path: to pick up on the way bits and pieces of market, private property, and democracy and use them out of context to make central planning and one–party dictatorship work at alleviating the economic problem and work better, that is, more efficiently. Unfortunately for China, this cannot be done — unfortunately, because such crazy-quilt borrowings are yet another waste of scarce resources in the long cycle of China's socialist self-abuse. They lead to a dead end.

Capitalism can help socialism become a modern economic system only by dissolving it. Parts and aspects of socialism can be mixed with market and private–property institutions and accommodated to market system theories — provided free markets, private property rights, and voluntary, competitive buyer-seller decisions unequivocally determine the rules of the game. The laws of the marketplace must under no circumstances be paralyzed by these admixtures of last resort. Free markets, private property, and automous competitive buyer-seller decisions must at the very least form a minimum critical mass of internally consistent, cooperating, and integrated institutions and principles that constitute a system and they must call the shots. No system is completely pure. What is crucial are the proportions of the actual mix.

The real issue is the relative strength of the components in the mixture. Although there are no exact measures, I venture the following proposition. The frequency and intensity of bureaucratic intervention into market processes have certain critical values. Once these critical values are exceeded, the market becomes emasculated and dominated by bureaucratic regulation.[4]

To survive and successfully evolve as a living social organism, the system of free markets, private property, and contractual buyer-seller transactions must operate within a legal order and in a politically democratic environment, both of which are totally alien to socialism. I would argue that China's post-Mao economic reform movement has failed to effectively tackle waste, inefficiency, and perverse motivation because it would not go all the way to the modern economic market system. To socialism's genetic problems, the partial and incomplete reform has added other troubles generated by truncated private property; deficient, highly imperfect, unlinked, and unharmonized markets; and bureaucratically circumscribed decision-making powers by consumers and firms. Other problems — principally runaway corruption — were contributed by the condition of dual dependence. Finally, what little progress had been made toward the establishment of the precondition of economic freedom was negated by the refusal of the power holders to give up monopoly power and create not just laws, but the rule of law and a pluralistic political environment leading to democracy. Given this situation, no amount of open-door foreign assistance will enable China to economize and modernize its system. It will quite simply be wasted at a not inconsiderable risk to the foreign lenders and merchant joint adventurers.

The half-finished job of marketizing, privatizing, and debureaucratizing agriculture and the less than half marketizing-privatizing job in industry gave birth to a Dr. Seusslike dialectical Thing, neither fish nor fowl, a bit of this and a bit of the opposite, an uncoordinated nonsystem with many gaping holes between weak markets and weakened plan regulation that swallowed what little there was left of allocative rationality and where bureaucratic cronyism, sloth, incompetence, feudalistic roguery, and old-fashioned squeeze bloomed like a hundred flowers. This latest newborn Thing, nourished by the Four Cardinal Principles, was to grow into 'socialism with Chinese characteristics,' a mythical creature taken seriously only in some American and West European centers of higher learning, and at the Australian National University.

To make the socialist system economic and modern at least three comprehensive measures have to be taken simultaneously. First, all markets — for consumer goods and factors of production — must be freed. The freeing of all markets implies freedom of entry into and exit from the market, which, in turn, implies competition (the unhindered presence of alternatives), individual financial responsibility (hard budget constraint on consumers and firms), and demonopolization (parcelization) of the agricultural and industrial structure. It also means that information, coordination, and motivation in the system take place through the agency of competitively formed, flexible, market prices that express the changing scarcity relationships in the economy (marginal social costs to producers and marginal social use values to consumers). In the most synthetic terms, there must be price system reform: the marketization (liberation) of all prices, which presupposes the monetization of what was under the plan a largely physical, administratively rationed process of resource allocation, and the removal of budgetary subsidies attaching to many existing prices.

Second, the bulk of property must be privatized. This means that very broad, legally sanctioned, and protected rights to use, transfer, and derive income from goods and services are vested in individuals and freely constituted associations of individuals (partnerships, corporations). Private property is a necessary precondition of economic freedom.

The bureaucratic class must be *denomenklaturized*, or in the simplest terms, decommunized. Its allocative prerogatives must be abolished. The *apparatchiki* have to be put out to pasture; or they should be vocationally retrained so they can use their newly acquired skills in higher value-added employments; or they can be given $100 each and a one-way ticket to Albania or North Korea. Like the denazification of Germany after World War II, the decommunization of socialism is the *sine qua non* of socialism's economic modernization. It is a Herculean but not an impossible task. As shown by Eastern Europe, a good 90 percent of communist power holders are opportunists ready to jump the ship when the going gets tough. They can learn market trades, adapt to market discipline, and even make profits from more honest labor for a change. But they cannot be left to operate the economy's structures. The structures must be taken out of their hands. Without that, there will be no reform, just obstructionism, stalling, tinkering, and eventually a comeback. Debureaucratization means, among others, fundamental change in the way the decommunized government intervenes in the economy (as intervene it must if only because of market failures). The market system requires that such intervention be primarily indirect, exercised at the economy's macro level. This necessitates the construction of fiscal and monetary instruments of public policy: the establishment of an independent banking system and a thorough reconstruction of socialism's tax system.

The freeing of markets and market prices in an economy of

chronic and acute shortages and fixed, immobile, heavily subsidized prices for basic, if often unavailable, consumer necessities and many producer goods will inevitably result in steep price increases. An inflationary surge will, in turn, cause significant income redistributions and much suffering for certain segments of the population, particularly urban fixed income earners. Marketization will also result in a hardening of the firms' budget constraint, profound changes in the economy's structure, the bankruptcy of many unprofitable enterprises, especially in the formerly protected state sector, and — in the context of large hidden unemployment — significant structural and frictional open unemployment. Inflation, visible money income disparities, erosion of many people's real living standards, and open unemployment will cause loss of popular enthusiasm for marketizing-type economic reform. They will strengthen the hand of those vested interests opposed to systemic change, even though the problems are the price that has to be paid to attain economic rationality and eventual prosperity, and even though the severity of the problems is in large part due to their having been suppressed, and left unattended for years in the name of centrally planned stability and socialist equity. To cushion the impact of these problems, it is necessary not only to have means of monetary and fiscal intervention in the changing system, but to keep a tight rein on the money supply, carry out a currency reform, construct institutional safety nets in the form of a national scheme of unemployment insurance, and secure external loans to help contain the short-term negative effects of the systemic changes.

Now, what has China done since 1978? First, it has not freed all markets, only some: those for selected agricultural but not many industrial goods, for some consumer but few producer goods, and not at all for factors. The freedom granted these disjointed, unintegrated goods markets is circumscribed by administrative rules and Party-bureaucratic microinterventions, including arbitrary, not to say capricious, local levies, taxes, and prohibitions of all kinds. There is no competition and continuing soft budget constraint (financial irresponsibility of firms) in the vast industrial state sector that continues to be dominated by large, quasi-ministerial oligopolies. Elsewhere, even in agriculture, competition is pervaded by the competitors' vertical-bureaucratic concerns. It takes the old socialist form of mutual exchange of favors, influence-peddling, power connections, and political backscratching. Physical rationing of key inputs has been somewhat reduced but not eliminated (e.g., 60 percent of capital goods are still bureaucratically allocated, and the share has been rising since 1988). The state remains the monopolistic supplier of essential industrial inputs to agriculture (chemical fertilizers, agricultural chemicals, plastics, machinery). The agricultural price system has been half-reformed, changed from the state's slave to a serf. Contractual deliveries to the state are paid for at 'negotiated' prices, the negotiation being between unequal parties (individual farm families and the state). Hence these purchase prices are in effect fixed by the state, although with fewer socialist sillies than before, and they are generally significantly below the free-market prices for equivalent above-contract surplus products. The 'free' prices for goods produced and sold over and above contractual deliveries are often tampered with by local Party zealots and bureaucratic micropotentates ever on the lookout for capitalist dirty tricks. Some industrial prices have been freed, but most remain state fixed or are permitted to move (mainly downward) within state-set limits. There are state-fixed vaguely cost-based prices for producer goods, and relatively free prices for whatever (not much) is left over after state orders are fulfilled. There are no free-market prices to speak of for factors, and free black market prices for practically everything, including currency. The two-track (or three-track, or four-track) price system remains extremely irrational. The first condition of making the socialist system economic and modern has been violated in China so monstrously as to make almost superfluous further analysis of how the other two conditions, privatization of property and debureaucratization have fared. For all practical purposes, there has been no genuine marketization of the system.

Neither in agriculture nor in industry has privatization been carried to any substantive lengths. This is not to deny that the decollectivization of agriculture after 1979 and the creation in its place of a system of tenant family farming, the state being the landlord, was a genuine structural reform. The reform, however, was partial and incomplete. It did not bring about the *de jure* vesting of land ownership in the private family unit. The responsibility contract is not voluntary — no contract, no land. Mandatory limitations are imposed on the size of family land plots, on private employment, and on land transfers, even on the use of land, both formally and informally through ad hoc harassments by zealous or simply envious cadres suffering from red-eye disease. The state keeps ordering the farmers what to grow, usually grain. It tacks family limitation requirements onto the production responsibility contracts (*baogan daohu*). In short, in agriculture, where the process had gone farthest, privatization remains for the most part confined to the expansion of family rights of use. There has been some increase in individual rights to income from land through the abolition of collectively determined work points, but practically no expansion of transfer rights. Despite the spectacular increase in the number of privately owned nonagricultural firms from near zero, state-collective property dominates industry and commerce. Since 1988 the trend toward privatization has been reversed.

There has been no decommunization, no debureaucratization at all, only a change of guard with the less savory geriatric characters noted for their inability to entertain complicated thoughts reasserting themselves at the top after June 1989. While central administrative controls over the economy have been weakened through reduction in their scope and numbers and a far-reaching administrative delegation of powers to the provinces, market-type levers of intervention in the economy have not been put in place, or only partially and imperfectly so. The banking system remains an administrative appendage of the government, there are no financial markets to speak of, and there has been no fundamental reconstruction of — only tinkering with — the tax system. The workplace (*danwei*) remains the basic producing and social welfare unit. Nothing has been done to replace it with a national system of social security. Nor has anything been done to tighten up the state firms' budget constraint. State sector firms remain financially irresponsible, and like old soldiers, they never die — they won't even fade away — but then neither do old PLA soldiers. The center appears unable to control the money supply by other means than sledgehammer administrative prohibitions. These create recurrent credit shortages and liquidity crises, supply bottlenecks as buyers are unable to pay for inputs, underutilization of industrial capacity, default on cash payments to peasants for contractual deliveries (the peasants are often paid with disincentive promissory notes or 'white slips'), and the settlement of a part of state sector workers' and employees wages in three-year government bonds without the wage earners' consent.

The institutional disarray grew worse as China's *perestroika* took longer and longer and as its indispensable elements — price system reform, property reform, political liberalization — were postponed again and again. The confusion has been heightened since the Tiananmen nastiness by the liquidation of most economic think tanks, the ending of relatively free debate on reform issues, reimposition of strict press censorship, the drafting of Beijing University students into the army, and the reintroduction of indoctrination courses in Marxist-Leninist quackery. Economic illiteracy and ideological schlock are once again in command. What after mid-1988 was a tactical retreat from reform, became after June 1989 a matter of unbending principle — the taboo domain of dogma. Marketization, privatization, and political democratization are no longer issues open to even the most circumspect public discussion. They are equated with counterrevolutionary rebellion.

Conclusion

The sad chronicle of China's post-Mao attempt to introduce a modern economic system contains a useful lesson, which others, notably the East Europeans, including communist quick-change artists, are taking to heart. China may yet one day learn from its own lesson, perhaps sooner than most people think, given the power struggles in the leadership, the bad news for most of the leading senior citizen contestants contained in actuarial tables, and the unworkability of the present 'economy.'

The lesson is that to address the economic problem in a modern way in the context of a low caliber, inefficient, slothful, wasteful, cronyfied socialist system, one must go all the way to the market system, do it quickly, and not stop anywhere on the way. To go part of the way slowly, 'crossing the river while groping for the stones' as the Dengists put it, is to end up the creek to nowhere. Most of the problems that have prompted the present retreat from reform are traceable to the nonviability — theoretical and practical — of intermediate systemic solutions consisting of the partial dismantling of one system and incomplete construction of another. What China has created is systemic disarray, a crazy concoction of unintegrated and antithetical institutions and principles where nothing works as it should: neither market nor plan.

While teaching in China in 1987–88 I had many interesting discussions with Chinese academic and government economists. The great majority of them agreed with the assessment presented above, which I developed at the time in a series of lectures and seminars and — with some surgery done by the censor on what must have struck him as malignant bourgeois politics — was published in the, as I understand it, restricted (*neibu*) Beijing journal *Comparative Social and Economic Systems* (No. 3, 1988). 'It's either now, or it's all over,' the economists concluded. 'We either move quickly all the way to the market system right now, or we fall back into planned nothingness. There is no third way.' The apprehension voiced by Chinese economists is echoed these days by those who have to clean up after the communist elephants in Eastern Europe. One repentant East German elephant who has harnessed himself to the cleansing task, Siegfrid Schiller, the communist deputy director of Dresden's economic research institute, says that 'every attempt to shore up a planned economy must be resisted.'

In 1988 China's communist leaders began to shore up their broken, planned economy. After June 1989 the shoring up operation was ideologically consecrated and the reform lapsed into a coma.

---

1. Jan S. Prybyla, *Market and Plan Under Socialism: The Bird in the Cage* (Stanford: Hoover Institution Press, 1987).

2. Nikolai Shmelev and Vladimir Popov, *The Turning Point: Revitalizing the Soviet Economy* (New York: Doubleday, 1989).

3. Janos Kornai, 'The Hungarian Economic Reform Process: Visions, Hopes, and Reality,' in Victor Nee and David Stark (Eds), *Remaking the Economic Institutions of Socialism: China and Eastern Europe* (Stanford: Stanford University Press, 1989), p. 49.

4. Kornai, *ibid.*, p. 48.

5. Jan S. Prybyla, 'Why China's Economic Reforms Fail,' *Asian Survey*, Vol. 39, No. 11, November 1989, pp. 1017–1032. On the general issue of marketization and privatization of socialism, see the essays in 'Privatizing and Marketizing Socialism,' *The Annals* of the American Academy of Political and Social Science (Philadelphia), January 1990.

Autonomy Versus Authoritarianism

THOMAS B. GOLD

IN 1989 China suffered through the bloodiest clash yet between the contradictory tendencies that have characterized the entire history of the Communist Party's relation with Chinese society: a drive toward autonomy and the effort to assert authority. Deng Xiaoping's reforms explicitly called for decentralization, enterprise autonomy, privatization, creativity, and individual initiative to stimulate economic development. But Deng also insisted that the Party must maintain total political and social dominance.

Chinese people see their nation's history since 1949 as an oscillation between two extremes of tightening (*shou*) and loosening (*fang*) of control over the economy, polity, and society by the Chinese Communist Party. By their nature, communist parties attempt to monopolize control over the societies they rule, and in China, this impetus was reinforced by a tradition of authoritarianism. Nonetheless, the Chinese Party never achieved total control, and on several occasions loosened its grip in order to address crises. The decade of reform beginning in 1979 was the longest sustained period of liberalization (*fang*) since the CCP took power in 1949, although it was punctuated by attempts to roll back. This chapter shows how 1989 embodies the legacy of these contradictory trends in the context both of Marxism-Leninism and of Chinese tradition.

Leninism and totalitarianism

A Leninist political party cannot tolerate autonomous action by social and political groups. Lenin created a type of political party which Philip Selznick called an 'organizational weapon.'[1] Based on the principle of 'democratic centralism,' Party members must submit to iron discipline and never question Party policy. The Party itself is a vanguard Party, in theory comprising only advanced members of society possessed of the highest consciousness of the laws of social development and totally committed to the lofty task of leading their society. This involves first the seizure of state power, then, for Leninist parties which adopt Marxism as their guiding ideology, as most do, building socialism.

In the Marxist-Leninist self-image, because Party members constantly study Marxism, they understand the direction of social development and where the long-term interests of the masses lie. The masses themselves, primarily workers and peasants, lack this comprehension; it is up to the vanguard to educate them about their long-term interests and to make policies that help achieve them. Consequently, after seizing state power, Party members must monopolize leadership of all organizations of the state, economy, and society (including the superstructure of education and the arts) using them as instruments to lead society toward the bright socialist future. Social groups cannot enjoy autonomy in organization, membership, leadership, or definition and pursuit of goals, because their backward, unenlightened practices and values risk obstructing or derailing society's progress. In China, the Communist Party attained a high level of control not only of institutions but also over the daily lives of Chinese citizens. This can be attributed to two factors. One is the Party's truly miraculous success at overthrowing Chiang Kai-shek's American-backed Nationalist Party, eliminating the old elite, then stabilizing, rehabilitating, and building the economy. China's communist movement was indigenous, unlike most Eastern European communist regimes, which were imposed and backed by the USSR.

The other reason for the success of the CCP in quickly gaining ascendancy over Chinese society is Leninism's affinity with central elements of the Chinese political tradition.[2] These include: 1) the rule of ideologically indoctrinated superior men rather than laws; 2) absence of a sense of tension between the individual and the state; 3) absence of intermediary institutions between state and society; 4) acceptance of an orthodox, 'correct' view of the world with bureaucrats as its moral exemplars exercising power linked to ethical ideals; 5) intolerance of heterodoxy and political power outside the formal governmental structure: 6) desire for order and fear of chaos; 7) legitimate hierarchy of personal relations with deference to and dependence on authority from the family up to the emperor; 8) perfectibility through study and self-cultivation.

I do not wish to draw too simplistic a line between Chinese tradition and Leninism, nor claim that Chinese are better suited to authoritarianism than to democracy. However, there is no question that the CCP was able to build upon elements of longstanding

legitimacy in Chinese society, and prevent the emergence of autonomous organizations until the end of the 1980s.

Although the CCP established a structure for totalitarian dominance, it never achieved total control, if indeed such a thing is even
possible. Instead, control has flowed between extremes of restriction (*shou*) and liberalization (*fang*). Why has this movement
between *shou* and *fang* occurred?

First, leaders manipulate the political environment as a tool in
their power struggles. For instance, in 1978, Deng Xiaoping ap-
plauded the use of big character posters and free expression of
grievances critical of the Cultural Revolution as a veiled way of
discrediting the still-Maoist regime headed by his rival Hua
Guofeng. Once it was clear that Hua and his cronies would have
to yield power, Deng cracked down on the Democracy Wall
movement. He turned *shou* and *fang* on and off like tap water.

Second, cadres can obstruct the implementation of policies because they oppose a particular policy, or fear that if they zealously
implement it, when the line (inevitably) changes, they will be
vulnerable to criticism. Hence, it is better to do nothing. Because
most Party members work in social units and not the Party
bureaucracy, they often adopt the viewpoint of their unit, and
obstruct the implementation of policies that will harm these
interests.

A third reason causing the shift between restriction and liberalization comes from the failure or success of previous policies.
For instance, direct Party leadership over the state and society
reached its zenith during the Cultural Revolution and brought
disaster upon the Chinese people. Under Deng, the reformers
realized they had to loosen up if the Party and nation were to
survive. Social and intellectual consequences of the liberalizing
economic reforms, in turn, led other leaders to try to reimpose
control.

Another related cause of the oscillation is the conflict between
trying to achieve both economic development and utopian communist goals.[3] Economic growth requires a certain amount of
freedom that engenders social changes that 'run counter to the
utopian vision,' thereby necessitating 'repeated "revolutions from
above",'[4] that is, renewed Party dominance to bring social developments back under its control.

Finally, the international environment can cause a movement
between *shou* and *fang*. As an example, in the early 1970s, when

the Chinese perceived that the U.S. no longer posed a direct threat to their security, they relaxed relations.

Tightening-loosening can take many forms. There might be economic liberalization with political restriction. There might be a clampdown in Beijing and liberalization in the provinces. Some social groups might experience restrictions while others escape untouched.

Liberalization does not mean autonomy. It means, adapting Chen Yun's famous simile referring to the economy, a roomier birdcage for people to fly around in; it does not mean no cage at all.[5] Party cadres grant people more scope to manage their affairs but do not grant them so much freedom that they might subvert Party control. It was when too many Chinese began to cross the line to true autonomy from the Party during 1988–89 that some members of the leadership realized they had to act decisively.

Eliminating the bases of autonomy

To better appreciate the trend toward autonomy after 1978, we must first look at how the CCP tried to eliminate the bases for such autonomous activity soon after taking national power.

There were only 4.5 million CCP members in a total population of 541 million when the Party established the People's Republic of China on 1 October 1949. A large percentage of Party members were peasants with at best only rudimentary education and little or no experience of a modern economy or urban life. Out of necessity, the CCP retained many bureaucrats from the former regime, but began to remove them as more trustworthy replacements could be found. The Party quickly began to establish its control over state and society, progressively eliminating enemies and potential competitors. It used terror and violence against counter-revolutionaries, some remnants of the old regime, landlords, and other 'disruptive' elements. It established a pervasive system of police and informers. It channeled citizens into mass organizations under Party control to monitor their activities and indoctrinate them in the new values and norms.

The Party began to restrict and remold intellectuals in the Ideological Reform Campaign in late 1951. Party cadres took over the entire educational system as well as the media and other cultural organizations. The activities of religious associations were monitored and, in the case of Christianity and Catholicism, the CCP forced them to sever their foreign links.

Through confiscation of the modern economic sector, the new regime inherited a large bloc of China's industrial workers and recruited them into Party-led unions. National capitalists and petit bourgeois businessmen became totally dependent on the state for utilities, capital, raw materials, and foodstuffs. By means of the Five-Anti Campaign[6] of 1952, the Party served notice on the private sector that its sphere of activity would be increasingly circumscribed. Bureaucratic job allocation replaced the labor market.

In the countryside, land reform eliminated the landlord class. Redistribution of land and property, followed by collectivization, brought peasants under Party leadership, and their output under state control. Stringent restriction on migration to the cities tied peasants to the land. Introducing Party-state control into old institutions and creating many new ones established an environment designed to reorient political, economic, social, and cultural activity in a new direction. At the same time, the CCP endeavored to remold all Chinese citizens as individuals. This involved ensuring that much of their waking life was spent in CCP-led organizations. Large state units (*danwei*) provided housing, schooling, health care, recreation, and rationed goods in addition to a job. People also had to participate in small groups at work or home where Party members or lay activists led them in studying official documents, monitored their thoughts and behavior, and pushed them to engage in criticism and self-criticism. The Party tried to revolutionize interpersonal relations as well, replacing former particularistic ties of friendship and family with universalistic ties of comradeship tied to the national mission of building socialism. Political messages dominated popular culture and the media. Restricted access to cultural artifacts and information from outside the communist bloc reoriented China's intellectual world.

Certainly, some measure of a private life continued, but it had to operate circumspectly. Particularly in the urban areas, people learned to ritualize public behavior, keeping their thoughts to themselves and a few trusted intimates.

Ironically, while the Cultural Revolution trumpeted that 'the Party must lead everything,' it simultaneously wreaked havoc on the Party as an organization. Constant power struggles, inconsistent policies, arbitrary exercise of power, and a wide gap between official values of asceticism and discipline and the reality of indulgence and corruption, left the Party with weak organization, low morale, and even lower prestige. The economy was stagnating and the standard of living declining.

In Deng Xiaoping's analysis, the Party's ability to retain power required a tactical retrenchment, ceding to the people more power over their own lives. The CCP had to win back the prestige it had lost by improving people's standard of living, introducing more predictability and stability into their lives, and restraining the arbitrary power of unpopular bureaucrats.[7]

The major thrust of this liberalization came in the economic realm, where Chinese were permitted and compelled to assume personal responsibility for their economic lot. Rapid decollectivization in the countryside brought about a return of family farming (without private land ownership) and a clear linkage between effort and reward through the market. Farmers were encouraged to diversify their economic activity; they could even leave agriculture altogether.

Economic liberalization in the urban areas came more slowly, but followed the same trends of Party retrenchment and increased autonomy. Control devolved from Beijing to localities and enterprises. The market began to replace the plan and prices for many goods were freed. In a revolutionary departure from orthodox Stalinism, the Chinese leaders began to encourage the consumer goods sector. To respond successfully to consumer demands required autonomy from rigid state plans. Enterprise directors had to be entrepreneurial and competent; this meant that they and not Party secretaries had to have decision-making power. These are all examples of the reformers' recognition of the need for *fang* in order to enliven the domestic economy.

Another example of Party-induced liberalization was the official encouragement of urban small-scale private business, in particular in the service sector. The CCP did this to solve a severe unemployment problem and also to stimulate production, enliven the market, and fill gaps in the economy. China's leaders anticipated that private businessmen would have to rely on the state for materials and capital, but wily entrepreneurs quickly established their own networks. What is more, they had permission to travel nationwide to purchase materials. Private businessmen were thus liberated to a large degree from the stifling womblike work-cum-residential units which most other urban Chinese are compelled to depend on.

The thousands of Chinese who found jobs in foreign-invested companies also enjoyed unprecedented autonomy from Party control. Those with access to telephone, telex, fax, and foreign travel suddenly gained direct contact with a world of information previously restricted to only the highest officials. Investors, tourists, experts, and students from abroad also revolutionized the world of Chinese they came into contact with. The fact that many of these visitors were ethnic Chinese from Hong Kong, Taiwan, and Southeast Asia opened the eyes of mainlanders to the momentous changes that had occurred in Chinese societies outside the socialist motherland, and suggested the potential benefits to themselves and the nation of a different type of system.

Party General Secretary Zhao Ziyang's speech at the Thirteenth National CCP Congress in October 1987, put forth the slogan, 'the primary stage of socialism.'[8] This gave an official blessing to a mixed economic system (under a dominant state sector) with a degree of tolerance for inequality and social diversity. Zhao claimed that China already was socialist, but because it had yet to achieve an advanced level of productive forces, had to permit a diverse range of economic activity in order to overcome the disadvantages of backwardness. Zhao's speech clearly downplayed politics. A legitimate second channel for upward mobility in China, outside the Party track, had emerged, based on individual initiative and effort. In other words, the CCP officially sanctioned autonomy in the economic realm.

Social scientists began to recognize that economic diversity was having an effect on social structure and values as well. Writers discussed the way that social values had changed as a result of reforms. Absolutism had given way to relativity, centralization to pluralism, theory to practice, and so on. People were no longer ascetics and the individual had emerged against the collective, some asserted.[9] A wave of opinion polling similarly turned up increased diversity of views on a range of subjects as a result of reforms.[10]

Intellectuals increasingly met on their own. George Soros, the Hungarian-American financier who had established the Soros Fund to support independent intellectual inquiry in Hungary, set up the China Fund for the same purpose in 1986 with Zhao Ziyang's blessing. The new pluralism was reflected as well in the arts. Drama, cinema, fiction, poetry, painting, sculpture, and so on entered a number of 'forbidden zones' to discuss formerly taboo subjects utilizing forms of artistic expression unknown in China. These included pure Western imports such as stream-of-consciousness, but also efforts to transform traditional Chinese forms.[11] China's Fifth Generation filmmakers attracted international attention.

Privatization of activity had a counterpart in privatization of values. Increasingly, Chinese opted out of Party-led political activity, concentrating their energies on making money, consuming, personal adornment, and the joys of family life. With the bankruptcy of official ideology, many searched for new sources of spiritual values. Religion experienced an unprecedented surge. Christian and Catholic churches enjoyed record attendance. In the countryside, Buddhism and a range of folk religions (branded 'superstition' by the authorities) also re-emerged.

In sum, the Party-initiated reforms had unintentionally created many potential social bases for autonomy: some state and collective enterprises, private business, foreign enterprises, cultural institutions, and ties with foreigners. China had no non-Party institutions with mass legitimacy, but the Party-state's retrenchment created an opening for many social groups to begin managing their own affairs. Scholars affiliated with the regime provided theoretical legitimacy for this trend.[12] It appeared that the supporters of economic liberalization were willing to tolerate attendant social and intellectual liberalization, and that they could prevent opponents from sabotaging this trend.

In fact, these trends had provoked fear and loathing among some elements of the Chinese leadership. They sensed that the CCP had lost control over major spheres of Chinese economic, cultural, and social life and appeared to be losing its grip on political life as well. As David Kelly notes elsewhere in this volume, the Party was becoming irrelevant to increasing numbers of Chinese.

To counter this tide, in 1981 conservatives attacked PLA writer Bai Hua's screenplay, *Unrequited Love*, whose central question, 'You love the motherland, but does the motherland love you?' voiced the frustration of many patriotic intellectuals. In the fall of 1983, conservative stalwarts such as Deng Liqun and Hu Qiaomu went after 'spiritual pollution,' initially defined as pornography, but then broadened to cover almost anything a particular official disliked,[13] including rural specialized households, urban private entrepreneurs, youthful criminals (thousands of whom were executed), and cultural figures.

University students in Hefei and Shanghai took to the streets late in 1986 demanding democracy and changes in the educational system. The vice president of the Hefei-based Chinese University of Science and Technology, Fang Lizhi, galvanized the students with a number of stirring pro-democracy speeches. In response, conservative leaders, including Deng Xiaoping, launched an attack against 'bourgeois liberalization,' which resulted in the sacking of Hu Yaobang from his post as CCP General Secretary, and the expulsion of Fang, Liu Binyan, and Wang Ruowang from the Party.[14] The students were rather handily suppressed with minimal violence.

The campaigns of 1983–84 and 1986–87 both fizzled out. Their conservative proponents suffered a humiliating loss of face and power as the Chinese masses and foreign opinion mocked their retrograde efforts. It also appeared that the increased involvement of foreign businesses, banks, and experts in China had helped to brake these Mao-style campaigns. The logical conclusion appeared to be that the moderate leaders had emerged victorious and that they were prepared to tolerate a great deal of diversity, even a bit of anarchy, in their headlong effort to modernize the economy.

In the winter of 1988–89, a curious debate signaled renewed fighting in Zhongnanhai. At conferences and in the press, scholars discussed the issue of 'neo-authoritarianism.'[15] Proponents of neo-authoritarianism argued that China needed a strong leader to push the reforms forward against continued unnamed resistance. The models of Japan and the Four Dragons (Taiwan, South Korea, Singapore, and Hong Kong) were cited as examples of successful economic development with strong authority. Once the situation stabilized, the argument ran, then the market economy would expand and political democracy could evolve based on newly emergent social forces. Opponents countered that democracy was not anarchic and that authoritarianism would shut off outlets for political expression, resulting in still greater instability.

Some observers realized that proponents of neo-authoritarianism were using this theory to shore up Zhao Ziyang's weakening position against attacks by Li Peng and other conservatives, especially aged retired revolutionaries, who wished to reimpose more controls over the economy and society.[16] Neo-authoritarians hoped to pre-empt Li and company by further institutionalizing the economic reforms while making temporary sacrifices on the sociopolitical front, although the theory could just as easily support the conservatives.[17]

Autonomy versus authority

The events of April and May 1989 strengthened the hands of Zhao's opponents. Not only did social chaos increase, but autonomous organizations began to appear. Many of these grew out of more or less formal discussion groups which students and others had attended.[18]

Significantly, virtually all of these groups included the word 'autonomous' (zizhi) in their name to stress that they were part of neither the state or Party. Most noticeable was the Beijing University Federation, comprising representatives of autonomous organizations established on many campuses. One of its heads was Beijing University history student Wang Dan, who had sponsored Wednesday afternoon democratic salons for more than a year with the backing of Fang Lizhi and Fang's wife, Li Shuxian.[19] Liu Xiaobo, the literary critic, worked with the Federation and also prepared to establish a Beijing Federation of All Circles, according to accusations against him.[20]

Autonomous student organizations were not limited to Beijing. Glancing through the Foreign Broadcast Information Service in the days after June 4, one sees, for instance, that students in Hefei (site of the 1986 demonstrations), Changchun, Chengdu, Shanghai, Liaoning, Xian, and Changsha organized similar associations. In addition to these new associations, students, as well as workers, journalists, and others, in some cases joined by their Party leaders, marched in protests carrying banners of their particular units.

Workers around China also formed autonomous associations with similar goals of engaging the leadership in dialogue over ways to solve problems such as inflation, corruption, inequality, and the stifling Party monopoly of power. In Hefei, the Hefei Municipal Self-Government Association of Workers, the Hefei Municipal Union of Workers, and the Hefei Municipal Association of Initiative-Taking Workers, paraded, distributed handbills, called for strikes by workers and students, and 'attempted to alienate the relations between trade unions and the Party and the government, divide the working class, and undermine the normal order in

Hefei.'[21] Members of Beijing's Workers Autonomous Federation stood accused of particularly aggressive violence.[22]

In many cities, citizens groups emerged in support of students and workers. According to Xinhua, the 'Beijing Citizens Hunger Strike Corps and Dare-To-Die Corps,' comprising mainly 'vagrants and idlers in society... were under the direct control and command of the "Beijing College Students Autonomous Federation," which funded them and supplied them with Molotov cocktails. They helped to erect the Goddess of Democracy as well.'[23] Private entrepreneurs in Beijing were actively involved in the Flying Tigers Team, using their motorcycles to run messages and supply goods.

Police in Tengzhou City, Shandong, reported the arrest of an activist of the Beijing Peasants Autonomous Union. He was accused of a variety of counterrevolutionary crimes in Beijing as well as several locations in Shandong.[24] The extent of peasant involvement in the movement is unclear.

Intellectuals also organized autonomous associations. Yan Jiaqi and Bao Zunxin of the Institute of Politics and the Institute of History of the Chinese Academy of Social Sciences headed the Beijing Association of Intellectuals. Another prominent organization, which predated the demonstrations, was the Social Development Research Institute of the private Stone Company headquartered in Beijing's 'Silicon Valley.' The company enjoyed the backing of reformers in the leadership. Hu Jiwei, former editor of the *People's Daily* who was sacked during the anti-spiritual pollution campaign, used Stone's think tank on two occasions to collect signatures of NPC members and others to convene a meeting to discuss martial law.[25] Stone's founder, Wan Runnan, provided financial and logistical support to the demonstrators and fled for his life after the crackdown. He emerged in Paris as one of the leaders of the Front for a Democratic China.[26]

Not all participants had the same motives. Certainly, some took advantage of the disorder purely for destructive ends. Many came to watch the action (*kan renao*). But the fact that so many social forces spontaneously organized on their own, giving names to their groups, to vent grievances and press one sort of demand or another, represented a significant change in China's political culture and an unprecedented challenge to the authorities. These were not naive students and workers organizing Red Guard groups to protect Chairman Mao as two decades before, but citizens of all stripes, tuned into global trends, especially the Soviet Union's *perestroika* and *glasnost*, demanding that the system reform itself in decidedly un-Leninist ways. But the response to it was decidedly Leninist.

At a morning meeting on April 25, Deng Xiaoping responded to reports by Li Peng, Yang Shangkun, and the Beijing Party Committee.[27] Deng called for decisive action, saying, 'We cannot let them have their way.' In his analysis, 'This is not an ordinary student movement, but turmoil.' He did not define what an 'ordinary student movement' is, but we can assume he meant activities initiated and led by the Communist Youth League, official student federations, or similar Party-led organizations in support of officially approved goals.

To Deng, 'Those people who have been influenced by the freedom elements of Yugoslavia, Poland, Hungary, and the Soviet Union have arisen to create turmoil.' That Mikhail Gorbachev was scheduled to arrive in Beijing three weeks hence made it even more imperative to end the turmoil. Referring again to events in Eastern Europe, Deng added, 'Concessions in Poland led to further concessions. The more they conceded, the more chaos.' Deng's remarks revealed frustration that the Party missed the chance to take early decisive action to nip this movement in the bud, tracing this failure back to Hu Yaobang's halfhearted efforts to stamp out bourgeois liberalization in 1986.

Furthermore, the students were using 'the rights of democracy and freedom in the Constitution to impose restrictions on us.' That is to say, the students demanded that the state implement its own Constitution. But Deng wanted to use the extralegal Four Cardinal Principles[28] to deal with the turmoil. He stated that 'This turmoil is entirely a planned conspiracy to transform a China with a bright future into a China without hope.'

Deng's Leninist view ultimately prevailed, with the quest for autonomy labeled a 'counterrevolutionary rebellion.'

Unresolved contradictions

June 4 signaled the reassertion of *shou*, but it leaves a schizophrenic, ultimately unstable mix. While calling for 'unity and stability,' the primacy of the Four Cardinal Principles, recentralization, and strengthened CCP leadership, the post-June 4 leadership also claims it has not abandoned economic reforms, the open door, or enlivening the domestic economy.

After purging universities and think tanks, the leadership has tightened control of students, intellectuals, and workers to prevent the resurgence of autonomous organizations. Cultural life has become a combination of mind-numbing political propaganda and inane bread-and-circus. Workers are organized to view museum exhibits on 'Pacifying the Counterrevolutionary Rebellion.'

The state is recentralizing economic control in Beijing, strengthening the role of Party secretaries in enterprises at the expense of directors, and closely regulating private business. It has made noises about solving some of the concerns voiced by the masses last spring,[29] but to date, only low- and medium-rank officials or allies of Zhao Ziyang have been punished for corruption. It has cooled the politically sensitive inflation rate but at the cost of shutting down thousands of state, collective, and private enterprises. It emphasizes that China's 'democratic parties' serve to advise the CCP but not to contest its hegemony. The upshot is a very cynical and pessimistic populace with little confidence in its leadership, which it sees as devoid of idealism, concerned only with preserving its own power and privileges.

Since June 4, the Eastern European dominoes have fallen one after the other, and the Chinese citizenry has been riveted by these events. In the Dengist-Leninist view, these are the inevitable consequences of loosening Party control. The East Germans and Czechs did try the 'Chinese solution,' beating and firing on demonstrators, acts which only motivated more demonstrations and the ultimate collapse of a once-hard-line regime. These countries, like Poland, had a legacy of civil society and nascent political parties, and their communist parties had never enjoyed popular legitimacy. As noted earlier, the Chinese Party had once enjoyed such popular support, but its subsequent actions have eroded this probably beyond repair.

The Christmas overthrow of China's close comrade-in-arms, Romania's Nicolae Ceausescu, who had gone the Chinese one better by shooting civilians from helicopters, even more clearly demonstrated the bankruptcy of the Chinese solution. China's decade of opening to the outside went much further than Romania's, a fact not lost on the inhabitants of Zhongnanhai. Their response has been even more *shou*, and warmer relations with the anti-reform regimes in Burma and Cuba.

The startling events of 1989 throughout the socialist world raise the question of whether Marxist-Leninist systems can be reformed without being dismantled. Once they permit autonomy they are compromised. Facts demonstrate that *fang* in one sphere inevitably expands to others. Marxism teaches that all social systems prior to communism are riddled with contradictions, and Mao taught that this includes socialism. China's tenacious gerontocratic Leninist leaders demonstrated their unwillingness to tolerate what they now vilify as 'peaceful evolution.' But the Party itself is seriously split, and the major question is the position of the successors. Some, such as Li Peng, who is a surrogate for the elders, would try to maintain power through suppression of pluralistic tendencies. This will only generate increased tensions and more violence. Should the chastised pro-reform neo-authoritarians regain power, there is a better chance of leaders recognizing the inevitability of change. Since their economic strategy includes a strong role for the market and consumer goods, they must grant competent factory managers decision-making power over their enterprises to satisfy demand. This entails flexibility in finding ways to improve productivity and lower costs, often through technological changes. These naturally have social consequences, and the question is whether the neo-authoritarians would be more willing and able to devise a strategy to guide social change and build a new consensus within society, and between the Party and society in order to avoid yet another outbreak of bloodshed on Tiananmen Square.

---

1. Philip Selznick, *The Organizational Weapon* (Glencoe: Free Press, 1960).

2. Some of the following elements are discussed in Lucian W. Pye, *Asian Power and Politics* (Cambridge: The Belknap Press of Harvard University Press, 1985), especially Chapter 3; and Franz Schurmann, *Ideology and Organization in Communist China,* second edition (Berkeley: University of California Press, 1968).

3. Richard Lowenthal, 'Development vs. Utopia in Communist Policy,' in Chalmers Johnson, ed., *Change in Communist Systems* (Stanford University Press, 1970), pp. 33–116.

4. *Ibid.*, p. 47.

5. David M. Bachman, *Chen Yun and the Chinese Political System* (Berkeley: Institute of East Asian Studies, Center for Chinese Studies, 1985).

6. The campaign was to eliminate the five vices of bribery, tax eva-

210 THE BROKEN MIRROR

sion, theft of state property, cheating on government contracts, and stealing state economic information.

7. Deng Xiaoping, 'On the Reform of the System of Party and State Leadership,' Deng Xiaoping, *Selected Works of Deng Xiaoping, 1975–1982* (Beijing: Foreign Languages Press, 1984), pp. 302–25.

8. Zhao Ziyang, 'Advance Along the Road of Socialism with Chinese Characteristics,' *Beijing Review* (North American Edition), (BR) 45, 9–15 November 1987, pp. 23–49.

9. Liu Yuejin, 'Shinian Gaigezhong Jiazhiguan di Shige Zhuanbian' (Ten Changes in Values in the Course of a Decade of Reforms), *Xinhua Wenzhai*, 1989, pp. 13–16.

10. Stanley Rosen, 'Public Opinion and Reform in the People's Republic of China,' *Studies in Comparative Communism*, XXII(2–3), Summer/Autumn, 1989, pp. 153–70.

11. A first-rate sampling can be found in Geremie Barme and John Minford, ed., *Seeds of Fire* (New York: Hill and Wang, 1988).

12. In the Eastern European context, this has been called the emergence of civil society. Some essays on this subject can be found in Part 3 of John Keane, ed., *Civil Society and the State* (London: Verso, 1988).

13. Thomas B. Gold, ' "Just in Time!" China Battles Spiritual Pollution on the Eve of 1984,' *Asian Survey* XXIV(9), September, 1984, pp. 947–74.

14. Orville Schell, *Discos and Democracy* (New York: Pantheon, 1988).

15. Xiao Gonggin, 'Checks and Balances by Authority: The Only Way to Success in China's Reform,' *Shijie Jinghi paobao* (World Economic Herald), 13 March 1989, p. 11. In *Foreign Broadcast Information Service* (FBIS), 24 March 1989, pp. 40–3.

16. For example, James L. Tyson and Ann Scott Tyson, 'Calls for a New Despotism in China,' *Christian Science Monitor*, 22 February 1989, pp. 1–2.

17. Thomas B. Gold, 'Neo-Authoritarianism Won't Create Economic Miracle,' *Los Angeles Times*, 30 June 1989, p. 119.

18. Craig Calhoun, 'The Beijing Spring, 1989: Notes on the Making of a Protest,' *Dissent*, Fall, 1989. Also, see essays by Jane Macartney, David Kelly, and Geremie Barmé in this volume.

19. 'Who Stirred Up the Turmoil,' *Beijing Review*, 10–16 July 1989, pp. 25–6.

20. 'Seize the Vicious Manipulator — Liu Xiaobo,' *ibid*, pp. 26–9.

21. 'Union Council Issues Statement,' FBIS, 13 June 1989, p. 39.

22. 'Security Organs Arrest Beijing Workers' Leaders', Xinhua, in FBIS, 16 June 1989, p. 50.

23. 'Sixteen Members of "Capital Workers Special Picket Corps" Arrested and Charged,' FBIS, 19 June 1989, p. 28.

24. 'Shandong City Arrests "Counterrevolutinary,"' FBIS, 20 June 1989, p. 41.

25. 'Signature Incident Discussed,' Xinhua, in FBIS, 5 July 1989, pp. 27–8.

26. Ye Guang, 'Wan Runnan Bangi "Shitou" Yao Za Shei?' 'Who Did

Wan Runnan Want to Smash By Throwing "Stones?"' *Renmin Ribao* (People's Daily), domestic, 17 August 1989, p. 1.

27. I have used the text as printed in *South China Morning Post*, 31 May 1989, p. 12.

28. Leadership of the CCP; the socialist road; dominant place of Marxism-Leninism-Mao Tse-tung thought; and dictatorship of the proletariat (softened as 'people's democratic dictatorship').

29. *'Jinqi Zuo Qijian Qunzhong Guanxin di Shi'* (In the near future, do 7 things the masses are concerned about), *Renmin Ribao* (People's Daily), 29 July 1989, p. 1. These include cleaning up companies associated with cadres and the business activities of their family members and a raft of other privileges.

The Ideology of Chinese Communism: Causes and Effects

Michael Lindsay

A FEW years ago this long essay on ideology might have seemed out of place in a book on contemporary China. With the launching of Deng Xiaoping's ambitious reform program in the late 1970s, the Chinese leadership seemed to have shifted away from Marxist-Leninist dogmatism toward a pragmatic, non-ideological approach to governance. Recently, however, renewed efforts in ideological indoctrination, the attack on 'bourgeois liberalization,' and the emphasis on Deng Xiaoping's Four Cardinal Principles have shown once again that Marxism-Leninism's staying power in China should never be underestimated.

An ideology need be no more than a guiding principle. Someone with no ideology would be a person who acts only for short-term and simple aims. Long-term aims involve some vision of the future; the action through which people try to attain their aims involves a process of reasoning based on assumptions about the nature of the world which can be described as ideological. Unfortunately, if actions are based on incorrect views about the nature of the world, results can all too easily differ from intentions. Few would dispute the fact that Mao had good intentions in launching his destructive Great Leap Forward, for example. However, his understanding of the economic potential of his country was so flawed as to give rise to a famine in which at least 30 million people are thought to have lost their lives. To give a simple example, doctors have always wished to cure their patients, yet until the latter part of the 19th century, a great deal of medical treatment actually harmed patients because it was based on erroneous theories about human physiology.

The long influence of Confucianism

Chinese methods of governance today are emblematic of the huge differences in political development between China and the West over hundreds of years. The West has had a long experience of differing political ideologies and systems of government. From 221 BC, when China was first unified, until the 20th century, Chinese government has for the most part been centralized, authoritarian, and bureaucratic, with Confucianism as the dominant ideology.

China became a hierarchical society with the emperor at the top, the high-ranking central government officials chosen through the examination system at the second level, the holders of lower degrees in the examination system at a third level, and farmers, artisans, and merchants (in that order) at a fourth level. Though merchants were theoretically at the bottom, many of them had obtained lower-level degrees, which were essential for a successful business. A degree also was of great advantage to a landowner. All this serves to illustrate how success in any walk of life was defined primarily in the government's terms. Success outside the realm of government and the examination system was effectively denied.

One consequence of the overwhelming preoccupation with the examination system was that anyone with an education was certain to have received indoctrination in Confucianism. Someone who won office through the highest degree, at the average age of 35, would have spent at least 20 years studying the Confucian classics. The ideal of Confucianism could be described as benevolent despotism, so the indoctrination inculcated a certain degree of public spirit. At the same time, however, Confucianism also inculcated the notion that rulers were to be respected. The ruled had no sense of 'rights' in their relations with their rulers. In fact, foreigners visiting China in the 18th century found that the Chinese language at that time had no word for 'rights.'

Confucianism had a long tenure in China because it ensured that the higher levels of government were filled by men of high intelligence. For a very long time, the Chinese could rightly pride themselves on having the most advanced civilization in the world. Thirteenth-century China was ahead of Europe in astronomy and mathematics and a good deal of technology. People in Europe refused to believe Marco Polo's accounts of the size and splendor of Chinese cities in the 14th century.

There was a decline under the Ming dynasty, but the Jesuit missionaries who went to China in the late 16th century made such favorable reports that by the early 18th century Europe had developed a fascination with all things Chinese. In addition to designing Chinese-style gardens and dressing themselves in

Chinese silks, European intellectuals also expressed admiration for the Chinese example of benevolent despotism in government.

The influence of Western ideas

By the 19th century, however, Confucianism found itself in crisis, seemingly unable to meet the military challenges posed by Western imperialism. Chinese intellectuals initially showed no interest in the West, resisted abandonment of their state ideology, and professed disdain even for Western technology. When the Chinese officials who had signed the Treaty of Nanking in 1842 visited the British fleet, they showed interest in British naval uniforms and drill but none at all in the engines, though naval steam power had been a major factor in the Chinese defeat. Later, the more intelligent officials realized that they must introduce Western military technology but thought that they could do this without changing the traditional society. The slogan of Zeng Guofan, who defeated the Taiping rebellion, was, 'Western culture for utility; Chinese culture as foundation.'

What finally discredited the traditional Confucian system was the defeat by Japan in 1895. It had been possible to think of the Western powers in the same terms as the Mongols or earlier barbarian invaders, societies which had military power but were not really civilized. However, the traditional view of Japan was that it had a certain degree of civilization, mostly learned from China. When this small country easily defeated China by learning from the West not only technology but also the organization of government, it became clear that there was something wrong with the Chinese system of government. Before 1895 some Chinese had learned something of Western political ideology — mostly people who had some contact with foreigners — but it was only after 1895 that such knowledge became at all widespread. Thousands of Chinese students went to Japan where a great deal of Western writing had been translated into Japanese. Many students returned from Japan to their home provinces in the interior, often to become teachers.

By now there are a large number of people who understand and admire the ideals of democracy, human rights, free expression and the rule of law, but this is a fairly recent development. I have discussed the traditional Chinese society at some length because I believe that its influences survived for a very long time and still exist. Chiang Kai-shek's hero was Zeng Guofan and Chiang's book, *China's Destiny*, published in 1943, said that communism and Western liberalism were both unsuitable for China. In 1989 a Chinese journalist said to me that what the Chinese people really wanted was a benevolent despotism. Foreigners teaching at Chinese universities report a survival of the traditional contempt for merchants.

Socialism and Marxism-Leninism

In the 19th century, the basic argument for socialism seemed plausible: Under capitalism decisions are made by people working for their private advantage whereas, under socialism, decisions would be made by people working for the interests of society as a whole. Two fallacies in this argument only became clear after socialism had been tried.

The famous mathematician Bertrand Russell visited the Soviet Union in 1920 and made a remarkably accurate prediction, 'This is what I believe to be likely to happen in Russia: the establishment of a bureaucratic aristocracy, concentrating authority in its own hands, and creating a regime just as oppressive and cruel as that of capitalism.'[1] By 1990 it had become clear that this was true for most countries under Marxist socialism.

The other fallacy was that it is possible for the decision makers in a large and complex centrally planned economy to make the right decisions. Even at the much smaller scale of private capitalist companies, the most efficient companies allow a great deal of decentralized decision-making.

Pure socialism and pure capitalism are extreme limits in a range of possible economic systems. Pure socialism has only existed in some small communities except for the brief period when the Soviet Union tried a moneyless economy soon after its founding. In the 19th century, the U.S. and the U.K. came near to pure capitalism and Hong Kong more recently came even nearer, but some controls by the government always remained.

A great deal of what might be called 'orthodox Marxism-Leninism' is not completely untrue but only grossly over-simplified. It often makes sense if one substitutes the word 'influences' where communists say 'determines.' It is true that the labor required to produce a commodity influences its value and that the mode of production influences the development of society but, in both cases, 'determines' is false. Orthodox Marxist-Leninists show a curious obsession with the number two. Choices are between two roads, though actual choices are often between a number of possibilities. Cause and effect are always a pair — any effect has a single cause and is not a function of several variables.

A good many communists have been reasonable enough to get away from this over-simplification but only a few have been reasonable enough to give up a basic fallacy — the claim that Marxism-Leninism is a science and that science gives final and certain knowledge.

This explains a good deal of communist behavior. If people are convinced that their beliefs are final and certain truth and give them infallible guidance about the action needed to produce the ideal human society, then they are only logical in using any means to win and retain power and in suppressing the advocacy of views they know to be false.

If they believe that ordinary people cannot understand what they really want without the guidance of a Marxist-Leninist leadership, then they are only logical in imposing what the Party has decided is good for society and in ignoring any expressions of opinion for the people except those induced by official indoctrination. The false belief that Marxism-Leninism has given them certain knowledge effectively prevents communists from realizing their proclaimed aim of producing a better human society.

Sun Yat-sen favored Western-style democracy, with a few reservations, and tried to establish a constitutional government. He did not, however, succeed in dealing with opponents who controlled military force. The result was degeneration into the warlord period of continual civil wars. Many intellectuals had rejected Confucianism and were also disillusioned about Western democracy. U.S. President Wilson agreed at Versailles that Japan could retain its control of Shantung and none of the Western powers were willing to give up their extraterritorrial rights or their concessions in major Chinese cities. Sun Yat-sen set up a rival government in Canton but was never able to get Western assistance. In 1946, my wife and I met Thomas Lamont, a J.P. Morgan partner who had been on the international banking consortium which made loans to China. He said that he had formed a low opinion of Sun Yat-sen, who had approached the consortium asking for a large loan. When asked what he proposed to do with the money, he replied that he would organize a large army to re-unify China. This was basically a good idea but the blunt approach was unlikely to impress a group of conservative bankers. When Sun visited Hong Kong in 1923 he asked the governor if he could borrow the services of some Hong Kong officials as advisers in the organization of his new government in Canton. The Hong Kong authorities wished to agree but were overruled by the Foreign Office in London. It is interesting to speculate on what would have happened if Sun's government had been organized with the advice of officials from the British colonial service instead of advisers from the Comintern.

This situation offered an opportunity to the new Soviet leaders. Before 1917 there was almost no Chinese interest in Marxism, which seemed irrelevant to China. In contrast to the Western powers, the Soviet Union denounced imperialism and offered to give up all Russian special rights in China. Agents sent to China worked to help the organization of a Chinese Communist Party, which was finally founded in 1921 with about 100 members.

A Soviet agent, Adolph Joffe, first approached Sun Yat-sen in 1921 but Sun was then hoping to succeed without Soviet assistance. He approached him again in January 1923 when Sun's fortunes were at a low point — his warlord ally had driven him from Canton and he was living in the foreign concessions in Shanghai. An agreement was reached that the Soviet Union would provide arms and military advisers. In return, members of the Communist Party would be allowed to join Sun's Kuomintang without giving up their Communist Party membership. Policy was to be based on Sun's Three People's Principles: nationalism, democracy, and economic security.

This was the period of Lenin's New Economic Policy, which allowed a large section of private enterprise, and Sun was inclined to believe that the Russians, having tried communism and found that it did not work, were moving to a position much closer to his own and could, therefore, be trusted as allies.

Sun Yat-sen returned to Canton with new warlord assistance and the new government was extremely effective. By the end of 1925 it controlled all of Guangdong province. The communists were rapidly increasing in numbers and influence. Sun Yat-sen died in 1925 and power shifted to Chiang Kai-shek, who was suspicious of the communists. Party membership continued to grow and reached 50,000 by early 1927, and the Communist Party claimed to control about 2.5 million organized workers and up to

10 million organized peasants, but Chiang ensured that communist power in the government, and still more in the army, was greatly reduced.

After Chiang Kai-shek's forces had captured Shanghai, he broke with the communists and tried to eliminate them. Several communist attempts at armed resistance were easily defeated. By the beginning of 1928 Communist Party membership had fallen to about 10,000 and communist military operations were confined to insurgency in mountain areas.

The Chinese Soviet Republic

Here Mao showed his real genius, which was in military affairs. There was a steady expansion of the communist forces and of the area they controlled. By January 1932, National Government sources reported that the Red Army had grown to 200,800 men with 151,600 rifles and some heavier weapons. A Chinese Soviet Republic was set up in December 1931 with Mao as chairman.

The policy derived from the Soviet Union classified all landlords and rich peasants as class enemies. The unreality of this was shown by the fact that the communists had to make elaborate regulations to deal with marriages between class enemies and non-rich peasants. The real class conflict at this time was against the rich landlords who had formed their own private armed forces and used their power to oppress and exploit everyone else, including small landlords. When communist insurgency started in North Shanxi the local leaders found that many small landlords supported them, but directives from the Central Committee denounced them for cooperating with class enemies.

The doctrinaire land policy would have weakened the communists greatly if they had faced competition for popular support. Chiang was always ready to fight the communists but never had been willing to compete with them until he had the psychological shock treatment of complete defeat on the mainland. In 1958, Chang Mon-lin, head of the Joint Commission on Rural Reconstruction in Taiwan, said to me that, if only they had carried out on the mainland the reforms they had carried out in Taiwan, the communists never would have won.

For some years, the National Government failed in its campaigns against the communist base areas. Finally, a new and better strategy made the communist position untenable and produced the famous Long March to Northwest China. This was a remarkable feat but the communists lost 80 to 90 percent of their original strength. In their new base area in North Shanxi the communists made some changes in policy. Land was still redistributed but landlords were given a share.

The Chinese Soviet Republic declared war on Japan in 1932 and the communists called for a united front against Japan but attacked the National Government leaders as collaborators. Following a change in the Soviet official line, the communists started negotiations with the National Government in 1936. A new united front was started after the war with Japan had started in 1937.

The communists agreed to work for the realization of Sun Yat-sen's Three People's Principles, to abandon their policy of confiscating land, to abolish the Soviet government, and to put the Red Army under the command of the National Military Council. The National Government agreed to recognize the Red Army as three divisions and to recognize the communist base areas as a special local government area. Some months later, it agreed to recognize the Shanxi-Chahar-Hebei base area as a special wartime area equivalent to a provincial government.

I have direct knowledge of the Chinese communists during the wartime period because my wife and I escaped from the Japanese-occupied area in December 1941 and I became technical adviser to the army communications department in Shanxi-Chahar-Hebei. I taught army technicians and traveled to sub-district headquarters helping to modernize their radio equipment. In 1944 we moved to Yenan, where I designed the equipment that enabled signals to reach the U.S. and became adviser to an English-language news service.

What struck me about the Chinese communists at this time was how different they were from communists I had known in England. One encountered some doctrinaires, more at Yenan than in the front-line base area, but most people were very reasonable, and the influence of Marxist-Leninist doctrine on practical policy was minimal. The proclaimed aim was a united front to resist Japan, and practical policies were effective in securing it.

My wife had lived in the countryside as a child and found it easy to get on good terms with the people in the villages where we stayed. The people said that, for the first time, they had a government that actually was trying to help them.

The Japanese made gains from 1941 to 1943 by using the fort and blockade line strategy that had enabled Chiang Kai-shek to defeat the communists in South China. At one time there were about 30,000 Japanese forts in North China. The 'mopping up' campaigns tried to make the base areas uninhabitable by burning villages, killing farm animals and seizing stocks of food. The ability to resist depended on active support from the local population.

This environment provided a strong process of natural selection against doctrinaire communists. Someone who believed that, because he understood Marxism-Leninism, he knew what the peasants wanted better than they did themselves, was not likely to win the strong support essential for the war.

If the sensible, moderate wartime policies had continued, Chinese development would have been different. The limitation of rent and the tax system with higher rates on unearned income made owning land less profitable. Landlords were starting to sell land to their tenants and to put their money into local trade and industry, which were encouraged by low taxation. If this had continued for another 10 years or so, the result would have been a rural society in which most farmers owned their land. Productivity would have been higher. Investment by former landlords would have produced a growth of local industry. What actually happened is described later in this chapter.

The efficiency of organization was much lower in the Yenan area than in the front-line bases. People who had come from the front line bases would complain in private conversations of the completely unnecessary bureaucratism that they encountered at Yenan. My diagnosis was that inefficiency came from organizations at Yenan being staffed almost entirely by Communist Party members; the doctrine of 'democratic centralism' inhibited criticism of anything that seemed to have the authority of the Central Committee behind it.

At the news agency, I heard an amusing illustration of blind reverence for Party authority. Mao gave a speech in which he used a four-character classical phrase meaning 'from masses win respect.' The news agency transmitted the text to its branches in the front-line areas. (Chinese is transmitted in four-figure groups.) In southeast Shanxi, the text was received with mistakes in two figures, which changed the meaning to 'from fog win treasure.' The editors of the local newspaper did not say to themselves, 'This must be garbled, we should ask for a repeat.' Instead they wrote an editorial on the deep inner meaning of winning treasure from fog.

This unwillingness to criticize was not found in Shanxi-Chahar-Hebei, where there were non-communists in the government. It was also noticeable that veteran communists were less inhibited than new recruits.

In July 1944 the National Government finally permitted U.S. army observers to go to Yenan. The members of the U.S. Army Observers Section were impressed by what they found and what they were able to see during visits to the front-line base areas. For several months, relations were cordial, and Mao said he hoped good relations would continue after the war because the U.S. would be the only country with the resources to help China in postwar reconstruction.

The Marshall mission

After the war ended, Gen. George Marshall went to China on behalf of U.S. President Harry Truman to try to mediate the looming civil war. Before leaving, however, Gen. Marshall said to President Truman that, even if Chiang Kai-shek refused to make reasonable concessions to secure a peaceful settlement, the U.S. would still have to support him because otherwise 'there would follow the tragic consequences of a divided China and of a probable Russian resumption of power in Manchuria.'[2]

The CCP had provided some basis for suspicion of Soviet control by its uncritical support in 1940 for the Soviet line on international affairs during the Stalin-Hitler pact. However, by 1945, the practical policies of the CCP had diverged very far indeed from the Soviet model and the State Department officials with the Observers Section could have done more to find out whether the CCP was still committed to blind support for the Soviet Union.

When it had become clear after a few months that Gen. Marshall was not an impartial mediator, the communists turned to the Soviet Union for assistance. The price for Soviet assistance was following the Soviet line. The result was a return to the policies of the Chinese Soviet Republic. The successful wartime agrarian policy gave way to class war in the countryside against landlords and rich peasants. In 1949, Mao declared that the Chinese Communists must take the Soviet Union as their model and the CPSU as their

teacher. In 1986, I asked friends in the CCP why they had changed
to a blindly pro-Soviet line in 1946. Their reply: 'We had no
alternative.'

'Liberation': the doctrinaires in control

When my wife and I visited China in 1949, we found that the
doctrinaires had become dominant. As many readers may never
have encountered a doctrinaire communist, I will give an example.
Talking with a cadre, I argued that the Soviet Union was not a
good model and that the NKVD (now KGB) was the same kind of
brutal and crooked organization as the Japanese Kempetai. The
cadre replied that these stories could not be true and that, if
I had read the works of Marx, Engels, and Lenin, I would have
known that it was theoretically impossible for the agents of a
socialist power to behave in the ways I had described.

After that visit and another with the British Labor Party delegation in 1954, I concluded that the communists were doing a good
job wherever their Marxist-Leninist doctrines were irrelevant. In
1949 people praised them for ending inflation and for rapid repair
of war damage to transport and public utilities, but even communist publications admitted that the class war in the countryside had
alienated large sections of the 'middle peasants.' By 1954, there had
been progress in irrigation and flood control and in extending
simple medical care and public health work. However, the Soviet
model led to completely centralized and inefficient management of
industry. A factory in central China had to refer every decision to
Beijing. The announced plan to collectivize agriculture was irrational. The attitude on population was completely doctrinaire.

In 1956 Mao departed slightly from Soviet orthodoxy by making a distinction between antagonistic and non-antagonistic contradictions. Antagonistic contradictions, arising from class conflict,
could only be settled by the complete victory of one party. Non-
antagonistic contradictions could exist in a socialist society and
could be resolved by discussion and compromise. (The Russians
denied the existence of any contradictions in the Soviet Union.)

By the end of 1956, landlords had been liquidated. Industry and
trade had been nationalized and their former owners and managers
're-educated.' It was logical to conclude that the remaining contradictions in China were non-antagonistic and that increased freedom for discussion and criticism would help to resolve them.

Mao's decision in 1957 to allow freedom of criticism, known as the 'Hundred Flowers' campaign, was logical if he believed that freedom of expression would reveal general support for the Communist Party, but criticism of defects that the Party was willing to correct.

Once a few people had dared to criticize and were not penalized, criticism grew exponentially both in volume and severity. A widespread criticism was that the Communist Party was becoming like the bureaucracy of the old empire. This was intolerable to the government and, after a few weeks, the critics were suppressed and penalized in the anti-rightist campaign.

Mao's next move, in 1958, was to change the mode of production by the organization of communes. This started in the agrarian sector, where the collectives were merged into much larger units that did away with what Marx had called 'bourgeois right' or payment by results. Commune members were organized into work brigades and were guaranteed a livelihood including such details as so many baths and so many hair cuts per year. Family cooking was replaced by communal mess halls. This was proclaimed as the beginning of the transition from socialism to communism.

The accompanying 'Great Leap Forward' came from the Marxist belief that labor is the only source of value and Mao's belief that mass enthusiasm could accomplish anything. People were told that a few years of austerity and extra hard work would produce a future of 'good clothes and enough to eat.'

There was a big increase in the input of labor but a great deal of the labor was unproductive or even counter-productive. In 1983, my wife and I were impressed by the elaborate irrigation works in Hebei with numerous tunnels and aqueducts. Someone who knew the area told us that this was a 'Great Leap Forward' project and that much of it was useless because its capacity far exceeded the available supply of water. In another case, local cadres ordered farmers to plant rice far more closely than usual. The rice plants grew very high but did not set seed. When the statistical service made some unfavorable reports, the head of the service was dismissed and its members were told that the proper aim of statistics was to rouse enthusiasm.

During the Great Leap Forward, the leaders in Beijing sent down two sets of targets, one specifying what should certainly be produced and a higher set specifying what they hoped for. Provincial governments passed down the 'hoped for' figures as what must be produced and still higher figures as 'hoped for.' The process was repeated at the county level. The officials in charge of production received impossible demands and could only avoid immediate trouble by making false reports. The leaders, having said that results should be spectacular, did not question reports that they were spectacular. By 1960, famine conditions had developed over large parts of China.

Mao resigned as president and was replaced by Liu Shaoqi, who decentralized the communes to the old collectives and made other sensible changes. The economy had started to recover by 1962. However, Mao retained a good deal of power. By 1965 he felt strong enough to start his last effort to transform Chinese society, the Great Proletarian Cultural Revolution.

In 1966, Mao wrote that, while in general the material determines the mental, we must also recognize that ideas can influence the economic base.[3] Mao could feel that he had failed in 1958 because he had tried to change the material mode of production without changing the superstructure of ideas. Some articles during the Cultural Revolution indicate a hope of returning to the communes.

Mao won enthusiastic support from young people; the Red Guards were able to defeat the bureaucracy but they were unable to provide an alternative government. Factional struggles escalated from lighting with sticks and stones to the use of machine guns and, in some cases, artillery. To restore order, Mao called in the army. The Cultural Revolution had failed.

The Cultural Revolution also damaged education. There was affirmative action in favor of professors and students with a proletarian or poor peasant class background. A few new professors were good but the great majority were useless. In 1973, a briefing at Beijing University for foreign visitors explained that undergraduate education had been reduced from four years to three and that students spent about half their time on practical work in factories or on farms. Allowing for the time spent on political indoctrination courses, this meant that students would graduate with perhaps one year of work on their main subject. All text books were being revised to eliminate everything not relevant for revolutionary reconstruction.

All this changed when Cultural Revolution supporters lost control of education in November 1977. A test of recent graduates doing scientific work in Shanghai showed that about two-thirds failed in elementary mathematics and about three-quarters in elementary physics and chemistry.

My wife and I visited China in 1973 and found it most depressing. There was a general atmosphere of fear. People in the streets did not speak to each other and even old friends were reluctant to talk with us. The only people who would talk were officials who tried to convert us but were usually ignorant. I knew more about Marxism than they did. We were allowed to visit my wife's old home town and so saw something of the countryside. There had been some improvements such as better roads and rural electrification, but most villages and small towns were no better than they had been in the late 1930s. There was little improvement in clothing.

The post-Mao era

Mao's death in 1976 was followed by a power struggle that ended with the victory of Deng Xiaoping and his supporters, who were less doctrinaire and more pragmatic. Big changes started in 1978 and were most successful in agriculture; family farming was again allowed. Collective activity remained where it was useful, such as in plowing large fields or starting small industries. The result was rapid rise in food production and in the income of farmers.

By 1983 the social atmosphere had become completely different from 1973. When we visited old family friends in Shanghai they asked us to stay with them and talked very freely, even in the presence of a son-in-law who was a Communist Party member. In 1973, they had been brought to see us at our hotel and obviously were afraid to talk.

In industry, there were some substantial difficulties hindering reform. Wages were low, but workers had almost complete security of employment. In 1983 we were told that there was one good restaurant in Shijiazhuang — its manager had been given the right to dismiss for incompetence.

The technical problems of the economy were compounded by a loss of trust in the government. In 1986, Communist Party members would speak of 'our 10 wasted years' (the Cultural Revolution). People who were not Party members would talk of 'our 30 wasted years.' Many people would say that, in the early 1950s, they had worked enthusiastically for the new government because they believed they were helping to produce a wonderful new society. This belief had been weakened by the anti-rightist campaign in 1957, weakened further by the Great Leap Forward in 1958 and destroyed by the Cultural Revolution.

The Communist Party could have recovered public trust if it had provided leadership by following up the great improvements produced by the policy changes of the late 1970s. In fact, it proved tolerant of the increasing defects that became more serious after the mid-1980s. There was steadily increasing corruption involving communist officials, and little was done to correct the irrational price structure left by the partial move toward the market economy, which made various forms of speculation very profitable. A great deal of money was simply squandered. Local governments even in small towns built luxury hotels that remained almost empty.

One obvious explanation for this failure to handle economic problems is the vested interest of the numerous officials who would have lost their jobs in a more efficient economy. However, there also has been an ideological influence from Deng Xiaoping's frequently announced determination to retain his 'Four Cardinal Principles': the socialist road, the dictatorship of the proletariat, the leading role of the Communist Party and Marxism-Leninism-Mao Tse-tung thought. It now seems that his reforms in 1978–79 were something like Lenin's New Economic Policy, which rescued the Soviet Union from economic collapse by allowing the growth of a considerable sector of private enterprise. This produced a few years of rapid economic growth but was seen as threatening socialism. Stalin liquidated the private entrepreneurs and collectivized agriculture.

Deng Xiaoping's reforms were a break with earlier orthodoxy. During the Cultural Revolution it had been stated that, in a proper socialist economy, all prices should be fixed by the central planning authority. It is likely that many people in the Party saw the rapid progress of the early 1980s as a revival of capitalism. They may even have welcomed the increasing economic difficulties after 1985 as evidence that China was taking the wrong road. They could point to the increases in speculation and corruption, the widening gap between rich and poor, the widespread unemployment among young people in the cities which was producing a rapid rise in crime, and the increasing rate of inflation. This could explain the reluctance to use the most effective method of dealing with the economic problems — expanding the market economy. The greater intellectual freedom of the early 1980s threatened Deng Xiaoping's fourth cardinal principle, Marxism-Leninism-Mao Tse-tung thought. Even quite high-ranking Party members started to express heretical views. The head of the Institute for Marxism-Leninism-Mao thought, Su Shaozhi, argued that Marxism was scientific *because* it was willing to change its theories in the light of new evidence. This was the heresy of revisionism.

Dissatisfaction with the trend of development produced a campaign against 'spiritual pollution' in 1983 and a campaign against 'bourgeois liberalization', which started in 1987 and continued into 1990. These campaigns showed the influence of those in the Party leadership with a quasi-religious faith in Marxism-Leninism.

There is clear evidence that some members actually favored developments that could be described as 'bourgeois liberalization.' As late as December 1988 an article in the *Beijing Review* said, 'At every stage of capitalism's economic development, corresponding achievements have been realized in ideology, culture, and politics, thus advancing civilization,' and concluded, 'It is necessary for us to systematically and critically study modern capitalism so that we can learn from and assimilate its achievements, adopting any that prove suitable for current conditions in China.' Such expressions of approval for capitalism must have infuriated those who were leading the campaign against 'bourgeois liberalization' and may well have convinced them that a purge in the Party was essential.

After Tiananmen

Respect of law is not only a requirement for democracy but also for an efficient economy. Efficient economic operations depend on coordination, and this becomes difficult if contracts cannot be relied on. A survey of foreign companies operating in Beijing found that their second most serious complaint was that government organizations did not observe contracts. (The first was that they could not choose their workers.)

Freedom of expression is another requirement for democracy. It is valuable for any society because a government that represses criticism greatly reduces its ability to discover and correct defects. The students who demonstrated at Tiananmen did not show any understanding of the difficulties of setting up a democratic government. No one seems to have told them that many countries during the past 50 or 60 years had started with excellent constitutions and elections by universal suffrage but had lapsed into military dictatorships and 'kleptocracies.'

A democratic system requires the development of public spirit in at least part of the population — a readiness to put the interests of society as a whole above private or sectional interests. It requires the development of a willingness to compromise. It requires an understanding of democratic procedures such as how to organize a meeting. Without these requirements a system that appears democratic on paper may perform worse than even a slightly benevolent despotism. In the 1950s, Taiwan gave power to elected village councils but, in a number of cases, these councils failed to take action that would have greatly benefited the village as a whole because people had not developed the ways of thinking needed for an effective democracy. The result was that villagers said, 'Things were better under the Japanese,' because a Japanese official would have imposed a solution.

Those who wish to promote freedom and democracy in China can be most effective in opposing the campaign against 'bourgeois liberalization' if they admit that there are some aspects of modern Western societies that China should not imitate. A great deal of modern Western thought has been influenced by ideologies that are at least as irrational as Marxism-Leninism-Mao Tse-tung thought, though they also claim to be scientific. These are positivism and behavioralism.

The basic doctrine of positivism is that our only certain knowledge is of our sense impressions, but we can describe and find regularities and correlations among our sense impressions but cannot have knowledge of an objective real world. The basic fallacy is the refusal to recognize that a great deal of knowledge can be objective though uncertain, that there is an important distinction between knowledge that is rational though uncertain and views that are simply a matter of opinion or taste. The working of a democracy depends on the assumption that a process of discussion and examining the evidence will tend to produce agreement on common action. If truth is a matter of taste, there is no reason why people should agree. Common action will be possible only if the tastes of one person or group are imposed on everyone else. This is the belief of totalitarian regimes.

Most behaviorists say quite explicitly that the scientific study of human behavior and thought must follow the same principles as studies of the non-human part of the world and rule out reason and free will as acceptable explanations. This is very like the exaggeration of 'influences' into 'determines' that can be found in Marxism. It is true that human behavior and thought are influenced by cultural, economic, psychological, and other factors but untrue to deny that human beings are exceptional in the degree to which they can use reason and exercise free will. The fallacy in the behaviorist position is the assumption that the behavioral scientist somehow can stay outside the system of determinism and use his reason to find out how other people's thought and behavior are determined and then use his knowledge to manipulate them. A consistent behaviorist would be like the mythical bird that runs around in ever–diminishing circles until finally it disappears up its own anus. Having shown that everyone else's thought was determined, he should go on to conclude that his own thought was equally determined by influences other than reason and free will.

These ideologies have caused a serious fall of standards in the social sciences, especially in the respect for truth. Progress in the natural sciences has depended on a world-wide consensus among scientists that they should be truthful. If a scientist could not trust the reports of other scientists he would have to repeat all their experiments and observations before he could do any original work of his own. When false reports have been made they have caused a large waste of time and resources, and the person responsible had lost status as a reputable scientist. In the social sciences, however, people who have made seriously false statements have retained a reputation as respected scholars. A very clear illustration was reporting about China. Some scholars have retained a high reputation in spite of making demonstrably false statements. Distorted views of the PRC received wide publicity in the U.S. during the 1960s and 1970s. Books giving seriously inaccurate information were used as text books in many schools and by study groups in the Methodist Church. These presented China during the Cultural Revolution as a model that should be copied.

Those who are trying to promote freedom and democracy in China could make use of the rational parts of Marxism. For example, Mao supported his contempt for law by quotations in which Marx said that law was a means to maintain the dominance of the ruling class. However, Engels expressed a completely different view. In a letter to August Bebel (a leader of the German Socialist Party), he criticized the Gotha Program of the Socialist Party because it did not contain '...the first condition of all functionaries should be responsible for all their official actions to every citizen before the ordinary courts and according to common law.'[4] One can also find quotations in which Marx violently denounced censorship of the press.

If these rational parts of Marxism became widely known in China through underground publications or foreign broadcasts they would seriously disturb the thinking of those who are still inclined to believe in Marxism-Leninism-Mao Tse-tung thought.

The most likely result of the present campaign of indoctrination is that people will learn to repeat passages from their indoctrination courses but will not believe them. Indoctrination sometimes produces strongly held beliefs but these are unstable because they depend on not asking certain questions, not following up certain lines of reasoning and not considering certain evidence. Once disturbed, the whole system of beliefs collapses.

------

1. Bertrand Russell, *The Theory and Practice of Bolshevism* (London: Allen & Unwin, 1921), p. 136.
2. *Foreign Relations of the United States,* 1945, Volume III, p. 768.
3. *Beijing Review,* 10 June 1966, p. 7.
4. *Critique of the Gotha Programme,* Marxist Library Vol. XI, edited by C.P. Dutt (New York, International Publishers, 1938), p. 31.

PART THREE
THE BROKEN MIRROR

The U.S. and China: Sanctioning Tiananmen Square

WILLIAM MCGURN

IN a television interview at his summer home in Maine, U.S. President George Bush acknowledged a critical shortcoming: his inability to inspire in times of crisis. 'I'm not good at expressing the concerns of a nation, in matters of national concern like that,' he confessed. 'I'm just not very good at it.'[1] He was referring to his response to the murder of Marine Lt. Col. William R. Higgins by Shi'a terrorists, but it could easily have been China. For Bush's reactions to the bloody events on Tiananmen Square have made him no friends. It has angered those on the left, who ask why the White House refrains from holding the People's Republic of China accountable to the criticisms it would never hesitate to apply to the Soviet Union. Nor has it pleased conservatives, who tend to favor Taiwan, and never trusted Deng Xiaoping or his reforms in the first place. Certainly it has not gone over well in Congress, which a few weeks after the massacre passed a sanctions bill in direct opposition to the president's wishes.

Even the students on the Square in Beijing were apparently more taken, at least initially, with Soviet leader Mikhail Gorbachev. At the heart of this irony lies Mr. Bush's WASPish diffidence. In some ways this has proved an asset: The opposition to Ronald Reagan was such that he couldn't help but polarize people with virtually his every utterance. But it is also a liability, and nowhere has it hurt him more than in his handling of China. Even his narrow victory over Congress in January on the Chinese students' bill was won on constitutional — not political — grounds, and the price was a public battle that revealed grave dissatisfaction with administration policy.

In responding to the events of June 3–4, for example, President Reagan would have done much less to more applause, simply because there would have been no doubt in anyone's mind on which side he stood of a line drawn between an unarmed assembly of people carrying a replica of the Statue of Liberty and a communist tyranny. In fact, Ronald Reagan did speak for most Americans when he stated simply at Oxford, 'You cannot massacre an idea.' Obviously, George Bush was as revolted as anyone by the events that weekend. But his position was open to more public doubt, if only because he had served as chief of the U.S. mission to Beijing in 1974–75 (before diplomatic relations) and knew many of the Party leadership personally. One of China's 'old friends,' the president trusts that his personal ties to, and knowledge of, leading Chinese communists will give him the edge.

At least in terms of generating the public and political capital he will need in the tough years ahead in dealing with the PRC, however, his ties with the Chinese leadership have been more hindrance than help. Newspaper columns and evening news shows have referred incorrectly to Deng Xiaoping as a one-time 'tennis partner' of Mr. Bush's, and the president's expressed determination not 'to see a total break in this relationship'[2] has been interpreted as a desire not to offend his buddies in the Chinese Communist Party leadership. Commentators also brought up the White House's refusal to make an issue out of the refusal by Chinese authorities to allow dissident Fang Lizhi from attending a dinner Bush had invited him to during the president's visit to Beijing just a few months before Tiananmen. In the midst of world outrage President Bush's calmness has come across as indifference.

Subsequent events have done little to overcome this, particularly in December when the president sent National Security Adviser Brent Scowcroft and Deputy Secretary of State Lawrence Eagleburger to Beijing, breaking his own ban on high-level trips, not to mention his word; in the midst of the shock the visit occasioned it soon came out that this was the *second* such trip. In any case, the December Eagleburger/Scowcroft trip was announced at 2:00 a.m. U.S. time, and coming on the heels of a Bush veto of a bill that would have permitted Chinese students who fear reprisals to remain in the U.S. indefinitely, it was greeted as a kowtow. The image etched in the public mind was Scowcroft clinking his champagne glass with the same people who only six months earlier had sent the tanks in, exclaiming 'We extend the hand of friendship and hope you will do the same.'[3]

Eagleburger and Scowcroft were controversial choices in themselves, inasmuch as they are former members of Kissinger Associates, a firm run by the former U.S. secretary of state Henry Kissinger involved in getting investment in countries such as

China. Kissinger had stirred controversy, not only by his own visit to the PRC post-Tiananmen, but also because of a newspaper article piece he published in the summer comparing the student protesters to the Red Guards and arguing that 'no government in the world would have tolerated'[4] such a demonstration. By choosing men prominently associated with Kissinger — and all evidence is that China policy is coming directly from President Bush — the impression Bush gives is of appeasement. The events at Tiananmen Square shattered the mirror through which the rest of the world sees China, but the administration appears to see the massacre as but a blip on China's long march to reform.

Consequently the worst twist has been put on Bush's statements, even when he was saying the right things. On May 21, as the students were still peacefully massed on the Square, Bush urged them in a press conference to 'stand up for what they believe in, fight for what you believe in,' adding, that 'I don't want to be gratuitous in giving advice, but I would encourage restraint.'[5] By itself the words were fine and the message full of support and common sense — 'Bush Backs Rebels' ran the headline in the next day's *New York Post* — regarding the push for democratic reforms. But Secretary of State James A. Baker III made it look as though Mr. Bush were directing his warnings to the students rather than the regime when he warned the same day that 'significant instability'[6] did not serve U.S. interests. Adding to the perception of White House neutrality was the conspicuous absence of an Oval Office invitation to a representative group of Chinese students, to bring home the president's expressions of solidarity with those on Tiananmen Square — this at a time when demonstrations in front of the Chinese Embassy in the American capital were attracting thousands. Does anyone doubt that Ronald Reagan would have instantly understood the importance of giving the students an audience?

This lack of symbolic appeal ensured that when the president did move — and he moved swiftly — to express American disapproval for the bloodletting, he received virtually no credit for the measures he did take. On 5 June 1989, just hours after the People's Liberation Army tanks rolled over the unarmed and still sleeping demonstrators, the president announced the following measures:

— the suspension of government–to–government sales and commercial exports of weapons;

— the suspension of visits between U.S. and Chinese military
 leaders;
— a sympathetic review of requests by Chinese students in the
 United States to extend their stay;
— an offer of humanitarian aid, via the Red Cross, for the
 wounded;
— a review of America's bilateral relationship with the PRC.

'I think it is very important that the Chinese leadership know it's
not going to be business as usual,' Bush explained.[7] Less than three
weeks later the administration would also end all high-level contacts with the PRC (until the Scowcroft visit) and suspend indefinitely $1.3 billion in international bank loans. Included in
these measures was opposition to further liberalization of the
Coordinating Committee for the Multilateral Export Controls
(COCOM) guidelines regarding technology transfers, a suspension
of export licenses for U.S. satellites to be launched by China, and a
stalling of the implementation of a Sino-American agreement
regarding nuclear energy.

It wasn't enough. On June 29 the House of Representatives,
over the objections of the administration, passed an amendment to
a foreign aid bill calling for economic sanctions. The vote passed
418–0. On July 14, the Senate voted for its own sanctions amendment, 81–10.

A year after the bloodletting on Tiananmen Square, U.S. foreign policy toward Beijing remains a jumble of legitimate geopolitical concerns, good intentions, and a profound lack of direction.
The benign feelings most Americans had toward China were forever changed in June 1989. To begin with, there remains the deeply
felt repugnance of the American people over what happened to the
Chinese students, only fueled by Beijing's brazenness in denying
what really happened and its concomitant attempt to paint the
demonstrators as unpatriotic troublemakers whipped up by
foreign instigators. Counterpoised against this are the clear U.S.
interests in China, as a balance against the Soviets and the Vietnamese in the Pacific, the same interests that compelled Richard
Nixon to send Henry Kissinger there in 1971, a breakthrough that
ultimately led to normalized relations and China's coming out of
its Maoist shell. President Bush has rightly argued that a PRC that
retreated back into isolation would serve the interests neither of
America nor of the Chinese people. Whether this is as much a
threat as the president believes is another question entirely.

There are other pressures here, too. Chief among them is America's relationship with Taiwan, expressed in the 1979 Taiwan Relations Act, which gives the U.S. special obligations to the Republic of China's security. Among America's right wing, the brutal course of events on the mainland have spurred calls to strengthen ties with Taipei. Indeed, it's at least curious that however much the image of the PRC has been shattered, the positive changes on Taiwan have done little to shake outside impressions of that China.

Finally, there is the PRC itself. On the one hand, Deng Xiaoping has made it clear that he expects modernization to continue despite his brutal actions on the political front; American business, American trade, and American capital are critical components in that equation. On the other hand, there is the historic lack of influence foreign nations have traditionally been able to exert on the Middle Kingdom, its communist phase not excepted. For the White House the dilemma is to walk the tightrope that fosters reform and maintains American geopolitical interests in the region without giving aid and comfort to a murderous regime. 'While salvaging the framework we must sustain indignation,' wrote former U.S. Ambassador to China Winston Lord. '. . . The impact of our policies may be modest, but it will be magnified if we can preserve unity between Congress and the administration at home and cohesion with our allies abroad.' Had President Bush been able to point to some real progress from his quiet diplomacy, he could count on this unity. But the PRC leaders have scarcely thrown him so much as a bone, and as a result has given Congress — always inclined to demagoguery when it comes to foreign affairs — the green light for some potentially disastrous but satisfying mischief.

The battle over sanctions crystallizes this problem. After the crackdown most of the voices of pro-democracy Chinese groups around the world called for just such sanctions against Beijing. The call came from all points on the political spectrum, and in America united for the first time an arch-conservative from the South, Sen. Jesse Helms, with an arch-liberal from the East, Stephen Solarz, both of whom chided the Bush administration for not cutting off all commerce with the PRC. Hong Kong politician Martin Lee, in testimony in July 1989 before the House Caucus on Human Rights, added his voice to the pro-sanction chorus, echoed by many students who came out of China via the underground.

The sanction lobby argues that trade with the West is critical for China's modernization of both its economy and its armed forces, and that continued dealings with China have only strengthened the hands of the authorities. The numbers give this credibility. Since the Chinese economy was first unshackled back in 1979, Sino-American trade has blossomed, growing at an annual rate of 20 percent over the last five years; in 1988 that amounted to US$14.3 billion. Investment, too, is up, to about US$2.6 billion, making the U.S. the second largest investor in China after Hong Kong.[8] All this makes China vulnerable. As the *Economist* put it, 'although troops and tanks can hold the center of China's cities, its factories and farms cannot be run at rifle point.'[9] The pro-sanctions people believe that given this need for Western capital and know-how, economic sanctions would bring unbearable pressure on Beijing, ultimately bringing it to collapse. They further argue that the Chinese public would be willing to endure any hardships that economic sanctions might cause if it would help bring down the regime.

No doubt they would, but economic sanctions have yet to demonstrate that they have the desired power to bring down anything. A full American embargo on Vietnam since 1976, for example, has not toppled Hanoi, as poor and backward as it is (also one of the few governments to endorse the PRC's suppression of the students). Arab-led sanctions have likewise failed to destroy Israel. Most notably, all the sanctions against South Africa have only substituted German and Japanese for American investment, hardly to the benefit of the blacks there. In all these cases, sanctions have failed because they come up against a hard reality of life: In a world economy there is always someone willing to sell.

Conversely, the dramatic changes of the past decade ought to be proof enough of the benefits of foreign trade and investment in the PRC. Since Richard Nixon's first visit to China more than 17 years ago, the number of Chinese entities conducting foreign trade has risen from eight to over 1,000.[10] About 550 American firms are doing business in China, most of them joint ventures involving Chinese partners,[11] all of which means more and more Chinese coming into contact with foreigners and foreign ideas. True, this has been accompanied by inflation and some public resentment over the relatively huge profits made by Chinese entrepreneurs. But average Chinese, as poor as they are, have much more in the way of consumer goods available to them than they did before.

The cultural effect has been no less significant. Back when Bush was head of the mission in Beijing, few Americans had been to China or even knew anything about it; as a result they were easily bamboozled into believing the most outlandish claims. One has only to recall the adulatory praise for the Chinese leadership at the height of the Cultural Revolution. Even in the cities there was precious little contact between the Middle Kingdom and the rest of the world, isolated as foreigners were in their own little ghettoes. In places such as Tibet, moreover, where Chinese imperialism and repression was strongest, as recently as the 1970s less than 3,000 Westerners had *ever* been there. Certainly the opening to foreigners changed the political equation there.

This is not to say that American trade and relations have made the Chinese people overnight Jeffersonians, but its influence has been felt. Today some 40,000 mainland Chinese are studying in the U.S., where they have first-hand experience of a democratic capitalist system and the rule of law; others come into touch with prosperous cousins from Hong Kong, Singapore, and Taiwan. It is impossible for mainlanders not to compare their own condition unfavorably with people from the outside, and this is precisely what worries the octogenarians in the Politburo. Certainly it has not escaped the regime's notice that in the U.S. the demonstrations against the government were led by these expatriate students, the privileged elite of China. In Washington, the sons and daughters of Communist Party elites planted a Statue of Liberty on the lawn in front of the Chinese Embassy.

Then there is the foreign press. If it's true that a tree falling in a forest doesn't make a noise unless someone is there to hear it, in today's world it is no less true that an event has not happened unless television was there to record it. The crackdowns in China and the USSR in the years up to Tiananmen, just as real, are virtually unknown in the West because there was no television present. Even with regard to the June 4 killings the extent of uprisings *outside* Beijing (in Chengdu, to name one) are still largely unknown because of the lack of foreign press on the scene. Like the midnight thief, the totalitarian fears the glare of the camera. In short, the nature of Chinese society has changed considerably since Henry Kissinger made his first secret visit there almost 20 years ago.

Even the side benefits of trade work to loosen the totalitarian grip. Fax machines alone proved their worth as an alternative to the government monopoly of news, as messages into and out of China produced a free flow of information the Chinese authorities simply could not keep up with. In George Orwell's *1984*, technology was thought to be a weapon of state control, and it's true that the state would like to maintain its monopoly of technology. But the example of the PRC provides eloquent testimony to the democratic nature of technology, inasmuch as lower and lower prices make advanced electronics ever more accessible to a wider (and thus harder to control) range of individuals.

Last, there are the people themselves. Little more than a decade ago, most Chinese had no future outside their dreary collectives or state factories. Today, in addition to the entrepreneurs who are making more and more goods available to the Chinese, others are working with foreign firms and growing in sophistication. It is a small but increasingly significant portion of the population, for these people are the true hope of China. Western trade and involvement is their lifeline. President Bush alluded to this when he noted that 'the budding of democracy which we have seen in recent weeks owes much to the relationship we have developed since 1972.'[12] Yet the Bush administration itself has not appreciated the dimension of these changes, and its main players — Eagleburger, Scowcroft, and the president himself — are still operating from the Nixon era which they all represent.

What does this mean for American policy? To the president, it meant the curtailment of military cooperation while holding the line on economic sanctions. '[It's] important at this time to act in a way that will encourage the further development and deepening of the positive elements of [the Sino-American relationship] and the process of democratization,' he said.[13] Toward this end he has rightly tried to fend off sanctions, which wouldn't work anyway because the U.S. does not have a monopoly on China trade. U.S. sanctions would not be joined by Hong Kong, the largest investor in China (which employs more people in the PRC than it does at home[14]), or Japan, the next largest investor after America.

Sanctions, however, should not become the be-all-and-end-all of American options toward China. At a time when Poland is instituting a market economy led by the communist world's first free trade union, when the Wall is down in Berlin, and when the head of the Communist Party in the Soviet Union comes hat in hand to the Pope in Rome, we ought to have learned a thing or two about lighting the candles of liberty in totalitarian lands. The events in Eastern Europe and the USSR are inconceivable without the Reagan Doctrine checking its expansionist designs in Afghanistan and Central America, as well as America's concomitant support for indigenous reform movements such as Solidarity to create pressures on the rulers.

There are lessons here for China, the chief one being that it is not the same country it was in 1972 or even 1988, and we therefore must modify our view of China, which in the past has all too often oscillated between unbridled enthusiasm and militant despair. A fundamental ingredient in any such revision must be to cease looking at Deng Xiaoping as the font from which all good things in China must trickle down; American policy ought to be looking to the long-term when Deng is no longer around. Keeping the lines of communication open is only part of the story. The operating principle ought to be to build up institutional forces outside government control that can in turn spawn other areas of (relatively) free activity. What China desperately needs is the creation of a dynamic middle class to replace an increasingly out of touch and xenophobic bureaucratic elite.

In other words, as opposed to looking for the one great leader who will singlehandedly pull the PRC from the brink, we need to realize that the Long March toward reform requires many small changes at the bottom as well. China-watcher Stephen Mosher, for example, argues persuasively for beefing up the Voice of America — which has an audience of some 60 million people in mainland China — to include regular instruction in what Fang Lizhi calls 'the ABCs of democracy': e.g., the rule of law, separation of powers, the relation between economic and political freedom.[15] Mosher also recommends that cultural exchanges between China and the U.S. be kept but privatized. Most American exchanges with other countries are arranged by private groups, but in the case of China the U.S. set up a committee to handle government-to-government exchange programs. Naturally this works to the advantage of the PRC, which is thus able to control (and thus limit) the interaction between foreigners and Chinese. On these fronts, President Bush has not been nearly as forceful as he needs to be.

An emphasis on the freedom of religion might help, too, particularly if it were more sophisticated than merely looking at the cleaning up of old churches and temples. Religion is much more than the right to worship, and it is no accident that Poland was the first country in the communist world to begin to transfer real power from the Communist Party to the people. What Poland had was the Roman Catholic Church, whose contribution to the whole demise of communism has yet to be fully appreciated. For although the faith of the Poles was of undoubted importance, the church's importance toward spurring political change was less religious than corporate. After all, many other countries under the communist thumb (Tibet, for example) have equally devout and determined populations.

What made Poland different was that it was the only country in the communist world where religion retained any institutional autonomy after World War II. The Catholic Church had its own university. It ran schools, hospitals, and co-ops. And it had an institutional structure that permitted it to pursue these corporate works. As a result, the church provided in Poland what no other communist people had: an *institutional* alternative to the state and an umbrella to other potential bases of independence, the chief example being Solidarity.

Friends of China ought to take heart from that. No other communist nation, with the exception of North Korea and Indochina, has as firm an institutional grip on daily life as the PRC. The churches are small and relatively powerless (though not without potential). But the lesson is adaptable to other sectors. There is, to begin with, the anomaly of Hong Kong, which after 1997 will be crucial to the future of the mainland. Any foreign policy directed at building a more open PRC will have to include a push for a more autonomous Hong Kong, fully in line with the promises outlined in the 1984 Sino-British Joint Declaration. A free-trade pact between America and Hong Kong would be one way to firm up Hong Kong's shaky institutional foundation to help it survive 1997.

With respect to the mainland itself, far from looking for restrictions U.S. policy needs to direct itself to creating thousands of little wedges against the centralizing tendency of all socialist governments. This is not to say that America should subsidize trade and pump more U.S. taxpayer money into the PRC; that has a way of being channeled through governments and shoring up the status quo. But anything that can be done to expand private contacts between Americans and Chinese weakens Beijing and prepares people there for running their own lives. In this regard the president should not oppose the PRC's entry into the General Agreement on Trade and Tariffs but should ensure that Chinese entry is consistent with the rules, linking membership to such market-opening measures as free pricing, copyright guarantees, and so forth. As Ambassador Lord argues, 'A China engaged in international markets and institutions will have greater incentives to pursue a responsible foreign policy.'[16]

Obviously Beijing does not see it this way. Nonetheless, it is handcuffed by its need to modernize. Along with a number of other Asian leaders, Deng Xiaoping apparently believes that this economic modernization can be divorced from political reform, and in the short run he is certainly right. Tiananmen Square showed the world that much.

But Tiananmen Square ought not to be treated as the end; it may also be a beginning. In the long run giving people more say over their economic lives inevitably leads to demands for more say in their political destiny, as everyone else in the region — Chun Doo Hwan, Lee Kuan Yew, even Mikhail Gorbachev — has found out. Contrary to all the purple prose in the newspapers about Tiananmen Square, there is nothing inevitable either way. Bursts of freedom have as often led to Napoleon as George Washington.

This makes the involvement of the outside world all the more imperative, and with regard to China there is no more important player than America, certainly not Gorbachev, who crystallizes all the traditional fears of chaos in the Chinese leadership. It's important not to exaggerate here, for it is not within Washington's power to decide change, or even the pace of change, in the PRC. But it's equally important not to underestimate America's role, secondary as it may be. The worst thing America could do would be to give the Chinese just enough trade, investment, and know-how to make marginal improvements without enough to bring pressure on the regime for even more. Like so many other things, Marx got his conclusions backward — if Deng Xiaoping and his cohorts are intent on hanging themselves through modernization, Washington should be there to make sure they have got plenty of rope.

For however much U.S. perceptions of China have changed, our interests remain and are remarkably congruent: keeping a check on Soviet ambitions; preserving a balance of power with Japan in the Pacific; watching India on the subcontinent, and so on. It's true that these are all important to Washington. But it's even more true that they are critical to the PRC: America has interests in Asia; China has *borders*. In some ways this puts the U.S. in an even a stronger position than it was when then-President Nixon first opened the door in 1972, for China today is much more involved with (and dependent on) the outside world. With events in the Soviet Union going America's way, China needs the U.S. much more than the U.S. needs China.

Based on his firsthand dealings with a Chinese leadership sensitive to slights and paranoid about the intentions of foreign powers, George Bush appreciates the need not to unduly offend them back into even more repression. Doubtless this is true. Nevertheless there is a groaning divide between having a healthy regard for Chinese face and publicly toasting men who only a few months before turned their army on their own people with all the world watching. Even in terms of *realpolitik*, a term often invoked by people to justify something distasteful and not necessarily practical, the desperate Eagleburger/Scowcroft gambit probably reduced Beijing's respect for the administration, a commodity much more critical to a successful U.S. policy than the PRC's goodwill.

More to the point, the crackdown in early June was not the only story at Tiananmen Square: For five glorious weeks the Chinese people showed where they stood and raised a Goddess of Democracy to show where they wanted to go. The final chapter has yet to be written. As necessary as it is to deal with Deng in the meantime, the U.S. needs to keep in mind that the future of China may well have much more to do with those now rotting in prison or hiding out in exile than those who, for the moment, sit triumphant atop the bloody heap.

---

1. 'David Frost Talks with the President and Mrs. Bush,' Public Broadcasting Service, 5 September 1989.

2. Excerpts of President Bush's News Conference, *The Washington Post*, June 6, p. A19.

3. 'Crawling back to the Great Hall,' by Patrick Buchanan, *The Washington Times*, 13 December 1989, p. F1.

4. 'The Caricature of Deng as a Tyrant Is Unfair,' by Henry Kissinger, *The Washington Post*, 1 August 1989, p. A18.

5. 'Bush Urges Students to "Stand Up for What You Believe In",' David Hoffman, *The Washington Post*, 22 May 1989.

6. 'The Utmost Caution,' by Robert Pear, *The New York Times*, 22 May 1989, p. 11.

7. Excerpts of President Bush's News Conference, *The Washington Post*, 6 June 1989, p. A19.

8. U.S. Chamber of Commerce, Fact Sheet on China Sanctions, July 1989.

9. 'In chaos divided,' The *Economist*, 10 June 1989.

10. 'The Bush administration and U.S.-China Trade,' The Heritage Foundation, 31 March 1989.

11. U.S. Chamber of Commerce, Fact Sheet on China Sanctions, July 1989.

12. Excerpts of President Bush's News Conference, *The Washington Post*, 6 June 1989, p. A18.

13. Ibid, p. A18.

14. 'How Inflation Figures Into China's Turmoil,' by Milton Friedman, *Human Events*, 22 July 1989, p. 14.

15. 'Promoting Democracy in China,' by Stephen W. Mosher, The Heritage Foundation, 7 December 1988.

16. Lord, p. 21.

The Romance of *Realpolitik*

MIRIAM LONDON

...man's love of truth is such that when he loves something which is not the truth, he pretends to himself that what he loves is the truth, and because he hates to be proved wrong, he will not allow himself to be convinced that he is deceiving himself...

St. Augustine, Confessions

LAST June in Beijing, the beast of communist totalitarianism suddenly stripped off its beguiling Oriental masquerade and showed itself, contemptuously naked, on the television screens of the world. Many will believe that the sight of this beast can never be denied or forgotten, but they will be mistaken. Scarcely had the shock of horror begun to recede when a few pundits on U.S.-China affairs, more collected and far-seeing than the rest of us, warned against an 'emotional' response by our country and reminded us of the strategic significance of the China 'relationship' to the U.S. This psychological counsel was offered in the name of realism.

'The true political realists in the West and East are only those who refuse to accept tyranny....' Milovan Djilas said several years ago. He was commenting on those realists of the time who regarded the 'destabilization' of Poland by the Solidarity movement as a threat to peace in Europe. Our China policy makers do not yet seem ready for Djilas's profound definition. Since the Nixon-Kissinger opening gambit almost two decades ago, U.S. policy toward the People's Republic of China has been premised on another, seemingly more hardboiled definition of political realism — that of shrewd players in a geopolitical game. This policy has been widely approved as necessary, clever, and correct. It may be all of these things, but even on its own terms, it has never been realistic. From the very beginning it has been marked not only by emotionalism and sentimentality, but by ignorance and fantasy.

Any possibility that overtures to Beijing would be combined with a cold eye on Chinese reality was virtually canceled by the architects of the new China policy. President Richard Nixon and his national security adviser, later secretary of state, Henry Kissinger, made it clear at the outset that China's internal situation was its own affair and irrelevant to relations between the two countries. This see-nothing attitude and moral neutrality proved unsustainable in practice and set the stage of self-delusion, not least because of the theatrical manner in which the new approach was initiated — in secrecy, followed by an international shock of surprise, like a triumphant master magician expecting applause, President Nixon pulled the new China policy out of a hat.

Americans, it seems, are not very good at *realpolitik*. When Nixon journeyed to the People's Republic of China in 1972, on what he regarded as an inspired, historic mission, and, with an emotional extravagance beyond the demands of protocol, gushingly offered toasts in the banquet hall of Chairman Mao Tse-tung, it became suddenly difficult to accept that this smiling old man, Mao, was in fact a cruel despot, an executioner of millions, still intent on perpetuating his reign of darkness. If this image of Sino-American accord in Beijing was not to be rejected as grotesque, then the image of China itself needed adjusting, in order to make sense of such extraordinary scenes.

China 'experts'

In fact, another China had already been invented, not by cynical propagandists but by eager scholars — namely, an influential group of Sinologists and their disciples in leading American universities. They were to become known respectfully as 'China experts,' especially to television interviewers, who appealed to them periodically as unravelers of Oriental mysteries and readers of green tea leaves.

The fictional land created by these China experts cannot be blamed on insufficient information at the time. The so-called bamboo curtain made information about the real China difficult but not at all impossible to obtain. For all their bristling academic credentials, the fact is that the China experts did not wish to know — but to believe. Like some Soviet experts before them, on whom they cast no backward glance, they were practitioners of the intellectual pseudo-faith of the century, dreaming up the City of Perfect Justice on earth. The bamboo curtain was indeed essential to the believing Sinologists, freeing them to elaborate their fantasies (in their esoteric way, with footnotes) unconcerned by the intrusion of messy reality or the possibility of verification on the scene.

Thus, in the 1970s, when the Chinese countryside was afflicted, as it had been for centuries, by periodic regional famine; when up to 200 million people were living in semi-starvation — as the Chinese press was later to admit — a number of prominent U.S. experts on the Chinese economy found that, under the Maoist system, the entire population enjoyed 'guaranteed' minimal subsistence. China's food problem, the refrain went, had been solved. At the time of the first Nixon visit, during the dark age of Maoist oppression and despair, the experts found a happy, relaxed, and motivated people, somewhat like our Pennsylvania Amish, only better. The reason for this, as explained by the 'dean' of American Sinology in 1972, was 'China's government by exemplary moral men, not laws,' which was clearly not the case in our own corrupt society. While factional battles still raged across a torn and disordered China, the experts noted that the Cultural Revolution had ended and all was calm and peaceful. It was the beginning of the myth of China's stability, which was to re-emerge in every lull between explosions. Two days after the 5 April 1976 massive popular riot against Maoist despotism on Tiananmen Square, a New York Times editorial expressed shock, for 'China had seemed to be so orderly, so completely controlled in recent years.'

Although these academic China experts were not instrumental in changing U.S. China policy, but seem rather to have been used by Washington once the new direction was set, they nevertheless had a role to play, especially in enhancing the new policy's credibility for the general public. Through the media they lent their authority to the growing illusion of a benign new China deservedly awaiting our recognition.

Nixon, Kissinger — Mao, Chou

It is a bit trickier to ascertain just what influence they may have had on the two chief policy makers themselves, men of no uncertain ego or easy suggestibility. It can be said, however, at the very least, that these experts never made Richard Nixon or Henry Kissinger uncomfortable with their own illusions, for which they demonstrated an independent talent. As in the works of these experts, the enormity of human suffering and death under Maoist rule, while not condoned by Nixon or Kissinger, became for them a bloodless abstraction, which did not, moreover, affect the pressing business at hand. Mao Zedong and Zhou Enlai were not a particularly merciless dictator and his wily supporter, but great 'statesmen,' whom an American president and his emissary could approach with awe, as if history had vouchsafed them the honor of being admitted into the presence of legendary figures. As recently as 1988, Nixon listed Mao, along with Winston Churchill, among the 'great leaders' he had met in the last 40 years.

To Henry Kissinger, Mao appeared a 'colossus,' who 'emanated vibrations of strength and power and will,' as indeed he might have. But Kissinger's boundless admiration and even a sort of affection went to Premier Zhou Enlai, by whom, like many other intellectuals before him, he was thoroughly seduced. For Kissinger, Zhou 'was one of the two or three most impressive men I have ever met. Urbane, infinitely patient, extraordinarily intelligent, subtle, he moved through our discussions with an easy grace that penetrated to the essence of our new relationship...'

Two eminent Sinologists have also described the urbane Chou. Father L. Ladany wrote: 'Zhou Enlai was one of those men who never tell the truth and never tell a lie. For them there is no distinction between the two. The speaker says what is appropriate to the circumstances. Zhou Enlai was a perfect gentleman; he was also a perfect communist.' Of the undeniably charming and witty Zhou, Simon Leys had this to say: 'He had a talent for telling blatant lies with angelic suavity. He was the kind of man who could stick a knife in your back and do it with such disarming grace that you would still feel compelled to thank him for the deed...He repeatedly and literally got away with murder. No wonder politicans from all over the world unanimously worshipped him.'

When Henry Kissinger in 1971 flew from Pakistan into what he called 'the land of mystery,' on his first secret mission to the communist court in Beijing he also crossed from *realpolitik* into romanticism. He cast, moreover, a peculiar aura around the relationship between Washington and Beijing, that was to persist through several administrations to this day and degenerate into a kind of sentimentality. After the June bloodbath on Tiananmen Square, President Bush appeared plainly reluctant to hold his 'old friend' Deng Xiaoping responsible. Secretary of State James Baker, who does not appear sentimental, passed off the President's hesitant and weak response as justifiable caution, alluding again to geopolitical reasons for maintaining our 'special relationship' with the regime — evidently any regime — in China. Whatever the reasons, Washington followed a pattern in Sino-American relations set almost two decades ago — of dealing delicately with ruthless men.

The rise of Deng Xiaoping's revisionism in 1978 gave fresh impetus to our China policy, but required a quick change of illusions behind the scenes. As China itself debunked the miracles of Maoism, a few China experts, to their credit, became thoroughly sober. In general, however, the believing China experts managed to switch one set of illusions for another, markedly different set, with astonishing ease and with no perceptible damage to their scholarly reputations.

In the People's Republic of China, where independence of mind is seldom a virtue, such experts are understood and valued. What matters is not that they erred on Maoism but that they conformed when it was proper to do so. They were wrong at the right time. Strangely enough, this also explains their survival as experts at home. As the sociologist Lewis Feuer once pointed out, academics get away with and even 'thrive on such blunders so long as they are congruent with the emotional currents' of what he called the 'Intellectual Elite' — a scholarly clique with status or influence in higher political circles. As for those scholars who had been accurate about Maoism, they could later be dismissed by the reigning experts as right for the wrong reasons — that is, because of some idiosyncratic tendency toward pessimism that paid off or even an accident of ideological bias.

Within China in the late '70s, the full realization that three decades of sacrifice and turmoil had gone for nothing, that China was still a poor beggar among modern nations, produced a 'crisis of confidence' in the Communist Party's ability to lead. Not so among the faithful China experts in the U.S. As if to compensate for the irreparability of their shattered Maoist dreams, they immediately displayed a neomissionary zeal to 'help' the new Dengist regime put China back together again. At first, this appeared to be a form of do-goodism, requiring no explanation. Inevitably, however, a rationale developed and a new myth emerged, of such appeal and verisimilitude that it was accepted by Americans generally, on both the political left and right.

In the Orwellian year of 1984, a Chinese émigré scholar who was invited to an international conservative conference on communism found that his presence was a meaningless formality. For the participants, China was already a solved problem of communism; it was 'going capitalist' and no longer a threat to the West, but, on the contrary, a useful ally against the Soviet Union.

Wish and reality

The new notion that China was 'going our way,' that Deng's economic reforms would of necessity lead to a democratized political system, reflected Western wishfulness, not Chinese reality. Careful observers of the China scene saw something far less benign. Through word and action, the Dengist strongmen made their objectives plain — to build a powerful communist state as rapidly as possible, by partly freeing the economy (still keeping 'the bird in the cage') and relying heavily on Western and Japanese aid. They looked not forward but backward to the Soviet China they had originally intended to build in the 1950s, before their plans were swept aside by Mao's irrational and deadly experiments. They were set on making up for lost time. By the mid-'80s, the German Sinologist Jürgen Domes saw in China 'no departure from communism,' but rather compromise rule by unsteady coalitions of 'enlightened Stalinist' and 'orthodox Stalinist forces.' As he and others discerned several years ago, the future toward which the Dengist regime seemed headed was 'the [pre-Gorbachev] political and organizational present of the Soviet Union.'

The attempt to apply modern economics to the pursuit of Stalinist goals had chaotic consequences. After the initial, successful reforms reached their predictable limit, new problems multiplied out of control. The economy had, in fact, been freed into a lawless environment, in which the Party bureaucrat, by virtue of his unrestrained power, became chief profiteer. As the authority on the Chinese and Eastern-bloc economies Jan Prybyla put it: 'Instead of socialism with Chinese characteristics [the officially coined phrase], what the Chinese on the mainland are getting is mercantilism with corrupt characteristics.' Indeed, the characteristics devoured the whole; corruption became the system.

In August 1988, China's *Gongren Ribao* (*Workers' Daily*) described the power of the new 'profiteer officials' over 'every important aspect of business,' including allocation of resources and market prices, and summed up the devastating effects: 'The bureaucrat-businessmen have used all their power to push the market's distortion to its furthest limit. This...has brought about a mock period of prosperity, and when the market erupts in the future, the cause of the ruin will be buried by the lack of order and market chaos.'

Beijing's response to successive economic crises was to retreat in alarm to administrative controls — and usually the wrong ones. Many Chinese became increasingly skeptical of the competence of the Party to proceed further with economic reforms. Moreover, the leftist-style suppression of the demonstrations of 1986–87 dispelled the last hope that the Dengist coalition would permit any of the political reforms regarded by most educated Chinese as essential to continued progress. Popular awareness of having reached a hopeless impasse seemed to intensify in 1988, when the regime floundered deeper into the economic morass.

All those trends were duly noted by Louise de Rosario, specialist contributor to the *Far Eastern Economic Review* (FEER), who in March 1989, little more than a month before the latest demonstrations began, was also to report a 'sense of chaos and breakdown of moral order...evident from many small details in everyday life in China today.' This was the 'stability' that the regime on June 4 sent out its killer-troops to restore.

Bush notions

Fond notions, however, die hard. During his June 8 news conference, President Bush disclosed a detail of his recent visit to Beijing.

...One of the Chinese leaders, very prominent name, told me we want change, but the people have to understand it's very complicated here how fast we move on these reforms. We've come a long way and indeed they did move, dramatically faster on economic reforms than I think any of us in this room would have thought possible.

What hasn't caught up is the political reform and reforms in terms of freedom of expression...But we were cautioned on that visit about how fast China could move. Some of it was economic and clearly some of the message had to do with how fast they could move politically.

Clearly, the message had been accepted by the American president who sincerely thought he understood China.

For our *realpolitikers*, the existence of a popular mood in China has always had a curious insubstantiality or, at least, irrelevance. For the communist leadership, real people do not exist, except as a fiction called 'the masses.' When the non-existent dramatically asserted itself as a million individuals on Tiananmen Square, the result was not only consternation in the power center of Beijing but surprise and discomfiture in Washington among those who had seen only a few Chinese communist officials as solidly real.

For what began last spring in China's capital as a peaceful student demonstration for 'dialogue' with the government on democratic rights and reforms swiftly turned into a popular movement, much like that sparked by Solidarity in Poland eight years ago. It was also the realization of the regime's worst fears. Deng and his aged cohorts have long shown an obsession with Poland's Solidarity movement and recognized the potential for a similar development in China. In January 1987 Deng praised the Polish government's use of martial law to crush the trade union movement and, in the summer of 1988, Chinese leaders reportedly consulted with visiting Polish leaders on 'how the security forces should deal with price-related unrest' (FEER, 21 July 1988). They understood well their own vulnerability in the face of such a threat.

As long ago as 1966, a Soviet internal dissident writer, F. Znakov, pointed to the Achilles' heel of Soviet-type totalitarian systems. His 'theory,' as elaborated in 1981 by a Lithuanian émigré scholar, Alexander Shtromas, assumes that every such system is 'in a state of permanent crisis' and riddled with various forms of dissent, only a small part of which may be overt. Under the controlled surface enormous pressures silently build — pressures of cumulative problems ignored, of injustices compounded by more injustice, of conflicts and grievances suppressed rather than resolved. If at a critical moment an organization voicing genuine popular interests and demands emerges into full public view, it becomes an 'outside body,' to which people can switch support. As more people become encouraged to join, the consciousness of no longer being alone and isolated increases and the switch-over snowballs with remarkable speed into a mass movement.

According to Znakov and Shtromas, should this organization, whatever it may be, have or acquire a recognized place within the system, it could then become a 'second pivot' of power, which could challenge the Party and 'split the system.' Barring military intervention, once this is allowed to occur, the unraveling or 'disintegration' of the totalitarian system is 'virtually unstoppable.'

During the Deng regime's earlier attempt to suppress the

burgeoning democratic movement in 1981, the Hong Kong journal *Cheng Ming* picked up an argument making the rounds in China — namely, that future reform would be possible only if the underground democratic organizations were to unite with reformists within the Communist Party. For a brief moment last May on Tiananmen Square, it almost seemed that this formation of a 'second pivot' of power was possible. However Deng actually perceived the situation, he acted on the basis of a mortal threat to the communist system and joined with the more rigid Stalinists in expelling his remaining reformist 'successor,' Zhao Ziyang. A document consisting of remarks made on May 24 by state President Yang Shangkun referred to Zhao, who had favored meeting the 'reasonable demands' of the students, as an unacceptable 'second voice' within the Party. Yang stated that anything short of firm opposition to the students would mean 'our collapse, the overthrow of the People's Republic, and the restoration of capitalism, which was the desire of the American [John Foster] Dulles.' The June massacre appeared deliberate — a terrorist action by the state intended to remove every trace of a popularly organized challenge to its power.

Even as the regime proceeded with its grisly mop-up operations, it hung out its business-as-usual sign to the world, for as Deng Xiaoping reportedly said with contempt in a June 9 speech, he fully expected that, once the situation was tidied, 'the foreigners are still going to come knocking on our door.' At the same time, a few veteran China experts, dusting off the debris of their latest illusions, reappeared as grim realists to explain why our country should meet these expectations. It was not easy to explain and thus understandably seemed confused. On the one hand, the experts stressed, the regime's odious massacre of its people — the failure of such a regime, as Richard Nixon phrased it, 'to live up to our standards' — should not be allowed to outweigh 'geopolitical considerations.' The latter appears to be an *idée fixe*, not subject to review in the light of events. On the other hand, strong economic sanctions would only 'hurt the Chinese people.' (It was not made clear who exactly would be hurt — the corrupt cadres lining their pockets on foreign business deals, Party Central with its brazen plan to shore up its power with foreign aid, or ordinary Chinese who once again have been trampled by their wildly erratic rulers and whose idea of 'hurt' may differ from that of the experts.)

Anyway, the experts concluded, there is nothing our government can really do to mitigate the repression in China.

The fact is that the U.S. government has never seriously tried to do so. On the contrary, since the establishment of relations with the People's Republic, each administration has refrained from using whatever real leverage it might have had to inhibit Beijing's repressive policies. As Roberta Cohen, deputy assistant secretary of state for human rights in the Carter administration, has well documented, China became 'the human-rights exception.'

This policy of sparing the 'sensitivities' of the communist court in Beijing was not only unwise but unnecessary. Certain evidence suggests that in 1979, the Deng regime — then a desperate suppliant for foreign economic aid — hesitated, with a wary eye on official U.S. reaction, before passing harsh sentence on the young advocate of democracy, Wei Jingsheng. The text of an internal speech in that year by old guard member and Vice-Chairman of the Central Committee Chen Yun surfaced later in Hong Kong. The speech included the following words by Chen Yun concerning the discussion of Wei's case within the Party:

I think it would have been much better to talk to him [Wei] and to persuade him gradually. Others were worried that [on account of Wei's condemnation] the human rights president, Carter, might change his policy toward China. I was not worried on this point. Carter has hundreds of reasons for normalizing Sino-U.S. relations, and human rights is not one of them.

Such an internal document, like a number of others that have surfaced since that time, cannot be verified, but its authenticity can be quite accurately judged by experienced China analysis. (The communist press in Hong Kong quickly declared the Chen Yun text to be false.) As a later document was to reveal, during the 1987 crackdown on student demonstrations, Deng Xiaoping himself referred to the Wei case as a test of Western reaction in his now-famous comment: 'Look at Wei Jingsheng. We put him behind bars and the democracy movement died. We haven't released him, but that did not raise much of an international uproar.' Indeed, very little was heard from the world when the Chinese police and military repeatedly crushed unrest in Tibet, using the same terrorist tactics that were later exhibited in Beijing, including random firing at houses and into crowds.

The Hungarian writer Miklos Haraszti, reflecting on the Tiananmen Square tragedy, summed up a few 'truths' that East Europeans have learned from experience: 'Oppression never eases without pressure from foreign governments; external pressure is never counterproductive, and in the case of countries that would like to keep advantageous relations with the West, such pressure always helps, at the very least, to halt the worsening of oppression.' The failure to apply these lessons of true political realism to China encouraged a ruthless regime to believe that it could get away with murder. As it evidently has.

This regime now sits in Beijing like an enemy occupying power, illegitimate and unstable, awaiting the next folly of the free world.

Reprinted by permission from Freedom at Issue, *where it appeared September–October 1989.*

Taiwan's Mainland Policy Before and After June 4

BYRON S.J. WENG

THE bloody military suppression of the democratic movement in mainland China on 4 June 1989 has set back China's political and economic development for years, maybe decades. In Hong Kong, it ushered in yet another confidence crisis. However, one Chinese community, Taiwan, may have benefited from that unfortunate event. Taipei has clearly gained the initiative while Beijing has become more defensive in their ongoing contest. This is evident not just in foreign affairs. In cross-straits relations, Taipei's options have opened up too.

The People's Republic of China's 40th anniversary celebration on October 1 in Beijing was a disheartening affair. Many members of the diplomatic corps boycotted the official soiree. The masses were subdued; it is hard to imagine just what they had to celebrate. By contrast, October 10, the 78th anniversary of the founding of the Republic of China (ROC), was a joyous occasion in Taipei. President Lee Teng-hui said in his National Day message, with more believability than at any time before, that the flame of China's hope was now burning brilliantly on the island and would one day illuminate the entire Chinese mainland.[1]

Readers of the October 12 issue of Taipei's *Free China Journal*[2] were informed that the mainland was shrouded in Party calls to revive the Maoist version of socialism and to tighten belts; that what freedom the people had come to enjoy in the days before the June 4 massacre had been abruptly taken away; that Beijing had sold US$1.3 billion of gold (about 120 tons) since May in order to cope with its mounting economic difficulties; and that Beijing, probably feeling insecure from the international chorus of criticisms and sanctions, had lodged a protest of interference against Norway for awarding the Nobel Peace Prize to the 14th Dalai Lama. In Taiwan, the same issue reported, the country was occupied with preparations for year-end elections, an exercise in the new game of democracy; the International Monetary Fund's world economic outlook report gave the island country a salient place among the world's developing creditor nations; and that Liberia re-established diplomatic relations.

In this chapter, we shall discuss briefly three key questions. First, what was Taipei's mainland policy before the Tiananmen massacre of 4 June 1989? Second, what were Taiwan's reactions to Beijing's democracy movement and the massacre? Third, in what ways have these events affected the development of Taiwan-mainland relations?

Since January 1979, when Beijing launched a more conciliatory policy toward Taiwan, the Taipei government had been on the defensive vis-a-vis its mainland rival. In answer to Beijing's call for three links (postal, commercial, and transport) and four exchanges (academic, cultural, sports, and scientific and technological), Taipei could only counter with the 'three-no's': no contact, no compromise, no negotiations. In the face of Beijing's tough stand against Taiwan's membership in international organizations and official diplomatic ties with other countries, Taipei stubbornly adhered to a rigid and passive position of 'no roof-sharing with the rebels.'[3]

During this period, the ruling Kuomintang (KMT) was constantly challenged by the opposing *Dang Wai* (later the Democratic Progressive Party or DPP) forces. They pointed out that Taipei's ostrichlike policies were self-serving to the KMT but self-defeating for Taiwan. While impressive economic growth was leading Taiwan to prominence among developing nations, diplomatically the island country had become even more isolated. Gradually, the people of Taiwan were losing patience with their government. More and more of them were ready to risk the wrath of the reigning power and respond to Beijing's overtures. They would not be denied the opportunities for reunion with long-separated families, potentially lucrative business deals, or tours of the motherland.[4]

Thanks to President Chiang Ching-kuo, decisive policy changes were introduced. In the two years before his death in January 1988, this wise, if dictatorial and aging, leader guided Taiwan onto a democratic track by carrying through a series of bold reforms. In September 1986, the DPP, the first real 'opposition party' in Chinese history, was allowed to come into existence. Though still technically illegal, it contested that year's elections and received 22 percent of the popular vote. On 15 July 1987, the 40-year-old martial law was lifted. In November 1987, Taiwan citizens, though not government officials, were allowed to visit their relations on the mainland. Some 350,000 persons traveled to the mainland in the first year alone.[5]

This visitation policy effectively tossed the ball back into Beijing's court. Without abandoning the 'three-no policy,' Taipei established a positive image for itself as a humanitarian and forward-looking government. To give concerted attention to various problems arising or anticipated from the new policy, the KMT Central established a working group. The government followed by establishing an Ad Hoc Committee on Mainland Affairs (ACMA), composed of the deputy premier and several ministers.

Under President Lee Teng-hui, Taipei's mainland policy has continued to unfold at a steady pace. In quick succession, controls over imports of herbal medicine, raw materials, indirect trade, exchange of publications, correspondence, and categories of persons permitted to visit the mainland were loosened. Regulations were promulgated to allow invitations of select students and distinguished individuals to visit Taiwan. Taiwanese soldiers stranded in the mainland in 1949 were allowed to return to live on the island.

Still, such measures seemed unable to keep pace with public demands for a faster and wider opening to the mainland. So much so that, in reaction, some leading scholars as well as the military and intelligence units raised concerns over communist traps, national security, and policy goals. They argued: (1) Communist intentions are not what they appear to be; to follow wishful thinking — (that reaching out is all that one needs to do to improve Taiwan-mainland relations) — will only lead to disappointment and danger. (2) It is important that the government and people of Taiwan do not forget their own policy goals and priorities; otherwise Taiwan's safety may be jeopardized. (3) Taiwan's policy toward the mainland must be cool and calculated, with acceptable *quid pro quos* from stage to stage; specifically, Beijing must cease to block Taiwan's return to international organizations and not prevent Taiwan from pursuing normal bilateral diplomatic relations.[6]

It was in light of this debate that Taipei adopted a new mainland policy in early 1989.[7] This policy can be characterized as a 'Taiwan experience' offensive.[8] It was designed to answer internal critics, to counter Beijing's loaded 'one country, two systems' scheme for reunification, and crucially, to improve relations with the mainland without undue security risk for Taiwan. The immediate task was to placate, if not persuade, Beijing to allow the status quo for an indefinite transitional period. The long-term rationale was to make Taiwan a model of success and a beacon of freedom for the mainland, and thereby win over the hearts and minds of the people there, without being swallowed up or squandering Taiwan's economic and military resources in the mainland's bottomless pit.

Strategically, the new mainland policy entailed the following significant aspects. In politics, the principle of one China and the eventual peaceful reunification of Taiwan with the mainland was upheld. Pending reunification (which must be based on the principles of freedom, democracy, and co-prosperity), the Taipei government was to relax its 'three-no policy' while people-to-people links were to be permitted under supervision. The recent democratic transformation in Taiwan was stressed and Beijing was challenged to respond in kind. This meant admission of opposition parties, release of political prisoners, open and free elections, freedom of the press, and freedom of association — in short, to move toward the rule of law.

In diplomacy, Taiwan would embark upon a 'pragmatic diplomacy.' Whether Beijing liked it or not, Taipei would seek bilateral ties with all who were willing and ready, and try to gain membership in international organizations. Such efforts would not be thwarted by 'the game of names' alone.[9]

In the cultural sphere, scholars, artists, athletes, and journalists were encouraged to visit the mainland to show the Taiwan way to their colleagues. Books, periodicals, movies, television and video programs, and music and fine arts were to be disseminated as widely as possible. However, this was to be a one-way operation: Going would be made easy, but not coming. Invitations of mainlanders to Taiwan were to be carefully screened and limited. Political propaganda from the mainland was still prohibited.

In the economic sphere, the policy aimed to transmit the 'Taiwan experience' to the mainland and, where necessary, indirect and limited financial and technical assistance to the mainland would be considered. Most analysts agreed that Taiwan's strength rested in its economy. Foreign currency reserves were large, about US$75 billion, and the manufacturing and trading sectors strong. But, to the pessimist, Taiwan's economy was beset with several major problems — appreciation of the New Taiwan dollar, a shortage of labor, sharp rises in wages, a decline in the work ethic, and the pressure for environmental protection. The vulnerability of Taiwan's relatively shallow economic base was hard to deny. Pitched against the mainland, Taiwan was small. Taipei's reading was realistic. As Shaw Yu-ming, director of the Government Information Office, put it, to become directly involved in the mainland's economic development was 'to squander Taiwan's strength or wealth.'[10] The idea of helping the communist-controlled mainland to develop into a modernized economy did not appeal to Taipei's rulers. Hence, Taiwan would play the role of model rather than invest or trade heavily in the mainland. However, the government realized that indirect trade and investment could not be effectively prohibited, so it closed an eye to such transactions.[11]

In military terms, Taipei's primary concern was national security. The preoccupation with security stemmed from at least six types of conceivable threat from Beijing: (1) a military campaign against Taiwan, whether an outright attack (by air or sea), a blockade (by warship, airplane, or missile), or harassment (by air raid, naval bombardment, etc.); (2) a diplomatic tightening aimed at squeezing Taiwan out of international organizations and to deny Taiwan diplomatic relations with other countries; (3) a border relaxation to flood Taiwan with mainland refugees; (4) a strategic commercial plan designed to lure and to trap Taiwan's businessmen in trade and investment; (5) a coastal smuggling operation putting guns and drugs onto the island via 'fishing' boats; and (6) a clandestine sabotage operation incapacitating Taiwan's infrastructure or inciting internal strife between different economic strata or language groups.

On the other hand, Taipei seemed to have given up whatever plans for a counterattack against the communists it might have had. Nor was it interested in intervening in the mainland's domestic turmoil. Within the island, growing pressure to bring the military budget and personnel matters into the political limelight was causing the hitherto well-shielded military apparatus to squirm. Vigilance in defense seemed to be slackening as economic prosperity brought on a new (perhaps false) sense of confidence. Greater emphasis was put, not on personnel training, but on sophisticated hardware, some of which could now be produced in Taiwan. It had been years since the armed forces were last engaged in a battle. Their defense capability was a matter to be tested anew. Still, most people on Taiwan were not too concerned. They did not see the

need to strengthen the military position of Taiwan since the likelihood of a communist military assault on the island was judged to
be small.

In early April 1989, just before the Beijing democracy movement was triggered by the death of Hu Yaobang, Taipei made
a number of unprecedented moves. On 6 April 1989, Taipei
announced its decision to send a high-level delegation, led by
Finance Minister Shirley Kuo, to the 22nd annual meeting of the
Asian Development Bank (ADB) being hosted by the PRC in
Beijing in May. On April 7, the world was informed that an
agreement had been reached between the two Chinese National
Olympic Committees accepting 'Zhonghua Taibei' as the Chinese
translation of 'Chinese-Taipei,' thereby enabling Taiwan to send
sports teams to compete on the mainland in international meets.
On April 9, Foreign Minister Lian Zhan let out a trial balloon
about a 'one country, two equal governments' formula. Implicitly,
Taipei was suggesting that it would recognize the legitimacy of the
PRC government if Beijing would reciprocate, a very significant
change in Taipei's official position.[12]

Beijing's rejection popped the trial balloon. But the first Taiwan
sports team in 40 years, a group of young gymnasts, went to
Beijing on April 17, two days after Hu Yaobang's death. On May
1, the delegation to the ADB meeting made history in turn, when
Shirley Kuo and fellow members arrived in the PRC capital. These
moves or, more accurately, the policy initiatives behind them, may
serve as an explanation for Taipei's strangely distant and lukewarm
support to Beijing's demonstrators throughout the first 30 days of
the democracy movement.

Taipei's first official response was on May 17, four days after
Beijing students started the mass hunger strike. On that day, the
KMT Central Committee issued a short statement[13] declaring that
the communist regime would be drowned by the historical tide
unless it abandoned the 'Four Cardinal Principles' (i.e. Party leadership, the dictatorship of the proletariat, Marxism-Leninism and
Mao Tse-tung thought and the socialist road). The statement also
hailed the student's month-long efforts for democracy and freedom. But instead of pledging any real support to that cause, the
statement merely reiterated the importance of spreading 'the
Taiwan experience' to the mainland. On May 21, the day after
martial law was imposed on parts of Beijing, the Taipei govern-

ment issued another statement backing the democracy movement. Thereafter, spokesmen from various units of both the KMT Central and the government voiced support for the democracy movement almost every day. However, the support given was more words than deeds and there was no animosity expressed toward the Beijing regime until after June 4. Concurrently, the Defense Ministry expressed its concern over the military implications of mainland developments for Taiwan.[14] Apparently, in the minds of Taipei's military leaders, a military operation against Taiwan by the frustrated Beijing rulers was not completely ruled out as the stand-off continued in the Tiananmen Square.

However, Taipei was compelled by events of June 4 and after to rethink its stand. The ruling few in Beijing, clinging to power and unwilling to take responsibility for their own mistakes, typically blamed the outside world for what went wrong: The U.S. had poked her nose into China's internal affairs; Hong Kong had not only smuggled bourgeois liberalism into the mainland but had put fuel on the fire; Taiwan's KMT agents had lighted the fire and incited demostrations. In the aftermath of the June 4 massacre, Taiwan 'spies' were rounded up and anti-KMT propaganda was stepped up.

Faced with such a grotesque reality, Taipei could no longer sustain its low-key approach to the democracy movement. On June 5, the day after the bloody suppression, President Lee Teng-hui denounced the Beijing massacre in a scathing press conference statement. 'This tyranny of the Chinese Communists is the shame of all Chinese people. With the greatest determination, the government and people of the Republic of China shall unite all patriotic, anti-communist forces in order to overthrow this tyranny, and shall not cease to do so until we reach our goal.'

An orchestrated propaganda barrage followed. Practically all government and KMT departments or organs expressed their anger and sadness over the event. On June 7, the Executive Yuan's ACMA adopted a draft resolution on 'Measures for Supporting the Democracy Movement on the Mainland.' It contained three main points: (1) to break through the mainland news blackout by strengthening broadcasting, air-drafting mail and leaflets, and opening up communications with the mainland by telephone, telex, fax, and post; (2) to provide emergency assistance to individuals involved in the democratic movement by supplying, indirectly, medicine, food, necessary funds and personnel, and granting passports, travel documents, scholarships, and other necessities to mainland students stranded overseas; and (3) to integrate anti-communist forces at home and abroad by organizing large-scale conferences and inviting deserving mainland scholars and students to visit Taiwan. The Ministry of Transport announced that, as of June 10, direct postal service and direct telephone dialling to the mainland were open. Many of the other measures adopted have since been implemented.[15] By June 16, more concrete measures were worked out by four ministries, Foreign Affairs, Internal Affairs, Education, and the Government Information Office.

The people of Taiwan were also moved by the extraordinary developments on the mainland after mid-May. The more liberal intellectuals and students led the way. At first, there were signature campaigns, rallies, and speeches. On May 23, thousands of professors and students from 21 tertiary institutions published a declaration strongly endorsing the Beijing democracy movement. On May 31, a million persons formed a 400-kilometer human chain stretching from one end of the island to the other to show their solidarity with the demonstrators on the mainland. Some 1,300,000 postcards expressing support for the demonstrators were sent to Quemoy for delivery to the mainland by air-drifting. On June 3, 10,000 persons staged an all-night vigil for their mainland compatriots at the Zhongzheng Memorial Hall.[16]

Immediately after learning of the massacre on June 4, people from all walks of life offered their help for the victims and their families. The Red Cross proposed sending a medical team to the mainland. Student groups organized a blood-donation campaign. The business community donated money as did many individuals. On June 6, all over Taiwan, there were services of 'national mourning' attended by tens of thousands. Directories of fax, telex, and telephone numbers of mainland Chinese enterprises were made available by the Institute of Modern History of the Academia Sinica so that those who had the means could transmit more accurate news reports to people on the mainland. Teachers and students of the National Institute of Fine Arts undertook the task of reproducing the Goddess of Democracy. On June 14, the whole country observed a day of mourning, with flags at half-mast and all churches and temples ringing their bells.[17] Taiwan's mass media, public and private, duly reported all the official measures as well as public responses to the Tiananmen massacre.

Still, critics, especially in Hong Kong, were quick to characterize official responses from Taipei as overly cautious. To them, such responses showed that the Taipei government had already lost its determination to vie for the right to rule the mainland.[18] Whatever the rhetoric, Taipei's real position now rested on the premise that existence of the two regimes was best accepted as a fact of life. Needless to say, any military action against Beijing was out of the question. The critics pointed out that Deputy Premier Shi Qiyang, who also served as the convenor of the ACMA, had said on June 4 that Taiwan's mainland policy would proceed along established lines and would not be affected by what happened at Tiananmen.[19] They noted also that the ACMA's draft resolution of June 7 made no mention of providing any concrete assistance to those being hunted by the Beijing regime after June 4 who were unable to escape from the mainland.

The impact of the June 4 massacre on Taiwan was clearly less striking than on Hong Kong. It should be remembered, however, that living under the Chinese Communist regime is a fate only eight years away for the latter, while for the former, any such question is remote. Moreover, after nearly four decades of anticommunist indoctrination, the people of Taiwan had become accustomed to reports of evil deeds by the communist government in Beijing. They might have been incensed by the June 4 massacre, but their basic attitudes toward the communist system on the mainland were not significantly altered by it. The KMT itself had had ample experience in dealing with the Communist Party and therefore harbored even fewer illusions about the Beijing regime. To their mind, the June 4 massacre was not the first or the worst of the communist regime's suppressions.

It is evident that authorities in the two Chinese capitals had drastically different preoccupations during the first half of 1989. Taipei was too wrapped up in its own plans and underestimated the potential impact of a major democracy movement on Beijing. On the mainland, the year 1989 was destined to be a year of confrontation and testing. Symbolic anniversaries abounded — the French Revolution's 200th, the May 4th movement's 70th, the PRC's 40th, Wei Jingsheng's[20] 10th year in prison and the conclusion of the first decade of Deng's post-Mao reforms.

Ten years of reforms and the open door policy, with their harvests and their hurdles, had given the Chinese people new anxiety as well as new hope. Impatient intellectuals, embittered by betrayal, persecution, and discrimination on the one hand, and emboldened by the unprecedented openness in the Soviet Union, Eastern Europe, and at home on the other, were determined to have their say. Fang Lizhi submitted his petition for Wei Jingsheng's release to Deng Xiaoping in February. Yan Jiaqi, Liu Binyan, Su Shaozhi and several younger thinkers quickly followed with their own petitions asking for democratic reforms. Overseas Chinese communities echoed them. The petitions became bolder and bolder. The options of the ruling elite in the face of such challenges were not easy or happy ones.

Beijing students initially planned to hold a May 4th demonstration on Tiananmen Square, with the regime's 'understanding.' The untimely death of Hu Yaobang on April 15 not only triggered student demonstrations three weeks ahead of schedule, but also brought forth a broad-based democratic movement. The insecure regime chose to denounce the movement as a *dong luan* (disturbance) and attempted to suppress it by the usual authoritarian means. When the official voice was drowned by even larger demonstrations of the people, the troops were called in.

On Taiwan, the primary concern as 1989 dawned, was how to return to the international community and be recognized. Throughout April and the first half of May, the mass media provided extensive coverage of the ADB meeting in Beijing and other news suggesting the prospects of a breakthrough in relations. By comparison, the events unfolding in the streets of Beijing received secondary treatment. Neither the KMT Central nor the ROC government issued any official statements in support of the democratic movement until May 17. The KMT Central Executive Committee did hear two reports, from the director of the Committee on Mainland Work, Xiao Changle, and the director of the Committee on Overseas Work, Zheng Xinxiong, and views sympathetic to the democratic movement were expressed by other members.[21] But there was no official statement. As for the general public, there were sporadic expressions of concern. A few legislators called on the government to show support and take meaningful action. A number of academics organized discussion meetings and voiced their support. But, by and large, greater attention was given to immediate domestic problems.

After the massacre, government spokesmen explained Taipei's reticence by saying that care was taken to avoid Beijing's accusation that they had incited the student movement. There were more important reasons. As suggested earlier, there was careful thinking and preparation before Taipei decided to send Shirley Kuo to Beijing in April 1989. Taipei was keen to see that its new mainland policy had a fair chance of success and did not want to defeat itself by open support for Beijing's demonstrators. At 10 a.m., May 4, while a massive demonstration was taking place on Tiananmen Square, inside the People's Hall, the Finance Minister of the ROC, Shirley Kuo, stood up along with other delegates to the ADB meeting when the PRC President Yang Shangkun entered the room and the PRC anthem was played.[22] This was a very unusual gesture, as meaningful as it was controversial.

Another reason for Taipei's low-key approach had to do with its concern over student demonstrations in Taiwan. Discouragement of student movements has been a long-standing policy of the KMT government. After the lifting of martial law in 1987, the political atmosphere in Taiwan became conducive to opposition activities and social agitation. The government did not want to invite criticisms to encourage troublesome student demonstrations within its own domain. The democratic movement by mainland students represented an unexpected, competing demand on the Taipei government for which Taipei's authorities were not prepared.

Among the citizenry, there was no lack of compassionate outcries and bitter condemnations, particularly from intellectuals. But the overall response was not as passionate and long-lasting as might be expected. There are two explanations for this. First, there was the fear of a reversal in the Taiwan-mainland relationship. For nearly 40 years, people had been denied access to the mainland, a denial encompassing not just travel access, but also information flow. Now that the route to the mainland was finally opening up, they did not wish to see it shut again. This was particularly important to older citizens whose relatives were still living on the other side of the Taiwan Strait.

Second, a new Taiwanese self-awareness also played a role. Most Taiwan natives never aspired to reunification. They distrust many of the ruling elders, for whom 'home' means the mainland and not Taiwan. They consider any prospect of being sold to the mainland communists in a political bargain intolerable. To them, getting tangled in a democratic cause on the mainland was a dubious endeavor. Instead, the correct goal was to secure an effective separation.[23]

Taipei's new mainland policy had been adopted not so much because Taipei wanted or needed to respond to Beijing's liberal reforms but because Taipei had finally come to terms with the fundamental political reality of the PRC. While the previous leaders, the two Chiangs, might have been emotionally charged and politically bound to pursue an 'either/or' policy vis-a-vis their communist rival, President Lee Teng-hui's government is relatively free from such a mentality or position. At the KMT's 13th Congress in July 1988, Lee spoke of the need 'to strive with a greater determination, pragmatism, flexibility, and vision in order to upgrade and break through a foreign policy based primarily on substantive relations.'[24] In March 1989, he paid a state visit to Singapore where the press referred to him as 'President Lee from Taiwan' rather than 'the President of the Republic of China' as his official title should be. Upon his return to Taipei, Lee told a press conference that he was not happy but found it acceptable. 'Whether someone called me "T.H.," "Teng," or "Hui," I'm still the same person,' he said. 'And if other countries, such as Japan, dare to invite me...then I would go with my head held high.'[25]

Such candor is refreshing. Without openly saying so, Taipei has let it be known that it is learning to live with the PRC. Like it or not, the prospect of a KMT return to the mainland is practically nil. A more liberal communist regime is welcome, of course. But, a more oppressive communist regime has to be faced too. Whatever happened in Tiananmen Square during April, May, and June 1989, Taiwan cannot simply dismiss the communist regime. Having recognized this fundamental reality, the new mainland policy was judged still appropriate. In Taipei's calculation, its own rational option was a steady course of cautious, unofficial links and exchanges that would help maintain a steady cross-straits relationship for the indefinite future.

The June 4 massacre and Beijing's new hard line drastically changed the mood of the moment and caused a slowdown of various movements across the Taiwan Straits. A long-lasting effect, however, does not appear probable. It has not significantly altered the direction of evolving Taiwan-mainland relations. Cross-straits relations will probably continue to improve, albeit at a slower pace and with a zig-zag pattern. Any talk of reunification within the foreseeable future is, of course, unrealistic; most likely, the status quo will be prolonged.

At the official level, the nature of the Taiwan-mainland relationship had been changing from hostile to competitive or even cooperative over the past 10 years.[26] Renewed mutual suspicion since the June 4 massacre has made cooperation more difficult, but by steering steadily along the line of its new mainland policy, Taipei has helped to prevent a worsening of the situation.

At the unofficial level, the flow of people and money contracted in the aftermath of the Tiananmen repression, although it has picked up again. There have been fewer moves based on wishful thinking on the part of Taiwan's businessmen and unification-advocates. The 'three links' and the 'four exchanges' will develop further, but not without hitches.

With respect to the various areas of developing Taiwan-mainland relations, the effect has been uneven. A good part of Taiwan's new investment has shifted to Southeast Asia, but cross-straits trade continues. Taiwan tourists suffer more mainland restrictions now, but not as many as Taiwan journalists.

In the area of trade, expectations were buoyant prior to June 4. The value of indirect trade through Hong Kong had increased from US$200 million in 1980 to US$2.7 billion in 1988. Another big year was expected for 1989. This trend was halted temporarily by Tiananmen and the crackdown. However, by August, optimism for a steady expansion in indirect trade was already being voiced.[27] According to Hong Kong's Wen Wei Po, some 600 Taiwanese merchants were present at the September 1989 trade fair in Fujian, accounting for 150 out of 534 contracts signed. One contract involved a plan by an investor to invest US$200 million in a synthetic fiber plant.[28]

Between 1979 and 1987, Taiwanese investment in the mainland had totaled only a little over US$1 billion; in 1988, it reached US$4 billion. Before June 4, owing to severe shortages in foreign exchange, bottlenecks in energy supply, unreliable workers, the inefficient bureaucracy, insufficient legal protection, unreasonable restrictions, and other undesirable system-related factors, many Taiwan businessmen already thought that terms for trade and investment in mainland China were less advantageous than those in some Southeast Asian countries. The June jolt awakened them to the political risks. Hence, a great deal of Taiwan money was shifted from mainland China to Thailand, the Philippines, Malaysia, and Indonesia.[29]

Taiwan travelers, at the rate of about 1,000 a day, going to the mainland for family reunions or tours were injecting an estimated

US$100 million in foreign exchange a month into the mainland's economy before June 1989. After June 4, this flow of people and money abruptly stopped. The loss to the PRC was considerable.

Ironically, Beijing's own paranoia might be responsible for a reduction in the future influx of Taiwan visitors and their money. In hunting for leaders of the democracy movement and opponents to the regime, Beijing's Public Security units conducted spot inspections of households with Taiwan or overseas connections to make sure that no individuals on the wanted lists were being harbored. In addition, new restrictions were imposed so that all Taiwan visitors were required to obtain a double-entry visa from Hong Kong before they could enter the mainland, making it impossible to transit through Hong Kong without stopping.

In the wake of the June 4 massacre, hundreds of PRC citizens abroad renounced their Communist Party membership and scores of defectors asked for political asylum in Western countries. Only a relatively small number asked to go to Taiwan but, unlike West Germany — where the gate was open for any East German compatriots — Taiwan exercised extreme caution in processing refugees from the mainland.[31] Population pressure is one reason, but fears of communist spies and the increasing gap in life experience and ideology are also pertinent. Some officials dreaded a wave of mainland refugees; none materialized since mainland border control remained tight. By the end of October 1989, only a handful had reached Taiwan with Taipei's blessing. A government spokesman explained that the existing law required that a mainlander must have at least four years of residence in a free country before his/her application for immigration could be accepted. Yet, an air force officer, Jiang Wenhao, who defected to Quemoy in a MiG-19 on September 6, was given a hero's welcome in Taiwan and rewarded with 2,000 liang of gold. A star swimmer, Yang Yang, who overstayed in Hong Kong and desperately pleaded for asylum in a press conference on August 23, was given a permit to go to Taiwan on September 27. In these cases, propaganda advantages or image costs, more than humanitarian or legal reasons, appeared to be the main consideration.[32]

Taipei apparently has not changed its intention to steer a better coordinated and steadier course in its approach toward Beijing. By and large, its mainland policy remains unchanged, except for minor adjustments in pace and timing. Recent indications are that the mainlanders very much appreciate the academic freedom, cultural products, and freedom of expression now enjoyed in Taiwan. Mainland products, on the other hand, are gradually losing their appeal among the citizens of Taiwan, with 'the exceptions of herbal medicine and works of art. Social science books from the mainland are actually producing negative impressions in Taiwan. The initial fascination with the forbidden items is quickly replaced by a sense of disgust; the forbidden fruits were not sweet after all. In Taiwan, as elsewhere, the standard Marxist jargon is hardly appealing to the thinking mind.

The Front for a Democratic China created in Paris by Chinese dissidents and many mainland scholars and students overseas has expressed a keen interest in the Taiwan experience.

Since June, Grenada, Liberia, and Belize have agreed to establish diplomatic ties and a number of countries have upgraded their unofficial relations with Taipei. Sympathetic voices are heard in many quarters, saying that Taiwan should be allowed to participate in the deliberations of various international bodies. Beijing is on the defensive and will be for some time to come.

Looking ahead, the government and people of Taiwan have reason to be cautious. Taipei may have gained the upper hand for the time being, but it faces two major worries: the Taiwan independence movement and Beijing's irrational moves. Both of these can be conducive to ugly emotion and unpredictable consequences.

For decades now, many native Taiwanese in exile have advocated independence for Taiwan under a Taiwanese government. Many of them are victims (along with their relatives) of political persecutions such as the February 28 Incident (1947), the Lei Zhen case (1960), and the Kaohsiung Incident (1979).[33] They speak of wresting power away from the oppressive intruders from the mainland. They want separate statehood for Taiwan, not reunification with the mainland.[34] In recent years, Beijing's transparent united front manipulations and its high-handed diplomatic maneuvers to isolate Taiwan have fed an increasingly visible political awareness among the islanders, particularly the young and educated. As a result, the idea of Taiwan independence, either under the continued rule of the KMT or under a newly constituted regime, has spread.

This independence movement has become very bold and visible since June 4. As the campaigns for the December 1989 elections gathered momentum, a number of candidates endorsed by the

DPP's radical New Tide faction openly embraced the slogan, 'A New State, A New Constitution.' The official registration of candidates closed on 30 October 1989. On November 2, the Central Elections Committee held an emergency meeting; the next day it announced that 'platforms' suspected of inciting treason were banned. However, the New Tide faction was determined to defy that ban. On November 6, the *Taiwan Times*, a newspaper sympathetic to the opposition, reported that some 32 candidates had joined together to form a 'Joint Front for a New State,' with the DPP's former Chairman, Yao Jiawen, as the convener and a former Provincial Assemblyman, Lin Yixiong, as an adviser. On November 6 and 7, the *Independent Evening Post* and a couple of other pro-DPP papers published the text of a 'Draft Basic Law of the Republic of Taiwan' prepared by Lin Yixiong.[35]

The 1989 election results produced conflicting signals. The 32 candidates of the DPP's Joint Front for a New State received approximately 15 percent of the total votes cast, which was good enough to elect 19 of them to office. This seems to indicate significant popular support for Taiwan independence. But, at the same time, Huang Erxuan, one of the 32, was soundly defeated by his opponent, the DPP's Zhu Gaozheng, who opposed Taiwan independence. All eight of the candidates belonging to the New KMT Joint Front were also elected as well as nine out of 10 candidates running with military support. These last two groups denounced Taiwan independence in no uncertain terms. After the elections, only a few token offenders 'suspected of inciting treason' were indicted. None of the successful candidates whose platforms might have gone beyond bounds were prosecuted.

Beijing sources reacted strongly to this development. The KMT government of Lee Teng-hui was blamed for nourishing the Taiwan independence movement through its 'flexible diplomacy' and the destruction of *Fa tong*, i.e., the basis of legitimacy for a government of the whole of China, as personified in the ROC's National Assembly.[36] Time and again, Beijing has threatened to use force against Taiwan should the latter declare independence.

Quite apart from the Taiwan independence issue, Beijing's difficulties worry Taiwan. Forty years of separation and animosity have created a real gap between them, a gap in life experience as well as in ideology, a gap of intentions as well as of communication. There is a danger of a reversion to Taiwan-mainland hostility should the post-June 4 regime in Beijing paint itself into a corner, deprive itself of the option of liberalization, and step up its anti-KMT campaign. Should the current mainland leadership remain in power but be unable to resolve its internal crises, the chance of Beijing being forced, or tempted, into using force against Taiwan would have to be very carefully considered.

Such worries notwithstanding, Taipei is still pushing ahead with its new mainland policy. One concrete evidence of Taipei's readiness to improve relations with the mainland is the adoption of the Draft Provisional Regulations Governing Relations Between Chinese People on the Two Sides of the Taiwan Straits by the Executive Yuan's ACMA on 9 October 1989.[37] This unprecedented draft law is based on the realization that once people of the two sides are allowed contact, certain cross-straits marriages and other leagal relations based on the laws of the PRC must be given legal protection under the ROC laws also. Realization of such a necessity is one thing but the decision to take the necessary legal measures to bring it about is quite another. There is a political price to pay. The draft law, if formalized, may be interpreted as constituting a de facto recognition of the Beijing regime as the 'government' of the mainland, rather than just a 'belligerent group' as the KMT authorities have maintained since 1949. Certain laws of the ROC would acquire a dual character and the judiciary would have to devote considerable resources to cases involving the application and interpretation of both ROC and PRC laws. Furthermore, Beijing's cooperation would be required if such a law was to be implemented effectively. That Taipei has chosen to take this route and to continue the process even after the June 4 massacre is certainly a meaningful indication of its policy stand.

The draft law as adopted by the Executive Yuan's ACMA broadly outlines the legality of cross-straits marriage, succession, patent, copyright, etc., defines the validity of public documents and judicial verdicts issued by the mainland authorities, and delineates the realm of permissible contacts and exchange, trade and investment, and communication and transportation. Beijing has criticized it as discriminatory against mainlanders in regard to inheritance. It will probably be adopted into law by the Legislative Yuan with amendments in 1990.

Come what may, Taipei is prepared to deal with the mainland in order to disseminate the Taiwan experience. Taipei's case for an improvement in relations with the mainland without undue security risks for Taiwan is certainly an imaginative, positive step. Its

'Taiwan experience' offensive — a mainland policy aiming to win over the hearts and minds of the people there — appears to be a sound one. Although there is a long way to go yet, the effort to make Taiwan a model of success and a beacon of freedom for the mainland is as plausible as it is laudable. The Tiananmen incident did not change that; it only strengthened Taipei's relative position. Nonetheless, the challenge confronting the government and people of Taiwan is not an easy one. They are going to need courage, wisdom, and time. The international democratic community will do well to give Taiwan its support.

---

1. See 'Lee Vows Taiwan to Light Way for Chinese People,' *The Free China Journal*, 12 October 1989, p. 2.

2. *The Free China Journal*, formerly under the name of *Free China Weekly*, is a semi-weekly in English, and has been published by the Government Information Office of the ROC since 1964.

3. In Chinese, the common usage of the phrase is 'Han zei bu liang li' which literally means 'the Han and the bandits do not stand side-by-side.' This policy position was closely associated with Shen Changhuan, former Foreign Minister and General Secretary of the Presidential Palace, who kept a tight hold on the ROC's foreign policy for a long time before he was forced to resign over the issue of Taiwan-Soviet relations in spring 1989.

4. See Byron S.J. Weng, 'Taiwan and Hong Kong, 1987: A Review,' in Anthony J. Kane, ed., *China Briefing, 1988*, N.Y.: Westview, Published in cooperation with the China Council of the Asia Society, 1988, pp. 121–43.

5. See Byron S.J. Weng, 'Political Liberalization In Taiwan,' *Jing Bao* (Mirror Monthly), No. 147, October 1989, pp. 66–70.

6. See Kau Ying-mao, 'A Critical Estimation of the Future Relations between the Shores,' in Zhu Ping, ed., *Yingjie Tiaozhan, Kaichuang Xinzheng — Yichi Haineiwai Zhishifenzi de Dabianlun* (Welcoming Challenges and Opening New Frontiers in Politics — A Grand Debate among Intellectuals at Home and Overseas), Taipei: China Times Cultural Publications, Ltd., 1988, pp. 331–46.

7. A case may be made that Taipei did not adopt a new mainland policy in early 1989, i.e., in essence, its current policy remains unchanged from that which was adopted by the 3rd Plenum of the 12th KMT in March 1986.

8. The 'Taiwan Experience' offensive may be said to have begun after the concept was incorporated in the 1989 New Year's Message of President Lee Teng-hui. It has since become a standard reference for Taipei officials. See Shaw Yu-ming, 'Refining A Creative Policy,' *Free China Review*, Vol. 39, No. 10, October 1989, pp. 40–43.

9. See Byron S.J. Weng, 'Divided China and the Question of Mem-

bership in International Economic Organizations,' a paper delivered at the Conference on Taiwan's Role in International Economic Organizations, co-sponsored by the Institute for National Policy Research (Taipei) and the Brookings Institution (Washington, D.C.), 10–12 September 1989, Washington, D.C.

10. See Shaw, supra, note 8. p. 42.

11. On June 23, barely three weeks after the June 4 Massacre, the Executive Yuan's ACMA adopted key provisions regarding indirect trade with the mainland. See *Xianggang Shibao* (Hong Kong Times), 24 June 1989, p. 3.

12. See Byron S.J. Weng, ' "One Country, Two Systems" and International Law: the Case of Hong Kong,' a paper delivered at the second conference of the Pacific Region and International Law, Fukuoka, Japan, 10–11 July 1989.

13. 'The KMT Supports Mainland Democracy Movement,' *Xianggang Shibao* (Hong Kong Times), 18 May 1989, pp. 1–14.

14. 'The President Orders Armed Forces to be on the Alert...,' *Xianggang Shibao* (Hong Kong Times), 5 June 1989, p. 1. Information regarding Taiwan's responses in the days following the Tiananmen Square incident are taken largely from this Hong Kong newspaper and from 'We Shall Return; a Special Issue on the Mainland Democracy Movement,' *Haihua* (Overseas China Magazine), No. 54, July 1989.

15. See Weng Songran (Byron S.J. Weng), 'The Great Suppression Puts Taipei's Mainland Policy into Disorder,' *Jiushi Niandai* (The Nineties), No. 234, July 1989, pp. 42–43.

16. See 'Chronicles of National Support to the Mainland Democracy Movement,' in 'We Shall Return...' supra, note 14, pp. 26ff.

17. *Ibid.*

18. See 'Taiwan — Your Name Is "Apathy"?' *Xinxinwen* (The Journalist), No. 117, June 5–11, pp. 6–7; 'Disorder in the Mainland Rekindles Debate about Reunification and Independence,' *Yazhou Zhoukan* (Asia Weekly), 25 June 1989, pp. 18–19; He Lihua, 'How Did Taiwan Support the Mainland Democracy Movement?' *Cheng Ming* Monthly, October, 1989, 91–93; and Weng, supra, note 15.

19. *Xianggang Shibao* (Hong Kong Times), 5 June 1989, p. 3.

20. Wei Jingsheng was the most daring and consistent critic of the Communist regime and of 'Deng Xiaoping, the dictator.' Symbolically, he represents the earliest true democratic spokesman in the PRC.

21. 'The KMT Central Executive Committee Discusses Mainland Democracy Movement,' *Xianggang Shibao* (Hong Kong Times), 27 April 1989, p. 1.

22. See the cover story of *Xinxinwen* (The Journalist Weekly), No. 113, May 8–14.

23. In the last few years, observers have noticed that, within Taipei's ruling circle, tacit support for Taiwan's de facto independence under continued KMT rule has been on the rise. A strong component of this support comes from the anti-Communist right wing. Analysts have dubbed this as 'Guodu' (Nationalist independence movement) which is to be distinguished from 'Taidu' (Taiwanese independence movement).

24. See Michael Y.M. Kau, 'The ROC's Diplomatic Impasse and New Policy Initiatives,' a paper delivered at the Conference on Taiwan's Role in International Economic Organizations, co-sponsored by the Institute for National Policy Research (Taipei) and the Brookings Institution (Washington, D.C.), 10–11 September 1989, Washington, D.C., p. 24.

25. *Ibid.*, p. 25.

26. See Weng Songran, 'Development of the Relationship between the Two Sides of the Taiwan Straits in the Coming Decade,' *Jiushi Niandai* (The Nineties), No. 193, February 1986, pp. 24–31.

27. See 'The Economic-Trade Relations that Are Not Only Economic-Trade Relations,' *Guojia Zhengche Jikan* (National Policy Quarterly), No. 2, June 1989, pp. 38–41; also articles by Zhang Rongfeng and Zhou Tiancheng in the same issue, pp. 22–31; 32–37. For a contrasting view from Beijing, see 'The Economic and Trade Conditions after the "June 4" Incident and Future Prospects,' *Liaowang* (Outlook Weekly, overseas edition), 16 October 1989, pp. 23–24.

28. *Wen Wei Po* (Hong Kong), 12 September 1989, p. 32.

29. See, e.g., 'Confidence in Investment Jolted, Taiwanese Business-men Shift to Southeast Asia,' *Wen Wei Po*, 13 July 1989, p. 32.

30. On the Huang Debei and Xu Lu cases, see first-hand reports and analyses in *Xinxinwen* (The Journalist), No. 122, 10–16 July 1989, pp. 30–51; and No. 123, 17–23 July 1989, pp. 68–83. See also, He Wentong, 'The Relative Positions of the Two Shores as Seen in the Huang Debei Incident,' *Jiushi Niandai* (The Nineties), No. 235, August 1989, pp. 76–77; and Wei Mingjian, 'Your Pen Can Become a Weapon Too!' *Jiushi Niandai* (The Nineties), No. 235, August 1989, pp. 78–80.

31. As of the end of October, 1989, out of some 60 reported democracy movement activists stranded in Hong Kong who wished to go to Taiwan, less than 10 had been given a positive nod by the Taipei authorities.

32. See Hua Yiwen, 'Embracing the Mainland Is Not at All Painful,' *Xinxinwen* (the Journalist), No. 131, 11–17 September 1989, pp. 44–52; and Zhang Jiefeng, 'The Knots among the Mainland, Taiwan, and Hong Kong in the Yang Yang Incident,' *Pai Shing Semi-monthly*, No. 202, 16 October 1989, pp. 7–8.

33. See George H. Kerr, *Formosa Betrayed*, Boston: Houghton Mifflin Co., 1965; *Lei Zhen Huiyilu* (The Memoire of Lei Zhen), H.K.: Qishi Niandai Zazhishe, 1978; and *Gaoxiong Shijian Zhuanji* (A Special Compendium on the Kaohsiung Incident), Hong Kong: 'Gaoxiong Shijian Zhuanji' Editorial Committee, n.d. (ca. 1980).

34. For a brief account of the major events in Taiwan, see Mao Jiaqi, ed., *Taiwan Sanshinian, 1949–79* (Taiwan over 30 years, 1949–79), Henan Renmin Chubanshe, 1988. For the positions and arguments of the independence advocates, see Wu Yuhui, ed., *Zijue yu Duli* (Self-Determination and Independence), Taipei: Xintai Zhenglun Zazhishe, n.d. (1985?)

35. Lin Yixiong, a former dang wai leader, was jailed for his leadership role in the 1979 Kaohsiung Incident. His mother and daughter were killed in what is suspected to have been a political assassination while he was incarcerated. To this day, Lin commands a good deal of respect and

receives much sympathy from the Taiwanese. His sudden return to Taiwan after more than four years of voluntary exile may well add an additional dimension to the already complicated election politics in Taiwan.

36. See the editorial of *Wen Wei Po* (Hong Kong), 8 November 1989.

37. The desirability for such a law on each side of the Taiwan Straits was first aired by scholars and lawyers from both shores attending an academic conference on the application of laws sponsored by the Chinese Law Programme, Chinese University of Hong Kong. This was in November 1987, soon after the visitation policy went into effect. In December 1988, a private draft commissioned by the Institute for Public Policy Research in Taipei was published. See *Draft Regulations on Inter-regional Relations Between the People of Taiwan and Mainland* drafted by Xu Zongli, Wei Fengheng and Lu Ronghai. Taiwan: Weli Legal Publications, 1989. In February 1989, the Executive Yuan's ACMA released a preliminary official draft. Full text in *Zili Zaobao* (Independent Morning Post), 25 February 1989. Criticisms came from both Taiwan's general public and the mainland's propaganda arms. On 9 October 1989, the amended draft law was adopted by the Executive Yuan's ACMA. The draft will become law when it is formally passed by the Legislative Yuan and signed by the President.

Prospects for Democracy in Hong Kong

JOSEPH Y.S. CHENG

IN the spring and summer of 1989, Hong Kong people established a very strong identity with their compatriots in China while intensely following the tragic events. There emerged a conviction that as long as freedom, human rights, and democracy cannot be guaranteed in China, they cannot be protected in Hong Kong after 1997. When over one million Hong Kong people marched for democracy and freedom in China and against the suppression of the student movement on 21 May 1989, a vast majority of the participants were marching for the first time in their lives. They were motivated by anger and shock at what was happening in China, and at the same time struck by a sense of despair and insecurity regarding their own future. Most of them marched again on the following two Sundays.

Before the massacre in Beijing, Hong Kong people's fragile confidence was largely based on the Chinese leadership's goal to modernize China. The Hong Kong community considered this a legitimate goal widely supported by the Chinese people, and believed that maintenance of the status quo in Hong Kong would enable the territory to contribute. This was the foundation of the confidence in the Sino-British Joint Declaration and various promises made by the Chinese leaders to Hong Kong. The developments in China in 1989 showed that power struggles within the Chinese leadership could totally disregard this goal. This has shaken Hong Kong people's trust in the Chinese leadership, the Sino-British Joint Declaration and the draft Basic Law. A confidence crisis has developed.

Promise of self-administration

During the Sino-British negotiations on Hong Kong's future, the Chinese leaders promised 'gangren zhigang' (self-administration) to the community. In its Green Paper: The Future Development of Representative Government in Hong Kong released in July 1984, the Hong Kong government pledged 'to develop progressively a system of government, the authority for which is firmly rooted in Hong Kong, which is able to represent authoritatively the views of the people of Hong Kong and which is more directly accountable to the people of Hong Kong.'[1] The respective positions of the Chinese and British governments were then a great boost to the morale of the advocates of democracy in Hong Kong. No one wanted Hong Kong to be ruled directly by Beijing.

The Sino-British Joint Declaration, negotiated in 1984 and ratified in 1985, promised that the 'current social and economic systems in Hong Kong will remain unchanged' for 50 years, a pledge welcomed by all parties.[2] Political reform, however, became a source of friction not only between Beijing and London, but within Hong Kong.

Some business leaders openly opposed direct elections to the Legislative Council, which the Green Paper had proposed. A few even said they would prefer Beijing's appointees to those directly elected to administer Hong Kong. These businessmen believed in the Chinese leadership's determination to maintain Hong Kong's stability and prosperity. They were therefore confident that the Chinese authorities would respect and promote their interests. An elected government, accountable to the electorate and hoping to win the next election, would find it difficult to resist the pressure to offer more social services, which in turn would hurt business interests.

Further, it was thought that a Beijing-appointed Hong Kong government would be more stable and predictable than an elected one. Many business leaders believed that they had the experience and ability to deal with Beijing's appointees, but lacked the confidence to bargain with an elected administration. They harbored deep suspicions of the leaders of grassroots pressure groups. Finally, these businessmen felt that a government appointed by Beijing would be in a better position to withstand pressures from Chinese officials seeking to take advantage of Hong Kong.

On the other hand, Hong Kong's younger generation and intelligentsia argued that only an elected administration could maintain the territory's international status and promote the interests of its citizens. After 1997, substantial coordination between the central government in Beijing and the government of the Hong Kong Special Administrative Region (SAR) will become essential. For this relationship, the people of Hong Kong, according to this view, needed a government directly accountable to them. Further, the territory's economic development depends on the maintenance of its present international identity. To maintain this status and to negotiate with other governments on economic and trade issues, Hong Kong, as an SAR under Chinese sovereignty, must be accepted by the international community.[3]

In 1982–85, concern for the future of the territory and the challenge posed by the development of representative government contributed to the development of many political and grassroots pressure groups. Their development was in turn boosted by the elections held in 1985–86. In the district board elections in March 1985, 476,500 Hong Kong citizens voted for 501 candidates, a milestone in Hong Kong's political development. These figures reflected a considerable degree of politicization.[4]

The September 1985 elections to the Legislative Council were based on the electoral college, comprising members of the district boards, the Urban Council and the Provisional Regional Council, and the functional constituencies.[5] Qualified voters therefore only numbered about 70,000; of these, 25,000 voted. The elections were nevertheless a significant step in Hong Kong's political development. Twenty-four of the 56 Legislative Councilors became accountable to their respective constituencies, unlike the appointed unofficial members, who were accountable to the governor of Hong Kong, who appointed them.

In preparation for the elections, middle-class political groups were prompted to develop their organizations and to establish close ties with the grassroots pressure groups. At the same time, they became concerned with social issues at the district level and took part in the related campaigns for citizens' rights. This process contributed to the expansion of almost all political groups.

The Chinese officials responsible for Hong Kong attempted to cool down the political fever. Their dissatisfaction with the rapid process of political reforms and their suspicions of the intent of the Hong Kong government finally led to the public warning issued by Xu Jiatun, head of the Hong Kong branch of the New China News Agency, in November 1985. Xu indicated that he 'did not want to see major changes in the 12 years (to come), transforming the fundamental system in Hong Kong, and then no more changes in 50 years.' He pointed out that the key to the maintenance of Hong Kong's stability and prosperity lay in 'following the text (of the Sino-British Joint Declaration),' and warned: 'Now we cannot help noticing a tendency of doing things deviating from the Joint

Declaration. If there are unexpected changes, I think one should pay attention to questions of this kind.'[6] Since then, London and the British administration in Hong Kong have abandoned the initiative regarding political reforms, emphasizing instead a convergence with the Basic Law.[7]

By the spring of 1987, it was clearly revealed that the first government and legislature of the Hong Kong SAR would be elected by an Election Committee formed by a Preparatory Committee appointed by the National People's Congress, thus giving Beijing a large measure of control. In the future Hong Kong SAR government, power would be concentrated in the hands of the chief executive.[8] In accordance with the Sino-British Joint Declaration, the Central People's Government in Beijing would appoint the chief executive and the principal officials of the Hong Kong SAR government, and the exercise of the power of the appointments would be 'substantial' rather than symbolic. The chief executive would be elected by a grand electoral college, which would also have the power of electing one-quarter of the seats in the legislature. A leader of the local democracy movement, Szeto Wah, attacked the system as 'dictatorship of the grand electoral college.' On the other hand, Ronald Li, then chairman of the Hong Kong Stock Exchange, made a statement at an international investment conference that perhaps best reflected the conservative business community's attitude. Li declared: 'Hong Kong is a colony. It is a dictatorship, although a benevolent one. It is and has been a British colony, and it's going to be a Chinese colony, and as such it will prosper. We do not need free elections here.'[9]

The community's response to Beijing's opposition to the development of representative government was another upsurge in emigration. On 16 May 1988, *Ming Pao* (a Hong Kong Chinese newspaper) published the results of an opinion survey which indicated that 24 percent of the respondents wanted to emigrate. Among those with tertiary education, the percentage was as high as 45.5 percent.[10] People emigrated because they felt, even if only vaguely, the pressure of China and consequently had no confidence in Hong Kong's future and China's promises.

Loss of confidence after the Beijing massacre

An opinion survey revealed that after the declaration of martial law in Beijing, only 52 percent of the respondents had confidence in the future of Hong Kong, whereas the corresponding indicator was 60 percent in April 1989, and 75 percent in January of the same year.[11] Another poll demonstrated that after the Beijing massacre, 37 percent of the respondents said that they were actively preparing to emigrate, or had family members residing abroad to secure the right of permanent residence in a foreign country.[12] (The same series of surveys in January 1989 reported that only 29 percent of the respondents were in the above categories.) The poll also indicated one-third of the 1.55 million families in Hong Kong was planning to emigrate. Among executives, professionals and entrepreneurs, 64 percent of them planned to leave Hong Kong, 18 percent more than in January 1989.

A survey by the Federation of Hong Kong Industries held three weeks after the Tiananmen crackdown showed that 75 percent of the manufacturers polled were either planning or considering emigration; a survey before the incident indicated that only 40 percent were in such a category.[13] Local manufacturers' confidence in the territory's future was directly affected by the changes in the Chinese political situation, and their investment horizons had become more short-term oriented.

Deng Xiaoping's speech on 9 June 1989 and the communique of the Fourth Plenum of the 13th Central Committee of the Communist Party of China demonstrated that the Party wanted to continue the open-door policy and economic reform, but to reimpose a conservative Marxist-Leninist political line. There is obviously a major contradiction at work.

When superficial calm was restored in Beijing, the regime turned its attention to Hong Kong. The initial reaction was criticism by name of Hong Kong's mass media by Beijing's *People's Daily* and other official media.[14] Then came the arrest in Beijing and subsequent release of Lee Cheuk-yan, representative of the Hong Kong Alliance in Support of the Patriotic Democratic Movement in China. Meanwhile, Chinese leaders and official media attacked Hong Kong as a 'counterrevolutionary base.' Beijing's mayor, Chen Xitong, in his report to the Standing Committee of the National People's Congress on the suppression of the student demonstrations, included a detailed account of the reports of the incident from Hong Kong's mass media as evidence of their 'collusion with foreign forces' in a conspiracy to make China 'give up the socialist road,' bring China 'under the rule of international monopoly capital,' and put China 'on the course of capitalism.'[15]

On 11 July 1989, when the new General Secretary of the Party, Jiang Zemin, met the leading figures of the Hong Kong Basic Law Drafting Committee (BLDC) and the Basic Law Consultative Committee (BLCC), he warned that Hong Kong should not interfere with China. Jiang considered that 'according to the principle of "one country, two systems," China practices socialism, Hong Kong practices capitalism. The well water should not interfere with the river water.'[16] The statements of Jiang and those previously made by Chinese officials responsible for Hong Kong affairs were basically aimed at providing assurances for Hong Kong's stability and prosperity, and at warning Hong Kong people to refrain from acts which would threaten the Chinese communist regime.

In June and July 1989, China's official media began to criticize the activities of the Hong Kong Alliance. On July 21, a signed article in the *People's Daily* criticized by clear implication the leaders of the Alliance, Martin Lee and Szeto Wah.[17] These accusations caused much concern. Pro-Beijing figures and leaders of the political establishment, such as the senior unofficial Legislative Councilor Allen Lee, appealed to the Hong Kong community to avoid confrontation with China. These accusations, conveyed through the local mass media, have certainly created a deterrent effect among the ordinary people and damaged their confidence on the territory's future.

Hong Kong affects China by its objective existence. Hong Kong's economic progress has certainly prompted the Chinese people on the mainland to doubt the superiority of socialism. Yet as long as the Chinese leaders want to make use of the territory's resources, they have to accept the compromise of 'one country, two systems.' It cannot work if Hong Kong people have to exercise various self-restraints in response to the Chinese leaders.

Hong Kong people were therefore alarmed to find that the political adviser of the Hong Kong government, in a letter to the Chinese authorities in October 1989, cited the prosecution of a radical group demonstrating outside the restaurant where the celebration of the 40th anniversary of the founding of the People's Republic of China was held, as evidence that there was no intention of allowing the territory to become a base for subversion.[18] The fear was that a legal decision was interpreted as having a political motivation, compromising the rule of law.

A similar cause for concern followed in December 1989 when

the Television and Entertainment Licensing Authority cut from a film, *Mainland China 1989*, a 16-minute series of interviews with Chinese student leaders Wang Dan and Wuerkaixi, and dissidents Fang Lizhi and Li Shuxian. A spokesman for the authority said the cuts had been made because the segment 'was propagandist in nature,' and was subject to a clause in the November 1988 Film Censorship Ordinance that requires the elimination of materials that would 'seriously damage good relations with other territories.'[19] Many in the local film industry, the legal profession, and the liberal political groups saw this as censorship and a concession to Beijing.

Consultation on the Basic Law

When the new Party general secretary, Jiang Zemin, received the leaders of the Basic Law Drafting and Consultative Committees, he indicated that the Basic Law would be promulgated as scheduled in spring 1990 at the third plenary session of the Seventh National People's Congress. The Standing Committee of the National People's Congress then decided to extend the period of consultation on the Basic Law by three months, until the end of October 1989. This was quite disappointing to Hong Kong people, because it implied that the Chinese authorities were reluctant to revise the draft Basic Law released in February 1989.

The recent political turmoil in Beijing has done much to promote the appreciation of democracy among Hong Kong people. To minimize Britain's responsibility for the territory, London and the local administration have supported an acceleration of the democratization process. In May 1989, the Executive and Legislative Councils reached a consensus on the direct election by universal suffrage of the chief executive and all seats of the legislature by 2003; on the election by the same means in 1997 of one-half of the seats of the legislature.[20] Senior Hong Kong government officials also reversed their position and indicated that the directly elected Legislative Council seats to be introduced in 1991 would be increased from 10 to 20. The report of the British House of Commons Foreign Affairs Select Committee released in late June 1989 even boldly suggested that by 1991, half of the Legislative Council seats should be directly elected; and by 1995, all seats should be directly elected.[21] This proposal was endorsed by the Joint Committee for the Promotion of Democratic Government, an umbrella organization representing the various groups of the democracy movement. The Joint Committee also demanded a 'through train' arrangement, which meant that the Legislative Councilors elected in 1995 should automatically become members of the first legislature of the Hong Kong SAR. As to the chief executive, the Joint Committee's position has been consistent in demanding that the post be directly elected by universal suffrage.[22]

According to an opinion poll, four out of five in the community favored speedier democratic reforms, even at the risk of confrontation with the Chinese government.[23] Moreover, 67 percent of the respondents supported the pace of reform for 1991 as advocated by the Hong Kong government. A later survey also revealed that 64 percent of those interviewed favored the creation of political parties to contest direct elections to the Legislative Council, while 17 percent were against and 19 percent had no opinion.[24] For the first time since the end of 1985, the British administration, the democracy movement, and public opinion were united. Nevertheless, Beijing's position is still the crucial factor; this the Thatcher government understands well.[25] In the drafting process of the Basic Law since 1985, it has been well-demonstrated that the Chinese leaders demand the final say on all vital issues.[26]

In response to the demand for accelerating the democratization process, local pro-Beijing political figures articulated the view that such a demand was 'naive' and might lead to greater confrontation with Beijing after 1997.[27] They also stepped up publicity activities to counterattack the demands for more democracy.[28] It is therefore not surprising that in January 1990, the political system sub-group of the BLDC endorsed a snail's pace for democratic reforms. It agreed during its final session to adhere to its earlier decision to limit the number of directly elected seats in the legislature in 1997 to 18. Of the remaining 42 seats, 30 percent would be elected by functional constituencies, while the other 12 would be chosen by an election committee. Beginning from the second legislature in 1999, the number of directly elected seats would be increased to 24. By the third legislature in 2003, the legislature would be constituted by an equal number of directly elected and functional group representatives.

Under this model all government bills and private members' bills would first be tabled for voting separately among legislators representing functional groups on one hand, and a combined group of members chosen through direct election and the election committee on the other. A bill can be passed only by a simple majority of the two groups of legislators at meetings with a legal quorum.[29] The effect is to make bills proposed by the directly elected members more difficult to pass.

After a final session in Beijing in February, the National People's congress rubber-stamped the Basic Law in March. There are a few cosmetic changes: 20 instead of 18 seats of the first post-1977 legislature will be directly elected; and the two-track voting system was slightly modified, but it still fell far short of democracy for Hong Kong.

These decisions disappointed the Hong Kong community, even though expectations were low given the political climate in Beijing. The Chinese leadership obviously felt very insecure in view of the Tiananmen incident and the following developments in Eastern Europe, the Soviet Union and even the Mongolian People's Republic. It looks upon Hong Kong with considerable suspicion as it was shocked by the territory's political awakening during the demonstrations in April–June 1989.

On the other hand, after the Beijing massacre, Hong Kong people feel that the autonomy for the Hong Kong SAR as defined by the Basic Law draft is inadequate. In a poll by the *South China Morning Post* in late June 1989, 18 percent indicated that the ideal option for Hong Kong people would be independence, and 31 percent opted for being an independent country within the British Commonwealth. Only 15 percent considered that the ideal choice would be an SAR under Chinese sovereignty.[30]

To seek some form of international guarantee has thus become an important issue. Since the second half of 1989, the Chinese authorities have reaffirmed their welcome for foreign investment. As China's US$40 billion foreign debt has become a serious burden, its need for foreign aid and foreign investment will become more urgent.[31] Foreign investors have the right to demand from the Chinese government guarantees of a satisfactory investment environment.

Western countries are Hong Kong's major trading partners. They have the right to ask Beijing to guarantee an attractive economic environment and investment climate in the territory. What Hong Kong people should ask of these countries is that the definition of 'an attractive economic environment and investment climate' should include the maintenance of the existing rule of law, freedoms, and human rights. On this basis, these governments can express their concerns and suggest measures for improvement.

If the Western governments can be persuaded to respond to the lobbying efforts on the part of the Brititsh government and the local groups, and promise to accept Hong Kong people should a violent crackdown take place in the territory, then some pressure can be brought to bear on China. These Western governments will then have all the more reason to be concerned with the rule of law, freedoms, and human rights in Hong Kong. The bill of rights that the British administration is now considering is a step in the right direction. Its effect will be limited, but it will attract the attention of the parties concerned.

Sino-British contradictions

Throughout the 1980s, the Communist Party of China stepped up its activities in the territory and sought to establish itself as the dominant political force.[32] It began publicly building its community network and influence in 1985 when the local branch of the New China News Agency opened three district offices. Pro-Beijing political forces mounted a campaign to block the introduction of direct elections to the Legislative Council in 1988. They also began to organize grassroots groups.

Since the conclusion of the Sino-British Joint Declaration, the local New China News Agency and pro-Beijing organizations have engaged in an all-embracing united front campaign to win the hearts of Hong Kong people. There have been numerous rounds of receptions, cocktail parties, and trips to China. To a certain extent, they were successful in co-opting businessmen, professionals, fledgling politicians, and grassroots community leaders, who were both flattered by the embrace of the Chinese motherland and afraid to reject it.

The Chinese authorities in Hong Kong also cultivated the media. Top officials of the local New China News Agency branch wined and dined the Hong Kong media proprietors; middle and lower ranking officials targeted editors and reporters. To be fair, the Chinese officials did not make any specific demands, but the operation ensured that, with the exception of a limited number of newspapers and news monthlies, few harsh criticisms were aired of China. The television stations were especially friendly.

These hitherto successful united front activities encountered a major setback during 1989. Hong Kong people's confidence in China was shattered. Worse still, the Chinese authorities also signaled their anger at Hong Kong for the anti-Beijing activities there.[33] A key element in the Chinese leaders' damage-control strategy in the aftermath of the Beijing massacre has been to portray the demonstration as a revolutionary rebellion. But Hong Kong news reports, in Chinese and accessible to many in mainland China, have seriously undermined the Chinese leaders' efforts to whitewash the massacre. Hence the Chinese authorities publicly rebuked the Hong Kong media for their coverage.

Relations with the local media deteriorated sharply in May and June, but united front activities since mid-June have achieved results. While reports of political suppression in China are still given prominent coverage in many newspapers in Hong Kong, they are also willing to carry publicity materials disseminated by the New China News Agency. Emphasis on the maintenance of stability and prosperity of the territory has become conspicuous again. Self-censorship, as existed in the past two or three years before May–June 1989, gradually returned.

Admittedly, Beijing's united front strategy is still considerably hampered by two factors. As pointed out by a former employee of a pro-Beijing organization in Hong Kong, since the Beijing massacre, and especially since the purge at *Wen Wei Po* (a local left-wing newspaper), 'Hong Kong's Left has been ripped apart, with many of its stalwarts fleeing and many of its organizations in a state of crisis.'[34] The continuing purge in pro-Beijing organizations in Hong Kong has caused much buried bitterness and resentment among both mainland and Hong Kong Chinese who work for them. More important still, the purge has resulted in the loss of many competent and enthusiastic local talents.

The second factor is the Chinese leadership's reluctance to make concessions to salvage the loss of confidence in Hong Kong after the Tiananmen massacre. Lu Ping, deputy director of State Council's Hong Kong and Macau Affairs Office, stated in Macau on 6 September 1989: 'They (the Hong Kong people) are just making unnecessary worries for themselves. The so-called confidence problem has been created by Hong Kong people, and should be solved by them because they are responsible for the problem.'[35]

Despite these two factors, China's united front work remains formidable because its 'unholy alliance' with the conservative business community remains largely intact. The latter is keen to maintain the status quo. It appreciates the Chinese leadership's maintenance of the open-door policy and is unwilling to accept the community's demand for an acceleration of democratic reforms.

In view of Hong Kong's emotional state, the conservative business community kept a very low profile in May and June 1989. But when Deng Xiaoping showed he was in control and when the Chinese media attacked the anti-Beijing activities in the territory, the conservative business community launched its campaign for a political system in the Hong Kong SAR that would best guarantee its interests. The New Hong Kong Alliance, a group of businessmen and supporters of the Chinese government, proposed in early September 1989 a bicameral legislature for the Hong Kong SAR, with the second chamber made up of members from key functional constituencies, i.e., the business, professional, and financial community.[36] Under the proposal, all legislation would require the approval of both chambers.

Meanwhile, some self-proclaimed 'middle-of-the-roaders' attempted to mediate between the democracy movement and the conservative business community. Leading figures in this group had strong links to pro-Beijing organizations and business groups. Such a scenario served to generate some discussions on the draft Basic Law, at least by the mass media, and thus enhanced the appeal and legitimacy of the consultative process. The emergence of several proposals on the political system of the Hong Kong SAR also eroded the consensus behind the reform package advocated by the Legislative and Executive Councils, which in any case were not recognized by Beijing as representing the Hong Kong people. A mainland member of the BLDC, Xiao Weiyun, indicated in early September 1989 that China would not consider the consensus model of the Legislative and Executive Councils for the development of Hong Kong's political structure.[37]

The decisions made by the BLDC in early 1990 have left little room for London and Hong Kong to maneuver. If the British government sticks to the policy of convergence, then it will have to slow political reform. This will make the British administration in Hong Kong a 'lame duck.' More important still, the Hong Kong government will find it difficult to retain the loyalty and dedication of the majority of Legislative and Executive Councilors who are pro-British and have been mobilized to support the acceleration of the pace of democratization. It is significant that Beijing even refused to make minor concessions to save London's face.

Will the British government stand firm? The answer appears to be no. In view of the increasing political apathy of the community, the Chinese leaders have little reason to concede. Hong Kong people think that it is futile to exert pressure on Beijing. While they desire democracy, they are largely unwilling to fight for it.[38]

The right of abode package offered by the Thatcher government for 50,000 Hong Kong families announced at the end of 1989 has become another bone of contention. While Hong Kong people perceived the reluctance of Britain to take anyone from Hong Kong, the Chinese attacked the package as a conspiracy to steal talent from Hong Kong, to threaten China with the departure of such talent; and to retain Britain's influence in Hong Kong after 1997. The BLDC decided in its January 1990 meeting that the number of foreign nationals should be limited to no more than 15 percent of the Hong Kong SAR legislature,[39] though in the final draft, it was raised to 20 percent. China has also threatened not to recognize as legitimate foreign passports after 1997, which can only accelerate the outflow of Hong Kong's best and brightest. Foreign nationals would not be allowed to hold a number of senior government positions.

Failures of the democracy movement

The democracy movement has failed in recent years to mobilize sufficient numbers of competent writers and speakers to explain its position while the wealth of the conservative business community enables it to employ prestigious public relations firms to manage its propaganda.

The small group of intellectuals who backed democracy in the territory and who were influential in the local mass media gradually lost enthusiasm for the cause. Some dropped out because of their pessimism and their sense of helplessness in view of the pressure from Beijing. But many of them turned their attention elsewhere. There are groups who plan to maintain their critical role overseas as they believe that freedom of speech and publication will become increasingly limited as Hong Kong approaches 1997. They see their contribution as critics of China's developments and they believe their strength lies in their ability to influence overseas Chinese opinion. The emigration of Hong Kong people to North America and the considerable number of scholars and students from China there create a potential readership, which may be large enough to support publications. The *Nineties* and *Cheng Ming*, the two most influential news magazines in Hong Kong, which are both highly critical of China, now sell thousands of copies in North America. *Cheng Ming* even prints an edition in the U.S. Many newspapers in Hong Kong publish overseas editions; the anti-communist ones may move overseas if they find it difficult to continue their operations in the territory.

Internal unity within the democracy movement is another problem. Despite two or three years of negotiations, the major democratic pressure groups have failed to agree to form a united political party. The split is between those who are openly critical of China and those who are keen to maintain a dialogue with the Chinese authorities. In many ways, this is the major difference between those who are less optimistic about Hong Kong's future, more inclined to emigrate before 1997 and have no intention of seeking public offices and those who are less pessimistic regarding the territory's future, more likely to stay and more eager to seek public office.

As the democracy movement's leadership is now dominated by activists (many of whom hold electoral offices), it lacks an overall view of the development of the movement and tends to respond to events as they emerge. This leadership is obviously over-burdened. In sum, the democracy movement has much to do before it can challenge the formidable strength of China's united front strategy.

Though the 'brain drain' makes the headlines, about five million people will have to stay in Hong Kong. From this point of view, the Sino-British Joint Declaration must be upheld, the drafting of the Basic Law must be taken seriously, the British administration must be supported, and contacts with the Chinese authorities must be maintained.

The present Chinese leadership's policy is to maintain economic reform while pursuing a conservative Marxist-Leninist line politically. The deteriorating economy and the shortage of foreign exchange will prompt the Chinese leadership to treat the maintenance of Hong Kong's stability and prosperity seriously. In many ways, their interests and those of the conservative business community are alike. However, the slowdown in the international economy and China's economic difficulties will hurt Hong Kong's economic growth considerably.

The sense of insecurity on the part of the Chinese communist regime has been challenged in an unprecedented way. The three demonstrations in Hong Kong in May–June 1989 in which over one million people participated, the defections of the Chinese organs in Hong Kong,[40] and the impact of the local mass media on China as well as its image abroad will most likely cause Beijing to strengthen its control over Hong Kong. This implies that the freedoms that Hong Kong people will continue to enjoy will be those restricted to dancing and horse-racing. The options are whether to acquiesce or to emigrate.

This is a testing period for the democracy movement. While it has to demonstrate leadership and provide guidance, developments in China are beyond its control. The Thatcher government wants an honorable retreat from Hong Kong, and is interested in continued cooperation with Beijing: It cannot be relied upon to staunchly support the development of representative government in the territory. The democracy movement will have to prepare for direct elections to the Legislative Council in 1991 and 1995, and it will have to perform in the bread-and-butter issues such as housing, medical care, transport, and education. While the movement's demand for more social services will remain popular, the danger is that it may have few achievements to boast of.[41]

In the long term, the democracy movement will have to count on its perseverance and integrity. It has to be prepared psychologically to remain in opposition for a decade and more, during which period it will have to strengthen its grassroots organization and demonstrate its commitment to Hong Kong's stability and prosperity. Above all, it must maintain its integrity under the pressure and temptation of China's united front strategy and the temptation of co-optation by the local establishment. These are no easy tasks. When the corrupt practices of China inevitably spread to Hong Kong, leaders of the movement may even have a better chance to reveal their superior moral fiber and win the hearts of the community.

A severe crisis is now looming in Hong Kong. In the early 1990s, the combined impact of a number of adverse factors will hit the territory. An economic slowdown, if not recession, is already apparent in many of Hong Kong's major overseas markets; China's economy is expected to deteriorate badly in the coming two or three years and its leadership succession problem remains.

The exodus of emigrants from the territory will also reach a peak in the first years of the decade. Under such circumstances, stability will be of greater importance than democracy to those who remain in Hong Kong. Many people expect the present Chinese communist regime to fall in the foreseeable future, but a period of chaos and instability will likely follow. While people in China are prepared to wait for democracy in the long term, the Hong Kong middle class is obviously reluctant to take such risks. When Hong Kong people who desire democracy and freedom seek them in the U.S., Canada and Australia, the prospects for democracy and freedom in the territory cannot be bright.

1. *Green Paper: The Further Development of Representative Government in Hong Kong*, Hong Kong: Government Printer, July 1984.

2. *A Draft Agreement between the Government of the U.K. of Great Britain and Northern Ireland and the Government of the People's Republic of China on the Future of Hong Kong*, Hong Kong: Government Printer, 26 September 1984, p. 12.

3. See the author's 'Cause for democracy,' *South China Morning Post*, 11 December 1986.

4. See the author's 'The 1985 District Board Elections in Hong Kong', in his edited work, *Hong Kong in Transition*, Hong Kong: Oxford University Press, 1986, pp. 67–87.

5. The nine functional constituencies returning 12 unofficial members comprised the commercial, industrial, financial, labor, social services, educational, legal, medical, and engineering and associated professions. See *White Paper: The Further Development of Representative Government in Hong Kong*, Hong Kong: Government Printer, November 1984, p. 17.

6. See *South China Morning Post*, 22 November 1985.

7. See the author's 'Hong Kong: the pressure to converge,' *International Affairs* (London), Vol. 63, No. 2, Spring 1987, pp. 271–283.

8. See the Drafting Committee for the Basic Law, *The Draft Basic Law of the Hong Kong Special Administrative Region of the People's Republic of China (for solicitation of opinions)*, 'Hong Kong: the Drafting Committee for the Basic Law,' April 1988.

9. *South China Morning Post*, 17 June 1987.

10. The survey was commissioned by the newspaper and conducted in early May 1988.

11. See *South China Morning Post*, 16 June 1989. The survey was conducted by Survey Research Hong Kong for the newspaper on 26–27 May 1989, and a random sample of 1,000 Hong Kong citizens was interviewed.

12. *Ibid.*, 4 July 1989. The survey was conducted by Survey Research Hong Kong for the newspaper during 22–30 June 1989.

13. See *Ming Pao*, 6 July 1989.

14. Louise do Rosario, 'Out of reach,' *Far Eastern Economic Review*, 20 July 1989, p. 19.

15. For the text of the report delivered on 30 June 1989, see *Beijing Review*, 17–23 July 1989, centerfold; see especially pp. I and II.

16. See *South China Morning Post*, 12 June 1989.

17. Ai Zhong, 'Sabotaging' One country, Two Systems' Will Not Be Allowed,' *People's Daily*, 21 July 1989. Regarding the responses of Martin Lee and Szeto Wah and other commentaries, see *Ming Pao*, 22 July 1989.

18. See Emily Lau, 'Shouting match,' *Far Eastern Economic Review*, Vol. 146, No. 44, 2 November 1989, pp. 10–11.

19. *South China Morning Post*, 20 December 1989.

20. *Ibid.*, 25 July 1989.

21. The report was published in full in *ibid.*, 1 July 1989.

22. *Ibid.*, 21 July 1989.

23. See *ibid.*, 3 August 1989. The survey was conducted by Inrasia Pacific Limited for the newspaper between 28 July and 1 August 1989, and a random sample of 619 respondents was interviewed.

24. See *Sunday Morning Post*, 20 August 1989. The survey was conducted by Inrasia Pacific Limited for the newspaper between 8 August and 14 August 1989, and a random sample of 602 households was interviewed.

25. For details of Sir Geoffrey Howe's visit to Hong Kong, see Emily Lau, 'Abide with me,' *Far Eastern Economic Review*, 13 July 1989, pp. 10–11.

26. See the author's 'The Draft Basic Law: Messages for Hong Kong People,' in Hungdah Chiu (ed.), *The Draft Basic Law of Hong Kong: Analysis and Documents*, Baltimore, Maryland: School of Law, University of Maryland, Occasional Papers/Reprint Series in Contemporary Asian Studies, No. 5 — 1988(88), pp. 7–48.

27. See *South China Morning Post*, 21 July 1989.

28. See *ibid.*, 29 July 1989.

29. *Sunday Morning Post*, 21 January 1990.

30. See *South China Morning Post*, 26 June 1989. The survey was conducted by Inrasia Pacific Limited three weeks after the Beijing massacre.

31. *China Daily* (Beijing) reported on 16 July 1989 that China's foreign debt amounted to US$42 billion at the end of March 1989.

32. Emily Lau, 'Positioning for power' and 'Grasping the grassroots,' *Far Eastern Economic Review*, 6 August 1987, pp. 26–9; see also Loon Sin (pseudonym), *A Shadow Government of Hong Kong* (in Chinese), Hong Kong: Haishan Tushu Gongsi, no publication date given, probably 1986.

33. Louise do Rosario, *op. cit.*

34. K.H. Lau (pseudonym for a former employee of a left-wing organization in Hong Kong), 'The purge next door,' *ibid.*, 7 September 1989, p. 77.

35. *South China Morning Post*, 7 September 1989.

36. See Emily Lau, 'Red herring,' *Far Eastern Economic Review*, 14 September 1989, pp. 26–27.

37. *South China Morning Post*, 7 September 1989.

38. *Ibid.*, 15 January 1990.

39. *Ibid.*

40. See Emily Lau, 'Waiting for the axe,' *Far Eastern Economic Review*, 22 July 1989, p. 19.

41. Margaret Ng, 'Democratic Leaders Have Lost Direction,' *South China Morning Post*, 6 December 1988.

Japan's China Policy — A Pattern of Consistency

Asai Motofumi

The upheaval on Tiananmen Square 4 June 1989 shattered the good image of China among many Japanese. That image was ruined once during the Cultural Revolution and was rehabilitated only after many years of painful efforts by both countries. Press reports and analyses of many China experts in Japan formed a de facto alliance in harshly criticizing the savagery committed by the Chinese leadership and have greatly contributed to Japanese ill-feeling, and lead to the appearance of such views as:

— China's reform and opening-up policy is finished;
— hard-liners are now in full command;
— democratization of the country is jeopardized;
— China cannot be a responsible member of the international society;
— Japan, as a responsible member of advanced democracies, should make clear, by concrete measures, its displeasure and indignation so that China may learn due lessons.

These presentations reflect the opinions of many Japanese, who were shocked and disgusted by the horrendous television footage carried live from Tiananmen. To be sure, an army opening fire against its own people cannot be justified by any reason or excuse. Here, adamant, unrepentant, and even defiant remarks by the Chinese leaders[1] only helped to inflame Japanese public opinion. This said, however, international relations cannot always be dictated exclusively by such moral values as democracy and human rights. True, in many advanced countries, democracy and human rights constitute the most fundamental values. Such violations offend the public's deepest beliefs and are therefore politically unsustainable. But the reactions of many developing countries to Tiananmen, especially Asian countries, suggest that such preoccupations may not be shared world-wide, and that such values are not yet universal — even though a majority of the countries, both developed and developing, are now committed to the 1948 U.N.

Declaration on Human Rights and/or two U.N. covenants on human rights. It may also be recalled that the record of advanced countries in their adherence and loyalty to such basic values is not unblemished. Their performances in the aftermath of the Tiananmen incident is regrettably no exception.

The purpose of this paper is to examine Japan's policy toward China after June 1989, and to suggest Japan's policy options.

Since its defeat in World War II, Japan has been torn by its self-destined dilemma of being both 'a member of the advanced democracies' and being 'a country in Asia.' Among the dilemmas are:

— whether Japan deserves to be called, 'an advanced democracy,' to the extent as to allow it to make judgments and criticisms about Tiananmen;

— whether Japan has liquidated its notorious past as a country and people who disregarded democracy and human rights and embarked upon aggressive war against neighboring countries, including China;

— how to resolve its legitimate geopolitical concerns vis-a-vis China in the Far East.

Before addressing these subjects, however, it seems appropriate to give a brief summary of what has happened between China and Japan since 4 June 1989.

As in the West, many Japanese people watched the live TV coverage of the horrifying suppression in Tiananmen Square with horror. Tremendous shock, combined with the outburst of condemnation in the West against the brutality of the Chinese leadership, led the Japanese public to demand that the Japanese government take as strong measures as possible, in order to align itself with the West in upholding human rights. The attitude of the Japanese government was far from straightforward. Its first reaction, expressed on June 6 only after the other Western governments' harsh attitude was made crystal clear, was,

— 'We do not have the slightest idea about taking punitive measures.'[2]

— 'The countries neighboring China (i.e. Japan) cannot be compared with remote countries (i.e. the U.S., Western Europe). Japan naturally has its won consideration and judgment.'[3]

— 'Japan still drags its past of military invasion (against China),

and is therefore doomed to extreme caution in making its attitude known';
— 'China's stability is a decisive factor for peace and stability of not only Asia but the whole international society, and friendly Sino-Japanese relations are indispensable for that purpose.'[4]

Under pressure both from within and outside, however, the Japanese government reluctantly announced 'emergency measures' on June 7. These measures were analogous to those announced by President Bush two days before, including humanitarian aid and extension of visas for Chinese in Japan. Military-related measures (which were included in the American decision) were not included, of course, for the obvious reason that no such relations exist between China and Japan.[5] On the same day, Prime Minister Sosuke Uno made restrained but definitely critical remarks in his answer to a question raised in the Diet.[6] 'It is very serious (for the Chinese army) to direct their guns against their own people. It cannot be justified,' he said. Asked what concrete steps he was considering, however, he replied, 'We must avoid to judge black or white.'

The measures and actions taken by the Western governments in protest against the Chinese leadership after June 4 may be divided into four phases.

Phase 1: June 4–June 15. Many Western countries lost no time in announcing their utmost anger and displeasure. On June 5, for instance, the European Community officially rejected a scheduled ministerial meeting with China. In clear contrast, the reaction of the Japanese government that day was lukewarm. The spokesman for the Ministry of Foreign Affairs was reported to have commented that the Japanese government was seriously concerned about the developments which brought about such bloodshed, and that it earnestly hoped the situation would not be aggravated. Patch-up operations were carried out on the next day cautiously and almost reluctantly. The mixed approach of the U.S. government, which was noticeable early on, must have influenced the Japanese government, which has had the notorious reputation of always looking to the U.S for its diplomatic course since the end of the World War II. On June 8 for instance, President Bush made known his intention not to downgrade U.S.-China relations despite his disappointment at the Chinese leadership.[7] (Although I have to confess to have no reliable information, my own experience within the Foreign Ministry leads me to think that frequent exchange of views and inquiries was under way between the two governments before Japanese decisions were taken.) On June 15, three Shanghai youths were sentenced to death for setting trains on fire; the West again lost no time in announcing its displeasure.

Phase 2: June 16–June 21. China's defiant sentencing of the Shanghai youths on June 15 stirred up international public opinion, which would have calmed down with Chinese restraint. On the next day, the White House condemned the sentence.[8] This time, Japan's reaction was considerably quicker. Foreign Minister Mitsuzuka criticized the sentences on June 16, saying that they ran counter to the basic values of Japan, and that the Chinese government should pay due regard to international public opinion and return to normalcy.[9] Later the same day, he warned Japanese industrialists to go slowly in their dealings with the Chinese, sensitively responding to then mounting criticisms from abroad of reckless activities of some Japanese businesses, which were condemned as fishing in troubled waters.[10]

Following harsh rhetorical remarks by President Bush on June 19,[11] the U.S. and Japan announced on the next day, separately but clearly after close consultation, further measures against China. The White House emergency statement revealed that high-ranking American officials would not, for the time being, be in contact with their Chinese counterparts, and that international financial organizations were requested to postpone provision of new loans to China.[12] According to press reports on June 21, the Japanese government decided on the previous day that new Overseas Development Agency assistance for Chinese projects be frozen until the situation in China calmed down.[13]

Phase 3: June 22–July 16. Curiously, after the Chinese executed those three Shanghai youths on June 21, both U.S. and Japanese attitudes switched to milder lines. Although U.S. Secretary of State James Baker immediately expressed his deep regret,[14] he retreated fundamentally when he appeared in the hearings before the Foreign Affairs Committee of the House of Representatives on June 22. After making clear that human rights are the keystone of U.S. diplomacy, he hastened to add that important geopolitical as well as economic considerations in the U.S.-China relationship should also be taken into account.[15] In a series of high-level consultations,[16] the two governments shared their views toward China, and agreed to take concerted action. This mild approach conspicuously contrasted with that of European countries. The EC summit meeting released a statement on June 27 repeating their condemnation against the savagery of the Chinese authority and unveiling several sanctions.[17] The measures did not include any harsher ones than those taken by the U.S. and Japan, however. What was important is rather that there emerged different approaches and policies within the Western democracies, and that these differences were intertwined with the basic problem pertaining to Western perception regarding China's importance in international politics at large and in the politics of the Asia Pacific region in particular.

Phase 4: July 16 onward: The enlarged ASEAN foreign ministerial meeting on July 6–8 held in Brunei and the Paris summit meeting in the same month provided the occasion where industrialized democracies sought face-saving accommodations. The outcome was the political declaration adopted on July 15, which only reconfirmed the measures so far taken but refrained from taking further actions. It was taken in Japan as a diplomatic victory of U.S.-Japan joint efforts.[18] At any rate, the attitudes and policies toward China of Western countries after the summit were greatly softened. Most symbolic of all were the successive meetings of the Chinese foreign minister, Qian Qichen, with counterparts from the U.S., the U.K., France, and Japan during the international conference on Cambodia held in Paris on July 30–August 1. Those meetings virtually nullified the EC summit political declaration, which called for boycotting high-level meetings with China. At the time of this writing, the postponement of new ODA assistance and suspension of new international financial arrangements, together with token measures related to military exchanges, are the remaining 'sanctions.' Even on economic measures, both the U.S. and Japan reached the understanding that sanctions could be softened if the Chinese showed signs of their sincerity.[19] In the meantime, China's diplomatic exchanges with foreign countries, including industrialized democracies, became more frequent in multilateral forums, for instance the U.N. General Assembly in New York.

With the background in mind, I would like to consider Japan's policy options, given its history and position.

First, is Japan really qualified as a country of advanced democracy to make free judgment and criticism about what is right or wrong in China? However fundamental and universal democracy and human rights are regarded in the West, can one impose such values upon any country, disregarding objective conditions? How does one resolve the contradiction between the internationally established principle of non-intervention in domestic affairs and the principles of democracy and human rights, the legality of which is increasingly accepted internationally but still with strong reservations in many developing countries?

It must be understood, first of all, that postwar Japan was given a legal framework for democratization, but the Cold War atmosphere in general and the outbreak of the Korean War in particular stopped the process short. In clear contrast to West Germany, postwar Japan was under one-man rule — Gen. Douglas MacArthur — of the U.S. The necessity of securing a stable and anti-communist regime in the region quickened the U.S. decision to release Japanese war-criminals. What the U.S. occupiers and these released war-criminals shared was strong anti-communism. Western forms of democracy were a distant second. Mainstream conservatism in Japan has therefore succeeded very easily in maintaining its traditional dual characters of anti-communism and indifference to Western forms of democracy.

More than 40 years of experience of political democratization in Japan have not completely eradicated such anti-democratic tendencies, but rather helped it to reproduce itself in a disguised manner — such as contempt for 'inferior' neighboring countries and peoples, emotional defenses of Japanese militarism, and the extravagant funeral ceremony for the late emperor, Hirohito, in 1989.

So far as Japan is concerned, it is questionable whether it is really qualified to make fair judgment about what has happened in China's political reform — what the Chinese call socialist democratization. To say the least, Japan has many things to do for its own housekeeping before engaging in others' business. Without having done this, Japan will always find itself vulnerable to possible counter-charges by China, which may easily find cause for making trouble. Of course, Japan cannot use its immature democratization as an excuse for it to ignore violations of values it regards as basic. However, considering that China and Japan interpret democracy differently, and as long as the true nature of the Tiananmen incident is still unclear, Japan's lukewarm approach cannot be totally reproached.

Second, has Japan really liquidated its notorious past vis-a-vis China? The Sino-Japanese Joint Communique in September 1972, which normalized diplomatic relations, settled the question legally and politically. It is one thing however, to have legal and political settlements but an entirely different one to soothe the badly hurt feelings of the Chinese people. Even if these emotions could be healed, utmost sensitivity is required for the Japanese, the offender, to make sure such feelings are not refueled by careless deeds or words. As the following examples show, this has not always been the case.

The text-book scandals. In Japan, Ministry of Education specialists examine the textbooks used in primary, middle, and high schools. In 1982, these specialists advised changing descriptions of the Sino-Japanese War. The main polemics centered on two subjects: the nature of Japan's military activities and the so-called Nanjing massacre. The original descriptions in many textbooks depicted the former as 'aggression' and the latter as costing hundreds of thousands of lives. The Education Ministry specialists claimed that it was premature to define the Japanese military activity as 'aggression,' and that the term 'massacre' was inappropriate, because the precise number killed was unknown.

When these opinions were made known, they immediately ignited an uproar of indignation and anger in China. The controversy not only reopened still-unhealed wounds, but equally important, struck the Chinese that Japan was unrepentant about its past. The Chinese may have quite naturally pondered that, if overlooked and forgiven, the Japanese would not learn due lessons from history. Further, as some Chinese newspapers pointed out, Japanese youths, without precise knowledge about the past, may nourish a quite twisted sense of history, which in turn may influence their thinking when they become responsible for the destiny of Japan. As a result, all available means, official and private, were mobilized to criticize, and change the course of, the Education Ministry's policy. After very tough negotiations, the Japanese government gave in and promised that the specialists would respect the opinions of neighboring countries in the future. The Chinese government expressed its appreciation but added that it would carefully watch if words were reflected in actual deeds.

The Chinese suspicions turned out to be correct. In 1985, the Education Ministry specialists repeated the mistake, prompting another round of tough diplomatic negotiations. The problem lies in the fact that these specialists in the Ministry are unrepentant ideologues and are strongly supported by the right wing in the ruling party. As long as this root cause remains, there is always the real and aggravating possibility of the recurrence of similar problems.

Official visit by prime minister to Yasukuni Shrine. Japan's Yasukuni Shrine is dedicated to the 2.4 million soldiers and civilians who lost their lives in wars. There are two reasons why official visits of cabinet ministers and especially of prime ministers invite political uproar at home and anxiety abroad.

First, and most fundamentally in Japanese politics, Japan's Constitution provides for separation of politics from religion. The main purpose of this provision is to deprive the emperorship of the claim to divinity and to prevent recurrence of political abuse by militarism and other ultra-rightists.

Nakasone, prime minister from 1982 until 1987, propagated the idea of 'settlement of postwar politics.' He felt Japanese politics, influenced by blind faith in Western democracy, had sacrificed many of the virtues and merits of Japanese tradition. It was therefore no surprise at all that he took the initiative to pay an official visit to Yasukuni Shrine in 1985.

Second, and more relevant for neighboring countries, among those enshrined at Yasukuni are those who were sentenced to death and executed for war crimes by the Far East Military Court after World War II. An official visit by a Japanese prime minister to the shrine is naturally regarded as insensitive, to say the least, and even arrogant. Some countries also sniffed reviving militancy.

Nakasone probably thought that he would not be challenged by the Chinese because of his relationship with then-Party Secretary Hu Yaobang, as well as Chinese reliance on Japan for the four modernizations. But he paid a heavy price for his miscalculation. Sino-Japanese relations turned sour; his successors have been forced to patch up such wounded relations. There have been no more official visits by the prime minister.

These two cases are but the tip of the iceberg but they are sufficient to reveal several important features in Sino-Japanese relations. First, the two incidents could not have happened if Japan's democracy was firmly rooted.

Second, they illustrate the difficulties and peculiarities of Sino-Japanese relations. Japan's inconsistent and guarded approach after Tiananmen can only be properly understood in light of this historical background. It is important to understand that Japan's approach to Chinese politics is not necessarily occupied exclusively by consideration of economics, or human rights.

The third subject to be dealt with relates to geopolitical considerations. Japan and China are the only two possible candidates for
regional superpower status. Asia-Pacific political stability will be
largely decided and influenced by the relations between them,
though the U.S. and the USSR will continue to be major players.
Although it is difficult to predict with any precision what will
happen to relations among these four major powers, judging from
what has happened in the last 10 years or so, it is more than likely
that the influence of Japan and China will increase while that of
the U.S. and the USSR will decline.

Chinese nuclear capability will emerge as a formidable factor in
relation to peace and stability of the whole region if the present
pace of development is not checked. The Chinese nuclear strategy
seems based on the theory of minimum deterrence similar to that
of France. Unless there are substantial cuts in U.S. and USSR
nuclear forces, the Chinese will very likely resist pressures to
revise its nuclear planning. As the Soviet threat is now perceived as
latent, the Chinese are confident that they can buy time up to the
turn of the century. They are scaling back modernization of expensive non-nuclear armaments, and focusing their military
resources on research and technical breakthroughs in nuclear
development.

Although still limited and less impressive if compared with the
superior nuclear forces of the two superpowers, Chinese nuclear
forces will certainly pose a considerable threat for Japan's security,
depending upon the variable political climate surrounding the two
countries. It will become critically important for Japan to take
pains so that normal and friendly relations can be maintained with
China.

The Chinese nuclear factor is also very important for its likely
influence on Japan's own security policy. The undercurrent of
rightist thinking in Japanese politics is far from negligible. If Sino-
Japanese relations deteriorate and the Chinese nuclear threat is
played up, no one can be sure that Japan will not go nuclear.

What diplomatic objectives should Japan pursue vis-a-vis
China? Should the Tiananmen incident change the course of
Japan's policy toward China? Neither Japan nor China can a
afford repetition of the enmity that characterized pre-war relations. The two countries cannot but base their respective policies
on mutual security and friendship. On this score, the Chinese took
the lead, setting out principles to guide Sino-Japanese relations in

the '80s and beyond. At the Twelfth Party Congress in September 1982, Hu Yaobang clearly conveyed the readiness of the Chinese leadership to develop solid relations with Japan. The simple fact that Sino-Japanese relations were addressed for the first time ahead of Sino-American and Sino-Soviet relations is significant. In the same address, Hu emphasized that such relations must be based upon Japan not allowing the resurgence of militarism. 'In present-day Japan, there are still some segments who try to beautify the historical facts of its invasion into China and other countries in East Asia,' Hu said. 'We, together with Japanese people and intelligent leaders both in power and in opposition, must repulse all the elements detrimental to the relations between the two countries.'

In Japan, almost all important foreign policy statements by prime ministers to the Diet have noted the importance of friendly and stable relations with China, but often too rhetorically to convey any serious meaning. In a typical message, then-Prime Minister Takeshita said in early 1989: 'China is an important neighboring country, the development of friendly relations with which constitutes one of the basic policies of Japan.'[21]

This lack of philosophical and political substance is not isolated to China policy. The fundamental ambiguity seems to stem from Japan's avowed commitment to two diplomatic principles, or 'pillars' in Japanese diplomatic jargon: to make contributions as a member of the advanced democracies and to play a role as a country in Asia. When the two pillars clash, the Asian pillar is always subordinated to the other.

Regarding China's case, Japanese postwar diplomacy has been handicapped by the American influence, to which successive ruling Liberal Democratic Party governments have paid high regard. When Prime Minister Tanaka visited China in 1972 for normalization talks, for example, he explained to Mao Tse-tung that for Japan, U.S.-Japanese relations are more important than Sino-Japanese relations. Successive prime ministers have loyally followed Tanaka's precedent, presumably without anticipating how contemptuously the latter listen to such remarks behind their gracious smiles. Japan's blind loyalty to the U.S. in its diplomatic dealings is now so well-known that even other East Asian countries tend to negotiate with the U.S. first over matters that involve Japan directly.

The obvious importance of friendly Sino-Japanese relations is understood by both sides, and China has long pursued its Japan policy based on such recognition. Even in those days of mutual suspicion and hatred in the 1950s and '60s, Chinese leaders were most eager to convey their willingness to improve relations. Japanese leaders turned a deaf ear to all appeals, official and unofficial. Therefore, it is no surprise that the Chinese became even more eager after 1978 to develop Sino-Japanese relations toward a very solid and even strategic partnership. Japan will continue to grope about in the dark, until primitive or instinctive understanding of the importance of Sino-Japanese relations is duly elevated and refined up to the policy level. Then, and only then, will the two countries really stand on an equal footing.

For China, economic construction, and reform and opening-up for that purpose, constitutes the primary and all-exclusive national objective whose importance has been unwaveringly emphasized even since Tiananmen. Only through such a course can they recover the people's confidence and retain their grip on power. Here arises a serious problem. For the mainstream of the Chinese leadership, political democracy and/or human rights cannot compete with economic development. Western-style democracy is not regarded as automatically adaptable to the Chinese soil, but must be transformed into the modern form of the 'mass' line. They recognize the importance of socialist democratization only as long as it serves the cause of modernization. In fairness, it should be remembered that China has never categorically denied the value of democratization. They even admit that, as economic conditions improve, so do political ones. What makes their case different and difficult for Westerners to understand is the difference of perceptions about values to be most basic. (To be precise, the term 'people' or 'renmin' in Chinese tends to have an aggregative connotation; in the West the term is almost synonymous with 'individual.')

The Chinese leadership insists that the sheer size of the country, poor traffic and communication networks, huge and ever increasing population, limited resources, stagnating standard of living, poor education, and low literacy rate must inevitably limit the pace and scope of political democratization. Under these conditions, the leadership insists that precipitous political democratization can only lead to chaos.

Here is not the place, I believe, to make any judgment for one or the other. Suffice it to point out that, in the aftermath of the Tiananmen incident, many Asian and other non-Western countries maintained very cautious attitudes, so as not to give the impression of intervening in Chinese internal affairs, a striking contrast with the forceful presentations of many Western countries.[22] The implication is that, where it may be theoretically possible to state basic norms required for a country to be a responsible member of the international community, it is rather difficult in concrete cases to establish beyond dispute whether or not a certain country really offended such norms, and even if so, how much.

To consider the Chinese case differently, what would have been Western reactions, if the Chinese had not opened up enough to allow full coverage by international mass media? Was it not disillusionment, amplified by exaggerated expectations about China's possibility of positive change consonant with Western values, which led the West to outrage and sanctions? To put the case rather ironically, was it not related to the Western sense of relief from the threat of the USSR? Would the harsh treatment of China have been possible or imaginable, if *perestroika* in the Soviet Union had not relieved the West's main cause of worry? The differences of approach of the U.S. and Japan on the one hand and the West European countries on the other notably indicate that such was the case. To put the case crudely, Western Europe may have felt free to criticize and demand harsh actions against China; the U.S. and Japan, Asian-Pacific powers doomed to have vital interests in a stable China, had second thoughts at every turn. The point is that even democracies are not necessarily consistent in upholding their most fundamental values, but are obliged to make compromises when political necessity demands it.

China and Japan have a heavy responsibility to develop productive relations, not only for their mutual benefit, but for the peace and prosperity of the Asia-Pacific region and international society as a whole. In recent years, China has begun to espouse the idea of a 'new international political order' based upon five principles of peaceful coexistence. China also has taken the lead in disarmament affairs after its successful rapprochement with the USSR. The Soviets have matched Chinese moves by reducing their own armaments in the region. These moves cannot be dismissed as tactical and deceptive, because it is obvious that both China and the USSR have serious economic problems. They cannot afford both military and economic construction. As these economic difficulties are doomed to last well into the next century, China's conciliatory approach to international affairs is also doomed to long duration.

Taking full account of the above, therefore, it should be Japan's turn to consider how to respond to these Chinese initiatives. Regrettably Japan has so far been quite unresponsive and even retrogressive. It has been forced to recognize, though quite reluctantly, that the international situation has changed substantially. But Soviet military improvement in qualitative terms is alleged to continue unabated, as justification for Japan (as well as the U.S.) to keep its vigilance and military preparedness. (Japanese policy is in full concert with the U.S., which has successfully resisted Soviet efforts to include maritime disarmament in overall disarmament negotiations.) As long as Japan is not prepared to re-examine its traditional Cold War perception about the 'communist threat,' and as long as the U.S. sticks to its policy of strengthening its war-fighting capability, an historically unprecedented opportunity will be wasted. The danger is that such stubbornness will discourage the two communist giants from pursuing their present mild and restrained approach, and thereby fail in bringing them into the Asian-Pacific politico-economic scene as constructive and stabilizing actors.

Japan must be urged to realize that the bigger and stronger its economy is, the greater its responsibility. Having grown accustomed to comfortable U.S. patronage, Japan now finds itself facing the task of identifying its position in the international order and looking for a strategy which may accommodate not merely its own needs but, more important, also the requirements of harmonizing its prosperity with that of the APR and the international community as a whole.

The China factor will become all the more important in this regard. Japan can hardly enjoy its long-term prosperity and security with a weak and unstable China as its close neighbor. China's tremendous economic difficulty poses a series of questions for Japan: Can China come out of its economic doldrums? Can Japan can satisfy the ever-increasing requests for aid from China and other Asian countries? Will the U.S. and other Western countries allow Japan to concentrate its major resources for China's development?

I do not pretend to know all the answers to the questions raised in this article: Sino-Japanese relations are not an easy business. The complexity has been further aggravated in recent years by developments in China, Japan, and internationally. The Tiananmen incident should, in my opinion, also be considered in a broader context, where considerations about democracy and human rights occupy a very important but not exclusive share.

---

1. See for instance, remarks of General Secretary Jiang Zemin at the press interview on 26 September 1989. Also see his speech on the occasion of the 40th anniversary meeting on 29 September 1989.

2. Premier Uno's remarks, as reported in the evening edition of Asahi Shimbun, 6 September 1989.

3. Remarks of Minister for International Trade and Industry, Mr. Kajikawa, as reported in Nihonkeizai Shimbun, evening edition, 6 June 1989.

4. Asahi Shimbun, 7 June 1989.

5. Nihonkeizai Shimbun, evening edition, 7 June 1989.

6. Asahi Shimbun, 8 June 1989.

7. Asahi Shimbun, evening edition, 9 June 1989.

8. Nihonkeizai Shimbun, evening edition, 9 December 1989.

9. Asahi Shimbun, evening edition, 17 June 1989.

10. Asahi Shimbun, evening edition, 16 June 1989.

11. Nihonkeizai Shimbun, 17 June 1989.

12. Asahi Shimbun, evening edition, 20 June 1989.

13. Nihonkeizai Shimbun, evening edition, 21 June 1989.

14. Asahi Shimbun, 21 June 1989.

15. Asahi Shimbun, evening edition, 22 June 1989.

16. Asahi Shimbun, 24 June 1989.

17. Foreign Minister Mitsuzuka visited the U.S. on 25–28 June 1989 and consulted with U.S. Secretary of State James Baker.

18. Asahi Shimbun, 28 June 1989.

19. Asahi Shimbun, 16 July 1989.

20. Nihonkeizai Shimbun, 30 December 1989.

21. Prime Minister Takeshita's political speech to the Diet, 10 February 1989.

22. As for Indonesia, see Nihonkeizai Shimbun, 14 June 1989; Singapore, Nihonkeizai Shimbun, 15 June 1989; India, Nihonkeizai Shimbun, evening edition, 22 June 1989; Malaysia, Asahi Shimbun, 24 June 1989; South Korea, Nihonkeizai Shimbun, 25 June 1989.

Death of a Dream in Rural China

ANDREW J. SPANO

WANG'S footsteps clicked on the cement floor. Many Chinese men wear hard plastic shoes. Street cobblers attach metal taps at the heel and toe to keep the sole from wearing — people are too poor to buy good, long-lasting shoes. The only strong leather shoes I saw in China were on Communist Party officials. It was fall of 1988. As we stepped out of the classroom building at Taian Teacher's College, we were discussing the catastrophe of the Cultural Revolution, in which perhaps 100 million people were touched by the violence unleashed by Mao Tse-tung. 'Things are much better now,' said Wang.

I had just left an English class where students debated whether a Chinese millionaire should be allowed to join the Communist Party. Though he had built many new schools at his own expense, the Party line was that he shouldn't be allowed to join. Most of my students agreed, saying, 'He is only trying to buy his way into the Party by doing such things.' Out of 50, only four thought the millionaire was qualified to join. (They would later be the most active in the pro-democracy movement.) 'After all,' the four argued, 'he earned his money honestly and doesn't need to abuse the privileges of his membership to become rich, as many Party officials do.' After this was said, the rest of the students squirmed. Despite a daring editorial in the English-language newspaper *China Daily* supporting the millionaire as an 'example to all of the goals of economic reform,' the Party turned him down, saying that he was instead an example of a 'bourgeois capitalist.'

This experience made me cynical. 'I know things are much better now,' I said to Wang, 'but it seems to me that people could go right back to thinking the way they did during the Cultural Revolution. All the Party has to do is throw the switch.' We walked without speaking, Wang's shoes tapping on the asphalt. Then he said, 'You're right.' We could not know that in six months the switch would be thrown, or that after the sudden death of former Communist Party General Secretary Hu Yaobang on April 15, we would hear the thunderous click of 10,000 hard shoes marching along the streets of Taian in defiance of the Communist Party.

Taian Teachers' College is a two-year teachers' training school funded jointly by the municipal government of Taian, and the provincial government of Shandong. Founded in 1958, the college has approximately 1,600 students and several hundred faculty. From August 1988 to June 1989, I was a 'foreign expert' in English and education. I was appalled at the state of China's higher education; and amazed at how my apathetic students turned into passionate activists during the democracy movement of 1989.

My students, many of them from rural villages, were conscripted to be teachers. In China, you study what you are assigned and submit to employment — usually for life — in the field chosen for you. The only possibility of escape is if relatives in high places can divert your destiny. The other legal route to a better life is to pass the university entrance examination. Of the 1,600 students at Taian Teachers' College only 16 were permitted to take the exam — though hundreds more would have liked the opportunity. Even this limited chance to rise above their circumstances is tainted with non-academic priorities — such as whose parents have the strongest *guanxi*. Aside from the small group that makes it through this political labyrinth, the other 99 percent teach for the rest of their lives. All of my students knew what a teacher's life is like in China and they dreaded it.

Their reasons are simple: low pay, terrible working conditions, no social respect, and no hope of anything better. I met two middle school teachers who told me they earned 55 yuan (US$15) a month. They would visit me at lunch time in the hope that I would invite them to eat with me. This was particularly true at the end of the month, when they had long since run out of money to buy groceries. One student from another department jumped off the roof of a building. She died instantly. In her suicide note left on her bed in the dormitory she said she couldn't face going back to her village to be a teacher.

The product of this force-fed education is almost complete apathy toward study. The students know they will not fail because the system needs these conscripted teachers. Any delay in their deployment and the local quota will not be filled. Allowing them to cheat on exams is a popular way to ensure that they pass. Their first experience with other ideas about test-taking etiquette led to many shredded exams in my class. 'Do not take it so seriously,' one professor told me. 'This sort of thing is common in China.'

'Hard-working' students may put in a total of 20 hours per week of study, class time, and organized extracurricular activities. Even with this light schedule, they are still exhausted because of their living conditions.

On our campus, 1,000 men lived in a huge cement hive, seven or eight to a room. There was no heat — though the temperature often dropped to below freezing for weeks on end. Many of the windows were shattered or had no panes. The electricity was often out, making it impossible to study at night. Students had to wash their clothes in the sinks, where the water came on only once or twice a month for a few hours. At night they used the sinks as urinals, since the only other toilet facility was a cement trench in the corner of the campus. Between 1958 and 1989 there was no place on campus to bathe. Then a shower was built which campus residents could use one night a week, when there was water. This facility was shared by the whole university. The summer I was in Taian there was no water on campus for five days in a row.

The classroom building where I taught was built six years ago, yet it looked like an abandoned factory from World War II. The hallways were filthy and dark. For one month a year water struggled up through the radiators, bringing the temperature in the classrooms to above freezing. Most of the time there was no heat at all. I taught in a winter coat, and my students wore gloves as they dipped their fountain pens into frozen ink wells. And despite all this, the students still had to rise at 5:30 a.m. for jogging, calisthenics, and propaganda via the public address system. Many of my 19- and 20-year-old students had gray hair and deeply lined faces. Most had bad teeth, or teeth missing, and were besieged with upper respiratory problems and devastating common colds.

These wretched conditions help to explain why the tragic drama in Beijing, by now so familiar to the West, found an echo in rural China, in Taian and dozens of places like it. Students, and the new and rising class of business owners, looked to the pro-democracy demonstrations in Beijing for definition of the struggle, for guidance and examples of behavior, and for a new language of democracy and freedom to replace the stale slogans of Leninist-Stalinist-Maoist communism.

In Taian, the students' primary contact with the idea of democratic freedom came from other students — usually older ones. The grapevine for seditious ideas, such as democracy, is well-developed. The prevalence of state-run or state-censored publications in China leaves intellectuals antagonistic or critical of the current regime no choice but to pass their ideas on orally. The state is well aware of this grapevine and has implemented an equally well-developed system of spies to ferret out dissent.

For instance, I once brought a Swedish photojournalist into an empty dormitory to show him my students' living conditions. Within a few hours, top Party officials at the college had already convened to discuss the matter and conduct an investigation which ended, oddly enough, with an all-night drinking session where the college Party chief interrogated the photojournalist. On another occasion, an American friend had his picture taken on his balcony with a female PLA soldier in uniform — who happened to be his Chinese tutor. The next day, she was brought before the commanding officer of her work unit, viciously reprimanded and reduced to tears — all for the offense of fraternizing with a foreigner while in uniform. In both cases, a passer-by had reported the activity to a Party official. With such an infrastructure of Party tattletales, there could be little open or printed discussion of democracy in rural areas.

At Taian Teachers' College, and at the other rural colleges and universities, older students who had traveled to Beijing, or had friends and relatives who had traveled abroad, carried the loosely concealed torch of democratic ideas and free-market principles that they were just beginning to understand. Cursory knowledge of 'Western' ideas led to an odd half-ignorance about the dangers of such thinking in a totalitarian state. It also led to a dim understanding of democracy and the free-market economy. Countries such as the U.S., once the reviled enemies of communism, were now seen as paradisical nations where all citizens lived a charmed life of wealth and freedom. Perhaps by comparison to China, it could be said that citizens of such countries do lead such lives. Unable to explore the nitty-gritty details of life in the West, these students had no idea of popular rule or the rigors of competing in a free-market economy. Instead, the West, democracy, and capitalism were lumped together into a single icon of hope for the future of China. This icon represented liberation from all of the modern sorrows of China — from engineering a solution to the flooding of the Yellow River to the ouster of the Long March gerontocracy.

Set in Shandong Province 400 miles southwest of Beijing, and 500 miles northwest of Shanghai, Taian was the center of Taoism before the communist revolution. Its main feature is the 5,500-foot Tai Shan mountain. Tai Shan is the most important of the five sacred Taoist mountains, and is still one of the chief destinations of Chinese pilgrims seeking assurances of having a male child and a long life. Here is where Mao Tse-tung, quoting an ancient Chinese poet, said, 'The East is Red.' Confucius, who lived in nearby Qiufu, revered the mountain. Mao's infamous last wife, Jiang Qing, was born in Taian and later moved to Jinan, the provincial capital 30 miles away.

When I arrived in China in August 1988, the political situation seemed fairly stable. That is, it seemed to have reached its lowest level of entropy, and could sink no further. People seemed to accept authoritarianism as they had for thousands of years. In conversations, the verdict was that things were bad but better than during the Cultural Revolution. The only upheaval I could see on the horizon was the possibility of mass starvation brought about by the terrible state of agriculture. But when I expressed my fears people rolled their eyes and said, 'It could never be as bad as the Great Leap Forward,' and tell me how they ate leaves off trees or plucked cicadas from branches.

Perhaps the impression was different at Beijing University, or at Nanjing University, where dissent was already brewing. But from the perspective of conservative Taian, submission to the mandates of government appeared to be the norm. The political environment was still tainted with the excesses of that brutal era; it seemed to me that the mere threat of another purge was enough to frighten people into complacency. The extreme political conservatism of western Shandong placed it firmly in the context of the Communist Party's plan for economic reform without political reform.

During the cold winter of 1989, the Party appeared entrenched and self-confident. I should have remembered that traditionally, it is precisely when the ruling powers are corrupt, complacent, and self-assured that it loses the 'Mandate of Heaven' — its divine right to rule the people. The result, typically, is chaos.

In Taian the spark for demonstrations came at the beginning of May, when the central Party office in Beijing asked for reports on uprisings in the countryside. President Tang of our college, without consulting students, sent a report that Taian students disagreed with those occupying Tiananmen Square. By midnight the news reached the dormitory and there was a riot. Students broke windows, dropped furniture from the fifth story, and smashed bottles on the quad below. ('Xiaoping' can be pronounced to mean 'small bottles.') When Party officials tried to talk with the students, they were repelled by flying bottles.

The next day my wife and I were awakened by cheers and the distinctive tapping of hard shoes. About 1,000 students were marching out of the campus gate with banners, chanting 'Down with corruption!' I grabbed my bicycle and camera and followed them. They cheered me as I went past, as if I suddenly symbolized something very important. As a Westerner, I was now, in a sense, part of the icon of hope that inspired the demonstrators on Tiananmen Square, where protesters from around the country gathered.

When we reached the center of the city, several other groups from Taian's other colleges and universities joined us until there were at least 5,000 beaming faces carrying huge banners and chanting: 'No democracy — no bread,' and 'Out with Li Peng and Zhao Ziyang.' Students all over the city had been secretly mobilized in the early hours of the morning; even the Public Security Bureau and the Party spies had been caught by surprise.

At Communist Party headquarters, the students chanted and cheered as their young leaders gave pep talks encouraging the protesters to 'oppose corruption' and make the leaders accountable. No one mentioned violence or overthrowing the government. I had never seen my usually glum students so animated. The anger of the earlier part of the march was gone from their voices and was replaced with the joy of the human spirit set free.

There seemed a kind of victory when a smiling Party official ran out of the building with news that a permit had been granted to the demonstrators. This unasked-for permission seemed to renew the students' trust — after the march some of them gushed to me that the Party officials were on their side! After that, there were daily marches and classes were canceled. Most of my students went to Beijing, returning with glowing stories of how they slept in tents on Tiananmen Square and carried the banner of Taian Teachers' College in demonstrations before the Great Hall of the People. 'The soldiers are on our side!' they said. It was just chance that all of them returned before the massacre.

On June 4 my wife and I went to the Ling Yan temple, a Buddhist shrine 20 miles away. We hadn't listened to the Voice of

America that morning, and it seemed that things had begun to cool off in Beijing and life in China would slowly drift back to its normally comatose state. The excitement of May was wearing off. After our return that evening, the old man from the gate house pounded on my door, his eyes wide with fright, to tell me I had an urgent phone call. Calmly, the voice of an American friend at the mining university across town told me, 'They've done it. They opened fire on them, and ran them over with tanks.'

I rode my bike to the mining university to talk with my American friends there. As I rode, I could tell that people on the street did not yet know what happened: There was a news blackout. After several hours of listening to the VOA and BBC, I rode home through the darkness. When I came to the intersection at the center of town, I saw a crowd of about 50 young people standing on the corner staring into the empty street. I asked, 'What are you doing?' A young man turned to me and said: 'Beijing.' The dream had turned into a nightmare.

Back at the college, on a long bench next to the gate sat President Tang, Party Secretary Song, Party Secretary Cui, the head of the propaganda office, and two huge thugs from the PSB who had become familiar faces around campus since the first march. I offered a grim hello; they replied with equally grim stares. Before this night I would always be greeted with the profuse head bobbing and toothy smiles with which foreign visitors are routinely cocooned.

When I entered the classroom the next morning, I asked: 'Do you know what happened in Beijing?' Sensing that it must have been bad, the students who had just returned from the countryside, where they were helping their parents plant peanuts, fell silent. I explained carefully, then played a BBC broadcast from the night before, which concluded: 'Hundreds and possibly thousands of demonstrators were killed.' Some of my students wept, their tears staining the floor's yellow Shandong dust.

That evening a huge crowd pressed against the bars of the college gates trying to get in. The news had finally spread to all the colleges and universities. The gate broke open and the crowd surged across the campus to the dormitory. There were no more slogans, just strangled cries of anger. (Only one teacher at our college brave enough to march with the students. The others had either been silent, or made a public show of denouncing the pro-democracy movement.)

The crowd roared in anger and hatred and started a small fire in the debris which had been thrown out of the six-story dormitory during several recent riots. A student from the Shandong Medical University in Jinan told me that young people were being arrested at the Jinan train station. Many students hid in the toilets when the train stopped in Jinan and continued on until Taian. (Later there would be an armored personnel carrier and troops with automatic weapons standing guard along the only road between the two cities, searching for students.) He also told me that he saw enraged residents of Beijing swarm an armored personnel carrier and kill the soldiers inside after a woman had been shot on her balcony. We watched for a hour. No one seemed to know what to do. The students howled and screeched in rage — I could see what would lead the people of Beijing to tear soldiers to pieces. Finally, a decision seemed to have been made, and the crowd surged out the gate. Returning to my house, I hid in some shrubs and watched the PSB men look into my windows.

After the massacre, a government news blackout forced people to turn to VOA and BBC broadcasts. The blackout finally ended June 8 when Premier Li Peng appeared on CCTV to deny reports of large-scale killing. On the same day the VOA, BBC, and Radio Taiwan all reported that the Chinese Red Cross estimated 2,600 dead. We waited in grim curiosity for the CCTV English news at 10 p.m. to tell us the latest government version. Instead of news, there was an eerie documentary detailing funeral rites of an ethnic minority. Five minutes into the program, the picture cut to a large red cross for a few seconds, perhaps a sign of continued resistance to Party censorship and propaganda.

Thus ended Taian Spring.

Since the communist revolution in 1949, the Chinese people have never had the freedom to choose from independent sources of information. Contrary to Deng Xiaoping's famous dictum, 'Seek truth from facts,' they must seek facts from wall posters, rumors, and the shadows and whispers of the government-controlled media.

When Beijing declared martial law on May 19, the news reader on the government-run China Central Television didn't look up from his script. Everyone in my work unit noticed. Before then, reports on CCTV and in newspapers about demonstrations in Beijing and elsewhere seemed more or less honest, even sympathetic to the demonstrations. Then the news suddenly turned into warnings from the Party against 'anti-revolutionary activity.' After troops occupied newspaper offices and television stations, there was no more honesty in reporting. The *China Daily* said June 3 that travel in the capital was 'normal' and that the 'personal safety of...tourists is guaranteed.'

In Taian and elsewhere before the massacre, students went to Beijing by free rail to gather unofficial information from big-character posters at Beijing University and Tiananmen. When they returned, they copied this information onto large posters and glued them to 'democracy walls' in a low-tech challenge to the official line. In Taian, students inked posters with names of Party officials involved in *guandao*, or profiteering. One showed caricatures of Deng Xiaoping and Li Peng gorging themselves from a banquet table shaped like China. Plainclothes police promptly tore it down.

Walls along the streets also became showplaces for poetry. This particular poem — a favorite with students at my college — appeared before the massacre:

> If you want to kill the people,
> you must have one billion bullets.
> If you imprison the students,
> you must have a jail the size of China.
> If you want to use tear gas
> don't lose your own consciousness.
> If you want to kill us with swords,
> please do,
> but don't build a big tomb for yourself.

Students also tried to spread the news by rigging loudspeakers in the cafeteria to broadcast Mandarin-language VOA during dinner. This outraged local Party officials, who removed the loudspeakers. (The students responsible for the broadcasts fled to the countryside.) Party members were forbidden to listen to radio from Taiwan, the VOA, or the BBC; English teachers who used the radio in their lessons were ordered to cancel their classes.

In the villages, students who had returned home to spread the word found that family and friends already were convinced of the Party's version of the 'truth' about the pro-democracy movement. Conditions are ideal for the rapid deployment of propaganda in China; in the evenings, dozens of villagers gather together to watch the news with a level of attention and credulity inconceivable to Westerners. It was easy enough for CCTV to show highly selective footage of violence against soldiers and government property and present that as the whole truth.

My students, however, believed China was in severe economic and political trouble, despite the propaganda. They saw no future for China under the current regime; democracy, they believed, was the only possible beginning on the road to solving China's problems. That belief will sow the seeds of another, perhaps more successful, Taian Spring.

PART FOUR
CHINA REACTS

Tiananmen and the Rule of Law

JEROME ALAN COHEN

ONE of the most significant costs of the June 1989 slaughter and subsequent repression in China has been the enormous harm done to the legal system that the People's Republic had been laboriously constructing since the death of Chairman Mao and the arrest of the 'Gang of Four' ended the Cultural Revolution in the autumn of 1976.

Achievements of 1979–89

Ironically, it was Deng Xiaoping's ascendancy to power in late 1978 that began to translate popular revulsion against the lawlessness of earlier eras into legislation that promised not only the suppression of crime but also the protection of individuals against arbitrary official actions. It was also Deng who recognized law's contribution to China's economic development and to the foreign business cooperation that is indispensable to the nation's modernization and to social progress. And he saw the need for government and Communist Party constitutions that would inspire confidence, both at home and abroad, in the rationality, predictability, and legitimacy of the leaders' exercise of political power.

There followed a remarkable decade of progress toward creating a credible rule of law.[1] In addition to constitutional and organizational reforms, a flood of criminal, commercial, and administrative laws emanated from a National People's Congress (NPC) that showed signs of abandoning its role as the Party's rubber stamp. Courts and arbitration institutions, judges, procurators, lawyers, and notaries, as well as legislative draftsmen, legal administrators, and enterprise counsel, tentatively groped toward professional autonomy, nourished by recently revived legal education and scholarship.

Judicial review of the legality of administrators' decisions — a truly revolutionary concept in Chinese society — was an idea whose time had come. Shortly before the spring demonstrations began, the PRC's first administrative procedure law was enacted, after many years of careful study and debate.[2] Even the feared public security agency could be taken to court, and this was hesitantly beginning to happen.[3] The NPC was even on the verge of abolishing the amorphous offense of 'counterrevolution,' as a courageous group of law reformers publicly proclaimed the dangers of such an arbitrary tool and its unsuitability for the new era.[4]

To be sure, there had been occasional serious setbacks. For example, not long after the enactment of the PRC's first codes of criminal law and procedure in 1979, the NPC Standing Committee adopted special rules to restrict some of the protections of the accused enshrined in the new codes.[5] Thus, before memories had faded of the Wei Jingsheng case and the other political trials that had immediately preceded the new codes, these special rules made it clear that the criminal codes did not preclude continuing Party use of the judicial weapon that is the prerequisite to the severest punishments and formal stigmatization as a 'counter-revolutionary' criminal.

Moreover, at the same time, the State Council reaffirmed the power of police-dominated local committees to ignore the criminal process and the courts and instead to confine people for up to four years for vaguely defined 'non-criminal' offenses. Legislation confirming continuation of the notorious *lao-jiao* (rehabilitation through labor) provided a 'safety valve' to officials who otherwise might have felt hampered by the criminal codes and a warning to citizens who otherwise might have sought to restore Democracy Wall.[6] And the manner in which Party General Secretary Hu Yaobang was forced to resign from office in 1987 raised significant doubts about whether the Party constitution had been respected.

Nevertheless, the overall direction was positive. Law reform was, on the whole, playing an important role in restoring popular support for the regime by reducing the scope of arbitrary political power, facilitating economic activity, promoting China's business cooperation with other countries, and enhancing social progress.

Manipulation of public law

The Tiananmen tragedy gravely damaged this nascent legal system, documenting the current leaders' low regard for law even while they professed to observe it. When their own political survival was at stake, they respected the rules of neither the Party nor the state.

Indeed, recent events revealed what the sacking of Hu Yaobang had implied — that, even after the death of Mao Tse-tung, the modern world's most famous proponent of lawlessness, the Party has secretly operated on an illegitimate basis. Perhaps the purged Party chief Zhao Ziyang's gravest offense was his confirmation to Mikhail Gorbachev and the rest of us in May that, contrary to the Party Constitution, Deng has enjoyed veto power over major decisions.

Further irregularities of Party rule soon surfaced as Deng moved to overcome the political paralysis induced by the popular demonstrations. It was apparently his ad hoc group of largely retired Party elders — not the badly divided but ostensibly all-powerful Politburo Standing Committee — that finally decided that martial law had to be declared.

In securing the necessary government declaration of martial law, the Deng group, despite a pretense of respecting formalities, showed little more concern for the government's rules of procedure than the Party's. Under the State Constitution, a decision of the NPC Standing Committee is required to place all of Beijing under martial law.[7] Although there was time to convene a meeting of the NPC Standing Committee, the Deng group could not be certain of the outcome. So it decided to invoke martial law in only parts of Beijing, an action that, under the Constitution, could be taken by the State Council, China's highest executive agency, which is more shielded from public view than the NPC.[8]

Actually, however, the martial law decree that was issued covered all of urban Beijing as well as several of its suburban districts but not its rural counties, complying with the letter of the Constitution but not its spirit.[9] Moreover, it is seriously open to question whether the decree signed by Premier Li Peng in the name of the State Council was approved as required by law. As far as outside observers can determine, neither the entire State Council nor its Executive Committee, consisting of the Premier, the Deputy Premiers, all of the State Councilors, and the Secretary General of the State Council, seem to have voted on the decree, again because of the difficulty of winning agreement from a properly constituted body.[10]

The NPC Standing Committee had the legal power to override the questionable State Council decree, and many in China hoped it would. Indeed, on three separate occasions members of the NPC Standing Committee petitioned its leadership to call a meeting to consider what action was appropriate to the crisis. Yet, despite NPC Chairman Wan Li's dramatic return to China on May 25 from his visit to the U.S., the NPC Standing Committee was not allowed to convene until June 29 because the Party Central Committee had not yet played its part in the drama. The Central Committee itself had not been allowed to meet until its reluctant members had been 'persuaded' to endorse Deng's decisions, including the ouster of Zhao Ziyang. By the time the Central Committee acted, the NPC Standing Committee was prepared to do Deng's bidding and did.

The process of persuading reluctant members of the Central Committee and the NPC Standing Committee was facilitated by their awareness that Party General Secretary Zhao himself had been detained, that a reign of terror already had begun to punish dissenters, including Party members, and that Zhao supporters within the elite, like Zhao himself, might well be branded 'counterrevolutionaries.'

Subtler pressures prevailed over other members of the elite, as Deng tried to stitch together a consensus among a fragmented leadership. For example, when one important member of the Party's influential Central Advisory Commission was consulted about whether he had any objections to the harsh measures Deng was proposing to end the crisis, he grudgingly decided to keep silent. 'What was my father to do?' one of his children later asked me rhetorically. 'He's an old, sick man. If he spoke out, he could have lost his pension, his house, his car, everything, and his children would have had no future.'

Abuses of the criminal process

The recent reign of terror has demonstrated how little the guarantees embodied in the 1979 codes of criminal law and procedure and China's adherence to the U.N. convention against torture can mean for those accused of 'counterrevolution.'[11] Deng, Peng Zhen, and other elderly leaders, who in the 1950s had mastered the techniques of cloaking political repression in forms of law lacking in substance, have reverted to familiar techniques.[12]

During the crucial pre-indictment detention and interrogation period, suspects have once again been unprotected against beating, torture, and public humiliation by the police.[13] Nor have they been guaranteed opportunity to consult with family, friends, or a lawyer while in custody. Endless repetition of the infamous maxim: 'Leniency for those who confess; severity for those who resist' has helped to break their resistance.

Once formally charged, the accused may have a lawyer assist him, but he and his counsel have frequently been given insufficient time to prepare a defense against 'facts' presented by a regime determined to blame the victims for the massacre. Overwhelming pressures have often been mobilized to convince the isolated defendant that exercise of his right to counsel at the trial would only assure him harsher punishment as a recalcitrant who refuses to mend his ways. And trials have generally been conducted in a coercive environment before judges who once again are being ordered to serve as instruments of the state and 'class struggle.'

Following conviction, the accused has a right to appeal. Yet, since appeal has often been portrayed by his jailers as the last refuge of a scoundrel and a futile, indeed counter-productive, gesture, it has not been unusual for defendants to be denied this right in practice.

In the period immediately after June 4, sentences have frequently been pronounced at mass rallies. After all, since the Constitution guarantees a public trial, what could be more public than parading an accused before 10,000 people in a stadium? Nevertheless, the actual trial of 'political' cases has often been held in secret or in front of a restricted audience. Although a senior spokesman for the PRC judiciary has denied this, he did not articulate his definition of 'public trial.' Since he also claimed that 'Chinese law has defined counter-revolutionary crime very precisely,' perhaps he was not using words in their commonly understood sense.[14]

The first few weeks after June 4 witnessed an enormous emphasis upon swift as well as harsh punishment. If, as the Anglo-American maxim goes, 'justice delayed is justice denied,' who can complain if only four days elapse between arrest and a death sentence? Certainly not the executed defendant. One had to bear in mind, after all, that many persons had been summarily gunned down on the street by a regime that has yet to enact legislation defining the contents of martial law.

This highly publicized judicial blitz — so reminiscent of the mass political movements of the '50s and '60s except for the increased intensity made possible by nationwide television — soon achieved the desired effect on a quickly cowed population. Then, as it became clear that the revamped leadership had literally engaged in 'overkill,' law enforcement quietly went underground in an effort to diminish shock and outrage at home and abroad.

Moreover, the nature of the regime's law enforcement concerns began to change. Emphasis gradually shifted from charges of violence by workers and the unemployed to cases of non-violent expression of 'counterrevolutionary' ideas by intellectuals, students, and workers who had been active as organizers, speakers, and writers during the spring demonstrations.

No one could condemn the PRC police for processing these cases of non-violent expression in undue haste. They have instead indulged in the opposite vice, detaining thousands of suspects for what at this writing is already more than half a year without bringing charges against them and thereby entitling them to make a defense with the assistance of counsel. Further, when under the pressure of the protests and economic sanctions imposed by Western governments, the Ministry of Public Security has released suspects instead of prosecuting them, PRC media have often erroneously identified these people as 'lawbreakers,' thereby unfairly complicating their return to jobs, education, and society.[15]

Tiananmen and legislation

Yet not all the gains made by the legal system since 1979 have been eroded. First of all, not only responsible judicial and legislative officials but also the nation's highest leaders, including the new Party General Secretary Jiang Zemin, have repeatedly stressed the importance of further developing the legal system. Even Prime Minister Li Peng, who at first seemed allergic to such references, has joined the chorus. In late November 1989, for example, he urged the nation's procurators to protect citizens' legal rights while cracking down on criminals,[16] and in January 1990 he encouraged directors of provincial judicial bureaus to strengthen legal training.[17] No People's Daily editorial writers of the current period have echoed the line taken by their Cultural Revolution predecessors 'in praise of lawlessness.' They oppose 'the search for paradise in bourgeois liberty, democracy, and law,' but they also oppose the lawlessness of the 'ultra-democracy or anarchism' of the Cultural Revolution.

The current leaders' definition of 'strengthening the legal system,' however, seems all too similar, for example, to that of Burma's repressive military rulers, who constantly promote law and

order the more ruthlessly to suppress free expression and democratic elections. Li Peng's idea of legal training for judges
would make them 'effective in understanding and settling issues
in keeping with the views of Marxism–Leninism–Mao Tse-tung
thought. Priority should be given to political quality in the
training of justice officials.'[18]

We should recall that, at the height of the Soviet Union's
bloodiest purges, Stalin solemnly proclaimed: 'Stability of the laws
we now need more than ever.'[19] Stalin was advocating a more
efficient legislative process, recognizing, as did Lenin and many
other dictators, the value of legislation in assuring nationwide
enforcement of their will.

Beginning with the spate of martial law decrees on May 19, the
Deng-Yang-Li leadership was quick to exploit the legislative
weapon to promote the restoration of superficial stability. After
June 4, one immediate product of their concerns was the NPC's
new national law, ostensibly designed to assure the masses full
power to engage in rallies and public demonstrations under
appropriate conditions, but which plainly lends itself to the frustration of this constitutionally guaranteed right.[20] The State Council promulgated a regulation that reaches the boundaries of the
absurd in circumscribing the legitimate activities of foreign journalists in order to further diminish their possibilities for learning
the true state of affairs in China.[21] Characteristically, the regime
advertised the regulation as necessary 'to promote international
exchanges and the spread of information, supervise the activities of
foreign journalists and resident foreign news organs on Chinese
territory, and help them carry out their assignments.'[22] After June
4, in accordance with guiding principles laid down by the Party's
Central Committee and the State Council, the Ministry of Culture
and the State Administration for News and Publications issued a
number of notices imposing strict new controls upon the publishing of books and periodicals under a law enacted in 1988.[23]
Local lawmaking organs, authorized by the national legislation to
issue implementing rules, have shown similar preoccupations in all
these matters.[24]

Yet the priorities of the legislative process have not entirely
shifted to repressive enactments. Much of the pre-Tiananmen lawmaking work of the NPC and the State Council has continued.
Efforts to draft new laws regulating urban residents' committees,
city planning, and environmental protection were well under way
long before their post-June 4 enactment.[25]

In certain respects, in fact, recent political events have stimulated progress with respect to drafts of business-related laws that had become mired in political/bureaucratic quicksand. For example, revisions to the 1979 Chinese-Foreign Equity Joint Venture Law that had been promised but failed to appear at the 1989 session of the NPC were finalized for promulgation at the 1990 session, in an effort to reinvigorate the sagging spirits of foreign investors and their governments.[26] Similarly, efforts have accelerated to complete the long-awaited and controversial copyright law in order to improve China's tarnished image as a responsible participant in the world's quickly expanding economic cooperation as well as win the support of Chinese authors.[27] Other new laws concerning foreign trade, amendments to the income tax regime affecting foreign firms, maritime matters, and foreign exchange control are also expected soon.[28]

Nor has previous interest disappeared in enacting other laws to stimulate domestic economic reforms. With occasional assistance from the World Bank, the U.N., and foreign legal experts, efforts continue to draft over 30 much-needed laws, including those to regulate companies, banks, railways, and unfair competition.[29] PRC specialists still meet regularly to develop plans for the establishment of full-fledged stock exchanges to replace the limited, simple experiments conducted to date. Obviously stimulated by recent events and an understandable concern that worsening economic conditions may lead to more widespread and severe demonstrations by China's urban workers, the PRC has announced that it is speeding up preparation of the country's first comprehensive set of labor laws in order to alleviate the many existing grievances of the proletariat and 'ensure that laborers enjoy the masters' role in the country.'[30]

Even more importantly, steps are being taken systematically to implement the administrative procedure law, the many foreign-related trade laws and other norms issued prior to Tiananmen. Concerning the administrative procedure law, the Bureau of Legal Affairs of the State Council recently announced that 'government officials across the country are alerting themselves to administrative malpractices which may bring them to court and are getting prepared to defend themselves.'[31] Even the Ministry of Public Security is reported to be conducting a thorough check of current police activity to correct illegal actions before the administrative procedure law takes effect 1 October 1990, a task so awesome that it presumably will leave little time for further pursuit of 'counter-revolutionaries!' And, obviously anticipating a flood of lawsuits by individuals denied their freedom, the ministry has instructed local Public Security Bureaus to establish reviewing offices to answer complaints and to hire legal consultants.[32]

So upset has the Ministry of Foreign Economic Relations and Trade (MOFERT) become by the widespread violations of the PRC's trade-related legislation by officials and state enterprises that at the end of 1989 it launched a campaign 'to instill a sense of law among the nation's almost 6,000 trade firms and thousands of provincial officials in charge of the businesses.' The campaign is supposed to awaken them to 'the possibility of a trade crisis if they continue to ignore laws and regulations in dealing with foreign business people.' Appropriately disturbed by the mind-boggling fact that 'only 60 percent of China's foreign trade contracts were actually carried out' in 1988, MOFERT officials inveighed against excessive administrative interference with existing laws and regulations and urged the Chinese business community to overcome its ignorance of the rules of the game.[33]

My own experience after Tiananmen has offered evidence that many officials have continued to take seriously their duty to apply new laws governing the conduct of their agencies. For example, the General Administration of Customs in Beijing investigated and criticized Shanghai customs authorities under their jurisdiction for erroneously accusing a foreigner of possessing illegal drugs, even before foreign lawyers complained about the matter. And the State Administration of Import and Export Commodity Inspection has welcomed a foreign request to investigate the issuance of a false inspection report by a provincial agency in its system.

Thus the post-June 4 experience with the preparation and implementation of legislation demonstrates that large areas of legal activity have continued to develop despite the leadership's distortion of the PRC's constitutional norms and its criminal laws in the hope of clinging to power. What can one say about the impact of Tiananmen upon the legal institutions that are supposed to have the principal burden of applying the laws?

Tiananmen and legal institutions

In the communist world the 'people's procuracy' is supposed to be the 'watchdog of legality,' not only deciding whether the state should institute criminal prosecutions but also generally supervising the conduct of government officials to ensure that their actions conform to constitutional and legislative provisions. The procuracy has plainly not fulfilled this role during the massive repression triggered by the Tiananmen massacre. Instead it has been an active participant in the continuing campaign.

Nevertheless, like the PRC's other legal institutions, it has not abandoned its goals. For example, in January 1990 the Supreme Peoples' Procuracy announced to the Beijing press corps that it had just issued an edict setting forth standards that would enhance the procuratorial department's protection of citizens' democratic rights and rights of the person. The procuracy's spokesman emphasized that, among the violations of individual rights that the procuracy is authorized to pursue directly, that is, without depending on the police, are cases of coerced confessions, false accusation and fabrication of evidence, unlawful confinement, illegal search of the person and the home, and interference with freedom of correspondence.[34]

Of course, one cannot take these assertions at face value, and much turns on the definitions accorded to these concepts. Yet, at least without greater knowledge of the actual situation — to be sure, knowledge that the regime does its best to deny its own people as well as foreign observers — it would probably be a mistake to dismiss these aspirations as merely hypocritical propaganda. Previous PRC experience suggests that the procuracy may well be striving to achieve these goals within the limits of political acceptability as prescribed by the controlling Party organization, that is, in ordinary criminal cases and to some extent even in sensitive political cases.

The people's courts are, of course, the vortex of the shifting pressures and tensions that have marked the always strained relations between politics and law in China. The sacking of Zhao Ziyang as the Party's General Secretary put an end to the most promising effort in PRC history to free the judiciary from Party domination and to give meaning to the constitutional prohibition against interference by any organization or person with the independent operation of the courts.

Prior to Zhao's ouster, as part of the reform of the political system launched by him and his group, an impressive effort was under way to remove the courts and the procuracy from the grasp of the political-legal committees and full-time Party secretaries responsible for behind-the-scenes coordination of the ostensibly independent legal institutions. Legal experts, even some associated with such traditional Party strongholds as People's University, openly condemned Party control as a violation of the Constitution, of legislation governing judicial procedures and of the principles of socialist democracy and legality.[35] By the beginning of 1989, most provincial and local political-legal committees were reportedly abolished.[36]

Just as the 1957–58 'anti-rightist' movement presided over by Deng Xiaoping put an end to the demands for legality voiced during the 'Hundred Flowers Bloom' period, so too the campaign to crush the 'turmoil' and 'rebellion' at Tiananmen shattered the hopes of those who had recently sought to achieve a genuine rule of law. Soon after June 4, events left no doubt that, according to the Party line, the pre-eminent task of the courts in the new era is swiftly and harshly to punish 'counterrevolution.' The judiciary's nominal chief, Supreme People's Court President Ren Jianxin, a member of the Party Central Committee, participates in the central Party political-legal committee together with the Procurator General, the Minister of Public Security and the Minister of State Security under the leadership of Qiao Shi, a member of the Standing Committee of the Politburo and also head of the Party's Central Commission for Disciplinary Inspection. President Ren lost no time in calling for merciless implementation of the new Party line in both public and unpublicized instructions, with consequences that were soon all too apparent.[37]

By the autumn, however, the leadership, as part of its damage limitation effort, wished to show a more benign, acceptable face to the world. Thus, in October 1989, President Ren gave an interview to the English-language *China Daily* summing up 40 years of judicial accomplishments. Innocent readers might have wondered whether Tiananmen had ever happened. 'At present, the People's Courts center their work on serving the economic construction and the reform program,' said the president, totally ignoring the ongoing campaign to use the criminal process against thousands of students, intellectuals, and workers whose only 'crime' in most cases was to have expressed their disapproval of government policies.[38] Nor would one have guessed that, in addition to their then unspoken but continuing preoccupation with the suppression of 'counterrevolution,' the courts were about to play a key role in a new campaign aginst 'the six evils' — prostitution, pornography, abduction of women and children, drugs, gambling, and superstition.

President Ren went on to tell his interlocutor: 'Our country is turning from one which is ruled mainly by government and Party policies to one chiefly administered by laws.' According to the *China Daily* reporter, Ren claimed that 'Chinese judges observe the rules, such as exercising their adjudicating powers independently, considering all citizens and nationalities as equal before the law, basing their judgments on facts, and regarding the Constitution and law as yardsticks.'[39] Nowhere in the long interview is there any reference to the Party political-legal committees that were being restored at every court level, nor did Ren mention the implications of the recently revived Maoist doctrine of 'class struggle' for the judges' guaranty of equality before the law.

In January 1990, however, when President Ren opened the 15th national judicial conference, the tone and content of his report to a home audience were very different. He took great pains to emphasize that, in exercising their power to conduct adjudication independently, the courts must do so under the leadership of the Party. Insisting on Party leadership of judicial work is the way to supervise and support the courts in their independent decision-making to guarantee the implementation of the law, he said, apparently without attempting to explain the logic of that assertion. Because there are hostile criminal forces not only at home but also abroad, including subversive elements advocating China's 'peaceful evolution,' Ren claimed that it is necessary to continue with the 'people's democratic dictatorship.' The People's Courts, he mentioned, are a major instrument of the people's democratic dictatorship that must never relax their struggle against 'counter-revolutionaries' and other serious offenders. The courts must never forget that, 'within certain perimeters, class struggle will exist for a long time.'[40]

In a masterpiece of understatement, Ren told his colleagues that 'the People's Courts' independent exercise of their power of adjudication in accordance with law is fundamentally different from the judicial independence of bourgeois countries.' The courts in China, he said, must accept Party leadership. 'It is a mistake to think that, because there is the law, justice can be executed without the guidance of the policies' of the party. Ren stated that 'in the course of last year's counterrevolutionary rebellion, some people hoisted the flag of "judicial independence." In actual fact, these people were advocating the concept of the "the tripartite division of power" of the bourgeois class. They were opposed to the principle of the Chinese Communist Party's leadership of judicial work.'[41]

This renewed emphasis on dictatorship, class struggle, and Party control of the courts is a return to principles that were clearly articulated more than 30 years ago by the victors in the 'anti-rightist' movement.[42] They were debated again during the halcyon days of 1978–79, as officials and scholars pondered the relationship between post-Mao reforms and continuing Party authority. At least during those periods of the 1980s when the reformers were in the ascendant, considerable progress was made toward acceptance of the idea that Party officials should not interfere in the determination of concrete court cases, and Zhao Ziyang's abolition of most political-legal committees seemed to be realizing that idea in practice.[43]

The full text of President Ren's report to the 1990 judicial conference has not been available. His published remarks did not explicitly endorse a return to Party dictation of specific court judgments. This was clearly implied, however, and indeed it is the obvious reason for reinstituting political-legal committees at every level. If judges are to be free to apply Party policies to the facts of each case, there would be no need for an apparatus on every court level that is evidently designed to deal with specific cases. Ren, who has spent most of his distinguished career not as a judge but as director of the Law Department of the China Council for the Promotion of International Trade, is too sensitive to the standards of foreign lawyers to discuss so indelicate a topic openly.

Nevertheless, his colleague in the central Party political-legal committee, Procurator General Liu Fuzhi, did not hesitate to state in his own report: 'For important circumstances and difficult cases, we must report to the Party and Government leadership.'[44] Although bourgeois lawyers can readily understand why judges should remain more aloof from the political leadership than procurators, the procuracy and the courts enjoy virtually similar positions in China's constitutional structure, and there is little doubt that in the current circumstances the courts, which like the procuracy are largely staffed by Party members, many of whom are former policemen or soldiers, similarly recognize the benefits of the Party's concrete guidance in important criminal cases.

Yet, just as the situation in the legislative and administrative organs and the procuracy does not represent a total setback for the legal system, the situation in the judiciary is not devoid of hope for growth of the rule of law in the many areas that are not bound up with the fragile political position of the leadership. As Ren's October 1989 interview with the *China Daily* made clear, the judiciary has made a genuine leap forward in recent years in the professional sophistication with which it handles civil, economic, administrative, and maritime cases, and even criminal cases of a non-political nature.[45] To be sure, prior to Tiananmen, apart from politics, the courts were struggling not only with the huge obstacles to quickly raising the knowledge and competence of China's 125,000 judges but also with the serious problems of cronyism and corruption. After Tiananmen those struggles continue, with only modest enduring distraction from the intensive political indoctrination to which all court officials, like all other officials, have been subjected.

Resort to the PRC courts was never an attractive prospect, even during the heyday of the Zhao Ziyang reforms, but, except for litigants suspected of opposition to the regime, it is not significantly less attractive since June 4. In fact, at least in cases involving foreigners and perhaps also in those involving ordinary Chinese, the felt need of judges to demonstrate that Tiananmen has not deprived them of all professional autonomy may give them an incentive to put their best foot forward in the new era, just as some administrative officials have done.

Whatever the role of the courts of late, from professional experience I can testify that the PRC's foremost institution for resolving foreign-related business disputes — the China International Economic and Trade Arbitration Commission (CIETAC) — has continued to function in an objective fashion. In one case, the final hearing of which was held just six weeks after Tiananmen, the conduct of the three Chinese arbitrators and their supporting staff could in no way be distinguished from their earlier competent performance, despite the audible presence of the martial law forces doing their physical exercises in a nearby courtyard. Subsequent experience with CIETAC has been equally impressive.

This is not to say that CIETAC is divorced from its environment. When after June 4 its Beijing headquarters belatedly implemented the PRC's welcome 1988 decision to invite a number of foreign lawyers to join its panel of potential arbitrators, it excluded from its final list certain specialists who have on occasion been deemed unduly critical of the PRC's legal progress.

The impact of Tiananmen on lawyers in PRC law firms has been considerably less than on their counterparts in the procuracy and the judiciary.[46] To be sure, lawyers, in the view of orthodox Party leaders, including Qiao Shi, have always been regarded as 'state legal workers,' despite the fact that they are not officials and have sought to develop an independent status during the decade since the revival of the legal profession. After June 4, members of law firms in urban areas where demonstrations had occurred had to undergo the same processes of investigation and indoctrination as those in all other units, as the Party sought to separate the goats from the sheep. Assuming that their activities during the spring events did not lead to their detention and that the process of *biaotai* (expressing their political attitude toward the upheaval by submitting written and oral statements concerning their conduct and viewpoint) did not lead the Ministry of Justice to doubt their loyalty to the current leaders of the Party and the state, lawyers have been able to pursue their professional business. For those who have not been involved in criminal defense work, this has meant that they were able to carry on as before June 4 in legal matters relating to property, family, inheritance, commercial transactions, administrative grievances, and other problems. Their daily work giving advice, negotiating contracts, mediating disputes, and taking part in lawsuits has remained largely unaffected by politics.

Lawyers who handle criminal defense work, however, have been exposed to the full force of the new Party line whenever they have participated in political cases. Called into a case only after criminal investigation has been completed and formal charges have been filed by the procuracy, given little time and facilities to prepare a defense, operating in a coercive arena on behalf of a client who has often been intimidated by his jailers, and aware of the hazards of waging too vigorous a defense, even the most conscientious lawyer has very limited scope if he wishes to retain his position. Their task is a formidable one not only in cases related to Tiananmen but also in those that may be the subject of any other political movement, such as the current campaign against 'the six evils.'

Tiananmen, legal education, and legal research

Turning from practice to theory, we find a similar situation prevailing in legal education and research. There is no doubt that certain aspects of this domain have been profoundly affected. Yet it is also clear that, thus far at least, some activities remain relatively untouched by the return to politics-in-command.[47]

A number of law faculty members and students, of course, were detained by the police on and after June 4. After months of incommunicado detention, some have been released, often still under a political cloud despite failure to prosecute them. Yet many others are still confined, their fate unknown. Certain younger instructors have been sacked or relieved of their duties, and school administrators have been valiantly struggling to retain both their positions and their self-respect as they mediate between political pressures from above and faculty and students below, amid great tension and uncertainty. Some law teachers, administrators, and students who were scheduled to return home from abroad decided to extend their foreign sojourns following the massacre. Some who had not intended to go abroad for the academic year 1989–90 were suddenly inspired to do so after June 4, and managed to get out. Some law teachers who had been accepted for foreign research and study prior to June 4 were not permitted to leave.

In the classroom, professors of constitutional law and legal theory and their students have plainly lost even their earlier restricted freedom to discuss and criticize. Those who insist on endorsing, for example, the application to China of Montesquieu's theory of the separation of powers, a view that Deng Xiaoping has long condemned as the class essence of bourgeois liberalism, now might risk unemployment or even life in a labor camp. Secret police 'spies' are thought to report on such classes.

Outside their individual classrooms, law students and faculty have been convened en masse for lengthy 'sober introspection' sessions concerning last spring's events, supposedly inspired by their compulsory study of the latest documents of the Party Central Committee and important speeches of the leadership. As reported in a major article in the *People's Daily* entitled 'Why Did Those Who Study the Law Violate the Law?' from this introspection students 'have come to realize the truth about the whole series of events, from the Student Movement, to the turmoil, to the counterrevolutionary riot. Drawing a lesson from a bitter experience, some students deeply felt that they themselves, as students of law, had failed the ultimate test in a political storm.' Describing the situation at the China University of Political Science and Law (CUPSL), which is under the direct supervision of the Ministry of Justice, the author of this article claimed that 'bourgeois liberalism has infiltrated the Marxist-Leninist legal front, weakened education and the study of Marxism and Leninism, and prevented people from using the class viewpoint to analyze the concepts of bourgeois democracy, liberty, and the legal system.'[48]

As this essay implies, not all students at CUPSL have seen the light, and steps have reportedly been taken to bar those who fail their political tests from moving from the undergraduate program to graduate study. By the same token, under new government rules, students who are regarded as politically deficient can also anticipate being denied the opportunity for study abroad, no matter how brilliant their academic records. Moreover, the president of CUPSL, Jiang Ping, one of China's leading law reformers, was sacked from his administrative position for reportedly refusing to make a self-criticism before the students regarding his opposition to the regime's repression.

Nevertheless, the bulk of law teaching, dealing with civil, economic, administrative, and even criminal law, remains largely untouched by Tiananmen, and much the same can be said about legal research. Books and articles continue to appear, discussing a plethora of important technical problems confronted by every developing legal system, although manuscripts on sensitive topics, including some challenging certain conservative attitudes toward the relation of law to economic as well as political reforms, remain in the author's study, awaiting the return of a more congenial climate.[49] Much research is still under way, a good deal of it of practical nature tied to law reform projects.

To be sure, as in other highly politicized periods, the post-June 4 law reviews make a bow to the new era by leading off with ideological pieces, often by high legal officials. Essays such as "In the realm of jurisprudence, strengthen the Four Cardinal Principles [of party domination] and oppose bourgeois liberalism'[50] hammer home the new Party line. The magazines then go on to present more substantive essays, usually avoiding anything that would challenge the prevailing orthodoxy in sensitive areas of public law. Since June 4, in publication as in teaching, the word has gone out to deal less with foreign legal systems, to refrain from praising them, and to avoid negative comparisons to China.

Conclusion

The implications of these sad actions are profound. By so belatedly and inadequately seeking to rationalize their exercise of raw power, China's current leaders have undermined their right to rule. By intimidating intellectuals and officials, they have denied their country the ideas and innovations of its most talented people and exacerbated already widespread feelings of injustice, hopelessness, and cynicism. By blatantly distorting facts and manipulating law and the legal system, they have devalued the currency of not only their country's domestic legislation and institutions but also its international agreements and made mockery of the Basic Law painstakingly debated and drafted to assure Hongkong's autonomy after 1997. And, in the eyes of foreign individuals, companies, and governments, all these actions make China a riskier place, a less trustworthy partner.

Yet Tiananmen has not undone all the achievements of the last decade's law reform efforts and turned back the clock to the nihilism and chaos of the Cultural Revolution. Much useful legislation continues to be enacted and implemented. Although legal institutions have been crippled, they continue to function and develop in non-political fields, and even today's truncated legal education and scholarship will keep alive legal ideas and goals despite the politicized environment.

China's current leaders, while ruthlessly manipulating the nation's public law and criminal justice systems to maintain themselves in power, have sought to contain the fallout from their actions by preserving the role of law in promoting economic growth, international business cooperation, and social stability. Moreover, the broad spectrum of China's elite that is unhappy with the tragic events of 1989 has been striving, often in subtle ways, to limit the damage to the extent possible without risking confrontation with the new Party line.

All these factors offer some consolation to those who, despite all the disappointments of China's modern experience, still hope for the establishment of a rule of law there. We should recall that, even during the darkest days of Stalin's terror, in non-political fields the legislative process, legal institutions, and education and research in law persisted to a surprising extent, laying the foundation for the demands and accomplishments of de-Stalinization and for the more significant law reforms at present under way in the Soviet Union. If a similar foundation can continue to be erected in China, when its political pendulum next swings in a more liberal direction, the legal system will be better prepared than in the past to support that trend.

An abbreviated version of this essay appeared as 'Law and leadership in China,' *Far Eastern Economic Review*, 19 July 1989, pp. 23–24.

1. For a summary of the legal accomplishments of that period, see Jerome A. Cohen, *Contract Laws of the People's Republic of China* (Hong Kong, Longman, 1988), pp. 3–11.

2. For an excellent study of this important law, see Susan Finder, 'Like Throwing an Egg Against A Stone? Administrative Litigation in the People's Republic of China,' *Journal of Chinese Law* Vol. 3, No. 1, 1989, pp. 1–29.

3. See, *e.g.*, the discussion in Jerome A. Cohen, 'Sex, Chinese Law, and the Foreigner,' *Hong Kong Law Journal*, Vol. 18, No. 1, 1988, pp. 102, 109–110.

4. See 'Criminal Law Called to Revise,' *Beijing Review* Vol. 32, No. 17, 24–30 April 1989, p. 7.

5. For English translations by Jerome A. Cohen, Timothy A. Gelatt, and Florence M.L. Li of the codes of criminal law and procedure and the subsequent amendments restricting their protections, see *The Criminal Law and the Criminal Procedure Law of the People's Republic of China* (Beijing Foreign Languages Press, 1984).

6. See '*Guowuyuan guanyu laodong jiaoyangde buchong guiding*,' (Supplementary Provisions of the State Council Concerning Rehabilitation Through Labor), promulgated 29 November 1979, in *Zhonghua renmin gongheguo gongan faqui xuanbian* (Selected Laws and Regulations on Public Security of the People's Republic of China) (Beijing, Legal Publishing House, 1981), p. 211.

7. See the Constitution of the People's Republic of China, promulgated on 4 December, 1982 (hereafter cited as the Constitution), Art. 67 (20).

8. See the Constitution, Art. 89 (16).

9. For an English translation of the State Council's martial law decree of 20 May 1989, see *China Law and Practice*, Vol. 3, No. 5, 5 June 1989, p. 5.

10. For the text of the relevant legislation enacted by the NPC, see *Zhonghua renmin gongheguo guowuyuan zuzhifa* (Organizational Law of the State Council), 10 December 1982, in *Zhonghua renmin gongheguo zuzhi faqui xuanbian* (Selected Organizational Laws and Regulations of

the People's Republic of China) (Beijing, Economy and Science Press, 1985), pp. 77–78.

11. The text of the U.N. convention may be found in General Assembly Resolution 39/46, Annex, U.N. Doc. A/39/51, p. 197 (1984) GEHRR, p. 259.

12. For a detailed study of the evolution of China's criminal justice system in the PRC's early years, see Jerome A. Cohen, *The Criminal Process in the People's Republic of China, 1949–1963: An Introduction* (Cambridge, MA, Harvard University Press, 1968).

13. The remainder of this section in based on a sifting of myriad dispatches that have appeared in the press inside and outside of China since June 4 and information gained in confidential discussions with relatives of detained dissidents. This portrait of the criminal process has been confirmed by several recent reports, e.g. Amnesty International; Asia Watch Committee, *Punishment Season: Human Rights in China After Martial Law* (New York, 1990).

14. See 'A Chinese judge rejects Washington Post story,' *China Daily*, 31 January 1990, p. 4. That many trials of protesters have not been 'open' in the usual sense is beyond question. See, *e.g.*, Richard Bernstein, 'As the Crackdown Continues, China Starts to Seem Just Like Old Times,' *N.Y. Times*, 20 June 1989, which points out how journalists who sought to attend the trials of protesters were told that it would be 'inconvenient at present,' a phrase familiar to all China hands.

15. See, *e.g.*, 'A Chinese judge etc.,' note 14 above.

16. See 'Party head stresses stability,' *China Daily*, 28 November 1989, p. 1.

17. 'Li meets justice directors,' *China Daily*, 15 January 1990, p. 1.

18. See 'Li meets justice directors,' note 17 above.

19. Stalin's speech, delivered on 25 November 1936 before a special meeting of the 8th All Union Congress of Soviets, on the subject of the Draft Constitution of the USSR, was printed in *Pravda*, 6 December 1936. I am grateful to Professor Robert Tucker of Princeton University for the translation.

20. See *Zhonghua renmin gongheguo jihui youxing shiweifa* (The Assembly and Demonstration Law of the People's Republic of China), promulgated 31 October 1989, in *Zhonghua renmin gongheguo quowuyuan gongbao* (Gazette of the State Council of the People's Republic of China), No. 22, 1989, p. 803.

21. For an English translation of the Regulations Governing Foreign Journalists and News Organizations in China, promulgated 11 January 1990, see B.B.C. Far East Broadcast Information Service Short Wave Broadcast (S.W.B.), (Reference No.) FE 10669 B 2/7, dated 23 January 1990.

22. See 'Council approves rules on foreign journalists,' *China Daily*, 13 January 1990, p. 1.

23. See, *e.g.*, '*Wenhuabu he xinwen chubanshe lianhe fachu tongzhi, yaoqui jiaqiang shukan shichang guanli gongzuo*' (Joint Notice of the Ministry of Culture and the State Administration of News and Publications Demanding Strengthening of the Work of Managing the Books and

Periodicals Markets), reported in *Xinhua Yuebao* (New China Monthly), No. 7, 1989, p. 123.

24. See, *e.g.*, 'Tiananmen rally rules outlined,' *China Daily*, 30 December 1989, p. 3, referring to the Beijing Local Regulations for Implementation of the Law on Rallies and Demonstrations of the People's Republic of China, adopted 28 December 1989 by the Standing Committee of the Beijing Municipal People's Congress.

25. These were adopted by the Standing Committee of the NPC on 26 December 1989. See 'NPC group approves three laws,' *China Daily*, 27 December 1989, p. 1.

26. See 'Revising business laws,' *China Daily*, *Business Weekly*, 27 December 1989, p. 1.

27. See, *e.g.*, '*Zhuzuo quanfa cao'an ying guangfan zhengqiu yijian*' (Opinions should be broadly collected on the draft copyright law), *Fazhi bao* (Legal Daily), 27 December 1989, p. 1.

28. See 'Revising business laws,' note 26 above.

29. Ibid.

30. See 'China will get its first labor laws next year,' *China Daily*, 28 November 1989, p. 1.

31. See 'Citizens can sue officials under new law,' *China Daily*, 10 January 1990, p. 3.

32. Ibid.

33. See 'China calls attention to trade regulations,' *China Daily*, *Business Weekly*, 11 December 1989, p. 1.

34. See '*Baohu gongmin minzhu renshen quanli bushou qinfan*' (Protect against violations of the democratic rights and rights of the person of citizens), *Renmin ribao* (People's Daily), overseas ed., 10 January 1990, p. 4. For the text of the edict, see *Fazhi ribao* (Legal Daily), 12 January 1990, p. 2.

35. See, *e.g.*, the essay by Wang Xinxin of Chinese People's University entitled '*Sifa duli shi zhengzhi tizhi gaige zucheng bufen*' (Judicial independence is a constituent part of reform of the political system), *Shijie jingji daobao* (World Economic Herald, Shanghai), 9 January 1989, reprinted in *Faxue yuekan* (Law Monthly), No. 2, February 1989, p. 152. Articles like this eventually led to the closing of this famous newspaper after June 4.

36. See Willy Wo-Lap Lam, 'Law still the rule, but power is the principle,' *South China Morning Post*, 10 January 1990, p. 19.

37. See, *e.g.*, *Zuigao renmin fayuan yuanzhang ren jianxin zhichu, yancheng baoluan fenzi buliu houhuan, chuanmian tixian dang he quojia zhengce* (Ren Jianxin, President of the Supreme People's Court, points out that mercilessly punishing rebellious elements avoids future trouble and fully manifests the policies of the Party and the State), *Renmin ribao* (People's Daily), 16 July 1989, p. 2.

38. See 'Top judge feels law has made big gains,' *China Daily*, 3 October 1989, p. 4.

39. Ibid.

40. See '*Fayuan yao zaidang lingdaoxia yifa duli xingshi shenpanquan*' (Under the leadership of the party the courts must independently exercise

their power of adjudication in accordance with laws), *Fazhi ribao* (Legal Daily), 5 January 1990, p. 1; '*Renmin fayuan yao zijue jieshou dangde lingdao jiaqiang shenpan gongzuo wei gaige kaifang fuwu*' (To serve reform and opening the people's courts should accept party leadership with full awareness and strengthen adjudication work), *Jenmin ribao* (People's Daily) overseas ed. 5 January 1990, p. ; Willy Wo-Lap Lam, 'China puts Communist Party above rule of law,' *South China Morning Post*, 5 January 1990, p. 1; *South China Morning Post*, 5 January, 1990, p. 1; and Willy Wo-Lap Lam, 'Law still, etc.,' note 36 above.

41. See sources cited note 40 above.

42. For a study of the impact of the anti-rightist movement upon the courts, see Jerome A. Cohen, 'The Chinese Communist Party and "Judicial Independence," 1949–1959,' *Harvard Law Review*, Vol. 82, March 1969, p. 967.

43. See Willy Wo-Lap Lam, 'Law still, etc.,' note 36 above.

44. Ibid.

45. See 'Top judge, etc.,' note 38 above.

46. The comments in this paragraph and the following one are based on the author's reading of the domestic and foreign press and confidential conversations with Chinese lawyers, relatives of detained dissidents, and other Chinese nationals.

47. The comments in this section are based on press monitoring and on confidential conversations with Chinese law teachers and scholars.

48. See Gu Zu, '*Xuefade wei shenma zuole weifa shi?*' (Why Did Those Who Study the Law Violate the Law?), *Renmin ribao* (People's Daily,), 23 October 1989, p. 4. Not long after June 4, Chinese state radio led its main evening news bulletin with long quotations from an article in the Guangming Daily, the newspaper for intellectuals, written by a law professor at Chinese People's University who advocated the restoration of ideological purity. 'Calls to intensify Marxist teaching,' *South China Morning Post*, 20 June 1989, p. 7.

49. Of course, even prior to June 4 there were political restraints upon the most outspoken writers on sensitive legal topics. See, *e.g.*, Willy Wo-Lap Lam, 'Officials move to gag top scholar,' *South China Morning Post*, 24 April 1989, p. 11, detailing the harassment of Mr. Yu Haocheng, a legal scholar, editor and publisher who had published many articles calling for the rule of law and revision of the Constitution along Western lines.

50. See Cai Cheng, Minister of Justice, '*Zai faxue lingyu jianchi sixiang jiben yuanze, fandui zichan jieji ziyouhua, Faxue*' (Law Science Monthly), No. 9, 1989, pp. 1–3.

Human-Rights Exception No Longer

NIHAL JAYAWICKRAMA

SINCE April 1989, the Chinese government has committed massive violations of the fundamental rights and freedoms of its citizens. When troops were permitted to kill unarmed civilians by firing at them either at random or deliberately, by beating them with lethal weapons, or crushing them with military vehicles, in order to facilitate passage through and into public places; when the death sentence was imposed, and summarily executed, for relatively minor offenses such as 'setting fire to a train' or 'attacking a soldier'; when persons suspected of involvement in the pro-democracy movement were picked up and liquidated in secret extra-judicial executions, the right to life was violated.

When tens of thousands of persons suspected of 'anti-socialist views,' 'being hooligans,' or 'beating, smashing and looting,' were subjected to indefinite administrative detention, the right to liberty and security of person was violated.

When detainees were severely beaten by security personnel with implements such as electric cattle prods, and subjected to degrading and humiliating treatment, such as being shackled to trees, made to bow 'airline style' (kneeling with head down and arms stretched backwards), or paraded in cattle trucks along the streets with shaven heads, bound, handcuffed, and with placards around their necks, the right to freedom from torture was violated.

When the Supreme People's Court, in a circular issued on 20 June 1989, requested judicial officers to study the government's version of the events surrounding the pro-democracy movement — 'act and think in line with comrade Deng Xiaoping' and 'fully understand, through studies, that the objective of the extremely small number of people in engineering the counterrevolutionary rebellion was to strike down the Communist Party, overthrow the socialist system and subvert the People's Republic of China' — and urged that those who organized the 'counterrevolutionary propaganda' be punished 'without leniency,' the right to a fair trial by an independent, impartial tribunal, was violated.

When a 1983 Decision of the Standing Committee of the

National People's Congress on the Procedure for Rapid Adjudication of Cases Involving Criminal Elements who Seriously Endan-
ger Public Security (e.g. by bringing defendants to trial without
giving them a copy of the indictment in advance, without giving
advance notice of the trial, and without affording access to a
lawyer before the trial begins, in cases where 'the main criminal
facts are clear, the evidence irrefutable, and the people's indignation is very great') was applied, the rights of accused persons were
also violated.

When the Beijing Workers Autonomous Federation, which represented over 100,000 workers in the city, was declared unlawful
and required to disband, and when its members were ordered to
'turn themselves in to their local public security organizations in
order to win more lenient punishment,' the right to freedom of
association was violated. If, as claimed by the Federation, many of
its representatives were killed by troops in Tiananmen Square,
along with demonstrating students, residents, and intellectuals,
then the right to freedom of assembly was violated in a most brutal
manner.

When the non-government federations of Beijing students,
which grew out of the student clubs of the mid-1980s, inspired by
concepts of democracy and civil liberty, were banned and their
members punished; when state-assigned employment was denied
to graduating students who had participated in demonstrations;
and when the student intake into universities was drastically reduced, the rights to education, academic freedom, and employment were violated.

When newspaper editors and reporters who failed to toe the
official line and reported events openly and accurately were fired;
when the sale of foreign newspapers and journals was banned, and
'subversive' books confiscated and destroyed; when telefax and
copying machines were monitored and satellite and wire transmis-
sions disrupted; when 'propagating and actively supporting the
spread of bourgeois liberalization' was declared punishable with
death; and when a man who spoke to American television of the
democracy movement was convicted of 'vilifying the righteous act
of the martial law troops,' and sentenced to 10 years' imprisonment, then the right to freedom of expression was violated.

By May 18, perhaps one million people had assembled in Beijing. But no riot or civil disorder broke out, and no threat to the
organized life of the community existed. On that day, Premier Li

Peng met with the students, and while refusing to discuss their demands, ordered them to cease their hunger strike. On the afternoon of May 19, Party General Secretary Zhao Ziyang visited Tiananmen Square to express his regret that the government had delayed for so long in meeting them, and urged them to end their hunger strike. Later that day, the Beijing Federation of Autonomous Student Unions announced that they would call off the hunger strike, but continue with a sit-in. It was at that stage that the Premier denounced the student demonstration as a 'conspiracy' and 'turmoil,' and imposed martial law in Beijing. The inference is irresistible that martial law was not imposed to deal with a serious threat of grave public disorder, and that, therefore, its imposition was unwarranted according to the norms and standards recognized by international human-rights law.

Acceptance of human-rights norms and standards

The internationalization of human-rights is a relatively new phenomenon. It manifested itself in the mid-20th century with the birth of the United Nations. Recoiling from the terror of Nazi Germany, the World War II victors sought to establish a new world order in which what a state did to its citizens within its territorial borders would no longer be its exclusive concern.

The charter of the United Nations was the first of several instruments that helped to create international human-rights law. Its preamble reaffirmed 'faith in fundamental human rights.' One of its principal objectives was the promotion and encouragement of 'respect for human rights and fundamental freedoms for all.' All its signatories pledged themselves to take joint and separate action, in cooperation with the U.N., to achieve that objective. In the view of the International Court of Justice, that pledge bound each member state of the U.N. to observe and respect human rights.[1] In 1945, the Republic of China was among the original signatories to the Charter. In 1971, the People's Republic of China made that same solemn commitment to the international community.

Since the charter neither catalogued nor defined the fundamental rights and freedoms to which it referred, the U.N. General Assembly unanimously proclaimed on 10 December 1948, the Universal Declaration of Human Rights. The Declaration was not the product of a single mind. Lebanese Ambassador Charles

Habib Malik presented the final text to the General Assembly and explained:

The Declaration is the composite product of all cultures and nations pooling their wisdom and their insight. The Atlantic world stressed principally civil, political, and personal liberties; the Soviet world advocated economic and social rights; the Latin American world concerned itself with the rule of law; the Scandinavians underlined equality between the sexes; India and China stood for non-discrimination, especially in relation to the downtrodden, underdeveloped, and underprivileged, and were also intensely interested in the right to education; others argued for the origin of these rights in the very nature of man itself; those with a dominant religious outlook wanted to safeguard religious freedoms. The study of how each nation and culture brought in the fundamental values of its cherished traditions to the common concern is a fascinating task.[2]

A committee of eight, one of whose members was a distinguished jurist from China, drafted the Declaration.

When the Universal Declaration was transformed into three international human-rights treaties, each with its own monitoring mechanism, the Republic of China was among their earliest signatories.[3] However, when the U.N. was at long last able to identify with accuracy the actual location of that enormous land mass known as China, and in 1971 admitted to its fold the representatives of the 22-year-old People's Republic of China, all multilateral human-rights treaties signed or ratified by 'the Chiang Kai-shek clique' by 'usurping the name of "China"' were immediately repudiated. The People's Republic said that it would need to study these treaties carefully before making a decision on whether or not to accede to them.[4] It was an understandable response from a government that had been wrongfully excluded from the conduct of mainstream international affairs for more than two decades. Unfortunately, no initiatives in this area were apparent for a very long time.

In 1980, China signed and ratified the recently adopted Convention on the Elimination of All Forms of Discrimination against Women. It was a treaty which sought to ensure the maximum participation of women on equal terms with men in all fields of activity. The following year, China acceded to the Convention on the Elimination of All Forms of Racial Discrimination. In so doing, it guaranteed the right of all Chinese people to equality before the law in the enjoyment of a variety of civil, political, economic, social, and cultural rights. In 1982, China undertook to conform to international law regarding the treatment of refugees, and in 1983, it accepted the obligation to punish both apartheid and genocide, now designated as crimes against humanity. In 1986, China signed the Convention, which seeks to outlaw torture and other cruel, inhuman, or degrading treatment or punishment.

By acceding to these human-rights treaties, China also submitted itself to scrutiny by the appropriate monitoring bodies. For instance, it is required to report regularly to the Committee on the Elimination of Racial Discrimination as well as to the Committee on the Elimination of Discrimination against Women. More significantly, it nominated an expert and secured his election to the U.N. Human Rights Sub-Commission, while seeking and obtaining membership in the U.N. Commission on Human Rights. Thereby, China not only recognized the existence of a human-rights regime, but also unequivocally acknowledged the right of the international community to scrutinize the human-rights performance of sovereign states. Indeed, China has repeatedly voted in favor of resolutions that sent U.N. investigators to examine allegations of human-rights violations in Chile, Afghanistan, and as recently as February 1989, to South Africa and the Israeli Occupied Territories.

A pattern of consistent violations

Despite these protestations of adherence to contemporary human-rights norms, no state has so conspicuously and so consistently violated them as the People's Republic of China. As the legitimacy which the revolution accorded to Mao Tse-tung and his fellow founders lapsed, and failed to be validated by the only known method in this age and time — the will of the people — China's continuing totalitarianism spawned increasing repression. The brutality of the past 40 years is now well-documented — the very antithesis of respect for human rights.[5]

For instance, the 1949 campaign to liquidate landlords, the 1950 campaign to liquidate counterrevolutionaries, and the 1952 'three-anti' and 'five-anti' movements directed against government officials and the national bourgeoisie, were all characterized by arbitrary mass trials before 'people's courts.' Mao Tse-tung reported to the Party Politburo that, during these exercises, 'two to three million counterrevolutionaries had been executed, imprisoned, or placed under control.' A contemporary historian asserts that the number killed was at least five million.[6]

In the 1957 anti-rightist campaign, principles such as judicial independence, equality before the law, and the presumption of innocence were denounced as bourgeois and reactionary.[7] In the first four months of that campaign, according to figures announced by the Minister of Public Security, 100,000 counterrevolutionaries were 'unmasked and dealt with,' 1,700,000 'subjected to police investigation,' and several million sent to the countryside for 're-education;'[8] euphemisms for death, arrest, and exile. The Great Proletarian Cultural Revolution unleashed in 1966 was character-ized by arbitrary arrests, torture, and summary executions. Ac-cording to Deng Xiaoping, a million people died by mob action, while the number persecuted has now been estimated at 100 million.[9] Simon Leys has documented a graphic account of an incident that was typical of this period:

In 1971, when Chen Jo-hsi [the noted Chinese writer] was living in Nanking, she was forced with thousands of other people to attend and participate in a public accusation meeting. The accused person's crime was the defacing of a portrait of Mao Tse-tung; the accused had been de-nounced by his own daughter, a 12-year-old child. On the basis of the child's testimony, he was convicted and sentenced to death; as was usually the case in these mass-accusation meetings, there was no right of appeal, and the sentence was carried out immediately, by firing squad. The child was officially extolled as a hero; she disclaimed any relationship with the dead man and proclaimed publicly her resolution to become from then on 'with her whole heart and her whole will, the good daughter of the Party.'[10]

If the brutality that characterized the first three decades of the People's Republic is explained as having occurred during a period when the Chinese government rejected contemporary norms and standards, no such defense can be pleaded in regard to the con-tinuing repression in post-Mao China. The 1978–79 Democracy Wall movement, which manifested itself in big-character posters, unofficial journals, and public demonstrations, and involved thousands of ordinary citizens advocating democratic reform and respect for human rights, was viewed as being opposed to social-ism, and was crushed with the same intensity as in the past. Scores of dissidents, writers, and human-rights advocates were beaten, imprisoned, or forced to undergo 're-education through labor' under harsh conditions.[11] Wei Jingsheng was brought to trial for 'counterrevolutionary crimes' and sentenced to 15 years imprisonment. An electrician and editor of an unofficial journal, Wei Jingsheng had the temerity to criticize China's leadership:

Everyone in China is well aware that the Chinese social system is not democratic and that this lack of democracy has severely stunted every aspect of the country's social development over the past 30 years...
    Does Deng Xiaoping want democracy? No, he does not. He is unwilling to comprehend the utter misery of the common people...He describes the struggle for democratic rights — a movement launched spontaneously by the people — as the actions of troublemakers and of people who want to destroy normal public order which must therefore be repressed...
    We cannot help asking Mr. Deng what his idea of democracy is. If the people have no right to express their opinions, or to enjoy freedom of speech and criticism, then how can we talk of democracy? If his idea of democracy is a democracy which does not allow others to criticize those in power, then how is such a democracy in the end any different from Mao Tse-tung's tyranny concealed behind the slogan 'The democracy of the dictatorship of the proletariat?'
    The people want to appeal against injustice, want to vent their grievances, and want democracy, and so they hold meetings. The people oppose famine and dictatorship and so they demonstrate...We consider that 'normal public order' is not total uniformity; particularly in politics, where a normal state of affairs only functions when there exists a great diversity of opinion. When there are no divergent opinions, no diverse discussion and publications, then it is clear that a dictatorship is in existence. Thus, when there is total uniformity, this must surely be called 'abnormal order'...
    So the crux of the matter is not who becomes master of the nation, but rather that...the people must maintain a firm control over their own nation, for this is the very essence of democracy. People entrusted with government positions...must be controlled by the people and be responsible to the people...Only a genuine general election can create a government and leaders ready to serve the interests of the electorate. If the government and the leaders are truly subject to the people's mandate and supervision, those two afflictions that leadership is prone to — personal ambition and megalomania — can be avoided.[12]

The Beijing Intermediate People's Court, after a seven-hour trial, convicted and sentenced Wei 'in order to consolidate the dictatorship of the proletariat, safeguard the socialist system, ensure the smooth progress of socialist modernization, and punish counterrevolutionary criminals.'[13]

In the Anti-Crime Campaign of 1983, an estimated 7,000–14,000 alleged counterrevolutionaries and common criminals were executed without due process.[14] The movement for democracy, which re-erupted in 1986 when tens of thousands of students took to the streets demanding greater political freedom, was also suppressed. Several intellectuals and writers who had supported the movement, including Fang Lizhi, Liu Binyan, and Wang Ruowang, were expelled from their academic positions. The general secretary of the Communist Party, Hu Yaobang, was held accountable for the event and forced out of office.[15] And in Tibet, China's policy since 1949 has been to arrest, detain, and torture any supporter of autonomy. There are severe restrictions on freedom of religion, expression, and association; over 800 people are estimated to have been killed by security forces in Lhasa in March 1989.

Immunity from international scrutiny

For 40 years, both before and after Mao, the People's Republic of China enjoyed within the post-war international human-rights regime an immunity granted to none other. As Roberta Cohen put it, China was 'the human-rights exception.' In the face of repeated, abominable violations, the silence maintained by the international community was deafening. It was this collective dumbness that led a sanguine Deng Xiaoping to remark, after the 1987 crackdown on intellectuals, 'Look at Wei Jingsheng. We put him behind bars and the democracy movement died. We haven't released him, but that did not raise much of an international uproar.'[16]

Non-governmental organizations at first suffered from an information gap,[17] particularly in the early Maoist years when travel into and within China was severely restricted. The few 'China experts' who were privileged to take a peak behind the mystical bamboo curtain were so mesmerized by the experience that, as Miriam London says, they 'did not wish to know — but to believe.' She refers to the 'myth of China's stability' that was created by some Sinologists from American universities who reported that China's food problem had been solved at a time when — as the Chinese press was later to admit — up to 200 million people were living in semi-starvation; that the people were 'happy, relaxed and motivated,' and governed by 'exemplary moral men, not laws,' during the dark age of Maoist oppression and despair;

that 'all was calm and peaceful' while factional battles raged across a torn and divided country.[18]

Some of the non-governmental organizations that did secure a foothold within China, notably religious groups, were extremely reticent lest they antagonize the authorities.[19] Information was also not forthcoming from Chinese living abroad. They had never really formed themselves into lobby or pressure groups, either because they did not wish to jeopardize the safety of friends and relatives at home, or because they did not wish to hurt national pride.[20] Even as China opened its borders to the world in the early 1980s, Maoist laws that prohibited the dissemination of information were revived,[21] and several investigative journalists and research-oriented academics were arrested and expelled. Deng Xiaoping warned that Chinese who had too many contacts with foreigners would be arrested; that threat was carried out. For instance, Liu Qing, the editor of an unofficial journal, was sentenced to three years' imprisonment for making available the transcript of the trial of Wei Jingsheng.[22] Consequently, it was only in late 1978 that a non-governmental organization published its first-ever report on a human-rights problem in China: Amnesty International's *Political Imprisonment in the People's Republic of China*.

Governments with embassies in Beijing could not plead an information gap. But pleading *realpolitik*, they too participated in a conspiracy of silence. When, in the late 1960s, the U.S. stepped in to take advantage of deteriorating Sino-Soviet relations, the least of its concerns was the human-rights situation in China. As then-U.S. Secretary of State Henry Kissinger noted in his memoirs, he did not even want to hear about the negative aspects of the Cultural Revolution.[23] Political and strategic consideration dictated rapprochement with China: Focusing on human-rights violations would not have contributed to that result.[24] Even the human-rights-conscious Carter administration turned a blind eye toward China pending the establishment of full diplomatic relations in December 1979. Thereafter, the Reagan administration sought to justify its willingness to overlook human-rights violations on the ground that, unlike other communist countries, 'China is not our adversary but a friendly, developing country.'[25] As for the United Kingdom, which had been one of the first European states to extend recognition to the People's Republic of China, it was continuously frustrated in its efforts to establish an embassy in

Beijing. Having been forced to break diplomatic relations with Taiwan and concede sovereignty over Hong Kong before the first British ambassador could present his credentials in Beijing,[26] it was hardly likely that Britain would initiate a debate on the human rights of Chinese people.

Economic factors also outweighed, and often eclipsed, concern for human rights. As then-Vice President George Bush explained in 1985, economic ties were central to the evolving Chinese-American relationship:

In 1972 our two-way trade came to less than $100 million. This year it will exceed $7 billion. In 1972 the United States had almost no investments in China. Today America is the largest foreign country investor. Americans have committed $150 million to more than 60 joint equity ventures and another $550 million in off-shore oil exploration.[27]

Therefore, it was not in the U.S. interest to publicly charge China with human-rights violations, or even to raise human-rights issues in bilateral talks. Indeed, as Assistant Secretary of State (now Ambassador) James Lilley explained, 'We don't necessarily see a great advantage in banging them over the head with it; they are a very sensitive people.'[28] As the United Kingdom prepared to hand over to China its colony of Hong Kong and its 5.5 million inhabitants and to create the necessary ambience for a significant British entry into the enormous, relatively untapped, Chinese market, it too asserted that 'it is not British government practice to raise human-rights issues with the Chinese; the PRC would find this offensive.'[29] The European Economic Community has also demonstrated considerable sensitivity in preferring to develop good relations with China rather than 'raise matters which were bound to prove a stumbling block.' As a European parliamentary delegation reported after a 1985 visit to China:

Having only recently emerged from isolationism, the Chinese authorities were not yet ready to agree to their laws, customs, and penal traditions being the subject of international debate, let alone in public.[30]

In the circumstances, the poor, developing countries of Africa and Asia, many of whom were grateful recipients of Chinese financial and technical assistance, and whose causes China had regularly espoused, could hardly have been expected to shoulder the burden of bringing China to judgment.

At the U.N., China has been treated with unique deference.

Whenever a representative of the People's Republic of China begins to speak, he holds center-stage in a hushed assembly hall, and the presiding officer is often willing to overlook time constraints and many other rules of procedure. Whether that deferential treatment is accorded because a PRC representative can claim to speak on behalf of a quarter of the human race, or as an inhabitant of the Middle Kingdom, is not clear. Perhaps it only results from a guilt complex toward a fellow member who had been wrongfully excluded for 22 years. Whatever the reason for this submissive attitude toward one of the most repressive regimes of this century, China has enjoyed for more than 40 years the immunity from scrutiny, which the international community has been willing to accord to the five permanent members of the Security Council. No resolution, report, or investigation had ever been presented, prepared, or initiated in respect of the human-rights performance of any of them. In August 1989, China forfeited that immunity. Its ethereal existence abruptly ended.

The breaking of the mold

The annual month-long meeting of the 26-member U.N. Sub-Commission on Human Rights[31] — a body of independent experts — is usually held in August at the Palais des Nations, Geneva. It is also attended by observers of member states of the U.N. and by representatives of duly accredited non-governmental organizations (NGOs).[32] One of its functions is to identify countries in which serious violations of human rights have occurred during the preceding year, so that the Commission on Human Rights — a political body comprising representatives of states — which usually meets in the following February, could consider how best to deal with situations which reveal a consistent pattern of violations. To perform that function, the Sub-Commission relies almost solely on NGOs for reliable information, usually gathered through their national networks, of such violations. At its 1988 session, the countries identified by the Sub-Commission as having violated human rights were South Africa, Namibia, Burundi, Israeli-occupied territories, E1 Salvador, Guatemala, Haiti, Chile, and Albania. On 31 August 1989, responding to the horror of the Beijing massacre, it took the unprecedented step of pulling aside the veil that had been spread for so long across the face of China. But it was perhaps in the nature of things that the initiative in respect of China was taken in a territory, Hong Kong, which was not represented in any U.N. human rights body, and by a group of individuals, the Ad Hoc Study Group on Human Rights in China, who did not themselves constitute a recognized non-governmental organization.

The Ad Hoc Study Group on Human Rights in China was spawned in the sprawling campus of the University of Hong Kong before the Beijing massacre actually took place. The idealism and fierce determination of the students on Tiananmen Square had inspired millions of ordinary people living in Hong Kong to shed their hitherto apolitical disposition and to take to the streets in repeated, massive, public demonstrations of solidarity. Groups of Hong Kong students joined their compatriots in Beijing, while others traveled to the mainland with financial and other material assistance. New organizations sprang up in the territory to extend support to the democratic movement in China. One of these was the Hong Kong University Staff Committee on Current Chinese Affairs which, following the declaration of martial law and the branding of the pro-democracy movement as 'counterrevolution-ary,' convened a meeting on May 29 to discuss what measures could be taken if the 'night of the long knives' were to descend upon the mainland. One of the suggestions was that the U.N. be activated through the Sub-Commission which, fortuitously, was due to meet shortly; and thereby focus its searchlight on Beijing. The fear of adverse publicity can sometimes work wonders, even with the most repressive regime, particularly if, like China, it is engaged in giving itself a cloak of respectability.

This suggestion was picked up enthusiastically by a young lecturer in architecture. At the age of 11, Dimon Liu had been smuggled into a train bound for the Chinese border by her mother who sensed the rapidly advancing Cultural Revolution. The cor-rupt Party cadre through whom the travel arrangements were made was determined to extract the maximum of the available resources, and it was 16 years before she and her parents could be reunited in secure surroundings. Meanwhile, the young girl who found herself deposited on a Kowloon pavement awaiting her unknown Hong Kong benefactor, would be sent to the U.S., and there pass through one strange family to another until she was eventually able, as a qualified architect, to return to Hong Kong. The wheel had gone a full circle and now, a decade later, the opportunity presented itself to strike an effective blow for freedom on behalf not only of numerous family members who were still on the mainland, but also of countless, nameless, less fortunate others. Dimon Liu was the prime mover behind the Ad Hoc Study Group on Human Rights in China which brought together a sprinkling of Hong Kong-based academics, journalists, professionals, and students. It had one immediate objective: to require China to account for the massacre of June 4. To achieve that objective, it would be necessary to break the mold.

Preliminary information from non-governmental organizations was disappointing. The International Commission of Jurists and Amnesty International both intended to refer to the Beijing massacre in their interventions before the Sub-Commission, but they did not seriously expect the issue to proceed beyond that body. China, apparently, was too formidable a factor to be encapsulated in a resolution. Others appeared surprisingly coy on the subject despite their activist stance on human-rights issues generally. They were either fearful of consequences for their branch organizations within China, or piqued at the students' lack of concern for causes such as Tibetan self-determination. On June 30, the Ad Hoc Group decided to send its own delegation to Geneva to lobby for a formal denunciation of the Chinese government. The delegates would include at least one of the Tiananmen Square student leaders then living abroad.

July was a month of feverish activity. What Hong Kong could offer the Sub-Commission was reliably attested, comprehensive information. Hundreds of eye-witnesses had entered the territory as they fled Beijing after the massacre, and a local lawyers' group had recorded many of their statements under oath. Unfortunately, the lawyers were unwilling to make this invaluable evidence available at short notice. Therefore, using as a basis statements recorded from Hong Kong journalists and students who had been among the last to leave Beijing, and other contemporaneous eye-witness accounts published in reliable Chinese-language newspapers in the territory, a comprehensive report was prepared on the events of June 3–4 and after. Entitled 'The Massacre in Beijing,' this 97-page document was the only one of its kind presented to the Sub-Commission at the commencement of its session.

Assembling a team to proceed to Geneva was another formidable task. Hong Kong had already been denounced by China for having engaged in 'counterrevolutionary' and 'subversive' activities. With every passing day bringing nearer 1 July 1997, the date fixed for transfer to China of sovereignty over the territory, many ethnic Chinese academics and professionals who belonged to the Ad Hoc Group were understandably unwilling to shed their anonymity. Consequently, besides the Chinese student leader now safely beyond the reach of his government, the team would comprise expatriates and ethnic Chinese who held foreign passports. The further problem of securing access to the Sub-Commission meetings began to be resolved when the New York-based International League for Human Rights, which had assisted in the preparation of the report, agreed not only to present the report, but also to include two members in its delegation. With the help of the Geneva-based International Commission of Jurists, the Paris-based International Federation of Human Rights, and the Bangkok-based Asian Cultural Forum on Development, the others were also assured of entry into the Palais des Nations.

China before the Human Rights Sub-Commission

In Geneva, at informal meetings convened by the International Human Rights Service, it was immediately apparent that the Beijing massacre and its tragic aftermath had aroused feelings of revulsion in non-governmental organizations throughout the world, and that there was tremendous support forthcoming for any effort at securing condemnation of China. Informal discussions with the experts revealed that while many of them were considerably distressed by the events of May and June, not all of them were independent agents free to act, each according to his own conscience. Several were subject, in varying degrees, to influence by their own governments, depending on the offices they held, or when their terms were due to end. Among the diplomatic community, ambassadors from Western Europe and Asia were agreed that while a great deal of heat might be generated on the issue by the NGOs, China would eventually not be the subject of a resolution: *realpolitik* would override any manifestations of idealism.

The discussion of agenda item 6: 'Violations of Human Rights and Fundamental Freedoms,' began on August 16 with China. The first intervention was made by one who was not only an eyewitness, but also an active participant in the events at Tiananmen Square. Nanjing University physics student Li Lu had been the deputy to Chai Ling at the Tiananmen Square Command Post as well as of the hunger strike committee, and had been one of the last to leave the Square on the morning of June 4. Speaking on behalf of the International Federation of Human Rights, he was able not only to explain the events that preceded the declaration of martial law, but also to testify to the attack that was launched on the 2,000 students who were making an orderly departure from the Square, and to the tanks that rolled over the tents crushing to death those too sick and weak to retreat. He also spoke of bodies being carted off and others being cremated where they lay. Mature beyond his 23 years, Li Lu's dignified presentation must have evoked memories among all who heard him of the fierce idealism of the brave new generation of Chinese so vividly transmitted to millions of homes throughout the world, thanks to modern technology and the coincidence of Mikhail Gorbachev's visit to Beijing.

One who did not hear him was the China observer, Yu Zhizhong. He walked out of the assembly hall as Li Lu commenced his statement, and returned when Li had finished, to castigate the U.N. for having permitted 'a criminal wanted by a member state,' 'a liar,' and 'one of the major organizers of the counterrevolution,' to 'spread rumors.' This outburst, however, did not go unchallenged. The French expert, Louis Joinet, joined issue with him:

Perhaps the observer for China could indicate the legal basis for his allegation and the international standard which allowed a peaceful demonstration witnessed by millions of television spectators, to be described as a crime. It was particularly serious to describe in that way opponents who were simply peaceful demonstrators. It was untrue to say that the demonstrators who were merely asking for a change in their country's institutions, were fostering rebellion or revolution. No international legal standard prohibited peaceful demonstrations.[33]

He challenged the Chinese authorities to issue an international warrant for the arrest of the student leader (on which Interpol would be obliged to act either by circulating the warrant, or by refusing to do so, as seemed more likely), or to refrain from using such language in the future. Indeed, if the Chinese contention was to be accepted, neither Yasser Arafat nor Nelson Mandela would ever have access to the United Nations.

Several non-governmental organizations, in particular Amnesty International, the International Confederation of Free Trade Unions, the World University Service, and the International Human

Rights Law Group, through their interventions and documentation, presented a formidable case against the Chinese government of serious and widespread violation of human rights. In a statement prepared by the Hong Kong group and read out by the secretary general of the International Commission of Jurists, Niall MacDermot, on behalf of his own and 13 other NGOs, ranging from the Arab Organization for Human Rights to the World Institute for Progressive Judaism, the facts and the law that formed the basis of the case were summarized in crisp, precise terms. The NGOs reminded the Sub-Commission of its duty

to ascertain accurately what happened and is still happening in China and to do what is possible and, in confirmity with accepted practice and procedure, to ensure that such a gross violation of international human-rights norms and standards — a tragedy of such depth and enormity — will not be allowed to occur again in China or elsewhere.

The observer from China disputed the facts. According to him, what his government crushed was a student demonstration that turned into a riot and ended up as a rebellion. It was not a spontaneous movement, but a 'pre-planned, organized, and premeditated political turmoil' which received financial and material help from 'forces abroad' and was 'instigated by the foreign mass media.' In quelling the rebellion, the government 'exercised great restraint.' Consequently, the army, the armed police, and the security officers suffered more than 6,000 injuries and 'dozens of deaths.' The students' withdrawal from Tiananmen Square 'was on the whole peaceful' and 'not a single person was killed by the troops or run over by military vehicles.' However, 'owing to the chaotic situation during the quelling of the rebellion, some innocent people and onlookers who were mixed together with the ruffians were accidently wounded.' After careful and repeated verification, it was estimated that about 3,000 civilians were wounded and more than 200 died, including 36 students. Immediately after the events, the departments concerned were instructed to make 'careful arrangements for their funeral affairs.' Having stated 'these facts,' the observer asserted that 'It is the internal affairs of a sovereign state to put down riots and quell rebellions in an effort to maintain law and order of the state. No foreign country or international organization has the right to intervene on whatever pretext.' One of the experts immediately rejected the implied suggestion that he was suffering from hallucinations; he preferred to believe that he had actually seen on television what he thought he had seen.

Under the rules of procedure, a state can intervene only on 'a matter of particular concern to that state.' When the observer of Australia began to 'demonstrate the depth of the Australian concern at the tragedy,' he was immediately interrupted on the grounds that the events in China were not of 'particular concern' to Australia. When others pointed out that the Syrian Arab Republic's observer had only just concluded berating the governments of South Africa and Israel, the objectors argued that to an Arab state, what happens in those two countries were always of particular concern. After the secretariat had ruled that human-rights violations anywhere could be a matter of particular concern to a state, the Australian observer was allowed to continue his statement. However, only two other observers — from the U.S. and Canada — chose to intervene in the discussion. None of the 80 other observers present expressed any views on the events in China.

On August 25, the end of the third week, nine members of the Sub-Commission from Norway, France, Netherlands, the United Kingdom, Mexico, Costa Rica, the U.S., the Philippines, and Japan — presented a draft resolution on China. Seven of them had previously spoken in favor of action against China, a measure that appeared to have the support of at least two others, Greece and Yugoslavia. Three others who spoke were non-committal: the Jordanian expert thought that 'it was difficult to judge' from the information received; the Algerian expert wondered whether a country ought to be judged 'on the basis of one single event'; and the Egyptian expert agreed that 'a country of one billion people could not be judged by what had taken place in one square.' He insisted, 'China should not be blacklisted, blackmailed, defamed, and condemned to a life sentence after a trial by the press and media.'

The only other references to China were the expressions of support by the Nigerian expert for 'the efforts of the Chinese government to carry out reforms' and the appeal by the Chinese expert to examine the human-rights situation in each country 'in a comprehensive way.' Excluding the Ethiopian chairman, who conducted the proceedings with competence and fairness, the remaining nine made no reference at all to the events in China. These were the experts from Togo, Somalia, Morocco, Cuba, India, the USSR, Romania, Argentina, and Colombia.

As the crucial final week began, the lobbies at the Palais were rife with rumors of tactical moves that might be employed to avoid a vote on the proposed resolution on China. The fear of a filibuster was overcome when the Sub-Commission resolved by a majority vote to give priority to resolutions on Item Six. Proposed by the Jordanian and opposed by the American, that move received the enthusiastic support of all the 'progressive forces' who obviously had in mind the ritual condemnation of Israel and South Africa. But unconfirmed whispers in the corridors suggested that the idea had in fact been put to the Jordanian expert by the sponsors of the China resolution. Old hands at the U.N. also commented on the unprecedented Chinese invasion. At times it seemed as if every table in the delegates' lounge had been commandeered by the Chinese mission, and there appeared no way in which a member of the Sub-Commission in need of a tea break could escape the diplomatic offensive. One of Hong Kong's group found herself cornered by a Chinese first secretary with the unnerving opening gambit: 'What passport do you hold?'

Twenty-four hours before the scheduled time for voting, Louis Joinet of France took the extraordinary step of moving the suspension of rules of procedure to enable voting on Item Six resolutions to be by secret ballot. It had never happened before, but it appeared to be the only protective device available to independent experts seeking to perform their legitimate functions under the U.N. Charter. At home, their foreign ministries were under pressure from the Chinese government to withhold their support to the resolution. Asian and Third World solidarity had in many cases been invoked to counter what was described as a 'Western conspiracy.' In Geneva, at least one African expert had been visited late at night by a contingent of Chinese diplomats who had threatened the suspension of economic assistance to his country if he voted for the resolution. The effect of China's brazen interference with the work of the Sub-Commission, with absolutely no regard or respect for its independent capacity, began to be seen when one of the sponsors of the resolution on China privately indicated to the others of that expert's intention to leave Geneva before the vote.

Stymied by the motion to hold a secret ballot, China's active 'friends' on the Sub-Commission — the experts from Cuba,

Romania, and India — invoked nearly every procedural ploy in the book to thwart it. After attempts to defer consideration of the motion pending an opinion on its validity from the Economic and Social Council — available perhaps in a year's time — and to refrain from taking action on the motion, had both been defeated, the Sub-Commission voted by 14 to 6, with 3 abstentions, to hold a secret ballot. The Algerian expert did not participate in the vote, while the Egyptian expert had already left Geneva. Those who voted against the motion were the experts from Cuba, India, the USSR, Romania, Somalia, and China. Togo, Jordan, and Nigeria abstained.

On the eve of the historic vote on the first U.N. resolution on human rights in China, Amnesty International released its preliminary findings on killings of unarmed civilians, arbitrary arrests, and summary executions in China since 3 June 1989. That 49-page report, based largely on eye-witness accounts and other reliable sources of information was, no doubt, a stark reminder to the experts of the measure of their responsibility. But before the secret vote could proceed, there were other hurdles. The Cuban expert wanted to explain his vote, and so did the Romanian, who also felt the need to place on record the reasons why he was voting against the resolution. A point of order raised, surprisingly, by the Algerian expert, which was upheld by the chair on the ground that there could be no explanation of votes in a secret ballot, abruptly ended a clever strategem aimed at identifying those who would vote for the resolution. At that stage, China's observer sought the floor to reiterate the facts. It was 4.20 p.m. on an unusually warm Geneva afternoon when the votes were counted and the chairman announced that the resolution on China had passed, 15 to 9. In a secret ballot, there was apparently no need for anyone to abstain.

The resolution expressed concern at the recent events in China and their consequences in the field of human rights. It requested the secretary general to transmit to the Commission information on those events provided by the Chinese government and by 'other reliable sources.' It appealed for clemency for those incarcerated in connection with the events. The language used by the Sub-Commission may seem to be unduly docile, and the resolution no more than a mild rebuke. Those who actively participated in the Chinese democracy movement and suffered in its tragic aftermath, and those millions of others who watched from the comfort and security of their homes the unfolding drama of the birth, growth, and then the abrupt abortion of youthful idealism, may well be mystified at the absence of any condemnation.

But the terms of a resolution, as the Chinese expert pointed out in a final, desperate appeal to his colleagues, are irrelevant. They are often the product of compromise, and are usually designed to attract the maximum possible support. The significance of a resolution lies in what it seeks to achieve. This resolution placed China on the Sub-Commission's list of states that had violated the human-rights of their citizens. It also placed China on the agenda of the Commission for consideration whether the material made available to it revealed a consistent pattern of human-rights violations, and if so, to initiate a thorough study of the human-rights situation in that country. In short, this resolution required the Chinese government to account to the international community for its treatment of its citizens. The mirror through which the awesome image of China had been reflected for four decades had finally cracked. That in itself was condemnation.

The future

The 1989 Beijing massacre was not an aberration in the 40-year history of the People's Republic of China. It was part of a consistent pattern of events that have occurred, and will continue to occur, as a totalitarian government seeks to subdue and liquidate dissident sections of its society. The fire of the revolution has long lost its glow. The Long Marchers and others who have crept or climbed to power under their patronage clearly lack the legitimacy to govern. That legitimacy can be derived only by the freely expressed will of the people. That is an essential element of international human-rights law. But in a totalitarian state such as China, the government is sustained primarily by the military, and violence is therefore the only option available to it whenever its authority is challenged by the popular will. Therefore, it is totalitarianism, not Confucianism or socialism, as some in the West would have us believe, that is inimical to respect for human rights.

With the incipient students' and workers' reform movements now effectively squashed, at least for the time being, there is no evidence of the emergence in China of an alternative nationwide force powerful enough to counter the superimposed ideological base of doctrinaire communism. There is no religious tradition that can act as a catalyst as in the Philippines or in Poland. There is no regular information network similar to that which offered the people of Eastern Europe an opportunity to imbibe the values and aspirations of the world that lay beyond their artificial barricades. Therefore, as people elsewhere in today's rapidly shrinking world become more assertive of their rights and freedoms, and China's economic liberalization program fails to be matched with political reform, another tragic Beijing Spring cannot be ruled out.

Yet, some developments may be significant. For the first time, a number of student leaders, intellectuals, and entrepreneurs have succeeded in escaping from China and have begun to mobilize support to mount a challenge from abroad. Simultaneously, expatriate Chinese have begun to organize themselves into activist groups, no longer inhibited by notions of national pride. Even the U.N. has been prevailed upon to explode the myth of Chinese immunity. These, however, appear to be minuscule efforts compared to the gigantic task that lies ahead.

That task has not been made any easier by the negative signs that are rapidly reappearing. Hong Kong, which exploded so spontaneously in a burst of popular democratic sentiment, has been intimidated into submission. Even the replica of the Goddess of Democracy now lies dismantled in a campus basement, forbidden by the British colonial administration from being publicly displayed.[34] A diplomatic offensive launched by the Chinese government in Asia, Africa, and in the Middle East, aimed at neutralizing many states which, in any event, were probably quite ambivalent in regard to events in China, has no doubt achieved firm commitments of support from those regions. And from the West comes the revelation that the human-rights rhetoric of the immediate post-Tiananmen weeks was only a cover behind which the U.S. and the United Kingdom continued high-level governmental contacts with the ostensibly ostracized Communist Party hierarchy in Beijing.

The events in and around Tiananmen Square were a clear message to the world that the youth of China had learned of a new ideology: human-rights. Spawned by the economic liberalization of the 1970s, they had grown up in a world in which traditional barriers could no longer stem the flow of information and ideas. The world must find ways of reaching out to them, of satisfying their intellectual needs, of sustaining them in their search for a new pragmatic philosophical base upon which their country could move into the new millenium. It is time to end the 41-year-old diplomatic conspiracy that has enabled the Chinese government to perpetuate its Jekyll and Hyde existence: a respectable member of international human-rights fora, even censuring some states and pontificating to others; an outlaw at home, killing, torturing and humiliating its own people. The longer the international community continues to nourish the corrupt and brutal dictatorship of the few, the longer will it deny a quarter of the human race the opportunity to assert their basic human attributes.

---

1. 'Legal Consequences for States of the Continued Presence of South Africa in Namibia (South West Africa) notwithstanding Security Council Resolution 276 (1970), Advisory Opinion,' *International Court of Justice Report, 1971*, p. 16.

2. Address of Ambassador Charles H. Malik, former President, United Nations General Assembly and former Chairman, Human Rights Commission, United Nations, at the opening plenary session of the Conference of Non-Governmental Organizations in Observance of the 25th Anniversary of the Universal Declaration of Human Rights, UN Headquarters, New York, 10 December 1973.

3. The International Covenant on Civil and Political Rights (ICCPR) and the International Covenant on Economic, Social and Cultural Rights (ICESCR) were adopted by the United Nations General Assembly in 1966 and came into force in 1976. China signed both Covenants and the Optional Protocol to the ICCPR on 5 October 1967.

4. See the communication sent to the United Nations Secretary-General by the Minister of Foreign Affairs of the People's Republic of China on 29 September 1972, which is reproduced in *Human Rights: Status of International Instruments* (New York, United Nations, 1987), p. 20. The Republic of China had signed or ratified several human-rights treaties. These included treaties relating to the abolition of slavery, servitude, and forced labor, and similar institutions and practices; the political rights of women, the age of and consent to marriage; the punishment of genocide; and the elimination of discrimination.

5. See, for example, Roberta Cohen, 'People's Republic of China: The Human Rights Exception,' *Human Rights Journal*, Vol. 9 (1987), p. 447; Simon Leys, *The Burning Forest: Essays on Chinese Culture and Politics* (New York: Holt, Rinehart and Winston, 1985), p. 113; Miriam London, 'China: The Romance of Realpolitik,' *Freedom at Issue*, September–October 1989, p. 9; Albert H.Y. Chen, 'Civil Liberties in China: Some Preliminary Observations, (in *Civil Liberty in Hong Kong*, Oxford University Press, 1987), p. 107; Amnesty International, *China: Violations of Human Rights* (1984); Amnesty International, *China: Torture and Ill-treatment of Prisoners* (1987).

6. Jacques Guillermez, *Le Parti Communiste Chinois an Pouvoir* (Paris Payot, 1972) 33, cited by Simon Leys, p. 124.

7. Albert Chan, p. 117.

8. Simon Leys, p. 125.

9. Roberta Cohen, pp. 448, 457.

10. Simon Leys, p. 115.

11. Roberta Cohen, p. 450.

12. Wei Jingsheng, 'Democracy or a New Dictatorship,' published in a special issue of *Exploration* (Beijing, March 1979); abbreviated, translated and reproduced in Amnesty International *China: Violations of Human Rights* (London, 1984), pp. 107–111.

13. New China News Agency, 16 October 1979, quoted in Amnesty International, *China: Violation of Human Rights* (London, 1984), p. 25.

14. A U.S. government estimate, cited in Roberta Cohen, p. 547.

15. Roberta Cohen, p. 520.

16. Roberta Cohen, p. 450.

17. For a fuller discussion, see Roberta Cohen, p. 451.

18. Miriam London, pp. 9–10.

19. See Roberta Cohen, pp. 503–504.

20. See Roberta Cohen, pp. 468–471.

21. For example, in 1980, the 1951 Regulations on Guarding State Secrets were republished.

22. Amnesty International, *China: Violations of Human Rights* (London, 1984), p. 27.

23. When on his first secret visit to China in July 1971, Premier Chou Enlai attempted to explain, somewhat critically, the significance of the Cultural Revolution, Kissinger insisted that that was China's internal affair and did not concern him. See Henry Kissinger, *The White House Years* (Boston: Little, Brown and Company, 1979), p. 750.

24. For a discussion of U.S. policy in respect to China's human-rights violations, see Roberta Cohen, pp. 474–485.

25. Statement of Assistant Secretary of State John Holdridge, before the Senate Foreign Relations Committee on 6 July 1981, cited in Roberta Cohen, p. 480.

26. Although the UK recognized the PRC on 6 January 1950, Beijing made it clear that diplomatic relations would have to be 'negotiated.' The decision to exchange ambassadors was announced only on 17 March 1972. Two events that immediately preceded that announcement were the letter dated 8 March 1972 to the chairman of the UN Special Committee on Decolonization from the Permanent Respresentative of China to the UN, Huang Hua, in which he asserted (with no protest from the UK) that the settlement of the question of Hong Kong was entirely within China's sovereign right; and the announcement by the Foreign Secretary, Sir Alec Douglas-Home, in the House of Commons on 13 March 1972 that official representation in Taiwan was being withdrawn since 'Taiwan is a province of the People's Republic of China.'

27. Department of State Bulletin 85 (December 1985), quoted by Roberta Cohen, p. 482.

28. Statement of James Lilley before the House Committee on Foreign Affairs in 1985, quoted by Roberta Cohen, p. 484.

29. Roberta Cohen, p. 485.

30. Roberta Cohen, p. 488.

31. Its proper name, the Sub-Commission on Prevention of Discrimination and Protection of Minorities, was dictated by its originally intended role. In 1967, its mandate was expanded to include a more general investigatory role into serious human-rights violations.

32. At the 41st session of the Sub-Commission, which commenced on 7 August 1989, 84 governments and 89 NGOs of various categories were represented.

33. Summary Record of the 16th meeting, 41st Session of the Sub-Commission on Prevention of Discrimination and Protection of Minorities, E/CN.4/Sub.2/1989/SR.16, paragraph 10.

34. In a letter to the Chinese government dated 23 October 1989, Hong Kong's political adviser, William Ehrman, confirmed that the government had rejected the proposal for a permanent site in the territory for the statue. This was intended to reassure the Chinese leadership that the Hong Kong government had no intention of allowing the territory to be 'used as a base for subversive activities against the PRC.'

Punishment Season: Human Rights in China After Martial Law

ASIA WATCH

Introduction

What are human rights? As understood by Western scholars, they are the innate rights of human beings, or the basic rights and freedoms enjoyed by a person as a human. They primarily consist of the rights to life, freedom, equality, property, self-defense, and happiness, and the right to oppose persecution. These rights are innate, permanent, universal, and nontransferrable. They cannot be taken away....

In the context of Marxism [however], such an interpretation of human rights is unscientific, incorrect, contrived, biased, and idealistically metaphysical...Human rights, like democracy and freedom, are concrete and class-oriented.

(*Guangming Daily*, 17 November 1989)

Since June 1989, the Chinese authorities have again been waging a war against the so-called 'class enemy' — an elastic term that has been used to stigmatize countless different groups of people in China over the past 40 years, but which currently denotes the students, workers, and intellectuals who actively promoted or took part in last year's pro-democracy movement. Several hundred and perhaps as many as a thousand of these 'counterrevolutionaries' were killed on the streets of Beijing by the Chinese army as it converged from all directions on Tiananmen Square on the night of June 3–4, and many thousands more have been hunted down and placed in incommunicado detention by the security forces since then. There have been at least 40 officially announced executions of pro-democracy demonstrators, and secret executions may also have occurred.[1] On 4 November 1989, Reuters quoted William Webster, head of the CIA, as saying that 'probably thousands of people have been killed' since the crackdown first began.

In late June or early July, following the international outcry over the scale and severity of the crackdown, the authorities issued a confidential directive sharply curtailing the open reporting of arrests and executions in the Chinese media, in an effort to convey the impression that it had somehow diminished. But the arrests have continued, largely in secret, right through to the present, and reports of further executions having recently been carried out continue to appear in the provincial press, to which foreign observers have only restricted access.

According to Asia Watch's information, most of those detained have neither been charged nor brought to trial, and often their families have not even been informed as to their place of detention. Those people who have been brought to trial have been subjected to expedited and summary trial proceedings, under a system of justice which specifically rejects the principle of the presumption of innocence and in which (according to the Chinese authorities themselves) verdicts are usually decided upon before the trial even begins.

The majority of those brought to trial have been convicted on charges of 'counterrevolution,' a blatantly political category of criminal offense, and the sentences handed down in such cases have generally ranged from 10 years to life imprisonment. Others have simply been sentenced without any trial at all — usually to three–year terms of 're-education through labor,' a form of incarceration that is dispensed solely on the authority of the police, and in which no appeal to the courts is possible. In addition, many of the detainees paraded on Chinese television last summer showed signs of severe physical abuse. As the Chinese authorities themselves have admitted in recent years, the use of beatings and torture to extract confessions is a common practice in Chinese jails.

In most cases, the prison sentences handed down by the courts have been entirely disproportionate to the alleged crimes. In July 1989 for example, three men accused of throwing ink and paint-filled eggshells at Mao's portrait in Tiananmen Square in May were sentenced to prison terms ranging from 16 years to life. And on 7 December 1989, a worker in Changsha was sentenced to 13 years' imprisonment for making pro-democracy speeches and engaging in independent labor union activity.

Evidence that the Chinese authorities are specifically trying to conceal from the outside world the fact that the political trials still continue was provided by the *Washington Post* in December 1989:

Two trial notices were posted outside the People's Intermediate Court in Beijing this week. One of the defendants was charged with 'counter-revolutionary sabotage;' the other with espionage and 'counterrevolution-ary propaganda and agitation.' Court officials, reached by telephone, declined to comment on the two cases. One of them told a foreign reporter, 'You know that it's not permitted to ask questions like that.' When the reporter went to the court to photograph the posted trial notices, a court official ripped them down.[2]

The question of how many people have been arrested or de-tained since last June is — like the question of how many died in the military crackdown — extremely difficult to answer with any precision, and estimates vary greatly. By adding up various scat-tered figures put out by the Chinese authorities themselves, West-ern journalists last summer arrived at a total official arrest figure of at least 6,000. In early December, *Beijing Youth News* disclosed that 2,578 people had been arrested in connection with the pro-democracy movement in Beijing in the 24-day period following June 4, and that only 190 have since been released; moreover, this total referred only to so-called 'ruffians' (or 'thugs'), and it ex-cludes all workers or students detained on non-violent and purely political charges.[3]

Other sources (cited by UPI) indicated that 6,000 people had been arrested in Beijing alone by the end of July, and the *Wash-ington Post* last October cited 'sources with access to internal government documents' as putting the figure at more than 10,000 nationwide. Western diplomats interviewed in Beijing last Novem-ber estimated that anywhere between 10,000 and 30,000 people had probably been arrested in China since the commencement of the crackdown. Citing 'well-placed Communist Party sources,' a recent article in the *Washington Post* (17 January 1990) reported that more than 800 of those involved in last year's movement had already been tried and sentenced to prison terms in recent months, many for 10 years on charges of divulging 'state secrets' or dis-seminating 'counterrevolutionary propaganda.'

Even those injured by government troops on the night of June 3–4 reportedly continue to be persecuted by the authorities. According to an interview conducted in China in October 1989:

Wang was on a Beijing street, a curious bystander, when a soldier's bullet shattered his bones and marked him with a label he may never shed. As

China continues its crackdown on the democracy movement that erupted in June, Wang and the other wounded are in great danger. The dead are beyond reach, the unmarked cannot be found, and so official wrath is focussed on the injured. Investigators have endless questions. Why was he out in the streets? What slogans did he shout? What banner did he wave? Who else was around him?[4]

In addition, large numbers of students and workers are currently under active investigation by the authorities, on campuses and in the workplace, for their alleged activities during the events of last summer; to facilitate the purge, people are being cajoled by the authorities to inform upon one another. At one of Beijing's elite universities recently, a teacher interviewed by the *New York Times* 'described a faculty meeting with the Party secretary, who complained that while some students had informed on others, no teachers had done so, behavior that set a bad example. . . . We felt he had no sense of shame.'[5] In at least two recent reported cases, students have committed suicide as a result of this intense official harassment and pressure.[6]

As for China's long-suffering intellectuals, who have been the target of repeated campaigns of persecution and intimidation since 1949, there are signs that their present plight may worsen still further. In December 1989, the Hong Kong journal *Bai Xing* reported that Wang Zhen, vice president of the PRC, had 'proposed at a recent Party meeting that 4,000 intellectuals in Beijing who stand opposed to the Party be sent into exile in Xinjiang,' the northwest frontier province where China's vast gulag lies, 'so that they could be transformed there.'[7]

Despite the crude severity of the government repression, China's pro-democracy movement has not been silenced completely. In a remarkable act of courage, 30 students from the Beijing Institute of Aeronautics on 9 December 1989 defied martial law by staging a protest march along central Changan Avenue and carrying banners saying 'Freedom and Democracy' and 'Why is China so poor?' They were promptly set upon and beaten by the police, and eight of them were taken into custody, though one later escaped. Onlookers, who had begged them to disperse, reportedly wept openly as the students were hauled away.[8] Revealing a striking — but characteristic — presumption of guilt, an Education Ministry spokesman later told Reuters: 'These students' illegal assembly and speeches. . . break martial law. They are detained and awaiting their sentences.'

Arrests

The Chinese authorities' relentless hunt for scapegoats to blame for their drastic recent loss of popular support and legitimacy continues. Asia Watch has documented several dozen further arrests and trials of pro-democracy individuals that took place between October 1989 and January 1990, and has received reliable reports that many others (though names are not yet known) were arrested or tried over the same period. The following examples convey the general flavor of the continuing repression in China.

*Wang Juntao and Chen Ziming, two intellectuals who headed one of the Chinese authorities 'most wanted lists,' together with Chen's pregnant wife, Wang Zhihong, were arrested near Canton last October while reportedly trying to escape to Hong Kong. Three Hong Kong residents, Luo Haixing, Li Peicheng, and Li Longqing, alleged to have been active in the underground rescue network, were also, between October and December, arrested in China in connection with the case. Wang Juntao and Chen Ziming are largely unknown in the West, but they were key figures in the 1989 pro-democracy movement. Indeed, both have played a major role in China's dissident movement ever since 1976, when they were arrested and jailed for helping to organize the popular mass demonstrations in Tiananmen Square against the regime of the 'Gang of Four.' During the Democracy Wall movement of 1978–80 (the forerunner of last year's movement), Wang Juntao founded and edited an unofficial pro-democracy magazine called *Beijing Spring*. And in 1980 he stood as an independent candidate for the local Beijing legislature, in the first openly contested elections ever to be held in the People's Republic.

Prior to last year's crackdown, Wang, 31, was a leading member of the Beijing Institute of Social and Economic Sciences and associate chief editor of the influential (and now banned) *Economic Studies Weekly*. Chen Ziming, 37 years old and from Zhejiang Province, is also a leading veteran of the Democracy Wall movement. Until June 4, he was director of the Beijing Institute of Social and Economic Sciences, a pioneering private research organization and think tank that worked closely with the Party's reform faction headed by Zhao Ziyang.

*On 5 November 1989, a man named Zhao Sujian was arrested in Henan Province for having allegedly spread 'counterrevolutionary slogans.' According to the *Henan Daily* of December 3:

On May 20 this year, more than 30 slogan posters with extremely reactionary contents were discovered on some main streets, the downtown district, and at the gates of some institutions, schools, and factories in Kaifeng City.... The Kaifeng Public Security Bureau organized nearly 100 cadres and policemen to handle this case. Through nearly five months' hard work, they eventually ferreted out the hidden criminal.

Criminal Zhao Sujian, male, 33 years of age, is a cadre in the Kaifeng Housing Construction Company. He began to write and put up counterrevolutionary slogans with extremely reactionary contents in 1987. In the spring and summer of this year, when turmoil and counterrevolutionary rebellion occurred in Beijing, Criminal Zhao took advantage of the opportunity and twice wrote and put up 36 counterrevolutionary posters on April 25 and May 20 [i.e., adding fuel to the flames in the counterrevolutionary rebellion.]

In the interrogation, Criminal Zhao confessed his crimes of writing counterrevolutionary slogans three times, organizing illegal demonstrations, giving counterrevolutionary speeches at Henan University, openly spreading what Voice of America broadcast in his own company, together with other illegal and criminal activities.[9]

Two points stand out clearly from this classic piece of demagoguery: first, that Zhao Sujian is being persecuted and charged with 'counterrevolution' — the most serious crime possible in China, and potentially a capital offense — purely on account of his exercise of the right to free expression; and second, that the release of such prejudicial pre-trial commentary on the case by the authorities, with its manifest presumption of guilt, erases all possibility of Zhao ever receiving a fair trial. Such strongly prejudicial commentary by the authorities is found in virtually all of the Chinese press reports on pro-democracy arrests seen by Asia Watch since last June.

Asia Watch has established the identities and documented the circumstances (where known) of more than 500 of those arrested by the Chinese authorities since last June on account of their involvement in the pro-democracy movement. According to all independent estimates, this total represents only a small fraction of the true number of arrests, most of which have never been publicly announced by the authorities. People from virtually all walks of life — students, professors, journalists, artists, engineers, government officials, businessmen and, above all, ordinary workers — have been arrested for their involvement in last year's pro-democracy movement. Many have been accused of committing acts of violence during and after the government's June 3–4 assault on Tiananmen Square. Many others, however, have been accused solely of non-violent activities relating to their free expression of political and other beliefs and on account of their involvement in peaceful protest demonstrations. The majority of those still held have, as far as is known, never been charged at all. The most recent reported arrests were of eight student activists in Lanzhou, northwest China, in early January 1990.[10]

The scope of the repression is immense. Asia Watch and other organizations have published details of many of those arrested from each of these groups since last June, and some of the more prominent of them are already fairly well-known outside of China. They include such people as Wang Dan, the student leader from Beijing University who helped originate the protest movement, and several other student leaders who were placed on the government's 'most-wanted list,' including Liu Gang and Zheng Xuguang; leading establishment intellectuals and theoreticians, such as Li Honglin, a prominent Party historian, and Bao Tong, the senior adviser to ousted Party leader Zhao Ziyang; outspoken pro-democracy journalists such as Dai Qing, who has perversely been accused by the authorities of inciting the students when in reality she tried to persuade them to quit while they were still ahead; Wang Ruowang, a 71-year old writer, expelled from the Party along with Fang Lizhi in 1987 following the student demonstrations of the previous winter; and the organizers of China's first independent labor movement since 1949, including Han Dongfang and Liu Qiang, both leaders of the Beijing Workers Autonomous Federation.

None of the above persons has yet been brought to trial or even, so far as is known, formally charged, and all have been held incommunicado since their initial detention. In both these respects, their continued detention — like that apparently of the vast majority of those held by the authorities since the crackdown began — is in violation of the Criminal Procedure Law of China, 1979, and hence unlawful.

Executions

Under Chinese law more than 40 different criminal offenses, notably that of 'counterrevolution,' may be punished by imposition of the death penalty, and executions are extremely common in China.[11] In 1983, the National People's Congress enacted legislative measures designed to speed up the adjudication of internal security cases and cases involving capital offenses, thereby reducing still further the already woefully inadequate procedural safeguards in Chinese law against the occurrence of wrongful execution. While not actually admitting to the latter, the Chinese legal press has in recent years (that is, the period of relative openness that preceded last June's crackdown) publicized a number of cases in which death sentences had been wrongfully imposed on people solely on the basis of confessions extorted through torture, and where the victims were spared execution only as a result of the fortuitous emergence of the truth or because of frantic last-minute efforts by defense lawyers.

A particularly serious case occurred [recently] in Anhui Province in which Xie Bingjin, chief of police and former deputy secretary of the Huanggang district Party committee in Funan County, together with Zhu Gui, the deputy chief of police, used torture to extract confessions from suspects. As a result, two people were subsequently given wrongful sentences of death at the trial of first instance, and one person received a suspended death sentence; another was given life imprisonment and ended up being unjustly jailed.[12]

It is likely that many of those executed for alleged violent offenses since June 1989 were in fact innocent, and had given confessions under duress or been convicted on the basis of grossly insufficient evidence. In addition, one man executed in Shanghai in late June 1989 on charges of setting fire to a train was said to be mentally retarded, and in the widely televised 'trial' proceedings he appeared not to understand what was going on.

The peremptory, almost sly casualness with which the Chinese legal system often seems to regard the question of judicial execution may be seen from the following statement, which is taken from a discussion in an official legal textbook of 1986 regarding the provision in Chinese law that pregnant women are to be exempted from capital punishment.[13] Reveals the author:

In the view of some [Chinese jurists], if the accused woman is given an abortion prior to the court hearing, then since she will no longer be pregnant by the time the trial began, she can be given the death penalty. And similarly, if the court (sic) performs an abortion on the accused at the time of the trial, then she will likewise become eligible for the death penalty.[14]

In Chinese criminal law, which is held by the authorities to be a mere 'tool of the dictatorship of the proletariat,' loopholes are always available when needed.

As mentioned, at least 40 people have already been executed in connection with the events of last June. Many of them had been convicted of crimes involving no use of violence against the person, but only of crimes against property — typically, such things as 'burning vehicles,' 'setting fire to trains,' and 'obstructing traffic.' Others were executed for having allegedly killed martial law troops and armed policemen on the night of June 3–4. Some soldiers and police were certainly killed (the government has so far identified only a dozen or so of them, though claiming much higher fatalities) but in at least some of those cases eye-witnesses report that the killings by crowds took place only after the soldiers and policemen had shot and killed unarmed civilians.

Reports of new death sentences and of judicial executions of pro-democracy activists recently carried out still continue to appear in the Chinese press. In view of China's past reporting practices on such matters, moreover, it is likely that those announced in the official press only represent a small portion of the total number of recent executions. The following are some of the cases that have been documented by Asia Watch from Chinese press and radio sources:

*A man named Sun Baohe was executed in Jinan, Shandong Province, on 14 October 1989, according to the *Jinan Masses Daily* of the following day. He had been charged only with the crime of having set fire to and burned a 'Shanghai-brand' vehicle in the course of a demonstration on June 6.

*Three men — Zhou Qi, He Xiaokang, and Chen Guangping — were executed on 7 November 1989 in Chengdu, Sichuan Province, following their conviction on charges of 'beating, smashing, looting and burning' during the period June 4–6. According to Chengdu Radio, the three had attacked the police, engaged in robbery, set fire to a movie theater, and destroyed shops. An official of the Chengdu External Affairs Department stated that they had been publicly paraded at a mass rally and then immediately executed.

*An execution that was carried out in Beijing on 30 November 1989 of a man named Liu Baode gives strong cause for concern that pro-democracy activists may have been tried and executed without the true reasons for their execution (namely their involvement in the protest demonstrations of last May and June) actually being made public. An article in the *Beijing Daily* of 1 December 1989 provided a detailed account of several cases of violent crime that had recently been brought to trial, giving the names of those charged, listing their precise criminal activities and stating what the court's sentences on the men had been. All these sentences were of various terms of imprisonment; there were no death sentences imposed.

The same report, however, stated that Liu Baode, whom it referred to merely as 'a hooligan,' had been executed by shooting after his sentencing on November 30 by the Beijing Intermediate People's Court. No further details, nor any indication of what the charges might have been, were given. Similarly, the report stated that Su Peng, also 'a hooligan,' had been sentenced to death with a two-year stay of execution, but again the charges were simply not mentioned. This is unique in Asia Watch's experience of monitoring the Chinese press, and given the particular context of this striking omission, one can only assume that the authorities had something to hide — or rather, that their aim was to 'inform' (the Chinese people) without 'revealing' (to the outside world).

Suppression of the workers' movement

The pro-democracy movement of 1989 was initiated by the students, through their mass occupation of Tiananmen Square and through the week-long hunger strike they conducted there. But at its height, the movement commanded active support from virtually all sectors of society, and particularly from the workers. By the end of May, independent labor organizations had sprung up spontaneously in numerous other major cities in China, including Shanghai, Nanjing, Changsha, Xi'an, Hangzhou, Guizhou, and Wuhan. This posed a formidable challenge to the Communist Party authorities, whose legitimacy rests upon their claim to be 'the vanguard of the proletariat.'

Not surprisingly therefore (although this has largely gone unnoticed in the West), it is the workers in China who have in fact borne the brunt of the recent and continuing repression. They form the great majority of those who have been detained, their conditions of detention ('30 to a cell,' according to UPI),[15] are much harsher than those of other groups, and they have been handed down exemplary prison sentences by the courts. They are also the ones most likely to be subjected to torture and other forms of gross ill-treatment during police interrogation. Significantly, all those known to have been executed since June 4 were either workers or unemployed.

The unsung nature of the independent labor movement in China is well illustrated by the fate since last June of Han Dongfang, 26-year-old leader of the Beijing Workers Autonomous Federation. Han, a railway maintenance worker who deserves to be better known as 'China's Lech Walesa,' has been held in secret incommunicado detention by the authorities in Beijing ever since late June 1989. Although his name, like those of the main student leaders from Tiananmen Square, such as Wang Dan and Wuerkaixi, topped the governement's 'most-wanted' lists just after the massacre in Beijing, the authorities have never announced or made public the fact of Han's arrest. According to sources inside the public security service, Han Dongfang is now gravely ill. Unable to hold down any food, he has just been hospitalized for the sixth time and is currently on an intravenous drip.

The Beijing Workers Autonomous Federation (BWAF) was formed by Han Dongfang and a small number of other workers on May 19, the eve of the declaration of martial law. Apart from a small, short-lived workers group that was set up in Taiyuan, Shanxi Province, in the winter of 1980, the BWAF is thought to have been the first truly independent labor organization in China since the founding of the People's Republic. Based in two small tents set up in the northwest corner of Tiananmen Square, the BWAF was a fledgling organization, but it appears to have enjoyed wide support from within key sections of the Beijing work force. Through its small broadcasting station on the Square, the organization gave out nightly programs of news, commentary, and political analysis, attracting enthusiastic audiences of several thousands, sometimes until dawn.

In its *Provisional Outline*, adopted in the Square on 25 May 1989, the BWAF made clear its intention to operate openly and in full conformity with the laws and constitution of the PRC. The main aims and principles of the BWAF were as follows:

The Federation shall be an entirely independent and autonomous organization, built up by the workers on a voluntary basis and through democratic processes; it should not be subject to control by other organizations.

The founding principle of the Federation shall be to address the political and economic demands of the workers, and it should not serve merely as a welfare body.

The Federation shall perform the role of monitoring the party of the proletariat — the Chinese Communist Party. Within the bounds of the law and constitution, it shall strive to protect all legal rights of its members.

On 2 June 1989, the BWAF was declared by the authorities to be a 'counterrevolutionary' organization. The Federation's tents were to be the first target of attack by the massive PLA force that arrived at the Square in the early hours of June 4, and many of its members were hunted down and arrested in the weeks and months thereafter. The day before the massacre in Beijing, Han Dongfang said:

We fully expect the authorities to take action against us. We've taken certain precautions. But if they use violence against us, well, we are unarmed and we will not resort to the use of violence against them. We are prepared to go to prison, and we are not afraid to die. I only hope that the international community will rally to our defense if the government does try to suppress us.

The reason for the unaccustomed discretion shown by the authorities, in their failure publicly to reveal the fact of Han's arrest, is plain enough, for China's leaders are above all concerned to prevent the emergence of what they refer to as the 'Polish disease' — namely, organized industrial unrest. Just after the declaration of martial law on May 20, Han Dongfang's BWAF proposed a general strike in support of the students in the Square. Had it transpired, Deng Xiaoping and his colleagues might now be collecting their retirement pensions, or worse.

Defects of the criminal justice system

Perhaps the most important human-rights concern in China today is the question of what is going to happen to all the thousands of people currently being held in police detention. Since most of them will probably be brought to trial eventually, it is worth examining in some detail the nature of the judicial system through which they must pass. Without doubt, China's criminal justice system is among the most deeply flawed in the world — indeed, it is essentially pre-modern.

First, there is no such thing as the presumption of innocence in China. The Chinese legal system, going against both the spirit and the letter of the Universal Declaration of Human Rights, explicitly rejects the principle that a detained person should be presumed innocent until proved guilty. In its place judicial officials are blandly instructed merely 'to take facts as the basis and use law as the yardstick' when handling criminal suspects. The argument given is that to presume people's innocence would be to prejudge the issue, and would mean that China's police would never be justified in arresting anyone at all.

Thus, although China claims not to presume guilt, the first thing detainees see when they enter police cells is a large sign on the wall saying: 'Lenience to those who confess, severity to those who resist.'[16] Penitence is essential, and any attempt to argue innocence is generally taken as evidence of a 'bad attitude' and as further proof of guilt. This stress on the importance of the prison confession accounts, in turn, for the authorities' frequent recourse to the baleful rituals of torture. Releases or acquittals are rare, for they imply that the judicial officers concerned have made some mistake, and this brings loss of face.

Second, the system of legal defense is woefully inadequate. Criminal detainees are expressly denied access to a lawyer throughout the period of pre-trial custody and interrogation, and may only seek legal counsel once the indictment has been issued and the case is ready to go to court — which is usually no more than two to three days before the start of trial. This more or less ensures that the lawyer has insufficient time in which to gather evidence and prepare a proper case. It also means that throughout the crucial period of the police interrogation, detainees have no one at hand to advise them of their rights or to ensure that they are not ill-treated, beaten, or tortured.

In addition, lawyers are subjected to blatant political control and interference in the execution of their duties. According to an article in *Faxue* (Law Studies) magazine in February 1988:

Some local justice departments have a regulation that if a lawyer wants to present a defense of 'not guilty' in a criminal case, then he must first of all obtain permission from the Party organization of the justice department concerned.

Evidently, the political authorities in China are even able to prevent defendants from trying to plead innocent.

Fourth, not only is there no independence of the judiciary in China (since judges are answerable to Party-dominated 'adjudication committees' and 'politics and law committees'), but the verdicts themselves are usually decided upon before the trial even begins. In fact, this unique system of justice — known in China (as in the topsy-turvy world of *Alice in Wonderland*) as 'verdict first, trial second' — is openly acknowledged to be the norm. As the Shanghai magazine *Minzhu Yu Fazhi* (Democracy and Law) explained in July 1988:

Our current trial practice in all cases, regardless of whether they are major or minor, criminal, civil, economic, or administrative ones, is that the adjudicative committee must first give its opinion on what the appropriate ruling should be, and this is then implemented [in court] by the panel of judges.

Continued the article:

'Verdict first, trial second' is tantamount to walking along a road on the top of one's head: It violates the law of proper procedure.... 'Brilliant luminaries,' who have not carried out any investigations or even read the case dossier, but have instead merely listened to an oral report on the case, are allowed to make the ruling in advance [of the trial]. Even if they reach an erroneous verdict, the panel of judges must submit to it completely and unconditionally; there is no room allowed for debate or disagreement.

And finally:

The practice of 'verdict first, trial second' can easily give rise to serious miscarriages of justice.... It gives the green light to those who seek to put their own word before the law.... It deprives the parties of their right of appeal.... It reduces the whole series of legally established procedures and principles to the level of an empty formality. All such things as 'public trial,' 'the judges' panel,' 'people's assessors,' ' legal defense,' and 'withdrawal' are stripped of all practical meaning and significance.

The prevalence of such practices demonstrates the full and bitter irony of the Chinese authorities' claim to be pursuing the current crackdown against dissent 'strictly in accordance with the rule of law.' For in reality, the 'rule of law' in China today is a one-edged sword that can only cut downward. The criminal justice system has always operated at the whim of the political authorities, but since last June it has been used as a direct instrument of wholesale political repression. So far as the many thousands of imprisoned

Chinese supporters of democracy now awaiting trial are concerned, there is simply no rule of law in China worth mentioning, and no justice can be expected.

Suppression of freedom of expression

The continued maintenance by the Chinese authorities of their false version of what actually happened last May and June has required strenuous efforts in the realm of press control. Party chief Jiang Zemin last November spelled out — though quite unintentionally — the true meaning and content of the Party's concept of press freedom in China.

Certainly, requiring propaganda and mass media to maintain political unity with the Party Central Committee propaganda does not mean mechanical parroting of political slogans. Rather, it requires them to keep to the stand of the Party and people and, by way of diverse forms, to accurately and vividly reflect and instill the Party's political standpoint, principles, and policies into news stories,[17] newsletters, commentaries, photos, headlines, and layout.

After the June 4 crackdown, propaganda officers of the PLA took over control of all the main newspapers in Beijing, and editorial departments were thoroughly overhauled. Qin Benli, chief editor of *Shijie Jingji Daobao* (World Economic Herald), the outspokenly pro-reform Shanghai newspaper, had been sacked even before the crackdown, and his Beijing deputy editor, Ruan Jianyun, was arrested last October. Yu Haocheng, former director of the Masses Publishing House (the organ of the public security authorities) and a leading advocate of legal reform, was arrested sometime last summer; and Dai Qing, China's most famous woman journalist, has been in prison since last July. Eleven other journalists or editors are known to have been arrested, but the true figure is probably much higher.

Many editors in China have been making strenuous efforts to shield and protect their journalists from the authorities' continuing purge of 'unreliable media elements.' Latest reports indicate, however, that a high-level decision has now been made to remove these editors themselves, so that the purge may proceed more smoothly. On 13 January 1990 Reuters reported the recent sacking of Guan Zhihao, director of *Law Daily* (and prime architect of the post-1985 period of 'judicial *glasnost*' referred to earlier), and also that of Xie Yongwang, liberal-minded editor of the Shanghai journal *Literature and Arts*. According to Reuters, the two have been sacked for seeking to protect their journalists from government retribution and for publishing articles last summer supportive of the students' demands.

On January 20, the Hong Kong newspaper *Ming Pao* reported that the CCP Propaganda Department had issued an order sometime after New Year calling for a renewed and intensified purge of the news media, so that editors who had failed to fall into line after June 4 could be replaced and the 'cleaning out' of journalistic ranks could begin properly. Mu Qing, director of the New China News Agency, and Zhou Bingde, deputy director of *Voice of China* and the niece of Premier Chou Enlai, head the list of senior press officials about to be sacked, according to the report.

Next in line for official 'cleansing' is the publishing world as a whole. On 6 December 1989, the New China News Agency reported that the Press and Publications Administration of China had decided to abolish or suspend the licenses of 10 percent of all existing publishing houses: 'Newspaper and magazine offices which publish pornographic stories or articles which run counter to the Party's line will be deprived of their licenses.' On 11 January 1990, the agency revealed that the Press and Publication Administration had issued a circular requiring all publishing houses to register anew between January 15 and the end of the month. 'The circular points out that in recent years publications with serious political errors and obscene and violent content have appeared despite repeated prohibitions.'[18]

The precise meaning of the terms 'anti-socialist' and 'reactionary,' as applied to writing and literature in China, have been formally codified by the authorities in recent weeks. According to Article 4 of the *Temporary Provisions of the Shanghai Municipality on the Banning of Harmful Publications*, enacted on 26 November 1989:

Reactionary publications refer to those opposing the people's democratic dictatorship and the socialist system, and include publications containing one of the following contents:
1. Opposing the Communist Party of China and its leadership.
2. Attacking the People's Republic of China and opposing taking the socialist road.
3. Attacking and vilifying the people's democratic dictatorship.

4. Denying the guiding position of Marxism-Leninism and Mao Tsetung thought.

5. Seriously distorting historical facts, advocating division of the state and people, and vilifying the Chinese people.[19]

The penalties for infringing these regulations range from a maximum fine of 30,000 *yuan* to criminal prosecution and unspecified terms of imprisonment.

Finally, on 22 December 1989 senior legislators meeting in Beijing to discuss a new draft law on authors' rights stated that henceforth 'any anti-socialist and anti-communist works should be banned in China.' According to the New China News Agency: 'The basic principle of anti-bourgeois liberalization should be spelled out in the draft...and the rights of authors who produce anti-socialist and anti-communist works should never be protected.'[20]

Only nine days after the lifting of martial law in Beijing the authorities saw fit to impose a fresh set of regulations on the news-reporting activities of foreign journalists, to replace those imposed as part of the post-June 4 clampdown. The new regulations ban all articles by foreigners that in the authorities' view 'distort facts' or 'violate the public interest,'[21] and journalists may be expelled if faulted on these counts. As was the case under the martial law rules, foreign journalists are prohibited from conducting interviews with any 'work unit' unless prior approval has been obtained from the authorities, and they may not deviate from the agreed program.[22] As one Western diplomat commented, regarding the new press regulations for foreigners: 'If they feel like it, they can get you on whatever they want.' Noted another: 'In real terms, nothing has changed.'[23]

In addition, restrictions on access by Chinese people to foreign television broadcasts have also been imposed recently. According to the *Hongkong Standard*, a municipal directive was issued by the authorities in Canton on 1 January 1990 banning the installation in the city of aerials capable of receiving television signals from outside of China. This ends a 10-year period during which the residents of Canton have been able to watch Hong Kong television programs freely. As a local cadre commented in the report: 'The authorities obviously want to stop people from being influenced by overseas reports on important issues, including the dramatic upheavals in Eastern Europe.'[24]

News censorship has been heavily evident in China throughout the recent events in Eastern Europe. Mandarin-language broadcasts of both the Voice of America and the British Broadcasting Corporation have been jammed by the authorities, and China's own press coverage of the major political turnarounds in the Eastern Bloc has been tightly controlled. Radical political change and moves toward democracy in the Eastern Bloc countries have been presented as being mainly the result of elite leadership decisions, rather than public pressure, and as constituting steps 'to perfect socialism' that ensure 'stability and unity.'[25] More generally, the upheavals in Eastern Europe have been presented by the Chinese authorities as merely proving their claim that the West is applying a 'capitalist strategy of peaceful evolution' against the socialist world.[26]

As mentioned above, a series of laws and regulations governing Chinese citizens' rights of assembly, demonstration, and association have been enacted in recent months and weeks. The net effect of these is to restrict still further the almost negligible prospects for free assembly, demonstration, and association in China, by formalizing the role and prerogatives of the state authorities in the regulation of these various types of civil activity. In the case of the *Regulations on the Registration of Social Organizations*, issued by the State Council in October 1989, for example, it is clear that a primary purpose of the document is to render unlawful any future formation of the kinds of student and worker organizations which sprang up all around the country last May and June.

The *Law of the PRC on Assemblies, Parades and Demonstrations*, adopted on 31 October 1989, is also clearly aimed at preventing the re-emergence of any sign or inkling of the kinds of mass public activity seen last summer in Beijing. Among other things, the law prohibits citizens from 'starting or organizing assemblies, parades, or demonstrations in cities where they are not residents, nor shall they participate in activities held by the local people;' and it forbids foreigners from taking part in all such activities without prior permission from the authorities. The police are granted sweeping powers to determine all aspects of any assemblies and demonstrations. In addition, the law pointedly bans all unauthorized parades and demonstrations within a 300-meter radius of a series of government institutions in central Beijing, the effect of which is to make it unlawful for any future protest demonstrations to be held in Tiananmen Square. Penalties of up to five years' imprisonment are laid down for those who violate the law.[28] On January 9, the Shanghai municipal authorities adopted a set of regulations for the law's specific enforcement, and the Beijing authorities did likewise on January 12, the day after martial law was lifted.[29]

One would think that such comprehensively restrictive measures, when viewed in the light of the current repression as a whole, would surely suffice to deter most potential 'counter-revolutionaries' from even trying to demonstrate openly. Astonishingly, however, it seems that Chinese workers and students have in fact been flocking to the authorities in the hundreds of thousands in recent months, in order to test the value of the new laws' promises regarding freedom of association and the right to demonstrate.

According to the *New York Times* of 8 January 1990, for example:

Party sources said groups representing thousands of workers across the country who have been suffering under the government's economic austerity program, which has reduced inflation but brought the country to the brink of recession, have sought permission to air their grievances.

Moreover:

The *South China Morning Post*...reported last week that workers in more than 30 Chinese cities had applied to carry out legal demonstrations involving a total of more than 500,000 workers. Party sources could not confirm the figure of 500,000, but said worker discontent was widespread and involved most of the country's provinces.

Clearly, the 'Polish disease' has already gone well past the merely incubatory stage in China today. The response of the Chinese authorities to these polite requests for the observance of their rights by workers was, however, predictably churlish:

According to the sources, the leadership issued an order to security forces that they use 'whatever force is necessary' to crush any demonstrations staged by workers.

The full shock-waves of the recent events in Eastern Europe are, of course, still to come.

These excerpts are reprinted by permission of Asia Watch. The report appeared in February 1990.

1. The Beijing correspondent of UPI reported on 27 July 1989 that more than 40 people had been secretly executed during the previous two weeks at Lugouqiao ('*Marco Polo Bridge*') in the suburbs of Beijing.

2. *Washington Post*, 3 December 1989.

3. *Agence France Press*, 5 December 1989; in *FBIS*, 3 January 1990.

4. *Star Tribune* (Minneapolis, Minn.), 24 December 1989.

5. *New York Times*, 2 January 1990. Reportedly: 'The Party secretary was particularly outraged because he had received anonymous letters purporting to inform on him.' According to another, slightly earlier interview: 'A professor, heaving a sigh, said: "*My students become cynical, suffer agonies, fall into despair, and are at a loss, and the school and sutdents are changed beyond recognition.*"' (*FBIS*, 27 December 1989)

6. Both were from Quinghua University, Beijing. According to the *Hongkong Standard* of 1 December 1989, a postgraduate student named Tang Zujie, 23, jumped from a sixth-floor window campus on October 1, China's National Day. An economics postgraduate named Guo Wei, 24, killed himself on November 2.

7. *Bai Xing*, 16 December 1989; in *FBIS*, December 19.

8. *Washington Post*, 14 December 1989.

9. In *FBIS*, 15 December 1989.

10. *Agence France Presse*, 8 January 1990; in *FBIS*, same day.

11. For example, *Hunan Radio* announced on 27 December 1989 that 18 criminals had been executed the previous day (*FBIS* 8 January 1989); and on 11 January 1990 the *China New Service* announced the execution the same day of no less than 31 criminals in Canton (*Ming Bao* January).

12. *China Law Daily*, 5 September 1988.

13. *Criminal Law of the PRC*, Article 154.

14. *Xin Zhongguo Xingfaxue Yanjiu Zongshu, 1949–1985* (A General Study of Criminological Research in New China), Gao Mingxuan (ed.), Henan People's Publishing House, p. 422.

15. UPI, in *South China Morning Post*, 5 November 1989.

16. The guidelines set by Ren Jianxin, president of the Supreme People's Court, for handling the trials of pro-democracy demonstrators forcefully reiterated this time-honored 'principle' of Chinese law: 'In the course of adjudication, we must combine punishment with leniency. We must deal with those who confess their crimes with leniency and inflict severe punishment on those who refuse to do so.' (*Beijing Television*, 15 July 1989; in *FBIS*, 17 July 1989)

17. 'Jiang Zemin gives speeches on mass media work,' *New China News Agency*, 29 November 1989; in *FBIS*, 7 December 1989.

18. *New China News Agency*, in *FBIS*, 11 January 1990.

19. *Jiefang Ribao*, 5 December 1989; in *FBIS*, 10 January 1990.

20. New China News Agency, 22 December 1989; in *FBIS*, December 27.

21. *FBIS*, 19 December 1989.

22. There are even signs that the English language itself is now considered to be subversive. Beijing's highly popular 'English Corner,' where Chinese of all ages used to come to practice their conversation, was just

recently closed down by the authorities. According to the *New York Times* of 19 December 1989: 'In mid-November, the area was cordoned off and notices went up, saying, 'English Corner has been withdrawn.' The university teachers, the notices said, no longer had the time.'

23. *Reuters*, 20 January 1990; *New York Times*, January 21; *Shijie Ribao*, January 22.

24. *Hongkong Standard*, 6 January 1990.

25. *New York Times*, 24 December 1989.

26. *New York Times*, 22 December 1989. The charge that the West is trying to make China 'peacefully evolve into a bourgeois republic' was first made by Deng Xiaoping, directly after the June 4 massacre. As the *People's Daily*, explained on 1 December 1989: 'The international reactionary forces...will work in coordination with the turmoil created in socialist countries in an attempt to force them to make concessions to them so that socialist countries may 'peacefully evolve' into capitalist countries, thus turning those socialist countries into their vassal states. Imperialists have openly declared that their principle is to implement political pluralism and market economy in socialist countries; in other words, they want to implement the bourgeois multiparty system and rotatory term of office, while driving the Communist Party out of office and eventually restoring capitalism.'

27. *China Daily*, 1 November 1989; in *FBIS*, same day.

28. Text of the law is in *FBIS*, 1 November 1989.

29. *FBIS*, 10 January 1989; *Shijie Ribao*, January 13.

Deng's 'Middle Kingdom' Strategy

RICHARD C. THORNTON

IN the wake of the Chinese government's massacre at Tiananmen Square and subsequent crackdown, many Western pundits have scrambled to make sense of what they believed was a major change in Chinese strategy. The fact is, however, that while a course correction has occurred, it is by no means a sea change. Indeed, post-Tiananmen policy is nothing less than a reaffirmation of the strategy Deng Xiaoping has pursued for more than 15 years. It can best be understood as the culmination of a two-year internal factional struggle, centering on the issues of the pace and content of China's modernization and geopolitical orientation between East and West.[1]

'Reformists' argued that China should continue to rely upon the West, principally the U.S., to provide the economic model, technological expertise, and resources for rapid movement toward a market-oriented economic system. Others, often termed 'conservatives,' pressed for the adoption of a slower developmental pace, with greater central control and planning, and rapprochement with Moscow and the Eastern bloc. From this perspective, the crackdown at Tiananmen indicated that the conservatives, for the time being at least, had won the leadership struggle.

A brief review of China's strategic options and recent history will help illuminate the larger significance of the decisions of June 3–4. If we assume that China's main priority is to become an independent, powerful, modern state, then given the country's backward condition, a sustained modernization effort is necessary. The problem has always been: how? From this perspective, the focal point of arguments within the Chinese leadership has been over the essential preconditions for modernization — that is, a long period of internal stability and external security.

As the Chinese leadership sees it, there are three possibilities: the American, the Soviet, and the independent.[2] The 'American option' offers a relatively fast-paced, high-tech oriented modernization program. But it would also require a substantial change in

China's economic system and political philosophy, as well as a substantial allocation of resources for defense against the Soviet threat. (China devotes at least 25 percent of its military budget to defense against the Soviet Union.) The chief concerns under this option are that the requirements for external security would consume too large a percentage of scarce resources, without guaranteeing it, and that the fast pace of Western-style modernization would threaten internal stability.

The 'Soviet option' required a full-scale political rapprochement with Moscow, including re-establishment of the alliance structure of 1950 in a more equitable form. The Soviet option clearly buys external security — but at a cost of significant loss of autonomy, no matter how nicely packaged. Chinese modernization under this option would proceed on a much slower pace, but under greater central control. The kinds of defense costs would, of course, be far different within an alliance with the Soviet Union than in opposition to it, and such an alliance would permit greater allocation of resources to domestic improvements. The loss of independence, however, is the real and probably unacceptable cost for Beijing.

The third possibility, the independent option, or the 'Middle Kingdom' strategy, is the approach Deng has advocated since his return to power in 1973. Deng first elaborated the independent approach in a speech delivered at the United Nations in April 1974.[3] Titled the 'three worlds' thesis, it called for an 'even-handed' treatment of Washington and Moscow, without leaning to either side. But Deng was unable to put his strategy into practice at the time because Mao Zedong still retained overall command of foreign policy. Indeed, Mao purged Deng again in 1976 a few months before his death. While Deng returned to power the following year, he did not ascend to a pre-eminent position until 1978. Nevertheless, the three worlds thesis indicated what he would do if and when he emerged as China's leader.

Under this strategy, China, as a Third World nation, would treat both superpowers more or less equally, while attempting to develop stronger ties with Europe — especially West Germany — and Japan, the key surplus nations of the second world. Adopting an 'even-handed' approach to the superpowers would, presumably, provide for external security by satisfying Moscow's concerns about an American-sponsored threat to its Asian security interests. It would also require ending the Sino-Soviet conflict and normalizing relations with the Soviet Union.

392 THE BROKEN MIRROR

At the same time, the independent approach would permit a moderately paced developmental scheme that would be consistent with Beijing's desire for internal stability and control. Drawing upon the resources of the European powers and Japan for basic developmental assistance, while accepting as much 'no strings' help as Washington and Moscow deigned to provide, Beijing could maximize its independence and security, and also reduce defense costs.

The difference between the independent and the American options centers on the kind of economic, and ultimately political, system China would develop as part of its modernization program. The former requires a fundamental turn away from the tightly controlled, communist system of central planning to a price-oriented, open market system with much less central control. There are obvious political implications as well. The latter would attempt, in traditional Chinese fashion, to incorporate Western technology without disrupting the existing political-economic system.

Deng's Middle Kingdom strategy in practice

Deng has sought to pursue his 'Middle Kingdom' strategy since his rise to power, but has been thwarted by developments beyond his control. The problem for Deng was that Moscow declined to cooperate. Since the late 1950s, when the Sino-Soviet split occurred, the Soviet Union had pursued an aggressive containment policy toward China even while professing a desire to heal the breach. Similarly, China under Mao had assiduously declined all Soviet offers — and there were several — for rapprochement.

In early 1979, following his victory over Mao's chosen successor, Hua Guofeng, Deng was in a position to change the anti-Soviet course set by Mao and implement his own Middle Kingdom strategy. A few weeks after the abortive invasion of Vietnam, in April 1979, Deng offered to normalize relations with Moscow as he had just done with Washington earlier that year.[4] While Moscow — after some hesitation — agreed to begin normalization talks, the Soviets stalled, and no progress had been made by the time the Soviet Union invaded Afghanistan, at which point the talks were suspended.

The cause for the Soviet delay had little to do with China, or Deng, per se. It had to do with a major geopolitical opportunity which the Soviets did not wish to complicate by normalizing relations with China.[5] That opening lay in the collapse of Iran in early 1979, which, from Moscow's perspective, opened up a geo-political opportunity at least as attractive as the revolution in China itself 40 years before. So Moscow procrastinated on China ties while positioning itself to attempt to draw Iran into its orbit.

The irony was that the collapse of the Shah came at virtually the identical historical moment that Deng had risen to pre-eminence in China. In any case, in the face of Moscow's disinclination to improve political ties, Deng was unable to pursue his Middle Kingdom strategy and moved gradually to develop relations with the U.S. and the West — the 'American option.'

Although diplomatic relations with the U.S. were established in 1979, Deng did not move toward the American option with alacrity. In fact, he procrastinated on economic reforms for almost three years before coming to terms, using Washington's determination to maintain ties with Taiwan, especially military ties, as the reason for delay.[6] Moreover, delay was made easier by the initial disinclination of the Reagan administration to undercut Taiwan. Finally, in the summer of 1982, the U.S. and China negotiated the basic document — the August communique — which governed their subsequent relations.

Deng then tried to open the door to Moscow one more time, perhaps assuming or hoping that the move toward the U.S. would prompt the Soviets to reply favorably. Following the 12th Party Congress in September 1982, which marked the final political rout of Hua Guofeng and his allies, Deng offered to normalize relations with Moscow once again. Low-level negotiations resumed, but Moscow's reaction was the same as three years before. The Soviets agreed to some improvement in economic ties, but stalled on the key question of political normalization.

The decision to proceed with the American option led to the emergence of a major constituency within the Chinese leadership. These 'reformers' demanded that initial steps toward reform, modernization, and development continue through introduction of a full-fledged market-oriented system, particularly with regard to loosening internal controls, both economic and then political. Deng and his supporters in the Chinese leadership were not ignorant of the dangers such broad-based reform could pose to continued Party rule and internal stability. At this point, however, they had no other choice.

Following Gorbachev's rise to power in 1985, however, Moscow changed its own strategy. In addition to improving relations with the U.S., Gorbachev offered to normalize relations with China.[7] The signal to Beijing came in Gorbachev's 28 July 1986 speech in Vladivostock. His speech marked the beginning of almost continuous high-level talks between the two countries, as well as a rapid increase in economic ties between the Soviet Union and China, and East European nations and China.[8]

Most importantly, the Vladivostock speech triggered the beginning of a policy debate within the Chinese leadership. Deng's Middle Kingdom approach, which would place limits on reform, increase central control, and include political rapprochement with Moscow, now looked viable.[9] The debate centered on the advisability of continued expansion of economic reform to encompass political reform, in the context of further development of the American option. Then-Party chairman Hu Yaobang argued the case for continued modernization and development along the lines of the American option. As Zhao Ziyang would in 1989, Hu gave support to student pro-democracy demonstrations in December 1986–January 1987 (although the demonstrations were of much smaller proportions than in 1989).

There were clearly grounds for debate. Through 1986, the reform program had produced big pluses, but also big minuses. Rapid foreign trade growth, made possible by the sale of petroleum, had led to a shortfall in domestic energy supplies and brought a slowdown in economic growth.[10] Moreover, petroleum prices had plummeted, making continued sales unprofitable. Direct foreign investment slowed markedly in 1986 and virtually all of China's accumulated foreign exchange reserves were used to reduce the cost of imports. This policy had been only partially successful. By year's end, the IMF estimated China's foreign debt to stand at more than US$27 billion, while China's overall budget deficit had reached nearly US$6 billion.[11]

Under these circumstances, Hu lost the internal debate and was subsequently purged in January 1987. The student demonstrations that accompanied the debate were ended, with minimal use of force. Deng then moved to constrict further development of the American option and opened the door wider to the Soviet bloc. In late 1986 Beijing concluded a major economic agreement with Moscow, which called for a fivefold expansion in trade from US$2 to US$10 billion by 1990 and opened discussions on trade and other bilateral questions with Hungary, Czechoslovakia, Poland, and East Germany.

According to Chen Yizi, after the 13th Party Congress in 1987, 'the reformers knew...they could not count on the full support of paramount leader Deng Xiaoping.'[12] Although Deng told the Congress that 'central planning and market forces both were necessary for China's future,' Chen said, he 'allowed conservatives to block the calls of Zhao...for liberalizing ownership of property.' Thus, while it appeared on the surface that the Congress had reaffirmed China's commitment to reform, conservatives were able to place their own supporters into key government positions to hinder or block it. This was possible because Deng's promotion of Zhao from the premiership to the Party chairmanship took control of the government — and therefore of the reform program — away from him.

Although the strategic issue was apparently resolved in early 1987, it was nevertheless clear that the substantial constituency within the Party-intellectual-student-entrepreneur strata continued to press for reform and Westernization, and that internal Party debate continued at high levels. Meanwhile, China's economy overheated as a result of too-rapid economic growth exacerbated by increasing official corruption. Through 1988, inflation soared to its highest level in the history of the People's Republic.[13]

At the September Party plenum, Deng moved to enact an austerity program to regain control over the economy. The retrenchment plan was also a turn away from the breakneck pace of reform of the previous five years. Market reforms were postponed indefinitely, plans to introduce price reform were shelved, capital investment was reduced by 20 percent, price controls were reimposed on selected raw materials, and to stimulate sagging agricultural output, state procurement prices for grain, sugar, and oil-seed crops were increased.[14]

With the December 1988 scheduling of Gorbachev's visit to Beijing for mid-May of 1989, the internal debate intensified. Zhao Ziyang, Hu's successor, took up the case for continued Westernization and expanded reform. Zhao urged on pro-democracy demonstrators in May 1989 in a last-gasp attempt to influence the leadership away from retrenchment. But he, too, lost the policy debate, and was purged (some say he resigned) before the crackdown.[15] The strategic issue, it would appear, had been decided in favor of Deng's Middle Kingdom course.

Given the nature of China's political system, resolution of the strategic issue also meant that the substantial constituency committed to the 'American option' had to be removed. The immediate question became how to deal with the demonstrators in Tiananmen Square. On this, there were clearly divisions within the military, and perhaps the Party as well, about the advisability of a harsh crackdown against the demonstrators. In this sense, the Tiananmen Square demonstrations were more product than cause of the division within the leadership.

It seems obvious that the Square could have been cleared without the degree of violence used. Consider the fact that between the imposition of martial law on May 20 and the massacre of June 3–4, the authorities, with considerable intimidation, but minimal physical coercion, had whittled the several hundred thousand demonstrators down to a few thousand. It is difficult to believe that removing the last few thousand holdouts could not have been done relatively peaceably, over the course of a few more days or weeks, as was done in 1987. Indeed, as we now know, the authorities had in fact reached agreement with the demonstrators to clear the Square.

From this perspective, the crackdown represented the decision to deliver a sharp blow to the pro-Westernizing constituency, while sending an unmistakable message to the West, and the U.S. in particular, that its influence would henceforth be strictly limited. China would not pursue the American option. In subsequent months, Beijing would take a tough line on relations with the U.S., denouncing Washington's position as 'interference in China's internal affairs' and accusing the U.S. of complicity in inciting the democracy movement,[16] even while denying that it had killed its own people.

Conclusion

Clearly, Deng hopes that China can have its *doufu* and eat it too, in pursuit of his Middle Kingdom ideal. He calculated that, after the dust settles, enough of a relationship with the West, particularly with Western Europe and Japan, will remain to allow China to continue on a moderately paced, centrally controlled modernization program.

He believes that political rapprochement with Moscow will, aside from an increase in economic agreements and trade, purchase external security and release substantial resources for reallocation to the modernization effort. (Indeed, barely six weeks after the Tiananmen events, Beijing and Moscow signed a protocol on long-term economic cooperation, covering industry, agriculture, science, and education.[17])

Soviet leader Gorbachev, during his visit to Beijing in May 1989, and reaffirmed since by Soviet spokesmen, reinforced the view of mutual border security, calling for 'demilitarizing the Soviet-Chinese border and turning it into a border of peace and good-neighborliness.'[18] In his speech, he declared that the Soviet Union would withdraw 11 Air Force regiments, 16 warships from the Pacific fleet, and 12 ground force divisions, representing 120,000 of the promised withdrawal of 200,000 troops from the border. (There are 600,000 troops deployed along the border in all.) Through 'joint efforts,' he said, withdrawal should proceed to the point where the only troops left would be those 'required for performing routine border guard duties.'

An intriguing question is whether Moscow seeks a *quid pro quo* in its own plan for rapprochement with Beijing. Could it be that in return for Soviet fulfillment of China's three conditions — reduction of the military buildup on the Chinese border, withdrawal from Afghanistan, and resolution of the Cambodian question — Beijing must fulfill one of Moscow's? That, of course, would relate to Moscow's long-standing fear of American military ties to Beijing. Is a condition for rapprochement and mutual security from Moscow's point of view a change in China's military ties with the U.S.? If so, Deng, and those who support him, must believe that given the level of China's development and its current needs, the gains from rapprochement will outweigh the losses from a cutback in U.S. military assistance.

Since Tiananmen, Deng has proceeded doggedly on his Middle Kingdom course. In November 1989, the Chinese leadership issued a series of directives, known as Central Committee Document Number 11, which went considerably beyond the 1988 austerity program. Belt-tightening measures were set in place to last 'for at least three years.'[19] Although calling for continuation of economic reforms and an 'even greater' opening to the outside world, private enterprises are to be subordinated to the state-run economy.

The directives seek to eliminate the two-tiered pricing system established earlier in the 1980s, in an effort to stamp out what the leadership terms a 'breeding ground for corruption,'[20] but which will effectively eliminate open market pricing for the economy. The main measures are to regain central control over prices, reinforce the lagging state enterprise sector of the economy, and increase taxes on the more productive private and collective enterprises.

Agriculture, described as based on a 'fragile foundation' and in 'serious condition,' would receive a greater infusion of state resources, particularly in the form of the 'organization of farm labor on a larger scale to build irrigation works.' The overall objective of the new retrenchment measures is to regain control over the economy and regulate it from above in an effort to pursue 'economic self-reliance.'[21]

If Deng believed that the West would soon return to business as usual, he was right. Within a month of the crackdown, Washington secretly sent emissaries to remonstrate with the Chinese leadership. And it took barely six months before Washington publicly backed away from the lukewarm sanctions imposed after the crackdown, sending secretly yet a second, high-level delegation to Beijing. The Bush administration's ostensible purpose was 'to resolve bilateral differences over human rights and to keep China from slipping into international isolation.'[22]

The missions produced no public agreements with the Chinese government on human rights and talk of China slipping into 'international isolation' seemed to have more to do with the Bush administration's self-perception than with Chinese reality. Indeed, it seems that it is the U.S. that is most concerned about being isolated, as West European nations and Japan showed little inclination to follow Washington's lead on sanctions. Perhaps this would help explain why the U.S. government had not placed any substantial penalties on Beijing for the Tiananmen massacre beyond a verbal wrist slap and brief suspension of ongoing projects.[23]

Although President Bush suspended export of military and military-related technology, Boeing was permitted to deliver four jetliners in July and August, and yet a fifth in October — even though the on-board navigational systems have obvious potential military uses.[24] The same is true for three communications satellites being built by Hughes Aircraft Company, two for AUSSAT, an Australian firm, and the third for AsiaSat, a British-Chinese consortium. The sale, described as coming under 'normal commercial exports,' rather than munitions, would be the first such technology transfer to a communist nation.[25] Finally, some 42 Chinese nationals being trained by Grumman Corporation to install and maintain an upgraded avionics package for China's F-8 fighter aircraft were briefly furloughed, but then permitted to return in the summer.[26]

From this analysis, it seems clear that Deng Xiaoping and his supporters have weathered a major challenge from a powerful faction within the Chinese Communist leadership elite, which pressed for the reform of China's economic and political systems along American lines. Deng's strategy, consistent since 1973, is for China to assume a position of self-reliance characterized by geo-political equidistance between the two superpowers — allying with neither, dealing with both.

Domestically, the strategy calls for economic growth to take place in a system that is both Chinese and socialist, not capitalist. Modernization and growth are to occur within clearly defined limits set by the Party, not by market forces. Whether it is realistic to revert to what is in essence the Soviet system of the 1950s — and a system that the Soviets themselves are casting aside — only time will tell. Whether Deng's strategy will survive his death, we will discover soon enough.

---

1. Chen Yizi, senior Chinese official and key adviser to Zhao Ziyang, who defected to France in June, declared in a rare on-the-record interview that 'the popular student-led demonstrations for democracy this spring brought to a head a two-year-old power struggle within the Politburo over the future of reform.' See Jim Hoagland, 'Senior Chinese Official Who Fled Emerges From Hiding,' *Washington Post*, 4 September 1989, p. A1.

2. I have touched on this developmental question elsewhere. See my *China: A Political History, 1917–1980* (Boulder: Westview Press, 1982), pp. 435–9.

3. *Beijing Review*, 19 April 1974.

4. *New China News Agency*, 3 April 1979. The offer came in the context of a denunciation of the 1950 treaty of Friendship and Alliance one year in advance as stipulated by the terms of the treaty.

5. For further discussion of the Soviet turnaround, see the author's *Soviet Asian Strategy in the Brezhnev Era and Beyond* (Washington: Washington Institute Press, 1985), pp. 63–71.

6. For the record of his delaying tactics, see A. Doak Barnett, *U.S. Arms Sales, The China-Taiwan Tangle* (Washington: The Brookings Institution, 1982).

7. I have treated the reasons for the change in Soviet strategy under

Gorbachev elsewhere. See, for example, 'Detente II — Salt III: American Dream or Nightmare?' *The World and I*, January 1987.

8. For more of the reaction to the speech, see my 'The Grand Strategy Behind Renewed Sino-Soviet Relations,' *The World and I*, December 1986.

9. See footnote 1.

10. Nicholas R. Lardy, *China's Entry Into The World Economy* (Lanham: University Press of America, 1987), p. 38.

11. *Ibid*.

12. See footnote 1.

13. Central Intelligence Agency, 'The Chinese Economy in 1988 and 1989: Reforms On Hold, Economic Problems Mount,' a report to the Subcommittee on Technology and National Security of the Joint Economic Committee, 7 July 1989, p. 1.

14. *Ibid*., pp. 4–5.

15. His removal was announced in late June. See Michael Weisskopf, 'Chinese Communist Party Ousts Zhao as Chief in Wide Shake-Up,' *Washington Post*, 25 June 1989, p. 1.

16. Don Oberdorfer, 'China Takes Tough Line on U.S. Relations,' *Washington Post*, 3 October 1989, p. 9, and Daniel Southerland, 'Deng Says U.S. Involved In Democracy Movement,' *Washington Post*, 1 November 1989, p. A40.

17. 'China and Soviets close economic deal,' *Washington Times*, 27 July 1989, p. A2.

18. 'Gorbachev wants "friendship" to protect Sino-Soviet border,' *Washington Times*, 18 May 1989, p. A7.

19. Daniel Southerland, 'China Sets Sharp Turn For Economic Policies,' *Washington Post*, 30 November 1989, p. A37.

20. *Ibid*.

21. *Ibid*.

22. Danial Southerland, 'Deng Meets With U.S. Delegation in Beijing,' *Washington Post*, 11 December 1989, p. 1.

23. George Lardner, Jr., 'U.S. Began Lifting Business, Military Sanctions on China Months Ago,' *Washington Post*, 12 December 1989, p. A20.

24. *Ibid*.

25. Frank J. Murray, 'Bush prepares to let China have satellites,' *Washington Times*, 13 December 1989, p. A1.

26. *Washington Post*, 12 December, 1989.

China's Post-Tiananmen Diplomacy

JOSEPH Y.S. CHENG

DENG Xiaoping emerged on 9 June 1989 to thank the People's Liberation Army for implementing martial law in Beijing. His reappearance left no doubt as to who was really in charge in China, and who had to take ultimate responsibility for the Beijing massacre. Nonetheless, his reappearance was a signal that the worst of the internal factional struggle had been avoided and at least temporary political stability had been restored, and this was welcomed by the people in China, as well as foreign governments.

Deng made an important speech on the occasion. He stated:

This storm was bound to come. This was determined by the international macro-climate and the micro-climate inside China itself. It was relatively good for us that it came now. The most important advantage was that we still have a large group of senior comrades who are still alive. They have experienced many storms, understood the pros and cons of the issues, and supported the use of resolute action to deal with the riots.[1]

Deng believed that those involved in the 'counterrevolutionary riots' had two basic slogans: 'One is to defeat the Communist Party, and the other is to overthrow the socialist system. Their goal is to establish a bourgeois republic completely attached to the West.'

Relations with the West

While the Chinese leadership now accuses Zhao Ziyang and his supporters of advocating 'complete Westernization,' the communique of the fourth plenum of the Thirteenth Central Committee of the Chinese Communist Party released on June 24 announced that the policies of reform and opening to the outside world 'will continue to be steadfastly carried out as before' and that China 'will never go back to the old closed-door path.'[2] Nevertheless, the Tiananmen massacre has much shaken China's status as the West's favorite partner in the socialist world. Under the pressure of public opinion, France, the Netherlands, and Sweden cut all links short of diplomatic relations with China in June 1989, while Britain and Switzerland confined their reaction to suspending arms sales and canceling formal visits between senior military personnel.

On June 5, President George Bush announced the U.S. response, which he described as 'reasoned, careful action that takes into account both our long-term interests and recognition of a complex internal situation in China.'[3] Bush's package included suspension of all government-to-government sales and commercial exports of weapons, suspension of all visits between senior U.S. and Chinese military officials, sympathetic review of requests by Chinese students in the U.S. to extend their stay, and the offer of humanitarian and medical assistance, through the Red Cross, to those injured during the fighting.

Reacting to criticisms and economic sanctions from the West, Beijing, typically, attacked the human rights advocates there for intervening in China's internal policies. An article in the *People's Daily* on 24 September 1989, for example, indicated that attempts by 'international policemen' in some Western countries to 'force China to change its domestic policy' amounted to instances of 'power politics and hegemonism.'[4] It went on to say that some Westerners even advocated 'granting economic cooperation in exchange for democracy.' Li Peng raised the theme of anti-hegemonism in a State Council meeting in mid-August 1989 when he elaborated on China's foreign policy and condemned the 'anti-China tide fanned by some Western countries.'[5] Though Li admitted that 'peace' and 'development' were still two major problems, he pointed out that the factors for war had not disappeared, and that anti-hegemonism and protecting world peace would be long-term struggles.

'Anti-hegemonism' had seldom been mentioned in recent years. Before the recent political turmoil, China maintained a very good relationship, sometimes described as a pseudo-alliance, with the U.S. Mikhail Gorbachev's visit to Beijing in May 1989 finally achieved full normalization of state-to-state and Party-to-Party relations with the USSR. The re-emergence of the theme of anti-hegemonism is largely an attempt on the part of Beijing to demonstrate its intention to keep a distance from the West and to reaffirm its status as a Third World country. This foreign policy shift is based on changes in the domestic political scene. The hard-liners in the leadership and the military have succeeded in turning China's foreign policy to the needs of domestic political struggles, and this factor will continue to shape Chinese foreign policy.

The communique of the fourth plenum of the Thirteenth Central Committee of the CCP reaffirmed that China's independent, self-reliant, and peaceful foreign policy would not change, and China would on the basis of the Five Principles of Peaceful Coexistence continue to develop friendly relations with other countries. [6] After a decade of close economic ties with the West, the Chinese leadership appreciates the capitalist world's contribution to China's modernization. It is prepared to adopt a business-as-usual attitude at the practical negotiation level, and in fact it is often willing to make concessions to come to agreements. The Chinese mass media have also taken care to continue to churn out success stories of foreign business ventures in China.

The CCP Political Bureau made the following three observations on the world situation after the Tiananmen massacre: a) the Party Central Committee had not changed its basic views on the global situation, the trends of detente between East and West had not changed, and likewise the triangular relationship among the U.S., the Soviet Union, and China; b) China would continue to improve relations with the Soviet Union and the Eastern European countries, but this improvement in relations could not surpass China's relations with the U.S., Japan, and Western countries; c) China in the past had been too close to the West and the rich countries, and had neglected the Third World and the old friends in Africa. In the crucial moments, as had been demonstrated in the recent disturbance, it was the old friends and the Third World that had shown China sympathy and support. China therefore should strive to resume and develop relations with these old friends. [7]

Soon after the Beijing massacre, the Chinese foreign minister, Qian Qichen, visited Africa in August and the Middle East in September. [8] These visits were designed to raise China's international profile among Third World countries and reassure them of its renewed commitment. No dramatic results were achieved, but they symbolize a significant shift in Beijing's pro-Western tilt since 1978, which had angered many of China's Third World friends.

During Qian's visit to Africa, he noted at a press conference in Harare, capital of Zimbabwe, that of the 137 countries that had established diplomatic relations with China, only some 20 had reacted adversely to what had happened in China; the majoritty, including African countries, neighboring Asian countries, Latin American countries, and socialist countries, considered it China's internal affair and that other countries should not poke their noses into it.[9]

Reviewing China's diplomacy in the past 40 years, Qian observed that 'the most fundamental experience is that a country must maintain state sovereignty and national dignity and uphold its independent foreign policy,' and he concluded by promising 'greater contributions to the struggle against hegemonism and for world peace.'[10]

Despite this rhetoric, the Chinese leaders have also been careful to maintain good ties with the major countries of the world. In late July and early August 1989, Qian launched an active diplomatic campaign while attending the Paris conference on Kampuchea. Qian achieved respectable results, which included the resumption of the Sino-British Joint Liaison Group meeting in September 1989, the beginning of mutual border troop reduction negotiations with the Soviet Union in the following November, the securing of a commitment from Japan to resume economic aid to China upon the normalization of the situation, the resumption of negotiations with Indonesia on the re-establishment of diplomatic relations by their permanent representatives at the United Nations, the securing of a promise from France not to allow anti-China activities in its territory, the resumption of a US$85 million loan to China from Canada, and the reaffirmation of importance attached to the bilateral relationship by the delegations from China and the U.S.[11] Qian again met the U.S. Secretary of State James Baker in New York while attending a meeting of the United Nations General Assembly in late September 1989. Baker defended the meeting and stated that the talks were needed to encourage Beijing to improve its human-rights record.[12]

The West certainly values China's modernization and it does not want to push China back into isolation. Western businessmen are keen to persuade their respective governments to avoid severe economic sanctions against China because they fear the loss of business opportunities. Japan has been especially eager to end economic sanctions because its strategic and commercial interests in China are enormous. (Japan's nightmare is soaring inflation and chaos in China, leading to inability to pay debts and an exodus of Chinese boat people to Japan.)[13] The arrival of Chinese in Japan posed as Vietnamese refugees in October 1989 marked the first time since 1949 that Chinese had fled other than to places like Hong Kong and Taiwan.

A few months after the Beijing massacre, a consensus gradually emerged among the Western countries that constructive engagement was better than a boycott and would produce a more influential China policy. In early October 1989, senior Japanese and American officials agreed that their two countries should unite to support China's modernization and its open-door policy, though they admitted that it was not possible in the near future to return to business with China as existed before June.[14] World Bank president Barber Conable indicated in September 1989 that the bank wanted to make loans to China as soon as possible; and the General Agreement on Tariffs and Trade resumed consideration of China's application to join in mid-December 1989.[15]

At the same time, cracks began to appear in the sanctions imposed by the West. Britain allowed the export of avionics equipment for Chinese fighter planes, and the British Foreign Office explained that as these items could not be used for internal repression, the deal did not break the embargo on arms sales.[16]

The Chinese leadership, however, still did not attempt to cultivate a more conciliatory public image in response to the friendly gestures from the West. The leadership instead chose to stick to the hard-line defined by Deng in June 1989. Fear of the developments in the Soviet Union and Eastern Europe may also be a contributing factor. The new leaders' joint press conference on 26 September 1989 at the Great Hall of the People clearly conveyed the message that the hard-line policies would persist for some time. CCP General Secretary Jiang Zemin declared that the Tiananmen incident was not a 'tragedy,' and refused to rule out more death sentences for the leaders of China's democracy movement.[17] China therefore missed the first opportunity to resume loans from the World Bank after its annual conference in late September 1989 in Washington, D.C.[18] The COCOM too decided to cancel preferential retreatment for China concerning the transfer of high technology.

Economic sanctions, though softened, continued simply because the Chinese leaders refused to compromise.[19] The Chinese mass media continue to attack the capitalist world for the use of trade, propaganda, war, and diplomacy to attack communisim.[20] The *Liberatio Army Daily*, for example, stated that the young Chinese who live in peace and prosperity find it difficult to understand 'the secret murder plan' behind the Western slogans of peace.[12] The same newspaper also attacked the imports of consumer goods from foreign countries, on the grounds they caused domestic factories to lose money, reduce production, and increase their stockpiles.[22]

In view of the instability in Eastern Europe and the Soviet Union, the Bush administration was eager to avoid severe damage to Sino-American ties. The visits by Brent Scowcroft, national security adviser, and Lawrence Eagleburger, deputy secretary of state, to Beijing in July and December 1989, demonstrated the president's desire not to further alienate China or exacerbate its isolation.[23] The Chinese leadeers were therefore able to claim that the West had made the first step, and were willing to respond by terminating martial law in January 1990. Economic ties between China and the West, particularly with the U.S. and Japan, will probably be resumed in 1990, though the confidence of the private sector will take much longer to recover.[2]

Relations with the socialist countries and the Third World

Sino-Soviet relations consolidated after Mikhail Gorbachev's visit to Beijing, and do not seem to have been affected by the Tiananmen massacre. Since May 1989, Chinese Vice-Premier Tian Jiyun and State Councilor Song Jian, head of the State Science and Technology Commission, have visited the Soviet Union. They were followed by Zhu Liang, head of the CCP International Liaison Department. During Zhu's visit in September 1989, Gorbachev invited Jiang Zemin to visit Moscow.[25] Gorbachev was the first foreign leader to extend an invitation to Jiang as CCP General Secretary. Though Jiang may not be able to visit the Soviet Union soon, Premier Li Peng will likely do so in the summer of 1990.

Trade between the two communist giants has been booming, with Soviet officials forecasting a 17% increase in 1989 to more than US$3 billion.[26] In the past decade, Sino-Soviet trade has risen six times, and the potential for further growth is substantial, though China at present accounts for only 3% of the Soviet Union's total trade. A new railway is now being built to connect Soviet Kazakhstan with the Xinjiang-Uigur Autonomus Region. The Soviet Union is interested in Chinese labor, foodstuffs, and consumer goods to develop Siberia and the Soviet Far East, while

China hopes its interior provinces will benefit from such economic exchanges, a compensation for the privileges enjoyed by its coastal provinces.

A senior Soviet parliamentary group arrived at China in September 1989, led by Analoly Lukyanov, a vice president of the Presidium of the Supreme Soviet. More significant still, a high-ranking Soviet military official was included in the delegation to initiate the first round of negotiations on setting up a demilitarized zone (DMZ) along the Sino-Soviet border.[27] In terms of today's modern military technology, a dozen kilometers from the border line will hardly have any impact on the military balance, but the political implications are considerable. The negotiations may eventually lead to the pulling back of the PLA from the Tibetan border with Nepal and India; this will underline China's desire for friendly ties with India.

Soviet troop reductions in Asia, announced by Gorbachev in December 1988, are under way. It is significant that most of the cuts have been made in border garrisons facing China, with so far little change in the line-up against Japanese and forces.[28] Gorbachev pledged a reduction of 200,000 troops from east of the Urals by the beginning of 1991, and this will certainly be closely monitored by China. Soviet defense analysts have indicated that they do not regard China as a threat to Soviet security. As both China and the Soviet Union badly need a peaceful international environment for their domestic reforms, their mutual perceptions of threat will become less significant in their strategic planning.

Ideology, however, has resumed its significance in Sino-Soviet relations. When Gorbachev visited Beijing, he was seen as a hero by the students at Tiananmen Square, and his request to address Beijing University was politely refused. The CCP leadership now obviously pursues a more orthodox approach to socialism, and it was alarmed by the events in Eastern Europe and the Soviet Union. In the internal documents of the CCP, Hungary has often been criticized. It is seen as no longer practicing communism, but as an example of a transformed bourgeois country. On the other hand, China's relations with the then-conservative socialist countries of East Germany, Romania, Bulgaria, North Korea, and Czechoslovakia improved in the second half of 1989. The East German and Cuban delegations were the only representatives from the Eastern Bloc to come to China to celebrate the 40th anniversary of the founding of the People's Republic of China. The

Beijing regime obviously feels threatened and isolated in view of the fall cf Erich Honecker and Nicolae Ceausescu as well as the stirrings in neighboring Mongolia.

Many conservative CCP cadres see what happened in Eastern Europe as a direct result of the misguided reforms of Mikhail Gorbachev. It was reported that Wang Zhen, vice president of the PRC, said that China should 'go public' with its criticisms of 'Soviet revisionism.' Since early August 1989, Chinese leaders and the official media have attacked 'hostile forces' in the West for trying to dilute the ideological purity of the socialist world through 'peaceful transformation.'

Despite China's renewed emphasis on diplomacy with the Third World, its achievements have been mixed. Since then-Prime Minister Rajiv Gandhi's visit to Beijing in December 1988, relations with India have improved. A joint Sino-Indian commission had its inaugural session in New Delhi in September 1989, which ended with the conclusion of a comprehensive trade protocol.[31] When Chinese Vice Premier Wu Xueqian visited India the following month, his host expressed hopes to open substantive talks on the Sino-Indian border dispute in 1990.[32] China also has a good chance to restore diplomatic relations with Indonesia.

Relations with Israel have improved markedly, and informal exchanges with Tel viv now appear possible. A delegation sponsored by the state Chinese International Tourism Service visited Tel Aviv in September 1989, with the aim of setting up an office there.[33] Obviously the small number of Israeli tourists to China would not justify such an act, and this was viewed by Israel as a step toward the establishment of consular relations.

China's trade with South Korea quietly increased to US$2 billion in 1988, and apparently has not been affected by the recent political turmoil in Beijing. A chartered Korean Air jetliner landed in China in August 1989, the first direct flight by a South Korean airliner between the two countries.[34] It has been suggested that China may look to South Korea as an alternative source of advanced technology embargoed by the West. But there remain major obstacles in the establishment of formalities between the two countries. The International Private Economic Council of Korea announced in late August that it had been informed by the China Council for the Promotion of International Trade that negotiations for the setting up of trade offices and a joint commission on economic cooperation would be shelved.[35] The difficulty seems to be opposition from North Korea.

In other areas, China has encountered difficulties. Taiwan hoped that the offer of generous economic aid and the international revulsion at the bloody suppression of the Chinese students' democracy movement would encourage some Third World countries to re-establish diplomatic relations with Taipei. The first breakthrough came in July 1989 when Grenada announced the establishment of diplomatic relations with Taipei while trying to maintain formal ties with Beijing. China responded by breaking off diplomatic relations with Grenada.[36] Grenada was followed by Liberia and Belize,[37] and Nigeria and Senegal may be next. Meanwhile, Taiwan officials are trying to find ways in which Taiwan can participate in the proposed scheme to reduce the debts of the developing world.[38]

Regarding Indochina, the Chinese leaders rejected Hanoi's offer to normalize relations following the failure of the Paris conference.[39] Instead, tension rose over the Spratlys. In response to Vietnam taking up position on three more atolls and shoals, Chinese warships have stepped up cruising in the South China Sea, and carried out a series of exercises for testing the preparedness of the navy and its air power.[40] There are as yet no signs that hostilities are about to break out, but a military victory will be more valuable to the Chinese leaders now as it will enhance the status of the PLA and divert the people's attention from the economic difficulties.

The domestic scene

Deng's reappearance on 9 June 1989 was accompanied by a propaganda campaign designed to convince the Chinese public that reports of a bloodbath in Beijing were fabrications. 'Troops did not kill or harm a single person when we cleared the [Tiananmen] Square,' according to Zhang Gong, deputy political commissar of the Beijing Military Region, at a televised press conference on June 6.[41]

The entire Chinese leadership rallied around Deng's speech on June 9. Party, government, and military organs conducted meetings at all levels to study what the People's Daily editorial termed 'a programmatic document for unifying the thinking of the entire Party.'[42] Beyond a few central points, however, Deng's speech was for a time subjected to widely differing interpretations, with some conservative extremist elements attempting to read into it support for a full-scale class struggle-oriented political campaign.[43]

While Deng occupies the center for now, the political landscape has been vastly altered. Deposing Zhao Ziyang has left a serious leadership vacuum around Deng, a vacuum which Jiang Zemin and Li Peng can hardly fill. Real power has returned to a group of eight or nine conservative veteran leaders, who were Deng's allies and supporters during the struggles against the Gang of Four in the late 1970s, but increasingly obstructed his reforms and his succession plans in the 1980s. Their retirement from active Party work in recent years was once considered one of Deng's most important political victories. Now the re-emergence of Chen Yun and Peng Zhen may be a threat to Deng, whose status and popularity have certainly eroded.

The fourth plenum of the Thirteenth Central Committee of the CCP in late June 1989 formally dismissed Zhao Ziyang and announced a new leadership lineup at the standing committee of the Political Bureau.[44] The communique of the plenum called for special attention to the following tasks:

a) to check turmoil thoroughly and quell the counterrevolutionary rebellion; b) to continue to improve the economic environment and straighten the economic order, to carry out the reform and open policies while seeking a sustained, steady and co-ordinated economic development; c) to carry out conscientiously ideological and political work and education in patriotism, socialism, independence, self-reliance, plain living, and hard work and to oppose earnestly bourgeois liberalization; and d) to enhance Party building, democracy, and legality, to eliminate corruption resolutely, and to accomplish matters of popular concern.[45]

The political climate in China has continued this shift to the left. The political views expressed in the mass media and theoretical journals are more conservative and extreme than during the short campaign against 'bourgeois liberalization' in 1987 and cover a wider range of issues, including economic policy, literature, education, and the media. The conservative leadership wants a return to the Stalinist model of the 1950s. This model involves more rigid planning, restricting the private and collective sectors of the economy and tighter Party control of the media. The model also calls for renewed efforts to inculcate the socialist values of self-sacrifice and submission to Party authority. Moderate forces within the leadership simply do not exist. Resistance mainly comes in the form of passive non-cooperation.

The Chinese authorities are intensifying political education among university students. Party and academic leaders are seeking to re-impose political tests as criteria in university admissions, faculty recruitment and promotions, and selection of candidates for overseas study. University students endured a month of political indoctrination, and the incoming freshmen class at Beijing University was required to take an entire year of political instruction under military supervision. Most the 35,000 students beginning graduate school in the liberal arts and social sciences in 1989 must first work for a year in factories and villages. 'Putting grades first' among students, and academic advancement 'depending entirely on writing books, publishing articles, and teaching' among university teachers have been publicly attacked.[46] The new emphasis on Marxism will certainly affect the morale of China's embittered intelligentsia, and further weaken China's higher-education system.

Meanwhile, the crackdown continues. It appears that the activists associated with the independent trade unions and student federations formed in the spring of 1989 have been hardest hit. Thousands were arrested and many were executed. Reorganization and purges started with the mass media, as the Chinese leadership is eager to reassert control in this vital sector. Liberal publications such as Beijing's *New Observer* and Shanghai's *World Economic Herald* have now disappeared.

By the end of 1989, the leadership's renewed emphasis on traditional Stalinist political orthodoxy was confirmed. At the fifth plenum of the 13th Central Committee held in November 1989, decisions were made to vastly increase the scope of state planning organs and to impose new restrictions on private business and collective rural enterprises. The plenum did not speak directly of abolishing reforms or eliminating market forces. However, it called for 'correcting and perfecting reforms' and preserving their 'socialist orientation.' This means combining the planned economy with market regulation, while maintaining overall control. Private enterprises would be permitted, but only within rigidly defined limits.[47]

General Secretary Jiang Zemin's National Day speech also provided some signals of China's new policy directions.[48] This speech was described by Yuan Mu, spokesman for the State Council, as 'the political manifesto of China's third generation collective leadership,'[49] and has been made study material for the entire CCP membership.[50] The most significant elements in Jiang's speech included: a) revival of the doctrines of working-class leadership and the worker-peasant alliance; b) establishing a distinction between 'two kinds of reform and opening' as a prelude to scaling back the reform and opening policies of the past decade; c) renewed assertions of the absolute superiority of socialism and the CCP's ultimate infallibility; and d) depicting an international environment in which China is besieged by hostile reactionary forces.

According to Jiang, the first kind of reform and opening are those which uphold the Four Cardinal Principles, while the second kind promotes 'bourgeois liberalization' and 'comprehensive Westernization.' The latter's basic nature is to make China part of the Western capitalist system. Jiang also warned that no attempt to implement a market economy that would weaken or negate the planned economy would be allowed.

Even before the formal approval of the 1989–91 retrenchment plan, the policy of tight credit aimed at bringing down inflation and cooling an over-heated economy had hit home. In the first eight months of 1989, fixed-asset investment by state enterprises declined by 8 percent compared with the same period in 1988, and total bank loans outstanding dropped by Rmb. 54.7 billion (in early 1990, US\$1 = Rmb. 4.7), compared with the double-digit growth of the year before. Meanwhile, growth of labor productivity of state enterprises slowed from 8.3 percent in 1988 to 3.1 percent in 1989.[51] The number of loss-making state enterprises has increased, while overall profitability of the state sector has fallen.

The alarm bell was sounded when national industrial output in September 1989 grew by only 0.9 percent over the previous year, and the output of light industries dropped 1.8 percent.[52] The dilemma for Chinese economic policy makers was how to find a balance between inflation and industrial growth. Inflation was one of the main factors behind the public dissatisfaction with the regime that provided support for the students' demonstrations in the spring of 1989. On the other hand, negative industrial growth would further cut revenue for the government. Tight control over credit has led to a considerable decline in retail sales. Products worth Rmb. 75 billion were piled up in warehouses in the first eight months of 1989, up 58% over the same period in 1988.[53] Domestic retail sales of consumer goods in August 1989 recorded the first year-to-year decline in a decade.

There are already signs that the central bank is willing to ease up on credit. A Rmb. 20 billion cash influx has been sent to agricultural banks to ensure that farmers were paid in cash for their grain sales to the state after the autumn harvest. The State Statistical Bureau also suggested that state banks should extend credit to the state retail network so that it 'can buy goods from producers, who can keep production going.'[54]

Conclusion

The domestic political turmoil and the developments in the international scene have certainly made the Chinese leaders feel insecure. Events in Eastern Europe and the Soviet Union on the one hand have confirmed the Chinese leadership's conviction that the military crackdown was justified, and on the other have prompted them to return to the Stalinist orthodoxy in the ideological and political spheres. The erosion of the legitimacy of the regime and the status of the leaders in the eyes of the people, the power struggles within the leadership and the purge of the moderate and liberal elements within the Party and government all serve to facilitate the return and consolidation of ideological conservatism. The coming to power of the Soviet-trained generation of cadres represented by Premier Li Peng may also help to strengthen the trend.

The regime as yet faces no effective domestic opposition. With the exception of a small minority of student activists and independent trade unionists, the majority of the urban population has retreated to the pursuit of individual material interests, cynicism, and political apathy. With the state media controlling the sources of information, the 800 million peasants cannot comprehend, nor are they interested in, the recent political turmoil and the struggle for democracy.

The present leadership has kept its control of the political machinery almost intact. The upper echelons of the political establishment have long been the beneficiaries of the status quo, and they strongly support stability. This is why Deng's reappearance on 9 June 1989 was largely welcomed. But the political machinery has been less effective because the communist regime lacks legitimacy and appeal. The regime is now trying to re-assert the significance of the state sector so as to strengthen its control over the population. The share of national income of the central government's budget dropped from 32.9% in 1979 to 22.4% in 1988.[55]

Beijing has indicated that this share will have to grow bigger. Compulsory purchase of treasury bonds and heavy taxation of rich individuals and units are measures to be adopted to accumulate wealth at the center; and when provincial budget contracts with the center come up for review, Beijing is expected to ask for a bigger slice of local revenue. Rural industries and the private sector will countenance less support and many more restrictions. To further ease the bottlenecks in transport, energy, and scarce raw materials and to speed up infrastructural development, the central government will allocate more resources to these areas through administrative methods such as preferential loans and more state-supplied resources. Similarly, large state enterprises will be given these privileges.[56]

Two crucial issues will test the present leadership. When economic difficulties generate dissatisfaction, will the regime make concessions by re-introducing liberal economic reform measures and soften its approach to the West, or will it further tighten its control, appeal for self-sacrifice and place the blame on the class enemies inside and outside China? The present crackdowns on corruption, crime, and pornography are measures typically adopted by authoritarian regimes to enhance prestige after their illegitimate usurpation of power, but its effect tends to have a limited time span. Already the Chinese leaders are eager to borrow and solicit aid from the West again.

The second test is the old political succession problem. Undeniably there are still intense power struggles within the present leadership after Deng's resignation from the chairmanship of the Central Military Affairs Commission. At any rate, most Chinese people expect a period of chaos and instability when the present gerontocratic leadership fades away in response to the call of nature. Such an expectation may create a self-fulfilling prophecy.

---

1. For the text of the speech, see *Tide Monthly* (a Chinese magazine published in Hong Kong), 15 July 1989, pp. 39–40.

2. For the text of the communique, see *Beijing Review*, 3–9 July 1989, pp. 9–10; and for an analysis of the plenum, see Robert Delfs, 'Purging the future,' *Far Eastern Economic Review*, 6 July 1989, pp. 10–11.

3. Nayan Chanda and Nigel Holloway, 'Links severed,' *ibid*, 15 June 1989, p. 10.

4. *People's Daily*, 24 September 1989; see also *South China Morning Post* (Hong Kong), 25 September 1989.

5. See *Ming Pao* (a Chinese language newspaper in Hong Kong), editorial, 25 August 1989.

6. See Note 2. The Five Principles of Peaceful Co-existence are: respect for each other's sovereignty and territorial integrity, non-interference in each other's domestic affairs, mutual non-aggression, equality and mutual benefit, and peaceful co-existence.

7. See Lo Bing, 'The Big Disaster in Chinese Communist Diplomacy,' *Cheng Ming* (a Chinese-language monthly in Hong Kong), October 1989, p. 8.

8. *South China Morning Post*, 9 September 1989.

9. Chang Qing, 'Chinese Foreign Minister Tours Africa,' *Beijing Review*, 28 August-3 September 1989, p. 10.

10. See Qian Qichen, 'New China's Diplomacy: 40 Years On,' *ibid*, 28 October 1989, pp. 11–15.

11. *Ming Pao*, 7 August 1989.

12. *Sunday Morning Post*, 1 October 1989.

13. *South China Morning Post*, 16 September 1989.

14. *Ibid.*, 6 October 1989.

15. *Ibid.*, 16 September 1989.

16. *Ibid.*

17. See Robert Delfs, 'Stuck in the groove,' *Far Eastern Economic Review*, 5 October 1989, pp. 14–15.

18. *Ming Pao*, 29 September 1989.

19. *Sing Tao Wan Pao* (a Chinese-language newspaper in Hong Kong), 6 October 1989.

20. *Ming Pao*, 9 October 1989.

21. *Liberation Army Daily*, 8 October 1989.

22. *Ming Pao*, 9 October 1989.

23. *South China Morning Post*, 20 and 21 December, 1989.

24. Susumu Awanshara and Charles Smith, 'Indecent haste,' *Far Eastern Economic Review*, 25 January 1990, pp. 10–11.

25. *South China Morning Post*, 13 September 1989.

26. *Ibid*, 18 September, 1989.

27. *Ibid*, 16 September, 1989.

28. Tai Ming Cheung, 'Opening gambit', *Far Eastern Economic Review*, 31 August 1989, pp. 28–30.

29. *South China Morning Post*, 20 January 1990.

30. *Ibid.*, 6 January 1990.

31. *Ibid.*, 22 September 1989.

32. *Ibid.*, 13 October 1989. For the background on developments in Sino-Indian relations in recent years, see Surjit Mansingh and Steven I. Levine, 'China and India: Moving Beyond Confrontation,' *Problems of Communism*, March-June 1989, pp. 30–49. *South China Morning Post*, 6 and 10 October 1989.

33. *South China Morning Post*, 21 September 1989.

34. *Ibid.*, 20 August 1989.

35. *Ming Pao*, 31 August 1989.

36. *South China Morning Post*, 8 August 1989.

37. *Ibid.*, 11 and 14 October 1989.

38. Susumu Awanohara, 'Political purse strings,' *Far Eastern Economic Review*, 19 October 1989, pp. 10–11. Michael Field, Rodney Tasker, and Murray Hiebert, 'No end in sight,' *ibid.*, 7 September 1989, pp. 14–16. *South China Morning Post*, 5 October 1989.

39. *Sunday Morning Post*, 3 September 1989.

40. *Ibid.*, 20 August 1989 and *South China Morning Post*, 5 October 1989.

41. Robert Delfs, 'Repression and reprisal,' *Far Eastern Economic Review*, 22 June 1989, p. 10.

42. *People's Daily* editorial, 16 June 1989.

43. See *ibid*, 14–16 June 1989 and *Economic Daily* (Beijing), June 14, 15 and 19.

44. 'CCP Central Committee Holds Plenum,' *Beijing Review*, 3–9 July 1989, p. 4.

45. 'Communique of the Fourth Plenary Session of the 13th CCP Central Committee,' *ibid.*, p. 10. *Ming Pao*, 14 October 1989.

46. Robert Delfs, 'Top Marx,' *Far Eastern Economic Review*, 24 August 1989, p. 13.

47. Robert Delfs, 'Power to the party,' *ibid.*, 7 December 1989, pp. 23–25.

48. For the text of the speech, see *Beijing Review*, 9–15 October 1989, pp. 11–24.

49. *People's Daily*, 10 October 1989.

50. *Ming Pao*, 5 October 1989.

51. Louise do Rosario, 'Quick step back,' *Far Eastern Economic Review*, 19 October 1989, p. 47.

52. *South China Morning Post*, 20 October 1989.

53. *China Daily* (Beijing), 19 October 1989.

54. *Ibid.*

55. Louise do Rosario, *op. cit.*, p. 48.

56. *Ming Pao*, 21 October 1989 and *Sunday Morning Post*, 22 October 1989.

PART FIVE
WHITHER CHINA?

The Re-emergence of the Realm of the Private In China

ORVILLE SCHELL

AFTER the debacle of 4 June 1989, China's aging leaders launched yet another Maoist political campaign to rein in the centrifugal forces let loose in their country. But their efforts succeeded in doing little more than creating a surface illusion of political order and stability. While they tried to put the blame for their country's ills on a 'small group' of malefactors whom they alleged had singlehandedly stirred up a 'counterrevolutionary rebellion' against them, the truth was that by the end of the 1980s so much had changed both in China and the world around it, that there was no turning back the clock. Not only had the Chinese Communist Party almost completely lost its own revolutionary idealism and self-confidence, but China itself now stood virtually alone on the world stage, bereft of almost every one of its former 'fraternal' socialist allies. China's 80-year-old senile vice president, Wang Zhen, might prattle on about 'the center' of international socialism now moving to Beijing, but few people anywhere were fooled.

For a decade in the 1980s we were regaled in our morning papers with news of one monumental change after another that embraced almost every aspect of Chinese life from culture and politics to the economy and environment. But there was one other change that, while not quite so palpable or directly measurable as the number of private vendors in the street, the variety of avant-garde pubications for sale at news stands, or the recrudescence of fashion in clothing, nonetheless had an impact on Chinese society of the most profound nature. This was a psychological change of heart that involved a transformation of the way Chinese began to feel about themselves. It was a transformation that changed the very chemistry of human and social relations.

When I visited Beijing in October 1989, martial law remained in effect and Tiananmen Square was still occupied by goose-stepping troops from the People's Liberation Army. Although I felt anxious to know firsthand how old friends and colleagues were faring under the crackdown, out of fear of causing them trouble, I decided not to look any of them up. Democracy movement suspects were still being detained, jailed and even executed, while ordinary people continued to be herded into study sessions, forced to write out detailed diaries of where they had been and what they had done during the crucial days of April, May, and June, and in many cases to write confessions.

Over the preceding years, as China opened up and relaxed, I had slowly become accustomed to moving about with more and more impunity; to visiting whomever I wished with little concern for either their safety or my welcome as a visitor. But, this time, with such free and open interchange suddenly denied me, on arrival I found myself feeling alien and isolated, very much as if I was back in the China I remembered from the latter days of the Cultural Revolution when Mao lived and the 'Gang of Four' still held away. Even now I remember with perfect vividness how perplexed I was upon arriving in Beijing in 1975 and finding that even though I spoke Mandarin and had spent years mixing with Chinese elsewhere in the world, I was now as unabsorbable as oil on water. No one, literally no one, was willing to speak with me as a foreigner, even to exchange pleasantries about the weather. The only exceptions were those officials deputized to do so by the state. And, like so many dump trucks, they unloaded on us interminable 'brief introductions' on how many kilos of *meng* beans their commune had produced per *mou* of land, or how many tons of lime their mine had exhumed 'under the guidance of Chairman Mao's correct line.' There was no possibility to establish one's own friendships or relationships outside this official cage. Even the hotel telephone, which in recent years has become a lifeline to friends and contacts, was useless. Simply put, there was no one to call. If one did make a spontaneous and unscripted advance toward some hapless Chinese, not only was a rebuke assured, but censure as well. The Party and the state did not shine kindly on unauthorized personal relationships. It goes without saying that in this environment of suspicion and mistrust where 'unofficial' contact with foreign 'imperialists' and 'capitalists' might land a Chinese in prison, a visitor did feel positively leprous.

As I later came to appreciate, however, it was not just foreigners who were kept at arm's reach. Chinese were also afraid of each other. For unprogrammed liaisons or spontaneous encounters between them also raised the specter of conspiracy and could portend disastrous consequences. In fact, it is not too much to say that during these bitter years a whole generation of Chinese lost touch not only with the outside world of foreigners, but with each other as well. So defoliated had the landscape become of trust, that almost any kind of personal friend with whom confidences could be safely shared became suspect.

Curiously, the distance between people was not maintained exclusively by secret police peering over shoulders and hectoring and bullying their charges into doing the bidding of the Party. Quite the contrary, as a measure of self-defense, most people learned how to police themselves. But, alas, by doing so, they slowly lost the habit of seeing themselves as separate and distinct human beings entitled to a private life free of state scutiny.

This dissolution of the realm of the private and of the self was aided and abetted by another compelling historical circumstance. The emphasis on the virtues of collectivized life and on 'serving the people' rather than oneself had been so prevalent in the early years of the Communist Revolution, that Chinese were provided with compelling rationalization for surrendering themselves to 'selflessness' and their country. Of course, these ideals were not only Maoist, but also enjoyed a good deal of resonance with older Confucian values of service and sacrifice to country and culture. Fragile enough in ordinary times even in the West where individualism is lionized, the boundary that ordinarily exists between the realms of the public and the private became even further eroded by this new exaggerated Chinese ethic of sacrifice and selflessness. It is no small wonder, then, that in the People's Republic, where service to the Party and 'people' was touted as the highest and most 'correct' aspiration, and where attention to oneself was deemed 'bourgeois' and antisocial, few people were able to maintain even a rudimentary sense of entitlement to the notion of a private life.

But perhaps the most powerful weapon the Party wielded in this collectivization of the Chinese psyche was guilt. By making its subjects feel responsible for their alleged 'ideological crimes,' the Party was able to manipulate them into blaming themselves even for those accusations that it chose to bring against them. This willingness — or perhaps it would be better to describe it as vulnerability — of intellectuals to blame themselves for charges leveled against them by the Party apparatus was perhaps the most destructive force of all to the preserve of a private world in which a 'self' might safely reside. In this Alice-in-Wonderland universe, the accused unwittingly and horribly became complicitors in their own downfall. By taking part in what the intellectual historian Sun Longji describes in his book *The Deep Structure of Chinese Culture* as the 'disorganization of the self,' they ended up becoming their own accusers. Rather than rejecting the charges of being 'rightists,' 'capitalist roaders,' or 'bourgeois individualists,' those who had been attacked and 'struggled against' tended to internalize the charges.

'The infallible Party cannot be wrong, therefore I must be wrong,' was the common presumption. Such self-judgment led the victims to draw the charges toward themselves as if they were magnets, and then, painstakingly to try to locate the seat of their alleged wrong-doing within themselves. The orgy of self-criticisms and confessions that China produced as a result of this perverted system is ample testament to a society that, having destroyed all vestiges of individualism, was left with an intellectually and morally defenseless populace passively accepting the Party's charges of ideological unhealth. The results were destructive and disastrous.

In his recent autobiography, Liu Binyan, one of China's most respected journalists, recalls his own long ordeal during the anti-rightist campaign of the late 1950s. Under repeated accusation, he writes:

I began to lose confidence. Was I without fault? Of course not. And all my faults, in the final analysis, boiled down to 'bourgeois individualism.' Could I honestly say that I had joined the Party solely for the liberation of the Chinese people with no ulterior motives? Of course not. There was at least some element of self-fulfillment. And then there was my writing. Could I honestly say that I never had any eye on publicity and profit? Of course not.

After repeated assertions that one is a 'rightist' with a 'wrong attitude' and a 'reactionary point of view,' even the most stalwart person begins to have grave doubts about his own innocence. 'All these [accusations] were very effective in adding to our load of guilt,' Liu writes of the reaction between the accused in his own group of exiled rightists.

In criticizing one another, we judged each other by the criteria of Communist Party members... Thus, the criteria we set out were grandiose, but in the end, it always boiled down to 'insufficient awareness of one's own guilt,' 'insufficient resolution to undergo thorough and complete reform of the self,' as was in keeping with our 'rightist' status.

The psychological effects of such incessant attack are obvious. As Sun Longji reminds us, 'This intrusion into and control of private lives has no other function than to eradicate individual personality.'

Looking back on all the political campaigns that he was forced to endure, Liu remembers being 'preoccupied with a sense of humiliation that silently reminded me that I was the lowest of the low. That I had injured my wife and children. That I had no hope of exoneration in this life.'

There were some notable exceptions of defiance in China. The writer Nien Cheng, author of *Life and Death In Shanghai*, comes to mind. But, it must be added that she had spent many years abroad and had a very highly evolved sense of self, not to say of justice and indignation. But she was the exception rather than the rule. The way in which most Chinese ended up surviving was by internalizing the guilt; by blaming themselves for those charges and accusations that the Party and revolution leveled against them. The fact that to most of these victims the charges now seem nothing short of bizarre and preposterous, suggests nothing other than the nightmarish world of Franz Kafka's fiction where characters labor eternally under vague but damning charges leveled against them by some apparat on high. Unable to understand the logic of their indictments, and thus unable to rebut them, they are left with no recourse other than guilty torment and the unsatisfying purgative powers of self-blame. That is, of course, the equivalent of mental self-immolation. In such a world, maintenance of a private reserve within which one's own psyche has any expectation of survival is unthinkable.

In *The Castle*, Kafka's anti-hero Land Surveyor K., and in *The Trial*, Joseph K., both find themselves in situations that most Chinese intellectuals would immediately recognize. Under a vague but menacing indictment, they are plunged into unfathomable circumstances that they are powerless either to understand or ameliorate. Rather than rebelling against the injustice of their plights — which would be useless and probably suicidal as well — both become paralyzed by confusion and uncertainty compounded by a sense of their own culpability. The Czech writer Milan Kundera, who became a refugee himself from a communist country after the failure of Prague Spring in 1968, has written a grimly insightful essay about this dilemma. Entitled 'Somewhere Behind,' from his collection *The Art of the Novel*, Kundera underscores the relevance of Kafka's fiction to modern communist totalitarianism. Describing Kafka's inverted heroes as being caught in an 'auto-culpabilization machine,' he analyzes how they seek to punish themselves as a last resort in order to expunge their overpowering if unfathomed sense of guilt for their alleged crimes.

'Raskolnikov cannot bear the weight of his guilt, and to find peace he consents to his punishment of his own free will,' writes Kundera.

It is the well-known situation where *the offense seeks the punishment*. In Kafka the logic is reversed. The punished person does not know the reason for the punishment. The absurdity of the punishment is so unbearable that to find peace the accused needs to find justification for his penalty: *the punishment seeks the offense*. [In fact,] in this pseudo-theological world, *the punished beg for recognition of their guilt*.

Once in such a mind-set, the burden of being jury, judge, and executioner is paradoxically shifted away from the accuser to the accused. Just to remind us that we are not dealing with any purely Kafka-esque literary abstractions here, Kundera reminds us that 'totalitarian states, as extreme concentrations of these tendencies, have brought out the close relationship between Kafka's novels and real life.' In short, it would not be too extreme to say that intellectuals in countries such as China have all too often found themselves as interchangeable with the likes of Joseph K. Having learned to internalize accusations against themselves, they live in a state of eternal guilt and self loathing; a bizarre state in which they are compelled to reject themselves much as the body sometimes finds itself seized by a violent allergic reaction.

Kundera describes these victims of the state who, robbed of all dignity and independence, have turned into their own enemies:

All their lives they had entirely identified themselves with the Party. When it suddenly became their prosecutor they agreed like Joseph K. to 'examine their whole lives, their entire pasts, down to the smallest details' to find the hidden offense and, in the end, to confess to imaginary crimes.

What Kafka's characters highlight is the understandable human yearning to have one's 'case' resolved, even if means to surrender to the accuser by way of confession to 'imaginary crimes.' What is important about this Kafka syndrome from the perspective of Chinese society is the way in which over the past few decades the Party's relentless scrutiny of individuals led to a virtual dissolution of the realm of the private. This 'rape of privacy,' as Kundera calls it, led to a helpless and supine attitude among the citizenry. It was a phenomena that ironically saved the Party many burdens of oversight. For when people have learned to control themselves by means of an internal psychological mechanism that turns them into their own suppressors, the state may justifiably feel a sense of triumph.

In this world, where there were and are no provisions against arbitrary mental search and seizure, where holding even any small part of the human self inviolate from official ideology is a crime, and where the prying arms of state are ubiquitous, it is impossible for an individual to maintain any meaningful sense of the self. Unless a person has a defiance made of steel, without the cushion and protection of a modicum of privacy, this aspect of a human being can only perish.

As Kundera bluntly puts it:

Totalitarian society, especially in its more extreme versions, tends to abolish the boundary between public and private; power, as it grows ever more opaque, requires the lives of citizens to be entirely transparent. The ideal of life without secrets corresponds to the ideal of the exemplary family: A citizen does not have the right to hide anything at all from the Party and state, just as a child has no right to keep any secret from his father or his mother.

What makes Kundera's notions about 'auto-culpabilization' and the 'rape of privacy' so important to an understanding of China in the 1990s, is that they help us comprehend the suppressive psychological mechanism against which Chinese intellectuals have been struggling to refoliate their lives with an interior dimension. During the past decade of reform, there has been a slow but steady process of incubation in which this dimension of life has at last been able to develop in a rudimentary way. And what was so important about the protests and demonstrations that rocked China during the spring of 1989 was not just their exterior political message, which was amazing enough, but their subliminal message. What they were announcing — without actually saying it — was that Chinese were now ready to resist further incursions by the Party and state into the legitimately private side of their lives.

So much has changed in China since I made my first visit there in early 1975 that it is doubtful that any Maoist-style political campaign or crackdown can now completely turn back the clock. Although the mood I encountered in Beijing during October 1989 did, at first, seem hauntingly reminiscent of what I remembered of earlier times, it soon became abundantly clear to me that the similarities were only superficial. Even though I had decided not to call up friends for fear of politically compromising them, by happenstance I began running into some of them in the streets and hotel lobbies anyway. I was astounded and relieved by their volubility. Far from being timid and fearful, as they had once been and as I feared they might once again have become, I found them not only willing to sit down and talk, but to be audaciously outspoken, even mocking and scornful about their government. It was as if once the habit of independent thinking which they had cultivated over the past decade, and which had reached a critical mass during the heady days of spring, had now been permanently ingrained in them. The longer I talked, the less it seemed likely to be scared out of them by any political campaign.

Something elemental had changed in their psychological attitude toward both themselves and their government. They might feign an outward appearance of submission to their leaders, present themselves for study sessions of Party documents, and even write confessions, but far fewer people were now inclined to submit themselves to the kind of guilty self-laceration that such Party campaigns had triggered in the past. A habit of thinking more critically and independently had clearly taken root enough so that individuals were now less ready to betray their friends and themselves in a rush to become reconnected with the Party. And, because of this important but elusive change of mind, even the Party's grave threats of intimidation and retribution were insufficient to terrorize everyone back into 'auto-culpabilization.' The fundamental chemistry both between people themselves, and between people and their government, had changed in a radical way.

What impressed me most was that in spite of the detentions, arrests, jailings, and even executions that were still going on, almost everyone I talked to was still able and willing to speak confidentially. Even though they were at considerable risk and I was a foreigner, they continued to speak from that private place which had slowly been expanding within them. It was a place that in spite of the chill, still acknowledged the sanctity of friendship, personal loyalty, and the primacy of bonds between individuals rather than those between a citizen and the state. The fact that this fragile realm of the private had been able to survive the aftermath of the massacre at all, suggested that, at least among these people, it had taken firmer root than anyone might have at first supposed. And, what makes these roots so important is that they represent the means of nourishment for the continuing transformation of an important psychological chemistry. It is a transformation away from the world of Franz Kafka toward a world where the rights of an individual to have a private life are slowly being staked out.

But what is perhaps most significant of all about this ongoing transformation is the recognition that this unique psychological change lies directly behind almost every one of the other monumental changes that we have been witnessing in China over the past decade. It is the life's blood of political liberalization, rock and roll, fashion, experimental film, entrepreneurial energy, avante-guard literature, and finally, of the kind of dissent that culminated in the democracy movement of spring 1989.

Chinese Bureaucracy:
An Historical Atavism

Wojtek Zafanolli

The historic visit to Beijing by Soviet leader Milkhail Gorbachev during 15–17 May 1989 was a godsend for the thousands of student demonstrators who had besieged Tiananmen Square in the previous month. As long as Gorbachev had not sealed the 30-year-old Sino-Soviet rift, the demonstrators knew they were safe from government reprisals. Better still, the presence of the man who symbolized political reform in the Soviet Union, reforms which the Chinese government so obstinately refused to consider, added considerable grist to their mill. Nor were the students alone in trying to turn the situation to their advantage: China's Party boss, Zhao Ziyang, used popular opinion to reverse his own delicate political situation (his star had been on the decline since the end of 1988).

At a reception for his illustrious guest on May 16, Zhao declared in front of Chinese TV cameras that 'in the interests of the Party, we still need Deng Xiaoping's wisdom and experience' — this despite the fact that Deng had resigned from all his posts with the exception of the chairmanship of the Military Commission. Zhao added in falsely deferential tones: 'We still need Deng Xiaoping to take the helm in important matters.'

For the Chinese, to whom this message was first and foremost addressed, this spelled proof that Zhao was a leader in name only, that he could be recalled at any time and that the power wielded by his superior was all the more absolute for being wielded entirely behind the scenes: Deng was not even a member of the Politburo. Zhao added that this situation was the result of a ruling by the 13th Congress of the Chinese Communist Party at the end of 1987, when he himself had been nominated General Secretary.[1] But this (obviously secret) ruling had, nonetheless, been tacitly enforced beforehand. Zhao's predecessor, Hu Yaobang, had learned this to his sorrow when, after trying to correlate the title of his job with its functions, he fell into semi-disgrace in November 1986. Two months later, with China already in the throes of student unrest, he was demoted following a highly irregular meeting of the Politburo.[2]

Zhao's public disclosure that Deng still pulled all the strings sparked an instantaneous reaction. On the following day, May 17, while in Czechoslovakia the dissident and future president, Vaclav Havel, was being released from jail, the Chinese Politburo convened a meeting in Beijing during which Zhao was deprived of his functions and martial law was declared. On the same day, hundreds of thousands of demonstrators took to the streets again, fired by Zhao's disclosure. They seriously perturbed the official program on the final day of Gorbachev's visit. At the last minute, the Chinese leaders were obliged to abandon the idea of taking him around Tiananmen Square because it was occupied by over 3,000 hunger strikers and their innumerable supporters. Neither could Gorbachev be taken to the Forbidden City, and he was only able to enter the Greco-Stalinist edifice of the National Assembly Hall by a humble side door.

This represented unprecedented loss of face for the oligarchs. Further affronts were to follow: For the first time since the student unrest, the hoards of people who had occupied central Beijing made a clear choice of sides in the power struggle that had been unleashed among the leadership. The entire population appeared to be clamoring for Deng's resignation. Many people added a touch of Chinese humor to their demands by waving twigs of bamboo and chicken feathers: The former represented Takeshita, the Japanese prime minister who had just resigned, and whose name is composed with the ideogram for bamboo, while the chicken feathers were often used of old in petitions to the Emperor because of the homophone in two Chinese characters for 'urgency' and 'chicken.'

With a General Secretary who is a supreme ruler in name only and mobs which willingly side with one faction of another of the communist oligarchy, it is difficult to apply ready-made categories to the Chinese political system. What then, is the true nature of this system and what are its main characteristics?

Let us first return to Zhao's revelation to Gorbachev.

In making his revelation, Zhao was attempting to thwart Premier Li Peng's conspiracy against him. The statement also revealed the paternalistic nature of the Chinese political régime. Superficially, the Chinese Party-state appears to be a simple national varia-

tion of the 'democratic centralism' of which the Eastern European
countries are (or rather were) models: The *nomenklatura*, com-
plemented by an all-pervasive bureaucracy, regulated by a rigid
grade system, enables the Party (itself an extremely hierarchic
organization), to control all the economic, political, social, and
cultural activities of the nation. But in China this undemocratic
but in no way arbitrary construction is pure window-dressing. In
reality, under the cover of a Stalinism with vague Maoist accoutre-
ments, there functions a system that operates on two axes: patronage and sponsorship. Contrary to all appearances, neither competence nor political/ideological conformity plays a determining role,
for the system is entirely founded on an age-old code of personal
loyalties. In the past, these principles were upheld by the secret
societies, artisans' guilds, associations of itinerant workers, etc.,
whose members were bound by oath. Today, the Party and the
bureaucracy have taken over, as indeed they did during the Cultural Revolution, which caricatured the principle of personal loyalty.
The Red Guards, remember, made individual vows of loyalty to
the Great Helmsman.

Deng Xiaoping's 'pragmatism' did away with this showy ritual.
Under his reign, students were able to study, workers to produce,
and peasants to cultivate their land without having to recall at
every moment that they were doing so according to the correct
Party line as dictated by a 'helmsman.' But Deng made sure this
'pragmatism' did not include any attack on the feudal concepts
which lie at the foundation of Chinese political life. As Zhao
Ziyang's revelations to Gorbachev signify, the octogenarian pat-
riarch had himself consecrated as a secret emperor of China or the
capo di capi of the communist regime.

There is no contradiction in these two appellations, for both are
steeped in ancient Chinese cultural tradition. As far as the former
is concerned, it should be remembered that it was by remaining
concealed from his subjects that the Emperor was supposed to
command social and cosmic order and harmonize the heavens
and the earth, according to the immutable cycles of the *Book of
Changes*. The second characteristic clearly fits into the clan concept of a society in which power is a natural prerogative of the
elders. A superficial examination of the Chinese communist oligarchy clearly reveals this type of order. After 1982, Deng Xiaoping
began to relegate the old guard of the regime to an institution
especially created for the purpose, the Committee of Sages.

However, contrary to all appearances and forecasts, this was not Deng's way of pushing them aside. From their position in the sidelines, these 'sages' (who incarnated as many as eight different factions and recognized Deng Xiaoping as their supreme arbitrator) continued to use their declining faculties to impose their (generally conservative and anti-'liberal') views on economic reforms. As recent events have shown, real power in China lies in this Committee of Sages.

The influence of these communist elders extends through an intricate web of alliances. The common denominator is allegiance, which, first and foremost, is personal, and only then ideological and political. Thus, as far as the second aspect is concerned, Yao Yilin, who joined the Permanent Committee of the Politburo at the 13th Congress, may be viewed as the accredited spokesman for economic matters of 89-year-old Chen Yun. Chen is Deng's principal rival and is of the opinion that a 'socialist market' is like a bird trapped in the cage of the Plan: The problem is to prevent it from escaping. The personal dimension to these allegiances is represented by the taciturn Qiao Shi, police 'super-boss,' who also became member of the Permanent Committee of the Politburo during the 13th Congress. Qiao is one of the 'Shanxi clique' under the 87-year-old Peng Zhen, mayor of Beijing until the Cultural Revolution and largely responsible for the legal reforms of the early 1980s. More mundanely, the president of the People's Republic of China, 84-year-old Yang Shangkun, has succeeded in making the high command of the army into a veritable family enterprise: Thanks to a brother, a son-in-law, and a nephew, he 'holds' the Political Department of the Armed Forces, the Logistics Department, and the High Command.

If the top rungs of the Party ladder are crisscrossed with networks of 'interpersonal relationships' (*guanxi*), much like the Mafia in Europe or the secret societies in pre-revolutionary China, it is easy to imagine the lower rungs. The nepotism of the Chinese bureaucracy is legendary, but nearly impossible to measure. Let us just say that according to the Chinese press, it's not infrequent that between 30–50 percent of employees in the various administrative departments of the rural counties (*xian*) are related to each other.[3] Anyone in a post which has not been obtained through family connections is bound to consider himself not so much a servant of the state as 'client' of the cadres (*ganbu*) who nominated him and who themselves answer only to their own direct superiors.

The networks of benefactors that imbue the Chinese bureaucracy (reminiscent of patriarchal and clan relationships among the
gentry before the revolution) generate informal links of solidarity
and render the bureaucracy opaque and impenetrable from the
outside. This may be seen from the 'rectification' campaigns —
those periodic attempts by the Party to regain the upper hand. The
scenario never varies. A team ('working group') is sent out from
the top of the bureaucratic pyramid to its base in order to investigate the 'style of work,' examine accounts, and eradicate 'indiscre-
tions.' The work units (*danwei*) being investigated organize festivities and vast banquets are given in honor of the guests.
Delicacies that are hardly seen in the average Chinese household
are copiously washed down with wines and alcohol in sufficient
quantities to wear down the determination of the most determined
'controllers.' Should they withstand the banquets and pursue their
duties, the controllers will be met with a wall of silence only
broken by the fearless or the very foolish. The reason for this is
obvious: The controllers, coming from outside, will move on,
while any local person testifying to them will remain behind, with
no shortage of opportunities for the local 'cadres' to get their own
back. Not all the blame is at the 'base': Consider the underdeveloped regions or those that have suffered from a natural
disaster and genuinely require aid but can only obtain it after
having wined and dined the cadres who have the power to grant
it. [4]

In a country where the principal means of production belong
to the state, a bureaucracy of 48 million Party members holds
formidable powers. This concentration of both economic and
political/administrative power leaves the door wide open to every
kind of abuse. At the bottom end of the scale are the special areas
in most department stores where string-pulling or a Party card
buys goods the average Chinese citizen can never aspire to obtain
— and at a discount. At the top end of the scale are the extraordinary cases of corruption that regularly made headlines in the early
1980s. The sensational scandals in which the sons and daughters of
the top Chinese leaders were involved reflect a compelling logic.
To put it simply, Deng's economic reforms consisted of organizing
a market at the heart of a system in which the principal economic
levers were still manipulated by the bureaucratic caste. One of the
main effects of this aberration has been to further blur the distinc-

tion between bureaucracy and trade, or between what is public and what is private.

Few things can better illustrate this lack of distinction than the 'collective ownership' (i.e. private) companies set up by cadres, often in their own names, which blossomed throughout the country after the mid-1980s. Here is a typical example. In 1984, the 84 employees and cadres of the state-owned Kunming Metallurgical Industries Company founded a 'development company,' in which they were the major 'shareholders,' and registered it with the local chamber of commerce. Their idea was quite simple. Donning their bureaucrats' hats, they went to the production units under their authority and bought steel at the 'unified' (i.e. state) price, which is extremely low. They then sold the steel to their own 'development' company at the same price. The wily cadres then donned their businessmen's hats and re-sold the steel at 'negotiated,' i.e. free, prices. Juggling in this way, they made profits of more than 50 times their initial investment within two months! It should be added that, thanks to a generous distribution of 'red envelopes' (*hong bao*), allocations, and 'special bonuses,' everyone was able to benefit from this ingenious business, including retired cadres from the state company and managers of the metal foundries under its jurisdiction.[5]

Another example shows both the nature and the scale of the financial and commercial speculation unleashed by reforms in the core of the bureaucracy: In November 1984, a company attached to the Aerospace Ministry ordered 180,000 televisions from a French company. Unfortunately, it had neither the foreign currency nor the import permits necessary to make such a transaction. The latter was easily solved, since the company bought the permits on the black market for a mere 18 million yuan. The foreign currency was taken care of through a subsidiary of the Bank of China in Shijiazhuang (Hebei province), which, for a modest premium of 15 million yuan, opened a credit line worth US$42 million, the remainder being supplied by the financial services of the Ministry. The minister concerned (Zhang Jun) was later removed from office, along with four high-level civil servants.[6]

It is possible to control such flagrant and widespread abuses. That is precisely what Hu Yaobang and then Zhao Ziyang attempted to do, under the general heading of 'political reforms.' This implied a certain degree of separation of the state from the Party, as well as of the bureaucracy's economic functions from its administrative ones. Most importantly, at the heart of these reforms, which were far more important than the various measures of economic liberalization gradually introduced after 1978, there lay the definition of a rule of law — a necessary framework for individual initiative to blossom outside the bureaucratic straightjacket. Such modifications to the political and social rules of the game, which had been under discussion since 1986, would have constituted a revolution in themselves. Clearly they were not to the taste of Deng Xiaoping, who on two occasions (when he fired Hu Yaobang and later, his successor, Zhao) dismissed them as manifestations of 'bourgeois liberalism.' Beneath this obstinacy lies the inability of a man, born at the turn of the century in Sichuan, one of the most remote regions of China, to understand what Montesquieu called the '*Esprit des Lois.*' For Deng, the law is not an imperative rule established by the authorities, the primary condition for which is that it must be immutable and universally applied. On the contrary, it is, in accordance with Chinese tradition, only considered for its dissuasive virtues. It is an aid to the sovereign power of the *guan*, the Mandarin-bureaucrat of yesteryear, of which the communist cadre is clearly a distant, albeit very poor, relative.

At the end of July 1983, it was made clear that the political ideas of the Chinese leaders and, first and foremost among them, Deng Xiaoping, were founded on an archaic and Confucian concept of the law. In 1979, after the Third Plenum of the 11th Congress, the National Assembly had adopted, with uncharacteristic speed, a penal code, a code of criminal procedure, and the organic laws governing prosecution and the courts. Despite numerous lacunae in the area of human rights (particularly the articles concerning 'counterrevolutionary crimes,' a euphemism for 'crimes' of opinion and politics), this nevertheless represented considerable progress in comparison with the Cultural Revolution. The principle of equality before the law was asserted, overruling the discriminatory practices against people with 'bad' social origins. The right to defense, though disgracefully restricted, was recognized and organized, and capital punishment, previously meted out at the drop of a hat, was regulated.

Unfortunately, at the first incident of any seriousness, namely a surge in crime in the major cities, this legal system tumbled like a house of cards. In the summer of 1983, on the personal intervention of Deng Xiaoping (who apparently had been greatly shocked by an armed attack on his official convoy), the authorities launched a campaign against crime, which immediately resulted in the biggest wave of executions since the one that followed the inauguration of the new régime in the 1950s. The police arrested tens of thousands of 'suspects' in surprise attacks: vandals, delinquents, or hapless passers-by. They were judged in court and 'swiftly and severely' condemned (i.e. according to exceptional procedures). Where previously sentences for crimes of this nature would have been limited to a few months or years in prison, now executions became the order of the day. The right to issue death sentences was suddenly decentralized to provincial and even, it seems, to regional level. Fabricated 'confessions' extracted by torture, which had nearly always been a feature of Chinese life, reappeared. Lastly, as during the peak of the Cultural Revolution, denunciation was officially encouraged and rewarded, while quotas (reminiscent of the Maoist campaigns) were established in police stations for the numbers of arrests and executions. As a consequence of the disintegration of the legal system, 965,000 people were arrested between August and October 1983 and 10,000 were executed. This zealous frenzy of activity on the part of the executioners only cooled off at Chinese New Year 1984 (by which time the total number of executions had reached 40,000).[7]

Since then, it has become a tradition in China to hold a massive 'clean up' operation against crime just before the national holiday on October 1, followed by a spate of summary executions. This is why the wave of repression against the 'counterrevolutionary rebellion' that followed the June 4 massacre was carried out with a kind of routine efficiency that surprised Westerners. The Chinese police are well practiced in this type of operation; only the 'target' had changed.

Chinese bureaucracy, impervious as it is to the *'Esprit des Lois'* and organized around a system of personal loyalties, presents a good image of the real backwardness of the People's Republic. It is, of course, a measure of the country's economic underdevelopment. But first and foremost it reveals a mentality. To take the Beijing police force as a random example: All witnesses of recent events concur that the orders received at dawn on June 4 were executed by the police with a savage, efficient ferocity. In China, the explanation for this blind obedience is that, for the most part, the force is made up of orphans from the terrible Tangshan earthquake of 1976. These children were raised by the state and subsequently taken over by the police force (some of them even underwent special training in West Germany). They are entirely devoted to their superiors.[8]

This situation, in which abstract moral values have not supplanted feudal notions of personal loyalty, also prevails in the army, with the possible exception of garrisons in cities where soldiers have come into contact with urban culture. The army is organized in a territorial system of military regions. It is largely composed of peasants whose mental universe is closer to the Neolithic age than the 20th century. For these poor people, snatched away from their ancestral villages, national service probably represents the unconditional allegiance which, in a previous generation, they would have granted their feudal lords. Despite a semblance of uniformity and unity imposed by communist jargon, the Chinese army is more a confederation of vassals than a professional army in the modern sense, i.e. an army devoted to national defense. That is why today, as in the time of Chiang Kai-shek, it is only prevented from splitting into clusters of armed groups under warlords intent on defending their own territory, by the political and diplomatic ability of its overall leader. Until 9 November 1989 this leader was Deng Xiaoping, chairman of the Military Commission. Today Jiang Zemin, a 'Deng creation', holds the post. The army first fragmented at the fall of the Manchu dynasty in 1911; it nearly did so again during the popular demonstrations which followed the death of Hu Yaobang in April 1989. Contrary to the convenient reports by most Western journalists, the fraternizing that took place between students and soldiers from certain PLA units, as well as the shots fired between units for and against the bloody crushing of the student demonstrations, were far less a sign of dissent over the degree of democracy compatible with Chinese political life, than the more prosaic effect of a serious disagreement concerning power-sharing at the summit of the military hierarchy.

China at the end of the 20th century, torn between its paternalistic bureaucracy and the latent 'warlordism' of its army, hardly differs from the China of old, with 3,000 years of cultural continuity. Hidden beneath the new political and social 'codes' generated by the communist takeover, lies the reality of this omnipresent immobility. Thus the bloodbath of June 4 and the world-wide protests that ensued have given rise to a resurgence of the xenophobia and isolationism which were prevalent during the 19th-century Qing dynasty.

Deng Xiaoping himself gave the signal for this leap backward which, since then, has taken the proportions of a major 'misinformation' campaign. He began early in July 1989 in a speech that could be a replica of a 1950s speech of Mao's. He condemned Zhao Ziyang's project for the integration of the coastal regions of China to the trade of the Asia-Pacific rim and declared, in all seriousness, that the boycott of China by certain Western nations was a good opportunity to put back into practice an old slogan of Yenan days, 'Rely on your own strength.' Worse still, in a true spirit of Maoist voluntarism from the Great Leap Forward, he anticipated that the forthcoming difficulties would be the best way to trigger the 'fierce struggle' which ultimately would overcome them.[9] This specious logic has already produced some results, albeit limited ones, as may be seen from the speech made on the 40th anniversary of the People's Republic (October 1989) by Jiang Zemin, the obscure new General Secretary and the third heir apparent in seven years. In this speech, Jiang proclaimed, as in the height of Maoist fervor, the advent of 'a new socialist man' as well as the inevitable fall of capitalism. Even in China, these hackneyed old phrases are of interest to nobody. Far more serious, however, was his announcement that, in accordance with Chen Yun's ideas, the market was only to serve the plan, and the government would slow down any expansion of this private sector, limited though it already was. Lastly, he accused some mysterious 'international reactionary forces' of working with the equally mysterious 'class enemies' within China to overthrow the 'socialist system.'[10]

Jiang Zemin could hardly expand on the last point, expressing himself as he did in a speech which was inevitably going to be scrutinized by China-watchers the world over. But as far as his Chinese audience was concerned, he didn't need to, for at the end of August 1989, a 200-page book was published under the aegis of the State Commission on Teaching, called *Retrospective and Reexamination of the Fifty Days*. This gem expands on the sybilline intuitions of Zhao Ziyang's successor. It bears the stamp 'for internal circulation only,' and was used as a textbook for a 20-day period of student indoctrination at the beginning of the term — in itself a return to the Maoist concept of 'education.' The book professes to lend credence to the theory of a 'counterrevolutionary plot' and is a veritable pack of lies. It states, for example, the 'all American governments' since John Foster Dulles, U.S. Secretary of State under President Eisenhower, 'have adopted his prime objective,' namely 'to place China under the domination of international monopolistic capital.' Where recent events are concerned, the U.S. is accused of leading 'psychological warfare' against China.

Thus in the last few years, American universities have welcomed a flood of Chinese students for the sole purpose of 'forming pro-American forces' in order to 'progressively tilt the Chinese government toward capitalism.' Continuing in a vein reminiscent of the tales concerning Chinese missionaries which sprung up in China during the Boxer rising of 1900, the anonymous but officially authorized compilers of this book firmly contend that the dozens of American teachers sent to China every year to teach, together with the American Embassy and the Voice of America, are working together 'to change China radically within a three-year period.' As for the Foundation for Reform in China, an organization financed with American money, it is no more than a hotbed of CIA agents attempting to recruit members of various 'think tanks' organized by Zhao Ziyang. Even the innocent training centers established by Washington in Beijing, Nanjing, Canton, and Dalian in order to teach modern management methods to Chinese company executives, are accused of 'the most serious attempts at subversion.' Because, in accordance with good Marxist theory, the economy is the nerve center of any war, Washington was seeking to 'obtain influence with the Chinese government and people, under cover of developing economic and technical cooperation between the USA and China' in order to 'make China economically dependent on the United States' and, ultimately, lead to its political submission as well.[11]

This xenophobic rubbish sets the Chinese clock back not just to the Cold War, but to the end of the Manchu dynasty. If we pursue this analogy to the end, it should follow that the revolution that will bring about the end of the communist rule in China should be close at hand. This would be unwise. In 1911, the Manchu government had been deserted by the elite, drained internally, weakened by division and the encroachment of Western imperialism. It was debilitated to such an extent that the handful of conspirators under Sun Yat-sen had only to give the *coup de grâce*. The 'father of the nation' (*guo fu*) would have a hard time reproducing this scenario today. The communists have added brute force to the immobility of the Manchu empire, a force more than sufficient to crush any attempt on the part of the populace to rebel. This brute force, first and foremost, is that of the army, as was seen during the June 4 massacre, and will continue to be so for as long as its unity is preserved. It is also that of the police; witness the efficient way in which they used Western journalism to make files on the Tiananmen Square demonstrators and pursue those who escaped the massacre. Lastly, and more importantly, the bureaucracy's hold on Chinese society has resulted in a total fragmentation of the latter. Despite centralized planning, the tentacles of the imperial administration never descended beneath county level. Below that, that is to say at township (*xiang*) and village level, custom and lineage leaders reigned. This division of power ensured that local communities and, in the limits allowed by tradition, individuals, were allowed a certain amount of autonomy. This changed totally with the arrival of the communists: Under their rule the tentacles of political and police power were extended from street to street and from house to house.

The power of the communists, which is infinitely more widespread than that of the bureaucracy which ruled the Empire for dynasty after dynasty, is nevertheless qualitatively very inferior. In the system installed during the 8th century, aspirants to the Imperial bureaucracy were recruited by examination after lengthy and extremely fastidious studies. It is true that the studies were only concerned with what might be termed 'Confucian humanities.' Nor were they of a nature to make scholars receptive to innovation or science. But, at the very least, they did offer some kind of guarantee that, in general, the reins of power were in the hands of people who held certain moral and intellectual values. This was particularly important when, faced with the superiority of Western technology, the Manchu dynasty was confronted with a dilemma: Modernize or die. At that time a number of remarkable men arose from the ranks of the mandarins and did their utmost to push the old empire into a Meiji-type direction. This resulted in the brief flowering of the New Culture movement in the second and third decade of the 20th century. The human 'raw material' with which the communist bureaucracy is composed, however, is of an entirely different nature. The few intellectuals who escaped Mao's pogroms are almost totally excluded. Positions of responsibility are in the hands of those who joined the Party ranks in the 1950s and early 1960s. This was the militant apogee of Chinese communism, meaning that selection was largely according to class origin and political conformity, and only secondarily for any skill or qualification. In the following period, that of the Cultural Revolution, the situation was to deteriorate still further: On a whim of the Ubu-Roi, it was declared that schools and universities would do better to teach how to plant cabbages the Chinese way than to impart any knowledge of science or technology. After 1978, Deng Xiaoping trimmed down the number of cadres of the 1966–1976 mold, but this did not succeed in raising the level of education of an over-abundant and near-sclerotic bureaucracy.

Under these circumstances it is hardly surprising that few bureaucrats supported the political reforms advocated first by Hu Yaobang and then by Zhao Ziyang, for they had everything to lose. Yet these reforms, limited though they were, were desperately needed; China would have benefited enormously Two anecdotes illustrate the prevalent mentality of the petty bureaucracy. Incredible though it may seem, in 1988, there was a minor revolution in a small mountain town, when, (such *lèse majesté!*) for the first time in the 40 years of the PRC's existence, a building was erected that was taller than the three storeys of the local Party secretary's palatial residence![12] In Hubei, county level cadres (*ganbu*) were accompanying a 'foreign expert' when their car was stopped by a group of peasants who asked them to take a pregnant woman on the point to giving birth to the nearest hospital. The *ganbu* curtly refused, giving their 'foreign guest' as a pretext, until the latter understood what was happening and intervened.[13] Generally speaking, the leadership style in communist China is that of authoritarian rule over subjects, not citizens. Conversely, the attitude of the led is marked by what the young authors of the controversial film series 'The River Dies Young' (shown on Chinese television in June 1988) called contemptuously 'the serf mentality.'[14] This is, of course, oversimplified, but it is true to say that few things have changed in China since the time when Confucius depicted the ideal relationship between a ruler and the populace as that of a benevolent father toward his child.

In view of the tacit consent linking a government that expects only obedience on the part of the population, and a population which, as an entity, cannot conceive that the government should have to account to it, the political situation in China is static. The minimum prerequisite for any development would be the creation of economically independent social elites within the state bureaucracy, capable of organizing themselves to defend their interests. This elite existed before 1949 even though, as in most Third World countries, it was weak and fragmented. But as soon as the communists came to power, it was systematically destroyed. First came the turn of the land owners (1950), who were exterminated as a social class by the massacres and expropriations of the land reforms. Then it was the turn of the craftsmen and 'national capitalists' (1955–1956) — those who made the mistake of trusting the new government instead of escaping to Hong Kong or Taiwan. They had all their assets confiscated during the movement to nationalize trade and industry. Lastly, in 1957, after the Hundred Flowers, the Party took hold of what was left of the intellectuals, and Deng Xiaoping, then General Secretary, brutally put them through their paces. Vast numbers had to bear the 'rightist' label for the next 20 years.

Not content with this devastation of the social elite, the communists set up a system of discrimination according to class origins, which were transmitted through the paternal line only. Thus all competence and know-how was excluded from the communist ranks. In the early 1980s, having continued in this vein for 30 years, the Party suddenly acknowledged the facts and made an about turn. Land was returned to the peasants and the ban on private enterprise lifted in the cities. But neither 'Marxism-Leninism' nor 'Mao Tse-tung thought' can raise the dead and today China finds itself in a strange social desert. This desert landscape is broken up by the occasional 'oasis,' for example, the handful of peasant 'millionaires' who were as praised by the propaganda press, as were the ragged peasants who were moving mountains single-handed not so long ago; or the 75 million people working in non-agricultural enterprises, or in the cities, the 15 million 'self-employed families' (geti hu) currently harassed by the tax man and under close political and police scrutiny. For a country the size of China, that's not much.

The amorphous social nature of the People's Republic of China and the absence of any interest groups sufficiently powerful to make themselves heard, explain the piecemeal and gradualist view of the Chinese democratization process held by the famous dissident, Fang Lizhi. Contrary to the far-fetched accusations made by the Chinese government, the astrophysicist's political views do not directly dispute the Party's monopoly of power. In fact, before the

tragic events of last June, with what was perhaps an exceedingly
realistic point of view, Fang anticipated a progressive revolution,
lasting perhaps for 20 or 30 years. At the end of this time, the
economic reforms would enable 'private entrepreneurs' to form a
'Third Estate,' or in other words, a real bourgeoisie. With an
independent economic base at its disposal, this new social category
could generate an opposition party which would, eventually, break
down the communist monopoly. But, until this process is
achieved, the liberal Chinese intellectuals should, according to
Fang Lizhi, content themselves with informing public opinion
about democracy, through the press in particular, and struggle as a
pressure group from within against the régime's autocratic
tendencies.[15] An example of this type of action, was the petition
launched on Fang's initiative in January 1989 to demand an amnesty for Chinese political prisoners, including Wei Jingsheng, the
advocate of the Fifth Modernization, imprisoned 10 years ago on
the orders of Deng Xiaoping. But, after the massacre of June 4,
even this moderate and pragmatic approach to political reform in
China is clearly too optimistic.

Under these circumstances, one might wonder what political
options remain open in China? Of course, it is not possible to
exclude the possibility of a return of the 'reformists' (with or
without Zhao Ziyang), and the open-door policy. Conversely,
there should be no illusions about the advanced old age of Deng
Xiaoping and the sages who are pulling the strings. Their replacements exist in the form of Li Peng, Jiang Zemin, Qiao Shi, and
Yao Yilin. Above all, there is a genuine correlation between the
realities of grassroots China and this type of autocracy. This is
why it is quite possible for the present regime to be perpetuated *ad
infinitum*, implying, at the very least, a partial withdrawal of China
into itself, as is currently the case on the political scene. This
would lead to a kind of 'soft Maoism,' without the exhausting
political campaigns that the Great Helmsman was wont to impose
on the country, but with a greater military presence than before
because the country is fraying at the edges and becoming increasingly ungovernable.

If the oligarchy behaves with common sense and makes a number of concessions to the increasingly stubborn urban population,
and if it does not get waylaid again by the illusions of collectivization, it might even succeed in putting an end to the severe crisis in
which China finds itself. Thus a long-lasting period of stagnation

could set in until such time as another eruption occurs. This scenario does not conform to the opinion that prevailed after the June 4 massacre, that the regime was under a suspended death sentence. One might say to supporters of this theory that the regime has survived other such events. After all, did it not survive the famine provoked by the Great Leap Forward, one of the worst in history? Did the government not succeed in regaining its position after the apocalyptic storm of the Cultural Revolution? Clearly, it is unlikely to fall, or even be shaken by the juvenile enthusiasms of non-violent student movement, a minority in the country at large, and uncertain as to its long-term objectives.

There does, however, exist an alternative scenario. It is, paradoxically, an optimistic one, and would occur in the event of a total disintegration of China as a consequence of insurmountable dissent within the oligarchy itself, following the death of its leader, for example, as Deng Xiaoping's hour of atonement is near. Freed from the burden of heavy political and bureaucratic leadership in Beijing, each of the vast provinces of the continent-country would then be more or less left to its own devices and free to follow its own destiny. The seaboard, for example, could pursue its economic development and realize its full potential which, prior to June 4, appeared to be extremely promising. This alternative scenario has a precedent in Shanghai's economic miracle following the dismemberment of the state after the fall of the Qing dynasty. Liberated from the government hold on trade, business flourished and pushed up China's economic growth by 14 percent per year for a 10-year period during the 1910s and early 1920s. In 1927, Chiang Kai-shek ended this long period of political anarchy and reunified China under a strong state leadership, he cut short this burgeoning and vigorous Chinese capitalism.

The manner in which this first industrial takeoff was terminated should put an end to the arguments of the 'neo-authoritarians' (numerous in China and in the Chinese diaspora), who hold that three of the 'Four Asian Tigers' (South Korea, Singapore, Taiwan, and the one pseudo-democratic exception, Hong Kong) owe their recently acquired prosperity to autocratic rule. According to their thesis, this model is better suited to Chinese culture than a Western-style democracy. But China, unlike the three 'tigers,' has no civil service worthy of that name, and the bureaucracy/bourgeoisie symbiosis was stretched by the communists to such an extent that the former alone manages the economy. Consequently, it is difficult to see what this model would produce if it were applied to China, except still greater corruption than under Chiang Kai-shek — which is probably already the case.

The conclusion that the only hope for China's salvation lies in its total disintegration is certainly upsetting, be it for base geographical reasons, vulgar nationalistic ones, or lofty humanitarian ones. But at least let us add, like Paul Valéry, that civilizations are not immortal, so why should China be an exception? And in the meantime, perhaps we should meditate on these words of Montesquieu: 'A vast empire must necessarily be governed by despotic authority.'

----

1. Special joint edition of *Zhengming* (Debates) and *Dongxiang* (Trends), June 1989, p. 24. Supplement of *Beijing Information*, 24 July 1989.

2. For further details, see W. Zafanolli, 'Les ambiguités d'une modernisation autoritaire,' and 'Un coup d'arrêt conservateur?' in *Encyclopaedia Universalis* 1988, pp. 119–131.

3. For a good example, see *Renmin Ribao* (People's Daily), 10 September 1985, p. 5.

4. According to Ba Shan, '*Si bai yi yuan hua wei niao you*' (40bn Yuan Reduced to Nothing) in *Dongxiang*, No. 56, September 1989, pp. 70–81. This is a reprint of a report that was published in China.

5. *Renmin Ribao*, 8 March 1985, p. 2.

6. *Renmin Ribao*, 7 February 1986, p. 1.

7. See W. Zafanolli, 'Pratiques légales et droits de l'homme en Chine' (Legal Practice and Human Rights in China) in *Le Cri des Hommes* (journal of the International Federation of Human Rights), No. 22, November 1984, pp. 18–34.

8. *Zhengming* No. 142, August 1989, p. 11.

9. *Ibid.*

10. *Renmin Ribao*, 30 September 1989, pp. 1–2.

11. *Zhengming*, No. 144, October 1989, pp. 20–23.

12. *Dongxiang*, No. 56, September 1989, p. 34.

13. *Ibid.*, p. 35.

14. This film, which triggered off a very lively debate, ascribes the backwardness of mainland China to its land-locked agricultural society and contrasts its characteristic peasant conservatism with the dynamism of the sea-faring nations which, eventually, led the latter into the industrial age. See Fr. Wakeman Jr., '*All the Rage in China*,' the New York Review, 2 March 1989.

15. *Zhengming*, No. 117, July 1987, p. 25 and No. 132, October 1988, p. 25.

16. See the excellent study by Marie-Claire Bergère, '*L'âge d'or de la bourgeoisie chinoise, 1911–1937*,' Flammarion, Paris 1986.

China and the Crisis of Communism

FRANZ MICHAEL

THE millions of people who demonstrated on Tiananmen Square in Beijing and in more than 80 other cities across China in May and June were the first massive protests against a communist regime in 1989, that remarkable year. The Beijing demonstration and the massacre that ended it preceded the collapse of communist regimes under the weight of similar mass protests in Berlin, Budapest, Prage, Sofia, and even Bucharest. Why did communism survive in China? And why did China use force, when Eastern Europe yielded?

The answer lies in the personalities and policies of two very different communist leaders, Deng Xiaoping and Mikhail Gorbachev. The Chinese students who started the avalanche of massive demonstrations assumed that the People's Liberation Army would not shoot the people; indeed, Beijing citizens put in a great deal of organized effort to dissuade PLA soldiers from carrying out the martial law orders of the communist radical elite. Finally, however, Deng ordered in the tanks to overrun and smash and shoot the protesters, ending, for a time, the drive for 'freedom and democracy.'

In Eastern Europe, the communist leaders did not dare to use tanks. This was a change in communist policy. In 1968, the 'Prague Spring' was crushed by a Soviet–led invasion of Warsaw Pact tank armies that deposed the reformist communist leader, Alexander Dubcek, and introduced a hard-line regime. Under the threat of mass strikes and demonstrations, and afraid to call in the troops, that same regime fell in November. In Hungary, the post-mortem honoring of Josef Nagy played a part in washing away the past, especially the brutal crushing of the 1956 uprising. There the Communist Party has renamed itself as a 'socialist' party, to form part of an anticipated pluralist regime. In Poland, the fear of Soviet invasion, and the imposition of martial law in the early 1980s, helped at first to hold down the free labor union, Solidarity. But in 1989, the first non-communist, Solidarity government, took office. In East Germany, Bulgaria, and Romania, hated communist regimes have fallen — due to the exact pressures that failed so bitterly in China.

This startling shift in Eastern Europe is the result of Gorbachev's policy of *glasnost*, a new openness that claims to allow the people of Soviet-bloc countries to decide their own destinies. *Glasnost* required a new policy of arms control and of cooperation with the West. Suppressing Eastern European demonstrations would have ended any such cooperation. Since World War II, Soviet armies have been the decisive power factor in Eastern Europe. Only guns held these governments together; without them, the regimes fell apart. The crucial difference is that in China, Deng was willing and able to send in a tank corps to smash and kill the protesters.

Between Eastern Europe and China, however, more is at stake than the use of troops to quell a massive popular uprising. What is at issue is the extent of the new revolutions themselves. Communist leaders in both Asia and Europe agreed that the Stalinist order had failed. They were ready to give up Stalin, but not Marx or Lenin. It is this final core of communism that is at stake in China, in the battle for Eastern Europe, and finally in the Soviet Union itself.

Marx assumed that human history must be seen as a class struggle over the means of production. His doctrine of 'dialectic materialism' claimed that throughout human history mankind was divided into exploiting and exploited classes, with the former holding a dictatorship over the means of production and the latter struggling to overthrow it and establish its own dictatorship; until, in Marx's time, the proletariat, the trained workers, would overthrow the 'capitalists' and would in turn gain control of all means of production. This worker class would then establish a 'dictatorship of the proletariat' that would somehow end the historical struggle and lead to a perfect society.

To this fantasy, Lenin added an institutional framework. If the workers did not act as they were supposed to, a special group of professional revolutionaries, the 'vanguard of the proletariat,' i.e. the Communist Party, must lead the way. In order to do so, it would impose an absolute dictatorship not only over society but over the 'proletariat' as well. This 'proletarian dictatorship' would bring about the desired millennium. This Leninist structure — with its pervasive control over mind and action — we call totalitarianism.

In this configuration the basic economic concepts of Marx are false. Marx's 'value theory' regarded human labor as the sole determinant for the price of goods; there was no understanding of supply and demand, nor of the role of private ownership of the means of production. No feasible price fixation can be obtained from this fallacy. Worse than its irrational economic concepts, Marxism as a 'materialist' philosophy cannot establish an ethical foundation. Nothing is more pitiful than the slogans propagated in China in 1982 to promote a 'spiritual socialism.' The Party called on a potpourri of institutions, ideals, and ideas to assert this 'ethical' background. 'Education, science, art, literature, the media, recreation, libraries, museums and public health' were to be combined with the 'Weltanschauung of the working class': scientific Marxism, communist ideals, morality and discipline to provide an answer to the search for something more than the material order.[1] The lack of such a spiritual or ethical base in China led to ruthless utilitarianism, exploitation, corruption, and total derangement of the economy and ethical standards. No wonder about the corruption of the Party in China and the arrest of the East German communist leadership for its parasitic life. For any reform of this system, the basics of Marx's doctrine have to be abandoned.

Lenin's heritage is of course much worse. Lenin is the father of the concept of total control by the Communist Party, the Orwellian order which, first established in the Soviet Union, created a power monopoly of the leading elite and of the leader himself. These precepts are still the basis of the communist system. Stalin created only a logical working order. He introduced a central command economy, with emphasis on heavy industry, agricultural collectivization, and complete bureaucratic control over the population. It was this order which was eventually copied by all communist countries, including China. The system was held together by terror, the secret police, and military power.

In the years of the war against Japan and the civil war in China, Mao Tse-tung was a skillful and ruthless leader who adapted the Soviets' prescribed policy for China. Mao was a Stalinist and China had a Stalinist order. The argument that there was 'the other communism,' or that Mao was a 'peasant leader,' often repeated in Western pro-Chinese communist propaganda, can no longer be taken seriously. It was Stalin who in March 1926 reaffirmed Lenin's policy in his directive to the Comintern: 'The most important task of the Chinese Communist Party is to win the peasant masses for active struggle on behalf of fighting slogans which link political and economic demands comprehensible to and important to the peasantry.'[2]

In Yenan, during the war years, Mao's speeches, the source of Mao Tse-tung thought, were derived from Soviet textbooks and encyclopedias, obviously sent to Mao by his protector in Moscow.[3] When he proclaimed the People's Republic of China in 1949, Mao asked Stalin to send an ambassador well-versed in Marxism-Leninism, of which Mao appears to have had only very limited knowledge. Stalin sent Pavel F. Yudin, former head of the Comintern who became Mao's confidant. When Stalin died, Mao indulged in an essay dedicated to Stalin under the title, 'The Greatest Friendship.'

It was, however, not this personal attachment between Mao and Stalin that determined China's communist policy. It was Chinese communism itself that was Stalinist. The establishment of a central command economy, the emphasis on heavy industry, the collectivization of agriculture, the political order, the five-year plans — all these introduced the Stalinist order. As in the Soviet Union, and indeed all communist countries, Mao eliminated, after the siege of power in 1949, the upper-class element in urban and rural China in the notorious five major drives in the first five years, killing 10 million people or more, to replace them with communist leadership.[4] It was this Stalinist order that separated the communist world, economically as well as politically, from the rest of the world. Behind the iron or bamboo curtains, a separate world of oppression and increasing impoverishment soon prevailed.

During the years of communist expansion after World War II, many people believed that the experiment, despite its obvious abuses, held out hope for a feasible future order. In our time when much of the communist leadership itself has come to realize that up till now communism has been a dead end, the first voices in the West proclaim the end of communism. China's communist leaders, however, do not think so. They want reform, but only within a continued, if undefined, communist order.

The reforms began in China with the death of Mao. It was urgent. A massive protest at Tiananmen Square in Beijing in April 1976, a few months before Mao died, had already indicated opposition within the Party and beyond against Mao's oppression and the purges of the Great Proletarian Cultural Revolution.

Though bloodily suppressed, this — later approved — Tiananmen uprising indicated mounting dissatisfaction with Maoist rule.

One of the leading foreign scholars on China, Father L. Ladany, once in despair questioned the chances for a Chinese revolution. He deplored Mao's destruction of the Chinese middle class, the presumed source of such a rising. As after all communist victories, this bloodletting in China had occurred; but among the communists themselves, a new middle class had emerged. Many of the protesters of 1976 were Communist Party members; and the Chinese students who led the protests for 'freedom and democracy' in 1989 were largely the children and grandchildren of Party members or Party members themselves. They were disillusioned by the economic stalemate, the corruption, and the dishonesty of the regime, the lies and the lack of freedom.

It was a communist leader, Deng Xiaoping, twice purged under Mao, who carried through his ideas of reform, economically and politically, upon his return to power in 1978. Deng realized that the impoverishment of China did not give credit to the communist regime and an improvement of living standards was desperately needed. He was willing to give up the centrally planned economy and even agricultural collectivization. At the same time, he wanted to affirm the leadership of the Communist Party. Perhaps it never occurred to Deng, who had made his career under Mao and contributed to the Stalinist measures that established the regime, that something within communism itself was basically wrong. Systemic change alone could help China to rise from the tragedy of its Maoist and Stalinist heritage. He wanted economic improvement without systemic change. Stalin could be abandoned, but not Lenin or Marx. In order to define the boundaries of reforms, Deng established, at the beginning of his new program, what he called the Four Cardinal Principles: the socialist way; the dictatorship of the proletariat; leadership by the Communist Party; and Marxism-Leninism-Mao Tse-tung thought. These principles were stressed over and over again. Speaking with young Chinese in Shanghai, I learned that many of them regarded the Four Cardinal Principles as empty propaganda. But to me it was clear that Deng meant them.

Many times Deng made his point. In January 1980, for instance, he addressed a meeting of Party cadres in Beijing to remind his audience: 'When did we ever say that we would tolerate the activities of counterrevolutionaries and saboteurs? When did we ever say that the dictatorship of the proletariat was to be abolished? There is no question that these activities should now be dealt with severely, because they are becoming outrageous. . . . By dealing sternly with these criminals now, we will be giving some kind of education not only to the overwhelming majority of offenders, but to the whole Party and people.'[5]

Deng's first problem — how to introduce economic reforms and still keep the state ownership of the means of production — led him to venture a compromise. Reform in agriculture was crucial. In the preceding years, peasant hunger marches had indicated the desperate plight of the agricultural population. Production had fallen in the communes and the collectives; peasants were impoverished. Deng decided to abolish the communes and to end collectivization. This was a major move away from the Maoist/Stalinist structure. But Deng did not dare to give the land back to the peasants; private ownership remained anathema to Chinese communist leaders.

Deng sought a middle way between 'socialist ownership' by the state or the community and 'capitalist' private ownership. He introduced a system of leasing the land through written contracts to peasant families over a fixed period. In this state-tenant relationship, land was distributed on the basis of the number of working members, on the average of one mou (about one-third of an acre) per family, first for three and eventually for 15 years. Each family was responsible for delivering to the state, at a fixed price, a certain amount of grain or other basic crops, but would be permitted to sell all surplus on the newly established free agricultural markets.

The immediate outcome of this policy of 'giving the land to the peasants' as one professor in Beijing called it, was a 250 percent increase in agricultural production between 1982 and 1985. It resulted in a great improvement of living standards not only of the rural but of the urban population as well.

In 1985, however, the system stalled. Agricultural production, especially grain production, stagnated. The peasants began to complain about government prices of fertilizer and equipment and the growing costs of other goods, such as bicycles, motorcycles, washing machines, and television sets. While some quick fortunes had been made, and visitors were shown some 10,000 yuan houses that rural leaders (usually cadres) had built for themselves, the agricultural economy had stopped progressing. Rural living standards in some successful areas like the south or the Yangtse region, had perhaps reached the level of 1937, but in the meantime population had, of course, more than doubled.

The reason for this stagnation was obvious. Tenancy, even for 15 years, does not equal ownership. The land, officially owned by the state, was cared for by nobody. Under the pre-communist system, not only small peasant owners (comprising on the whole about 50 percent of the farming population) but also small landlords (there were no large ones) had a vested interest in the long-run profitability of their land and other needed facilities. With no owners, this long-range interest was lacking. Public works were not taken care of and the uncertainty about future government policy supported the rush to quick returns of income.[6]

In 1985, at the time when the new agricultural policy seemed to have paid off, the regime decided to apply the same contract system to state-owned industries. There had been during the last years a development of Western, joint, and small-scale Chinese private industries. The idea was that Western capital investment and technical know–how would stimulate China's own industry. Chinese small-scale private industry in the cities was permitted to lap up the growing unemployment. Despite this private enterprise, by far the largest part of Chinese industry was state industry or, to a lesser degree, cooperative enterprise.

Special zones for foreign investment were established in the coastal areas, especially in Shenzen, near Hong Kong. The privileges that foreign investors enjoyed in these zones have sometimes been compared with the treaty ports of old, though the new zones remain under Chinese sovereignty. In the new zones and some cities on the coast, standards of living became much higher than those of the inland areas, causing considerable jealousy.

Shenzen, the SEZ near Hong Kong has, for instance, developed a life of its own. Foreign, particularly Hong Kong Chinese, investments have improved not only living conditions, but have created a new lifestyle that has become more opulent than that of most of the mainland. Though Beijing has succeeded in purging some local leaders and Beijing's pronouncements indicate an intention to curb the autonomy of the SEZs, such a policy may become counterproductive. It would further reduce what is left of foreign investment. Beijing cannot have it both ways: Curb reform and at the same time open up toward the West. Whatever Beijing decides, the SEZs remain disgruntled and could, with some others, serve as autonomous regions in a coming leadership struggle.

The leadership intended, of course, to maintain government-managed industries, overstaffed and debt-ridden as they were, to protect China's 'socialist character.' To do so, however, a basic reform appeared essential to improve the efficiency and management of these enterprises, far behind in technical development and bureaucratized to an incredible degree.

To these state industrial plants, Deng attempted to apply the contract system, which had seemed to salvage agriculture. Deng's plan was to place the plant director in a contract relationship to the local government authorities. Under this contract, the director was to make his decisions on the basis of his assessment of local and overseas market conditions. In this way, it was hoped, he would produce a certain quantity of commodities at 'a profit.' These state industry directors were thought to be comparable to Western entrepreneurs.

In practice the whole system was entirely different. There was, after all, no price structure on which these directors could base their planning. They had to relate their judgment on the chance decisions of local or central government; they had to have therefore connections with government officials — guanxi. It was still Party policy that determined economic decisions. Moreover, the large majority of the directors were Party members, as such already obliged to carry out Party policy; and those who were not, had to be Party-approved. It was the Party which proposed all candidates to director positions and could fire them at will. The contract which the directors signed already outlined Party policy. They were supervised by the Party and had to deal with a Party labor organization. The Party also controlled energy, raw material, transportation, and most prices; and though in theory the directors could fire workers for gross neglect, in reality they would be prevented from doing so. A Party member himself, or even if in a few cases not, the 'independent' manager remained a fiction.

This presumed new role of decentralized management of industry was part of Deng Xiaoping's plan for reforming the political structure. Deng was aware that economic reform required a political change as well, but he was not going to allow it to threaten the leadership of the Communist Party. Instead of Stalin's system of central planning of the command economy by central ministries, the Party structure was to be loosened up. First, there should be a separation within the Party of the supervisory and the actual executive functions; second, there should be a delegation of central authority to local communist agencies, including the establishment of industrial 'independent' directors. This separation between supervision and management was at least attempted and reported in many cases, but in practice resulted chiefly in a further complication of bureaucratic management. It demonstrated at the beginning how little trained the communist leadership was for its newly assigned professional management of government and industry. In the long run, even a trained group of managers could do little in the economic confusion that the reforms created. The only certain outcome was a growth of bureaucracy.

Since the new emphasis was on modernization, stressing profitability and money making, the Party leadership, centrally and locally, was in an extraordinary position to profit, particularly from the many opportunities which a dual price system between government-controlled prices and free market prices provided. The corruption by Party members and by their offspring — always important — expanded massively. It was one of the major complaints of the student protesters in 1989. The Party itself admitted it, and, after the massacre at Tiananmen, it thought it necessary to introduce large-scale purges of corrupted officials. These purges appear to have affected mainly the families of the inner-Party opposition, Zhao Ziyang's group, and not the families of the hard-liners, now in power.

What happened at Tiananmen in May 1989 was a massive and spontaneous explosion of popular indignation. When the hundreds of thousands of students from Beijing universities and other cities broke by sheer weight of numbers through the police lines and congregated at Tiananmen, the city of Beijing erupted. Over a million people on the Square and in the streets jubilantly joined the chorus shouting for 'freedom and democracy,' the chief slogans of the demonstration.

It has been said that the students had only vague notions of their goals. I disagree. During the demonstrations at Tiananmen Square, there were banners calling on Lech Walesa and the Polish Solidarity movement. The students wanted their own, independently elected organization to have a dialogue with the Party. Similar independent organizations of workers and of professionals were rapidly being formed. This was in fact an attempt to change the system peacefully.

Even if these demands at the time were unacceptable to the Party leadership of the five octogenarians under Deng Xiaoping, there were clearly many ways to negotiate on some of the points, especially on corruption. Yet Deng, in particular, wanted a bloody suppression of the demonstration to give vent to his fury and provide a lesson for the future. He had, after all, condemned the 'too soft' handling of unrest in Poland and Hungary and had suggested that in the Chinese demonstrations 'blood would have to be shed.'

It was Deng's bad luck that the uprising coincided with the visit of Soviet leader Mikhail Gorbachev, a meeting Deng regarded as his crowning success. The visit was ruined by the students' occupation of Tiananmen Square and their protests in Shanghai. It prevented Gorbachev's obligatory laying of a wreath at the memorial column at the Square. And it sharpened the intra-Party Chinese conflict when Zhao Ziyang, explaining the situation to Gorbachev, pointed to Deng and the five octogenarians as holding the power of decision. Deng must have been furious, sitting in the Great Hall of the People and seeing outside the hundred of thousands of protesters and perhaps pondering the threat to his regime. Yet he had to wait. In the presence of the Soviet visitor he could not use the violent action he intended. In the meantime, the world press arrived to witness the historic summit meeting and was surprised to find itself in the midst of a revolutionary uprising. They were to televise and report the spectacle, producing pictures, films, and reports that aroused many people who held a total misconception of the Chinese reform movement and Deng Xiaoping.

It was not a 'tragedy' for Deng, as a leading American former official regretfully declared; Deng lived up to his own standards. His Four Cardinal Principles had to be maintained at all costs, and bloodshed was the method he believed he needed. Not only was the idea of elected student representatives, let alone other such independent organizations, unacceptable to him, he wanted to reassert the Party's authority as powerfully as possible. Thus we had the brutal military suppression, the killing of hundreds or thousands of citizens, wounding many more; and, after that, dozens of executions and thousands of arrests.

What lies in the future? The present regime of hard-liners

cannot last. Many reforms are halted, some are being reduced; but reform or no reform, without systemic change, the system is bound to fail. There is one major advantage for the hard-line communist regime in Beijing: the apparent unwillingness of President Bush to see the parallel between the mass demonstrations in Berlin, Leipzig, Wenceslas Square, and Tiananmen. The missions of Anna Chennault, Richard Nixon, Brent Scowcroft, and Lawrence Eagleburger, whom the president sent to Beijing to stress Sino-U.S. 'friendship,' are obviously going to strengthen the regime and presumably open the way for American, Japanese, German, and World Bank financial support. This presidential policy, if not cut short, will prolong the agony but not affect the final outcome.

There is still disunity among the Party leaders, between those in power and those discredited. There is an unknown factor of disunity within the military. Someday, could or would a man like Zhao Ziyang play the role of a Jaruzelski? Or would future leaders call for a change as the Hungarians did? The Chinese communists, unlike the now-unemployed despots of Eastern Europe, have proved they are willing to pull the trigger on their own people to protect their monopoly on power. For a time, this willingness to shoot will work to the regime's advantage, but as the example of executed Romanian dictator Nicolae Ceausescu shows, no one can guarantee the guns will not someday be turned the other way. One can only wonder. In China for the moment, the opportunity has passed; the future struggle could prove even more violent than the tragedy of Tiananmen.

---

1. *Beijing Review*, 2 May 1983, pp. 18–19.

2. Jane Degras, ed., *The Communist International, 1919–1943*, Vol. 2, New York, 1964, p. 279.

3. Nakajima Mineo, *Gendai Chugoku-ron*, Tokyo Skoka, 1964, pp. 44–53.

4. Richard Walker, *China Under Communism; The First Five Years*, New Haven, Conn., 1955.

5. See *Selected Works of Deng Xiaoping (1975–1982)*, Beijing, 1984, p. 239.

6. See article by Feng-hwa Mah, ' "Primary Stage" Leasing and Ownership: Mainland Chinese Economy at the Crossroads,' in *Issues and Studies*, Vol. 25, No. 1, January 1989, Taipei.

The Next Power Struggle

RAMON H. MYERS

ON 18 May 1989, 10,000 students, workers, and professionals marched in Yining city of remote Qinghai province, shouting: 'Mama, we are not wrong'; 'Get rid of old-man politics'; and 'Unless the official profiteers are toppled, the state will collapse.'[1] All over China, from Liaoning and Inner Mongolia in the far north, through the northern provinces, and as far south as Guangdong, great crowds demonstrated to express their grievances about the way the country was being managed by the Chinese Communist Party.[2] A day later, Party General Secretary Zhao Ziyang offered to resign after being unable to persuade his colleagues in the Politburo's Central Committee to deal more leniently with the student activists in Beijing and elsewhere.[3]

These urban demonstrations had become inextricably mixed with a major power struggle among the Party's top leaders. That struggle, under way for over a year or so, had divided the Party into two major factions: One faction, under Zhao Ziyang, opted for reform, and the other, under Li Peng and the old cadres, merely wanted gradual change with CCP control intact. Power struggle within the CCP was not new. Ever since the Party had formed in July 1921, its leaders had quarreled. Only temporarily, under Mao Tse-tung and Deng Xiaoping, had the power struggles ceased. The slaughter of unarmed students and civilians by PLA troops on 3–4 June 1989, however, showed how violent such power struggles could become. How will this influence the Party's ability to rule and control China in the next decade? Can the Party remain unified and retain its present power?

The pattern of Party power struggle

China's internal Party power struggles are incomprehensible to outsiders; even their patterns are unclear. We simply lack evidence about the origins of these struggles and how they evolve. Historically, some common elements exist. When conflict erupted, the protagonists knew each other fairly well; they had experienced the same privations; they shared the same doctrinal views of Marxism and Leninism; they were of the same generation, although their social backgrounds varied. Another element was that personal differences and dislikes often made consensus among the top leaders difficult to achieve. Mao, it is rumored, disliked Liu Shaochi's distant bearing; Mao also resented the theoretical astuteness of Wang Ming. But exceptions existed. While Mao and Chou Enlai had serious differences between 1928 and 1934 in the Jingangshan Soviet base period, they later were close partners.

At the root of most power struggles, however, were different views about Party strategy and policies. In the mid-1920s, Chen Duxiu kept the Party 'oriented to the urban proletariat,' whereas Peng Pai and Mao Tse-tung concentrated their efforts in the countryside.[4] In the Soviet Republic base area of Jingangshan in Jiangsi, Mao and Zhu De quarreled over Party strategy and military tactics with Li Li-san, Chou Enlai, and the 28 Bolsheviks sent by Moscow.[5] Between 1936 and 1941 in Yenan, Mao struggled against Wang Ming and his faction, eventually aligning with Zhu De and Chou Enlai to defeat Wang and his supporters and emerge as the Party's paramount leader in 1942–43. He was then able to impose his strategy, or 'line,' and policies.

After the founding the People's Republic of China on 1 October 1949, the CCP leadership failed to establish a constitutional form of governance that would eliminate power struggles and instead produce consensus and an orderly succession of leaders. At the Eighth Party Congress in September 1956, disagreements surfaced between Liu Shaochi and Mao. These differences deepened as Mao pressed for more radical policies; he wanted to create ever-larger collective units to run the economy and remold people's behavior. So he destroyed the Liu faction in 1966–67 by aligning with the military commander Lin Biao, and in 1971–1972 turned on Lin Biao and eliminated him. Then in 1977, Deng Xiaoping fought Hua Guofeng, Mao's designated heir, for Party control over how to revitalize the sick economy and restore the Party's credibility, and won. Again in 1988–89, disagreement between General Secretary Zhao Ziyang and Premier Li Peng worsened over which policies could effectively control inflation, reduce corruption, allow more information, and terminate the student 'democracy' movement. Zhao lost.

In all these cases, Party debates centered on which strategy, or 'line,' the CCP would adopt and the necessary policies to carry out that strategy. As top leaders quarreled, they also fought each other on whom they wanted selected and promoted or demoted within the Party and government. A leader might lose his life, be humiliated, or be expelled from the Party. The Tiananmen tragedy set the stage for yet another Party leadership struggle.[6]

Time for a transfer of power

Since shortly after the death of Mao Tse-tung, the indisputable leader of the Party and, therefore, of China, has been Deng Xiaoping, a man of Mao's generation and background. Mao, Deng, and their colleagues all participated in the Long March, the Yenan years, the anti-Japanese war, the civil war, the socialization of China in the 1950s, and the Cultural Revolution. Deng's connections with various regional military commanders, his popular standing among the Party rank and file, and his ideological genius had qualified him to be the Party's supreme ruler. He was also supported by leaders of his own age who had built their personal networks of power throughout the Party, the bureaucracy, the security system, and the military: They were Peng Zhen, Bo Yibo, Yang Shangkun, Wang Zhen, Chen Yun, Li Xiannian, and others.

These leading cadres not only had held top posts in the Politburo and government for many years, but in the mid-1980s Deng had given them positions in the committees he had created to monitor the CCP, to resolve Party disputes, and to ensure the maintenance of the Party 'line': the Central Military Commission, the Central Advisory Committee, and the Central Committee for Discipline Inspection.[7] These octogenarian cadres, so supportive of Deng, have spent over a half-century working and suffering together for the Chinese Revolution. Even their children have intermarried. They never quarreled in public and shared the same 'socialist' vision for China. They are the legitimate leaders of the Party.

As the first leadership echelon, they still governed the country, even though a younger generation of leaders ran the Politburo, the Central Committee, and the top government positions. When critical decisions had to be made, when a major debate had to be resolved, and when a crisis threatened, these octogenarians, especially Deng, still called the shots. For example, when the extraordinary events of spring 1989 unfolded after Hu Yaobang's death on April 15, these leaders supported Deng in the decisions to impose martial law in Beijing, to suppress the student movement, to seize control of the city, and to remove Zhao Ziyang and Hu Qili from the Standing Committee of the Politburo.

All are in their 80s; these leaders cannot be expected to hold their power beyond another five years. Inevitably, power will slip from Deng and his colleagues to force the transfer of power to the second echelon of leaders.

The new Standing Committee of the Politburo now consists of Jiang Zemin (63), Song Ping (72), Li Ruihuan (55), Li Peng (61), Qiao Shi (64) and Yao Yilin (72). These men, along with roughly another 10 members of the Politburo, now run the Party.

The six Standing Committee members share similar backgrounds.[8] Unlike the first-generation leadership, they are educated: Jiang Zemin graduated from the electrical machinery department of Jiaotong University in Shanghai; Li Peng studied at the Moscow Power Institute; Song Ping studied at the Agricultural College of Beijing University and at Qinghua University. All of them have managed factories, industrial divisions of ministries, industrial institutes, and departments in the State Council related to economic affairs. Many have had experience managing large cities: Jiang Zemin was mayor of Shanghai; Li Ruihuan was mayor of Tianjin. Song Ping served as first political commissar of the Gansu Military Command Area. All have performed Party work in the Central Committee and its organs at one time or another.

These powerful new leaders are skilled technocrats, experienced bureaucrats, and orthodox Party cadres. One or more among them or of their generation and experience might have the vision or leadership capability of a Gorbachev, but we simply do not know. In spite of their more impressive technocratic leadership experience than the old veterans of the first echelon, they do not have extensive connections with the military, nor do they have extensive personal links or client network supporters in the Party, as did Hu Yaobang and Zhao Ziyang. None of them have displayed any theoretical skill concerning Party strategy and organization. It is interesting to note that only Deng's selected writings, not the writings of any current Politburo members, have been published in the past year for Party membership study.[9] While Jiang Zemin has been designated as the heir apparent to Deng, he appears to have none of the qualifications for that task: He has no friends among the military; he has no theoretical writings worthy of eliciting agreement and respect by other top leaders; and he lacks Party connections.

Since Zhao Ziyang and his supporters were sacked from the Politburo and Central Committee, this new leadership team has tried to consolidate its control in the Party.[10] They vigorously suppressed the 'counterrevolutionary' movement of last spring; launched a Party rectification campaign; imposed restrictions on universities to achieve ideological conformity; restricted the number of students going abroad; and tried to maintain tight controls over the economy by issuing bonds to absorb purchasing power of urban workers, extending more regulations over private enterprises, and tightening controls over money supply and state subsidies.

Adopting the conventional policies of despots, these leaders have merely endorsed the Deng 'line.' Yet they have been groomed by the old veterans to lead China into the 21st century in which Deng's philosophy of cultivating the 'enterprising spirit in hard struggle and plain living' should serve as the credo at a time when the country faces staggering problems.

First, these problems must be placed in the historical context of a society that has experienced no long-term period of stability and calm since 1949. Each decade has been punctuated by violent social and economic upheavals that produced an enormous loss of life — a ballpark figure of between 50 million and 80 million people is not far from the mark — great psychological trauma and misery for hundreds of millions, widespread social divisiveness and lost opportunities to build a stable, creative society worthy of the rich heritage of the Chinese people.

The CCP remains seriously divided, especially since the power struggle between Li Peng and Zhao Ziyang came to a head in the spring of 1989. This Party split still exists in the provincial and sub-provincial Party committees governing the cities as well as the 'free' economic zones along the coast. The ideological side of this split relates to what kind of strategy or 'line' the Party should adopt. Should there be political reforms to liberalize the nation's press as reflected in the demands of over 1,000 journalists in spring 1989?[12] Should Party and state be separated — as both Deng and Zhao wanted? Should Marxism–Leninism–Mao Tse-tung thought be the only doctrine? These and other salient issues formed part of the great ideological debate in 1988–89. Central to the Deng 'line' was the Party's adherence to the Four Cardinal Principles: the dictatorship of the proletariat; the leading role of the Communist Party; the socialist road; and Marxism–Leninism–Mao Tse-tung thought. The reforms backed by Zhao, Hu, and their allies only paid lip service to the Four Cardinal Principles. If enacted, their program would certainly have diluted and ultimately replaced that orthodoxy.[13]

Second, the public is bitter about the Party's failure to solve the country's social and educational problems. Workers in state and collective enterprises see their entitlements threatened by inflation and the economic reforms and feel deprivation. Party members and state functionaries are increasingly disillusioned by corruption and falling living standards. The unemployed and new riffraff (liu-mang) account for more crime in every large Chinese city. Finally, many youths are thoroughly disenchanted with the Communist Party, and they doubt that education can provide an escape from their dreary existence. They are frustrated by their inability to have a life in China like that observed through television and videotapes of the capitalist West or the East Asian countries.

Third, serious economic difficulties confront the country: acute scarcities of energy, fresh water, transportation, telecommunications, skilled labor, scientists, and so on. Inflation and urban and rural pollution have worsened.

Fourth, severe cleavages exist in society. A young generation has high expectations for its future and will become impatient if these cannot be fulfilled. A 'lost generation' of people in their 40s and early 50s were denied education during the Cultural Revolution and are still bitter. An older generation remembers the high hopes of the 'revolution.' It yearns for the stability and egalitarianism of those years and resents the emerging affluence that is perceived as being distributed unequally.

Finally, a spiritual and cultural frustration now grips Chinese society, arising in part from the disappointments suffered from previous decades of upheaval and the promises that were never fulfilled. At times, China is depicted as having lost its cultural bearings, as reflected in the 1988 television epic, 'The River Dies Young.' That film depicted China's backwardness and missed opportunities in recent centuries and blamed those failings on its cultural legacy. It was banned in August–September 1989 and severely criticized thereafter.

These problems can be looked at as entwined and vicious circles that the Party must break if grievances in cities are to be checked and moderated. From the Party's point of view, none of the policy options is attractive. Liberalizing prices to enable enterprises to raise productivity only produces more inflation and unemployment, which quickly transmits into more urban social grievances. Pursuing a more vigorous open-door policy to entice foreign investment and technology transfer soon brings more corruption, producing envy and bitterness among those who do not directly benefit. More liberalization of information to improve decision-making and efficiency only brings public debate and eventually criticisms of the Party and its leaders, leading to more repression and restoring tight control over information. Expanding higher education merely raises the expectations of the youth to choose their careers, study abroad, and avoid blue-collar work. If the Party resists their demands, these youth become 'alienated' and potential trouble makers; if the Party complies, these educated youth then challenge Party orthodoxy.

These vicious circles have produced a pattern of CCP loosening of controls followed by severe repression: Reforms between 1979 and 1982 meant CCP relaxation of its levers of control over information followed by a clampdown with the Party's 'anti-bourgeois liberalization' campaign of 1983; relaxing of CCP controls again followed, culminating in the university student demonstrations of December 1986 and January 1987, again followed by the Party's crackdown on 'bourgeois thinking'; reforms continued with more free debate in 1988–89, followed by the Tiananmen affair and despotism ever since. The CCP has reversed reform with suppression, especially controls over information and ideas, for fear of losing power altogether.

China's urban population, around 30 percent of the population, or some 300 million people, now constitutes the greatest source of grievances. Moreover, as tensions continue to mount, the cities have become a tinderbox ready to ignite into flames should some event bring tens of thousands into the streets.

The political decay of the Party

Can the Party still retain control over society after the inevitable transfer of power? Furthermore, can the Party deal with the difficulties just mentioned without losing power and plunging China into anarchy? The Party's history suggests that a leader needs charisma, military support, and a 'line.' A Leninist Party requires a paramount leader, like a Mao or a Deng, to uphold 'democratic centralism' and to maintain the Party's absolute control. As the first echelon of Party leaders dies off, there does not appear to be anyone in the second echelon of leadership who qualifies.

The current Deng 'line' already has been severely discredited within the Party, and it cannot be upheld for very long. Many Party members and intellectuals now contend that Marxist-Leninist-Mao Tse-tung thought must be greatly modified to accord with China's new conditions. So far, no ideological consensus for a new doctrine has evolved; nor is there any strong consensus in favor of the current, Dengist 'line.' Without such a unifying ideology, the Communist Party cannot maintain its legitimacy and retain its present control over the levers of power. Therefore, the CCP will soon split into factions, and very likely some CCP members will even want to form new parties and lead the country.

Second, as Deng weakens and eventually dies, no top Communist except Zhao Ziyang, who is now 73, appears to have sufficient charisma and respect from enough segments of Party, government, and military to hold power for long.[14] Any emerging strongman, moreover, must deal with the vicious circles and urban grievances now widespread in China. The Chinese are not likely to be patient and give any new leader much time to legitimize his authority unless he produces remarkable results, and quickly. A political leader in Chinese society must possess awesome authority to silence his critics. Moreover, many Party leaders and intellectuals still seem to share a vision of history in which China must advance toward socialism and then move to communism. Any leader who opposes such a vision will be challenged on ideological grounds. The iconoclastic, transformative mode of thinking shared by most Chinese leaders can only exacerbate existing Party factionalism.[15]

Therefore, if Deng is not followed by a charismatic leader, the CCP will be rent by factions and a fierce power struggle. The power struggle already taking place within the Standing Committee of the Politburo will simmer and persist. Should Li Peng and Yang Shangkun still remain aligned, their clique could gain and hold power for a brief period. Without strong Party support throughout the country, however, they will not last for long.

When that clique or another, perhaps under Jiang Zemin, begins to lose power, more political power will devolve to provincial leaders. That could lead to new regional coalitions to challenge the political center, and further factionalize the Party. Under these pressures, the second echelon of Party leaders are not likely to be able to offer new ideas and policies to legitimize the CCP and build popular support for the Party. If urban grievances cannot be minimized by Party reforms, and the Party becomes progressively weaker and factionalized, then the CCP will collapse.

Leadership is always an unknown factor. Can China produce a Gorbachev or another Deng Xiaoping? Possibly, but not likely. This much can be said for the early 1990s. Political struggle will continue; the Party will weaken and fragment. Urban grievances will get worse. These are the prospects awaiting the Party's second-generation leadership as the top echelon of old cadres dies off.

Caught in the web of its own history, and without leaders of charisma and theoretical skills, the Chinese Communist Party sits on a political powderkeg.

---

1. Foreign Broadcast Information Service, *Daily Report: China*, 19 May 1989, p. 32.

2. *Ibid.*, pp. 27–34.

3. *South China Morning Post*, 20 May 1989, p. 1.

4. Stephen Uhalley, Jr., *A History of the Chinese Communist Party* (Stanford, California: Hoover Institution Press, 1988), p. 28.

5. *Ibid.*, pp. 46–47.

6. It is rumored that Li Peng wants Zhao Ziyang placed on trial and thoroughly humiliated, perhaps even sent to prison. Jiang Zemin prefers that not be done. As he still has Deng's backing, Zhao's trial has not taken place, although virulent articles appeared in August and September in the press demanding such a trial.

7. For example, Deng Xiaoping until November headed the powerful Military Affairs Commission; Chen Yun heads the Central Advisory Committee (200 members); Qiao Shi heads the Central Committee for Discipline Inspection (69 members). These three committees have exerted a powerful, stabilizing influence on the CCP's Central Committee, which comprises roughly 175 full members and 110 alternate members. See Richard F. Staar (ed.), *Yearbook on International Communist Affairs, 1989* (Stanford, California: Hoover Institution Press, 1989), p. 189.

8. For a brief biographical background of the Standing Committee leaders, see 'Profiles of the Party's Leaders,' *Beijing Review*, 10–16 July 1989, pp. 21–25.

9. Examples can be found in *Beijing Review*, 18–24 September 1989, p. 18 and *Beijing Review*, September 25–October 2, p. 20.

10. A review of the country's provincial press during the months of June, July, and August finds arrests, censoring of Party officials, rectifica-

tion campaigns, and a variety of other means being used to crush the Hu–Zhao faction.

11. This important phrase can be found in the speech delivered by Deng Xiaoping on 9 June 1989 at the Martial Law Headquarters and circulated to CCP members for study. See 'This Storm Was Bound to Happen,' *South China Morning Post*, 20 June 1989, p. 8.

12. See Wang Xingwu, 'The Crying Need for Press Reform,' *Beijing Review*, 22–26 May 1989, p. 7, which indicates liberalization of the press was strongly demanded by Chinese journalists. At this time, the journal *Beijing Review* was controlled by Zhao's faction, but after 4 June 1989 Li Peng and Jiang Zemin, *inter alios*, had regained control over the press and all information.

13. Zhao, however, very likely believed he could uphold orthodoxy and still be a reformist like Deng. Zhao Ziyang had gone public on many occasions to support the Deng 'line.' See his remarks in the *People's Daily*, 10 June 1987, pp. 1 and 4; as well as his *Work Report* to the CCP congress on 26 October 1987. Deng seems to have honestly believed that China could be opened up to foreign investment, trade, and new ideas, yet he and others could uphold the purity of the CCP orthodoxy and rebuff all ideological challenges to the 'Four Cardinal Principles.' For a good description of the ideological schizophrenia of Deng (and probably of Zhao as well), see Chang Chen-pang, 'The Dual Nature of Teng Hsiao-ping's Thought,' *Issues & Studies*, July 1989, pp. 11–26.

14. The following leadership scenario cannot be ruled out. Jiang Zemin, with Deng's backing, becomes a permanent vice chairman of the Military Advisory Commission and develops a modest power base in the military, then boldly restores Zhao Ziyang to the Politburo. By teaming with Zhao, both men shore up their Party power temporarily to defeat the Li Peng-conservative faction. The new Jiang–Zhao team then initiates more liberal policies. The likelihood of these policies successfully solving the country's problems is not high unless those leaders had unusual good luck to avoid serious crises. Even so, this seesaw struggle between reformers and conservatives would continue through the early 1990s. The party, however, would have lost its Leninist features and begun to fragment into factions demanding greater Party democracy. The time might eventually come, then, when some Party members demanded the right to form new parties to challenge the Communist Party. Such a complex process could evolve with stability and gradual expansion of prosperity, provided the leaders had implemented successful policies and were spared nasty crises.

15. Even Party reformers who now press for democracy adhere to iconoclastic and 'transformative thinking,' to use the apt term coined by Thomas A. Metzger to describe the patterns of traditional Confucian cognitive thinking.

Four Ways Communism Could Die in China

JÜRGEN DOMES

THE continuation of Marxist-Leninist single-party rule in China into the next century has, since the spring crisis of 1989, become entirely unlikely. To assume a very long continuation of communist rule in the People's Republic of China is a delusion, and to base projections of future political perspectives and policy recommendations on it reveals nothing but incompetence in social science analysis.

The future of communist single-party rule in China is indeed predictable: New crises will deepen the rifts and sharpen the contradictions between the rulers and ruled, Party and public. The Beijing massacre made this gap unbridgeable. The future points unmistakably toward a collapse of communist rule, toward the emergence of a new, no longer communist China. It is, however, by no means clear how long the agony of Marxist-Leninist rule may last.

The seizure of power by totalistic elites, and the stability of political systems established and dominated by them, depends upon the forging of social coalitions and the ability to block organized dissent. Citizens in any society develop hopes and expectations. Elites are only able to seize power if they manage to respond to these desires. In order to stay in power, they must, at least occasionally, renew such responsiveness (The term 'social coalition' is defined here as a loose alliance that accumulates the demands of different strata of the society.)

Before inflation and the ensuing disintegration of Chinese society in 1987–88, the central government's policies were generally supported by a social coalition of leading cadres, a sizable group of the mid-level cadres, the majority of the technological and scientific intelligentsia, engineers, the higher-paid industrial workers, and the newly emerging private sector. Those peasants who profited from the decollectivization of agriculture — about two-thirds of the peasantry or approximately 47 to 48 percent of the

PRC — tolerated the current ruling elite as long as it guaranteed the continuation of its rural policies.

Yet during 1988 and until the spring of 1989, one group after another left the social coalition. Thus, a rather formidable new coalition has evolved — one which has displayed an increasing propensity toward active opposition. It is now composed of almost the whole younger intelligentsia in the humanities, the majority of the technological and scientific intelligentsia, students, many apprentices and young workers, most of industrial labor, the majority of employees in commerce and services, artists, writers, many journalists, and most of the owners of small enterprises. In other words, during the last two years, almost the entire urban society of the PRC has emancipated itself from the Party. The basic political tension today is no longer between rulers and opposition, but between the rulers and the urban citizenry.

Indeed, the process of separation between the Party and society arrived at a quite advanced stage during and after the spring crisis of 1989. Yet there remains the question of to what an extent the 78 percent of the PRC's population who live in the countryside (and particularly the 71 percent of the population who make their living by farming) have been affected by these fundamental social developments. Are they on the verge of a nationwide peasant rebellion? No. Despite more than three decades of political campaigns, mobilization attempts, passive and even active resistance between 1950 and 1980–81, the Chinese countryside is still divided into approximately four to five million uncoordinated political societies (hamlets, villages, and small towns) with nearly pure parochial political cultures. These minuscule polities have time and again successfully resisted all attempts at inclusion into a nationwide subject culture, but they so far have not been able to generate the momentum for a drive toward systemic change. There is not even a nucleus for an organization that can articulate peasant interests above the village level.

This does not mean that the countryside may not be affected by social unrest. The quest of the peasants for title deeds to the land they now till individually under contracts, will become very strong. Another peasant demand is freedom of childbirth. If the peasants were to confront the Marxist-Leninist rulers with these two demands, the crisis of the political system of the PRC, now confined to the cities, would spread to the countryside.

Yet even if the countryside in the PRC did not develop unrest within the next few years, the process of emancipation of the urban society from the Party already has meant revolutionary change. We cannot expect a return to 'normalcy.' Under the burden of increased repression, the people will try to circumvent the political system and the demands of the ruling elite to an even higher degree. They will use the cadres' corruption to mellow the grip of the regime by bribing its representatives. To give one example: Less than four weeks after the Beijing massacre, the special exit permits, which citizens of the PRC must now obtain before they can apply for foreign visas, could be bought from corrupt cadres for 7,500 yuan (US$1,900) in Shanghai. In Canton, where the national currency obviously is no longer held in any esteem, the price was US$2,000 (or HK$15,000). Moreover, the people will increasingly try to move out of the socialist economy into an ever-expanding parallel or second economy of moonlighting, black marketeering, illegal exchange of foreign currency, and underground banking and production. These trends are bound to further weaken the structures of social control, even though those of political control may be strengthened. This means that social policies in general will be more and more difficult to implement. In particular, the birth-control and family-planning policies, which have shown major deficiences since 1986, and were verging toward failure in 1988, will most probably collapse. Education and the public health system will continue to deteriorate. The social and economic trends that can be expected for the next decade do not leave much room for optimism for the ruling elite.

In April 1989, the official figure given for the population passed 1.1 billion. This figure, however, does not include between 25 and 35 million 'black babies,' i.e. children born in defiance of the ruling elite's family-planning rules and hidden from the authorities. Even if population growth should stay at the official rate of 1.43 percent in 1988 until the mid-1990s, and then drop to 1.3 and further to 1.2 percent, the PRC would have between 1.29 and 1.3 billion inhabitants by the year 2000 — about 100 million more than originally planned. This figure could grow to between 1.35 and 1.4 billion. Population growth puts severe strains on economic development. The current ruling elite, during the early 1980s, had set the goal of achieving a per capita GNP of US$800 (in 1985 value) by 2000. This goal appeared realistic, but in order to reach it, real per capita growth of the GNP must remain constant at 7 percent right through 2000. If it should stand at 8 percent — a rather unlikely long-term projection over 11 years — the goal could be surpassed, and the per capita GNP could reach US$895. At 6 percent real growth annually, it would only reach US$757 by 2000, and at five percent, only US$670. Yet even if an annual per capita growth rate of 7 percent could be sustained, this would bring the PRC only to the level which South Yemen and Nicaragua had reached in 1985. Moreover, it is not very likely that within the next few years, the ruling elite, ridden with political and social problems, will be able to solve the PRC's three major economic problems: inflation, shortage of energy, and shortages of raw and semi-processed materials.

In terms of social development, the prospects are also bleak. In 2000, at least 70 percent of the populace will still live in hamlets, villages, and rural towns; between 60 percent and two-thirds will still derive most of their income from farming. Income differentials between city and village will probably widen, as well as the gap between more well-to-do and poor regions.

Yet despite the assumption of Karl Marx that developments in the social and economic base determine developments in the ideological and political 'superstructure,' the history of the PRC has so far strongly suggested that the economic and social perspectives of the country depend upon its political development much more than the political development depends upon those of the economy and the society. It is, therefore, of central importance to address the political trends that can be expected during the next decade.

One theoretical possibility is the triumph of the ruling elite over dissent, i.e. a stabilized system of bureaucratic socialism. In this case, the ruling elite would definitely try to continue the policies of selective opening toward the outside world, but it would also, domestically, freeze the economic reforms at the position of 1988.

There are four other possible scenarios.

First, a comparatively long-term, though fragile, stabilization of the structures of domestic control. This would mean a long period of repression under an orthodox leadership, somewhat mellowed by corruption and an expansion of the parallel economy. But it would also mean freezing economic reform, state enterprise autonomy, and decollectivized agricultural production on the level of 1988. Demands to widen them would be refused; in order to sustain this refusal, the bureaucratic elements of the economy would have to be strengthened. As a consequence, social tensions would increase, exploding in consecutive manifestations of ever more violent dissent. The ruling elite could probably suppress a number of such manifestations, but finally, China would move into a large-scale, extremely violent confrontation. Communist rule would drown in a veritable ocean of blood.

Second, the return of reform-oriented revisionists, who would assume control of the Party and state. In this case, the new leadership would try to push ahead with economic liberalization, including price reform, property rights, expansion of private enterprise, and a decentralized public sector. These daring reforms would be accompanied by political change. (That could mean raising the level of direct election from the county, where it stands today, first to the provincial and finally to the national level; the granting of considerable autonomy to social organizations; and the introduction of a free choice between several candidates in elections.) But since the expansion of economic reforms would necessarily result in high inflation and a further increase in income differentials, the Party would have to bear the brunt of public discontent. This, in turn, would lead to a gradual edging of the Party out of power and, hence, to a comparatively peaceful transition from the communist to a more pluralistic political system.

Third, the return of reform-oriented revisionists, who would be able to assume control of the decision-making organs of Party and state, and start to develop policies of economic and political reform. In this scenario, such policies would prompt a backlash from the orthodox forces, more likely than not in the form of a coup d'etat backed by parts of the PLA. Such a coup would then provoke reaction from the society in the form of a nationwide revolutionary movement, which, with the support of other parts of the PLA, would finally result in a violent overthrow of communist rule.

Fourth, the speedy aggravation of the current economic crisis, which would then combine with a leadership crisis after the death of Deng Xiaoping, Chen Yun, and other veteran revolutionaries. Under these circumstances, which could develop quickly, the opposition would rise again on an even larger scale than in the spring of 1989. Considerable parts of the PLA would no longer be willing to protect the rulers and fight the people, and the control structures would disintegrate, as would the whole system of CCP rule. Without large-scale bloodshed, the transition to another political system would then evolve, leaving China under the rule of non-communist elites well before the end of this century.

No one can tell which of these four scenarios will be played out, or when. Yet given the scope of the delegitimation of Party rule since spring 1989, the swell of popular discontent, and the composition of the ruling elite, one can assume that the first and the fourth scenarios are more probable than the others. At any rate, the world should prepare itself for the rise of a new, non-communist China.

But what could follow the period of communist rule over China? There are two alternatives: First, the beginning of a long period of regional autonomy, if not independence, of four to seven major regions of the country. This would not mean a return to a system of 'warlordism,' but rather the emergence of a commonwealth-type network. Second, a coalition of revolutionary elites from mainland China, the ruling elite of the Republic of China on Taiwan, and the political and intellectual elites of Hong Kong initiate the transition to a pluralistic representative system, including guarantees of freedom of speech, information, association, and assembly, the gradual introduction of a rule of law, and competitive elections. This would be the implementation of the platform that the democracy movement developed during the spring of 1989.

In this context, it would be a grave mistake to underrate the role of the ROC. Many observers of the Chinese political scene tend to dismiss all too easily the importance of the alternative political system of Taiwan for the development of politics in the PRC. The process of pluralization and even incipient democratization in Taiwan has strongly influenced the quest for democracy in the PRC. The ROC is not going to 'return to the mainland' in terms of a takeover after the collapse of communist rule. If this collapse should come about, those who will have engineered it will not step aside in favor of the current government in Taipei. But the ROC has to offer a canon of legal codes, including rather liberal laws on the press and political parties; it has highly trained administrative and managerial personnel, and also a still faulty, yet, as compared to the PRC, nevertheless quite advanced system of education. With these it seems obvious that the ROC will play quite an important part in any political equation for China after the end of CCP rule.

This speculation on the future of China must end on a note of caution. While the representative democracies in the world today may be impressed by the extent to which the 1989 democracy movement in China shared their values, their governments and their citizens should be aware that the evolution of a democratic political system is not the only alternative to communist rule. There could develop other, nativist or even atavistic alternatives, which might substitute a communist totalitistic rule by a totalitistic rule of a different persuasion.

Democratic governments, businesses, and citizens therefore should not indulge in the delusion that we have already won the sympathy of the future China. Even after the end of communist rule, whenever it comes, the West in general, and the U.S. in particular, will have to strive for a close and fruitful cooperation with the newly emerging political system — or systems — in China. If our governments and our business world, in a short-sighted effort to please the country's current rulers, give too much comfort to today's Marxist-Leninist ruling elite, we might well lose the contact to the future of China. For the next decade, because of its domestic difficulties, the PRC will only play a marginal role in international politics. It cannot be used as a balancing force against whatever opponent we may perceive in any international system of competition, confrontation, or cooperation. The PRC is one of the most overestimated factors on the international scene; China may need the West's support desperately, but the West does not need China's.

If we start from the clear recognition of these facts, we should then try to keep as many gates into China as open as possible without compromising our support for change there. But the most important task is to realize that China is not identical with the current ruling elite of the PRC, and to devise strategies to continue and deepen our contacts with the forces of the future. If the Western powers concentrate their efforts on this task, they may be able to win the cooperation and even the friendship of 21st–century China. And that should not be too small a goal for policy makers, even today.

APPENDICES

A Chronology of Selected Documents and Statements

JOSEPH Y.S. CHENG

ON 22 April 1989, China's top leaders, including Zhao Ziyang, Deng Xiaoping, and Li Peng, joined more than 4,000 people in mourning Hu Yaobang, former General Secretary of the Chinese Communist Party (CCP). Hu died on April 15, and his death triggered off student demonstrators in Beijing. Zhao Ziyang, General Secretary of the CCP, delivered the memorial speech:

As a Marxist, Hu Yaobang led a glorious life, Zhao said. As one of the principal leaders of the CCP since the third plenum of the 11th CCP Central Committee held in 1978, Hu devoted himself to the integration of the fundamental tenets of Marxism with China's modernization drive. Hu made significant contributions in adhering to the Four Cardinal Principles, in persisting in the policies of reform and opening to the outside world and in building socialism with Chinese characteristics...

Comrade Hu Yaobang dedicated all his energy to our great cause. He cherished a deep love for the Party and the people who in turn loved him deeply, Zhao stated. (*Beijing Review*, 1–7 May 1989, pp. 5–6.)

Taking advantage of the situation, an extremely small number of people spread rumors, attacked Party and state leaders by name, and instigated the masses to break into the Xinhuamen Gate to Zhongnanhai, where the Party Central Committee and the State Council are located. Some people even shouted such reactionary slogans as 'Down with the Communist Party.' In Xian and Changsha, there have been serious incidents in which some lawbreakers carried out beating, smashing, looting, and burning....

An extremely small number of people with ulterior purposes continued to take advantage of the young students' feelings of grief for Comrade Hu Yaobang to spread all kinds of rumors to poison and confuse people's minds. Using posters of both big and small characters, they vilified, hurled invective at, and attacked Party and state leaders. Blatantly violating the Constitution, they called for opposition to the leadership by the Communist Party and the socialist system. In some of the institutions of higher learning, illegal organizations were formed to seize power from the student unions. In some cases, they even forcibly took over the broadcasting rooms on the campuses. In some institutions of higher learning, they instigated the students and teachers to go on strike and even went to the extent of forcibly preventing students from going to classes, usurped the name of the workers' organizations to distribute reactionary handbills, and established ties everywhere in an attempt to create even more serious incidents....

This is a planned conspiracy and a disturbance. Its essence is to once and for all negate the leadership of the Party and the socialist system. This is a serious political struggle confronting the whole Party and the people of all nationalities throughout the country.

The whole Party and the people nationwide should fully understand the seriousness of this struggle, unite to take a clear-cut stand to oppose the disturbance, and firmly preserve the hard-earned situation of political stability and unity, the Constitution, socialist democracy, and the legal system. Under no circumstances should the establishment of illegal organizations be allowed. It is imperative to firmly stop any acts that use any excuse to infringe upon the rights and interests of legitimate organizations of students. Those who have deliberately fabricated rumors and framed others should be investigated to determine their criminal liabilities according to law. Bans should be placed on unlawful parades and demonstrations and on such acts as going to factories, rural areas, and schools to establish ties. Beating, smashing, looting, and burning should be punished according to law. It is necessary to protect the legitimate rights of students to study in the class. The broad masses of students sincerely hope that corruption will be eliminated and democracy will be promoted. These, too, are the demands of the Party and the government. These demands can only be realized by strengthening the efforts for improvement and rectification, vigorously pushing forward the reform, and making perfect our socialist democracy and our legal system under the Party leadership ...(Editorial in the *People's Daily*, 26 April 1989)

On 1 May 1989, the Beijing College Students Autonomous Federation issued a statement, emphasizing that ' "the spontaneous students" patriotic movement is the process of promoting democratization in China through the means of peaceful petition.' The statement demanded 'a dialogue with the authorities,' and the principles of dialogue had to be 'sincere, equal, open, and direct.' The statement upheld the right of protest and demonstration, and it listed the following seven demands:

1. Open, objective assessment of the contributions and mistakes of Hu Yaobang;
2. Fair reporting of the student movement;
3. Protection of the civil rights granted by the Constitution;
4. Anti-bribery, anti-corruption, punishment of speculative activities by officials, especially concerning the Kanghua Company (believed to be associated with Deng Xiaoping's son);

5. Promulgation of a law on journalism, permission for newspapers run by the people;
6. Raising of government expenditure on education, improvement of the conditions of service for teachers, publication of the reports by the three survey teams of the Chinese People's Political Consultative Conference on the revenues of 10 tertiary institutions in Beijing, and survey of the conditions of primary and secondary schools as well as publishing its results;
7. Review of the serious policy mistakes on the part of the government, investigation of the causes of inflation by a team of experts from the 'Chinese People's Political Consultative Conference.' (Chinese text from *Tide Monthly*, Hong Kong, 15 May 1989, p. 38)

On 2 May 1989, a group of prominent intellectuals in Beijing released an open letter in Beijing in commemoration of the May Fourth movement advocating democratic reforms.

The young students are sincere. They want democracy, support reforms, oppose authoritarianism, and hate corruption. These are most valuable patriotic acts, a strong force for the promotion of socialist modernization, and the continuation of the spirit of the May Fourth movement in a new era.

The students held peaceful demonstrations, and raised their political demands in an open and above-board manner. This is in accord with the common practice of democratic politics throughout the world, and is a civil right guaranteed by the Chinese Constitution. Moreover, what they demanded has already been written into the Constitution. If repeating the language of the Constitution is not allowed, and even accused of 'a planned conspiracy' or 'turmoil created by a small minority,' then is there any democracy to speak of? And where will the Constitution be placed? We earnestly hope for stability and oppose turmoil; but democracy and stability must not be treated as opposites. In fact, only democracy can eliminate all the causes for turmoil, and bring about long-term stability and good government for the country.

Democracy certainly cannot be achieved immediately. But we cannot agree to the strange argument that the qualities of the Chinese people are too low so that the implementation of democracy has to be delayed. It has been demonstrated in fact that it is exactly those officials fearful of democracy that lack the qualities of democracy.

Democracy, freedom, human rights, and rule of law are the valuable achievements of human civilization as well as the pre-conditions for the building of socialism. We oppose the rejection of such civilization on the pretext of 'the conditions of China,' which is another version of 'Chinese learning as the essence, Western learning for utilitarian purpose.'

We must resolutely uphold reform, and cannot allow it to be abandoned half-way. For this purpose, we must firmly establish democracy and the authority of the legal system, promote reform with the spirit of the rule of law, effectively guarantee the civil rights stipulated by the Constitution, especially the freedom of speech, freedom of the mass media and publication, and freedom of assembly, association, and demonstration.

Reform must be comprehensive and cover all aspects. Political reforms cannot be delayed. We have to separate the Party from the government effectively, resolve the issue of replacing the government with the Party, hold really free elections so that people's congresses at all levels will become genuine organs of state power, and realize the independence of the judiciary.

The world is moving forward. Reform is related to the destiny of China. We cannot afford to lose another chance. (Chinese text from *Tide Monthly*, Hong Kong, 15 May 1989, pp. 36–37)

On 18 May 1989, Premier Li Peng met representatives of the striking students for an hour at the Great Hall of the People upon the sixth day of the hunger strike.

Li Peng: I am glad to see you. Today, we will talk only about one thing: how to get the fasting students out of their present plight....

You are all young, no more than 22 or 23 years of age. My youngest son is older than you.

I have three children. None of them engage in official profiteering. To us, you are like our own children.

Wuerkaixi (a student leader from Beijing Teacher's University): Premier Li, if we go on like this, it seems we won't have enough time. We should enter into substantial talks as soon as possible. Just now you said we would discuss only one thing, but in fact it was not you who invited us to be here and rather it was so many people on Tiananmen Square who asked you to come out and talk with us. So, as to how many questions we should discuss, it is for us to decide. (*Beijing Review*, 29 May–4 June 1989, p. 16)

On 19 May 1989, Premier Li Peng called for resolute and powerful measures to curb what he termed 'turmoil' and restore order in a midnight speech which was immediately followed by a declaration of martial law.

Li Peng made the call at a meeting of cadres from the Party, government, and army organs at the central and Beijing municipal levels held by the CCP Central Committee and the State Council in Beijing.

He said the meeting, held according to a decision of the Standing Committee of the Political Bureau of the CCP Central Committee, was aimed at mobilizing all to maintain stability and unity in order to ensure the smooth progress of the reform, the open policy, and socialist modernization.

The premier said that the briefing by the Beijing Municipal Party Committee Secretary Li Ximing showed that the capital was in a critical situation. The anarchic state was turning from bad to worse, and law and discipline were being violated. Before the beginning of May, the situation was cooling down as a result of great efforts. But after that the turmoil revived again. More and more students and other people were involved in demonstrations and many colleges and universities had come to a standstill. Traffic was jammed everywhere, Party and government offices were affected, and public security was deteriorating. All these seriously disturbed the normal order of production, work, study and everyday life of the local people.

Under these circumstances, we were forced to take decisive measures to put an end to the turmoil, he said. (*Beijing Review*, 29 May–4 June 1989, pp. 15–16)

On 5 June 1989, the Central Committee of the CCP and the State Council issued a joint message to all Party members and the people of the whole country, saying that the Chinese capital was then in a 'critical state' as a result of the 'shocking counterrevolutionary riot' instigated by a handful of people with ulterior motives.

According to the message, the riot was aimed at 'negating the leadership of the Communist Party, destroying the socialist system and overthrowing the People's Republic.'

It was under such circumstances that the People's Liberation Army was compelled to take action to quell the riot. In the course of the action, the People's Liberation Army martial law units 'tried their best to avoid bloodshed, but some casualties, nevertheless, occurred, mostly involving military personnel,' the message said.

'An initial victory had been won in putting down the riot, but the counterrevolutionary riot had not been completely quelled,' the message continued.

It urged all Communist Party members, Chinese people from all walks of life and other compatriots to support the Party and government in opposing the riot and help maintain law and order in the city, 'and not let themselves be misled by rumors.' (*Beijing Review*, 12–25 June 1989, p. 5)

On 7 June 1989, a press conference was held for Chinese journalists. State Council spokesman Yuan Mu disclosed that over 5,000 officers and

*men of the People's Liberation Army were wounded in the action which
began on June 3. Also wounded were over 2,000 civilians (including rioters
who committed crimes and onlookers who did not know the truth).*

'As for the death toll,' Yuan said, 'the initial calculation was nearly 300,
including army men and civilians. The dead students from all Beijing
universities and colleges numbered 23,' he added. Yuan said China was
not afraid of world opinion's 'condemnation' or 'sanctions.' 'Before I
came to this conference,' the spokesman said, 'I asked the leading comrade
of the State Council for instructions and he asked me to make two points
through the media. First, we are not afraid. No matter what means they
use — condemnation or sanction — the Chinese government and people
will never allow them to interfere in China's internal affairs. The struggle
we are waging to curb the turmoil is one that decides the fate of the Party
and the country; if concessions are made on this question, you will not
dare to take actions, and the People's Republic will be overturned,' he
said, adding 'then, what use is there for you to take loans and technology
from them? Second,' he said, 'we hope world opinion, foreign statesmen,
and governments will not be so short-sighted... Although we are in
difficulties, and the Party and the state are at a critical moment, the
Chinese Party and government have the ability, measures, and determination to overcome these difficulties,' he said. *(Beijing Review*, 12–25 June
1989, p. 5)

On 7 June 1989, in response to U.S. President George Bush's statement
against China concerning its domestic political turmoil and declaring
suspension of all U.S. arms sales and commercial arms experts to China at
the governmental level, as well as suspension of mutual visits by military
leaders of the two countries, the Chinese foreign ministry expressed 'its
profound regret.'

The Chinese foreign ministry announcement said that the U.S. government made flagrant accusations against China regarding something that
was exclusively China's affair. It was apparent that Washington had taken
unilateral action to bring about the deterioration of relations and was
exerting pressure upon the Chinese government, which China found
completely unacceptable.

The Chinese government expressed the hope that the U.S. would
refrain from any action that could harm bilateral relations in view of the
overall interests of U.S.-Chinese relations, and its own long-term interests. The Chinese government announcement said that 'what is happening in China is China's internal affair,' and that the 'Chinese government
is completely capable of quelling the current rebellion in Beijing.'

According to *Beijing Review*, the announcement, though mostly concerning the U.S. reaction, was in essence addressed to all other countries, setting out the hope that all foreign countries, organizations, and individuals, who had friendly relations with China, would refrain from any kind of interference into China's internal affair. (*Beijing Review*, 12–25 June 1989, p. 7)

On 9 June 1989, Deng Xiaoping re-emerged and spoke in Beijing to commanders above the corps level of the martial law enforcement troops.

The April 26 editorial of the *People's Daily* classified the problem as turmoil. The word was appropriate, but some people objected to the word and tried to amend it. But what has happened shows that this verdict was right. It was also inevitable that the turmoil would develop into a counter-revolutionary rebellion. . . . Some comrades didn't understand this point. They thought it was simply a matter of how to treat the masses. Actually, what we faced was not just some ordinary people who were misguided, but also a rebellious clique and a large number of the dregs of society. The key point is that they wanted to overthrow our state and the Party. Failing to understand this means failing to understand the nature of the matter.

The crux of the current incident was basically the confrontation between the Four Cardinal Principles and bourgeois liberalization. It isn't that we have not talked about such things as the Four Cardinal Principles, worked on political concepts, and opposed bourgeois liberalization and spiritual pollution. What we haven't done is maintain continuity in these talks. There has been no action and sometimes even hardly any talk.

The fault does not lie in the Four Cardinal Principles themselves, but in wavering in upholding these principles, and in the very poor work done to persist in political work and education.

I once told foreigners that our worst omission of the past 10 years was in education. What I meant was chiefly political education, and this doesn't apply to schools and students alone, but to the masses as a whole. And we have not said much about plain living and the enterprising spirit, about what kind of a country China is and how it is going to turn out. This is our biggest omission. . .

This incident has compelled us to think over the future as well as the past soberly. It will enable us to carry forward our cause more steadily, better and even faster, to correct our mistakes faster and better carry forward our strong points. The political line, principles and policies formulated at the Third Plenum of the 11th Central Committee of the Chinese Communist Party are correct.

Adherence to the Four Cardinal Principles (the socialist road, the people's democratic dictatorship, the leadership by the Chinese Communist Party and Marxism-Leninism-Mao Tse-tung thought) and adherence to the policies of reforms and opening to the outside world with the modernization construction as the central task for the Party are all correct and should be firmly carried forward. The basic political line and the basic policies and principles will remain unchanged.

However, we should seriously sum up our experience and carry on what is right, correct the errors and make great efforts to improve what is unsatisfactory. In a word, sum up the present and see the future. (*Beijing Review*, 12–25 June 1989, p. 4, and 10–16 July 1989, pp. 14–17)

Since mid-April, the Voice of America (VOA) has shown unusual enthusiasm for the turmoil and counterrevolutionary rebellion that occurred in Beijing, China's capital. It allocated more than 10 hours every day in three programs to cover these events. Unfortunately, its reports do not hold water. Aside from its instigations, attacks, and slanders, fabrication of rumors by VOA has reached a surprising peak in its career. For an official media organ that has long claimed objectivity, fairness, and strict observance of journalistic ethics in news reporting, such acts are really a disgrace....It reported on June 5 that the Chinese troops' bloody slaughter caused thousands of deaths and that at least 1,400 people were believed dead in the massacre in Tiananmen Square by the People's Liberation Army. What was really true? The comments of many eyewitnesses in Tiananmen Square and videotapes that have been broadcast have laid bare this lie. There was no 'massacre' of the sit-in students in the Square, and no one died there. As for the death toll of army men and civilians during the advance of the troops into the city, State Council spokesman Yuan Mu had put it clearly at a press conference. The VOA's exaggeration has its ulterior motives. (*Beijing Daily*, 12 June 1989)

On 17 June 1989, Yuan Mu, spokesman for the State Council, in a televised interview with Tom Brokaw, anchorman of the U.S. National Broadcasting Company, said that most Chinese people supported the leadership of the CCP and did not want to see the government subverted. In answer to a question on what happened the night of June 3 on Tiananmen Square, Yuan replied:

The PLA troops marched into Tiananmen Square to enforce martial law and restore order in the capital. In the whole process of clearing the Square, there was no casualty. No one was shot down or crushed under the wheels of armored vehicles. The reports abroad that there was a bloodbath and many people were crushed were incorrect. The students then occupying the Square withdrew peacefully in rows and waving banners.

I did not say that no casualties resulted from our efforts to put down the counterrevolutionary rebellion. I only said that no one died when the PLA cleared Tiananmen Square. As for the entire process of putting down the counterrevolutionary rebellion, some thugs were shot dead and some onlookers were accidentally killed or wounded. The PLA suffered great casualties.

I already made these facts clear at the press conference on behalf of the State Council on June 6. The number of wounded PLA officers and men exceeded 5,000 and the number of wounded people including thugs and onlookers exceeded 2,000. The total death toll is about 300.

Nowadays there are widespread reports in the foreign media that during China's efforts to put down the counterrevolutionary rebellion, thousands — even tens of thousands — of people died. This is not the correct situation but an exaggeration and distortion. (*Beijing Review*, 3–9 July 1989, pp. 11–14)

I am an intellectual and my home is near Beijing Normal University. Since the establishment of the external broadcasting station of the 'students' autonomous union' of the university at the beginning of May, nearby residents have all suffered from the noise of the broadcasts. The station was an important propaganda and agitation point for the 'Beijing College Students Autonomous Federation,' and also a rumormaking place. Every day, they made many broadcasts over loudspeakers, frequently past midnight and even to three o'clock one morning. They completely ignored the regulations of the Beijing municipal government on controlling noise and protecting the environment and they wantonly trampled on the right of residents to enjoy peaceful lives. They attacked the Party and government with extremely demagogic words and maligned leaders of the Party and government by spreading rumors.

They often broadcast news which was said to come from the Voice of America and other Western mass media. News, such as 'more than 30 countries have decided not to recognize the Chinese government' and 'the Chinese Foreign Ministry has announced that it has broken away from the central government' was so far-fetched that people who had some basic knowledge could not believe it. (Letter from a reader, *Beijing Daily*, 17 June 1989)

On 21 June 1989, Premier Li Peng met a Pakistan delegation headed by Foreign Secretary Humayun Khan who was in Beijing for Sino-Pakistani vice-foreign ministerial consultations. This was the first time Li had met foreign guests since the suppression of the rebellion in Beijing. Li said some countries had tried to exert diplomatic and economic pressure on

China. 'This only showed that they are short-sighted and unwise,' he said, adding that once they got to know the truth of the matter, these countries would change their viewpoints. In times of difficulty, it is very clear who are true friends, Li Peng stated. (*Beijing Review*, 3–9 July 1989, p. 5)

Firstly, they (the students) have little knowledge of how to build a democratic political system at the elementary stage of socialism, and where to start. As their knowledge about China is limited to books, their plan for a democratic political system for present-day China is not practical. They do not understand that the elementary stage of socialism can only accommodate a low degree of democracy and that we have a long way to go before we can have a highly developed democratic system.

Secondly, since the opening to the outside world, students have been exposed to a great deal of Western ideas and culture, which they have absorbed without discrimination. The overflow of bourgeois liberal ideas has aggravated their blind worship of the bourgeois democratic systems.

Thirdly, social and family environment as well as public opinion, for a time, made young students regard themselves as 'born national elite,' 'pride of the heaven,' and 'favorite of the society.' A handful of plotters with ulterior motives took advantage of this, 'killing' the students with excessive praise in order to achieve their own covert ends. (*Liberation Army Daily*, 21 June 1989, 'Meditation after the Disturbance — Why the Situation Runs Counter to the Wishes of the Students' by Zheng Yanshi)

From 23–24 June 1989, the fourth plenum of the 13th Central Committee of the CCP was convened in Beijing.

A communique was issued announcing that Party General Secretary Zhao Ziyang had been dismissed from all leading posts in the Party for 'supporting the turmoil and splitting the Party.' His case would be further looked into, the communique said. Jiang Zemin, former Party chief of Shanghai, was elected to replace him.

'The Four Cardinal Principles were the foundation of the country and must be implemented unhesitantly and consistently,' the communique said, adding that 'reform and opening to the outside world, which led the country to strength and prosperity, must be steadfastly carried out as usual. China will never go back to the old closed-door path.'

The plenum reiterated that 'China's independent foreign policy for peace remains unchanged. China will continue to develop friendly relations with other countries on the basis of the Five Principles of Peaceful Coexistence and continue to contribute to world peace.'

The communique called for special attention to the following tasks: to check turmoil thoroughly and quell the counterrevolutionary rebellion while making a clear distinction between two different types of contradictions and further stabilizing the situation nationwide; and to carry out conscientiously ideological and political work and education in patriotism, socialism, independence, self-reliance, plain living, and hard work and to oppose earnestly bourgeois liberalization. (*Beijing Review*, 3–9 July, 1989, pp. 9–10)

During the university students' hunger strike, the 'Beijing College Students Autonomous Federation' announced its refusal to keep any contact with the Beijing municipal government. At the same time, to ensure the safety of the hunger strikers' lives, the Red Cross Society of China, Beijing Branch (BRCS) sent medical workers to the Square to give the students first-aid treatment, so that, in the end, there were no health complications and not one died. At the same time, medical workers of the BRCS were in contact with the chiefs of the 'federation,' doing preparations for mollifying the event. However, these people, with ulterior motives, paid no attention to hunger strikers' health and deliberately obstructed medical workers' efforts to give first aid. Their apparent purpose was to exacerbate the situation, befuddle public opinion, and mislead those unfamiliar with the situation. (*Beijing Daily*, 27 June 1989)

On 30 June 1989, Chen Xitong, mayor of Beijing and a State Council-or, delivered a report at the Eighth Session of the Seventh National People's Congress Standing Committee on checking the turmoil and quell-ing the counterrevolutionary rebellion.

Some political forces in the West have always attempted to make the socialist countries, including China, give up the socialist road, eventually bring these countries under the rule of international monopoly capital, and put them on the course of capitalism. This is their long-term, fundamental strategy. In recent years, they stepped up the implementation of this strategy by making use of some policy mistakes and temporary economic difficulties in socialist countries. In our country, there was a tiny handful of people both inside and outside the Party who stubbornly clung to their position of bourgeois liberalization and went in for political conspiracy. Echoing the strategy of Western countries, they colluded with foreign forces, ganged up themselves at home and made ideological, public opinion, and organizational preparations for years to stir up turmoils in China, overthrow the leadership by the Communist Party and subvert the socialist People's Republic. That is why the entire course of brewing, premeditating, and launching the turmoil, including the use of varied means such as creating public opinion, distorting facts, and spreading rumors, bore the salient feature of mutual support and coordination between a handful of people at home and abroad.

To safeguard the social stability in the city of Beijing, to protect the safety of the lives and property of the citizens and ensure the normal functioning of the Party and government departments at the central level and of the Beijing Municipal Government, the State Council had no alternative but to declare martial law in parts of Beijing as empowered by Clause 16 of Article 89 of the Constitution of the People's Republic of China and at a time when police forces in Beijing were inadequate to maintain the normal production, work, and living order. This was a resolute and correct decision.

The decision on taking resolute measures to stop the turmoil was announced at a meeting called by the central authorities and attended by cadres from the Party, government, and military institutions in Beijing on May 19. Comrade Zhao Ziyang, persisting in his erroneous stand against the correct decision of the central authorities, neither agreed to speak at the meeting together with Comrade Li Peng, nor agreed to preside over the meeting. He even didn't agree to attend the meeting. By doing so, he openly revealed his attitude of separating himself from the Party before the whole Party, the whole country, and the whole world. (*Beijing Review*, 17–23 July 1989, pp. i–xx)

The G-7 summit made a miscalculation in continuing to exert pressure on China in a bid to force it to drop the just struggle against rebellion and subversion. It is necessary to point out that the actions taken by the Chinese government have in no way affected the West or any other countries. The problem arises simply because certain countries, out of their own likes and dislikes and their concept of values, have directly and extensively damaged China's interests and dignity with words and deeds. Any action that aims to meddle in China's internal affairs will be of no avail. The Chinese government and people will never give it to any pressure, whatever its form and whichever nation it may come from. On the contrary, such pressure will only encourage the Chinese people to develop the spirit of hard work and self-reliance to place their own country in an even better position.

The political declaration also mentioned restoring confidence in Hong Kong. Not long ago, the British government made it clear that it would continue to observe the Sino-British Joint Declaration on the future of Hong Kong. We expressed appreciation of this stance. China will continue to adhere to the principle of 'one country, two systems' and will abide by the agreement not to change the capitalist system in Hong Kong. You carry out your capitalism and we carry out our socialism, and neither side should poke its nose into the other's affairs. We believe that as long as both sides strictly observe the agreement, the restoration of confidence in Hong Kong can be accomplished. The current problem is that some people are attempting to use Hong Kong as a base to interfere in or even change the socialist system on the mainland. This cannot be allowed. We advise those people not to lift a rock only to crush their own feet. We hope that the so-called 'continuous support by the international community,' as claimed by the G-7 summit on the issue of Hong Kong, will not turn out to be a factor detrimental to stability there. (*People's Daily*, 17 July 1989: 'China's Internal Affairs Brook No Interference — On the Political Declaration Adopted at the Summit of the Seven Western Nations')

On 19 July 1989, the Foreign Affairs Committee of China's National People's Congress issued a statement and expressed indignation over the U.S. Congress' interference in China's internal affairs. The statement said:

On June 29 and July 14, the House of Representatives and the Senate of the United States adopted respectively amendments on sanctions against China which wilfully distorted the facts about China's efforts to put an end to turmoil and quell the counterrevolutionary rebellion in Beijing, slandered and attacked the Chinese government in a groundless manner, and set forth a series of measures of sanctions against China.

We hereby express our utmost indignation at such acts by the U.S. Congress of grossly interfering in China's internal affairs and seriously hurting the national feeling of the Chinese people.

Ample facts have shown that the disturbances in Beijing between April and June this year were in no way ordinary activities for democracy and human rights. They were a planned, organized, and pre-meditated political turmoil started by a tiny number of people in collusion with some hostile forces abroad through taking advantage of student demonstrations. The turmoil later escalated into a counterrevolutionary rebellion in Beijing.

The U.S. Congress based itself on rumors and in the amendments adopted called the rebellion a 'pro-democracy movement' and the handful of ruffians who seriously disrupted public order and attempted to overthrow the Chinese government 'peaceful pro-democracy demonstrators.' On the other hand, the U.S. Congress slanders the Chinese government, describing its lawful punishment of criminals who have violated the Chinese law as 'repression of peaceful demonstration.' Such acts of the U.S. Congress are not at all a serious approach and have behind them ulterior motives.

China has a most firm and clear-cut position and will never yield to any outside pressure when it comes to safeguarding China's sovereignty, independence, and dignity. Any attempt to use sanctions to pressure China into changing its policy is futile. Such an attempt, like lifting a rock only to drop it on one's own feet, will ultimately hurt the interests of the United States itself. (*Beijing Review*, 31 July–6 August 1989, p. 6)

On 19 July 1989, the People's Daily *(overseas edition) published an article by Yi Jiayan entitled 'What Does* The River Dies Young *Advocate?' The editor of the paper attached a note to the article, indicating that it was completed in October 1988 but suppressed by Zhao Ziyang. Here are excerpts:*

'The River Dies Young' has tried hard to extol and beautify Western civilization, i.e., the capitalist civilization. It says: 'Capitalism, by moving the two wheels of industrial revolution and free trade, has developed by leaps and bounds and started the dual historical cantata of science and democracy.' But, it does not say a word about the sanguinary and criminal history of old-line imperialism which invaded, plundered, and trampled China underfoot for more than a century under the signboard of free trade. This history of imperialism was completely removed in the TV series.

'The River Dies Young' has propagated the 'theory of Eurocentrism,' claiming that only capitalism can save China and that 'complete' Westernization and taking the road of 'blue-civilization' has been regarded by the TV series as the 'new dawn.' To save the 'wane of civilization,' the only way is to 'open the country's door wide to the outside world' and 'usher in the new dawn of science and democracy.' It also claims that it is the 'only choice' which should not be rejected. This 'choice' is meant to change the 'color' of our civilization. The reform advocated in the TV series is, in fact, aimed to replace the so-called 'yellow civilization' with the 'blue civilization' by 'letting the continuous, heavy rain of the blue ocean civilization fall on the dried yellow land.' Besides this, it holds that the foreign 'concessions' in China were not 'a hotbed of crime,' but the 'pioneer of civilization.'

Although 'The River Dies Young' has talked much about the reform and opening up, its stance does not comply with the Party Central Committee and Comrade Deng Xiaoping's policy of reform and opening to the outside world, and it also runs counter to the target of building China into a Chinese-style powerful, modern, socialist country. Reform and opening up do not mean 'total acceptance of Westernization' and following the capitalist road. As early as 1979, Comrade Deng Xiaoping pointed out: 'Some people have spread the view that socialism is not better than capitalism. We should refute this view.' This admonishment is still valid.

Against the coming waves of bourgeois liberalization, students were at a loss where to steer themselves. Since 1979, students have been greatly intrigued by an assortment of theoretical debates. Social problems like corruption, economic slowdown, unfair distribution, loose morals, and educational crises led them to realize the emptiness of 'traditional teaching.'

After 1985, student confidence in the reforms began to waver. During the student unrest that year, students spoke out on their discontent with the government's unscientific decision-making process, economic crimes, and corruption inside the Party and government. They also compared the social system in China with that in Western countries.

Stimulated by debates on political reform and academic seminars comparing Chinese and Western cultures, they voiced ambiguous demands for 'political democratization' and advocated 'freedom of the press' in the Western style. In demonstrations at the end of 1986, some students even resorted to 'wholesale Westernization' to reform Chinese culture.

In the recent turmoil, some students pinned hopes on a 'multi-party system' and private ownership. This change in political focus has best shown their deviation from the Four Cardinal Principles of adhering to socialism, Party leadership, proletarian dictatorship, and Marxism-Leninism and Mao Tse-tung thought.

The introduction of Western ideas into China has notably imbued Chinese university students with individualism. On the one hand, students have grown increasingly conscious of their independent values; on the other hand, they find it baffling to be adapted to the demands of society.

Over the past 10 years, intellectuals have constantly looked back at the Cultural Revolution and, in the process, have negated 'leftist' ideology and slogans. When this tendency became uncontrolled, it led to nihilistic views of Chinese culture.

The unchecked negativism cultivated among students a strong antagonism toward political teachings by the Party. The students opposed Chinese culture and favored Western culture. They dismissed Party leadership as corrupt and pointed to socialism as an impediment to productive forces. With this unscientific and biased way of analyzing society, discontent became rife and had to find an extreme outlet, eventually at Tiananmen Square. (From an analysis by the Theoretical Study Group of the Communist Youth League Beijing Committee, 'Aping Western Ways Resulted in Turmoil,' quoted in *China Daily*, 22 July 1989)

The rapidly developing economy in the past several years has brought about an importing craze — a craze of imported cars, color televisions, and computers, which has cost an excessive amount of foreign exchange and has dealt domestic industry a severe blow.

In the past couple of years, China has imported cars worth millions of U.S. dollars. Now most units above the county level in China have luxury foreign cars. When the Second Session of the Seventh National People's

Congress was held in the Great Hall of the People, one reporter spent one hour outside the hall and found that of the 556 cars parked there, 519 were foreign ones. If one stands in Tiananmen Square to count the passing cars, he will find that at least 90 percent of them are foreign made.

China has more than 40 color television factories, probably more than any other country in the world. Yet in 1988 alone, it spent US$237 million importing foreign color TVs...To change the situation, the country should tightly control the import of consumer goods, and spend foreign exchange rationally to reinforce its industry and agriculture.

Among the 1.1 billion people in China, over 200 million are illiterate. Its productive force is so backward that its GNP ranks 120th in the world. It is impossible to realize the four modernizations — modernization of industry, agriculture, science and technology, and national defense — in the country if we do not have the spirit of hard work and plain living. (From an article in *China Youth News*, reprinted in *China Daily*, 12 August 1989)

On 19 September 1989, Deng Xiaoping met Masayoshi Ito, leader of the Parliamentarians League for Japan-China Friendship, and expressed the belief that no matter what would happen, 'Sino-Japanese friendly ties must not change and will not change.'

Speaking of the world situation and international relations, Deng said that it had been proved that hegemonism and bloc politics did not work. At present, not only a new world economic order should be established but also a new world political order, he added.

Deng criticized the summit of seven Western nations held in Paris during the summer. The meeting's resolution concerning China was based on 'lies and distortions' and was 'too shallow' in dealing with matters, he said. The resolution represented interference in China's internal affairs which China found unacceptable, he continued.

Deng told the Japanese delegation that the Chinese government noticed 'some differences' in attitude between Japan and other nations at the Paris meeting. 'China is not afraid of sanctions, which in the long run will backfire at those imposing them,' Deng said. (*Beijing Review*, 2–8 October 1989, p. 5)

On 25 September 1989, the Chinese government lodged a strong protest with the French government for granting permission to the Front for a Democratic China (FDC) to hold its founding congress in Paris when an official of the Chinese Foreign Ministry's Department of West European Affairs met the French ambassador to China, Charles Malo.

The Chinese official pointed out that the French government, disregarding the solemn representations made by China, had gone so far as to allow the FDC to hold its founding congress in Paris.

Such action by Paris constituted serious encroachment upon China's sovereignty and gross interference in its internal affairs, the official said, expressing China's 'profound indignation' at France's action.

The Chinese official said that it was indeed a rare case in international relations that the government of one country brazenly supported activities on its territory by a handful of foreigners aimed at opposing and subverting the government of a foreign country with which it had normal diplomatic relations. (*Beijing Review*, 2–8 October, 1989, p. 4)

Over the past 40 years...China's diplomacy has undergone many adjustments. Especially since the 1980s, major adjustments have been made under the personal guidance of Comrade Deng Xiaoping. With China's independent foreign policy of peace being enriched and perfected, a complete line guiding foreign affairs and a unique diplomatic style have gradually taken shape. They have met with brilliant successes in safeguarding China's sovereignty, opposing egomanias, and safeguarding world peace, and made due contributions to the enhancement of international friendship and cooperation and the promotion of human progress.

Looking back on the course of New China's diplomatic practice, the most fundamental experience is that a country must maintain state sovereignty and national dignity and uphold its independent foreign policy...

Regrettably, willful interference in other countries' internal affairs is still a common occurrence in today's world. Some Western countries regard their values as absolute truth. So long as they don't like what is happening, they will interfere, exert political pressure, and apply economic sanctions. They keep on talking about 'freedom,' 'equality,' and 'democracy,' but they brazenly pursue egomanias in handling state-to-state relations. The Chinese people, who have stood up, certainly will not submit to outside pressure. We adopt an attitude which is intended to safeguard not only our Motherland's dignity but also the Five Principles of Peaceful Co-existence and the norms of international relations. (From an article by Foreign Minister Qian Qichen, 'New China's Diplomacy; 40 Years On,' in the *Beijing Review*, 25 September–1 October 1989, pp. 11–15)

On 26 September 1989, Jiang Zemin, Li Peng, Qiao Shi, Yao Yilin, Song Ping, and Li Ruihuan answered questions on China's internal and external affairs at a press conference in Beijing attended by more than 300 Chinese and foreign reporters.

In response to an Italian correspondent who asked 'whether the Tiananmen tragedy could have been avoided and how,' Jiang Zemin said, 'First I'd like to correct you in using the word "tragedy." We hold that it was a counterrevolutionary rebellion aimed at opposing the leadership of the Communist Party of China and overthrowing the socialist system.'

Premier Li Peng said that the State Council would soon issue new regulations controlling public funds used to entertain guests in public activities. Li disclosed this when a reporter from New China News Agency asked how to build a clean government and what further measures the government would take in this regard.

Li said that since the new leadership of the Chinese Communist Party had been formed, children of the Political Bureau members, Secretariat members, and the State Council officials were told to withdraw from companies engaged in circulations; senior officials' luxurious imported cars were replaced; and special preferential treatment for central leaders in food supply were removed.

Jiang Zemin also said that Deng Xiaoping's retirement from the chairmanships of the Central Military Commission would have to be decided by the CCP Central Committee and the National People's Congress respectively. Deng had on several occasions expressed his hope that the new CCP leadership would shoulder full responsibility, Jiang added. Jiang said that this matter was very important, and the question of when Deng would retire and who would succeed him should be decided by the Party and the state. (the *People's Daily* (overseas edition), 27 September 1989)

On 29 September 1989, CCP General Secretary Jiang Zemin made a speech at the meeting in celebration of the 40th anniversary of the founding of the People's Republic of China. This speech has been made important study material for the whole Party. Here are highlights:

To give full play to the spirit of patriotism and uphold the principle of independence and self-reliance is a fundamental conclusion from the successful experience of the Chinese revolution and of China's socialist construction. In modern China, patriotism and socialism are essentially united. History has proved that, in most cases, patriots who resolutely defend the dignity of the Chinese nation and yearn for our country's prosperity finally become faithful socialists or the dependable friends of socialism. Patriotism and the self-reliant spirit of the Chinese people lend major strength to our socialist modernization. Our socialist cause is consolidated and developed in the process of breaking through the efforts of antagonistic foreign forces to isolate, blockade, and provoke our country. The Chinese people have never bowed to any foreign pressure and never will, nor will China give up the road of socialism and national independence in return for others' alms.

The Communist Party of China. . .shoulders the supremely important responsibility for China's independence and development. The correct choice of the Communist Party of China as the leading core of the Chinese revolution and construction was made by the Chinese people in a protracted process of practice. The Party has gradually matured in the process of overcoming difficulties, correcting mistakes, and summing up the experience of history. The achievements of the last 40 years were made under the correct leadership of our Party, relying on the efforts by our whole people. The root cause of our mistakes and setbacks also frequently lies within our Party. The condition of our Party is of decisive significance for the fate of our country and nation.

To build democracy and a legal system, we must proceed from the realities in China and carry it out under leadership, in an orderly way, step by step, along the orientation and within the orbit of socialism. In this process, some of the practices in capitalist countries can serve us as reference, but they must not be copied indiscriminately. We must clearly distinguish between socialist democracy and capitalist democracy, between socialist democracy on the one hand and extreme democratization and anarchism on the other. The essence of the politics of 'the elite,' political pluralism and the multi-party system, advocated by a small handful of people is to push the broad masses of people out of the scope of democracy, negate the leading position of the Communist Party, and substitute a bourgeois republic for our socialist People's Republic. The tendency of extreme democratization and anarchism has a wide social basis in China, and is very destructive to our cause and is liable to be exploited by a small handful of reactionaries. We must maintain sharp vigilance and resolutely prevent this trend from running rampant. We do so precisely to guarantee the democratic rights of the majority, and to guarantee the healthy development of socialist democracy and the socialist legal system. Democracy towards the people and dictatorship towards hostile elements and anti-social elements are closely linked with each other and complement each other. The function of dictatorship cannot be weakened so long as class struggle exists in some areas of life.

It should be stressed here that the international reactionary forces have never given up their basic stand of hostility towards the socialist system and their attempts to subvert it. Beginning in the late 1950s, after the failure of their military interventions, they shifted the focus of their policy to 'peaceful evolution.' They adopt political, economic, and cultural means to infiltrate and influence socialist countries, exploiting their temporary difficulties and reforms. They support and buy over so-called dissidents through whom they foster blind worship of the Western world and propagate the political and economic patterns, sense of values, decadent ideas, and life-style of the Western capitalist world. When they feel there is an opportunity to be seized, they fabricate rumors, provoke incidents, plot turmoil, and engage in subversive activities against socialist countries. Class struggle is now no longer the major contradiction in Chinese society, but still exists within a certain sphere, and may sharpen under certain conditions. And it is precisely on this point that the international hostile forces have sought grounds for carrying out their strategy of 'peaceful evolution.' The struggle between infiltration and counter-infiltration, subversion and counter-subversion, 'peaceful evolution' and counter-'peaceful evolution' will last a long time. (*Beijing Review*, 9–15 October 1989, pp. 11–24)

The nature of our labor camps is completely different from prisons of capitalist countries. Labor camps use the weapon of the law to strike a blow against enemies of socialism and all types of serious criminals. As long ago as the 1950s and 1960s, labor and re-education camps successfully reformed large numbers of war criminals, counterrevolutionary enemies of new China, and common criminals. They won renown at home and abroad as a miracle on earth. According to preliminary statistics, more than two million people have been sent to reform camps and re-education camps over the past 10 years. (*Legal Daily*, Beijing, 12 October 1989)

On 12 October 1989, the Economic Daily, *Beijing, compared the threat of capitalism with the danger of AIDS, saying that its material attractiveness was an infectious disease in China and was partly to blame for the pro-democracy movement. A commentary in the newspaper used the unseemly comparison to coin a phrase 'loving capitalism disease,' which in Chinese is pronounced as 'aizibing' the same sound as the term for AIDS. Here is a summary:*

'The disease destroys a person's ability to distinguish, remember and compare,' the commentary said. 'In the eye of the patient, if something is named capitalism, everything will be good.' The 'infectious disease,' the commentary added, makes those afflicted believe 'commodities in foreign countries are good, white skin is wiser than yellow skin, individualism that ignores national interest is freedom and human rights.'

The commentary said that people who 'appeared brave' in fighting the PLA's suppression of the pro-democracy protests were actually 'patients' of the 'loving capitalism disease.'

'The turbulence that has just passed can be said to have shown the large impact of loving capitalism disease on some persons,' it said. 'AIDS has been warned of in the world,' the commentary added. 'Loving capitalism disease should also cause us to be vigilant.'

Capital, power, and transport are all inadequate. Sanctions against us by some countries are having a definite effect on our economy, Premier Li Peng said. We face several years of hard living. We must build up confidence and go all out to overcome the hardships. (Premier Li Peng, quoted in the *People's Daily*, 13 October 1989)

The leadership certainly has made mistakes. We cannot avoid responsibility, and we cannot condemn the demonstrators...From kindergartens to tertiary institutions, we have not done enough to educate our young people. It is very difficult to rectify these mistakes now. We should not bear grudges against the demonstrators, the signatories on the anti-government materials, and the hunger strikers. (Deng Xiaoping, quoted in *Ming Pao*, Hong Kong, 19 October 1989)

At a meeting of the UN Third Committee on social issues, the Chinese Ambassador Ding Yuanhong defended China and warned the West against pressuring China on human rights.

Some people may disagree with us, but it does not matter. All we hope is that they will not try to impose their views on us, still less take any actions detrimental to China's interest...

To have adequate food and clothing, and to stay healthy from illness, to us Chinese, are more important than prattling human rights slogans...

Certain major Western countries have been deeply involved in China's internal affairs by supporting and fostering forces opposed to the legal national government and engaging in subversive activities in an attempt to alter the socialist system in the country. It is they, rather than China, that should be condemned...

Some people, finding an excuse of showing concern about human rights, make unwarranted criticism of the political systems and ideologies of other countries, put pressure on and impose sanctions or blockade against a country simply because they are not happy with a particular event inside its borders.

(Quoted in the *South China Morning Post*, Hong Kong, 26 November 1989)

There are two determining factors behind China's choice of the socialist system. One is historical conditions, the other is the national characteristics of China. China cannot adopt a total market economy. Just because China does not pursue a market economy, it cannot be said that it is giving up reform.

Socialism has the support of the great majority of Chinese. If another system like capitalism is practiced in China, which has a huge population and an underdeveloped economy, polarization of the rich and poor and social injustice will occur...

It will not do if, as in the past, we implement an entirely planned economy. What we are pursuing is a synthesis of a planned economy and adjustment by the market.

(Premier Li Peng, quoted in the *South China Morning Post*, Hong Kong, 4 January 1990)

We should strongly criticize Soviet revisionism. What the Soviet Union has pursued is not reform, but revisionism. We should thoroughly express our views to the outside world.

(Vice President Wang Zhen, quoted in the *South China Morning Post* Hong Kong, 6 January 1989)

On 11 January 1990, a People's Daily editorial warned that 'unstable factors still exist,' and that the government would not relax its guard against 'foreign and domestic subversive elements who persist in bourgeois liberalization and do not resign themselves to defeat.' The editorial called for a 'further deepening of the struggle and education against bourgeois liberalization' and 'effective combat against the disruptive activities of enemy forces.'

The day following the lifting of martial law, stricter rules were imposed, banning 'illegal' gatherings in several areas in Beijing, including Tiananmen Square, the Zhongnanhai compound where China's leaders reside, central government offices, and military installations.

Who Was Who During Beijing Spring

JOSEPH Y.S. CHENG

Bao Tong: trusted aide of Zhao Ziyang. He was arrested on 28 May 1989, when he was secretary to the Politburo Standing Committee and director of the Political Structure Reform Research Office of the Party Central Committee. Bao's major crime was to organize four research institutes in Beijing to issue a six-point statement asking the Standing Committee of the National People's Congress to meet to resolve the student demonstrations, thus negating the line defined by the *People's Daily* editorial on 26 April 1989. Bao also was believed to be the writer of Zhao Ziyang's speeches in early May 1989, which adopted a soft line on the student demonstrations.

Bao Zunxin: deputy research fellow of the History Institute of the Chinese Academy of Social Sciences, editor-in-chief of the 'Towards the Future' book series, and organizer of the May 16 statement signed by a group of leading intellectuals, appealing for a just assessment of the students' democracy movement and the implementation of political reforms. Bao was among the first arrested after the Beijing massacre.

Cao Siyuan: director of the Stone Social Development Research Center under the Stone Company, China's largest private company. Cao was an expert on the Chinese Constitution and a pioneer in the development of the bankruptcy law. He was arrested in early June.

Chai Ling: a 23-year-old postgraduate student in psychology at Beijing Normal University. She was the commander-in-chief at Tiananmen Square and a Standing Committee member of the Beijing Federation of Autonomous Student Unions. Chai was probably the most popular of the student leaders. She escaped to France in April and is high on the 'wanted' list.

Chen Xitong: mayor of Beijing and a state councilor. Together with Li Ximing and others, Chen firmly supported Premier Li Peng in suppressing the student movement. The group also was responsible for sending negative reports to the leadership discrediting Zhao Ziyang and others who attempted to take a soft line on the student movement. Chen delivered a report at the eighth session of the seventh National People's Congress Standing Committee on 'quelling the counterrevolutionary rebellion' in June 1989. There are rumors that he and others in Beijing are unhappy with the promotion of Jiang Zemin from Shanghai and Li Ruihuan from Tianjin while they have not been promoted.

Chen Ziming: director of the Beijing Social and Economic development Research Institute, a private research organization in Beijing. He was among the 'most wanted' after the Beijing massacre, and was believed to have been arrested in Guangdong in November 1989 when he attempted to escape to Hong Kong. Ironically, Chen played an active role in the demonstrations against the Gang of Four in April 1976 upon the death of Chou Enlai.

Chi Haotian: chief of the general staff of the People's Liberation Army since 1987 and member of the Party Central Committee. He became deputy political commissar of the Beijing Military Region in 1973, and took part in the coup against the Gang of Four in 1976 when he assumed control of the *People's Daily*. Chi was believed to be the commander of the martial law troops in Beijing in 1989. He began his career with the 27th Army, the most-hated troops in the massacre, rising from ordinary soldier to head of the political department. It has been reported that Chi was the son-in-law of Yang Shangkun, but Chinese authorities denied this.

Deng Xiaoping: China's paramount leader and chairman of the Central Military Commission from June 1981 to November 1989. He was political commissar of the Second Field Army during the Civil War and enjoyed a respectable status among the first-generation military leaders. He was elected general secretary of the Party Central Committee in 1956 but lost power in the Cultural Revolution and was placed under house arrest. He became deputy premier in 1973 and was groomed by Chou Enlai to be his successor. He was purged again by the Gang of Four in April 1976 and re-emerged as a senior leader in July 1977. At the end of 1978, Deng established himself as China's leader and assumed leadership of the modernization drive. He purged Hu Yaobang and Zhao Ziyang, his two hand-picked successors, when they went too far in promoting political reforms or in conceding to forces for such reforms. He ultimately was responsible for the suppression of the student movement in 1989, and his status in the Chinese people's mind and in Chinese history will suffer as a result. Deng's children are widely believed to have been involved in corruption scandals in the past decade. He gave up the chairmanship of the Central Military Commission in November 1989, but few believe that he genuinely has retired from Chinese politics.

Fang Lizhi: former deputy president and professor of the Chinese University of Science and Technology. Fang is an astrophysicist better known for his advocacy of democracy and political reforms in China; he has been compared with Andrei Sakharov of the Soviet Union. Among the prominent intellectuals, he probably went furthest in challenging the communist system in China. As a result, he was harassed by the Chinese authorities even before the student movement in 1989. He and his wife, Li Shuxian, an associate professor of Beijing University's Physics Department and an elected deputy to the People's Congress of the Haidian district (where Beijing University is located), took shelter at the U.S. Embassy after the Beijing massacre.

Feng Congde: a 22-year-old postgraduate student of the physics department of Beijing University. Feng is Chai Ling's husband, and he was a deputy commander-in-chief at Tiananmen Square and a Standing Committee member of the Beijing Federation of Autonomous Student Unions. He escaped to France in April with Chai Ling.

Han Dongfang: a 26-year-old worker of the Beijing Railway Bureau. Han was a Standing Committee member of the Beijing Workers Autonomous Federation. He was sometimes compared to Lech Walesa of Poland and is now high on the 'wanted' list.

Hong Xuezhi: deputy secretary general of the Central Military Commission until his ouster in November 1989. Hong became head of the General Logistics Department of the People's Liberation Army in 1956, but was purged in 1959 for criticizing Mao Tse-tung's failure in the Great Leap Forward campaign. He resumed his position in 1980 and was elected a member of the Party Central Committee. He became deputy secretary general of the Central Military Commission in early 1985. Hong showed sympathy for the student movement in 1989, and was rumored to be allied with Zhao Ziyang.

Hu Qili: removed from the Standing Committee of the Politburo, the Politburo, and the Secretariat of the Party Central Committee at the fourth plenum of the 13th Central Committee in June 1989 for his relatively liberal attitude toward the student movement. He was a key supporter of Hu Yaobang, and was believed to have betrayed Hu Yaobang in order to keep his own position. Before Tiananmen, he was considered a rising star and a key member of the collective leadership to succeed Deng. The purge of leaders like Hu Qili means there is no one with liberal inclinations in the present top leadership. Also purged at the fourth plenum for the same reason were Rui Xingwen and Yan Mingfu, who were both removed from the Secretariat of the Party Central Committee. Rui was previously in charge of ideological matters, and Yan was head of the United Front Department of the Party Central Committee and had overall responsibility for negotiations with the demonstrating students prior to the imposition of martial law.

Hu Yaobang: chairman of the CCP Central Committee between June 1981 and September 1982; general secretary of the CCP Central Committee from September 1982 to January 1987 when he was forced to resign. He retained his membership of the Politburo until his death. Hu was a key supporter of Deng when Deng re-emerged after the fall of the Gang of Four, and in the mid-1980s was regarded as Deng's successor. Hu was respected for his genuine support for political reforms. His forced resignation was prompted by student demonstrations at the end of 1986, and his death on 15 April 1989 triggered the student demonstrations leading to the Beijing massacre.

Jiang Zemin: elected general secretary of the CCP Central Committee in June 1989, and chairman of the Central Military Commission in November 1989. Before that, he had been minister of the electronics industry and mayor of Shanghai; and in 1988, he became secretary of the Shanghai Municipal Party Committee and a Politburo member. Typical of his generation of leaders, Jiang joined the Party when he was a university student in Shanghai, was an outstanding activist in the student movement, has an engineering background, and was trained for one year in the Soviet Union in the 1950s. Jiang has experience in economic work, but took a hard line in suppressing student demonstrations in Shanghai and thereby won the confidence of Deng and other conservative leaders.

Li Jijun: former commander of the 38th Group Army, which appeared to be more sympathetic to the student movement in 1989. The 38th Group Army was said to have clashed with the brutal 27th Group Army, though this could not be verified. Li was put in jail for disobeying orders to move on the students in the initial period of the student movement. He was replaced by Xu Jingguang, and it was under Xu that the 38th Group Army moved on the students and workers on 3 June 1989. Li was given the rank of lieutenant-general in 1988 and was generally liked by his men. The 38th Group Army was the unit to which many Beijing university students were attached for brief military training periods.

Li Lu: a 20-year old student at Nanjing University. Li was a deputy commander-in-chief at the Tiananmen Square and an active member of the Non-Beijing Tertiary Students Autonomous Federation. He fled to France after the Tiananmen massacre.

Li Peng: member of the Standing Committee of the Politburo since 1987. He was appointed premier at the same time Zhao became general secretary of the Party. It is generally believed that Li heads the Foreign Affairs Group of the Party Central Committee. Li was the son of a revolutionary martyr and was raised by Zhou Enlai and his wife. As a typical descendant of senior cadres, Li was educated in the Soviet Union in 1948–55 and moved up the leadership hierarchy as a technocrat in the Ministry of Water Resources and Electric Power. Family background was a major factor for his meteoric rise, and he was generally regarded as mediocre. Together with Li, a group of descendants of senior cadres with Soviet training are now in key positions, and their formative experience may well be an important factor affecting the policy orientations of the future Chinese leadership. Li made use of the student demonstrations in the spring of 1989 to attack Zhao Ziyang; and at the direction of Deng Xiaoping and Yang Shangkun, he was directly responsible for the military crackdown on the student movement. Many observers believe Li has become a political liability of the present Chinese leadership because he is much hated by the Chinese population. He may be dumped in the future to win the goodwill of the people.

Li Ruihuan: elected member of the Standing Committee of the Politburo at the fourth plenum of the 13th Central Committee in June 1989. He has been in charge of united-front work. He was only 55 years old then and was secretary of the Tianjin municipal Party committee as well as a member of the Politburo. Before that, he was deputy mayor and mayor of Tianjin and had served as secretary of the Central Committee of the Communist Youth League of China. He was tipped as a rival to Li Peng to succeed Zhao Ziyang as premier in 1987. Like Jiang Zemin, he was very tough with the student demonstrations in Tianjin in late 1986 and had ample experience in economic work and dealing with foreign investors. He once was a carpenter and therefore can claim to have a proletarian background.

Li Xiannian: an expert in financial and economic work in the State Council for almost three decades. He was not purged during the Cultural Revolution and is one of the few leaders who has always managed to keep his position in various political movements. In 1977, he was elected a vice chairman of the Party Central Committee, and became head of state in 1983. In 1987 and 1988, he retired from all important Party and state posts, and was elected chairman of the Chinese People's Political Consultative Conference in April 1988. Li, as one of the conservative elder leaders, actively supported the suppression of the student movement and the purge of Zhao Ziyang.

Li Ximing: secretary of the Beijing municipal Party committee and member of the Politburo since 1987. Li was a colleague of Li Peng when the latter headed the ministry of electric power industry. Following the instructions of Li Peng, he presented materials to the top Party leadership on the student movement in spring 1989, describing the students and masses as engaged in riots. Li Ximing also mobilized peasants in the suburbs of Beijing to take part in pro-government rallies. Extremely unpopular with the people of Beijing, he was not promoted to the Standing Committee of the Politburo at the fourth plenum of the 13th Central Committee in June 1989.

Liu Binyan: probably the most famous journalist for the *People's Daily*. His reports on the corruption and abuse of power among Chinese officials have won him great respect. Liu was a communist who believed in the reform of the Party; he was ejected from the Party in January 1987. He has traveled overseas extensively since the mid-1980s. He is now living in exile in the U.S.; he was visiting the U.S. during the Tiananmen demonstrations and is reluctant to return to China.

Liu Huaqing: deputy political commissar of the navy before the Cultural Revolution. He was transferred to the post of deputy chief of staff of the navy in 1972 and promoted to deputy chief of staff of the People's Liberation Army in 1980, and then commander of the navy as well as member of the Party Central Committee in 1982. He became deputy secretary general of the Central Military Commission in 1987. There were unconfirmed reports that Liu was sympathetic toward the student movement in 1989, and the navy indicated its support for martial law and military suppression only belatedly. Liu, however, was promoted to vice-chairman of the Central Military Commission in November 1989; it is generally believed that he is intended to be a balancing force against the Yang Shangkun faction in the Central Military Commission.

Liu Xiaobo: a Chinese literature specialist. He was 34 years old in 1989 and a part-time lecturer at the Chinese Department of Beijing Normal University. In recent years, his publications attracted considerable attention. During the student demonstrations in spring 1989, he was doing research in the U.S. He returned to Beijing because he felt he could not 'depart from the masses.' He was on hunger strike at Tiananmen Square (together with Hou Dejian, a famous singer and songwriter from Taiwan, and Zhou Duo, a senior executive of the Stone Company) and was arrested. Liu subsequently appeared on television and acknowledged that he did not see anyone killed at Tiananmen Square the night of 3 June 1989.

Liu Yongchuan: a 29-year-old Ph.D student in sociology at Stanford University, California, specializing in theories of social democracy. He was elected chairman of the All-America Chinese Students and Scholars Autonomous Federation, which was established at the First All-America Chinese Students and Scholars Congress held in Chicago in July 1989. The federation is composed of Chinese students and scholars in the U.S. and Canada who support the democracy movement in China.

Peng Zhen: a conservative elder political leader retired from the Chinese political scene. A key supporter of Liu Shaoqi, the No. 2 man in the leadership before the Cultural Revolution, Peng consequently suffered severely in the political turmoil. Peng was 'liberated' in early 1979 and elected a Politburo member later that year. He assumed a leading role in the drafting of the 1982 Constitution. He became chairman of the Standing Committee of the National People's Congress in 1983 and retired in April 1988. He has considerable influence in the Party's political-legal system (the public security and judicial organs), and played an active part, together with the other conservative elders, in the downfall of Hu Yaobang and Zhao Ziyang.

Qin Benli: editor-in-chief of the *World Economic Herald* in Shanghai. The weekly, first published in 1980, was also the first newspaper in China to be financially self-sufficient. The *World Economic Herald* in recent years established its position as the most liberal newspaper in China and enjoyed a high reputation overseas. Jiang Zemin took over the newspaper on 26 April 1989 and removed Qin from his post. The immediate cause for such action was a report by the newspaper of a forum in memory of Hu Yaobang, which contained statements concerning the 'unjust treatment of Hu.'

Qin Jiwei: close ally of Deng since the civil war, when he served under Deng in the Second Field Army. He suffered from attacks by Red Guards in the Cultural Revolution, but emerged in 1975 as second political commissar of the Beijing Military Region. He was commander of the Beijing Military Region in 1980–87 before he became minister of national defense and a member of the Politburo. Qin and Yang Shangkun were considered Deng's most–trusted military leaders. Qin, however, is reported to have been sympathetic to the student movement in 1989 and to have opposed the military's entry into Beijing. Since the Beijing massacre, there have been constant rumors of power struggles between Qin and Yang.

Senior cadres who are believed to be in trouble for taking a liberal stand regarding political reforms and the student movement include:

Au Zhiwen: adviser to the Structural Reform Commission of the State Council, and formerly deputy head of the commission.

Gao Shangquan: deputy head of the Structural Reform Commission of the State Council. Gao is generally considered to be close to Zhao Ziyang and was behind many of Zhao's economic reform proposals.

Gao Zhanxiang: deputy minister of culture. He is believed to have lost his post.

Gong Yuzhi: deputy head of the Propaganda Department and the Party Literature Research Centre of the Party Central Committee.

Hu Jiwei: member of the Standing Committee of the National People's Congress, vice-chairman of the Education, Science, Culture and Health Committee of the National People's Congress and former editor-in-chief of the *People's Daily*. In May 1989, Hu attempted to mobilize Standing Committee members of the National People's Congress to propose an emergency meeting of the Standing Committee to discuss the student movement, thus antagonizing Li Peng and his supporters.

Li Honglin: a famous theoretician who took part in the debate in 1978 supporting 'practice as the sole criterion of testing the truth.' His subsequent publications were in support of democracy and against authoritarianism and a personality cult. He was thus removed from his post as head of the Theory Bureau of the Propaganda Department of the Party Central Committee in 1985. He became head of the Fujian provincial Academy of Social Sciences, but again lost his job after the fall of Hu Yaobang. Li was arrested in July 1989 at his home in Fuzhou.

Liu Yandong: secretary of the Central Committee of the Communist Youth League of China and chairman of the All-China Youth Federation.

Mu Qing: head of the New China News Agency and member of the Party Central Committee. He was removed from his post at the New China News Agency.

Qian Liren: former head of the *People's Daily* and secretary of its Party group.

Qin Chuan: former editor-in-chief of the *People's Daily* and member of the Standing Committee of the National People's Congress. He participated in the signature campaign for an emergency meeting of the Standing Committee of the National People's Congress to discuss the handling of the student movement.

Tan Wenrui: former editor-in-chief of the *People's Daily*.

Tong Dalin: adviser to the Structural Reform Commission of the State Council, and formerly deputy head of the commission.

Wang Meng: member of the Party Central Committee and minister of culture. Wang himself is a famous novelist. He pretended to be sick after the Tiananmen massacre and refused to appear with the other leaders to demonstrate solidarity and support for the crackdown. He is believed to have lost his post.

Wang Yuanhua: former head of the Propaganda Department of the Shanghai municipal Party committee, he also was editor-in-chief of the 'Xin Qimeng' series of books.

Wu Mingyu: deputy director of the Technological, Economic and Social Development Research Center of the State Council.

Yu Guangyuan: member of the Party Central Advisory Commission and adviser of the Chinese Academy of Social Sciences. Yu is best known for his advocacy of a major overhaul of Marxism.

Seven senior retired military figures sent to the martial law authorities and the Party Central Military Commission a letter that was circulated in Beijing on 22 May 1989. 'The People's Army belongs to the people,' the letter said. 'It cannot stand in opposition to the people, much less oppress the people, and it absolutely cannot open fire on the people or create a blood-shedding incident. In order to prevent further worsening of the situation, troops should not enter the city (of Beijing).' The seven authors were: former commander of the navy **Ye Fei**, former minister of national defense; **Zhang Aiping**, former chief of general staff of the People's Liberation Army and deputy secretary general of the Party Central Military Commission; **Yang Dezhi**, former president of the People's Liberation Army Academy of Military Sciences; **Song Shilun**, former vice minister of national defense; **Xiao Ke**, former commander of the railway corps of the People's Liberation Army; **Chen Zaidao**, former political commissar of the General Logistics Department of the People's

Liberation Army; and **Li Jukai**, an adviser to the Party Central Military Commission.

Song Ping: elected to the Standing Committee of the Politburo at the fourth plenum of the 13th Central Committee in June 1989. He was 72 years old then and was head of the Organization Department of the Party Central Committee. Song was Chou Enlai's political secretary in Nanjing during the 1940s, and served as a vice minister of labor and of the State Planning Commission in the 1950s. He again became a vice minister of the State Planning Commission in 1981 and its minister in 1983. Song is now believed to be in charge of the rectification of the Party.

Su Shaozhi: famous Marxist theoretican and former head of the Institute of Marxism-Leninism of the Chinese Academy of Social Science. Like Yan Jiaqi, in recent years he gradually moved from being a member of the official think tank to becoming a dissident intellectual. His writings had an important influence on the student movement in 1989. Su now lives in exile in the U.S. and was a founder of the Front for Democracy in China.

Su Xiaokang: chief author of the controversial TV series 'The River Dies Young.' The TV series advocated the replacement of the 'yellow civilization' with the 'blue civilization,' i.e., for complete Westernization. How to evaluate traditional Chinese civilization and whether to accept Western civilization completely or selectively have been controversies among Chinese intellectuals since the opium wars. The TV series attracted considerable attention in China and in overseas Chinese communities, and subsequently was severely criticized by the official Chinese mass media after the Tiananmen incident. Su escaped from China to Hong Kong in early September 1989 and is now in France. Su's father, Su Xing, was deputy head of the Central Party School.

Wan Li: Politburo member since 1982 and chairman of the Standing Committee of the National People's Congress since 1988. He has been a trusted ally of Deng since the Civil War. Like Zhao Ziyang, he achieved spectacular results with agricultural reforms when he was first secretary of the Anhui provincial Party committee in 1977–1980. In May 1989, Wan was visiting the U.S. and Canada. There was speculation he might return and be persuaded to mobilize the National People's Congress machinery to remove Li Peng from his premiership. Wan did cut short his overseas trip and returned to Shanghai on May 25, but two days later he released a statement supporting the position of Yang Shangkun and Li Peng. Unconfirmed reports, however, indicate that he still resists the hard-line measures taken after the Beijing massacre.

Wan Runnan: founder in 1984 of the Stone Company, China's largest private firm. Chinese authorities accused the Stone Company of providing more than 400,000 yuan in support of the student movement in April–May 1989. Wan fled to France after the Beijing massacre and together with other emigres, began to organize in Paris the Front for Democracy in China, which was formally established in September. Wan was an intellectual turned entrepreneur, and was keen to support independent research. He was believed to be quite close to Zhao Ziyang.

Wang Dan: a 24-year-old student in the history department of Beijing University. Wang was one of the most prominent leaders of the student movement and a Standing Committee member of the Beijing Federation of Autonomous Student Unions. Wang's father was an associate professor at Beijing University and Wang himself was quite close to Fang Lizhi. He was arrested in Beijing in July 1989.

Wang Juntao: a young economist, an alternate Central Committee member of the Communist Youth League of China and deputy editor-in-chief of *Economic Studies Weekly*, an influential liberal publication that advocated economic reforms. Wang was close to Chen Ziming and was believed to have been arrested with him. Wang also is remembered for a famous poem written in the demonstrations against the Gang of Four in April 1976.

Wang Ruoshui: former deputy editor-in-chief of the *People's Daily*. He engaged in polemics with the conservative Party leaders in charge of the ideological front on the issues of 'socialist alienation' and humanitarianism, thus becoming a target of the anti-spiritual pollution campaign in 1983–84. He also was the editor of the liberal 'Xin Qimeng' series of books. Wang enjoys a high reputation among intellectuals in China and in overseas Chinese communities.

Wang Ruowang: a famous intellectual in Shanghai. Since the mid-1980s, he has been a major target of the conservative Party leaders because of his liberal views. Wang, then 71, took part in the student rallies in Shanghai in spring 1989. He was later arrested and jailed. The Shanghai municipal Party committee mobilized the literary circle to criticize him, calling him 'Shanghai's Fang Lizhi' and 'the origin of the disaster of the Shanghai riots.'

Wang Zhen: vice chairman of the People's Republic of China since April 1988, and a Standing Committee member of the Central Military

Commission in the late 1970s and early 1980s. Wang was the most senior military leader among those from the First Field Army, and he has been a loyal supporter of Deng. He is typical of the conservative old guard military leaders who often reveal a strong anti-intellectual bias. Wang attacked the TV series 'The River Dies Young' in 1988 and played a key role in the military suppression of the student movement in 1989.

Wuerkaixi: a 21-year-old Xinjiang Uygur student from the Education Department of Beijing Normal University. He was a Standing Committee member of the Beijing Federation of Autonomous Student Unions. He attracted much media attention because he was outspoken and arrogant. He escaped to France via Hong Kong in mid-June 1989, was elected vice chairman of the FDC, now a student at Harvard University. His allegedly luxurious life-style has attracted much criticism and has caused concern for the development of the FDC.

Yang Baibing: a cousin of Yang Shangkun; their fathers were brothers. Yang Baibing was deputy political commissar of the Beijing Military Region in 1982, promoted to political commissar in 1985, and appointed head of the General Political Department of the People's Liberation Army in 1987. He became secretary general of the Central Military Commission and member of the Secretariat of the Party Central Committee in November 1989. It is generally believed that his rapid rise was based on the backing of Yang Shangkun, who in turn received firm support from his cousin in the suppression of the student movement. There is much fear that the Yang family may control the People's Liberation Army and present a major obstacle to political and economic reforms in China.

Yang Shangkun: elected head of state in 1988. He had been executive vice chairman of the Central Military Commission of the Party since 1982, and was elected first vice chairman of the commission in November 1989. Yang was educated at the Sun Yat-sen University in Moscow in the 1920s, and became an alternate secretary of the Secretariat of the Party Central Committee in 1956. During the Cultural Revolution, he was severely attacked, and his case was not settled until December 1978. In the 1980s, he firmly supported Deng in the Central Military Commission and at the same time created a faction of loyal supporters within the People's Liberation Army. He fully backed Li Peng's declaration of martial law in May 1989, and he probably was responsible for ordering troops into Beijing. His influence within the PLA has made him a powerful figure in the present leadership. Upon Deng's death, he will be a leading contender to Peng have caused much anxiety concerning leadership succession in China.

Yan Jiaqi: a leading political scientist in China, formerly director of the Political Studies Institute of the Chinese Academy of Social Sciences. He resigned from the position even before the student movement in 1989, and increasingly moved from an official think tank specialist to become a critic outside the establishment. He was close to Zhao Ziyang and until 1987–88 was the designer of many official political reform proposals. A book on the history of the Cultural Revolution by Yan and his wife has been a bestseller. Yan is now among the most prominent emigres and has been elected head of the Front for Democracy in China.

Yuan Mu: spokesman for the State Council. He became the infamous symbol of post-Tiananmen massacre propaganda when in a televised interview of 17 June 1989 he stated that 'there were no casualties' in the process of clearing Tiananmen Square the night of 3 June 1989. Yuan was close to the ultra-leftists in the Cultural Revolution. He was then secretary to Ji Dengkui, a member of the Politburo, deputy premier and first political commissar of the Beijing Military Region.

Zhao Ziyang: former general secretary of the Party, purged in 1989, Zhao was first secretary of Guangdong provincial Party committee when the Cultural Revolution began. He was 'liberated' in 1971 and became first secretary of the Sichuan provincial Party committee in 1975. His economic reform program in Sichuan, especially the responsibility system in agriculture, achieved spectacular results. In 1980, he was elected member of the Standing Committee of the Politburo and replaced Hua Guofeng as premier. Zhao became general secretary of the Party upon Hu Yaobang's forced resignation in January 1987; he in turn was relieved of all Party posts after Tiananmen because of his sympathy for the student demonstrations. Since then, he has been criticized for supporting the riots and splitting the Party.

Zhu Houze: vice chairman of the All-China Federation of Trade Unions and first secretary of its secretariat. He was formerly secretary of the Guizhou provincial Party committee and head of the Propaganda Department of the Party Central Committee. Zhu had close connections with Hu Yaobang, and he supported Hu's liberal policies, especially when he was head of the Propaganda Department. Zhu lost the Party propaganda portfolio after Hu's fall from power, but re-emerged in autumn 1988 as a leader of the All-China Federation of Trade Unions. The federation not only showed support for the student movement in 1989, but provided 100,000 yuan of food and medical supplies for the students at Tiananmen Square.

About the Authors

ASAI MOTOFUMI

Asai Motofumi graduated from Tokyo University and joined the diplomatic service in 1963, serving in Australia, the Soviet Union, and the U.K. He served in China from 1980 to 1983. From 1983 to 1986, he was director for China and Regional Policy Planning Sections of the Asian Affairs Bureau. He is the author of *Japan's Diplomacy, Reflections and Change* (Twanami, 1989). Mr. Asai is currently a professor-designate of the faculty of law at Nihon University.

GEREMIE BARMÉ

Geremie Barmé did his undergraduate training in Sanskrit, Classical Chinese and Modern Chinese at the Australian National University, Canberra, then studied literature and politics in China. He worked as an editor and translator for the Hong Kong monthly *The Seventies* (now *The Nineties*) from 1977–79. He finished his doctoral thesis on 20th-century Chinese intellectual history in 1989, and is currently a research fellow in the department of Far Eastern History of the Australian National University. He is coordinator of the Australian National University's Tiananmen Square Documentation Project. Recent publications include: *Seeds of Fire: Chinese Voices of Conscience*, edited with Professor John Minford (New York: Noonday Press, 1989, 3rd edition); and with Yang Jiang, *Lost in the Crowd: A Cultural Revolution Memoir*, translation (Melbourne: McPhee Gribble, 1989). Barme is presently editing with Linda Jaivin a sequel to *Seeds of Fire* entitled *New Ghosts, Old Dreams: Voices from Tiananmen Square*, to be published in 1990 by Farrar, Straus & Giroux, New York.

MICHAEL T. BYRNES

Michael T. Byrnes is a colonel in the U.S. Army currently assigned as a U.S. Army Fellow to the U.S. Naval War College in Newport, R.I. A member of the Army's foreign area officers program, he has served three tours in the Far East, including a recent tour as a military attache in Hong Kong. Colonel Byrnes has traveled extensively in China.

JOSEPH Y.S. CHENG

Joseph Y.S. Cheng is dean of the School of Arts and Social Sciences at the Open Learning Institute of Hong Kong. He graduated from the University of Hong Kong and received his Ph.D. from the Flinders University of South Australia. He has published extensively on Hong Kong politics, Chinese politics, and Chinese foreign policy. His recent work includes *China: Modernization in the 1980s.*

JEROME ALAN COHEN

Jerome Alan Cohen is a partner in the international law firm of Paul, Weiss, Rifkind, Wharton & Garrison. He is a specialist in business and public law relating to China and he has long represented foreign investors and traders in their contract negotiations and dispute resolution in China. Mr. Cohen formerly served as professor, director of the East Asian Legal Studies, and associate dean at Harvard Law School, where he still teaches courses on 'Legal Problems of Doing Business with China' and 'China and International Law.' He has published books on the administration of criminal justice in China and Beijing's record in international law as well as many articles on Chinese law and a general book, *China Today*, co-authored with his wife, Joan Lebold Cohen.

JÜRGEN DOMES

Jürgen Domes received his doctorate in political science from Heidelberg University and passed his professorial examination in political science and modern Chinese history at the Free University of Berlin in 1967. Since 1975, he has been professor of political science and director of Research Unit on Chinese and East Asian Politics, Faculty of Law and Economics, The Saar University at Saarbrucken. He has so far published, edited or co-edited 24 books, 38 contributions to symposium volumes, and 42 articles in academic journals on Chinese politics. His latest books are: *Taiwan im Wandel* (1982), *The Government and Politics of the PRC: A Time of Transition* (1985) and *P'eng Te-huai, The Man and the Image* (1985).

FANG LIZHI

Fang Lizhi was born in Beijing in 1936, and graduated from the Beijing University Department of Physics in 1956. From 1958 until 1987 he taught physics and astrophysics at the University of Science and Technology in Hefei, Anhui Province, where he served as teaching assistant (1955–1963), lecturer (1963–78), professor (1978–87), and vice president (1984–87). From 1987 to 1989, he was a professor at the Beijing Astronomical Observatory of the Chinese Academy of Sciences. He specializes in relativistic astrophysics and cosmology, and has published more than 150 articles in international journals, as well as 12 books. In the 1980s Fang became widely known for his advocacy of human rights and democracy in China. He was a leading spirit behind the Chinese student movement in

1986, and was expelled from the Communist Party in 1987. He took refuge in the American Embassy after the Beijing massacre.

THOMAS B. GOLD

Thomas B. Gold is associate professor of sociology at the University of California, Berkeley, where he has taught since receiving his Ph.D. from Harvard University in 1981. In 1986 he published *State and Society in the Taiwan Miracle* (M.E. Sharpe). He is currently writing a book on urban private business and the emergence of civil society in China. He has conducted fieldwork numerous times in mainland China and Taiwan.

GEORGE HICKS

George Hicks is an economist, a survivor of countless business trips to China, and a longtime observer of the East Asian scene. He is the author of *Hong Kong Countdown* (1989).

NIHAL JAYAWICKRAMA

Nihal Jayawickrama is a senior lecturer in law at the University of Hong Kong. A graduate of the University of Ceylon, he received his doctorate from the University of London for research on international human rights law. He is a member of the Sri Lanka Bar, and has held positions as Attorney General, Secretary for Justice, and Vice Chairman of the Sri Lanka Delegation to the U.N. General Assembly. He has served on the legal staff of the International Commission of Jurists and the Commonwealth Secretariat, and was recently associated in research into the human rights of scientists in the Helsinki Act countries. He is a member of the Hong Kong-based Ad Hoc Study Group on Human Rights in China.

CHALMERS JOHNSON

Chalmers Johnson is the Rohr Professor of Pacific International Relations within the Graduate School of International Relations and Pacific Studies at the San Diego campus of the University of California. He is the former chairman of Berkeley's Center for Chinese Studies and its department of political science. His books include *Peasant Nationalism and Communist Power, An Instance of Treason, Revolutionary Change, Conspiracy at Matsukawa, Autopsy on People's War, Japan Public Policy Companies, MITI and the Japanese Miracle*. He is a fellow of the American Academy of Arts and Sciences, and a member of the Council on Foreign Relations.

DAVID KELLY

David Kelly is a member of the Contemporary China Centre, Research School of Pacific Studies, Australian National University. His work centers on intellectual and social trends in the post-Mao era. A book written in collaboration with Bill Brugger, *Chinese Marxism in the Post-Mao Era*, will be published by Stanford University Press in 1990.

MICHAEL LINDSAY

Michael Lindsay, professor emeritus at The American University in Washington, D.C., taught at Yenching University in Beijing from 1937 to 1941. He also served as a press attache at the British Embassy and became involved in the anti-Japanese underground movement during the same period. During World War II, he was a technical adviser to the army communications department of the Shanxi-Chahar-Hebei Military District. He has taught at Australian National University, Yale, Harvard and the University of Washington. He is the author of *China, a Handbook* (Praeger, 1973), *The Unknown War: North China 1937–1945* (Bergstrom & Boyle 1975, Beijing edition, 1987), and numerous other books and articles.

PERRY LINK

Perry Link is a professor of Chinese at Princeton University. In 1988–89 he was director of the Beijing office of the National Academy of Sciences / Committee on Scholarly Communication with the People's Republic of China. He has written extensively on modern China, including *Mandarin Ducks and Butterflies: Popular Fiction in Early Twentieth Century Chinese Cities* (University of California Press, 1981) and *Roses and Thorns: The Second Blooming of the Hundred Flowers in Chinese Fiction, 1979–80* (University of California Press, 1984).

JANE MACARTNEY

Jane Macartney graduated in Sinology from Durham University in 1979. After language training in Taiwan, she took reporting assignments there for *Newsweek* and several business publications in Hong Kong. She joined United Press International as Taiwan correspondent in 1985, transferring to China as UPI correspondent in Beijing from early 1986 through December 1988. While there, she covered the student protests in Shanghai in December 1986 and subsequent demonstrations in Beijing. She returned to China in April 1989 to cover the student demonstrations for *Asiaweek* magazine, a Hong Kong-based subsidiary of Time.

WILLIAM MCGURN

William McGurn graduated with a B.A. in Philosophy from the University of Notre Dame and an M.S. in Communications from Boston University. He has worked as assistant managing editor for *The American Specta-*

tor, managing editor for *This World*, and deputy editorial page editor for both *The Wall Street Journal/Europe* and *The Asian Wall Street Journal*. He is author of the monograph *Terrorism or Freedom Fighter* (Institute for European Defense and Strategic Studies, London, 1987) and editor of *Basic Law, Basic Questions: The Debate Continues* (Review Publishing Co., Hong Kong, 1988). Today he is Washington bureau chief for *National Review* and is working on a book about Hong Kong.

FRANZ MICHAEL

Franz Michael is professor emeritus at George Washington University, where he was associate director and director of the Institute for Sino-Soviet Studies from 1964 to 1972 and professor until 1977. His publications include: *Rule by Incarnation: Tibetan Buddhism and Its Role in Society and State* (Westview 1982); *The Taiping Rebellion*, 3 vols (1971); *Mao and The Perpetual Revolution* (1977); *China Through The Ages; History of a Civilization* (Westview 1986); *Human Rights in the People's Republic of China* (Westview 1987), co-author with Y.L. Wu, John Copper, Ta-ling Lee, Maria Hsia Chang, A. James Gregor; *China and the Crisis of Marxism-Leninism* (Westview 1990, editor and co-author with Carl Linden, Jan Prybyla, Jürgen Domes), and many other books and articles.

RAMON H. MYERS

Ramon H. Myers is Senior Fellow at the Hoover Institution and curator of the East Asian Studies Collection. He was associate editor of *The Journal of Asian Studies* between 1969–72 and edited *Ch'ing-shih wen-t'i (Studies in Ching History)*. In 1980, Garland Publishing, Inc., issued a 44-volume series that Myers selected and edited, entitled *The Modern Chinese Economy*. His publications include *The Chinese Peasant Economy* (Harvard University Press, 1970) and contribution to the Cambridge History of China (volume 13, part 2, 1986), *Two Chinese States* (Hoover Institution Press, 1978), *A U.S. Foreign Policy for Asia in the 1980s and Beyond* (Hoover Institution Press, 1982), and *Understanding Communist China* (co-authored with Dr. Esther Kuo, Hoover Institution Press, 1986).

JAN S. PRYBYLA

Jan S. Prybyla is professor of economics and fellow of the Center for East Asian Studies at Pennsylvania State University. He is the author of numerous articles on socialist economies with special reference to China, and of several books, including *The Political Economy of Communist China* (1970), *The Chinese Economy: Problems and Policies* (1978, 1981), *Issues in Socialist Economic Modernization* (1980), *Market and Plan*

Under Socialism: The Bird in the Cage (1987), and of a forthcoming collection of essays, *Reform in China and Other Socialist Economies*, which will be published by the American Enterprise Institute. He has taught at Nankai University's Institute of Economics (1987–88) and lectured at the Shanghai Academy of Social Sciences (1988). He was visiting scholar at the Institute of International Relations, National Chengchi University, Taipei, Taiwan, in 1989.

LUCIAN W. PYE

Lucian W. Pye is Ford Professor of Political Science at the Massachusetts Institute of Technology. He was born in 1921 in Fenchow, Shansi, China. A specialist in comparative politics, he has been a leader in developing the fields of political culture and political psychology, with a general focus on Asia and a particular concentration on Chinese political behavior. He is a past president of the American Political Science Association; he has played a leading role in numerous scholarly and citizens' organizations; and he has been elected to the American Academy of Arts and Sciences, the American Philosophical Society, and a Fellow of the Center for the Advanced Study in the Behavioral Sciences. He is the author or editor of 21 books, the most recent being *The Mandarin and the Cadre: China's Political Cultures*, and *Asian Power and Politics*.

ORVILLE SCHELL

Orville Schell is a journalist, a Guggenheim Fellow working on a project in contemporary Chinese intellectual history and a research associate at the Center for Chinese Studies at the University of California/Berkeley. He has written extensively on China, including *Discos and Democracy* and *To Get Rich is Glorious: China in the 80s*.

ANDREW J. SPANO

Andrew J. Spano was a visiting lecturer in English and education at Taian Teachers' College in Shandong Province, China, during 1988 and 1989. His articles have appeared in the *South China Morning Post*, *The Asian Wall Street Journal*, the *Vermont Quarterly*, the *Salem Evening News*, and the Chinese government publication *Bridge for Communication and Mutual Understanding*. Currently, he is a free-lance writer teaching journalism, American literature, and writing as a visiting lecturer at Salem State College and Quincy Junior College in Massachusetts.

RICHARD C. THORNTON

Richard C. Thornton is professor of history and international affairs at the Elliott School of International Affairs, George Washington University. He is the author of *China: A Political History, 1917–1980* (Boulder: Westview Press, 1982) and *The Nixon-Kissinger Years, Reshaping America's Foreign Policy* (New York: Paragon House, November 1989).

BYRON S.J. WENG

Byron S.J. Weng is a reader in government and public administration at the Chinese University of Hong Kong. Born in Taiwan, he received his B.A. in Law from the National Taiwan University, and his M.S., and Ph.D. in political science from the University of Wisconsin/Madison. He authored *Peking's U.N. Policy: Continuity and Change*, and edited *Studies on the Constitutional Law of the People's Republic of China*, *Essays on China's Economic Law*, and *Introduction to Chinese Law*. He has also written extensively on Chinese politics and foreign relations.

WOJTEK ZAFANOLLI

Wojtek Zafanolli is a pen name for Jacques Andrieu. Born in France in 1949, he came to Sinology from a scientific/economic educational background. After studying the Chinese language in Paris he spent several years in the PRC and in Hong Kong at the crucial time of the transition between Maoist legacy and Dengist legitimacy. He has written extensively on modern China, his main interests being the second economy and issues related to corruption as well as the history of thought, literature, and politics. He currently holds a research post with the Centre National de la Recherche Scientifique in Paris.

Index